THE NATURE OF THE ENGLISH REVOLUTION

The Nature of the English Revolution

Essays by
JOHN MORRILL

Longman
London and New York

Longman Group Limited,
Longman House, Burnt Mill,
Harlow, Essex CM20 2JE, England
and Associated Companies throughout the world.

Published in the United States of America
by Longman Publishing, New York

This edition © Longman Group UK Limited 1993

First published 1993
Second impression 1994

ISBN 0 582 08941 7 CSD
ISBN 0 582 08942 5 PPR

British Library Cataloguing-in-Publication Data

A catalogue record for this book is available from the British Library

Library of Congress Cataloging in Publication Data

Includes bibliographical references and index.
ISBN 0-582-08941-7. – ISBN 0-582-08942-5 (pbk.)
Morrill, J.S. (John Stephen), 1946–
    The nature of the English Revolution: essays / by John Morrill.
    p. cm.
    1. Great Britain–History–Puritan Revolution, 1642–1660.
2. Great Britain–History, Military–Stuarts, 1603–1714.
3. Great Britain–Politics and government–1603–1714. I. Title.
DA405. M67 1993
941.06-dc20   92-25941
                                                                         CIP

Set by 5B in Bembo 10/12 pt
Produced by Longman Singapore Publishers (Pte) Ltd.
Printed in Singapore

Contents

Preface

I was appointed to my first academic job at the age of 23, and have a contract of employment which could keep me employed until I am 67. My 45th birthday (June 1991) – the mid-point – therefore seemed an appropriate moment to take stock. I have taught, studied, ate and slept the English Civil Wars/Great Rebellion/Revolution/Wars of Religion (or whatever we are to call the blasted *thing*) for all those twenty-two years and more. Time for a public academic appraisal, perhaps.

This is a combination of essays which I have written over the past twenty years with some additional material. It consists of twenty items. Fourteen have appeared in accessible places hitherto; two (chs. 1, 15) have appeared in inaccessible places (ch. 1 only in Chinese!); and a third (ch. 19) has appeared only in a truncated form. Five items (chs. 9–11, 13–14) are review articles and represent considered responses to the major works on the period to have appeared over the period. For this collection I have provided three new essays, one introducing each of the three sections. I have left all the essays as I first wrote them, bar the removal of typographical errors which marred their earlier incarnation and the updating of references to works not published at the time of original publication. I have by-and-large stuck by this rule not to 'modernize' these essays even in the case of those items which will not be familiar to readers (chs. 1, 15, 19). I toyed with the idea of removing questionable statements or such factual inaccuracies as have been pointed out to me; but I concluded that this would put me on a slippery slope or at least on a sliding scale without any natural breaking point on it; that such a procedure would produce curious hybrids; and that any tampering at all would probably involve me in degrees of rewriting and adaptation which would change the whole nature of the book. I did however decide to write introductions to each section, introductions that would indicate how I myself would now sort out the wheat from the chaff of my earlier work. I hope I have achieved honesty without an unedifying display of either self-congratulation or self-chastisement.

I am deeply grateful to all my friends and colleagues for their encouragement with this project. I asked Colin Davis, Anthony Fletcher, Jonathan Scott and David Smith whether they thought it mere vanity to undertake this 'retrospective'. All gave me good and reassuring reasons for proceeding and guided me as to which of the fifty or so pieces would make a reasonably coherent package. I am also deeply grateful to my daughter Rachel for her skilful help in the compiling of the index.

I believe that we understand ourselves better if we understand the past that shaped us. And I think we can recover – imperfectly but actually – the reality of that past through those surviving fragments that are susceptible to analysis by trained observers. That training is continuous, and in my case continues in a wonderfully conducive environment. Over the past decade I have had responsibility at any given moment for something like 12–18 graduate students, and close links with others working with colleagues on fields adjacent to my own. I owe more to each and every one of them than they will ever realize. They have all stretched me intellectually over the years and it would be invidious to single out any particular students and otiose to fill many columns with all their names. But they are all inscribed in my heart and I dedicate this book to them for sharing their striving with me, for listening to my speculations and for their proper scepticism mingled with a belief in the possibility of making the past yield up its secrets.

JOHN MORRILL
Feast of the Annunciation 1992

Acknowledgements

We are grateful to the following copyright holders for permission to reproduce pieces by John Morrill: the Royal Historical Society for the article 'The Religious Context of the English Civil War' in *Transactions of the Royal Historical Society*, 5th series, 34 (1984); Cambridge University Press for the following chapters: 'The Attack on the Church of England in the Long Parliament' in *History, Society and the Churches* eds. D. Beales and G. Best (1985), 'Order and Disorder in the English Revolution' in *Order and Disorder in Early Modern Britain* eds. A. Fletcher and J. Stevenson (1985), 'The Sensible Revolution' in *The Anglo-Dutch Moment* ed. J. Israel (1991); Edinburgh University Press for the chapter 'The Scottish National Covenant of 1638 in its British Context' in *The Scottish National Covenant in its British Context, 1638–51* J.M. Morrill (1990); The Macmillan Press Ltd for the chapter 'The Church in England 1642–1649' in *Reactions to the English Civil War* ed. J.M. Morrill (1982); the editor of *Northern History* for the article 'The Northern Gentry and the Great Rebellion' in *Northern History*, XV (1979); the University of Chicago Press, and the editor of *Journal of British Studies* for the article 'The Ecology of Allegiance in the English Civil War' in the *Journal of British Studies*, 26 (1987), © 1987 by The North American Conference on British Studies; the Historical Association for the article 'Christopher Hill's Revolution' in *History*, 27, No. 241 (1989); The Folger Shakespeare Library for the chapter 'Charles I, Tyranny and the English Civil War' in *Religion, Resistance and the Civil War* ed. W. Lamont (1990); Stenfert Kroese/Martinus Nijhoff Publishers for the chapter 'The Army Revolt of 1647' in *Britain and the Netherlands*, vol. 6, eds. A. Duke and C. Tamse (1977); the editors of *Past and Present* for the article 'Mutiny and Discontent in English Provincial Armies,

1645–1647' in *Past and Present: A Journal of Historical Studies*, 56 (1972), world copyright: The Past and Present Society, 175 Banbury Road, Oxford; the editor of *History Today* for the article 'Restoring the Balance' which was the basis for chapter 19.

CHAPTER ONE

The Nature of the English Revolution[1]

I

This introduction seeks to do three things: first, to show why a particular kind of civil war took place in England in the 1640s; second, to examine the aims of those who challenged the authority of King Charles I in the 1640s; and third, to examine why a limited civil war turned into a revolution with profound effects on the subsequent history of the British Isles.

II

Early modern England was a personal monarchy in which the King or Queen exercised personal authority over the most sensitive issues of politics and statecraft and in which he or she personally selected (and dismissed) councillors, judges and bishops. In such a polity the personal weaknesses of the monarch could in themselves cause the collapse of order; certainly the particular weaknesses of particular monarchs were always likely to determine the kind of collapse of order that might occur.

It is worth beginning with this assertion because England had a civil war in the 1640s just when the danger had appeared to recede. There are at least five ways in which England seemed to be moving away

---

1. This paper was written for the Sino-British Historical Symposium in Nanjing in May 1987 and subsequently published in the record of that Symposium – in Chinese! It was aimed at a highly intelligent but not especially well-informed audience. In revising it for publication here I have left most of it untouched; but I have removed some short sections of explanation designed for a Chinese audience and slightly expanded a few sections. I could not have included reference to work I had not read at the time of writing without breaching the conventions of this volume and starting effectively from scratch.

from rather than towards internal collapse in the early seventeenth century.[2]

First of all, there was far greater security of title to the throne and an end to disputed successions. After chronic instability and civil war for much of the fifteenth century (the consequence of the complicated marital affairs of Edward III and John of Gaunt and the consequence of the Lancastrian *coup d'etat* of 1399), the country teetered on the brink of civil war for much of the sixteenth century as the doubtful legitimacy of Henry VIII's daughters and the childlessness of all three of his children made a War of the English Succession an ever-present threat. In 1559 a heretic bastard Queen (three damning qualities) was trying to secure the throne and was faced by a formidable rival in Mary of Scotland, married to King Francis II of France. If Francis had fathered a child by Mary before he died unexpectedly of an ear infection at the age of nineteen, there would have been a single heir to the thrones of France, Scotland and England, a circumstance that would have ensured that the great Habsburg/Valois struggle would have been fought out on British soil. If Elizabeth had died at any point before 1587, it seems clear that Mary, backed by legitimist and religious-conservative forces in England and abroad, would have plunged England into civil war.

Less certainly, if James I's elder son Henry, a blinkered and determined evangelical Protestant, had lived and acceded to the throne, it is quite possible that he would have plunged England into the maelstrom of European warfare, stretching the resources of the Crown to breaking point and presiding over the collapse of order which characterized so much of Western Europe.

By the mid-1630s, however, Charles I was the undisputed King with a quiverful of children. The civil war of 1642 was not the product of dynastic rivalry. Indeed England would have had a far less messy civil war with a far less violent outcome if it had been possible to depose Charles I and replace him by someone with a reversionary claim on the throne.

Secondly, in England – as throughout Europe – the Reformation divided the nation. The hybrid, compromise Church established by Elizabeth (reformed in doctrine, traditionalist in government and discipline, a mixture of 'catholic' and 'protestant' elements in

---

2. What follows is based on a large number of sources. Among the best and most accessible are C. Russell, *The Crisis of Parliaments* (1971); D. Hirst, *Authority and Conflict* (1986); P. Williams, *The Tudor Regime* (1979); J.P. Kenyon, *Stuart England* (rev. ed. 1986); J.C.D. Clark, *Revolution and Rebellion* (1986).

its ceremonies and forms of worship) was accepted by the mass of the people, but it haemorrhaged on the one side a minority loyal to the Pope, and on the other side a minority determined to complete the re-formation of religion. Both these minorities had, by the 1580s, set up embryonic organizations (one outside and the other within the Church) comparable with the revolutionary parties in Western Europe,[3] the Catholics in particular developing a radical political thought justifying resistance and regicide.[4] By the 1620s, both the 'Puritan' militants and Catholic recusants had abandoned their organizational and intellectual challenges to the state and had opted for passive disobedience in the face of an increasingly indulgent, if not officially tolerant, state – an uneasy freedom of worship occasionally stamped on, but at the expense of civil rights (exclusion from office, heavier tax burdens, etc.). It was not far short of the kind of accommodation that made eighteenth-century England so free from religious strife.

Thirdly, the centre of gravity of Habsburg/Valois rivalry shifted during the sixteenth century from Italy to the Atlantic seaboard; and that, together with dynastic entanglements, made England a potential arena for the working out of their rivalries. In the late sixteenth century there was a constant threat of Spanish invasion of England or of Ireland, especially if Elizabeth died with the succession issue unresolved. By the 1620s, the centre of gravity of European power politics had moved eastward again, to the Rhineland and to Bohemia: invasions of the British Isles, even assistance to rebels, were not on the agenda of over-committed continental monarchs.[5]

Fourthly, the century from 1540 to 1640 saw major social and economic shifts. The root cause was a population steadily growing faster than the food supply. This produced severe underemployment, falling wages, occasional (localized) dearth. It also led to the consolidation of those who produced and marketed scarce goods (larger farmers, master craftsmen, merchants) and a *relative* decline of the

3. The key word here is 'embryonic'. There are clearly Catholic militants; but the thrust of Patrick Collinson's work ever since *The Elizabethan Puritan Movement* (1967) has been to show how well-assimilated most 'Puritans' are. I simply wish to point out that had a major Catholic threat arisen – such as the assassination of Elizabeth – then the clandestine classical structures were capable of adaptation for revolutionary purposes. See H.G. Koenigsberger, 'The Origins of Revolutionary Parties in France and the Netherlands during the Sixteenth Century', in idem., *Estates and Revolutions* (1971).
4. P. Holmes, *Resistance and Compromise: the Political Thought of Elizabethan Catholics* (1981).
5. See G. Parker, *The Thirty Years War* (1987), index, *sub* England.

greater (rentier) landlords. Yet by 1640 the pressures were easing. For the one hundred years after 1640 there were to be stable prices, fuller employment, and (from the 1670s) grain surpluses. The Stuarts had weathered the storm largely because the political system had proved supple enough to adapt to the major changes.[6] Thus there was a dispersal of political power. In part this was a reaction against the lawlessness of the fifteenth century when a militarized peerage had run amok, and law and order had collapsed. The peerage had not been destroyed by the Tudors, but it had been systematically demilitarized and stripped of its inherent power to run the provinces. Instead of exercising full jurisdiction over particular regions by hereditary grant from the Crown, they found themselves appointed on a revocable basis to carry out specified duties under conciliar supervision. More importantly, an ever-increasing range of regulatory and judicial responsibilities were entrusted to the gentry who looked more and more to one another for support. Their advancement came more and more through the mediation of the King's councillors and courtiers and less and less through provincial magnates.

It is of the utmost importance that no *noblesse de robe* or *hidalgo* class developed in England. There were no *intendants* and no hereditary civil service posts. Less than one in ten of the judges were the sons of lawyers; less than one in five of all civil servants were the sons of civil servants. Most salaried or fee'd officials of the Crown were first-generation officials who either retired to, or set their sons up in, the provinces. The 'Court' consisted largely of men on loan from the 'country'[7]. In addition, the problems of lawlessness, the social ills occasioned by population growth and inflation, the policing of religious uniformity, all brought about a massive increase in state power. But while the Crown acquired new supervisory powers, the administration of those powers was entrusted to local elites – the peerage and (more generally) the gentry. This growth of royal

6. Cf. here L. Stone, *The Causes of the English Revolution* (1972), the book which sparked off the revisionist revolt from the mid 1970s. Looking back over the past ten years, I think I was too hard on Stone's attempt to look for the structural weaknesses of the English state as well as at the largely unexceptional 'precipitants' and 'triggers' of the particular crisis of 1640–2. But it seems ever clearer to me that his attempt to find a dysfunction between social-structural change and political-structural atrophy misrepresents the dynamism of the latter.
7. See, for example, the figures in G.E. Aylmer, *The King's Servants* (1961), pp. 264–5 and table 16, which indicate that in the sample of all Caroline officeholders whose surnames begin with the letters A–C less than one in five were the sons of officeholders. Those Household Departments waiting upon the king's person – such as the Royal Bedchamber – are a partial but important exception.

power was shaped and sanctioned by Parliament. The key to an understanding of sixteenth-century government is to see it as the enhancement of royal authority by consent, a story of the recognition of the mutual benefits to be derived from a controlled growth in the responsibilities and power of the monarch. Tudor Parliaments did not seek to reduce royal power. They sought to shape its growth.

One powerful testimony to the way political institutions had adapted to new social realities is the very low level of violence in early Stuart England. The period from 1569 to 1642 was the longest period ever without a major rebellion;[8] the period 1605 to 1641 the longest without the conviction of a peer of the realm for treason;[9] the number of trials for treasons declined decade by decade from the late sixteenth century through to the 1630s. Where else in the early seventeenth century were few or no royal officials killed in discharging their duties? Was not England alone in not having no-go areas for unaccompanied tax-collectors? Were there not more dead bodies on stage at the end of a production of *Hamlet* than following any collective act of violence in the period up to 1642? Where else was the arbitration of the royal courts so completely accepted? Riots declined in number, in the number of those involved and in intensity after the turn of the sixteenth century.[10] Englishmen were notorious throughout Europe for being litigious. They were litigious because they were law-abiding.

Fifthly, we need to bear in mind Marc Bloch's judgement on medieval England: 'England was a truly unified state much earlier than any continental kingdom.' To linguistic, commercial, legal and fiscal unity unique among the states of late medieval and early modern Europe, the Tudors added greater administrative unity. The 'regionalism' which lay at the heart of so much rebellion in western and central Europe between 1560 and 1660 was absent.[11]

III

The stability of early Stuart *England* made civil war unlikely; it was the instability of early modern *Britain* that first made the war of 1642 possible. It was paradoxically the strength of Tudor England which

8. I am here assuming that the attempted putsch of the earl of Essex in 1601 does not count.
9. Only one peer of the realm was tried in the whole reign of Charles I to 1640 – Lord Castlehaven for most known sexual offences in 1631; State Trials records only one case of treason for the same period – Hugh Pyne's unkind comments on Charles' kingcraft which the judges found not to be treasonable.
10. See below, pp. 373–9.
11. Quoted and discussed in P. Corrigan and D. Sayer, *The Great Arch* (1985), pp. 2ff.

allowed it to extend its claims to sovereign power in Ireland[12] and it was the dynastic roulette that created the union of the Crowns of England and Scotland in 1603 that set up that problem. Multiple kingship led to tension and jealousies within political elites, exposed less easily controlled peripheries to incompetent and overbearing kingship and created a billiard-ball effect between the events of the three kingdoms. England, Ireland and Scotland all experienced authoritarian government in the 1630s and the rebellions in Scotland and then in Ireland and then in England reflect variant responses to a shared problem – the incompetence and authoritarianism of Charles I. Thus his attempts to force a surrender of title to all grants made by the Crown of Scotland between 1541 and 1625 and his attempt to ram major reforms of the Scottish Church down the throats and past the consciences of the Scottish people without bothering to consult a Scottish Parliament, a Scottish General Assembly, the Scottish Council or even the Scottish bi-shops in conclave was breathtakingly inept. And Charles's determination to bring the resources of England, Ireland and Highland Scotland against the Scottish Lowlands elite initiated a struggle he was doomed to lose.[13]

IV

In the 1630s, England appeared to be a stable polity. There were, of course, persistent weaknesses in the state system. Political elites expected the Crown to administer the realm and to uphold the Protestant cause abroad, but on a shoestring budget. The Crown had thus to accept the limitations on its resources and underachieve in foreign policy; or it had to use provocative means to increase revenues so as to fulfil expectations. It is also clear that while there was massive coincidence of interest between the Crown and the political elites, the Crown could not attack what the latter believed to be its intrinsic interests without finding itself obstructed and rendered powerless. It was Charles's disastrously partisan challenge to many cherished values and beliefs which made civil war possible.

At one level, given the scale of Charles's assault on political liberties and religious values, it is surprising that he secured as much support

---

12. B. Bradshaw, *The Irish Constitutional Revolution of the Sixteenth Century* (1979), parts II and III; S. Ellis, *Tudor Ireland, 1470–1603* (1987), chs. 5–8.
13. Important recent studies of the 'British' Revolution include M. Lee, *The Road to Revolution* (1985); D. Stevenson, *The Scottish Revolution* (1978); D. Stevenson, *Scottish Covenanters and Irish Confederates* (1981); A. Clarke, 'The Genesis of the Irish Rebellion of 1641' in P. Roebuck, (ed.), *From Plantation to Partition* (1981). For work published since this article was written in 1987, see below, ch. 13.

as he did in the 1640s. On the other hand, it took some spectacular miscalculation on his part to create the circumstances in which resistance became feasible. England lacked a focal point around which resistance could gather: the flag of a Pretender or a militarized nobility; or provincial institutions (such as the Estates of the Dutch provinces or the French Parlements).

Indeed it is striking that the administrative unity of England made organized resistance unthinkable in the absence of a Parliament; and the recall of Parliament was in the king's gift. He chose to recall it in the spring of 1640 because he wanted to continue his fight with the Scots, but he dismissed it again (with ease) when he found it insufficiently cooperative. He could have chosen to make a painful deal with Parliament so as to secure the money to deal with the Scots; or to make a painful deal with the Scots in order to resume his personal rule in England. That choice remained his in the aftermath of the Short Parliament. Only when he made an absurd choice – to fight the Scots without proper resources – did he lose control of the situation.[14] The Scots occupied the north-east of England and made it clear that they would not return home until their demands had been negotiated with an English Parliament. Charles was forced to do something unforeseeable – summon a Parliament without the freedom to dismiss it at will. That Long Parliament had a once-for-all opportunity to redress the grievances accumulated since the beginning of the reign.[15] But it was only when Charles proved unchastened and when he made it apparent to many that he intended to dishonour the concessions he had made in 1641, and when (and only when) he voluntarily withdrew from London and initiated a sequence of military provocations, that resistance to him became unexpectedly necessary and feasible.[16]

When war came, most people sought to distance themselves from it – by ignoring the orders of both sides, or by obeying the orders of both sides, or by taking the line of least resistance and doing what they were told, or by organizing themselves to raise citizen armies to

14. He hoped for Spanish and papal money to finance his campaign. But the outbreak of rebellion in Portugal, Catalonia and Spanish Italy made this unlikely hope impossible. See J.H. Elliott, 'The year of the three ambassadors', in H. Lloyd-Jones, V. Pearl and A.B. Worden (eds), *History and Imagination* (1982).

15. It is worth noting that there was no interest in redressing secular grievances that predated the accession of Charles I. See, for example, the Grand Remonstrance, a catalogue of 180 grievances drawn up in 1641, which begins in 1625 (S.R. Gardiner, *Constitutional Documents of the Puritan Revolution* [3rd edn., 1906], pp. 202–31).

16. See C. Russell, 'Why Did Charles I fight the Civil War?', *History Today*, May 1984 (unhappily not included in his collected essays, *Unrevolutionary England* [1991]).

keep *both* sides out their region.[17] But, manifestly, militant minorities did believe that there were issues worth fighting for; and they found others who – whether or not they had private views on those issues – were prepared to receive pay to further those causes. Most historians would now agree that the 'activists' (those who believed that there were issues worth fighting for) were drawn on each side in similar numbers from each social group. (It is an important corollary to this that men of all social groups had a good deal of freedom of choice, even though many exercised this freedom to take the line of least resistance.) There was popular royalism as well as popular parliamentarianism[18].

V

Those who wished to criticize Charles or his government had to use euphemisms or circumlocutions. Two phrases newly coined during the 1620s and 1630s sum up the anxieties of the period: the first was 'new counsels'[19] and the other was 'the piety of the times'.[20] Both are mild terms concealing a sense of menace to civil and religious liberties. James I often regretted that his predecessors had (voluntarily but irrevocably) bound themselves to act in certain ways but he did see himself as so bound.[21] Charles I did not hold himself to be so bound. One of his ministers, speaking for the young king in 1626, advised Parliament that

> Move not His Majesty with trenching upon his prerogatives lest you bring him out of love with his Parliaments. . . . In all Christian kingdoms . . . monarchs . . . seeing the turbulent spirit of their parliaments, at length . . . began to stand upon their prerogatives, and at last overthrew the parliaments throughout Christendom except here only with us.[22]

17. J.S. Morrill, *The Revolt of the Provinces* (1976), ch. 1; A.M. Fletcher, *The Outbreak of the English Civil War* (1979).
18. For a debate on these issues see D.E. Underdown, *Revel, Riot and Rebellion* (1985) and the debate between David Underdown and myself in *Jnl. Brit. Studs.* 26 (1987), and below, ch. 11.
19. For a discussion of this term, see R. Cust, 'Charles I and the Forced Loan of 1627', *Jnl. Brit. Studs.* 24 (1985).
20. For a discussion of this term, see S.P. Salt, 'The Origins of Sir Edward Dering's Attack on the Ecclesiastical Hierarchy', *Historical Journal (HJ)*, 30 (1987).
21. As in his famous dictum to the Spanish ambassador concerning the English Parliament, 'I am surprised that my predecessors let such an institution come into existence . . ., I am obliged to put up with what I cannot get rid of' (S.R. Gardiner, *History of England . . . 1603–1642* [10 vols., 1864–86], II, 251n). This is more usually cited with the crucial second clause left out (as in J.P. Kenyon, *The Stuart Constitution* [1962], p. 62).
22. Kenyon, *Stuart Constitution*, pp. 50–1.

Charles could never accept that men could sincerely hold principled opinions different from his own. Those who did not obey his orders were, necessarily, unprincipled and factious. Throughout his life he attributed obstruction to the wilful, unscrupulous and sectional interests of a minority. He saw his early Parliament as a flock of sheep blindly following some wily wolves.[23] If he was unable to gain that to which he was entitled by following 'constitutional' courses, he believed he had a residual right to fall back on a naked authoritarianism. This included the imprisonment of opponents without showing cause, impressment of those who would not lend voluntarily and many other abuses of the rule of law.[24] Charles himself referred to such expedients as 'new counsels' and it was a term taken up by his critics.

Charles and his ecclesiastical advisers, notably William Laud and Matthew Wren,[25] played down England's status as a member of the Protestant communion and played up her status as a Church which combined an unbroken apostolic tradition parallel to that of the Church of Rome, with a purity of teaching and practice that the latter had lost. They viewed Rome not as an antichristian church, a force of evil in the world, but as an errant sister-church. Determined to bring a largely illiterate population into greater obedience to the will of God, the Caroline Church shifted the weight of worship from the pulpit to the altar, from preaching to the sacraments; and it sought to restore the wealth of the clergy and to restore clerical jurisdiction and to impose sanctions on laymen who intruded themselves into the preserves of the clergy.[26] That is what was meant by 'the piety of the times'.

23. Much of the material in C. Daniels and J. Morrill, *Charles I* (1988), is devoted to this. See also Charles's Declaration of March 1629, printed in Gardiner, *Constitutional Documents*, pp. 93–108.
24. See e.g. J. Guy, 'The Origins of the Petition of Right', *HJ*, 25 (1982); L.J. Reeve, 'Arguments in King's Bench in 1629 Concerning the Imprisonment of Members of the House of Commons', *Jnl. Brit. Studs.* 25 (1986); R. Cust, *The Forced Loan and English Politics 1626–1628* (1988). Also below, ch. 15, pp. 289–91.
25. I am increasingly persuaded that Matthew Wren, dean of the Chapel Royal as well as bishop of Norwich (1637–40) and Ely (1640+) was more important in shaping Charles's policies in the later 1630s than was Laud. Laud shared Charles's goals but seems increasingly to have felt that Charles was going too far too fast. I was persuaded to consider this possibility by Dr Julian Davies.
26. There is a vast recent literature on this subject. I still find W.H. Hutton, *Archbishop Laud* (1900), an excellent introduction, and that J.S. McGee, 'William Laud and the Outward Face of Religion' in R. de Molen (ed.), *Leaders of the Reformation* (1985) and A. Foster, 'Church Policies in the 1630s', in R. Cust and A. Hughes (eds.), *Conflict in Early Stuart England* (1987) are the best modern introductions. See also below, chs. 2–7.

Within fifteen years of coming to the throne, Charles had alienated the great majority of his subjects. There was no large or powerful class or interest group which had benefited from his rule and which he could call upon to support him when resistance began.

Instead, the years 1640–2 saw a sudden and dramatic collapse of royal power. Once Charles had blundered away his initiative, he became a petulant spectator as his critics fell out among themselves. Most of the secular grievances were remedied by agreement within the Parliament, but fatal splits appeared over the remedies to Charles's religious changes. The Houses divided into two groups. On the one side stood those who wished to restore the pattern of church government and worship that had evolved during the reigns of Elizabeth and James I (the true reformed Protestant religion by law established without any connivance of popery or innovation, as they put it). On the other side stood those who believed that a church so easily subverted by English popery as the Laudian Church had been was an intrinsically unsound church. The latter persuaded themselves that the opportunity now existed to introduce a pattern of church government and discipline more closely modelled on the scriptures and on the example of the best reformed Churches – which to some of them meant the strict Calvinist Churches of Scotland and Geneva and to others the example of the English Puritan diaspora in the Netherlands and New England.[27] The paralysis of government at the centre led to a collapse of social order in London and, more spasmodically, in the provinces.[28] For some this indicated the urgency of creating a reformed church and state that would provide an efficient paternalism to dissolve social and economic ills; for others this indicated the imminence of anarchy and the need rapidly to back away from confrontation and to rally to the *natural* focus of obedience, the king. We must never forget that while there was a widespread and sophisticated notion of tyranny, and a fear of it, there was an equally widespread if less sophisticated notion of anarchy, and a greater fear and hatred of it.[29] There was no easy recourse to violence in 1642.

VI

My own sense is that there was no great militancy about the constitutional demands of the parliamentary activists in 1642. The

27. Fletcher, *Outbreak*, chs. 3, 6, 8; W. Hunt, *The Puritan Moment* (1982), chs. 10–11.
28. For accounts of these disturbances, see B. Manning, *The English People and the English Revolution* (1976), pp. 163–227.
29. E.g. W. Lamont, *Richard Baxter and the Millenium* (1979), ch. 2. Below, ch. 3, pp. 49–52.

reforms of the first eighteen months of the Long Parliament had certainly reduced the king's capacity for arbitrary government. But those reforms had been achieved by constitutional means and they had not, by and large, divided the king's future friends from his future enemies. Obviously there was populist agitation in 1641 – organized crowds used to intimidate the House of Lords into passing the Attainder of Strafford, for example; but the extraordinary thing about the constitutional deadlock of 1642 was that it concerned issues not of parliamentary sovereignty, still less of popular liberties; it was concerned with the restoration of the ancient peerage to its dominant role around the Crown. At one level, the civil war began as an aristocratic coup.

Parliament's war aims are set forth in two documents: the Militia Ordinance and the Nineteen Propositions.[30] The Militia Ordinance certainly appropriates to the two Houses the right to nominate Lords Lieutenant, but it merely names the men who were to control local defence forces throughout England. In almost every case the Lords Lieutenant were to be peers of the realm. Those newly created included twice as many men whose family gained their titles before 1559 as there were in the group they replaced. Almost no men whose titles had been created since 1603 were appointed.[31] It was these men, not the two Houses, who were to nominate the deputy lieutenants, and together they were given greater freedom and responsibility for the training and deployment of the militia than had existed before 1640.

The Nineteen Propositions laid out the terms designed to ensure that Charles could not escape from the framework of limitations he had accepted in 1641. The Propositions claimed for the two Houses the right to veto all royal appointments to the Privy Council and to senior offices of state and in the Household; they made councillors accountable to Parliament for the advice they gave; they allowed the Houses the right to vet those appointed to educate the king's children; they strengthened the laws against Roman Catholics; and they sought to commit the king to accept whatever reform of the Church was proposed by an assembly of Puritan ministers and laymen to be established by the Houses. No attempt was made

30. Readily (but, as we will see, in some ways unhelpfully) to be found in Gardiner, *Constitutional Documents*, pp. 245–7, 249–54.
31. For the royal appointees, see J.L. Sainty, *Lords Lieutenant of English Counties, 1559–1642* (List and Index Society, 1970). For the appointments made in the Militia Ordinance (but not included in modern editions), see *Lords Journal (LJ)*, IV, 587.

to formalize Parliament's role in the administration of the country, to make permanent that range of duties which the Houses had assumed on an *ad hoc* basis during and since the crisis of 1641 – supervising the levying and disbursing of taxes, direct involvement in the negotiation of treaties and alliances – or to institutionalize the standing committee of estates between sessions as practised in 1641 and urged upon them by the Scots.[32] Even the claim to vet royal appointments to high office – usually seen as an attempt to enhance a 'parliamentary constitution' – was really little more than the lever by which an aristocratic coup could be completed. These proposals were not designed disingenuously, in a void. Those who proposed them knew just who they wished to see placed in each of the major offices. It is noteworthy that those offices named were dominated by those traditionally held by the peerage. The reformed Council with a new maximum membership would be dominated by those officeholders. And the list contains one major oddity – the restoration of the ancient office of Constable, an office effectively defunct since 1521, and one with a unique history. According to medieval claims, the Constable had the authority to arrest the king if he violated his coronation oath and to bring him before his Parliament.[33] It evokes the Ordinances of 1311 and the *Modus Tenendi Parliamentum* (c. 1322) which sought to make wayward monarchs accountable to the Estates of the Realm and especially to the great officers. More generally it evokes a general late medieval tradition of 'representative Council'.[34] For 250 years before 1536, the advantages for and against a 'bureaucratic' as against a 'representative' council had been freely aired in discussions of the nature of English government. Some felt that efficient and active government depended upon the king's ability to select his advisers from among his peerage and Household; others held that that king was best advised who received his counsel from representatives of the Estates of the Realm. Thus he would readily discover the limits of his enforceable will. Numerous schemes were propounded (as by such loyal Crown servants as Sir John Fortescue,

---

32. For some of these developments, see D.H. Pennington, 'The Making of War', in D.H. Pennington and K.V. Thomas (eds.), *Puritans and Revolutionaries* (1979).
33. K.M. Sharpe, *Sir Robert Cotton* (1979); and *ex info* John Guy.
34. My approach to the Nineteen Propositions was stimulated by reading an early draft of J. Guy, 'Privy Council, Revolution or Evolution?' in D. Starkey and C. Coleman (eds.), *Revolution Reassessed* (1986) and to many stimulating conversations with John Guy. Since this was written, John Adamson has independently developed a similar thesis. See his 'The Baronial Context of the English Civil War', *TRHS*, 40 (1990).

Christopher St German, Thomas Starkey) for the selection of such 'representative councillors'. Henry VIII's reorganization in 1536–40 settled the question for a century. But faced by an incompetent king who chose bad counsellors and went beyond even their advice, it is not surprising to find the alternative tradition being re-examined during the crisis of 1641–2.

I do not think the civil war was essentially a baronial revolt. There was no great debate on the issues contained in the Nineteen Propositions. The armies were not recruited in 1642 to the cry of 'support your local baron'. But for one crucial group of men, the ancient peerage, this was a very live issue; and it is unlikely that Charles himself failed to see the significance of what was being demanded. Certainly while first-generation peers were fairly solidly for Charles in 1642, the pre-Elizabethan peerage were, by a clear majority, for Parliament and the Nineteen Propositions. And not many of them were hard-core Puritans.

When civil war broke out, the senior positions within the parliamentarian army were given mainly to peers. At the battle of Edgehill, the first battle of the civil war, more than half the colonels of both cavalry and infantry regiments were peers or sons of peers (on the royalist side the figure was less than one third; and none of those royalist peers were pre-Stuart creations). As Parliament created its regional armies during the winter of 1642–3 most of the commands went to peers.[35]

The English civil war was politically a war between a king who – imitating his fellow-monarchs throughout Europe – was striving to enhance royal authority, who was an innovative, dynamic king; and a parliamentarian movement that was *reactive,* putting its faith in traditions of noble paternalism. Although the Houses received much popular support, where this was not religious in character (see below), it too was conservative. The Nineteen Propositions evoked neither criticism nor enthusiastic endorsement from supporters in the provinces. Petitions from the provinces in the six months before war broke out almost without exception called for a negotiated settlement.[36] Insofar as there was a 'political' programme in the provinces, it aimed to settle for the reforms of 1641 (which had themselves been designed to restabilize the constitution). Furthermore

---

35. P. Young, *Edgehill, 1642* (1967), pp. 62–70; C.H. Firth and R.S. Rait, *Acts and Ordinances of the Interregnum* (3 vols. 1911), I, *passim.*
36. Fletcher, *Outbreak,* chs. 5, 6, 8.

(although this is a statement with which many historians would disagree), what evidence we have generally supports the view that popular political attitudes expressed confidence in the existing social and political order. Theirs was a protest against the way in which those around the king had abused their trust. Men fought to free themselves from bad governors, not from a bad system of government.[37] There was no popular demand in 1642 for an extension of the franchise; or for the popular election of magistrates and juries, or for the redistribution of property. All of these demands were being made by 1649.

VII

Yet while the civil war was a *defensive* political operation, a defence of existing liberties against an arbitrary king, it was an *aggressive* religious operation, a challenge to the whole of the existing structure and practice.[38] The men who were most strenuous in raising troops for the defence of Parliament (I am thinking here of those in the provinces rather than those at Westminster) were those obsessed by a fear of 'popery' (the international Catholic conspiracy) and by the need to seize the opportunity to realize a more godly reformation (that is to create church structures and patterns of worship and discipline more wholeheartedly based on a Protestant understanding of the commands of the Bible). This meant the repeal of the Elizabethan statutes setting up the Church of England; the abolition of Bishops and the system of church courts which had survived from pre-Reformation days; the abolition of the Book of Common Prayer, which was full of ceremonies and prayers which were Catholic in origin; and a ban on the celebration of Jesus's birth (Christmas), and of his death and resurrection (the Easter Triduum) as of all Saints' Days and 'superstitious' observances (with a contrasting emphasis on a more solemn and austere observance of the Sabbath day [Sunday]). This 'puritan' drive was not common to all parliamentarians, but it was characteristic of most parliamentarian activists. It was also largely a preoccupation with removing one coercive, unitary national church and replacing it by another. Freedom of individual conscience, the key issue ten years later, was not a major issue in 1642. The Puritans

---

37. K. Lindley, *Fenland Riots in the English Revolution* (1981), pp. 138–9; B. Sharp, *In Contempt of All Authority* (1980), pp. 263–4 and n. 9; D. Underdown, *Revel, Riot and Rebellion* (1985), chs. 5–6; 'Order and Disorder in the English Revolution', below, ch. 18; but cf. Manning, *English People*, esp. chs. 6–7.
38. See below, especially ch. 3 and 4.

were so bound together by hatred of the existing Church that they failed to recognize the difficulties they were likely to encounter once they tried to agree on what to put in its place.[39]

In order to understand the militancy of puritanism in 1642, we have to understand men like the town clerk of Northampton, Robert Woodford, or the Warwick schoolmaster, Thomas Dugard, whose diaries have been dissected by John Fielding[40] and Ann Hughes.[41] We sense the build-up of tension, or internalized anger, among the godly in the years before 1642 – what I would call *the coiled spring effect*. Unless we grasp the bitterness of those years, of the sense that the Protestant cause and therefore God was being betrayed, then the release of pent-up energy in the early 1640s cannot be understood. I am currently undertaking studies of a series of such men, ranging from the leading Cheshire magistrate Sir William Brereton to an obscure Suffolk yeoman-farmer, William Dowsing.[42]

Brereton was probably the most active of all the Cheshire justices in the 1630s. He certainly disliked much that Charles I did in the period 1625–41, but he stayed in office, paid his taxes, and complained quietly and privately. In 1640–2, he went along with all the secular reforms without ever taking a lead in them. Meanwhile, he had been rethinking his attitude to the Established Church. Trips to Holland and Scotland persuaded him that the gospel could be preached more purely and was being lived out more exactly in Churches less compromised in their government and liturgy than was the Church of England. When he was returned to the Long Parliament, he became a tireless critic of the Laudian regime and of episcopacy, and he gathered round him in his home county enough like-minded men to be able, at the outbreak of war, to launch a small but effective army. The men who gathered that army were almost all men who had led the campaign against bishops and the Prayer Book in Cheshire in 1641.[43]

By contrast, William Dowsing was a humble East Anglian farmer who was to be appointed by the earl of Manchester to visit all the

---

39. For a guide to my subsequent thinking about the spiritual diaspora of puritanism in the 1640s see my 'The Impact on Puritanism' in J.S. Morrill (ed.), *The Impact of the English Civil War* (1991), pp. 50–66.
40. John Fielding, 'Puritan opposition to Charles I: the diary of Robert Woodford, 1637–1641', *HJ*, 31 (1988), 769–88.
41. Ann Hughes, 'Thomas Dugard and his circle: a puritan-parliamentarian connection', *HJ*, 29 (1986), 771–94.
42. For a third case study, see below, ch. 6.
43. J.S. Morrill, *Cheshire, 1630–1660* (1974), ch. 2; as revised by J.S. Morrill, 'Sir William Brereton and England's "Wars of Religion"', *Jnl. Brit. Studs.* 24 (1985).

churches in Cambridgeshire and Suffolk to remove all 'monuments of idolatry and superstition' (medieval carvings in wood and stone, stained glass windows, altar rails etc.). The register which he kept of his activities reveals a man at once methodical and fanatical, with a burning hatred of idolatry and a belief that God would punish the English until such time as all the churches in the land had been cleansed. He was also a man who month-by-month bought the printed versions of the sermons preached to the two Houses at their monthly Fast Days, and filled the margins with his own glosses as he watched with growing dismay the collapse of Puritan unity. It is clear that he pushed himself forward, driven by an inner conviction that the godly were being offered a once-for-all opportunity to set up gospel ordinances in England. Like Brereton and like Thomas Woodford, he no doubt hated himself for paying the hateful Ship Money. But he *had* paid it. It was the vision of Zion that spurred him on.[44]

Both Brereton and Dowsing were worried that this great period of transition could breed 'a liberty running to license' but both (in the early 1640s) felt that the risks were worth taking. What comes through the rhetoric of such men, and even more through the sermons of the preachers who thundered from their pulpits about the ways God was leading the English (His new Chosen People) towards a Promised Land just as He guided the People of Israel in the stories recounted in the Old Testament, was a genuine conviction that the civil war was a religious crusade to drive out old corruptions, and to establish new patterns of evangelism. In 1642, there was a self-confidence and energizing faith in religious renewal for which there is no secular equivalent.

VIII

The parliamentarians fought the English civil war not to abolish monarchy but to control it; not to weaken the power of existing elites but to institutionalize it; not to redistribute land and wealth, but to protect the rights of those in possession; not to destroy the right of the state to define religious truth and to impose moral standards, but to change what the state prescribed and imposed.

Yet by 1649 all this had changed: monarchy and House of Lords had been abolished; there was a campaign backed by powerful elements

---

44. Since writing this I have written up my researches on Dowsing: see 'William Dowsing, the Bureaucratic Puritan' in J.S. Morrill, P.S. Slack and D. Woolf, (eds.), *Public Men and Private Conscience in Seventeenth-Century England* (1993). For a further case study, see below, ch. 6.

among those who were running the state for a radical democratization of legislature, executive and judiciary; attacks on primogeniture and other key aspects of property right; and perhaps most remarkably of all, a surrender by the state of the right to determine and impose on all citizens a uniformity of religious belief, observance and practice. In 1642, men had fought about which monopolies to impose on one another. From 1647 onwards, both in theory and practice, the state abandoned the attempt to make all men belong to the state church.

The English Revolution was not, in any simple or obvious sense, the completion of a process begun in 1642. It was more the product of the traumas of civil war.[45] In order to win the war, the two Houses had had to abandon their commitment to the very civil liberties which they had maintained that they were fighting to preserve: one in four adult males were mobilized in the war – one in ten at any given time during the campaigning seasons of 1643, 1644, 1645. The taxation necessary to pay and supply such armies was beyond the resources of the community: direct taxation alone was at ten times the level of parliamentary grants for the war years of the 1590s or 1620s. Yet on top of the 'assessments' (a quota tax modelled on the hated Ship Money assessments), Parliament imposed unprecedented internal duties ('excise') on basic commodities such as meat, beer and salt; quartered soldiers on civilian families without meeting the cost of board of lodging; and confiscated the estates of political opponents. Despite all this, the pay of its armies fell heavily into arrears. By 1647 the Houses faced a disillusioned civilian population and a discontented soldiery. In order to maximize its resources, Parliament also set up committees in every part of the country, and conferred upon those committees powers of arrest, imprisonment and distraint; they introduced conscription and martial law; and they used troops to assist committeemen which led to clashes between soldiers and civilians, especially with respect to the collection of the excise.[46]

45. R. Ashton, *The English Civil War, 1603–1649* (1978), chs. 7, 10; D. Hirst, *Authority and Conflict 1603–1658* (1985), chs. 8–9; Morrill, *Revolt*, ch. 3; chapters by Ashton, Morrill and Pennington in J.S. Morrill (ed.), *Reactions to the English Civil War* (1982).
46. Fully described in Morrill, *Revolt*, ch. 2. The most vivid evocation of wartime taxation, of its cost and yet its insufficiency, is to be found in C. Holmes, *The Eastern Association in the English Civil War* (1974), pp. 127–161. My thinking about excise has been transformed by the work of Mike Braddick, whose article, 'Popular Politics and Public Policy: the excise riot at Smithfield in February 1647 and its Aftermath', *HJ*, 34 (1991), is the harbinger of a book on *The Roots of the Tax State*, to be published in 1993.

During the civil war, ecclesiastical discipline collapsed. The Houses suspended and paralysed the old system of church government and proscribed many of its practices. In addition, one in four of all ministers were dismissed from their livings, sometimes by official commissioners, sometimes as a result of the intimidatory behaviour of zealous minorities of parishioners; and there was a similar combination of official and unofficial activity to destroy superstitious statues, stained glass windows and altars in parish churches. But the hoped-for 'purer' Protestant church was not introduced. When it came to agreeing on what should be introduced rather than what should be abolished, the Westminster Assembly of laymen and ministers set up to advise Parliament made painfully slow and bitterly contested progress, and godly laymen in Parliament itself set out to remove from all the Assembly's schemes any enhanced authority for the clergy. By the time that a scheme was approved in 1647, it was too late.[47] Religious anarchy prevailed. In many parishes, even in areas that had appeared heavily 'puritan' before the war, there was a strong reaction in favour of the old Church; in others the whole notion of a state church to which all must belong was rejected in favour of the notion of a 'gathered' church, an exclusive gathering of the 'godly' free from all external control by the state or centralized ecclesiastical authority. Many more men who would have preferred a state church found that they disliked the one on offer in 1647 so heartily that they came reluctantly to demand freedom for themselves outside that church. By the end of 1647, it was clear that a substantial minority in both Houses, and in the country at large, had no will to make the proposed national church work.[48]

As the landmarks of the political and religious order collapsed, more and more men came to yearn for a return to old certainties, while a hardening minority became more and more convinced that God was making all things malleable, that He was preparing England for yet greater changes. This led some to believe that they were about to witness the fulfilment of those biblical prophecies about God bringing the world of flesh and blood to an end, and inaugurating a 1,000-year personal reign of Christ which would culminate in the Day of Judgement. Others came to believe that just as God was willing the overthrow of the political and religious order, so He was guiding

---

47. The story is told in two works: Robert Paul, *The Assembly of the Lord* (1985), and G. Yule, *Puritans in Politics* (1981).
48. See below, ch. 7; also the introduction to J. MacGregor and B. Reay (eds.), *Radical Religion in the English Revolution* (1982).

them to challenge the inequities and oppressions of the social order.[49] Campaigns (mainly peaceful and impractical) were launched for the abolition of the rights of primogeniture, for granting security of tenure to tenant farmers, for the return to common use of the ancient common lands which had been enclosed over the previous century by landlords and larger farmers, and for strengthening the position of independent small producers and craftsmen at the expense of entrepreneurs and proto-capitalist merchants. Underpinning such demands for social reform was a radical extension of notions of social contract. The leaders of the Levellers argued that rulers were not appointed by God (as Charles I had argued) nor in agreement between king and people (as many Parliamentarians had argued) but in an agreement among the people themselves. The Levellers asserted that abuses of power by all existing institutions (the standing Parliament as well as the king) invalidated their right to govern. What was needed was a new social contract – what they called (in a very literal sense) the Agreement of the People – by which all who wished to enjoy political rights opted into an agreement by which limited powers to maintain order would be accorded to *elected* governors. The mechanism of selection (the extent of democracy) was less important than the end – the accountability of all who exercised authority, the rigidly fixed and non-renewable terms of office which would prevent the concentration of power in particular hands, a hatred of 'professionals' in government (e.g. lawyers and judges who claimed to be able to mediate justice through their mastery of arcane legal language and procedures).[50]

Yet we must not exaggerate the numerical strength of the Levellers and their supporters, nor their ability to shape events. Indeed, it may well be that their significance lies more in the fears they generated within the ruling elites than in their direct contribution to the shaping of events.[51] And we should not forget that what they represent is one aspect of the freeing up of the human mind. As the most fixed and daunting structures of the external world – monarchy, Lords, Church – crumbled, so the internal pillars of thought crumbled. Men were freed to think hitherto unthinkable thoughts.

49. The best introductions to the thought of the Levellers are G.E. Aylmer, *The Levellers in the English Revolution* (1975); J. Frank, *The Levellers* (1944); and Manning, *English People*, ch. 10. For Gerrard Winstanley see Christopher Hill, *Gerrard Winstanley, 'The Law of Freedom' and Other Writings* (1968), which should be read in the light of J.C. Davis, *Utopia and the Ideal Society* (1981), pp. 169–204.
50. The classic on these themes remains M. James, *Social Problems and Policy during the Puritan Revolution* (1940). My views are now more fully explored in 'The Impact on Society' in J.S. Morrill, (ed.), *The Consequences of the English Revolution* (1992).
51. See below, ch. 18, pp. 385–8.

Before we bring all this to bear on the question of the Regicide, two other factors need to be mentioned. The first is the intensification of the British problem in the later 1640s. The Scots had been a strong military presence in Ireland, alongside English troops, some loyal to Charles I and others to Parliament, Anglo-Irish troops, some loyal to Charles I and others to Parliament, and the armies of the Irish Confederacy, loyal to the Pope and the *patria*. Almost every group fought every other group at some stage. Meanwhile, after initially staying out of the war in England, the Scots had agreed to send 20,000 men south in the autumn and winter of 1643 in exchange for an English commitment to create a federal political structure in Britain and a common system of church government and worship throughout the British Isles. The Parliamentarians were united on the need for Scottish support in 1643, but many disliked the price exacted by the Scots and by 1647 many were prepared to disown it. In the winter of 1646–7, as the Scots army returned home, the parliamentary executive planned a reconquest of Ireland by an exclusively English army, they were busy sabotaging the Presbyterian system and dismantling the confessional state, and they were stalling on all moves towards a federal Britain. The consequence was a collapse of Covenanter power in Scotland and the return of a coalition headed by of disaffected pro-royalist peers. The second civil war combined a series of regional revolts by those in England who were sickened by the costs of war – a revolt of the provinces indeed – with an invasion by non-Covenanted Scots. Meanwhile the king's representative in Ireland, the marquis of Ormonde, was able to make common cause with the hitherto pro-Parliamentarian Lord President of Munster, Lord Inchiquin. The likelihood of an Irish invasion of England grew throughout the year.[52]

The final part of the jigsaw was Charles himself. Militarily crushed in 1646, he refuse to negotiate seriously. He appeared indifferent to everything except the prospect of waiting for his opponents to fall out among themselves so that he could launch a counter-coup.

In 1648, all the pieces came together.[53] The king allied himself to

---

52. *New History of Ireland*, vol. III, *1534–1691* (1981); D. Stevenson, *Revolution and Counter-Revolution in Scotland, 1644–1651* (1977); D. Stevenson, *Scottish Covenanters and Irish Confederates* (1981). The papers calendared in H.M.C. Egmont, I, pp. 287–485 are especially important, and deserve to be more fully used.
53. Robert Ashton has a study of the second civil war in preparation. Meanwhile see his *English Civil War*, ch. 10; J.P. Kenyon, *The Civil Wars in England* (1988), ch. 9; and B. Lyndon, 'The South and the Coming of the Second Civil War', *History* (1986).

the powerful sections of the Scottish nobility and he appealed to those Parliamentarians disillusioned with the administrative tyranny, the religious anarchy, and with the Houses' failure to rid themselves of an expensive and radicalized New Model Army.[54] Those who stood by Parliament and Army were a combination of pragmatists who saw no hope of avoiding the reimposition of all the tyrannies of the past but by further bloodshed, and a minority who saw the second civil war as even more of a crusade than the first. Many officers and soldiers were convinced that God was responsible for their victory in the first civil war: that it was, in a sense, a trial by battle in which both sides put themselves under the judgement of God. For such men, the king's decision to begin a new war was no less than sacrilege – an attempt to challenge God's decision. It left the way clear to his trial and execution. He had delegitimized himself and his office: he was a 'Man of Blood',[55] one who had so offended God that he had to be destroyed. Only by expressing a total revulsion against him could the English people continue to enjoy divine favour. After all the major engagements of the second civil war – after the sieges of Colchester and Pembroke, for example, or after the battle of Preston – the leading royalists were tried and executed. There was no parallel for this in the first war. The charge was treason, but the offence was sacrilege. If those who represented the king at those engagements needed to be called to account, how much more did the arch-royalist, the king himself, need to be called to account. His fate was sealed, in my judgement, from the time of the Army Prayer Meetings at Windsor in April 1648.[56] Only by accepting their role as the instrument of divine justice could the army leaders cause the English people to remain under divine favour.

---

54. On which see now, A. Woolrych, *Soldiers and Statesmen: The General Council of the Army in 1647 and its Debates* (1987); I. Gentles, *The New Model Army in England, Ireland and Scotland, 1645–1653* (1991), chs. 7–8.
55. See especially P. Crawford, '"Charles Stuart, That Man of Blood"', *Jnl. Brit. Stud.*, 16 (1977).
56. This is a controversial view, especially since the army leaders sent fresh negotiators to him even after Pride's Purge in early December. But it seems to me that the point of Denbigh's mission was to demonstrate that God had so hardened the king's heart that he would not see sense and negotiate seriously even in those extreme circumstances. The aim was to demonstrate to the many who still had not got the point that he was a man incapable of reason and being driven to destruction by his own folly.

IX

It is probable that no more than one in ten of all MPs and perhaps less than one in ten of all regional governors approved of the Regicide; but it was supported by a majority of army officers and it was they who effected the coup that led to the establishment of the High Court of Justice that put the king on trial and ordered his execution. Clearly a much larger proportion of the Parliamentarian movement endorsed what had happened after the event: the king could not be brought to life again. One had to live in a world in which regicide had taken place. Various *de factoist* arguments, which proceeded less from a defence of the legitimacy of the regime than from the stark fact of its existence and its ability to command obedience, led a proportion of all social groups to accept office. Many did so in order to dilute the power of religious radicals. They did not retrospectively approve the execution of the king: they sought to limit its consequences.[57]

I suspect that much of our confusion about the 1650s arises from our failure to distinguish support for the Regicide from support for republicanism. To endorse the execution of Charles I did not logically imply support for the abolition of monarchy; neither did support for kingless rule imply support for the Regicide. For example, Algernon Sidney, Henry Vane and the Leveller leaders appear to have deplored the public trial and execution of the king but to have embraced the political possibilities which it created.[58] One major problem is that while support for regicide was very much an either/or choice, support for republicanism covered a spectrum of possibilities. At the time, of course, the term for supporters of kingless rule was 'Commonwealthsmen' rather than 'Republicans'. 'Republicanism' generally refers to a location of sovereignty in the people rather than in a God-given ruler; and more specifically evoked the constitutions of ancient Rome between the end of the monarchy and the coming of the Emperors, or else the constitutions of Renaissance Venice or of the United Provinces of the northern Netherlands. The looser and more

---

57. D.E. Underdown, *Pride's Purge* (1970); A.B. Worden, *The Rump Parliament* (1974); J. Scott, *Algernon Sidney and the English Republic* (1988), ch. 5; A.B. Worden, 'The Politics of Marvell's Horatian Ode', *H J*, 27 (1984); Q. Skinner, 'Conquest and Settlement' in G.E. Aylmer (ed.), *The Interregnum: The Quest for Settlement* (1972).
58. A.B. Worden, 'Classical Republicanism in the Puritan Revolution' in H. Lloyd-Jones, V. Pearl and A.B. Worden (eds.), *History and Imagination* (1981). I am grateful to Sarah Barber, Glenn Burgess and Jonathan Scott for discussions of this subject.

common term 'Commonwealthsmen' has resonances in that tradition too, but more specifically in notions of government bound up with the 'common weal', a government committed to, even established by, the will of the community. Both are terms concerned with problems of accountability and with the preservation of natural rights, the location of sovereignty in the people at large, entrusted – directly or indirectly – to representative bodies. Such thinking did not preclude the appointment of a single person as chief magistrate; it might not rule out calling that single person 'king'. But it was predicated upon that the magistracy being, in meaningful ways, circumscribed in what he, she or it could do, and accountable in some way to the community at large.

Such general ideas frequently went along with an acceptance of the view that the particular arrangements in any state at any time were subject to evolution and change, but that a people who wished to avoid tyranny and to enjoy liberty would so establish patterns of government that usurpation of *their* rights would be difficult. Thus some men were convinced that, in England, monarchy had proved too dangerous and that the restraining bonds set up by successive generations too weak to hold a purposeful tyrant. Therefore the abolition of *Stuart* monarchy left all options open, including the creation of a new constitution which entrusted supreme administrative power to a single person who might not make law or control the judiciary and who would be accountable to others. Indeed as early as 1651 we have clear evidence that there was talk of making Cromwell king.[59]

Politically, then, the English Revolution saw a violent act carried out by a fairly isolated band of well-placed soldiers and civilians, mainly driven by religious fanaticism (the regicides) which gave rise to a political programme supported by a wider and more pragmatic group (the republicans). Both had the support of a minority of all social groups, but the crucial backing of the army. One is left with the feeling that for many, even of those groups, the English Revolution was based on the politics of regret: most of its supporters, even, were making the best of a bad job.

59. In addition to the long-known but doubtful testimony of Ludlow, Whitlocke and others (reviewed by C.H. Firth, 'Cromwell and the Crown', *Eng. Hist. Rvw.* (1902). But see the startling evidence recently unearthed by Leo Miller in the contemporary diaries of a German envoy who recorded conversations in September with leading politicians in which Cromwell was hailed as *unus instar in omnium, et in effectu rex* ('a man set above the rest, and in effect our King'). See L. Miller, *John Milton and the Oldenburg Safeguard* (1985), p. 49.

Furthermore, at the heart of the rhetoric of those who made the Revolution lay a profound contradiction. Much of the intellectual background to republican theory lay in the language of natural rights and of consent. Kings had to be destroyed or restrained because they had challenged the liberties and property of the people in their charge. Yet the one thing none of the constitutional experiments of the 1650s could claim was consent. Any form of free election or plebiscite at any point during the Interregnum would have resulted in a vote for a Restoration of the Stuarts. However much the social definition of the right to political participation had been broadened or narrowed, the result would have been the same. Yet those willing to support 'Commonwealth' government were too amorphous in their thinking to form the cadres of a successful vanguard state. A system built around the right of an enlightened minority (in Calvinist terms, the elect) to govern in the interests of the fleshy, unregenerate majority,[60] that mass of grossly sinful men and women who had not been redeemed by Christ's passion, could not be vigorously developed, because of the disappearance of all consensus among the godly as to who were the godly! Successive regimes, then, had a general theory but no ability to generate positive proposals for effective state-building.

Many – and perhaps it was most – of those who exercised power after 1649 saw the Revolution not as a beginning but as an end; not as the dawn of liberty, but as a desperate expedient to prevent the loss of traditional liberties, either to a vengeful king or to social visionaries such as the Levellers. The regimes of the 1650s were radical only in the circumstances that brought them into existence. In most other respects, there was a rush to restoration: a return to familiar forms of central and local government (the central courts, the revival of Exchequer control of revenue collection and audit; the consolidation of gentry power in the localities; the silencing of radical demands for land reform or greater commercial freedom; a renewed social paternalism).[61]

The social system experienced an earth tremor in the late 1640s, but then settled back on its foundations.[62] Furthermore, the political

60. The classic formulation is Cromwell's: 'government', he told Parliament in 1655, 'is for the people's good, not what pleases them' (W.C. Abbott, *Writings and Speeches of Oliver Cromwell* (4 vols. 1937–47), III, 583.
61. G. Aylmer, *The State's Servants* (1975), part I.
62. In England, but not in Ireland and Scotland where the 1650s did see a massive transfer of the social distribution of power, I would now want to say: see my essay, 'The Impact on Society', in J.S. Morrill, *Revolution and Restoration* (1992).

24

institutions were as conservative as anything that can be envisaged in the wake of regicide (the Nominated Assembly of July–December 1653 is an exception to this).[63]

X

Only in relation to religion can those in authority still be said to have some fire in their belly. Indeed, among the sects, the only coherent movements outside the army, it was those with specifically religious visions that thrived (Baptists and Quakers especially), while those whose religious ends led them to seek to control the state (e.g. the Levellers) dissolve before our eyes. Indeed it is striking that the 1650s sees no political sects or movements (or even milieux) except as aspects of essentially religious groups. Certainly the self-confidence of the 1640s largely disappears at all levels of the puritan movement. The preachers to Parliament in the 1650s had none of the elemental confidence of the preachers of the years 1640–5 that the old must be torn up root-and-branch to be replaced by a church whose blueprint God would make known in due time. Despite a fear of backsliding, a fear that men might lack the courage to follow the route God had chosen, they had no doubt as to the route and the destination. England was to be delivered from popery and superstition and brought to a new condition of peace, tranquillity and obedience to biblical precepts – in a very literal sense a repetition of the deliverance of the people of Israel from slavery and bondage as described in the Old Testament. By the early 1650s the tone of the preachers was hesitant and their advice muted: their appeal was for unity among the godly and for 'waiting upon the Lord' (that is, God's immediate purpose was no longer self-evident to them).[64]

This failure of nerve was the result both of the experience of internal disunity, the disintegration of puritanism as a dogmatic, ecclesiological and ethical system; and a recognition of failure on the ground. Ten years after the fall of the old religion, attachment to its practices, beliefs and 'superstitions' was proving remarkably resilient. In the chaos that followed the failure to implement an agreed 'godly' programme in the mid 1640s, a small minority walked out of their parish churches and set up in religious assemblies of their own; but far more (from all social groups) purposefully set out to recreate the practice of the old religion – forcing out the ministers put in during

63. A. Woolrych, *From Commonwealth to Protectorate* (1987).
64. M. Seymour, 'Pro-Government propaganda in Interregnum England', University of Cambridge PhD thesis (1987), pp. 26–52.

the civil war and restoring the ministers ejected for their anti-puritan or anti-Parliamentarian views, using the proscribed Anglican Prayer Books (especially for the sacraments and for the rites of passage), celebrating the banned festivals of Christmas and Easter, and so on.[65]

If puritanism did not attract the mass of converts that its adherents in the early 1640s had assumed that it would, it had also lost many of its activists along the way. Both of our earlier representative figures – Sir William Brereton and William Dowsing – abandoned active service of the Commonwealth: for them Christian liberty had turned to licence. They had fought to liberate the nation from ignorance and superstition, and to impose a godly discipline. Both welcomed greater freedom in forms of worship, but both found their spiritual energy sapped. Like men cast overboard in a storm at sea, their bodies succumbed to cold and they gave up struggling some time before death came to them.

Yet for many others, the disintegration of puritanism was a source of strength and opportunity, not of disillusionment. For them, religious freedom became *the* essential gain of the 1640s. At one extreme stood groups who rejected not only the right of the state to define religious truth, but also the authority of a professional caste of preaching ministers to interpret the scriptures and even the authority of the scriptures themselves. In its stead they placed the direct action of God entering and dwelling in the hearts of those who opened themselves to Him. A number of sects claiming a variety of revealed truths became established in this way, the most important being the Quakers.[66] Other groups looked to particular passages in scripture to predict the imminent Second Coming of Christ, the end of the world, the Day of Judgement on the living and the dead.[67] All such groups experienced intermittent or persistent persecution: Christian liberty was never extended by the state to those who rejected the scriptures and the creeds.[68] None of these groups had ambitions to set up particular constitutional forms, and they were all essentially politically anarchistic: even if some of them did dabble from time

65. See below, ch. 7; MacGregor and Reay, *Radical Religion* pp. 8–11; C. Cross, 'The Church in England 1646–1660' in Aylmer (ed.), *The Interregnum*, pp. 99–120.
66. MacGregor and Reay, *Radical Religion,* ch. 6; B. Reay, *The Quakers in the English Revolution* (1984). See also C. Hill, B. Reay and W. Lamont, *The World of the Muggletonians* (1983) and J.C. Davis, *Fear, Myth and History: The Ranters and the Historians* (1986).
67. E.g. B. Capp, *The Fifth Monarchy Men* (1972), chs. 6 and 8.
68. A.B. Worden, 'Cromwell and Toleration', in W. Sheils (ed.), *Studies in Church History* 21 (1984).

to time in insurrectionary politics, they were under no illusion that a Stuart Restoration would be much worse for them.

At the other extreme, sheltering under the wing of the Protectorate, was a more ambivalent group of intellectuals whom one historian has characterized as 'politiques'.[69] These were men who had supported Parliament in the wars but who had deplored the Regicide. Accepting that it had happened, they would work to mitigate its effects. We have already looked at their political preferences. In religion they were equally pragmatic: they deplored the violence and bigotry of Presbyterianism and of the sects, but they displayed 'a willingness to understand and to permit beliefs on premises very different from their own'. They were the heirs of the Erasmian spirit of religion – practical, rational, sceptical, tolerant. For them, the defeat of Laudianism and of Presbyterianism spelt an end to clericalism and the abandonment of dogmatic precision for the sake of moral precepts. In that sense they were as much precursors of the Enlightenment as heirs of the Humanists.[70]

But the principal proponents of religious liberty in the 1650s were neither the sects nor these early latitudinarians. They were men for whom paradoxically religious liberty was a means to a deeper unity. The supreme representative of this view, as he was the supreme examplar of all the ambiguities of the Revolution, was Oliver Cromwell.

Cromwell was a man who accepted that all existing political and religious institutions had been discredited by the civil wars.[71] All human institutions were 'dross and dung in comparison with Christ', he said.[72] He was not a man 'wedded and glued to forms of government.'[73] All human political, religious and legal institutions,

69. Worden, *Cromwell and Toleration,* p. 230.
70. A. Cromartie, 'Sir Matthew Hale', University of Cambridge PhD thesis (1991), part II, is a splendid case study.
71. For Cromwell, the literature is inexhaustible. For me, the classic biographies are those of C.H. Firth, *Oliver Cromwell and the Rule of the Puritans* (1900); R.S. Paul, *The Lord Protector* (1955) and C. Hill, *God's Englishman* (1970), together with three essential articles by Blair Worden: 'Cromwell and Toleration', loc. cit.; 'Oliver Cromwell and the sin of Achan', in D. Beales and G. Best (eds.), *History, Society and the Churches* (1985); and 'Providence and Politics in Cromwellian England', *Past and Present,* no. 109 (1985). There is a very important essay by Colin Davis, 'Cromwell's Religion' in J.S. Morrill (ed.), *Oliver Cromwell and the English Revolution* (1990). What follows would have been sharper if I had read that essay when I wrote these paragraphs.
72. Ed. T. Carlyle (rev. S.C. Lomas), *The Letters and Speeches of Oliver Cromwell* (3 vols., 1894) III, 373.
73. Carlyle/Lomas, *Cromwell,* III, 362.

because they were human, were subject to human frailty. There was no simple way to improve mankind by improving the institutions that disciplined its members. The civil war had destroyed a tyrannical king only to set up a tyrannical Parliament; it had destroyed one kind of priestcraft only to see another seek to take its place. Yet all was not lost. God was visible in the affairs of men. Everything was following His plan. He had 'winnowed'[74] the English people. He had marked out the instruments of His will. They belonged to no single church or sect. No man had been vouchsafed the whole of His plan. Many men had 'the root of the matter in them', a deep piety and religious energy that Cromwell believed he could identify in men as diverse as former bishops, Presbyterians, Congregationalists, Baptists and even in George Fox the Quaker. God's truth, 'in the several forms of it', lay divided among such men.[75] Only by creating a context within which such men could debate together, and witness in their way, could sinful man be brought to recognize the common ground, to perceive something close to God's whole plan for His new chosen people. Thus Cromwell was not wedded and glued to *forms* of government because he was wedded and glued to the *ends* of government, the gradual building up of a state and of a church through careful attention to what God was revealing in each and every one of His saints. Much of this was conventional providentialist Calvinism. What makes it remarkable was that Cromwell looked for the saints across all social and religious groups. Such pragmatism over forms, combined with a belief that anything was justified that he could convince himself was God's will as demonstrated through His saints, made his period as Lord Protector a destabilizing one. At what he took to be God's behest, he levied taxation without parliamentary consent, he imprisoned men without trial or cause shown and he generally undermined the confidence of the elite that they and their property were secured by the rule of law.

Cromwell believed that the Old Testament told of God offering choices to the people of Israel – a choice of obedience (which would see them enter into a land of milk and honey) or of disobedience (which would cause them to endure servitude in Egypt or Babylon). God offered similar choices to His new chosen people of England. It was this visionary teleology which made Cromwell a great revolutionary leader. There was a brutal and arbitrary side to his pursuit of this vision, but there was a noble side to it, too. The 'cruel necessity'

74. Carlyle/Lomas, *Cromwell,* II, 275.
75. Carlyle/Lomas, *Cromwell,* II, 538.

of regicide was to be the prelude to a great transformation of the moral and spiritual order.

Cromwell failed. His revolution had too narrow a social base, his religious vision sought to unite too diffuse a movement, while the political programme predicated by that religious vision was too disturbing to those conservative revolutionaries for whom regicide was a desperate act intended to safeguard ancient liberties. Once Cromwell was dead, the centripetal tendencies within the revolution intensified. The alienated majority clamoured for the restoration of the House of Stuart, and the fragile hold of the supporters of the republic collapsed. The Restoration brought back all the old structures in church and state. The political legacy of the Revolution was almost wholly negative – memories of it sending a shiver down the spine of elites for many generations to come. Malcontents among the elite would never again take the risks that the men of 1640–2 had taken.

The religious legacy was more complex. Both the authoritarian puritanism of the early 1640s and the visionary dreams of religious liberty as a stage towards a new kind of unity were largely abandoned. But that irenic, tolerant, sceptical spirit that we saw sheltering under the wing of the Protectorate survived and thrived. Despite some serious gestures in that direction, the Restoration did not witness any effective attempt to realize the authoritarian dreams of earlier kings and bishops. By the end of the century it was accepted – joyfully by some, sulkily by others – that, in an imperfect world, men and women should be left to make the most of their opportunities, and it was the task of the state to protect them in the free enjoyment of inherited and acquired goods and values. From the wreckage of England's religious wars, the liberal-democratic state was gradually to emerge.

PART ONE
England's Wars of Religion

CHAPTER TWO

Introduction: England's Wars of Religion[1]

I

Each of the three main sections of this book will begin with a short commentary on the works chosen for inclusion. I have tried hard to be straightforward in acknowledging how time has moved on, how I have continued to develop my own thinking and how I have continued to learn from others. As time passes, the best of any historian's ideas and the riper fruits of his or her researches get absorbed into the general understanding, leaving behind a chaff of eccentric and plain wrong ideas. Hence the hazard of collections such as these. In addition, the shape of many a piece of historical writing is partly determined by the targets it is aimed at. Years later, it is unclear to new readers why particular pieces of historical writing take the form they do. They seem, quixotically enough, to be tilting at windmills. The point is that the windmills were real enough when the essays were written, but they have become dilapidated and have collapsed between the time of original publication and the present.

II

The theme of the first section of the book is religion. Although one historian found it surprising and an 'irony worth savouring' that I and other 'revisionists' had in the 1980s 'rediscover[ed] the centrality of religion', I have in fact never had any doubt of it.[2] As I remind

---

1. This essay draws on material from the introductory paper I gave at a Conference I was asked to arrange at the Folger Institute for Early Modern Political Thought in March 1990. The theme of the conference was 'England's Wars of Religion'. And it benefits from pondering the commentaries on that theme given at the conference by Peter Lake, Johann Sommerville and others.
2. G. Eley and W. Hunt (eds), *Reviving the English Revolution* (1988), pp. 4, 9; and for my response, below, pp. 274–6.

readers below, even when I was analyzing the way a national struggle was being diffracted into a series of unique patterns in each region, I had no doubt that the beam of light entering the prism was essentially religious in character.[3] In the 1970s I was primarily concerned to explain the complexity of individual choices in, through, and after the civil wars; and I wanted to draw attention to the way anti-war sentiment and a politics of regret were important constituents in the dynamics of change through the whole period. 'Neutralism' and the other myriad forms of panic, dismay, anger against the war were not inert, passive forces which played no part in the struggles for power between king and Parliamentarians or within the 'victorious' Parliamentarian movement. By 1981, it was clear to me that I had said all I wanted to say about 'neutralism' and 'localism'. And I began to analyse more closely what it was that overcame the natural reluctance of the political elite to confront an overwhelmingly unpopular king.

I was working on a book, now laid aside, which I was having problems with. The book was to be a general survey of the period 1637–62. By 1983 I envisaged it as a book in four sections of four chapters each, the sections covering the periods 1637–42, 1642–9, 1649–58 and 1658–62. Each section would have a narrative chapter and parallel chapters on social, political and religious developments. The more I worked on the first two sections of that book, the more I became convinced of two things. The first was that there was a difference between the role of religious ideas and the role of secular-constitutional ideas in the dynamics of the crisis; and the second was the need to set the crisis in England much more into a *British* and into a European context. In 1983, I made a decision to call the book *England's Wars of Religion*, and I trailered that title in the peroration to a paper to the Royal Historical Society (below, ch. 3). It is a decision I have sometimes regretted because it was not as thought out as it might have been and it has helped to create some misunderstandings of my position.

I can now see that the deployment of the term 'England's Wars of Religion' was a quintessentially revisionist statement. By locating the mid seventeenth-century crisis in an early modern context away from what I took to be misleading and unhelpful comparisons with modern revolutions from 1789 on, I was seeking to reject a fundamentally anachronistic approach to the seventeenth century, one designed to render the event explicable by assimilating it to a category

3. See below, pp. 187–9.

familiar to modern experience and social theory. It represented and
represents what I still believe to be a salutary reaction against
various forms of modernization theory. It was an essential part
of the revisionist claim for the particularity of past experience, and
for the gulf between our mental world and that of the seventeenth
century. Thus I was consciously seeking to assimilate the events
in seventeenth-century England to a class of events which belong
distinctively to the period under study and not to the social and
secular divisions alleged to underlie most modern revolutions.[4] And
yet, paradoxically, one aim was to enhance the claims of the 1640s and
1650s to be a great turning-point by suggesting that the overthrow
of monarchy, House of Lords and confessional state constituted a
fundamental transformation which – even without the social transformation sought by the model-builders and even given the reversals
of 1660 – changed political consciousness.[5] As I put it recently, the
present may not have been determined by these events, but it tastes
of them.[6]

I had another reason for calling the crisis *England's* wars of religion:
I wanted to leave the way clear to see them as England's wars with
Scotland and Ireland as well as within itself. Can anyone deny that
the Anglo-Scottish wars of 1639–51 and the Anglo-Irish wars of
1641–64 were wars of religion in a purer sense than the English
civil war? Thus the Scottish National Covenant was a religious
document in form and content, and neither it, nor the supporting
documents, represent a Scottish Grand Remonstrance. The Scots
were preoccupied from 1641 onwards with a redefinition of the
Union of the Kingdoms and the creation of a federal union; and
that preoccupation was overwhelmingly the result of a need to
protect the Kirk from further anglicization. As Robert Baillie put
it in 1644 following the Solemn League and Covenant, the English
had wanted a civil league and the Scots a religious union.[7] Can

---

4. I am grateful to Peter Lake for discussions which sorted out my thinking on this.
5. This discussion raises the question of why I have given this book this title. My
motives are mixed. I decided against calling it *England's Wars of Religion* because
it would have confused those expecting my systematic account of the period
1637–62 long promised under that title, but now mothballed; I needed a title
that would indicate the sort of book it was; and I hope that the contents of
the book will sufficiently indicate what sort of transformation took place in
seventeenth-century England. Whether the nature of those changes makes the
term 'revolution' appropriate can then be decided by each reader!
6. Article in *The Times Saturday Review*, 4 Apr. 1992, marking the 350th anniversary
of the outbreak of the English Civil War.
7. D. Laing (ed.), *The Letters and Journals of Robert Baillie* (3 vols., Edinburgh,
1841–2), II, 90.

anyone doubt that the Irish rebellion of 1641 resulted from Irish Catholic fears for the freedom to practise their religion and of civil persecution as a result of their religious commitments? The events of the 1640s turned Ireland into a seventeenth-century Lebanon, but with a fundamentally Protestant/Catholic alignment which most sixteenth-century Europeans would have had no difficulty in recognizing.

Having located the crisis in an early modern context, I hoped the term England's Wars of Religion would also distance it from the General Crisis context.[8] Most European states were convulsed in the 1640s by a collapse of (or at least challenge to) central authority generated by the formidable efforts of the state to appropriate revenues and resources to maintain total war and the consequent bureaucratization and challenge to particularisms. I wanted to suggest that Charles I's failures in the 1620s and 1630s were simply not part of that experience. Rather, what England suffered in the 1640s was its delayed, or deferred, wars of religion. They had been delayed, or deferred, in England because of Elizabeth's success (against the odds) in establishing a hybrid church – sufficiently traditional in government and discipline, sufficiently reformed in belief, sufficiently confused in its liturgies – to bamboozle the overwhelming majority into accepting it as offering something to them. And it had been delayed, or deferred, because of the successful bribing of a high proportion of the elite with church lands, because of the integration of the elite into the structures of power by the transformations of government, and an institutional suppleness that accommodated the social redistribution of power that took place in the sixteenth century. James I had proved just as successful as Elizabeth in holding the religious centre together; but after that all the other Stuart kings were to risk destabilizing their thrones by devious if not deviant religious policies. If the worst that could be said of James I by his puritan critics was that he was moving the Church of England too slowly in the right direction, then Charles I was all too generally seen as frogmarching it Romewards. Together with his abandonment of the political latitudinarianism essential to stable government, his reckless authoritarianism and his corruption of justice, England finally experienced its reformation crisis.

What this makes clear is that I never thought or claimed that the crisis of the 1640s was 'only' about religion. No scholar thinks

8. For this see T. Aston (ed.), *Crisis in Europe 1560–1660* (1965), and works therein cited.

that the European wars of religion were only about religion. The crises in Germany, France and the Netherlands concerned competing visions of state formation (especially the creation of effective national institutions) and the social distribution of power at a time of economic and demographic change; but many historians have concluded that religious poles are the ones around which most other discontents formed; that religious arguments dominated the debate on the choices people made; and that religious dynamism determined the stages through which the wars run.

I would still think there was virtue in these arguments, and in the term 'England's Wars of Religion'. But there are drawbacks too. The most obvious is that (except in Ireland) the poles in Britain in the 1640s were not straightforwardly Catholic/Protestant ones. In England and in Scotland the struggle was within Protestantism, although there is no reason to doubt that for the godly, there was a Popish Plot to subvert the Protestant identity of the Church of England as a prelude to the reclamation of Britain for Catholicism. Charles I was the dupe, and Laud at best the dupe and at worst the agent, of a Catholic conspiracy at the heart of government. The Laudian programme was believed to be one that dethroned the scriptures, restored idolatry and superstition, and recreated a dualism of church and state that had been rejected by the Tutors. But it is not quite the same thing.

More importantly, the term has proved unhelpful in several, untidily overlapping, respects. As far as I know, there are no historians nowadays who would deny that religion was *an* important cause of the civil war and an important dynamic within it. But many would suggest that the use of the term 'religion' itself is unhelpful. On the one hand religion is so interpenetrated into every aspect of early modern thought, that to say that it is the religious aspect of their thought that matters in making and shaping the conflict is a tautology. The opposite but not incompatible criticism is that there are few purely 'religious' disputes, and those that are essentially religious (such as disputes about Grace) are unimportant in causing civil war and causing people to take sides. For example, Johann Sommerville argued, with direct reference to the ecclesiastical disputes in the Long Parliament, that 'debate about such topics as ceremonies, the Prayer Book, the canons of 1640, and episcopacy, were by no means purely religious in nature'.[9] John Adamson has suggested that much of

9. J. Sommerville, unpublished paper at the Folger Institute Conference on England's Wars of Religion, March 1990.

the assault on episcopacy in the Long Parliament arose from a determination of the Junto of royal critics in the Lords to get the bishops out of the Lords in order to allow them to achieve a numerical ascendancy in the Upper House.[10] Finally, there is the commonly asserted claim that divisions on constitutional questions were themselves sufficiently marked to create the collapse of royal authority in the early 1640s.

Now I find all these unexceptionable statements. However often I have asserted the opposite, I am told that I created a monocausal explanation of the civil war, and that it is contrary of me to put religious causes on a pedestal. It is clear that I have consistently failed to make clear what it is I am claiming. What follows is, I would hope, borne out in the essays that follow.

The crisis in 1640 was a general crisis of confidence in the government of Charles I. Because the rebellion in Scotland had arisen from Charles's attempts to change how Scots worshipped God, religious issues were high on the agenda, but they are far from the only ones. Those – and they are many – who tried to work out what had gone wrong drew on many traditions of thought and discourses, and I have little argument with the way Johann Sommerville, for example, has characterized them in his *Politics and Ideology in England, 1603–1640* (note the terminal date). His book, together with the work of Richard Cust and Ann Hughes,[11] has done much to elucidate how those trained up in the common law, or simply with a decent grounding in the classics, would and could articulate their disquiet – and in many cases their anger – at the attempted suppression of Parliament, abuses of prerogative and the rule of law, heavy-handed centralism of Charles's rule. In so far as some revisionists, myself included, stressed too much the areas of political consensus in the early seventeenth century and played down the depth of feeling resulting from alternative accounts of the ancient constitution, this more recent work is to be valued. But how does it explain the crisis of 1642 as against the crisis of 1640? That within a highly sophisticated political culture such as that of early modern England there should be alternative and sharply distinguished political languages, different and sharply distinguished accounts of the origins and nature of royal power, different and sharply distinguished views

10. J.S.A. Adamson, 'Parliamentary Management, Men of Business and the House of Lords, 1640–1649', in C. Jones (ed.), *A Pillar of the Constitution: the House of Lords in British Politics, 1640–1784* (1989), pp. 24–9.

11. R. Cust and A. Hughes, *Conflict in Early Stuart England: Studies in Religion and Politics, 1603–1642* (1989), esp. chs. 1, 2 and 5.

of the limits of the subjects' obedience is hardly surprising. But it is not sufficient to show that there were such differences within the political culture. Cataloguing firmly held and angrily expressed differences of theory and the applications of those theories to the particular events of the period does *not* constitute an explanation of why there is a civil war. What we need is an explanation of under what circumstances those differences caused particular men to withhold their allegiance either to the king or to those who represent them in Parliament. When does the belief that injustice and misgovernment can be and must be remedied by actions sanctioned within a shared political culture (petitioning, lobbying through Court and Council, recourse to the courts, parliamentary action, passive disobedience) give way to a belief that violent resistance is possible and necessary? There is almost nothing in the work of Sommerville or Cust and Hughes that explains that transition. Labelling attempts at statutory control of royal powers, labelling the exercise of long-established legal rights to make the king demonstrate to the satisfaction of his judges that he had the right to do what he wished to do, or labelling a refusal to pay loans or, other prerogative charges as acts of 'opposition' turns them into explanations of the crisis of 1640. It does not turn them into causes of the civil war of 1642. What proved the solvent to resistance to resistance theory? What turned constitutional opposition to an unconstitutional taking up of arms? What made men throughout England in 1642 decide to *impose* terms upon the king by force, rather than using the leverage of parliamentary supply to get the best settlement the king would grant? It is those questions which underlie my concern with the *psychology* of protest – the belief that while many distrusted the king in 1642 and wanted further guarantees of his future conduct, it was principally those who *also* believed in the necessity of a second Reformation who determined to fight.

What the chapters that follow have in common, then, is a concern to chronicle the dynamism of religious language and argument in the years before the outbreak of the war and to compare that dynamism with the reticence and hesitancy of much legal and constitutional argument. I am concerned with the viciousness of the attack on the bishops and the Laudian clergy unmatched in the attacks on lay advisers of the king; the sheer scale and relentlessness of the complaints against the Church and the calls for a transformation of religious values that caused the middle ground in ecclesiastical matters to collapse while the search for the middle ground in secular politics continued – re-formation of the Church, restoration of the balanced constitution; the deafening silences of 1641–2 in precisely those concerns which would have unlocked secular arguments for taking up arms against a tyrannical ruler.

III

The essays in this section all substantiate the claims of this introductory essay. Chapter 3 ('The Religious Context of the English Civil War') establishes the case more fully. Readers might like to read it alongside chapter 15 ('Charles I, Tyranny and the English Civil War').[12] This latter develops the point about the reticence of the king's opponents in developing a secular-constitutionalist case for taking up arms against him in 1642. The closer the country came to civil war, the more reticent MPs became about sticking the label of tyrant on him. Many of those who remained at Westminster in 1642 were at least as much concerned by the security of their secular liberties and about the king's long-term commitment to honour the constitutional reforms of 1642 as they were by the religious issues. My point has always been that there was little constitutional militancy in 1642; that in sorting out those who went to war wringing their hands and looking for the earliest possible negotiated peace from those committed to settling the disputes by the necessary application of force, we need to look at religious militancy.

I hope readers will recognize that the article makes clear the range of dissatisfactions with the government and what I termed the three modes of opposition. Each had its own part to play in determining the sort of civil war England had. Localist perceptions helped to shape the form of the war; legal-constitutionalist perceptions determined the way many acted once a choice of sides was forced upon them. My point is simply that most men would not have had to make those choices if those for whom the conflict centred around religion had not brought the issues – secular and religious – to the point of conflict.

Chapters 4 ('The Attack on the Church of England in the Long Parliament') and 6 ('The Making of Oliver Cromwell') seek to analyse the nature and extent of religious militancy in the early 1640s. The latter is just one of a series of case studies I have been engaged in, three

---

12. The latter was first written immediately before I wrote the first draft of 'The Religious Context' (which appears here more or less as written), whereas the latter went through many revisions before reaching the form printed here in 1988.

of which are now in print.[13] I hope chapter 6 speaks for itself. Chapter 4 was written for a festschrift and against a very tight deadline. The result was that some clumsy thinking and poor use of evidence slipped through. The main problem is that I failed to note how little progress was made by the Houses on the great volume of religious business brought before them. Those imprisoned by Star Chamber and High Commission for religious offences in the 1630s were released quickly enough by the Houses, but after that their claims for compensation and calls for the punishment of their oppressors made much slower progress than I implied.[14] I greatly overstated the powers of summary jurisdiction assumed by the Commons;[15] and similarly failed to note the dilatoriness of the Committee for Scandalous Ministers under the chairmanship of John White.[16] I could and should have noted the failure of the Houses to make progress with respect to nullifying the canons of 1640[17] and I could and should have clarified exactly

13. 'Sir William Brereton and "England's Wars of Religion"', *Jour. Brit. Stud.*, 24 (1985), pp. 311–32; 'William Dowsing: the Bureaucratic Puritan' in J.S. Morrill, P. Slack and D. Woolf (eds.), *Public Men and Private Conscience in seventeenth-century England* (Oxford, 1993). In some ways the Brereton study would have been the most appropriate, but it contains more overlap of text and content with chapters 3 and 4 than the later study of Cromwell. Having completed studies of a greater gentleman, a 'mere' gentleman and a working farmer, I hope to add studies of a leading minister and a working lawyer.

14. For example, Burton, Bastwick, Prynne and Lilburne were still, individually or collectively, petitioning against their fines in the years 1644–6 *LJ*, VII, 21, 713; VIII, 18, 62, 286).

15. I say at p. 71, n. 11, that of the 800 petitions presented to the Commons, more than 100 had been reported back by September 1642 and later, p. 86, n. 80, state that this led to 70 losing their livings. This was based on a careless reading of a misleading heading to an appendix in W.A. Shaw, *A History of the English Church during the Civil Wars and under the Commonwealth* (2 vols., 1900) II, pp. 295–300, where I was taken in by the term 'dealt with by the Long Parliament', by which Shaw can have meant no more than 'petitions handled by'. I am deeply grateful to Dr Sheila Lambert for pointing out to me privately this and many of the other errors in this piece.

16. I should have noted that this pamphlet (Wing W. 1777) was not published until November 1643 and that the accuracy of its account is hard to assess and not self-evident.

17. The debate on the canons ran from 10 Nov. to 16 Dec. 1640 with many postponements, then a committee was set up to draw up votes for the House of Lords which dragged on until 2 March 1641, when the matter was dropped (*CJ*, II, 95). After several more false starts, it finally passed the Commons and was sent to the Lords on 7 June 1641 (*CJ*, II, 130, 147, 163). The Lords then sat on the proposals for over a year. The canons were never 'annulled' by the Commons.

what happened to the impeached bishops.[18] It is, then, a piece which needs to be read with great care. But I have decided to include it in this volume because, flawed though it is, I do not think that the main thrust of the argument is vitiated by the sloppiness at the edges. Against those who argue for the pressure for religious reform in 1641 and 1642 coming principally from Scotland, or from those whose main purpose was to get the bishops out of the Lords in order to secure their political control, and who see the petitioning campaigns as rigged and controlled from the centre,[19] I still present my body of evidence of widespread, spontaneous and venomous anger and I still present my case that many MPs – and specifically those who made the war happen – felt impelled by a spiritual imperative for which there was no constitutional parallel.

Chapter 5 ('The Scottish National Covenant of 1638 in its British Context') explores the relationship between the crisis in England and the crisis in Scotland in the reign of Charles I, taking the story down to the coronation of Charles II as King of Britain at Scone in January 1651. It represents my recognition of the importance of the *British* dimension of the English civil wars.[20] It is also the harbinger of a more general study I have in hand of the relationship of the English, Irish and Scottish Reformations from 1559 and 1689.

Chapter 7 represents a different aspect of the problem. In 'The Religious Context of the English Civil War' I suggested a symmetry between the forces driving individuals to choose between king and Parliament. There were as many reasons for being royalists as there were royalists, and many royalists may have put allegiance to the Established Church second. Brian Wormald's normative account of

18. I was in error to say (p. 81) that the bishops were impeached over the canons in December 1640; it was only in August 1641 (LJ, IV, 340); and little was done to make it stick until the separate impeachment of an overlapping group of bishops for their action in December 1641 in claiming that votes taken by the Lords during their absence caused by mob action were null and void.
19. For an outstanding account of the petitioning on episcopacy in 1641 and 1642, including a meticulous analysis of the signatories from individual parishes in Cheshire, see J.D. Maltby, 'Approaches to the study of Religious Conformity in Late Elizabethan and Early Stuart England: with special reference to Cheshire and the Diocese of Lincoln', University of Cambridge PhD thesis (1991), chapters 4–5.
20. See also below, chapter 13 ('The Causes of Britain's Civil Wars'). Chapter 5 was written before I had read Conrad Russell's major discussion of the British problem. Together with chapter 13 it indicates the convergence and divergence of our thinking. Conrad Russell is concerned with the British dimension of English history; I am moving towards a study of the English, Scottish and Irish dimensions of British history. See my 'A British Patriarchy? Ecclesiastical Imperialism under the early Stuarts', forthcoming 1993 or 1994, in a festschrift.

Edward Hyde, for example, sees constitutionalist concerns as taking precedence over religious ones in determining his behaviour in 1642.[21] But then Hyde was one of those who knew by the spring of 1642 which side he would be on if it came to blows, and who strained every muscle to prevent a descent to arms. The best I could say is that those at Westminster who were precocious in identifying a threat to episcopacy, and in deploring that threat, and those who can be identified as the organizers of petitions for and on behalf of bishops and the Prayer Book in 1641 and 1642, are amongst the earliest and most active organizers of armed royalism in 1642. Just as John Adamson has presented a cogent argument for seeing a baronial conspiracy and a baronial preoccupation with the seizure of power around the Crown as being part of what mobilized the Parliamentarian movement in 1642,[22] so it has become clear to me that in the course of the 1640s personal loyalty to the king and a deep anger at and fear of Parliamentarian populism drove many to arms for the king in 1642. While I would still argue for a spiritual imperative impelling most of those who made others make intolerable choices for Parliament in 1642, I would no longer claim that things were so straightforward on the royalist side. Meanwhile chapter 7 demonstrates the extent to which the forms of the worship, the kalendar and the sacramental practice of the Elizabethan and Jacobean Church had sunk roots in English culture such that the attack on it in the 1640s was fiercely and widely resisted. When the godly tried to reform the Reformation, they found not a sea of indifference but a bed-rock of affection for the established order which they confronted counter-productively. I think some of my reliance on churchwardens' accounts was rather unsophisticated,[23] but in the last decade I have come across a vast amount of additional evidence in court records which strongly supports the basic thesis of a Prayer Book rebellion in the period between the end of the civil war and the execution of the king.

This section represents then, a view of the 1640s which restates the centrality of religion in destabilizing Britain, in which it was religious arguments which proved to be the solvents of resistance to resistance theory. I have not suggested that most people determined their choice about which side to support on religious grounds. I have

---

21. B.H.G. Wormald, *Clarendon* (1951), part I.
22. J.S.A. Adamson, 'The Baronial Context of the English Civil War', *TRHS*, 40 (1990), 95–120.
23. See now J. Craig, 'The Use of Churchwardens and Parish Accounts: a Suffolk Study', forthcoming.

suggested that they were driven to make those choices by men driven by religious imperatives. The civil war was fought to restrain an untrustworthy king and to release the forces of reformation. But what made men throughout England who wished to impose further constraints upon Charles I in addition to those which he had accepted in 1641 (to the rapture of most future royalists as well as most future Parliamentarians) also wish to impose those constraints *by force*? Was it not that such men had – in addition – a fire in their belly that made them see religion not simply as an academic squabble about dogma, ritual and about how the primitive Church was governed, but as about how people related to one another, about how the ideal Christian community was to be constructed, and about how, under the Providence of God, it could be and *must* be constructed?

CHAPTER THREE
The Religious Context of the English Civil War

Lengthy reports survive of speeches by several members of the Long Parliament for 9 November 1640, at the end of the first week of the session. The future royalist militant, George Lord Digby, is reported to have begun his address by saying that:

> you have received now a solemn account from most of the shires of England of the several Grievances and Oppressions they sustain, and nothing as yet from Dorsetshire: Sir I would not have you think that I serve for a Land of Goshen, and that we live there in sunshine, whilst darkness and plagues overspread the rest of the land . . .[1]

The future royalist moderate Sir John Culpepper is reported to have begun: 'I stand not up with a Petition in my hand, I have it in my mouth', and he enumerated the grievances of his shire beginning with 'the great increase of papists' and the 'obtruding and countenancing of divers new ceremonies in matters of religion'.[2] The future Parliamentarian moderate, Harbottle Grimston, said that 'these petitions which have been read, they are all remonstrances of the general and universal grievances and distempers that are now in the state and Government of the Church and Commonwealth'.[3] The future Parliamentarian radical Sir John Wray said:

> All in this renowned senate, I am confident, is fully fixed upon the true Reformation of all Disorders and Innovations in Church or Religion, and upon the well uniting and close rejoining of the poor dislocated Great Britain. For, let me tell you Mr Speaker, that God be thanked, it is but out of joint and may be well set by the skilful chyrurgeons of this Honourable House.[4]

1. J. Rushworth, *Historical Collections* (7 vols., 1659–1701), IV, 30.
2. Ibid., IV, 33.
3. Ibid., IV, 34.
4. Ibid., IV, 40.

In November 1640 there was apparent unity of purpose amongst the members of the Long Parliament. Fortified by petitions signed by their county establishments at Michaelmas Quarter Sessions or at the county court on election day, they arrived determined to take the once-for-all opportunity which had presented itself to set things right. For this Parliament met in unique circumstances. The military defeat of the king by his Scottish subjects and the latter's occupation of north-east England guaranteed that this would be no addled parliament as in the spring, for the Scots had made it clear that they would not go home without reparations voted by the English Parliament, a Parliament which could make that supply dependent upon the redress of grievance. There was no expectation of civil war, nor even of constitutional aggression. As Sheila Lambert says:

> the opening of the parliament following the traditional pattern: the earl of Essex carrying the cap of state in the opening procession. The proceedings of Parliament during the first few weeks were entirely in accordance with the precedents of the early Stuart Parliaments.[5]

But while the *form* of the Parliament was familiar enough, and while the expectation was that the remedy of grievance would follow established practice, the mood and context of the Parliament were unprecedented. This is most obviously seen in the contrast between the rhetoric and the agenda of the Long Parliament in its early weeks and those of the Short Parliament. When the latter had assembled, the king had retained the initiative, the freedom to dissolve them at will and resume the Personal Rule. He could reach an understanding with them and continue his war with Scotland, or he could make painful concessions to the Scots and be rid of Parliament, or he could be tempted to seek an understanding with Philip IV and the Pope and to resume both the Personal Rule and the Bishops' War. Conscious that the initiative lay with the king, both Houses set their sights low.[6] In the autumn, the king had lost effective freedom, and the managers of the Parliament set their sights high.

It is true that one crucial dimension to the history of the Long Parliament is the working out of factional rivalries and the struggle for office. But while this forms a necessary dimension of any rounded account of the collapse of royal authority, it does not offer a sufficient

5. S. Lambert, 'The Opening of the Long Parliament', *Hist. Jnl.*, 27 (1984), 265–88.
6. Existing impressions of the Short Parliament have been transformed by the availability of the very full parliamentary diary of Sir Thomas Aston. I am grateful to Judith Maltby for allowing me to see her full transcript of this very important diary prior to publication. It is the property of Mr Howard Talbot. It has now appeared as *The Short Parliament (1640) Diary of Sir Thomas Aston* (Camden Soc., 4th ser., vol. 35, 1988).

explanation – any more than it does of the parliamentary clashes of the 1620s.[7]

My argument will be that there was in 1640 an ideological crisis as well as a functional crisis. But I wish to argue that, however jumbled together they were in the hectic early days of the Long Parliament, there were three quite distinct and separable perceptions of misgovernment or modes of opposition – what will be called the *localist*, the *legal-constitutionalist*, and the *religious*. One man could hold two or three of them; but many did not do so. It was possible for an individual to see links between royal secular and religious misgovernment, but not necessary or usual for him to do so. Too often in the past we have assumed that those who opposed most vigorously the Caroline religious experiment would also be in the forefront of the protest against forced loans or ship money. There are notable examples of those who did oppose both (though the link is stronger in the case of the forced loans) and who saw a connection between them. But there were many more who were prominent in their protest against either fiscal feudalism or Laudianism and who risked their careers and their liberty in protesting against one of them, but who fell in with the other. Many notable puritans paid ship money without protest, and some were even effective ship money sheriffs; many notable protesters against secular misgovernment proved to be loyal defenders of the established church in 1641–2.

The argument of the paper will be that the localist and the legal-constitutionalist perceptions of misgovernment lacked the momentum, the passion, to bring about the kind of civil war which England experienced after 1642. It was the force of religion that drove minorities to fight, and forced majorities to make reluctant choices.

The localist perception of misgovernment need not detain us. Recent work drawing attention to localism has much to teach us about the nature of the civil war, but little to tell us about why civil war broke out.[8] It will probably be widely accepted that the decline of other *loci* of political and social action – the baronial

7. E.g. B.S. Manning, 'The Aristocracy and the Downfall of Charles I', in *Politics, Religion and the English Civil War*, ed. B.S. Manning (Manchester, 1973), pp. 37–82; C. Roberts, 'The Earl of Bedford and the Coming of the English Revolution', *Jnl. Mod. Hist.*, 49 (1977); P. Christianson, 'The Peers, the People and Parliamentary Management in the First Six Months of the Long Parliament', *Jnl. Mod. Hist.*, 49 (1977); Lambert, 'Opening of Long Parliament'.
8. The recent critique by Clive Holmes, 'The County Community in Stuart Historiography', *Jnl. Brit. Stud.*, 19 (1980), 54–73 lists the main corpus of recent work. What follows is based on that corpus, bearing Holmes' strictures in mind.

household, the liberty and franchise etc – and the expansion of the duties and responsibilities of royal commissions of which the sphere of operations was the shire, and the development of distinctive and valued patterns of local government (unique administrative arrangements, customary procedures etc.) made the county a focus of loyalty and identity. The leading families in each county had a greater or lesser degree of attachment to their 'county community'. Not all gentry put the coats-of-arms of the families of their shire on or around the ceilings of their great halls, but many did so. It is not claimed that this made for a cosy world of purring, contented squires, enjoying one another's company and getting cross only when the Crown made demands on them. Quite the contrary. The social and political institutions of the county were arenas within which rivalries were worked out, disputes arbitrated, prestige and honour won and lost. Frequently the institutions of the county were respected or powerful enough to resolve such issues. But often they were not so, and appeals downward to the electorate or upward to the Court were necessary extensions of the system. It was precisely the ability to arbitrate between rival groups or individuals within particular counties and boroughs or between rival counties and boroughs which gave privy councillors or courtiers their chance to ensure that the price of their arbitration was obedience to the Crown's wishes.

There was a dual allegiance, and therefore alarm, anger, frustration when those dual allegiances were in conflict. This occurred with the collapse of the delicate patronage system in the 1620s, when powerful groups in many counties found that they had no friends at Court, or none able to help them against the power of Buckingham, and it also occurred with the intrusive drive for 'unity through uniformity' in the 1630s.[9] Local traditions and customs were challenged, local men set aside, more demanded and less conceded than hitherto. Some of Charles's fiscal expedients – ship money for example – exacerbated or resurrected jurisdictional disputes, led to charges of unfairness and arbitrariness of distribution. Some articulated their protest in legal and constitutional terms; many more saw it as a source of needless local disputes and conflict.[10] By 1640 there was a widespread

---

9. For a recent survey of work on Caroline 'patronage' and 'faction' see K. Sharpe, 'Faction at the Early Stuart Court', *History Today*, 33 (1983), 39–46. The last phrase is from Ivan Roots, 'The Central Government and the Local Community' in *The English Revolution 1600–1660*, ed. E.W. Ives (1968), p. 42.
10. J.S. Morrill *The Revolt of the Provinces* (1976), pp. 24–30, 144–50; Holmes, 'County Community', pp. 65–8.

demand for a return to the older forms of local self-determination. Such a mood can be found in the addresses brought up by MPs, or reaching them from their constituents in the early months of the Long Parliament.[11] This perception – a strongly held but ultimately mild perception of arbitrary government, of innovation and externally induced disruption – helps to explain the mood of the electorate in 1640 and of the pressure for reform in 1641. But it does not explain the pressure for war in 1642. Localism in the 1630s or in 1640 leads naturally into neutralism in 1642. Indeed Anthony Fletcher has argued that what has been taken as neutralism in 1642 is in fact an advanced form of localism, with leading magistrates and others seeking either to keep both sides out of their shire, or seeking to minimize the level of commitment to one side or the other for the preservation of the local peace.[12] That mentality which continued to see war as an unmitigated disaster, which could not decide between a loyalty to both king and parliament, is vital to an understanding of the *nature* of the war and of its outcome, but not to the explanation of its outbreak.

Derek Hirst and others have reminded us that there was more to the debates of the 1610s, 1620s and 1630s than a factional struggle for power and a dislike of centralizing tendencies imposed on the Crown by the need to finance itself.[13] There were major and deeply-held differences of opinion and belief about the nature and extent of the royal prerogative, about the accountability of the king's servants, and even (for some) about the origins and nature of kingly power. Such disagreements are natural in all sophisticated political cultures, and to identify such differences is not to identify the source of inevitable political collapse. Many of the issues were keenly felt, but everyone most of the time did accept that there were clear and unquestioned ways of expressing dissent: in and through parliament, in petitions of the king-in-council, *in extremis* by passive disobedience. What is remarkable about early Stuart England is the absence of political violence: virtually no treason trials, no rebellions, a decreasing and localized incidence of riot, no brigandage.[14] The English civil war certainly did not grow out of a gradual and inexorable collapse in the state's ability to compel obedience. Those who preached passive obedience to the Catholics in the late sixteenth and first decade of

11. E.g. Morrill, *Revolt*, pp. 147–52.
12. A. Fletcher, *The Outbreak of the English Civil War* (1981), pp. 369–406.
13. D. Hirst, 'Revisionism Revised: Early Stuart Parliamentary History – The Place of Principle', *Past & Present*, 92 (1981), is the most cogent of many recent critiques of the 'revisionist' approach.
14. See 'Order and Disorder in the English Revolution', below, ch. 18.

the seventeenth centuries could not, or at any rate did not, bring themselves to contemplate the right violently to resist wicked kings. This was in part because of the intellectual bonds in which they had wrapped themselves, but it was also in part because the area of constitutional dissent and alarm was still limited. What bound them together was far greater than what divided them. We must beware of two tendencies: to overlook the undebated common ground which united the political nation; and the habit of lumping together every complaint on every issue raised by any critic of royal policy and then to assume that anyone who articulated any of them accepted all of them. There is clear evidence that by 1640 very large numbers of men, in the gentry and beyond, had a limited but clear and firm belief in a partial royal tyranny. The king, albeit as a consequence of wicked counsel, was misusing his powers. But let us be clear what we mean. There was no criticism of monarchy itself; there was no criticism of the long-term development of the early modern state; there was no demand for fundamental change in the nature of royal power. The complaints were very specifically about the misgovernment of a single man, Charles I, and about the misuse of agreed powers, not about the attempt to usurp fresh powers. The king was not accused of trying to make law outside parliament, nor of claiming new prerogatives or emergency powers. What was widely asserted and believed was that the king was using approved powers in inappropriate circumstances, powers which he possessed *pro bono publico*, for the public welfare, *pro bono suo*, for his own benefit. He was most criticized for raising emergency taxation in non-emergency situations, for allowing private individuals to profit from the use of powers reserved to the king himself, and for corruption of justice.

This limited perception of royal tyranny produced a grim determination in the members of the Long Parliament to secure remedy and guarantees against the abuse of power. Yet the tale told by the Journals of the Houses and the diaries of MPs is not one of headlong constitutional action, but of sluggishness and hesitancy.[15] In contrast to the debates on religion, the rhetoric of the constitutional debates was conservative, restorative. Whatever the actual cumulative effect of the remedial legislation of 1641, the declared purpose, and, as far

---

15. Lambert, 'Opening of the Long Parliament', pp. 265–75. Her account of the slowness of the Houses to take up legislative redress of grievance is very telling. But I cannot agree with her that this is evidence of a house deeply divided over the need for such redress from the outset.

as we can determine, the undeclared purpose, of those who devised, spoke to, and approved those reforms was to maintain the rights and liberties of the subject by amputating diseased limbs of government, pruning back those emergency powers which had been so readily subverted for corrupt purposes, in order to preserve the essence of the ancient and established political order. There was no will to model the constitution anew, to reform it root and branch, let alone to create parliamentary sovereignty.[16] It was the failings of Charles I, not of the political system, which had to be rectified. In all the political debates down to and beyond the Grand Remonstrance, nothing was presented as a grievance which predated the accession of Charles I. The constitutional problem was a problem with a particular monarch. In contrast, an increasing number of ecclesiastical reformers argued for a fundamental reform of the Church. The Elizabethan settlement was to be dismantled and reconstituted.

The most puzzling aspect of the Long Parliament's first session is the lack of urgency about legislative remedies. Although early speakers laid out an agenda for reform, little attempt was made to enshrine that programme in statute until after the execution of Strafford in May 1641. By that time, it is true, the Triennial Act and the Act which gave the Long Parliament control over its own dissolution had been enacted. But the substantive attack on the conciliar and prerogative courts, and the statutory pruning of royal emergency powers, only passed through the Houses in the summer months. This may reveal supreme self-confidence in the inability of the king to wriggle free, but to defer conclusive action until long after that parliamentary session had become the longest in history may also indicate that concern over the remedies were less obsessive than is often supposed.

By contrast, the attack on evil counsellors was immediate and effective. Within a few weeks, most leading privy councillors and principal officers of state were in the Tower, in exile or in disgrace. Less than half those who attended meetings of the Council in the second half of 1641 had been members of it in November 1640.[17] But while the king's principal advisers were hounded from office, there

---

16. This is based principally upon a reading of the following: Rushworth, IV, *passim*; J. Nalson, *An Impartial Collection of the great affairs of State from the beginning of the Scotch Rebellion in the year 1639* (2 vols, 1682–3), *passim*; and the parliamentary journal of Sir Simonds d'Ewes (BL, Harl. MS 163–5, for which the period up to March 1641 and for the period November 1641 to March 1642 have been published in three separate volumes).

17. Fourteen of the thirty (reconstructed from the facsimile edition of the Privy Council Registers, PRO, PC 2/52–54).

was no wider harrying of those responsible for civil misgovernment. In addition to the councillors, six judges were impeached but allowed to preside over their courts while on bail,[18] and there was a fitful pursuit of monopolists.[19] But there it ended. Those lords lieutenant who had vigorously supported unpopular royal policies, those who had exceeded their powers during the Bishops' Wars, those zealous ship money sheriffs, were exempt from investigation and penalty.[20] There was no call for the removal or persecution of those who enforced the forest laws or knighthood fines; no weeding out of JPs who had openly and brazenly extolled royal policies. We will see how stark is the contrast between this and the Long Parliament's pursuit of churchmen.

The legal-constitutionalist perception of misgovernment was thus one of a limited tyranny, and it led to an unhurried and largely uncontroversial programme of remedial legislation consciously intended to restore a lost balance, to conserve the ancient constitution. There was no recognition either that the old system was unworkable or intrinsically tyrannical, or that the remedial legislation was making it unworkable or intrinsically unstable. There was no intellectual ferment in the period November 1640 to August 1641 creating new theories of government and new constitutional imperatives. If the king's behaviour left many unsatisfied with the achievements of the first session, there was no new rhetoric of popular or parliamentary sovereignty spurring members on to self-confident constitutional demands. All this is in stark contrast to the progress of religious concerns.

Unlike some recent commentators, I believe that it is almost impossible to overestimate the damage caused by the Laudians. I see no reason to doubt that most 'hotter sort of protestants' were integrated into the Jacobean church and state. Puritan magistrates and churchwardens abound, and can be found arguing for and working for an evangelical drive to instruct the ignorant, and all alliance of minister and magistrate to impose godly discipline. There was no incompatibility between serving God and the Crown. Such men found comfort in St John's letter to the true believers in Laodicea,

---

18. W.J. Jones, *Politics and The Bench* (1972), pp. 137–43, 199–214; *Somers Tracts*, ed. Sir Walter Scott (13 vols., 1809–15), IV, 130, 300–8; Rushworth, V, 318–44.
19. *The Journal of Sir Simonds d'Ewes from the Beginning of the Long Parliament to the Opening of the Trial of Earl of Strafford*, ed. W. Notestein (New Haven, 1923), pp. 19–20 and *passim*.
20. A committee was set up to investigate complaints against Lords Lieutenant and their deputies, but it appears never to have reported (Rushworth, IV, 98–9).

a church pure in doctrine but not in worship, in which he urged them to work for reform from within. They yearned for a new Constantine, a godly prince who would put the power of the state at the service of the church. The godly magistrate and parish notable yearned for more to do rather than for less. They saw James I and even more Charles I as *abdicating* their responsibilities under God to promote true religion. But while they saw James I as moving too slowly but in the right direction, they found in Charles I a negligent king who was oblivious to the threat of popery at home, abroad, and within the church of which he was supreme governor.[21]

It remains uncertain how and how far Laud's doctrine of grace departed sharply from the spectrum of predestinarian views maintained by successive generations of bishops and theologians since 1559.[22] Certainly his ecclesiology does not appear to make sense except as the expression of a belief that man, morally and intellectually depraved, could only be reconciled to God and brought to sustain a saving faith by and through the sacramental grace mediated to him by the church.[23] Be that as it may, the programme of Charles and Laud was profoundly offensive to most lay and much clerical opinion. It rested upon a narrow and literal enforcement of the observances and practices of the Book of Common Prayer and early injunctions of the Elizabethan church.[24] This prohibited the penumbra of observances and practices which had grown up around the Prayer Book, which for many represented the kernel of their witness, as the prayer book ceremonies represented the husk. This penumbra did not constitute a challenge to the church until Laud chose to make it one, by a narrow reading of the Prayer Book which treated its forms and rubrics not

21. This paragraph and the succeeding ones are a synthesis of much reading in primary and secondary sources. The most influential of the latter include Professor P. Collinson's *The Religion of Protestants* (Oxford, 1982), *Godly People* (1983), especially chapters 4, 6, 20, and his Birkbeck lectures in Cambridge of Lent 1981 (as yet unpublished).
22. N.R.N. Tyacke, 'Arminianism in England in Religion and Politics', University of Oxford D.Phil. thesis (1968), and cf. P. White, 'The Rise of Arminianism Reconsidered', *Past & Present*, 101 (1983), 34–54. The best work on Laud's own thought remains W.H. Hutton, *William Laud* (1895).
23. See also his statement, in reply to Lord Saye and Sele, that 'almost all of them [the Puritans] say that God from all eternity reprobates by far the greater part of mankind to eternal fire, without any eye to their sins. Which opinion my very soul abominates.' *The Works of the Most Reverend Father in God William Laud*, ed. J. Bliss (7 vols, 1853), VI, 133.
24. K. Sharpe, 'Archbishop Laud', *History Today*, 33 (1983) is correct to see Laud as consciously a 'traditionalist'; but by all evaluations, except Laud's own, he was stressing and imposing (often neglected) aspects of the Elizabethan church at the expense of other traditions and much established practice.

only as necessary, but as sufficient.[25] The heavy task Charles and Laud gave themselves, of bringing conformity to religion and of bringing sinful man to a due regard for the things of God mediated through His church, rested upon a profound clericism. The church had to be freed to evangelize, to convert, to impose order, and had to be freed from the cloying, stifling, corrupting intrusions upon its wealth and jurisdiction which had grown up over the previous century: the invasion by 'common law cormorants'; the secularization of church lands and assets; lay appropriations and impropriations; and so on. In all of his kingdoms, Charles and Laud set out to restore the autonomy of the church.[26] Whatever they thought they were doing, by 1640 their programme had aroused disenchantment amongst its committed and its critical members, a disenchantment which gave rise to a debate more passionate than the debate on the constitution. In November 1640, Wentworth was the most feared man in England; but Laud was the most detested – 'the sty of all pestilential filth', according to Harbottle Grimston, 'like a busie angry wasp, his sting is in the tayl of everything'.[27]

The religious perception of misgovernment differed from the localist and the legal–constitutionalist perception first in its intensity. It spilled over into everything in the early weeks of the Long Parliament.[28] It saturates the language of the petitions to Parliament; it crops up with greater regularity and persistence in the business of both Houses than do secular grievances.[29] The first positive achievement carried through was the annulment of the canons[30] of convocation approved during the spring of 1640 (canons which gave full force to the Laudian programme).[31] But the religious perception is more complex than the others. It too, at the outset, was in part a perception of tyranny. Laud was accused of promoting false doctrine which

---

25. This view owes much to the ideas of Patrick Collinson in his Birkbeck lectures.
26. For key letters and instructions of Laud in relation to these issues, see *Laud's Works*, ed. Bliss, V, 321, 324, 337, 345, 351, 355, 361, and VI, 310, 330, 332, 338, 341.
27. Rushworth, IV, 122–3.
28. It is not true, as has been often asserted, that the managers of the Parliament sought to keep contentious ecclesiastical issues out of the Houses until after the secular reforms were achieved. See, for example, the willingness to escalate religious issues in *Journal of the House of Commons* (henceforth *CJ*), II, 25, 26–7, 35, 41, 52, 54, 71 etc.; *d'Ewes*, ed. Notestein, pp. 4, 5, 16, 17, 18, 22, 24–5, etc.
29. For a full discussion of this, see, 'The Attack on the Church of England in the Long Parliament', below, ch. 4.
30. *Synodalia: A Collection of Articles of Religion, Canons and proceedings in Convocation in the Province of Canterbury*, ed. E. Cardwell (2 vols., Oxford, 1842), I, 380–406.
31. *CJ*, II, 30–3, 41–52; *d'Ewes*, ed. Notestein, pp. 21, 70–2, 125, 149, 152–7.

lent support to the king's arbitrary actions; and of abusing his own jurisdiction and that of other courts to impose unlawful observance and to silence 'professors' of the true religion.[32] But this was not simply a matter of the arbitrary use of power. Indeed, the scale of religious persecution under Laud was in fact quite limited: there were fewer deprivations and suspensions in the 1630s than in most other decades since the Reformation.[33] It was not his persecutions which caused most outrage. The religious perception was paradoxically also one of royal weakness, abdication, failure to halt the advance of popery. The attack on the bishops was built around their usurpation of the royal supremacy.[34] There were long debates in early 1641 about whether the bishops who had promoted the canons and prosecuted Bastwick were guilty of treason or *praemunire*, of derogating from the king's title and dignity.[35] In the words of Laud's impeachment: 'the said archbishop claims the king's ecclesiastical jurisdiction as incident to his episcopal office . . . and doth deny the same to be derived from the Crown of England'.[36] Laud had a plausible defence to the charge, but his own words in High Commission in the case of Sir Giles Allington[37] and the alleged words of John Cosin, that 'the king had no more power over the church than the man who rubs my horse's heels',[38] leave us in little doubt why his defence was unheeded. One of the most heated exchanges in the early months of the Long Parliament was over a report of a sermon by Dr Chaffin at the metropolitical visitation of Salisbury. Chaffin, referring to Laud as 'our little Aaron', had compared him favourably with 'the blessed archbishop Arundel'. He may have had in mind Arundel's silencing of preaching and harrying of Lollards, but d'Ewes was quick to remind the house that Arundel had been impeached for treason in 1397 for usurping the king's regality, dignity and Crown.[39] Laud's usurpation had been intended to weaken the church: 'these are the men that should have fed Christ's flock, but they are the wolves

32. Rushworth, IV, 196
33. Hutton, *Laud*, pp. 98–102.
34. W. Lamont, *Marginal Prynne* (1963), pp. 11–27; W. Lamont, *Godly Rule* (1969), pp. 44–52.
35. *D'Ewes*, ed. Notestein, 70–2, 152–163, 427–8.
36. Rushworth, IV, 197.
37. Quoted in Hutton, *Laud*, p. 103.
38. Rushworth, IV, 210.
39. For the impeachment articles brought against Arundel in 1397, see *Select Documents of English Constitutional History, 1307–1485*, eds. S.B. Chrimes and A.L. Brown (1961), pp. 170–1. Arundel was impeached for issuing commissions 'en prejudice du roy et overtement encontre sa regalie, sa dignite, et sa corone'. For the debate, see *d'Ewes*, ed. Notestein, pp. 276, 419–20.

that have devoured them'.[40] As Lord Falkland put it, they sought 'to introduce an English, though not a Roman, popery'.[41]

The remedies to the constitutional ills of the 1630s were widely agreed, leisurely pursued, based upon a conservative rhetoric. From the outset, the reform of the church was more contentious, more impulsive, and more divisive, because there quickly emerged a radical rhetoric which many could not accept. It is true that Laud and Laudianism were quickly swept away and without dissent. But within eight weeks of the opening of Parliament, the Houses were subjected to a pulpit oratory and to a petitioning campaign that called not for the restoration of the pre-Laudian order, not for the conserving of the 'pure religion of Elizabeth and James', but for the abolition of the entire ecclesiastical order and its reconstitution along pure biblical lines. Edward Calamy called upon Parliament to 'reform the reformation', and Stephen Marshall called upon them to 'throw to the moals and the bats every rag that hath not God's stamp upon it'.[42]

In the late 1620s, most critics of Arminianism spoke as defenders of the established church against novelty and innovation; even in late 1640 the number who appear to have anticipated the need to overturn the church of Elizabeth was small.[43] But whereas the events of 1641 reinforced constitutional conservatism, they polarized the religious views of members of both Houses. In part, this resulted from their response to the sermons, the tracts, the lobbying. In part, it was a response to Scottish pressure.[44] But in large part it was a response to the level of ecclesiastical corruption revealed by the Houses' enquiries.

The attack on churchmen was far wider than the attack on the laity. In addition to the thirteen bishops impeached in December 1640, and the overlapping group of twelve impeached in December 1641,

---

40. Rushworth, IV, 122.
41. Lucius Cary, Viscount Falkand, *A Speech Made to the House of Commons Concerning Episcopacy* (1641), p. 4. For a discussion, see M.L. Schwartz, 'Lay Anglicanism and the Crisis of the English Church in the Early Seventeenth Century', *Albion*, 14 (1982), 1–5.
42. E. Calamy, *England's Looking Glass* (22 December 1641), p. 48; S. Marshall, *A Sermon Before the House of Commons* (17 November 1640), p. 40. It should be said that the Fast Sermons as a whole displayed an indifference amounting to contempt for secular injustices, and focussed with increasing clarity on the prospects for building a New Jerusalem. I am grateful to Mr S. Baskerville for his comments on this question.
43. W.M. Abbott, 'The Issue of Episcopacy in the Long Parliament', Univ. of Oxford D.Phil. thesis (1981), ch. 2.
44. C.L. Hamilton, 'The Basis of Scottish Efforts to Create a Reformed Church in England 1640–1', *Church Hist.*, 30 (1961), 171–8; P. Crawford, *Denzil, First Lord Holles* (1979), pp. 42–51.

there was a steady stream of complaints against individual ministers, especially from within London, East Anglia and the Midlands. The Commons sent more than twenty such complaints to committees by the end of November 1640 and a steady flow thereafter.[45] In those early weeks they also undertook long reviews of the trials of Burton, Bastwick, Prynne, Leighton and Lilburne, set aside their conviction and sentence, and awarded them damages against their persecutors. This was far more aggressive than anything done for the victims of secular tyranny.[46] In those early weeks when more than twenty clerics were hounded, only two civil officers, a sheriff and an under-sheriff, were investigated.[47] By the summer of 1641 the Commons were happily depriving ministers of their freehold, banning them from future preferment, imprisoning them in the Tower or elsewhere, or otherwise punishing them for ceremonialism or preaching up Laudianism. Those ecclesiastics responsible for ordering the parish of Waddesdon in Buckinghamshire to repair its organ and pay for an organist found themselves covering all the consequent costs by order of the Lower House.[48] As early as January 1641, the Commons declared that the judges in High Commission had acted *ultra vires* in ordering the parishioners of St Bartholomew's London to pay the wages of the parish clerk; they themselves acted *ultra vires* in setting aside the order and requiring the judges to pay the parishioners' fines and costs.[49] Such highhandedness soon produced a reaction amongst the members themselves. A study of the 700 and more cases taken on appeal by the House of Lords in the early 1640s leads to the same conclusion. Far more and worse abuses of ecclesiastical authority were revealed than of secular authority. The Lords were far more resolute in the pursuit of ecclesiastical officials than of secular ones.[50]

At the very time that the Houses expressed alarm at the abuses within the church, the Commons were willing to wink at breaches of ecclesiastical law. In June 1641, 'mechanicall' lay preachers were called before the House but merely gently reprimanded and protected from the rigours of the law',[51] rather later, the JPs of Monmouthshire were ordered not to prosecute those who absented themselves from

---

45. *CJ*, II, 24–40; *d'Ewes*, ed. Notestein, pp. 4–40, *passim*.
46. *CJ*, II, 24–52, 102, 124, 134; *d'Ewes*, ed. Notestein, pp. 4, 17, 130, 172–4, 232–3, 240–9, 386, 400–1, 424–9.
47. *CJ*, II, 23, 32.
48. *d'Ewes*, ed. Notestein, p. 306.
49. Ibid., pp. 281–2.
50. J. Hart, 'The House of Lords and the Reformation of Justice 1640–3', Univ. of Cambridge PhD thesis (1985), chapter 3.
51. BL, Harl. MS 163 ff. 662, 669.

their parish churches in order to hear sermons elsewhere,[52] in a bitter ten-hour debate in early September 1641 the Commons issued instructions to local governors to take the law into their own hands to demolish 'innovations', and rejected an amendment which would have 'provided a remedy against such as did vilify and contemn the common prayer book'.[53]

The point is that by the end of the first session of the Long Parliament, not only had a militancy of rhetoric and action led to a militancy of conduct in religion different in kind from that generated by the constitutional debate; but that militancy had led to a decisive shift in perception amongst many MPs who had begun the Parliament looking for a pruning and cleansing exercise in the church similar to that enacted for the state, but who now saw that the established church had to be abolished, reconstituted. For many, the existing order had been shown to be intrinsically unstable. For reasons of prudence, and for reasons of Providence (God's judgement appearing upon the order as well as upon the individuals who composed it), episcopacy had to be destroyed. Many accepted the necessity, fewer *embraced* the necessity, seeing it as the breaking of the mould, the opportunity of renewal and of the millennium. Yet the same militancy which had forged this new religious radicalism produced a reaction which created, or at any rate crystallized, a theoretical and practical defence of non-Laudian episcopacy and of the Anglicanism of the prayer book and of the Thirty Nine articles. The debates on church government in the spring and summer of 1641, culminating in the resolutions of the Commons in the final days of the session, witnessed a gradual polarization of the members.[54] By the time of the recess there was no royalist party; but there was an anglican party.

The constitutional reform of 1641 was largely uncontroversial and created no major division, generated no major public debate. The perceived tyranny of the 1630s was remedied. No issue left over from the past remained on the agenda in late 1641. The renewed constitutional concern arose from the king's fresh misbehaviour. It is, of course, true that in 1642 questions of trust generated new constitutional demands which proved non-negotiable and which

52. *The Private Journals of the Long Parliament 3 January to 5 March 1642*, eds. W.H. Coates, A.S. Young, V.F. Snow (New Haven, 1982), pp. 302–3.
53. BL, Harl. MS 164, ff. 887–90, 895, 914; and for the rumbling battle over the declaration in the autumn, *The Journal of Sir Simonds d'Ewes from the First Recess of the Long Parliament to the withdrawal of King Charles from London*, ed. W.H. Coates (New Haven, 1942), pp. 1–66.
54. W.A. Shaw, *A History of the English Church during the Civil War and under the Commonwealth* (2 vols. 1900), I, 1–121; Abbott, 'Episcopacy', *passim*.

became the *occasions* of civil war. A review of the Militia Ordinance and the Nineteen Propositions, however, must keep in mind a number of easily forgotten points.[55]

The first is that Parliament's defence of its actions remains basically conservative. A reading of the exchanges over the Militia Ordinance, over the king's attempt on Hull, over the Nineteen Propositions, leaves little doubt that the moves towards war were reluctantly taken. No such self-doubt can be found amongst those who pushed forward towards godly reformation in 1642, as iconoclasts, as the protectors of illegal gathered churches, as campaigners for presbyterianism. A reading of the debates, at least up to the battle of Edgehill, tells not of a radical group leading a quailing majority gently onwards, but of a leadership picking its way through a minefield, full of self-doubt, seeing the hazards of turning back as worse than the perils of pursuing their passage.[56] This impression is reinforced in two further ways. First the logic of events forced the Houses to make claims and then to justify them[57] that is, the claims to exercise unprecedented control over the militia and the executive were not the inexorable working out of a clarified constitutionalism, but were desperate rationalizations of pragmatic responses to a king increasingly seen as deranged and incapable of governing, no longer a tyrant but a man incapable of discharging his trust. Secondly, the new claims made by the Houses were advanced piecemeal and tentatively. The so-called 'legislative' ordinances of 1642 were in fact astonishingly hesitant and half-hearted. The most aggressive and assertive were those which dealt with religion, as that of June 1641 which extended local governors' powers to collect recusancy fines and amended the legal definition of

---

55. The following is based not simply on the documents themselves (for which see *Constitutional Documents of the Puritan Revolution*, ed. S.R. Gardiner (3rd edn, Oxford, 1906), pp. 245–7, 249–54), but also on the debates which arose from them (see *Private Journals*, eds. Coates *et al.*, 291–5, 313–15, 334–50, 544–50; BL, Harl. MS 163, ff. 427–8; Rushworth, IV, 516–50, 691–735.

56. I recognize that this is a highly contestable view. Might not the prospective leaders of the parliamentary cause have deliberately played down their radicalism for tactical reasons, for fear of alienating moderate opinion and losing the initiative? This is the very influential view of J.H. Hexter, *The Reign of King Pym* (New Haven, 1940), pp. 1–30 and *passim*. I prefer the view expressed here because (1) they displayed no such reticence on religious matters despite the fact that it cost them moderate support; (2) their private thoughts appear to reflect their public statements; (3) their rhetorical reticence led to a reticence of action which threatened the success of the military operations.

57. E.g. L. Schwoerer, '"The Fittest Subject for a King's Quarrel": an essay on the Militia Controversy', *Jnl. Brit. Studs.*, II (1971); R. Tuck, '"The Ancient Law of Freedom": John Selden and the Civil War', in *Reactions to the English Civil War*, ed. J.S. Morrill (1982), pp. 137–64.

recusancy.[58] In early August 1642, by contrast, Parliament desperately needed money to raise an army to defend itself. The sixth and last of the Long Parliament's acts for the collection of tonnage and poundage had lapsed and there was no prospect of the royal assent to another one. Yet the Houses could not bring themselves to claim the right to vote themselves taxation. They appealed to all those liable to pay customs, asking them voluntarily to hand over their dues to Parliament's treasurers, promising them a fifteen per cent discount and threatening refusers that when king and Parliament once more worked in harmony, retroactive legislation would contain a clause 'for the forfeiture of the value of all such goods as shall not be duly entered'.[59] Similarly the Militia Ordinance possessed no legal force. The Houses specifically laid down that no action at law could follow from non-compliance. As d'Ewes said, the form of the ordinance was moral and not legal, telling the people how they ought to look to their own defence, not requiring them to do so.[60]

Most importantly, the constitutional issues of 1642 were means to an end, not ends in themselves. They were a controversial means to protect the uncontroversial settlement of 1641 and to deal with a king no longer trusted to keep his word. I shall argue below that that lack of trust grew out of a religious perception.

Finally, the Militia Ordinance and the Nineteen Propositions may have been the *occasion* of armed conflict, may have provided the non-negotiable issues which required men to take sides, but they were not the issues which determined which side most men would be on. This is a point which is particularly true of the provinces, as I shall argue at the end of the paper.

Once more, in 1642, a comparison of the constitutional and religious dynamics is suggestive. The presses remained remarkably silent on the theoretical issues underpinning constitutional issues. As Michael Mendle has written, there was 'no public debate on the major constitutional questions until mid 1642.'[61] Yet there was a vast and

---

58. BL, Harl. MS 164, ff. 858, 876; *Journal of the House of Lords* (henceforth *LJ*), IV, 384–7; Fletcher, *Outbreak*, pp. 76–7.
59. *Acts and Ordinances of the Interregnum*, eds. C.H. Firth and R.S. Rait (3 vols. pp. 1911), I, 16–20.
60. Gardiner, *Constitutional Documents*, 247; BL, Harl. MS 163, f. 247, viz. 'That all men ought to obey the ordinance it is not thereby implied that an ordinance of parliament hath the same vertue and efficacie that an Act hath . . . by those words that they ought to obey, is intended that . . . every man ought voluntarily, willingly and cheerfully to obey.'
61. M. Mendle, 'Politics and Political Thought, 1640–1642', in *Origins of the English Civil War*, ed. C. Russell (1973), pp. 219–46; idem 'Mixed Government, the Estates, and the Bishops', Washington Univ., St Louis, PhD thesis (1977), pp. 396–432; G.K. Fortescue, *Catalogue of the Thomason Tracts* (2 vols., 1908), pp. 1–116.

growing literature on the nature of the church and of episcopacy. The contribution of Lord Brooke, of John Milton, of the Smectymnuans and of others against episcopacy, and of Joseph Hall, James Ussher, Sir Thomas Aston and others in its defence is well-known, but they constitute only a tithe of the works which poured out on the subject[62] Even the most important constitutional developments were swamped by literature on religious ones; in January 1642 four times as many pamphlets were devoted to the impeachment of the bishops as to the Attempt on the Five Members.[63] The great issues of church government were fully rehearsed in print for months before the substantive debates on the issue. Recent studies of a number of MPs, including Sir Robert Harley, Sir John Wray, Sir William Brereton and Sir Thomas Barrington, all show a dramatic process of radicalization, a conversion to the necessity of root-and-branch reform.[64] That radicalization grew out of a considered review of the possibilities; it grew out of a fundamental reappraisal and a belief in the need for a fresh start. As we have just seen, majorities in the Commons, if not in the Lords, consistently grasped the nettle of acting to promote and to protect those who challenged not merely Laudian innovation, but the very basis of the established church. Finally, the demand for a godly reformation was an end in itself, a vision. As Jacqueline Levy has recently written of the Harleys: '[They] viewed the civil war primarily as a war to establish true religion, in defiance of a catholic-inspired plot against church and state'.[65] She here points, as others have recently done, to the widespread belief in a Popish Plot about the king's person, which was seen as the only credible explanation of his behaviour.[66] It was not claimed that Charles I was a papist; but it was believed that he had ceased to be responsible

62. The best discussion is probably in *The Prose Works of John Milton* (8 vols., 1953–82), vol. I, ed. D.M. Wolfe, 48–151; Fletcher, *Outbreak*, pp. 91–124 and *passim*.
63. Fortescue, *Thomason*. I, 57–73; similarly in March 1642 there was more discussion of the prayer book than of the militia (ibid., pp. 86–97).
64. J. Levy, 'Perceptions and Beliefs: The Harleys of Brampton Bryan and the Origins and Outbreak of the Civil War', Univ. of London PhD thesis (1983), *passim*; R.N. Dore, 'The Early Life of Sir William Brereton', *Trans. Lancs and Cheshire Antiq. Soc.,* 63 (1954), 1–26; J.S. Morrill, 'Puritans and the Church in the Diocese of Chester', *Northern Hist.,* 12 (1975), 151–5; W. Hunt, *The Puritan Moment* (Cambridge, Mass., 1983).
65. Levy, 'Harleys', p. 175.
66. C. Hibbard, *Charles I and the Popish Plot* (Chapel Hill, 1983), *passim*; G. Albion, *Charles I and the Court of Rome* (1935), *passim*; W. Lamont, *Richard Baxter and the Millennium* (1979), pp. 76–123; M. Finlayson, *Historians, Puritanism and the English Revolution* (Toronto, 1983), pp. 79–119; Fletcher, *Outbreak, passim*.

for his actions, had ceased to govern. It was, in modern parlance, as though he had been got at by the Moonies, had been brainwashed, programmed; or in a metaphor more appropriate to the seventeenth century, that he had been insidiously and deliberately poisoned, so that he had gradually become disoriented, distracted. The Nineteen Propositions were designed for such a circumstance: not to deal with a tyrant or a despot, but with a deranged king, one who needed to be rescued from the contagion of popery, to be shielded and deprogrammed, to be decontaminated. The historical precedents to be pursued were those of the senile Edward III or the catatonic Henry VI, not the wicked Edward II or Richard II.[67]

The principal elements of the Popish Plot are well-known: the penetration of the court and household by known and suspected Catholics; the activities of papal envoys; the ascendency of the Queen over the King; the use and projected use in 1639 and 1640 of Highland and Irish Catholic troops alongside an English army containing many Catholic officers, all to be subsidized by Rome and Madrid, the ostensible purpose of which was to impose Charles's religious preferences upon the Protestant Church of Scotland. No wonder the papist threat to the state was seen to parallel the infiltration and subversion of the English church. While lay papists schemed to take over the state, the church was to be fatally weakened by the activities of the episcopal wolfpack.[68]

Yet not everyone shared this belief in the popish plot; or more importantly, not everyone continued to see it as the principal danger. This was partly the result of the excesses of those who most fully believed in it, and was partly the result of the wildly inconsistent signals sent out by the king. On the one hand, he was, or seemed to be, implicated in the Army Plots, the Incident, the Attempt on the

---

67. I owe this point to conversations with Conrad Russell and to ideas contained in his unpublished paper 'The Causes of the English Civil War'. The notion that the king had been 'poisoned' is a common one, but more specific was the declaration of the Houses that they proceeded as though the king was suffering from nonage, natural disability or captivity (BL, Thomason Tract E 241 (I), pp. 207–8). Dr Ian Roy tells me that Sir Ralph Verney's (hitherto undeciphered) notes on the debate of 28 February 1642 show MPs considered the king in the position of a suicidal maniac, from whom the power of the sword must be removed. *Verney Papers: Notes of Proceedings in the Long Parliament by Sir Ralph Verney* (Camden Ist series, 31, 1845), pp. 184. I am very grateful to Dr Roy for this reference.
68. See n. 66; also D. Stevenson, *Alasdair MacColla and the Highland Problem of the Seventeenth Century* (Edinburgh, 1981), ch. 1; J.H. Elliott, 'The year of the Three Ambassadors', in *History and Imagination,* eds. H. Lloyd-Jones, V. Pearl and A.B. Worden (1981).

Five Members, and, in the midst of all these, and most damagingly, the Irish Rebellion.[69] Those who knew of Charles's negotiations with the earl of Antrim in 1639 had little reason to doubt the authenticity of the warrant which Catholic rebel leaders produced to vindicate their rising.[70] Yet Charles also projected another image of himself. He accepted all the remedies for grievance put to him; he pointedly and heartlessly abandoned Laud and his policies and promoted to the episcopate moderate men, or at any rate men who were Laud's enemies.[71] And he publicly associated himself with the slogans and values of non-Laudian Anglicanism.[72] Just as Pym and his colleagues were increasingly obsessed[73] by the stranglehold of popery at court and beyond, so the reinvigorated Anglicans became preoccupied with the indulgence given by the Commons to fanatic preachers, to unlawful religious assemblies, to mass picketing. The very measures which religious perceptions led a majority of the Commons to adopt as a defensive means to the end of safeguarding themselves and the nation from the threat of popery led an increasing minority to back away. Fresh constitutional priorities were evaluated from the perspective of increasingly polarized religious assessments.

Talk of 'popery' is not a form of 'white noise', a constant fuzzy background in the rhetoric and argument of the time against which significant changes in secular thought were taking place. This has been a fundamental error in the intellectual historians of the English Revolution. This falsifies the passionate belief, the passionate belief that is the ground of action, that England was in the process of being subjected to the forces of Antichrist, that the prospects were of anarchy, chaos, the dissolution of government and liberties; and

---

69. Hibbard, *Popish Plot, passim.*
70. D. Stevenson, *Scottish Covenanters and Irish Confederates* (Belfast, 1981), pp. 43–65; A. Clarke. 'The Genesis of the Ulster Rising of 1641' in *Plantation to Partition*, ed. P. Roebuck (Belfast, 1981), pp. 40–61; Lamont, *Baxter*, pp. 77–87, 116–19, 230–2.
71. J.S. Morrill, 'The Chruch in England 1642–9' in *Reactions*, ed. Morrill, pp. 98–100; P. King, 'The Episcopate during the English Civil War', *Eng. Hist. Rev.*, LXXXIII (1968), 526–30.
72. B.H.G. Wormald, *Clarendon* (Cambridge, 1951), p. 18; *Bibliotheca Lindesiana: A Bibliography of Royal Proclamations of Tudor and Stuart Sovereigns*, ed. R.R. Steele (2 vols., Oxford 1910), I, 295.
73. There was a generalized anxiety about the growth of popery in and around the Court from the beginning of Charles's reign, but few saw it as the principal hazard until the events of 1641. For John Pym's precociousness in this respect, see C. Russell, 'The Parliamentary career of John Pym, 1621–1629', in *The English Commonwealth*, eds. P. Clark, A.G.R. Smith and N.R.N. Tyacke (Leicester, 1979).

the equally passionate belief that disobedience to the king, carried to
the point of violent resistance, could only lead to chaos and anarchy;
and to the conviction of most men that both dangers were equally
real, a conviction which led to panic and a yearning for settlement.

There is a steady but inexorable shift from the muffled fears in
the early months of the Long Parliament to the outpourings of
apprehension of imminent Armageddon to be found in the declarations of 1642; from Mr Thomas's call, during a debate on cathedral
chapters in 1641, for the abolition of church music:

> For I do find in my reading that anno 666, the year that was designed
> and computed for the coming of Antichrist, Vitalian, bishop of Rome,
> brought to the church singing of service and the use of organs,[74]

and from Sir John Wray's introduction of the Protestation as being

> first . . . to preserve our religion entire and pure without the least
> compound of superstition or idolatry; next to defend the defender of the
> faith, his royal Crown and Dignity . . . thus doing, Mr Speaker, and
> making Jerusalem our chiefest Joy, we shall be a blessed nation;[75]

from these to the exchanges of 1642, with Pym speaking of evil
counsellors, who like 'diseases of the brain are most dangerous', and
of a plot to destroy all liberties, privileges and the rule of law.[76] Gone
were the accusations of a tendency to arbitrary government; in their
place is the language of anarchy and destruction, brought about by
those whose 'devilish purpose was the better destruction of the true
reformed religion'.[77]

If we read the sequence of parliamentary defences of its actions in
1642[78] to find out *to what end* they acted, rather than *by what right*, we
find the same primacy of religious argument.

William Lamont's brilliant reconstruction of Richard Baxter's account of his decision to resist the king's authority lays emphasis on
the King's responsibility for the Irish Rebellion and his abdication of
the duty to protect his subjects from the forces of Antichrist. It was
not royal tyranny but royal abdication which forced the people to look
to their own defence.[79] At a stroke, decades of intellectualizing about
how subjects were bound to obey wicked kings as scourges sent by

74. Rushworth, IV, 287.
75. Ibid., IV, 240–1.
76. *LJ*, IV, 540–3.
77. *LJ*, IV, 512.
78. Rushworth, IV, 398–421 (since the pagination is awry at this point, 385–415 being
    used twice, this reference is to 398–415 and then 385–421), 516–50, 565–601,
    691–739. A good starting point is 'the Declaration of Causes and Remedies' (*CJ*,
    II, 443–6, reprinted in *Private Journals*, eds. Coates *et al.*, pp. 543–50).
79. Lamont, *Baxter*, pp. 88–98.

God were set aside; and at a stroke we can see how the constitutional issues of 1642 differed from those of 1640. The issue in 1642 was not the king's past tyranny; it was his present moral and political incapacity. This was precisely the argument of the Declaration of Lords and Commons sent to the North (11 July 1642)[80] and of the Declaration for Taking Up Arms (2 August 1642)[81] It is also the increasingly dominant theme in the work of Henry Parker, whose thought evolved under the impact of providentialist argument and a growing recognition that the king's will had been seduced by 'those execrable instruments which steal the king's heart from us, but they think the religion of protestants too tame and the nation of the English insensible to injuries'.[82] In the *Contra-Replicant*, for example, Charles was portrayed not as a tyrant but as a man helpless to prevent lawyers, corrupt clergy or soldiers from 'spoyling above the general law'.[83]

In 1640 and 1641 there is and was no way to distinguish 'moderate' and 'radical' constitutionalism. Future royalists like Hyde, Falkland, Dering and even George Digby, were no less 'hardline' than future Parliamentarians like Pym, Selden and d'Ewes. What distinguished them was the gradual unfolding of the religious debate and the religiously-conditioned response to a new constitutional situation which was only indirectly related to the debates of 1640. None of those who defended the pre-Laudian church order in the debates of mid 1641 subsequently became a parliamentarian; few of those who demanded a fresh start supported the king. Defence of the established order, shorn of recent innovations, was partly a social perception: the defence of hierarchy in society and government. But it also owed much to affection for the practice and rhythms of a church of which they were third-or fourth-generation members; and to the claims for the superiority of the 'catholic and reformed' church as set forth by its apologists following Jewel and Hooker.[84]

80. *LJ*, V, 201–2.
81. *LJ*, V, 257–60.
82. H. Parker, *Observations on His Majesties late Answers and Addresses* (1642), p. 15.
83. H. Parker, *The Contra-Replicant His Complaint to his Majestie* (1642). See also his comments on the 'absolute and unlimitable power of the king's sword and sceptre' controlled by the Queen who is in turn controlled by 'the Romish vice-god' (bid., pp. 10–15). Parker's thought was dramatically affected by the Irish Rebellion. My reading of Parker has been enormously helped by discussions with Howard Moss, and by supervising his admirable BA dissertation.
84. Fletcher, *Outbreak, passim*; Morrill, *Revolt*, pp. 46–50; Morrill, 'Church in England', pp. 89–114; See also the forthcoming Cambridge PhD thesis by Judith Maltby. For the growing articulation of the case for episcopacy within the Commons, see the debates on the Grand Remonstrance (the most heated exchanges before the final vote all concerned the church) in *d'Ewes*, ed. Coates, pp. 117, 149–52, 165–6.

The party which withdrew from Westminster during the winter of 1641–2 and during the spring of 1642 was the Anglican party. Those who remained were more or less unanimous in approving the Militia Ordinance, and the final form of the Nineteen Propositions, but they were far from unanimous on the need to wage war to implement them. While sources for religious commitment at that juncture are hard to come by, it seems likely that what distinguished those willing to raise armies to impose the new guarantees on the king, from those who voted against the escalation of the conflict, was the level of commitment to the godly cause. Robert Harley, William Brereton, Alexander Rigby are examples of men who had modest records of standing up to secular misgovernment; but all were men who were fired by the vision not simply of ecclesiastical reconstruction, but of building a godly commonwealth. By contrast, many of those with an impeccable record of standing up to legal and constitutional misgovernment but whose commitment to ecclesiastical reform was more cool, prudential, erastian, got cold feet in 1642. They felt that they had no choice but to stay at Westminster and to work for fresh guarantees of the constitutional settlement, but they could not bring themselves to support the means which alone could in fact achieve these guarantees. No one who reads the works of d'Ewes, Selden, Rudyard or Whitelocke can have much doubt that constitutionalism, however deeply felt, was inadequate as a ground for militant action. They would be parliamentarians in the war; but they did not will that war.[85]

Pressure of space has led me to an uncharacteristic concentration on the centre rather than on the provinces. What follows is the merest sketch of how the points made above can help to make as much sense of the provinces as of Westminster politics. MPs were too much in the limelight, too much on the spot, too much in the know, to be able to avoid making decisions which typecast them and limited their options. In the provinces, decisions were more easily hedged, fudged, deferred. It is quite clear that a majority of the gentry and of all social groups, whether they had a preference or not between king and parliament, had an absolute preference for peace, and the attempts of individuals and of county establishments to prevent or

85. Innumerable works could be cited here. See, for example, Fletcher, *Outbreak*, pp. 228–82; Gardiner, *History*, X, 152–219; Hexter, *King Pym*, pp. 1–30; Rushworth, IV, 754–5; B. Whitelocke, *Memorials of the English Affairs* (4 vols. Oxford, 1853), I, 148–90; R. Spalding, *The Improbable Puritan* (1979), pp. 78–97.

to limit the coming of the war to their communities are well enough known. Localism in 1640 led naturally to neutralism in 1642.[86]

Anthony Fletcher's study of the petitioning campaigns of 1640–2 is very telling. In the autumn of 1640, all three 'perceptions of misgovernment' can be found in the petitions, jostling side by side and sometimes inconsistently. By late 1641 and the first half or 1642, petitions on constitutional issues were beginning to show a lack of comprehension of developments at the centre. Fletcher discusses the petitions sent up by thirty-eight counties and characterizes them as containing paeans of praise for the achievements of the parliament in putting an end to arbitrary government; but he also argues that while 'at Westminster there was a sense of outright confrontation with the Crown . . . this is entirely absent in the provinces'. While some petitions showed an interest in the Militia Ordinance and a desire for regular musters, this was purely defensive and grew out of a concern with papist risings and local order. They remain suffused with a loyalty to Charles as well as to Parliament.[87]

More dramatic still was the wave of petitions in the summer of 1642 which called for peace and accommodation and which refused to acknowledge the non-negotiability of the differences between Charles and the Houses. There was no great wave of petitions for and against the Nineteen Propositions, no great debate on its constitutional claims. Contemporaries took rather less interest than have historians in the exchanges of Culpepper and Parker.

Yet at the same time the religious issues were being stirred, the source of division and polarization. The wave of anti-episcopal petitions in the spring of 1641 was followed by widespread icono-clasm, by 'swarms of conventicles' and by anti-Catholic mobs, all winked at and countenanced by some in authority. Throughout the provinces this led, just as it did in parliament, to a reaction in favour of the established order, to movements to defend episcopacy and the Prayer Book. More than half the counties sent up petitions in the period pleading for the established church.[88] The bitterness of the language of the religious petitions of 1642 contrasts with the yearning for settlement and the increasingly forlorn pleading for peace which comes out of the constitutional petitions. Yet again,

86. Fletcher, *Outbreak*. pp. 369–406.
87. Ibid., pp. 191–227, 369–407. See how well this account fits the sequence of petitions in Kent, as discussed in A.S.P. Woods, *Prelude to Civil War* (Salisbury, 1981), pp. 30–62, 95–119, 141–4, 153–7.
88. Sir Thomas Aston, *A Collection of Sundry Petitions* (1642); Fletcher, *Outbreak*, pp. 283–96.

we find that the dynamism of religious argument contrasts with a shrinking away from constitutional choices.

The civil war broke out because small minorities thrust themselves forward, volunteered, took to arms. Neither the militia nor the array were the instruments of war. It was individual captains and colonels, recruiting their own companies and regiments, who created the armies that went to war.[89] Many of the rank and file volunteered, doubtless because they expected a short campaign in the slack season after the harvest or to escape the trade slump in London. But many, especially amongst the officers, were motivated by a cause. And here for the last time, we find the familiar contrast. In Cheshire the royalist activists in 1642, who created the war effort and dragged the reluctant county establishment into the war, were led by Sir Thomas Aston, campaigner against ship money and for episcopacy; and the parliamentarian war effort was led by Sir William Brereton, constitutional quietist and sponsor of the anti-espiscopal petition.[90] In Herefordshire Jacqueline Levy finds that 'religious issues lay at the heart of divided opinion . . . contemporaries were writing of "parties" in connection with espiscopacy as early as January 1641'. She finds in 1642 reluctance to divide over the militia, but an increasing polarization over the religious issues.[91] A similar conclusion was reached by Liam Hunt in his recent study of Essex.[92] If we go back to other county studies and distinguish between the issues which required men to make choices, and the grounds upon which they made their choices, I believe we will find that only where there was strong and distinctive and developed religious commitments will we find militancy. There were no constitutional militants.

On 10 September 1642 the Houses told the Scottish General Assembly that 'their chiefest aim' was 'the Truth and Purity of the Reformed Religion, not only against Popery but against all other superstitious sects and innovations whatsoever'.[93] Have we been so confused in seeking parallels between the British Crisis of the 1640s and the wave of rebellions on the Continent (brought on by war and the centralizing imperatives of war), or between the English Revolution and the events of 1789 and 1917, that we have missed an obvious point? The English civil war was not the first European revolution: it was the last of the Wars of Religion.

89. R. Hutton, *The Royalist War Effort* (1981), pp. 22–32.
90. J.S. Morrill, *Cheshire 1630–1660* (Oxford, 1974), pp. 31–74.
91. J. Levy, 'Harleys', ch. 4–6.
92. Hunt, *Puritan Moment*, pp. 235–313, especially pp. 311–12.
93. *LJ*, V, 348–50.

CHAPTER FOUR
The Attack on the Church of England in the Long Parliament

The problems of England in the 1630s stemmed from having a strong monarchy and a weak king. With a secure title, an effective and ubiquitous legal system, declining levels of public violence, a balanced (peacetime) budget and strong and pervasive ideologies of order and obedience, Charles had many advantages over his predecessors. But he was a wholly incompetent king, mishandling patronage in such a way as unnecessarily to alienate powerful figures amongst the peerage and gentry, interfering in due process of law, breaking his solemn word when it suited him, blundering away his political initiatives in a self-imposed war with the Scots. But his greatest folly was to put himself at the head of a faction in the Church whose aims jarred significantly with the preferences and beliefs of the greater part of his subjects. By 1640, Charles's government was profoundly unpopular, and above all for its religious policies. Innovation in religion was even more compulsively listed in the petitions and addresses to the Long Parliament than was ship money. Yet England was psychologically far from civil war in 1640. The absence of a pretender made the simple remedy to his misgovernment (a *coup* on the precedents of 1399, 1461, 1485 or as a foreshadowing of 1688) impossible. It made civil war less likely; but it meant that if it did come, it would be a far more radical experience. It would involve a questioning of far deeper values, beliefs, certainties.

It is my contention that what made civil war possible in 1642 was a crisis of religion. Elsewhere I have argued that there were three linked but separable 'perceptions of misgovernment' in the 1630s and 1640s,[1] each playing a different role in the shaping of the civil war: the

---

1. J.S. Morrill, 'The Religious Context of the English Civil War'; above, ch. 3.

'localist', the 'legal-constitutionalist' and the 'religious'; and that while the first two created political stalemate, the third proved to have the ideological dynamism to drive minorities to arms. The momentum of 'constitutionalist' argument in 1642 was not sufficient. In this essay, I want to look more closely at how religious issues presented themselves to the Long Parliament.

In its first session (November 1640 to September 1641) the constitutional debates were conducted within a rhetorical and intellectual framework little different from that of the 1620s. No one who had attended the debates on the Petition of Right could be shocked by the arguments used against ship money, the prerogative courts, the evil counsellors.[2] Yet there was already a significant shift in the whole framework of reference within which the religious issues were discussed and this was causing an irrevocable division within the House of Commons.

Jacobean Parliaments had been little troubled by religious disputes.[3] The regular bills against pluralism, and for stricter observance of the sabbath, were in no sense 'puritan' bills, and the bishops would have said Amen to their pious intentions.[4] There was some anxiety about the legislative status (rather than the content) of the canons of 1604 and about the powers of High Commission, but this stemmed as much from the common law mind as from puritanism, and we no longer make easy connections between those two influences.[5]

But in the very last parliamentary session of the reign, and in the sessions from 1625 to 1629, religion returned as a major and increasingly bitter issue.[6] The cause was not a reawakening of puritan militancy but Court sponsorship of a group of divines whose writings appeared to depart sharply from the evolving spectrum of liberal Protestant beliefs which had formed the agenda of the Jacobean debates. Some of these writings were sharply critical of predestinarian beliefs; others challenged the status of the *ecclesia*

---

2. See, for example, the case made for the 'normality' of the Long Parliament by Sheila Lambert, 'The Opening of the Long Parliament', *HJ*, 27 (1984), 265–88. Lambert concentrates on constitutional and financial questions.
3. E.g. C. Russell, *Parliaments and English Politics 1621–1629* (Oxford, 1979), pp. 26–32 and *passim*.
4. K. Parker, 'English Sabbatarianism, 1558–1642' (Univ. of Cambridge PhD thesis, 1984), chs. 5 and 6.
5. J.P. Kenyon, *The Stuart Constitution* (Cambridge, 1962), pp. 126–9, 176–8. James in 1611 adjusted the membership and powers of the Court to take account of parliamentary criticisms.
6. Russell, *Parliaments and Politics*, pp. 29–32, 167–8, 230–3, 404–14, and *passim*; N.R.N. Tyacke, 'Arminianism in England in Religion and Politics, 1603–1640' (Univ. of Oxford D.Phil. thesis, 1968), *passim*.

anglicana as on the Protestant side of the unbridgeable gulf between
the Christian reformed and antichristian Roman churches; or they
sought to exalt the power of the king and to decry the power
of parliaments, so that 'the subjects' goods must be arbitrarily
disposed'.[7] Yet those who denounced these 'Arminians' did so for
impeccably conservative reasons; to protect the Church of England
from innovation and subversion.[8] None of the debates led to calls for
change in a more Protestant direction: for restrictions on episcopal
power, for the reform of the Prayer Book or the abolition of
'superstitious' furnishings and fixtures in the church, all matters
pursued by the Long Parliament in its first eighteen months. It cannot
be doubted that the religious temper was raised by aggressive Court
sponsorship of new opinions.[9] The reactions in the Commons and, to
a lesser extent, in the Lords were not the reactions of MPs speaking
to briefs or mandates from their constituents so much as reactions to
what they found while present at the political centre. Only twenty
petitions relating to religious issues were presented to the House in all
the Parliamentary sessions of the 1620s.[10] From the outset, the Long
Parliament was inundated by petitions from individual parishes, from
counties, from groups of ministers. Probably 800 parishes petitioned
in the first two years of the Parliament denouncing their ministries as
scandalous in life, doctrine or liturgical fashion.[11] All counties sent in
addresses for and/or against episcopacy, the book of Common Prayer,
and many took other religious issues.[12] The pressure on MPs was
thus now largely from without. While the pressure grew out of
the perceived threat to the established church, that threat was no
longer seen as emanating from a handful of clerics puffed up by

7. *Complete Collection of State Trials*, eds. W. Cobbett and T.B. Howells, 33 vols. (London, 1809–26), IV, 26.
8. M. Finlayson, *Historians, Puritanism and the English Revolution* (Toronto, 1983), pp. 79–104. For reasons which will become clear I do not share Finlayson's account of the religious dynamics of 1640–1.
9. As in the promotion of Montagu and Mainwaring shortly after they had been attacked in Parliament: and in the imposition of Buckingham as Chancellor of Cambridge, a move closely linked to the theological disputes there and to Buckingham's espousal of the Arminian position at the York House Conference; V. Morgan, 'Court, Country and Cambridge University: The Making of a Political Culture 1558–1642' (Univ. of East Anglia PhD thesis, 1984), ch. I.
10. An approximate figure reached by browsing the *Commons Journal* but confirmed in a private communication from Dr W. Abbott.
11. W.A. Shaw, *A History of the Church During the Civil Wars and Under the Commonwealth*, 2 vols. (London, 1900), II, 177. For the 100 + reported back to the House by September 1642, ibid., II, 295–304.
12. A. Fletcher, *The Outbreak of the English Civil War* (London, 1981), pp. 91–124, 191–227, etc.

the patronage of Buckingham. It stemmed from an 'army of priests which doth many ways advance the design and plot of popery', an army commanded by the archbishop of Canterbury himself.[13] As Harbottle Grimston put it: Laud

> is the only man, the only man that hath raised and advanced all those that, together with himself, have been the authors and causes of all our ruins, miseries, and calamities we now groan under that hath sat at the helm, to steer and manage all the projects that have been set on foot in this kingdom this ten years last past.[14]

It soon became clear to an increasing number of MPs that the threat to the Protestant foundations of the Church of England was so great, and the penetration so deep, that remedial action was insufficient. Only the total demolition of the existing edifice, only the sterilization of the site and the erection of a new Temple could protect the nation from Antichrist.[15] This is the all-important point: the fact that there was much hazy talk of 'primitive' episcopacy,[16] much imprecision about the future form of the church, that there is little evidence of committed Presbyterianism has led historians to speak of the 'moderation' of 1641–2. Two things in particular are often stressed: that no bill against episcopacy was approved until the summer of 1642 and that the managers of the Long Parliament played down potentially divisive religious issues in the first session in order to allow less divisive constitutional reforms to be effected. It is hoped to demonstrate that this latter point is simply incorrect, and that there were very straightforward reasons why no bill could be approved. But principally the essay seeks to argue that ecclesiological indecision is not the same thing as religious moderation. In 1641 religious issues polarized the House of Commons into those who stood by the pre-Laudian church and those who were acting *de facto* to replace it; in 1642 religious issues divided those who remained at Westminster into

---

13. From Francis Rous' speech carrying up the impeachment articles against John Cosin to the House of Lords, *State Trials*, IV, 26.
14. Ibid., IV, 318. It is not being asserted here that the allegations were true. Nor that there is a coherent 'Arminianism' to which all 'Laudians' subscribed. Our concern is with what was said and believed at the time. For wise words on how the actions of the Laudians did constitute an affront to mainstream Protestant opinion, see W. Lamont, *Godly Rule* (London, 1969), pp. 56–68.
15. See below, pp. 83–5.
16. Historians commonly conflate two distinct forms of 'primitive' episcopacy – the 'reduction' of the powers of bishops within the existing structure; and the establishment of preaching superintendants within an entirely new ecclesiastical order established in the wake of the abolition of the old order.

those committed to seek fresh guarantees of the settlement of 1641 and those committed to fight for those guarantees.[17]

Between November 1640 and the spring of 1642 little legislative progress was made despite the best intentions of the managers of the Commons, but this did not prevent them from crippling the old religious order and adumbrating a new one by virtue of an assumption of unwonted judicial and administrative powers.[18] Laud and his henchmen were incarcerated, suspended, silenced; the church courts stilled; the parish clergy made accountable to committees of the House; religious literature licensed by another committee; liturgical *laissez-faire* encouraged; iconoclasm permitted. The House of Commons was depriving ministers of their freehold; restoring those silenced by Star Chamber or High Commission; endorsing arrangements for lectureships; claiming the jurisdiction of the ordinary over church furnishings, etc. Note the emphasis on the House of Commons. A principal reason for the failure to proceed by legislation, for acting on what has been termed 'the dictatorial assertion of a semi-political, semi-judicial court exercising an authority which can only be described and justified as revolutionary',[19] was that there was no majority for radical reform within the Lords. A majority in the Upper House remained stubbornly committed to the programme of 1628 – the defence of the Elizabethan settlement from 'Arminian' innovation.

A good example of the contrast between the sentiment of the two Houses can be found in their attitude to iconoclasm. On 23 January 1641 the Commons determined to act summarily to select commissioners in each county to deface, demolish or otherwise get rid of *all* 'images, altars or tables turned altarwise, crucifixes, superstitious pictures, ornaments and relics of idolatry' from all churches.[20] This was to go far beyond the reversal of recent innovations; it was to 'throw to the moals and the bats every rag that hath not God's stamp and name upon it',[21] to complete that left incomplete

17. Morrill, 'Religious Context', pp. 164–78.
18. The standard accounts are Shaw, *English Church*, I, 1–122, II, 175–85, and the splendid recent study by Fletcher, *Outbreak*, pp. 91–124, and *passim*. A recent thesis by W. Abbott, 'The Issue of Episcopacy in the Long Parliament' (Univ. of Oxford D.Phil. thesis, 1982), is valuable on one aspect of the question. I am grateful to Dr Abbott for showing me a draft of his thesis some time before it was submitted. I have not seen the final version. The theological issues are explored in G. Yule, *The Puritans in Power* (Sutton Courtney, 1981), ch. 5.
19. Shaw, *English Church*, II, 175–6.
20. *Commons Journal*, II, 72. (hereafter *CJ*).
21. The call of Stephen Marshall in his sermon to the House of Commons at their Fast on 17 November 1640, Brit. Lib., Thomason Tracts (hereafter TT), E 204(9), p. 40.

in the first Reformation. Yet only days earlier, the Lords ordered that 'the parsons, vicars, and curates in the several parishes shall forbear to introduce any rites or ceremonies that may give offence otherwise than those which are established by the law of the land.[22] Their concern, as throughout the next twelve months, was that 'divine service should be performed as appointed by the Acts of Parliament of the Realm, and all disturbers of the same severely punished'.[23] In individual cases where innovations by ministers were uncovered, as with east-end railed-in altars, the Lords ordered a restoration so that the tables stood in 'the ancient place where they ought to do by the law, and as it hath done for the greater part of these three score years last past'[24] There was no point in trying to press a bill for a wider iconoclasm through such a House (as the events of early September 1641, discussed below, also demonstrate). Equally the limited progress of anti-episcopal legislation may owe as much to the certainty that it would fail in the Lords as to lack of zeal in the Commons. The simple bill against the temporal authority of the bishops (and especially against their seats in the Lords) was comfortably defeated in the Upper House in the first session,[25] and ignored by it in the second session after a similar bill had passed all stages in the Commons within a week of the end of the recess.[26] Only the suicidal petition of the twelve bishops on 30 December against decisions taken after they were intimidated from taking their seats by the mass picket around Westminster Hall revived the peers' interest in the bill.[27]

The House of Lords, then, constituted a legislative stymie upon the House of Commons, at least until the expulsion of the bishops and the haemorrhage of royalist peers to York in the spring of 1642 gave the radicals their chance to bring the two Houses into line. Almost immediately the series of bills which had been marking time in the Commons – bills for abolishing superstition and idolatry, for uprooting scandalous ministers for stricter sabbath observance and

22. *Lords Journal*, IV, 134 (hereafter *LJ*).
23. *LJ*, IV, 100–1, 107, 113, 133, 225.
24. *LJ*, IV, 174.
25. *CJ*, II, 114, 127; *LJ*, IV, 256.
26. *CJ*, II, 291–3 (21/23 October); 1st reading in the House of Lords, 23 October, but no second reading until 4 February 1642, after which it quickly passed all remaining stages (*LJ*, IV, 402, 562, 564, 580); Shaw, *English Church*, I, 117–19.
27. J. Rushworth, *Historical Collections*, 7 vols. (London, 1659–1701), IV, 466–8; S.R. Gardiner, *The History of England from the Accession of James I to the Outbreak of the Civil War*, 10 vols. (London, 1884), x, 120–6; B.S. Manning, *The English People and the English Revolution 1640–1649* (London, 1976), pp. 74–94.

against pluralism and non-residence – were sent up and passed in the Upper House,[28] to be included in the Nineteen Propositions sent to the king in early June.[29] This legislative block had not, however, prevented the managers of the Commons from ensuring that such bills were in the pipeline. It was not fear of dividing the Commons but certainty of defeat in the Lords which had slowed down legislative progress. Those actually or potentially divisive ecclesiastical bills had been read before or at the same time as the less controversial remedial constitutional legislation.[30]

The Commons were thus forced into 'arbitrary' action to achieve reform; intense external pressures constantly reinforced the need for that reform. That pressure came in part from the waves of petitions, in part from the full discovery of the transgressions of the clergy in recent times, in part from the urgings of the preachers and pamphleteers.

We have already noted the contrast between the paucity of religious petitions to the Parliaments of the 1620s and the wealth of such petitions to the Long Parliament. Several hundred petitions poured in from parishioners alleging ceremonialism, unsound preaching (or no preaching at all) and moral laxity in their ministers.[31] Francis Rous, carrying up the impeachment articles against Cosin to the Lords, said that 'when a great man is coming, his sumpters, his furniture, his provisions, go before him: the pope's furniture, altars, copes, pictures and images are come before him; and if we believe Mr Cosin the very substance of the Mass; a certain sign that the pope is not far off'.[32] The House of Commons cannot but have been rattled by the evidence of enthusiastic espousal of popish ceremonialism by hundreds of the clergy. These were not the lone fanatics pursuing some private religious vision who had troubled Parliaments in the past. Here were men taking their cue from the bishops and not merely railing off the altar on a raised dais at the east end, or bowing to it

28. Bill for Abolishing Superstition, *CJ*, II, 79, 84, 162, 183, 199, 212, 246, 278; replaced by a different bill in February 1642, *CJ*, II, 436, 437, 465, 476, 493, *LJ*, IV, 669, 679, V, 210, 212, 248; Bill against Scandalous Ministers, *CJ* II, 109, 162, 183–4, 208–11, 491, 516; *LJ*, V, 19, 35, 156; Bill for Stricter Sabbath Observance, *CJ* II, 348, 356.
29. *LJ*, V, pp. 97–9; Kenyon, *Stuart Constitution*, pp. 244–7.
30. Indeed one can say that legislatively there was more activity in terms of ecclesiastical legislation in the first few months than in terms of constitutional legislation, and the two sorts of bill jostle one another in June and July 1641.
31. For some examples, see *CJ*, II, 35, 139, 149; *The Journal of Sir Simonds D'Ewes from the Beginning of the Long Parliament to the Opening of the Trial of the Earl of Strafford*, ed. W. Notestein (New Haven, 1927), pp. 65, 77, 270, 276, 281, 419.
32. *State Trials*, IV, 27.

and refusing communion to those who would not kneel before it, but who preached, as the rector of All Hallows, Barking, did: 'that they are black toads, spotted toads and venomous toads, like Jack Straw and Watt Tyler, that speak against the ceremonies of the Church; and that they were in the state of damnation'.[33] By no means a majority of the petitions were ever read in the House or reported from the committees to the House. But many members were well aware of the magnitude of the outcry: Sir Edward Dering had more than seventy such petitions against Kentish ministers in his papers.[34] W.A. Shaw suggests that the total number of parish petitions may have been around 800.[35] Something of the pressure they must have exerted can be seen from the business at just one meeting of the committee of religion, held on 16 November 1640.[36] The committee received a petition from Lincolnshire clergymen against the increase in popery, 'idle and frivolous ceremonies', the canons and for fresh laws against fornication, adultery and sabbath-breaking; several petitions against the imposition of altars and organs; against ministers who would not communicate those who refused to kneel; against the pulling down of an ancient parish church in the shadow of St Paul's to provide building materials for the cathedral; and a report of the excommunication of a man who had proceeded against his minister for 'false doctrine'. Day in and day out MPs were inundated with stories of a spreading cancer in the church, promoted and nourished by its leaders.

There is some evidence that the petitioning was orchestrated. One of Sir Edward Hyde's correspondents told how John Lilburne had come down with warrants to get signatures for a petition against him as a persecuting or innovating minister. Archdeacon Marler, in another letter to Hyde, reported how

> your House hath sent forth encouradgements and derections for busy men to traduce at such as be not of the faction . . . wherein such as ar zealous in the cause both of the clergy and layty . . . have mett together and consulted how to informe against such as we orthodox and obedient clergymen and to furnish your house with arguments for the overthrow of the hierarchy of the church.[37]

33. *CJ*, II, 35.
34. 'Proceedings Principally in the County of Kent in Connection with the Parliaments Called in 1640', ed. L.B. Larking, *Camden Society* (1862), pp. 101–240.
35. Shaw, *English Church*, II, 38.
36. *D'Ewes*, ed. Notestein, p. 38.
37. Bodl. Lib., MS Clarendon 19, fo. 281; MS Clarendon 20, fo. 13.

In January 1641, indeed, the Commons called for a survey of scandalous clergy from each county: the draft reply of five Herefordshire clergy survives, giving the great majority of the 193 ministers surveyed as scandalous, and pinning responsibility on the bishops, 'the main atlases which upholds the babel of confusion in church and commonwealth'.[38] Mrs Pearl finds evidence that the timing and content of London petitions was organized within the House.[39] One consequence of all this, according to a friend of Sir Edward Dering's, was 'the Monstrous Easye receipt of Petitions att the Standing Committees makes Authoritye declyne'.[40]

The flood of petitions was, then, both sustained by radical MPs wishing to reinforce the threat, as they saw it, of 'the army of priests' to the integrity of English Protestantism, and was intended to soften up the concerned middle ground by constantly reinforcing the scale of that threat. This in turn was further strengthened by wider petitions on the urgent need for radical reform.

The most important of these were the London petition for root-and-branch reform (presented with 15,000 signatures on 11 December 1640),[41] a digest of county petitions subscribed by 750 clergy in all and presented to the House of Commons in late January 1641;[42] and the wave of county root-and-branch petitions (nineteen in all) which were launched with those from Kent and Essex in mid-January:[43] Cumulatively, these were an even more stunning indictment of the state to which the Laudians had reduced the Church. Despite the reluctance of some historians to accept it, the aim of the petitions was unambiguously to be rid not only of the Laudians but of a church order so easily subverted by them. Certainly, as Mr Fletcher has suggested, there was only a limited comprehension of what the radical rhetoric would lead to. Sir Edward Dering, in a telling rewriting of the Ministers' Remonstrance, recorded that 'this hierarchical power may be totally abrogated, if the wisdom of this honourable House shall find it cannot be maintained by God's Word and to his glory'.[44] It must remain an open question just how soon a majority in the Commons wished to uproot episcopacy: it is clear that from early

38. Bodl. Lib., MS 206 Corpus Christi. I am grateful to Paul Gladwish for lending me his microfilm copy of this manuscript and for his comments on it.
39. V. Pearl, *London and the Outbreak of the Puritan Revolution* (Oxford, 1964), pp. 212–16.
40. Quoted in P. Zagorin, *The Court and the Country* (London, 1969), pp. 229–30.
41. Rushworth, *Historical Collections*, IV, 93–7.
42. No copy of this petition survives. See Shaw, *English Church*, I, 23–7.
43. Fletcher, *Outbreak*, pp. 92–6.
44. *Ibid.*, Lamont, *Godly Rule*, pp. 83–8.

on in the Parliament a growing number accepted the need to uproot the Elizabethan settlement. Primitive episcopacy could either be a 'reduction' of the existing system, or part of a new system. Since the overwhelming concern of MPs was *religious* renewal, not *ecclesiastical* renewal, their flexibility and lack of precision on this point is not the problem which has worried historians. Lack of zeal for an articulated presbyterianism is not evidence of religious 'moderation'. Some have argued that the adoption of a more radical language was intended to placate the Scots, and disguised continuing religious conservatism; it is more likely that it revealed a growing commitment to *a* fresh start but not *a particular* fresh start.[45] Thus, when the Commons voted in early February to refer the substance of the Ministers' Remonstrance to a committee, it reserved to itself debate on the future of episcopacy. This has usually been taken as evidence of caution, a refusal to commit so sensitive an issue to a committee of the kind so readily packed. But the fact that the question was already accepted as an open one, and to be aired where it could create greatest heat, is just as significant. On 25 January 1641, John Pyne, the Somerset radical, wrote to Thomas Smyth of Ashton Court that 'the heat in the lower House increases . . . [the Remonstrance] will require great consideration and time, especially episcopacy which hath so many advocates and so strong a party in our House'. In such circumstances, the managers were grasping nettles, not avoiding them.[46]

Petitions formed the first source of pressure on MPs, reinforcing the need for radical reform. The revelations of committees of enquiry into ecclesiastical misgovernment constituted a second, allied source. The most obvious of those was the Committee for Scandalous Ministers, which looked into the petitions alleging 'vitiousness of life, errors in doctrine, contrary to the Articles of our Religion, and for the Practising and Pressing superstitious innovations contrary to Law'.[47] The reports of the committee merely reinforced the message of the petitions themselves, but they also made a pattern out of them. When John White, chairman of the committee, celebrated the expulsion of the one hundredth delinquent minister in a tract, he called it *The First Century of Scandalous Ministers, Malignant Priests, Made and Admitted unto Benefices By the Prelates, in whose hands the Ordination of Ministers*

45. E.g. P. Crawford, *Denzil Holles, First Lord Holles* (London, 1979), pp. 43–52; C.L. Hamilton, 'The Basis of Scottish Efforts to Create a Reformed Church in England, 1640–1', *Church History*, XXX (1961), 171–88; Yule, *Puritans in Power*, pp. 118–20.
46. Fletcher, *Outbreak*, p. 97; Bristol Rec. Off., MS 36074, fo. 139.
47. Shaw, *English Church*, II, 177–85.

The Attack on the Church of England

and government of the Church hath been.[48] It was not episcopal neglect but episcopal design which had created the pollution in the church.

Very few committee papers survive from the Commons.[49] But one important report from the committee set up to establish 'abuses of the universities in matters of religion' does survive to reveal an alarming picture, at least at Cambridge. The principal concern of the report was to investigate six preachers whose sermons reveal a startling range of theological speculation and also suggest deep divisions within the *Caput*, or committee of college Heads. None of the errant preachers had been punished and some had been aided by the intervention of the archbishop's chaplain. Some of the sermons were palpably in breach of the articles of religion, notably the eleventh on Justification. As late as August 1640, the Commons committee were told, William Norwich, Fellow of Peterhouse, preached in the University Church defending the need for works of satisfaction, recommending private confession, declaring that works had to accompany faith in the process of justification and urging the use of ceremonies. The Vice-Chancellor (John Cosin), with the support of a bare majority of the Heads, dismissed charges against him. While the University Church resounded to such preaching, the committee found that godly preachers had been silenced and that the Heads had encouraged not only popish teaching but also popish ceremonies: there were decorated altars, bowing and turning to the east in twelve of the sixteen colleges.[50] Dr Morgan has recently pointed out that after 1600 the Crown had taken an increasing interest in the elections to Cambridge Fellowships, and specifically to Headships, viewing the colleges more as cathedral chapters than as independent corporations. The subversion of Cambridge followed the extended use of royal *congés d'élire*.[51]

Amongst the very earliest acts of the Long Parliament was the release from prison of the principal victims of the Laudian regime: Burton, Bastwicke and Prynne; Leighton; Lilburne; Smart; and Thomas Wilson.[52] Committees were set up to investigate the

48. Brit Lib., TT, E 76(21).
49. Except in brief summaries in some of the parliamentary diaries (e.g. *D'Ewes*, ed. Notestein, pp. 38–9, 150) and extracts from the Committee of Religion, of which Dering was chairman, 'Proceedings in Kent', ed. Larking, pp. 80–100.
50. BL, Harl. MS 7019, pp. 52–93, especially pp. 53, 61, 71, 73, 76–85. I owe my knowledge of this manuscript to David Hoyle who also kindly showed me a copy of his unpublished paper based upon it. See also J.D. Twigg, 'The University of Cambridge and the English Revolution' (Univ. of Cambridge PhD thesis, 1983), ch. 2.
51. Morgan 'Court, Country and Cambridge University', *passim*.
52. *CJ*, II, 22, 24, 25, 40.

circumstances of their trial and punishment, the reports of their committees coming in at intervals. These reports consistently emphasized not only that they had suffered for upholding ortho-doxy, but that proceedings against them had been arbitrary or in breach of the rule of law.[53] This was a much more prominent theme in the investigations of the Lords' committees which in the 1640s reviewed several hundred cases from the lower courts. Dr Hart, who has investigated this process, is in no doubt that many of the worst instances of the abuse of due process lay in the church courts. Several ministers had been ejected on flimsy or trumped-up simony charges to make way for Laudians like Dr William Beale; ministers were ejected or suspended on the evidence of a single witness; the Court of Arches refused to hear appeals from a number of churchwardens or others in cases relating to altar rails, apparently because Laud 'had given order that no inhibitions should go into Northamptonshire, Bedfordshire or Buckinghamshire without his special knowledge'.[54]

There can be little doubt that it was the intention of the parliamentary managers to exploit this flow of information that linked together the ills of the church into a grand conspiracy. Far from playing down religious issues, they amplified and focussed them. While it is possible to exaggerate the importance of 'king' Pym in the early months of the Long Parliament,[55] his role was an important one. Nowhere is this more evident than in his promotion of religious issues in the early weeks. On 7 November it was Pym who presented the petitions of the wives of Burton and Bastwicke to the Lower House; on the 9th he sought a committee 'to see that papists depart from town'; on the 10th, when Peter Smart revived his petition from the Short Parliament

53. E.g. *CJ*, II, 90, 102, 123, 124, 134; *D'Ewes*, ed. Notestein, pp. 83, 240–1; Rushworth, *Historical Collections*, IV, 253.
54. J. Hart, 'The House of Lords and the Reformation of Justice' (Univ. of Cambridge PhD thesis, 1985), ch. 4; see Farren vs. Clarke, H.L.R.O., Main Papers for 6 February 1641; Garfield vs. Clarke, H.L.R.O., Main Papers for 22 December 1640; Bloxam vs. Sandiland, H.L.R.O., Main Papers for 5 January 1641 and 10 March 1641; *LJ*, N, 155, 181; also H.L.R.O., Main Papers, 8 February 1641, *LJ*, IV, 181.
55. Lambert, 'Opening of the Long Parliament', argues that Pym's role has been greatly exaggerated. Many of her points are of substance, but it seems to me that it reduces Pym from the most important manager of the Commons into being one of the most important, especially with regard to religion. The article also rightly stresses the important role of the peerage in the events of 1640–2. It is vital, however, to distinguish the role of individual peers from the role of the House of Lords.

about Cosin's innovations at Durham Cathedral, 'Mr Pym desired to consider who promoted Dr Cusons to be dean', a clear escalation. In the following days and weeks, he brought in three petitions against unjust proceedings in the Court of High Commission; he was one of those who spoke against the canons; and he was the first MP to suggest that Laud should be impeached for treason. He was appointed to most committees on religion, and was active in the Grand Committee and in the more specific enquiries into the cases of Leighton and Lilburne.[56] This is not compatible with the common view of him as putting religious issues on a back burner until the less controversial measures to remedy the secular ills of the commonwealth had been approved.[57]

It is, perhaps, worth stressing the virulence of the attack on the leading churchmen, more violent in tone than the attacks on counsellors and judges. Laud was impeached in December 1640, Wren bailed pending the drawing up of articles, committees set to work to draw up charges against Piers of Bath and Wells and that majority of the bishops who had supported the canons of 1640. Cosin, Master of Peterhouse, and a number of officials of the church courts were also investigated. This was a wider trawl than amongst the lay authors of misgovernment. Once again, however, the Commons ran into a stone wall in the Lords who simply failed to take action on any of the impeachments.[58]

It is true that there is no reference to 'Arminianism' in any of the impeachment articles (in comparison with the debates of the late 1620s).[59] But the articles against Laud speak of his espousal of 'divers doctrines and opinions contrary to the articles of religion'[60] Furthermore, the innovating ceremonialism of which all were accused was intended to exalt the altar and subdue the pulpit, to emphasize the sacramental grace of the communion promiscuously offered to all who would kneel to receive it. One obsessive theme, however, runs through all the Commons investigations: the usurpation of the royal supremacy: Laud 'traiterously assumed to himself a papal and

---

56. *CJ*, II, 24; *D'Ewes*, ed. Notestein, pp. 4, 17, 21, 136, 149, 162, 163, 169.
57. See also the dominant position accorded to religious issues in his major address to the Commons on 7 November, *Speeches and Passages of this most Happy Parliament* (1641), pp. 458–60 (mostly in J.P. Kenyon, *Stuart Constitution* (Cambridge, 1966) pp. 203–6.
58. State Trials, IV, 22–41, 63–82, 315ff. For the Commons' appeals to the Lords to take up the cases, see, e.g., *CJ*, II, 292, 333–4.
59. Russell, *Parliaments and Politics*, pp. 404–14, and *passim*; H. Schwartz, 'Arminianism and the English Parliament 1624–1629', *Jnl.Brit.Studs.*, XII (1973).
60. *State Trials*, IV, 327.

tyrannical power, both in ecclesiastical and temporal matters . . . to the disinheron of the Crown, dishonour of his Majesty and derogation of his supreme authority in matters ecclesiastical'[61] (as Pym glossed it, 'he hath made the king's throne a footstool for his own and their pride');[62] Wren 'assumed to himself an arbitrary power;[63] Cosin was alleged to have said that 'the king hath no more power over the church than the boy who rubs my horse's heels';[64] Montagu is supposed to have written to Laud that 'the bishoprick of Norwich, since the total desolation and dissolution of the former bishoprick by King Henry the eighth, who stole the sheep and gave not so much as the trotters for God's sake, is a meane thing';[65] and Sergeant Wilde, moving the impeachment of the thirteen bishops for their role in the making of the canons, described the latter as containing 'in them divers matters contrary to the king's prerogative'.[66]

The attack on the clergy was intended to demonstrate the existence of a popish conspiracy against the commonwealth. The king had been seduced by the papists at Court and the spawn of the papists in the Church into surrendering his power into their hands. Much of the rhetoric of 1640–2 was apocalyptic: Sir John Wray's speech on 25 November 1640 is often quoted but infrequently glossed:

> What must we do then to preserve our Religion safe and sound to us and our posterity, that our golden candlestick be not removed? Why, the only way is to fall to our work in earnest and lay the Axe to the Root, to unloose the long and deep Fangs of Superstition and Popery, which being done the Bark will soon fall down.[67]

The Church of England is here identified with one of the seven golden candle sticks described in the Book of Revelation. The struggle against popery was matched by the struggle for a New Jerusalem. The deeper the perception of a Popish Plot – as it unravelled itself in 1641 through the machinations of army plots, the Irish Rebellion, the Attempt on the Five Members – the greater the need to push forward to complete the Reformation, to fall in with God's Will that His work

61. Ibid., p. 326
62. Ibid., p. 322.
63. Ibid., p. 35.
64. Ibid., p. 25.
65. W. Prynne, *A Breviate of the Late William, Archbishop of Canterbury* (London, 1645), p. 555.
66. *CJ*, II, 233.
67. J. Nalson, *An Impartial Collection of the Great Affairs of State From the Beginning of the Scotch Rebellion in the Year 1639 to the Murder of King Charles I*, 2 vols. (London, 1682–3), I, 513. For a fuller discussion of the theme of 'protestant apocalyptic imperialism', see P. Christianson, *Reformers and Babylon* (Toronto, 1978), and Lamont, *Godly Rule*, both *passim*.

be done.[68] Here the conviction, the rhetoric, the authority of the preachers was all-important. We know that those who delivered Fast Sermons to the Long Parliament were carefully chosen and that they preached to encourage the godly. Their sermons were emphatic on the need for Reformation, but less clear on the means. They reinforced the split between the political conservatism of emergent parliamentarianism and the religious commitment – 'Consider what some say of Solomon', said Edmund Calamy, 'that it was his great fault, that he bestowed more time in building of his owne house, than he did in building the house of God.'[69]

In his study of the Fast Sermons, John Wilson distinguishes the 'prophetic' from the 'apocalyptic' tradition of preaching. In the former – espoused by the preachers of 1640–2 – the minister 'delivered' the 'word' from the Lord, a 'word' embodying judgement and mercy contingent upon the people turning or returning to Him. It emphasized 'human ability to exercise agency'. (The 'apocalyptic' tradition emphasized not an offer from God requiring human acquiescence, but God's irresistible action quite independently of human agency. This style of preaching was taken up by other preachers later in the 1640s.)[70] This is a crucial distinction. Preachers like Cornelius Burges, Stephen Marshall, Edmund Calamy and Thomas Goodwin all took Old Testament stories of God's offers to Israel and the consequences of human acceptance or rejection of those offers.[71] The history of Israel was precisely and literally matched to the history of Britain. The terrible choices were hammered home:

> If a Nation doth evil in God's sight, God will repent of the good he intended . . . when God begins to draw back his mercies from a Nation, that Nation is in a wofull plight. . . . But on the contrary, if we turn

68. For the widespread belief that there *was* a Popish Plot and for evidence that, in a sense, there was, see the excellent recent book of C. Hibbard, *Charles I and the Popish Plot* (Chapel Hill, 1983), chs. 8 and 9, taken up and developed throughout Fletcher, *Outbreak*.
69. BL, TT, E 133(18), p. 50 (E. Calamy, *God's Free Mercy to England*).
70. J.F. Wilson, *Pulpit in Parliament* (Princeton, 1969), pp. 198–200, and *passim*. More generally, see H.R. Trevor-Roper, 'The Fast Sermons of the Long Parliament', in *Religion, the Reformation and Social Change*, ed. H.R. Trevor-Roper (London, 1967), pp. 294–314. These sermons were only the most immediate and pressing of the advices offered to Parliament. Both Christianson, *Reformers and Babylon*, and the introduction to *Milton Prose Works*, ed. D.M. Wolfe, 8 vols. (New Haven, 1956–83), I (1956), discuss the wider literature.
71. E.g. BL, TT, E 204(8), C. Burges, *The First Sermon Preached to the Honourable House of Commons*; TT, E 133(9), S. Marshall, *Meroz Cursed*; TT, E 131(29), E. Calamy, *England's Looking Glass*; TT, E 147(13), T. Goodwin, *Zerubbabel's Encouragement to Finish the Temple*.

from our evil ways, God will perfect his building, and finish his plantation, he will make us a glorious Paradise, an habitation fit for Himself to dwell in.[72]

Thomas Goodwin reminded the Commons how the Israelites were freed to 'build the Temple and restore God's worship' after 'the Babilonian Monarchy [Rome's type] had trod downe the holy city, and laid waste the Temple and worship of God'. But after laying the foundations and establishing the principal ceremonies of the faith, they found themselves hampered by 'a company of Samaritans that were adversaries of the Jewes . . . a generation of men who were not heathens in their profession for that they professed the same religion with the Jewes . . . and yet were not true Jewes either, nor perfectly of the same religion, but a mungrell and mixt kind . . . intermingling heathenish idolatries with Jewish worship'. These Samaritans were initially 'but underhand adversaries, for they friendly offer to build with them but so as with an intent to have defiled and spoiled the work', but later they openly opposed it: 'they troubled them (all they could) in building. And they ceased not here, but further, they incensed and made the Court against them . . . both by hiring counsellors . . . and also by insinuating to those mighty Persian kings . . .'. Only with the appearance of the prophet Zachariah many years after the release from Babylon was Zerubbabel encouraged to drive out the Samaritans and bring the people back to their task. The application to English history since the Reformation is self-evident.[73]

The spiritual imperatives were clear. As the managers of the Commons ducked and weaved in the constitutional debate, responding to royal escalations of the conflict, making the minimum claims to a share in power compatible with self-preservation and the protection of the reforms achieved by due legislative process, they thrust forward with ecclesiastical revolution. We have seen how, until the spring of 1642, legislative remedy was denied to them. We have seen how the revelations in petitions, in the investigations of the Houses and their committees, opened the eyes of members to the apparent magnitude and central coordination of a plot against the protestant foundation of the church. The preachers warned them, with terrible historical examples, of the consequences of deferring or withholding action. For those with a dualistic view of the world, as the battleground of immanent forces of Good and Evil, the years

---

72. BL, TT, E 131(29), Calamy, *Looking Glass*, p. 58.
73. BL, TT, E 147(13), Goodwin, *Zerubbabel's Encouragement*, pp. 3–6.

1640–2 saw the mists clear, the future certain.[74] It became less and less a question of tinkering with the Elizabethan settlement in order to render it safe from another William Laud: there was a necessity to build such a church as would make all men obedient to God's word and turn them into His loving servants. Then indeed would the fruits of peace and prosperity flourish. The political struggles over the church in these years were not in essence sterile debates over ecclesiology: they were an attempt to realize a transformation in Man. For the next twenty years, those driven on to lead the Revolution were caught up with that elusive task, to hold onto their glimpse of Zion's glory.

Yet such language and such rhetoric repelled as many as it attracted.[75] While it was possible, all too possible, to see Charles I in 1641 as mendacious, or as the tool of a papist conspiracy, it was also possible to see him as a chastened and wiser king: as a man who had accepted constitutional reform, remodelled his Council, abandoned the Laudians, appointed moderate bishops. It was also possible to lay alongside the threat of popish risings the reality of popular disturbances in London and elsewhere, a perceived collapse of social order which the parliamentary leadership at the least condoned. A great many of those who denounced most bitterly the innovations of the Laudians did so out of concern for and love of the evolving practice and piety of the Elizabethan and Jacobean church. They were not unmoved by the revelations of 1641, but they put them into a different context. Less obsessive in their anxieties about Catholicism, they looked harder and less indulgently at the fissures within radical Protestantism, at the spread of separatism and at doctrines of social levelling preached by some of the separatists.

These were the circumstances in which the attack on the Church of England took place: from an apparent unity in 1640 against the Laudian experiment with a general rhetorical appeal for reform to the confrontation of 1642 between 'the true reformed protestant religion by law established without any connivance of popery or innovation' and 'the godly reformation'. It was this which made civil war necessary.

Between the summoning of the Long Parliament and the outbreak of the civil war, then, notwithstanding the failure of its attempts at legislation, the two Houses had toppled the Church of England

---

74. The powerful hold of apocalyptic anti–catholicism is explored by Hibbard, *Charles I and the Popish Plot, passim.*
75. Morrill, 'Religious Context', pp. 63–5.

and had equipped themselves to turn it into a department of state under gentry control. Few bishops by the summer of 1642 retained any authority in their dioceses; most church courts had ceased to function; there was no mechanism to enforce, and parliamentary encouragement to modify, the liturgy and formal worship of the church; the outward and visible sign of Laudian innovation – the altar rail – had vanished in most parishes far more speedily than it had gone up. A vacuum had been created which the Houses were proceeding to fill.

From early in 1641 ministers were deprived of their livings and freehold by order of one or other of the Houses: the assumption of this quasi-judicial, quasi-executive power was wholly without precedent and went undefended. No comparable assertion in the civil sphere is to be found before 1643.[76] Early examples included Edward Finch of Christchurch, London, too drunk to take communion to the sick, a whoremonger and an innovator (and, perhaps most to the point, brother of the disgraced Lord Keeper);[77] Immanuel Uty, for popery in teaching and ceremony, for haunting alehouses and saying that the bishops not the king headed the church;[78] and George Preston of Rotherthorpe, Northamptonshire, who thought that 'Parliaments in England never did any good nor never would, but that his hogs were fit to make Parliament men of, and their sty a place fit for them to sit in', and that those who gadded to sermons were 'like jackdaws that hopped from twig to twig; and that they did go to several churches to commit whoredom'.[79] By 1642 the number was escalating: over seventy were dispossessed between February and July 1642.[80]

At the same time the House of Commons was setting aside judgements in Star Chamber and High Commission against puritan martyrs of the 1630s. A special committee was set up to consider abuses of ecclesiastical jurisdiction in Lincolnshire;[81] in the case of Peter Smart, the prebend of Durham who had tangled with John Cosin, the proceedings in High Commission were adjudged 'illegal and unjust and ought not to bind'. His degradation from the ministry

---

76. D.H. Pennington, 'The Making of the War, 1640–2', in *Puritans and Revolutionaries*, eds. D. Pennington and K. Thomas (Oxford, 1978), pp. 161–85, examines the growth of parliamentary executive control of finance which is much more hesitant and circumspect in questions of legality; see also Morrill, 'Religious Context', above pp. 57–62.
77. *CJ*, II, 139; BL, Harl. MS 163 (*D'Ewes'* Journal), fo. 537.
78. *CJ*, II, 65, 148; BL, Harl. MS 163, fo. 190; *D'Ewes*, ed. Notestein, pp. 232–3.
79. *D'Ewes*, ed. Notestein, p. 270.
80. Shaw, *English Church*, II, 295–300.
81. *CJ*, II, 56.

was reversed and his livings (in plurality) restored, and Cosin and his judges ordered to pay damages and costs. While the Commons proceeded in many such cases by committee fiat, the Lords proceeded in another fashion, building on but greatly expanding their formal procedures of judicial review.[82]

On 14 June 1641, the Commons ordered that there be sermons every Sunday afternoon in every cathedral church;[83] on 8 September, they went further: 'It shall be lawful for the parishioners of any parish . . . to set up a lecture and to maintain an orthodox minister at their own charge, to preach every Lord's day where there is no preaching, and to preach one day in every week when there is no weekly lecture.'[84] From the end of the summer onwards, the Commons spent much time ratifying appointments in particular parishes, creating lectureships by combination and imposing sanctions on vicars and rectors resisting 'men thrusting their sickles into another man's harvest'.[85]

By the summer of 1641 the Commons had assumed power to license sermons and other books, and the fact that this activity grew out of powers granted to a sub-committee of the Grand Committee of Religion displays the importance of the licensing of religious works. The committee, initially chaired by Sir Edward Dering, also investigated the publication of 'unsound' works.[86]

These developments helped to polarize the House of Commons; the assumption of such powers and the pursuit of ends so hostile to the sustaining of the established religion were bitterly resented. The greatest disputes, however, on the eve of the summer recess, in Houses thinned by departures for the country after a ten-month session, concerned the orders against innovations. By a resolution on 1 September, altar rails were to be removed, chancels levelled, communion tables settled in the nave, crucifixes, candles and images taken away, bowing banned and sabbatarianism strictly enforced. Church wardens had full authority to put this into practice, justices of the peace and mayors the duty to report those who disobeyed to

82. Ibid., p. 71, and cf. ibid., p. 90 (Bastwicke), p. 102 (Burton), p. 123 (Prynne), p. 124 (Leighton), p. 134 (Lilburne).
83. Ibid., p. 174.
84. Ibid., pp. 281–3, and cf. p. 206.
85. Ibid., pp. 381, 484, 485, 488, 491, 492, etc. (over fifty between March and June 1642 alone). See also *Private Journals of the Long Parliament*, eds. W.H. Coates, A.S. Young and V.F. Snow (New Haven, 1982), p. 355.
86. S. Lambert, 'The Beginning of Printing for the House of Commons, 1640–1642', *The Library*', 6th ser., III (1981), 43–61; 'Proceedings in Kent', ed. Larking, pp. 80–100.

Parliament after the recess. The device was a controversial addition to the growing stock of assumed executive powers; but it met a double (and related) challenge. In the Commons, Culpepper successfully moved that 'we would likewise provide a remedy against such as did villifie and contemne the common prayer book established by act of parliament' and it was referred to a committee how this might be phrased. The resultant draft was then rejected after a long and acrimonious debate on 6 September. The issue was then taken up by the Lords who also sought to protect the prayer book and to reiterate their commitment to the 'religion as by law established'. In issuing its declaration on its own, the Commons made the astonishing claim about the Lords' statement:

> which being presented to the House of Commons, it was thought unseasonable at this time, to urge the severe execution of the said Laws: whereupon it was voted that they do not consent to those orders . . . [and] that it may be understood that the last order of the Lords was made with the consent of 11 Lords. . . . We expect that the Commons . . . quietly attend the Reformation intended without any tumultuous disturbance of the worship of God.[87]

Not surprisingly, the House found itself with many problems arising from the declaration and much recrimination after the recess.[88]

This decisive debate revealed fully the basic split within the Long Parliament: there was an anglican party before there was a royalist party and a commitment to 'the reformation intended' before any recognition that non-negotiable constitutional issues would arise. The radicals who won the day 'expected' that 'the reformation intended' (i.e. licensed iconoclasm) would not occasion tumult. But they had already exonerated lay preachers and were soon to stay proceedings at common law against those who absented themselves from their own parish church.[89]

These assumptions of power over religion were, of course, pragmatic and piecemeal. But in debates that were often long and acrimonious, they were to lay the groundwork for a future church permanently and explicitly under gentry control. In June

---

87. *CJ*, II, 279–87; BL, Harl. MS 164, fos. 888–90, 895–914. Rushworth, *Historical Collections*, IV, 385.
88. *The Journal of Sir Simonds D'Ewes From the First Recess of the Long Parliament to the Withdrawal of King Charles from London*, ed. W.H. Coates (New Haven, 1942), pp. 5–6, 11, 12, 19–20, 35, 41; *Private Journals*, eds. Coates *et al.*, pp. 136–7. See the pointed reiteration of the Lords' declaration and of Culpepper's amendment in the royal declaration on religion on 10 December 1641, Rushworth, *Historical Collections*, IV, 392, 456–7.
89. *Private Journals*, eds. Coates *et al.*, pp. 302–3; BL, Harl. MS 163, fo. 669.

1641, the Commons approved a scheme to set up a synod which would propose a permanent settlement of religion: meanwhile the Houses were to empower nine lay commissioners in every county, chosen by its parliamentary representatives, to discharge all ecclesiastical jurisdiction, and both to run the church and to supervise a massive redistribution of episcopal and capitular wealth. Clergy who resisted the authority of these commissioners would incur the penalties of *praemunire*. Nominated clergy would ordain and assist in determining cases of heresy and schism. But powers of excommunication would lie exclusively with Parliament itself. At other times in 1641, the Commons proposed bodies of lay commissioners in each county to proceed against scandalous ministers (through jury trial), and to establish lay feoffees to handle alienated church land and impropriations.[90]

Not all parliamentarians were erastians;[91] but it is hard to believe that those who pushed through the bill 'for the abolition of arch-bishops, bishops', etc., on second reading on 27 May 1641 by 139 to 108 envisaged surrendering this gentrified church. In the spring of 1642, they did set up an assembly of divines to advise on a permanent solution.[92] This hand-picked assembly was as dependent on the Houses for the fate of its proposals as it was for its summons. The lack of commitment to a presbyterian scheme and the determination on secular control of the means to effect the building of Jerusalem does not make the religious imperatives any less vital.

Between 1640 and 1642 the Church of England collapsed, its leaders reviled and discredited, its structures paralysed, its practice if not yet proscribed, at least inhibited. In the years to follow, yet worse was to befall it. And yet in every year of its persecution after 1646, new shoots sprang up out of the fallen timber: bereft of episcopal leadership, lacking any power of coercion, its observances illegal, anglicanism thrived.[93] As memories of the 1630s faded and were overlaid by the tyrannies of the 1640s, by the attempts of Zerubbabel and Zachariah to frogmarch the nation to the site of the Temple, the deeper rhythms of the Kalendar and the ingrained perfections of Cranmer's liturgies bound a growing majority together. In April

---

90. A. Fletcher, 'Concern for Renewal in the Root and Branch Debates of 1641', *Studies in Church History*, XIV (1977).
91. Yule, *Puritans in Power*, pp. 149–208.
92. *CJ*, II, 159, 579; LJ, IV, 595, 672–3; *Private Journals*, eds. Coates *et al.*, pp. 133–9; BL, Harl. MS 163, fos. 475, 514.
93. J.S. Morrill, 'The Church of England 1642–9', below, ch. 7.

1660, three weeks before the Declaration of Breda and the proclamation of Charles II, Easter, a forbidden Festival, was celebrated
in most parish churches up and down the country. It was the collapse
of the old church which presaged the downfall of the monarchy: and
it was to be the church's survival which was to herald the Restoration.

CHAPTER FIVE

The Scottish National Covenant of 1638 in its British Context[1]

I

The signing of the National Covenant in February 1638 has always
and rightly been recognized as an event of great importance in
the history of Scotland. Like so many of the great 'constitutional
documents' that shape the cultural identity of particular peoples, its
ultimate importance lies as much in subsequent misrepresentations
as in the retrievable historical reality of the purposes and aspirations
of those who made it.[2] That said, no one seriously doubts that the
National Covenant, of itself and in the bitter wars that were fought
in the twenty years after its formulation to uphold and to export it,
crystallized out a set of beliefs and practices that have determined the
ecclesiastical and religious if not necessarily the political history of
Scotland over the past three hundred and fifty years. But the Scottish
National Covenant has been less well studied as a critical document in
British history. English historians have noticed it in so far as it caused
Charles I to lose control of his metropolitan kingdom but have seen
it principally as an exogenous factor, a contingent and unpredictable
happenstance that gave his critics a chance to halt his Personal
Rule. Scottish historians have certainly noted its importance as an
expression of national alarm at the effective subordination of Scotland

---

1. I am grateful to Peter Donald, John Scally and David Smith for their comments
on and criticisms of drafts of this article.
2. See D. Stevenson, *The Covenanters: the National Covenant in Scotland* (Saltire
Society, 1988), pp. 70–84, for a cool evaluation of its legacy; J.C. Johnson,
Treasury of the Scottish Covenant (1887), for a cross-section of the myths.

to England through the Union of the Crowns. But the extent to which it went beyond being a little-Scotlander reflex to anglicization (and angli*caniz*ation) into representing a considered answer to the problems of multiple kingdoms in the early modern period remains much less fully considered. I would suggest that Scottish historians have considered the *English* context of the Covenant, but not the *British* context. This volume takes up that issue. It looks at the impact of the early covenanting movement on the whole of what John Pocock has called the Atlantic archipelago in the years during which the Covenant itself became established deep in the Scottish psyche. In this introductory chapter, I will seek to suggest that both the nature and the consequences of the Scottish National Covenant need a British context.

The central point I want to make can be neatly encapsulated in a study of the dramatically different Scottish coronations of Charles I and Charles II. The coronation of Charles I in the abbey church adjacent to Holyroodhouse in 1633 shows why the Scots needed a National Covenant; the coronation of his son at Scone in 1651 shows why the National Covenant failed. This essay will be framed by consideration of those two events.

II

Fifteenth- and sixteenth-century England was afflicted by an uncertain succession law which enabled the enthronement of a series of monarchs whose titles were open to challenge. In these circumstances, the importance of coronation and anointing took on particular significance. Fifteenth- and sixteenth-century Scotland saw few challenges to the house of Stewart. Each monarch left an heir of his or her body (and, almost as importantly, did not leave too many heirs); but one after another, the Stewarts died leaving the throne to a child. The result was that Scottish coronations, especially in the sixteenth century, were invariably rushed and improvised affairs through which a given faction sought to legitimize its kidnapping of an infant monarch. Charles I was crowned in the coronation robes of James IV[3] because he was the first Scottish monarch for one hundred and fifty years to ascend the throne as an adult.

The lack of any collective memory of how Scottish coronations were conducted may have made the way Charles chose to be crowned

3. J. Haig (ed.), *The Historical Works of Sir James Balfour* (4 vols., Edinburgh, 1825), IV, 396: C. Rogers (ed.), *The Earl of Stirling's register of Royal Letters . . . 1615–1635* (2 vols., Edinburgh, 1885), I, 660.

a shade less offensive to the Scottish nation. But only a shade. It represented the epitome of his indifference to Scottish sensibilities. It took place not at one of the two places where Scottish coronations normally had taken place (Scone or, more recently, Stirling) but in the abbey kirk of Holyrood.[4] Worse, the abbey kirk had been reordered for the occasion with the erection of a stage twenty-four foot square and 'railled aboute', at the east end of which, reached by a further flight of stairs, was a communion table.[5] One observer tells us:

> it is to be marked that there was a four-nooked taffil in manner of an *altar*, standing within the kirk, having standing thereupon two books . . . with two chandlers and two wax candles, whilk were on light. . . . [A]t the back of the altar . . . there was a rich tapestry wherein the crucifix was curiously wrought, and as thir bishops who were in service past the crucifix, they were seen to bow their knee and beck.[6]

In iconophobic Scotland this was provocation indeed, and it is not surprising to find John Spalding commenting that it 'bred great fear of inbringing of popery.'[7] The Scottish bishops were all present at the coronation (if only to swear fealty) but they were in two distinct groups. John Spottiswoode, the archbishop of St Andrews, David Lindsay of Brechin, Adam Bellenden of Dunblane, Alexander Lindsay of Dunkeld, John Guthrie of Moray and John Maxwell of Ross all appeared on the dais 'with white rockets [rochets] and white sleeves and loops [?coops = copes] of gold, having blue silk to their foot'.[8] The other bishops, including Archbishop Lindsay of Glasgow, sat in the body of the kirk in their black gowns. (Did some or all of them refuse to wear the popish rags? Was the Scottish episcopate visibly split? It seems a question worth further investigation.)[9] If the

---

4. Charles seems to have been wilfully ignorant on this point. He could write in 1626 to the Scottish Council, ordering the repair of the abbey kirk, and describing it as 'the buriall place of some of our royall antecessours and the usuall place for the solemnitie of coronatiouns' (*Stirling's register*, I, 96–7). Four years later he asked the Council to choose between St Giles and the abbey kirk (ibid., II, 416–17). I am grateful to John Scally for these references.
5. *Works of Balfour*, IV, 384.
6. Spalding, *History of the Troubles and Memorable Transactions in Scotland from the years 1624 to 1645* (2 vols., Aberdeen, 1792), I, 23. The reasons why this was such an affront can be found by comparing this extract with the discussion in G.B. Burnett, *The Holy Communion in the Reformed Church of Scotland* (Edinburgh, 1960), esp. pp. 25–43, 64–87. See also W. Forbes-Leith. *Memoirs of the Scottish Catholics* (2 vols., 1909), I. 162–4.
7. Spalding, *History of Troubles*, I, 23.
8. Ibid.
9. A later anecdote, quoted by John Rushworth, points in the same direction, though its authenticity must be suspect. Rushworth has Laud sneer at Archbishop Lindsay of Glasgow as he attended the king, 'are you a churchman and wants the coat of your order?' (cited in J.K. Hewison, *The Covenanters* [2 vols., Edinburgh, 1908], I, 219).

physical spectacle which the Scottish elite encountered as it entered the kirk were not bad enough. the service could only confirm their worst fears. The coronation took place within the context of the Holy Communion service according to the rite of the English Prayer Book and appears to have been modelled closely on the English coronation of 1625,[10] while the coronation oath taken by Charles, although based on that prescribed by the Act of Parliament of 1567, added significantly to it. Charles swore to uphold 'the trew religions of Christe, nou preached and professed within this realme'; to rule 'according to the lawes and constitutions receaued within this realme': and 'to preserve and keipe inviolated the preuilidges, rights and rents of the croune of Scotland, and not to transfer and alienat the same in aney sorte'. All these promises derive from the Act of 1567 and echo its precise wording. But Charles then added a fourth promise: 'to grant and preserue wnto ws of the clergie, and to the churches committed to our charge, all canonical prewilidges: . . . and that you vill . . . defend [the] Bischopes, and the churches vnder ther governiment.' It is noticeable that this final and additional oath met a fuller and more emphatic response from the king.[11] In calling upon him to accept the abolition of episcopacy in 1639, the Covenanters sought not only to set aside a body of statute; they sought to make the king violate his coronation oath.[12]

At least he was crowned king of Scotland. Despite the presence of the eight English heralds and two English earls (Suffolk and Holland, in their capacities as Captains of the Gentlemen Pensioners and of the Yeomen of the Guard) in the coronation procession, and despite Laud's presence on the coronation dais (as Dean of the English Chapel Royal), this was an essentially Scottish event. Charles had not sought to be crowned as king of Britain back in 1625/6; his crowning in 1633 was exclusively as king of Scotland, and the gold and silver coins showered upon the commons as they stood around the entrance to the kirk at the king's exit bore the legend 'Carolus Dei Gratia, Scotia, Angl:, Fran: et Hyb: Rex'.[13] (This is significant, for since

10. For the English coronation of 1625, see Sir William Sanderson, *The Compleat History of the Life and Raigne of King Charles . . .* (1658), pp. 25–7.
11. The wording of this additional clause closely echoes that of Charles's addition to his *English* coronation oath: Sanderson, *Compleat History*, p. 27.
12. The text of the coronation oath is printed in *Works of Balfour* IV, 392–3. The 1567 Act is in *The Acts of the Parliament of Scotland* (12 vols., 1814), III, 23–4. This oath was created by Act *following* James's coronation at Stirling. For an interesting account of that coronation, see Hewinson, *Covenanters*, I, 66–7.
13. *Historical Works of Balfour*, IV, 405.

1604 all coins in both kingdoms bore the legend 'Jacobus [Carolus] DG Mag. Brit. Fra. et Hib. Rex'.) But it was small consolation. The Scottish elite were confronted by a king who cared nothing for their traditions, customs, values, even laws. In part this was an anglicized coronation; but, as we shall see, it is never possible to describe Charles's government straightforwardly as anglicization, as colonial, as Unionist. There was a naked authoritarianism and a disregard for tradition which transcended or only partially involved an assertion of Englishness.

III

In order to establish the British context of the National Covenant we must look back to the Union of the Crowns and to the trajectories of change that had become established in the generation before 1638. It was typical of James that he recognized the challenge and the opportunity to make more of the whole of Dual Monarchy than a sum of its parts. But it was also the story of his government of England that he let things drift and achieved little.

It is, however, difficult to establish the precise nature of that commitment to the Union of the kingdoms. Bruce Galloway and Brian Levack have recently and separately argued that James was more gradualistic than used to be thought, that he wished to proceed through a 'union of hearts and minds' and through a melding of peoples and cultures towards an eventual integration of the institutions.[14] But there is no reason to doubt that he was telling Robert Cecil the truth in a private letter of November 1604 in relation to the commission of the two Parliaments established to promote greater union. In it he expressed the hope that once a small start was made to 'this great work' by the commission, the two peoples, 'more ruled with shadows than substances' would come to see 'that the Union is already made', and that the commissioners had made

> such a pretty reference for the full accomplishment of all other points which fault of leisure could not now permit you to end as it may appear that working in this errand shall never be left off till it be fully accomplished. I mean specially by the uniting of both laws and parliaments of both the nations.[15]

This seems emphatic enough; and James had no reason to dissimulate to Cecil at that stage. If he was as clear about his target as this, he

---

14. B. Galloway, *The Union of England and Scotland, 1603–1608* (Edinburgh, 1986), esp. pp. 15–16, 165–6: B.P. Levack. *The Formation of the British State* (Oxford, 1987), esp. pp. 7–8.
15. *HMC Salisbury* XVI, 362–4.

was all too quickly and totally dispirited by the hostility of the English Parliament in 1606/7 to the limited proposals relating to trade, nationality and the Borders. I suspect he had not adjusted to the very different conditions in his kingdoms. James, whose technique in Scotland was to put legislation on to the statute book and then frequently to delay enforcement until an opportune time, was too quickly discouraged at falling at what in Scotland would have been the lowest hurdle. He never recognized that in England monarchs had to work hard to get Acts passed, but then found that these Acts often enforced themselves. Dispirited by the setback in 1607, James permitted twenty years of drift.

Certainly James's ambitions shrank after 1607; but equally clearly the bitter memory of the small-mindedness of English MPs and the hankerings after a great uniting of his peoples remained with him to the end. The Star Chamber speech of 1616[16] and the Rubens ceiling for the Banqueting House[17] represent the negative and positive aspects of that lingering passion. There was, then, no move towards 'perfect Union' (a full integration of the institutions and laws respectful of the traditions and interests of both kingdoms); no move towards federal Union (the greater coordination of sovereign Parliaments. Councils etc.); perhaps a creeping incorporative Union as the Scottish Council lost its deliberative function, becoming an ill-consulted executive body, and as more and more decisions affecting Scotland were made at the English court by a mixture of anglicized Scots and non-scottified Englishmen.[18] Indeed the most *British* thing to emerge by the 1630s was an Anglo-Scottish, *British* nobility, with English wives, English-educated sons and estates and offices on both sides of the Border. Edward Cowan has drawn attention to the fact that this group – in attesting the Cross Petition – actually described themselves as 'we British subjects', and sought a strengthening of the civil Union.[19]

There is no need to credit Charles with any Unionist vision. His father's fine words about the sum of his kingdoms being greater than the parts, about the ways each could learn from the other,

16. C.H. McIlwain (ed.), *The Political Works of James I* (Cambridge, Mass., 1918), pp. 329–32.
17. G. Parry, *The Golden Age Restored* (Manchester, 1981), pp. 32–7.
18. But, contrary to a common misapprehension, there was no formal Scottish Committee of the English Privy Council until 1638.
19. Edward J. Cowan, 'The Union of the Crowns and the Crisis of the Constitution in 17th century Scotland', in S. Dyrvik. K. Myklund and J. Oldervoll, (eds.), *The Satellite State in the 17th and 18th centuries* (Oslo, 1980), p. 131.

about the merits of 'a perfect Union'[20] meant as little to him as did his father's recognition that politics was the art of the possible. Charles I may have had some policies that were common to all his kingdoms (the most obvious being the re-endowment of the churches with sufficient of the lands plundered from them at the Reformation to allow them to plan their evangelisms free from lay control, and – concurrently – a determination to ensure that the laity lost all ability to interfere in ecclesiastical government),[21] but they were not a *British* policy. What is striking about Charles's policies towards Scotland is not anglicization but a naked authoritarianism. Charles was an unimaginative man, who governed Scotland with a greater indifference to its laws, customs and traditions because he failed to study and to understand what those might be. The years, even decades, of drift did not, as far as I can determine, produce much systematic thinking and planning behind the scenes. One thing which is clear about Charles's government in the 1630s is that it was not based (as, arguably, English policy in Ireland regularly was) upon a clear sense of the relationship between the kingdoms, or upon any developed plan to alter that relationship.[22] Equally, the National Covenant, however much made necessary by absentee kingship, did not provide any remedy that took cognizance of the need to develop a Unionist (presumably federal Unionist) strategy for the future. The Covenanters seem to have considered that a king of Scotland, faced by the bonding of by far the greater part of their nobility and lairds,

---

20. As in the opening speech to his first Parliament, McIlwain, *Political Works*, pp. 269–80.
21. For the Laudian programme in England, Ireland and Scotland on these issues, see W. Scott and J. Bliss (eds.), *The Works of William Laud* (7 vols., 1847–60), III, 253; IV, 176–7, 299–304; and numerous letters in VI and VII. See the encomium of English secretary of state Coke on Laud at the latter's installation as Chancellor of Oxford University: 'this worthy prelate maketh it his chief work to recover to the church for the furtherance of God's service what may be restored . . . under his majesty's great and powerful order, not [in] England alone, but Scotland and Ireland', V, 128. See also [W. Balcanquhal]. *A Large Declaration* (1639), esp. pp. 8,424. For England, see C. Hill, *The Economic Problems of the Church* (Oxford, 1956), esp. pp. 307–36: for Ireland, see H.F. Kearney, *Strafford in Ireland* (Manchester, 1959), pp. 122–9. For Scotland, M. Lee, *The Road to Revolution: Scotland Under Charles I, 1625–1637* (Urbana, 1985), pp. 44–62 is the clearest account we have until Allan Macinnes's major study of the effects of the Revocation fracas is published.
22. For Wentworth's determined plans to anglicize Scotland, cold-shouldered by Charles, see T. Knowler, *The Earl of Strafford's Letters and Despatches* (2 vols., Dublin, 1740), II, 190–2.

would have no capacity within Scotland to impose his will.[23] They seem not to have considered that Charles might use English and Irish resources to impose his will on the Scots. Only in 1639–41 did the covenanting leaders work out a British solution to their problem: extensive and feasible proposals for federal Union. Once worked out, these remained the essence of Scottish constitutionalism for the remainder of the century (and beyond). But the English never showed the slightest interest in federal Union. The Scots should have learnt their lesson in 1641 as the Long Parliament put the proposals for *conservatores pacis* on a back burner and turned off the heat.[24] At no point, even in 1639–40 while he still had reason to believe that he commanded events, does Charles I appear to have seen the solution to his Scottish problems to lie in an incorporative Union. He wanted a separate Scotland with weak institutions which he could control. It was left to the Rump of the Long Parliament and to Cromwell to articulate and to effect a ruthless subjugation and incorporation of Scotland. If the National Covenant is, then, to some extent a response to problems created by the Union of the Crowns, it did not, of itself, suggest a remedy to those problems.

IV

The National Covenant unquestionably arose from a whole series of challenges Charles had delivered to Scots religion, law and property.[25] But its *occasion* was the series of innovations Charles attempted in the government, discipline and practice of the Kirk. We need to look particularly at the ecclesiastical dimensions of Dual Monarchy.

It is odd that James's letter to Cecil in November 1604 should contain no reference to the Union of the Churches.[26] This is significant because after the failure of the limited Union legislation in 1607, the area in which James might be thought most effectively

---

23. For the history and significance of Bonding in Stewart History, see J. Wormald, *Lands and Men in Scotland: Bonds of Manrent, 1442–1603* (Edinburgh, 1985); K.M. Brown, *Bloodfeud in Scotland, 1583–1625* (Edinburgh, 1986). For the theological background, see M. Steele, 'The "Politick Christian"' in J.S. Morrill (ed.), *The Scottish National Covenant in its British Context 1638–51* (Edinburgh 1990), pp. 31–67.
24. P. Donald, 'The King and the Scottish Troubles, 1637–1641', University of Cambridge PhD thesis (1988), ch. 6; C.L. Hamilton, 'The Anglo-Scottish Negotiations, 1640–1', Sc.H.R., XLI (1962), 84–96.
25. For some introductions to this vast topic, see Lee, *Road to Revolution*, pp. 43–249; D. Stevenson. *The Scottish Revolution 1637–1644: the Triumph of the Covenanters* (Newton Abbott, 1973), pp. 29–55.
26. *HMC Salisbury*, XVI, 363–4.

to have continued to work towards Union was in relation to the Churches (for example, in the English consecration of Scottish bishops in 1611 and in the Five Articles of Perth).[27]

James was quite capable of clumsily ignoring the right procedures and of permitting an apparent subordination of Scotland to England, as in issuing the mandate for the consecration of three Scottish bishops by four English diocesans under the Great Seal of England,[28] or as in instructing Archbishop Abbott to release Huntly from the excommunication declared by his kirk session when the earl had settled in London.[29] But these represented slipshodness, not calculation. In the case of Huntly, for example, the aim was not to override the authority of the Kirk, still less to allow the earl – a stubborn recusant – to take Holy Communion in the Church of England, but to protect him from the secular penalties of excommunication in English law so long as he resided south of the Border.[30] At heart, James remained a Scot and proud of it, telling the Scottish Council in 1617 of the 'salmonlyke instinct' that had drawn him back to where he had been spawned.[31] If he admired the reverence and richness of developed Anglican liturgy, he admired (as much as Elizabeth disparaged) preaching and sought to make good sermonizing as ubiquitous in England as it was in (at any rate Lowland) Scotland, James's preoccupation was with developing mutual respect amongst his peoples, and in relation to religion this

---

27. J. Spottiswoode, *History of the Church of Scotland* (1655), pp. 528–40, gives the core texts: M. Lee, *Government By Pen: Scotland Under King James VI and I* (Urbana, 1980), pp. 170–89 offers a clear account; and D.G. Mullan, *Episcopacy in Scotland: The History of an Idea, 1560–1637* (Edinburgh, 1986), pp. 152–62, is an interesting gloss; I.A. Dunlop, 'The Polity of the Scottish Church 1600–1637', *Rec.Sc.Ch.Hist.Soc.*, XII (1958), 162–82; I.B. Cowan, 'The Five Articles of Perth', in D. Shaw (ed.), *Reformation and Revolution* (Edinburgh, 1967), pp. 160–77; P.H.R. Mackay, 'The Reception Given to the Five Articles of Perth', *Rec.Sc.Ch.Hist.Soc.*, XIX (1973), 185–201.

28. A.I. Dunlop, 'John Spottiswoode, 1565–1639' in R.S. Wright (ed.) *Fathers of the Kirk* (Oxford, 1960), p. 53. It is ironic that James should casually proceed by English letters patent after he had taken such pains to ensure that no claim to jurisdiction was implied: neither archbishop and no bishop of the Northern Province – which had historically laid claim to jurisdiction over Scotland – was permitted to attend, let alone take part in, the consecration. For James's reasons for these consecrations, see below, pp. 100–1.

29. Spottiswoode, *History*, pp. 525–8. The emollient letter of explanation from Abbott to Spottiswoode contained in this account makes clear that no jurisdiction within Scotland was implied: the order merely released Huntly from the penalties of excommunication in England so long as he resided there. But it was a tactless act by James, nonetheless.

30. Spottiswoode, *History*, pp. 525–8.

31. *Register of the Privy Council of Scotland*, 2nd ser., X, 685.

meant principally establishing the full catholicity of the two Churches. He sought to provide for each of his national Churches all those marks which their respective leaders believed to be necessary marks of all branches of the True and Visible Church. The English Church had been defective in its preaching; the Scottish Church was defective in its preaching; the Scottish Church was defective in that it lacked an apostolic succession. It was this desire to raise the status of the Scottish Church, not any attempt to subordinate it to the English Church, that surely explains the consecrations of 1611 (and the manner in which they were carried out).[32] This, too, may form part of the explanation of James's determined actions to restore the Scottish episcopate in the years 1596–1612. But that restoration cannot be seen principally as a prelude to Union of the Churches, either in the sense of their integration or of their federation. Scottish bishops remained very different from English ones. There is no evidence of any intention to move beyond episcopacy-in-presbytery. The bishops were to monitor and to supervise (but not to supplant) the authority of kirk session and presbytery as constant moderators, not as autocratic prelates with intrinsic power.[33] The restoration of bishops probably had three primary purposes for James: first, to strengthen his control of Parliament,[34] secondly, to deliver a grievous blow to Melvillian political theory (when James said at the Hampton Court Conference 'no bishop, no king' he clearly did not mean no bishop, no monarchy, but no bishop, no effective secular ruler – the king being a royal eunuch waiting upon the orders of churchmen?),[35] thirdly, to give the Crown, through personally-appointed bishops, that very inspectorate without which his ignorance and impotence with regard to what was happening in the Scottish regions would be even greater. These were reasons enough why Scottish kings would always prefer a centralizing episcopate to any kind of presbyterian ecclesiastical structure. Anglicization need not be invoked as the primary reason for James's policies.[36]

In trying to find a term to describe James's policy towards the two Churches, I have struggled to capture some of these ambiguities. It

32. For a discussion of notions of catholicity and visibility in the early Stuart Church, see A. Milton, 'The Laudians and the Church of Rome', University of Cambridge PhD thesis (1989), esp. chs 2 and 6.
33. For an emphasis on continuity rather than discontinuity in the early seventeenth century, see W.R. Foster, *The Church before the Covenant* (Edinburgh, 1975) and 'The Operation of the Presbyteries in Scotland, 1600–1638' in *Rec.Sc.Ch.Hist.Soc.* (1964), 21–33.
34. James restored their parliamentary titles in 1596 before attempting anything else.
35. For James's remark, see D.H. Willson, *King James VI and I* (London, 1956), p. 207, for a full transcript of James's speech which gives the context for James's remark.
36. This extends the discussion in Mullan, *Episcopacy in Scotland*, pp. 98–103, 122–3.

is necessary to abandon notions of Union and uniformity; but also to recognize that James's knowledge of both Churches did inform his policy towards each of them. The best term I can come up with is *congruity*. James was concerned to make the two Churches more congruous, to remove, as it were, all 'hostile laws' from their relations, but not to plan either a merger of them or a takeover of the Northern Church by the Southern.

It is possible that Charles's policies might also be incorporated within this concept of congruity. Charles was a man concerned above all with *order*. In England and in Ireland. Laud's aim was less to impose new ceremonies and innovations than to compel all men to conformity with (an admittedly narrow) reading of the established liturgy, and where there were defects in ecclesiastical discipline to supply remedies through new canons. What mattered most to Charles in relation to Scotland was not to anglicize its discipline and liturgy but to provide clear rules and to insist on uniformity of practice.[37] If Charles's method of introducing the Prayer Book represented foolhardy authoritarianism, it was based upon an inability to think in terms of Scottish law and custom, not upon a determination to subordinate Scotland to English ways. It showed a sheer lack of imagination and empathy. If he had tried to impose a new prayer book on *England* without consulting Parliament, Convocation, the Privy Council or (to quote John Row) 'even a conventicle of bishops and doctors', William Laud would have been amongst the first to shriek out at the violation of the rights of the Church.[38]

The Scottish canons[39] show a lack of concern with a narrow uniformity but a preoccupation with order: they may well have maintained an ominous silence about presbyteries and enjoined placing communion tables 'at the upper end of the chancel',[40] but

---

37. G. Donaldson, *The Making of the Scotland Prayer Book of 1637* (Edinburgh, 1954) remains the best account, superceding and incorporating all others. Lee, *Road to Revolution*, pp. 184–222, is a useful summary.
38. Lee. *Road to Revolution*, pp. 201–4 is the most forthright writer on the inanity of Charles's methods. For John Row's comment, see his *History of the Kirk of Scotland from 1558 to 1637*, ed. D. Laing (Wodrow Society, 1842), p. 394. Charles did of course consult what he (disingenuously) referred to as the 'representative body of the church', i.e. *some* of the bishops: but he did so individually and not (Row's point) in conclave; and not all of them.
39. The canons are in *Works of William Laud*, V, 583–607.
40. Curiously this went further than in England where the placing of the communion table in each church was left to the discretion of the ordinary (which led in many cases, even in Laud's diocese, to an order placing it elsewhere than at the east end): see Julian Davies, *The Caroline Captivity of the Church* (Oxford, forthcoming), ch. 4. But note that the Scottish canon did not insist on (or mention) the railing-in of the Holy Table, something Laud was more insistent on in England.

they also laid down rules for ordination much more respectful of Scottish traditions than of English ones, and were clearly not based in any significant way on English models.[41] In their defence, Walter Balcanquhal (not without a certain disingenuousness) wrote that:

> because there was no booke extant containing any rules of such govern-ment, so that neither the clergie nor laity had any certaine rule either of the one's power, or of the other's practice and obedience, and con-sidering that the Acts of their General Assemblies were but written, and not printed, and so large and voluminous . . . we had them reduced to . . . such a paucitie of canons and those published.[42]

Well, yes and no. At least this suggests that there were good reasons for a king obsessed with order to impose canons. But his aim was to improve royal control and not English control of the Scottish Church.

In Charles's view, sinful man could best be brought to an inner obedience to the will of God by learning an outer conformity. As William Laud put it:

> It is true, the inward worship of the heart is the great service of God, and no service acceptable without it; but the external worship of God in His Church is the great witness to the world, that our heart stands right in that service of God. . . . Now, no external action in the world can be uniform without some ceremonies: and those in religion, the ancienter they be the better.[43]

These are sentiments shared in large part by several of the Scottish bishops, including Spottiswoode, who stated that

> In things indifferent we must always esteeme to be best and most seemly which seemeth so in the eyes of publike authority; neither is it for private men to control public judgments.[44]

And later that

> for matters of rite and government, my judgment is and hath been, that the most simple, decent, and humble rites should be chused, such as is the bowing of the knee in resaving the holy sacrament, and others of that kinde, prophanenesse being as dangerouse to religion as superstition.[45]

41. The canons (and the Prayer Book) are discussed at much greater length in my paper 'Ecclesiastical Imperialism under the early Stuart', forthcoming.
42. *A Large Declaration*, pp. 44–5.
43. *The Works of William Laud*, II, xvi (from the Epistle Dedicatory to *A Relation of the Conference . . . with Mr Fisher the Jesuit*, and cited in W.H. Hutton, *Archbishop Laud* [1900], pp. 69–70).
44. Quoted in G. Gillespie, *A Dispute Against the English Popish Ceremonies Obtruded on the Church of Scotland* (1637), p. 2.
45. Quoted in M. Ash, 'Dairsie and Archbishop Spottiswoode', *Rec.Sc.Ch.Hist.Soc.*, XIX (1976), 131. This article also describes the crucifixes, east-end altar with kneelers, and chancel screen which Spottiswoode installed in the church he built in his home parish.

The Scottish Church certainly lacked the ordered liturgy that Charles craved. The Book of Common Order lacked statutory force; rather than prescribing a set form, it gave instruction on how to construct a liturgy and was admired by contemporary Scottish ministers precisely because, as Calderwood put it, 'none are tyed to the prayers of that book; but the prayers are set down as samplers.'[46]

Charles's explanation of his Scottish Prayer Book was both unambiguous and convincing. The Preface recalls the words of the Lords of the Congregation in 1559:

> Religion was not then placed in rites and gestures, nor men taken with the fancy of extemporary prayers. Sure, the Public Worship of God, being the most solemn action of us his poor creatures here below, ought to be performed by a Liturgy advisedly set and framed, and not according to the sudden and various fancies of men.[47]

Order, not uniformity with England, was intended. Walter Balcanquhal recalled James's growing concern at 'that diversitie, nay deformitie which was used in Scotland, where no set or publike forme of prayer was used' which had led him to start the process that led to the 1637 Liturgy. But Charles had taken special care to ensure such differences from the English Prayer Book

> as we had reason to thinke would best comply with the mindes and dispositions of our subjects of that Kingdome: for we supposing that they might have taken some offence, if we should have tendered them the English service book *totidem verbis*, and that some factious spirits would have endevoured to have misconstrued it as a badge of dependance of that church upon this of England.[48]

The Liturgy was based on the English one, 'so that the Roman party might not upbraid us with any weightie or materiall differences in our Liturgies.'[49]

I see no reason to doubt this description of Charles's *intentions*. For him, a want of order in worship and a lack of clear authority emanating from the Crown and exercised through the bishops cast doubts upon the catholicity of the Scottish Church in the same way that the lack of an apostolic priesthood in the Scottish Church or the want of a full preaching ministry in England had troubled his

---

46. See the excellent discussion in Hewison, *Covenanters*, I, 43–5.
47. G. Donaldson, *The Making of the Scottish Prayer Book of 1637* (Edinburgh, 1954), p. 102.
48. *A Large Declaration*, p. 18.
49. Ibid.; Donaldson, *Making*, p. 102.

father. Once again, a concern with congruity might better account for Charles's policy than a concern with uniformity or anglicanization.[50]

V

The National Covenant was at once a very precise and an infuriatingly imprecise document.[51] Although tedious, it is easy to understand: but it is horrifically difficult to interpret. It begins by recalling the 1581 Confession of Faith ('Negative Confession') subscribed by the king, his council and household, and 'by persons of all ranks', and resubscribed in 1590 'with a general band for the maintenance of the true religion and the King's person.' Half of the document is then taken up with the Negative Confession and with a list of all those Acts of Parliament which established true religion in Scotland and drove out popery, and the bulk of the rest with describing a 'general band to be made and subscribed by his Majesty's subjects, of all ranks, for two causes: one was, for defending the true religion [as defined above]. . . . The other cause was for maintaining the King's Majesty, His Person and Estate.' Signatories would 'labour by all meanes lawfull to recover the purity and Liberty, as it was stablished and professed before . . . the Innovations and evils contained in our Supplications, Complaints and Protestations.' In the meantime, they would forbear all 'novations, already introduced in the matters of the worship of God, or approbation of the corruptions of the publicke Government of the Kirk, or civil places and power of Kirkmen, till they be tryed & allowed in *free assemblies*, and in Parliaments.'[52] In relation to the king's power, 'we shall, to the uttermost of our power . . . stand to the defence of our dread Soveraigne, the Kings majesty, his Person, and Authority, in the defence and preservation of the foresaid true Religion, Liberties and Lawes of the Kingdome.'

---

50. If space permitted, I would argue that the history of the High Commission and of the Scottish Ordinal make the same point. See Morrill, 'Ecclesiastical Imperialism', forthcoming. See also G.I.R. McMahon, 'The Scottish Court of High Commission, 1610–38', *Rec.Sc.Ch.Hist.Soc.*, XV (1966), 195–209.
51. I have relied upon the text in G. Donaldson and W.C. Dickenson, *A Source Book of Scottish History* (3 vols.), III, 95–104, which derives its text from *The Acts of the Parliament of Scotland*, V, 272–6. For an especially helpful discussion of the bibliography of the Covenant see Stevenson, *The Covenanters, passim.* There are especially stimulating commentaries in W. Makey, *The Church of the Covenant* (Edinburgh, 1979), pp. 26–31; D. Stevenson, 'The Early Covenanters and the Federal Union of Britain' in R. Mason (ed.), *Scotland and England* (Edinburgh, 1987), pp. 165–81; and A. Williamson, *Scottish National Consciousness in the Reign of James VI* (Edinburgh, 1979), ch. 7. For a fuller analysis of the Covenant, especially in its theological context, see Steele, 'Politick Christian'.
52. Emphasis added, see ibid., pp. 48–53.

This Covenant represents a very specific and clear commitment to a particular form of evangelical Protestantism: if it only cross-refers to those royal ecclesiastical policies which constituted innovation, no one at the English court or anywhere in Scotland in 1637 can have been left in any doubt as to what was meant; and it is unambiguous on how those who subscribed it intended to render the king's will ineffective – by a campaign of corporate passive disobedience. The Covenant is infuriatingly unspecific about the fate of the bishops: was the office itself antithetical to the Negative Confession?[53] There is a menacing ambiguity by the reference to 'free' General Assemblies, implying that there had been unfree ones whose acts might be declared void. Indeed, predicating itself on the assumption that everything which could be construed as a violation of the Negative Confession of 1581 was null and void, it brought into question many Acts of both the General Assembly and of Parliament throughout the reigns of James VI and Charles I. This willingness to deny the force of the positive law of Scotland can be traced back to even earlier than 1581: at the General Assembly held in 1567, early in the civil war, the noble subscribers of the so-called 'Edinburgh Covenant' bound themselves to obstruct parliamentary legislation until 'the faithfull Kirk of Jesus Chryst profest within this realm salbe put in full libertie of the patrimonie of the Kirk . . . the matters of the Kirk forsaid be first considerit, approvit and establishit.'[54] This is echoed in the National Covenant and, while there is no reason to doubt that it was a yearning for presbyterian forms that lay behind these claims, it demonstrates a willingness to use arguments shocking in their implications for secular rulers. While it may demonstrate the immaturity of parliamentary institutions in Scotland, it also represents a willingness to challenge positive law which was not to be found in England until the Levellers. There is also silence in the Covenant over the civil grievances that most of those who subscribed the Covenant undoubtedly harboured. Perhaps above all there was silence about where their allegiance would lie if they had to choose between their 'dread Soveraigne' and 'the true Religion, Liberties and Lawes of the Kingdome'. Were they simply trying to avoid alienating their more timid supporters, avoiding giving the king an easy opportunity to call them traitors, or were

---

53. This needs far fuller treatment than it can receive here. Many of the conundrums are solved in Peter Donald, 'King and the Troubles'; ch. 2 admirably sums up thus: 'The protest movement, of which the convinced presbyterians were only a part, came instead fairly quickly to attack the bishops, because they were seen to represent an ill-liked manner of government in church and state, and furthermore because the true religion was threatened through them' (p. 79).

54. J.K. Hewison, *The Covenanters* (2 vols. Glasgow, 1908), I, 68.

they unable to recognize that they might have to choose? Similar problems of interpretation have flummoxed historians of the first eighteen months of the English Long Parliament.[55] My suggestion is that in the period between the attempted introduction of the Prayer Book and the signing of the Covenant, the leaders did not contemplate that choice. They had come up with a traditional Scottish remedy against a king pursuing an unpopular policy.[56] What the proponents of the National Covenant most obviously ignored was the possibility that Charles would use traditional *English* methods for dealing with a recalcitrant Scotland: if Henry VIII believed in Rough Wooing, then Charles I believed in Wife-Beating.

VI

When the Long Parliament met in 1640, it was the abuses of power by a particular monarch, not the whole system of government, that came under attack. The Grand Remonstrance was a critique of Charles's reign alone.[57] The National Covenant, by contrast, is a critique of a system of government. The drift towards popery and tyranny is specifically dated back to the reign of James VI, and even to Parliaments and General Assemblies which predated James's move to England.

The Covenant is no Grand Remonstrance in a second sense: its obsessive concern is with religious issues. This has not stopped many commentators from arguing strongly and effectively that the covenanting *movement* was not primarily religious in character or purpose. This case rests, for me, less in a study of the document itself and in the apologias for it (as far as I can determine, almost all the apologias produced by the Covenanters[58] dwelt on the religious crusade; constitutional issues, if dealt with at all, were seen as a means to the end of securing true religion) than in the canards of opponents. (Canards are not always based on falsehood.) Typically, when the Covenanters presented their articles of complaint against Laud to the Long Parliament, they categorically stated that 'novations in religion . . . are universally acknowledged to be the

---

55. Morrill, 'Charles I, Tyranny and the Origins of the English Civil War', below, pp. 285–306.
56. For comments on the traditions behind the Covenant and a conservative reading of what was intended, see Stevenson, *Covenanters*, pp. 28–42.
57. I have argued this case in 'The Religious Context of the English Civil War', and in 'Charles I, Tyranny', above pp. 49–52, below pp. 294–5.
58. In preparing this paper I read fifty-two pamphlets and tracts listed either (a) in the bibliography of Peter Donald, 'The King and the Scottish Troubles', University of Cambridge PhD thesis (1987) or (b) under 'Scotland, Covenant' in *The Short Title Catalogue . . . 1485–1641*; I supplemented this with a check of the author index in the S.T.C. for all authors identified in (a) or (b).

main cause of commotions in kingdoms and states, and are known to be the true cause of our present troubles'. Laud, in response, equally firmly ascribed 'the present troubles . . . [to] temporal discontents, and several ambitions of the great men, which have been long a-working'.[59] Someone closer to home, John Spalding, from his eyrie in Aberdeen, could observe that 'here you may see they began at religion as the ground of their quarrel, whereas their intention was only bent against the King's majesty and his royal prerogative'.[60]

It may be. And yet the *passivity* of the Scots prior to 1637; the rapidity with which revolt grew once the Prayer Book appeared; the clarity with which the threats to the Reformed Religion were articulated within the Covenant and the lack of clarity over threats to property and civil liberties; the absence throughout the succeeding period of any Scottish equivalent to the Grand Remonstrance; the lack of any large-scale campaign to prevent anything like the Act of Revocation or the Commission on Teinds for the future; all these things suggest that religion did matter most and was the ameliorating bond bringing together different groups, different interests. Behind the Covenant, of course, lay the Supplication and Complaint of October 1637, attested by 400 nobles and lairds, the representatives of 21 burghs and 120 ministers, the core of the future covenanting movement. *Its* content was exclusively concerned with the Prayer Book and the canons, which 'sowen the seeds of divers superstitions, idolatrie and false doctrine' and which 'ar imposed contrair to order or law appointed in this realme for establishing of maters ecclesiastick'. It ends with a more explicit challenge to the authority of those 'prelats, who have so farr abused ther credite with so gude a King as thus to insnare his subjects, rent our Kirk, undermynde religion.'[61]

If, as seems probable, those who organized the Supplication and then the Covenant had *assumed* that the king would have to give way to a people bonded and banded against him, then the self-sufficiency of the religious concessions demanded in the Supplication is striking. As I have already suggested, there is nothing in the Covenant which would lead to a redefinition of the Union, so that even if the Covenanting lords had gained control of the Scottish Council it would avail them little so long as Scottish policy was made

59. *Works of Laud*, III, 298.
60. J. Spalding, *The History of the Troubles* (2 vols., Aberdeen, 1792), I, 58.
61. D.H. Fleming (ed.), *Scotland's Supplication and Complaint* (1927), pp. 60–6: D.H. Ogilvie, 'The National Petition to the Scottish Privy Council', *Scottish Historical Review*, XXII (1925), 241–8.

elsewhere.[62] The Scots, unlike the English, could not expect to be able to promote remedial legislation in any parliament which might be called. There seems little reason to me to doubt that what they asked for was what they wanted.

VII

The sum total of what I have argued above is that the Scots had not yet seen their problem fully in British terms. A National Covenant, a bonding together of the Scottish nation, was an effective way of dealing with a Scottish king but not with a king of Britain.

The extent to which it *was* a 'National Covenant' in that sense can, of course, be doubted: Keith Brown points out the amazing loyalty to Charles of the Scots who dwelt at the royal court; the Aberdeen region had to be coerced into acceptance.[63] John Spalding's account (albeit from the standpoint of one living in Aberdeen) was of the widespread use of intimidation needed to impose the Covenant in a much wider region.[64] Even if one does not believe that the Covenant was a self-consciously fudged compromise between those determined to be rid of bishops and those who wanted an end to innovation but who could see the benefits of a Jacobean ecclesiastical polity, one has to accept that by 1640 the unity of those who had subscribed in 1638 was severely eroded. No fewer than nineteen peers resident in Scotland signed the Cumbernauld Bond in August 1640, for example.[65] While the problem of collating attested copies of the Covenant is enormous,[66] it is surprising that no attempt has been made to calculate precisely what proportion of the Scottish peerage and how many other men in certain defined groups failed to subscribe. (Given how much they owed to the monarchy in the past, and the extent to which recent policies had been directed at them, the Lords of Erection would be one obvious group; how many known to have served for the shires and burghs in past parliaments, how many ministers, *failed* to take the Covenant?[67] There exist lists in the

62. For the powerlessness of the Scottish Council, see e.g. Stevenson, *Scottish Revolution*, pp. 29–33.
63. K. Brown, 'Courtiers and Cavaliers', in J.S. Morrill (ed.), *The Scottish National Covenant* pp. 155–92. See also D. Stevenson, *Scottish Revolution*, pp. 101–2, 138–48.
64. *History of Troubles*, pp. 100–21.
65. Hewison, *Covenanters*, I, 357.
66. A task made simpler by the appearance of D. Stevenson, 'The National Covenant, a list of known copies', *Rec.Sc.Ch.Hist.Soc.* (1989).
67. For a range of comment on the social implications of the Covenant, see the arguments of Allan Macinnes, 'The Scottish Constitution, 1637–1651' in Morrill (ed.), *Scottish National Covenant*, pp. 106–33. W. Makey, *The Church of the Covenant, 1637–1651* (Edinburgh, 1983), pp. 1–25; and Stevenson, *Covenanters*, pp. 36–42.

Hamilton Papers[68] and elsewhere of nobles '*pro Rege & contra Regem*' which divide them almost equally in half. One especially interesting list, transcribed into the Nalson Manuscripts, has 1 duke, 2 marquise, 23 earls, 5 viscounts, 11 barons (a total of 42 peers) *pro rege*, 22 earls, 1 viscount and 16 barons (a total of 39) *contra regem*. Even though a third of the loyalists were the court group discussed by Keith Brown, these are striking figures.[69] The pressure on all to subscribe (at least in the Lowlands) must have been enormous.[70] The appeals of the Aberdeen doctors to the acts of James VI against banding without royal licence, the self-contradictions they discovered in the formularies of the Covenant, the allegation that the Covenant made a 'perpetuall law concerning the externall rites of the Church' struck against the self-interest of most Scotsmen: but this does not mean that many of them did not stop and think.[71]

Nonetheless, we must conclude that the Covenant was, in aspiration and in effect, a document of the Scottish nation.[72] Most men took it and few resisted it. But was it a document *only* for and of the people of Scotland? Peter Donald argues in this volume and elsewhere that the English critics of Charles I's government took a keen interest in the Covenant and in the covenanting movement from early on. By the summer of 1639 we can uncover traces of quite close, furtive links between members of groups seeking to change the direction of English fiscal, ecclesiastical and foreign policies and the Covenanters,

68. Discussed by Peter Donald, 'King and the Troubles', p. 118 and n. 138.
69. Brown, 'Courtiers and Cavaliers', pp. 155–92. Bodl. Lib., MS Dep.c. 172, fo. 11. (I am grateful to Ian Atherton for preparing a transcript for me.) This list, with some variant spellings, was printed in Zachary Grey, *An Impartial Examination of the Third Volume of Daniel Neal's History of the Puritans* (London, 1737), pp. 110–12. Both Conrad Russell and Peter Donald, who have studied this document, believe it is an authentic copy of a list drawn up in mid-1638; but its purpose and reliability are uncertain. While it is probably less accurate than the list in the Hamilton Papers, the latter only contains a list of those seen as supporters of the Crown. (It consists of 1 duke, 3 marquises, 28 earls and 12 lords.) It may, however, have been the wishful thinking of someone in Hamilton's entourage rather than an accurate statement of opinion. I am grateful to Peter Donald for detailed comment on this point.
70. Stevenson, *Scottish Revolution*, pp. 83–7; Donald, 'King and the Troubles', pp. 58–80. As for the Highlands, I cannot improve upon Ian Cowan's cautionary note against *assuming* that the Covenant failed there (I.B. Cowan, 'The Covenanters: a Revision Article', *S.H.R.*, XLVII [1968], 39 and n. 7).
71. *The Generall Demands Concerning the Late Covenant Propounded by the Ministers and Professors of Divinity in Aberdeene . . .* (1638), giving the grounds of their dissent, deserves further study. Meanwhile see G.D. Henderson, 'The Aberdeen Doctors' in his collection of essays, *The Burning Bush* (Edinburgh, 1957), pp. 75–93.
72. For a good account of the circulation and subscription of the Covenant, see Stevenson, *Scottish Revolution*, pp. 83–7.

links which also had an Irish dimension.[73] By 1640, the Scots had
clearly committed themselves to exporting the Covenant: to cleansing
the Augean stables by diverting the waters of presbytery through the
accumulated filth of English prelacy. They now preached – as they
had not done in 1637 and the first half of 1638[74] – that there could
be no security for the Kirk so long as prelacy prospered in England
or Ireland; and no security for the constitutional guarantees exacted
in 1639 unless the king was bound by similar restraints in those
other kingdoms. All this is well established.[75] Did this dawn on the
Covenanters only with time? Everything we have seen so far would
suggest as much. But there are some tantalizing glimpses that suggest
that secret contacts between the Scots and disaffected Englishmen
might have predated the Covenant. William Laud, writing from the
Tower once things had fallen apart, commenting on reactions to the
Scottish Prayer Book, wrote:

> Then they grew up into a formal mutiny; and the Scottish subjects
> began to petition with arms, in their mouths first, and soon in their
> hands. His Majesty was often told, that *these northern commotions had their
> root in England* . . . which was most true of a powerful faction in both.[76]

I cannot think of any strong reason why Laud would have needed to
invent such an allegation. Although he offers no evidence, what he
alleged is independently confirmed by John Spalding who wrote, *of
pre-covenanting days* (after a discussion of the Balmerino affair, threats
to the Lordships of Erection and to lay interest in teinds):

> whereupon followed a clandestine band drawn up, and subscribed
> secretly betwixt the malcontents, or rather malignants, of Scotland and
> England: that each one should concur and assist others while they got
> their wills both in church and policy, and so bring both kingdoms under
> one reformed religion, and to that effect to root out the bishops of both
> kingdoms, whereby His Majesty should loose one of his three estates,
> and likewise that they should draw the king to dispense with divers
> points of his royal prerogative, in such degree as he should not have
> arbitrary government, as all his predecessors ever had [and] conform to
> the established laws of both kingdoms.[77]

73. Donald, 'King and the Troubles', pp. 179–82; P. Donald, 'New Light on the
    Anglo-Scottish Contacts of 1640', *Historical Research* LXII (1989), 221–9. I am also
    grateful to John Adamson for discussions on this point. See also P. Donald, 'The
    Scottish National Covenant and British Politics', in Morrill (ed.), *Scottish
    Covenant* pp. 95–101.
74. Below, pp. 112–14.
75. Stevenson, *Scottish Revolution*, ch. 7: Donald, 'King and the Troubles', chs. 4–6;
    C. Russell, 'The British Problem and the English Civil War', *History* (1987),
    pp. 395–415.
76. *Works of William Laud*, III 279.
77. *History of Troubles*, pp. 55–6.

Although none of the English members of this 'clandestine band' are named, nine Scots are listed. The presence of Traquair and Lorne along with Rothes, Cassilis, Glencairn, Loudoun, Lindsay, Balmerino, and Cowper does not inspire confidence. Nor does the statement that the group was 'not without advice from the Marquis of Hamilton'. The list precedes a discussion of the offensive policies and is not necessarily a list of the 'clandestine band'. In a subsequent passage,[78] also about a period prior to the introduction of the Prayer Book, Spalding again speaks specifically of a 'privy meeting' convened by Lorne and drawn from the same group 'and others, of whom the marquis of Hamilton was one, together with a menzie of miscontented persons' including (as ringleaders among the clergy) Alexander Henderson, David Dickson and Andrew Cant). This is a combination of highly plausible and highly implausible names and is worrying. It has led some historians to dismiss the whole story out of hand.[79] But can so firm and detailed an account constitute smoke without fire? I am troubled rather than convinced by these accounts. On the one hand, there clearly *were* clandestine contacts among members of the group Spalding names from 1634 on (as Rutherford's correspondence shows); the speed with which the Covenant was drawn up, disseminated and promoted is striking, as is the evidence of close collusion among most of those Spalding named in the course of 1638; above all, there is the evidence that Eleazor Borthwick was acting as an agent in England for leading Scottish malcontents even before the Covenant was signed.[80] Yet three things point another way. The first, which we have already examined, is the failure of the Covenant itself to propose solutions to the crisis in *British* terms: the second is that covenanting propaganda took so long to address an English audience on the need for reform in England: the third is that it was palpably Charles I himself who first treated his Scottish crisis as a British problem – indeed, the Covenanters can be seen scrambling in response to *his* broadening of the issues. Thus, within weeks of hearing about the Covenant, Charles was laying down contingency plans for a military invasion of Scotland by English and Irish troops;[81] the Scots did not begin to consider military preparations until they became aware of Charles's

78. *History of Troubles*, p. 56.
79. Stevenson, *Scottish Revolution*, p. 56.
80. H. Guthry, *Memoirs* (2nd edn, Glasgow, 1747), p. 15. (See also Stevenson, *Scottish Revolution*, p. 57.)
81. Donald 'Scottish Covenant', pp. 97–100.

plans.[82] Similarly, it was Charles who saw the challenge to episcopacy in Scotland as undermining the authority of the bishops (as an Estate in Parliament and as a separate order within the Church).[83]

Early Scots propaganda both played down English responsibility for their plight and also denied that the Covenant had implications for England. The 1637 *Petition of the Noblemen, Barons, Ministers, Burgesses and Commons* against the canons and Prayer Book not only found in the latter

> the seeds of divers superstitions, Idolatrie, and false doctrine . . . but also the Service Booke of England is abused, especially in the matter of communion, by additions, subtractions, interchanging of words . . . to the disadvantage of Reformation as the Romish Masse is, in the more substantial points, made up therein . . . for reversing the gracious intention of the blessed reformers of Religion in England.[84]

Thus there was no need to intervene in English affairs. The Covenanters' *Answer to the Profession and Declaration Made by James, Marquis of Hamilton*, issued as late as December 1638, contained the following assurance:

> We doe not meddle with the Kirks of England or Ireland . . . all our argument and proceedings being for the Kirk of Scotland, where, from the time of her more pure Reformation than of her sister kirks, Episcopacie heth been ever abolished, till the latter time of corruption. . . .[85]

Not only was the Covenant non-exportable, but the problem was perceived in Scottish terms. It was the fault of the prelatical cuckoos in the presbyterian nest; it was their reintrusion via packed and improperly-constituted General Assemblies that had created the problem. As Andrew Cant and his colleagues toured Scotland in 1638 explaining and justifying the Covenant, the account they gave of the coming of the Troubles was an internal history of Scotland since 1596. Not once, in his sermons at St Andrews, Inverness, Glasgow or Edinburgh, did Cant blame the English.[86] The nearest he came was at Glasgow, where he appealed to his congregation to think on the sufferings of the poor Scots in Ireland, under the lash of 'the

82. E.M. Furgol, 'Scotland Turned Sweden' in Morrill (ed.), *Scottish Covenant*, pp. 138–48.
83. M. Mendle, *Dangerous Positions* (Alabama, 1985), pp. 115–27. For a similar conclusion, that the Scots were not initially anti-English, see W. Ferguson, *Scotland's Relations with England to 1707* (Edinburgh, 1977), p. 116.
84. *A Large Declaration.* p. 42.
85. Printed in *A Large Declaration* at p. 348.
86. His sermons are printed in *Covenants and Covenanters*, pp. 54–128.

proud prelates' there.[87] More typical is his narration at Inverness of
how God had singled out Scotland, 'a dark, obscure island, inferior
to many' and 'planted a vineyard there' so that other nations 'had
more of antichrist than she, she more of Christ than they'. Recently,
however, 'Satan envied our happiness, brake our ranks, poisoned our
fountains, muddied and defiled our streams: and while the watchmen
slept, the wicked one sowed his tares.'[88]

Even the angriest and fiercest of the apologists for the Covenant in
1637. George Gillespie, while he scorned Hooker and other 'English
formalists' for their errors, did not see the problem of Scotland in
1637 in British terms. The nearest he comes is in this passage:

It is not this day feared, but felt, that the rotten dreggs of poperie,
which were never purged away from England and Ireland, and having
once been spewed out with detestation, are licked up again in Scotland,
prove to be the unhappy occasions of a woeful recidivation. . . . What
doleful and disastrous mutation . . . hath happened to the Church and
spouse of Christ in these dominions? Her comely countenance is mis-
coloured with the fading lustre of the mother of harlotts: her shame-
faced forehead hath received the mark of the Beast: her lovely-locks
are frizled with the crisping pins of antichristian fashions: her chaste
ears are made to listen to the friends of the great Whore, who bring
the bewitching doctrine of enchanting traditions; her dove eyes looke
pleasantly upon the well-attired harlot; her sweet voice is mumming and
muttering some missall and magical liturgies: her fair necke beareth the
halter-like tokens of her former captivity, even a burdensome chain of
superfluous and superstitious ceremonies. . . . Oh transformed virgin.[89]

The blame for the many innovations – those 'best wares which the
big hulk of conformity, favoured by the prosperous gale of mighty
authority, hath imported upon us – is very indirect.'[90]

As late as February 1639, the Scots could deny anglicization as
the root of their problem. Rather than claiming that an anglicized
worship was being rammed down their throats, they claimed that
Scotland was being used as a laboratory for experimental liturgies:

The churchmen of greatest power in England . . . sent down to their
associats the pretended Arch-bishops and Bishops of this Kingdome, to
bee printed and pressed upon the whole Church here, without order
or consent as the only forme of divine worship and government of the
Church, to make us a leading case to England.[91]

87. *Covenants and Covenanters*, p. 97.
88. *Covenants and Covenanters*, pp. 78–9.
89. G. Gillespie, *A Dispute Against the English Popish Ceremonies* [sig. A 3].
90. Ibid.
91. *An Information to All Good Christians within the Kingdome of England, from the Noblemen, Barrons, Borrows, Ministers and Commons of the Kingdome of Scotland, for vindicating their intentions and actions* . . . (Edinburgh, 1639), pp. 6–7.

But this document does represent a first shift: it was Englishmen (specifically and exclusively Churchmen) who were to blame for the Scottish Troubles. A strengthening sense of the antichristian nature of the episcopal office (one can see this strengthening and clarifying in the minds of writers like Baillie), which clearly had implications for Scottish attitudes to those national churches which retained bishops, combined with an ever greater recognition that the Scottish bishops were but the tools and instruments of the English hierarchy. These are features of the propaganda in late 1639 and 1640. There is no language before April 1640 to match the fury of Robert Baillie's *The Canterburian's Self-Conviction*, in which he alleged that Laud and his 'dependencies' intended to substitute the Mass for the Bible, the laws of Castile for Magna Carta, and to send nobility and gentry to the chain-gangs of Peru or the galleys of the Mediterranean.[92] And, in comparison with the examples cited above from 1638, the blame is squarely removed to England, 'to the Prelacy in England, the fountaine whence all the Babylonish streams issued unto us'. The Scots had come to realize that they needed to trace the streams of corruption back to their source south of the Border.[93] From then on, as Peter Donald, Conrad Russell, David Stevenson and others have amply shown, the Scots determined both to seize the military initiative from Charles and to ensure that antichristian bishops were removed and godly order and discipline established throughout the king's dominions.[94]

VIII

In the event, of course, the struggle for the Covenant led inexorably on to the War of Three Kingdoms, in which the affairs of each became inextricably bound up with the affairs of the others. English and Irish troops were called upon to impose the king's will in Scotland;[95] the defeat of those armies brought a Scots invasion of England and direct intervention by the Scots in the settlement of England in 1641;[96] the

92. [R. Baillie], *The Canterburian's Self-Conviction* (Edinburgh, 1640), preface [sig. A 4].
93. *The Lawfullness of Our expedition into England Manifested* (1640), p. 4.
94. See above, n. 64.
95. Donald, 'King and the Troubles', esp. pp. 194–215; D. Stevenson, *Scottish Covenanters and Irish Confederates* (Belfast, 1981), pp. 1–42. And see the comments of M. Perceval-Maxwell, 'Ireland and the Monarchy', *Historical Journal* XXXIV (1991), 279–98; M. Fissel, '*Bellum Episcopale:* The Bishops' Wars and the end of the "Personal Rule" in England, 1638–1640', University of Berkeley PhD thesis (1983).
96. Stevenson, *Scottish Revolution*, pp. 214–42; Donald, 'King and the Troubles', ch. 6; Hamilton, 'Negotiation', pp. 84–96; C.L. Hamilton, 'The basis of Scottish efforts to create a Reformed Church of England, 1640–1', *Church History*, XXX (1961), 171–7.

Irish Rebellion in November of that year speedily brought Scottish as well as English armies into Ulster and Leinster,[97] the Scots invaded England again in 1643, provoked in large part by the king's machinations in Ireland,[98] and a crucial dimension of the campaigns of Montrose in 1644–5 was the renewed interest of Ulster Macdonnells in their ancestral lands in the west of Scotland.[99] Scottish disaffection with their English allies, culminating in the Engagement, was inflamed by the latter's betrayal of the interests of the Scots in Ulster. By 1648, most of those involved in public affairs in Scotland recognized that there could be no security for Scotland unless a federal constitution and a uniformity of religion had been achieved in all three kingdoms.[100] In 1641, in the Solemn League and Covenant of 1643, in the peace negotiations at Uxbridge and Newcastle, Scot proposals for ecclesiastical unity and mechanisms for coordinating the governments at least of England and Scotland were at the fore. But as, north of the Border, the conditions for constitutional cohabitation became clearer and clearer, so in England, indifference to a formal arrangement turned to hostility. The Long Parliament deferred discussion of the Eighth article of the Treaty of London,[101] dragged its feet over the appointment of *conservatores pacis* in 1643–5, unilaterally shut down the Committee of Both Kingdoms, tampered with the ecclesiastical proposals produced by the (Anglo-Scottish) Westminster Assembly without consulting their partners,[102] and, under pressure from the army, paved the way for religious toleration in 1647.[103] This was indifference more than malice. When the Scots Engagers invaded England in 1648, Cromwell chased them out and moved north to Edinburgh in the aftermath of the battle of Preston. But neither Parliament nor the generals had any stomach for an occupation or conquest of Scotland. Cromwell was delighted when a putsch by Argyll restored power to the anti-Engagers, and was happy to leave

97. Stevenson, *Covenanters and Confederates*, pp. 103–61.
98. Stevenson, *Covenanters and Confederates*, pp. 137–50.
99. D. Stevenson, *Alisdair MacColla and the Highland Problem in the Seventeenth Century* (Edinburgh, 1980), *passim*: Stevenson, *Covenanters and Confederates*, pp. 137–50.
100. D. Stevenson, *Revolution and Counter-Revolution in Scotland, 1644–1651* (1977), pp. 82–122; Stevenson, *Covenanters and Confederates*, pp. 253–84.
101. Donald, 'King and the Troubles', ch. 6.
102. Most fully discussed in L. Kaplan, *Politics and Religion during the English Revolution: The Scots and the Long Parliament, 1643–1645* (New York, 1976). The best discussion of the Westminster Assembly and of the Scots' part in it is now R. Paul, *The Assembly of the Lord* (1985).
103. Stevenson, *Counter-Revolution*, pp. 82–94.

them in charge.[104] The English had still to work out a British policy. But while the Scots might agree on the necessity of federal Union, they were split about how best to achieve it. By the spring of 1648, the covenanting movement, which, despite the Montrose schism, was still substantially intact, was sundered. Over the next three years it disintegrated into fragments as disaster followed disaster and as unpalatable solutions to intractable difficulties presented themselves: Engagers, Whiggamores, Resolutioners, Remonstrants, Protesters – so many possible responses to events in England.[105]

IX

The coronation of Charles II at Scone on 1 January 1651 brings home the transformations of the years since 1637.[106] After the grim harangue from the Moderator of the General Assembly, during which Charles was both reminded of the public shortcomings and private vices of his predecessors, and given a lecture in political thought that Buchanan would have been proud of, Charles took the Covenants, was acclaimed, took the coronation oath, and was crowned.[107] Two aspects of the ceremony sum up my argument. The first is that Charles was being crowned as head of a faction, not a nation: in no way could anyone delude themselves that the nation was united behind the imposition of the Covenants on this manifestly unworthy and unbelieving king. The second is that those who imposed the National Covenant and the Solemn League and Covenant upon him no longer believed that this was or could be simply a Scottish monarch. The words with which Charles took the Covenants are revealing indeed:

> I Charles, King of Great Britain, France and Ireland, do assure and declare, by my solemn Oath, in the presence of Almighty God, the searcher of hearts, my allowance and approbation of the Nationall Covenant and of the Solemn League and Covenant above written, and faithfully oblige myself, to prosecute the ends thereof . . . and that I

104. D. Stevenson, 'Cromwell, Scotland and Ireland', in J.S. Morrill (ed.), *Oliver Cromwell and the English Revolution* (Harlow, 1990), pp. 153–5.
105. Stevenson, *Counter-Revolution*, pp. 115–29.
106. *The Forme and Coronation of Charles the Second, King of Scotland, England, France and Ireland* (Aberdeen, 1651), I have used an original copy. There is an accessible and generally reliable transcript in Kerr (ed.), *Covenants and Covenanters*, pp. 349–99, based on a 1741 edition of this account.
107. The order is of course highly significant: the acclamation (election by and contract with his people) *followed* his taking of the Covenants (and his election was thus made conditional upon the Covenants), whereas the taking of the coronation oath *followed* the acclamation and was not a condition of election. (For the sequence, see Kerr (ed.), *Covenants and Covenanters*, pp. 386–9).

shall give my royal assent to acts and ordinances of parliament passed, or to be passed, enjoining the same in my other dominions.[108]

This was no less than sticking by the commitment to British monarchy demonstrated in the solemn proclamation of Charles II as king of Great Britain, France and Ireland by Chancellor Loudoun on behalf of the Scottish government on 5 February 1649, the day news of Charles I's execution reached Edinburgh.[109] While the English had not consulted the Scots over the trial and execution of Charles I, the Rump's Ordinance abolishing monarchy had referred to England and Ireland, but had pointedly avoided any reference to Scotland.[110] The decision in Edinburgh to declare Charles king not only of Scotland but of Britain was provocation indeed.[111]

Thus, if the coronation of Charles I taught the Scots the need to covenant together against an authoritarian, unfeeling, foreign king, the coronation of Charles II showed that the price to be paid for the struggle against that king was a double denial of the National Covenant: no longer a covenant of all the nation, neither was it a document exclusively for that nation.

108. Ibid., p. 386. It is curious, in view of this form of words, that the title of the pamphlet should describe him as King of Scotland, England, France and Ireland (the form used at the coronation of James in Westminster Abbey in 1603 – for which see Ferguson, *Scotland's Relations with England*, p. 97). The difference did, of course, matter.
109. *Acts of the Parliament of Scotland*, VI:ii, 156–7; Stevenson, *Counter-Revolution*, pp. 131–3.
110. S.R. Gardiner, *Constitutional Documents of the Puritan Revolution* (3rd edn, 1906), pp. 384–7.
111. Stevenson, *Counter-Revolution*, pp. 129–34.

CHAPTER SIX

The Making of Oliver Cromwell

I

For the first forty of his fifty-eight years, Oliver Cromwell lived in obscurity.[1] He and his immediate family can be found in parish records as they were baptized, married and buried. We can trace him from his first family home in Huntingdon, via an unsettled period in neighbouring St Ives to the cathedral city of Ely. We can trace his tax returns. We can glimpse him in local disputes which brought him under the scrutiny of the Privy Council. We have three accounts of what appears to have been his only speech to the parliament of 1628–29. We have a few rich but tantalizingly decontextualized letters. But there is much darkness and the beams of light are pencil thin and of low wattage.

Nevertheless, I want to suggest that his invisibility is itself a clue to his early identity. This chapter will re-examine the shreds of evidence and will suggest that he was a man in humbler circumstances, a meaner man, than has usually been allowed; that he spent the 1620s and 1630s in largely silent pain at his personal lot and at the drift of public affairs; and that any understanding of his later life needs to begin from a rather different sense of that early life.

The firm pieces of evidence about him, along with the more or less malicious stories gathered together by biographers in the decade or

---

1. This essay involves building a model with needles from many haystacks. For much help in finding the needles, and some in assembling them, I am grateful to Tim Wales, a marvellous researcher, and to John Adamson, Michael Berlin, Anthony Milton, Conrad Russell, David Smith, Christopher Thompson and many habitués of the Cambridge University Library tearoom.

so after his death[2] have given rise to a fairly universal modern image of the young Cromwell: the 'mere' country gentleman of solid but not substantial wealth ('by birth a gentleman, living neither in any considerable height, nor yet in obscurity', as he himself put it),[3] a man of magisterial experience, accustomed to governing local communities if not the nation; a man firmly rooted in an extensive cousinage of families prominent in their criticism of royal policies; a man who sowed wild oats in his youth but who, returning belatedly but wholeheartedly to the firm puritan teaching he had received at the hands of Dr Thomas Beard in the local grammar school in Huntingdon and of Dr Samuel Ward and the tutors of Sidney Sussex College Cambridge, underwent an archetypal puritan conversion experience at some time in the later 1620s; a man whose intuitive egalitarianism made him stand up for the freemen of Huntingdon dispossessed of their rights in the town's new and oligarchic charter in 1630 and also stand up for the rights of commoners against aristocratic fendrainers in the later 1630s.

Very little of this picture survives close scrutiny. This chapter will consider in turn Cromwell's family background and his economic and social status; his intellectual formation; and the handful of key incidents known to us. It will conclude with a review of the circumstances of his return as MP for the city of Cambridge in 1640 and his participation in the debates of the first two years of the Long Parliament.

II

Oliver Cromwell was the eldest (surviving) son of the younger son of a knight. In consequence his social status was very ill-defined and his economic situation precarious. The wealth of the Cromwells rested upon former church lands, and the revival of Oliver's economic fortunes was to rest upon the acquisition of preferential leases on cathedral properties. It may indeed be that some of the obsessive anti-popery of the English landed groups in the 1620s and 1630s derived from a residual fear that their titles to land might become

<hr>

2. I have made little use of two very jaundiced Restoration authorities – James Heath, *Flagellum* (1663, 1674) and Sir William Dugdale, *A Short View of the Late Troubles* (1681). To rely on them, as many biographers have, whenever they are uncorroborated is irresponsible, since they are so unreliable whenever they can be checked. See J.S. Morrill, 'Textualizing and contextualizing Cromwell', *HJ*, XXXIII (1990), 629–40.
3. W.C. Abbott, *Writings and Speeches of Oliver Cromwell* (4 vols., Cambridge, Mass., 1937–47), III, 453.

insecure if a popish or popishly-inclined king sought to unmake the Reformation. Charles I's challenges to the holders of former church property in Scotland and Ireland, and the adumbration of such a challenge in England would have reinforced the suspicions of men in Cromwell's position.[4]

Oliver's grandfather (Sir Henry) and then his uncle (Sir Oliver) lived in the grand Elizabethan style in his substantial modern house at Hinchingbrook, built on the site of a pre-reformation nunnery, just outside Huntingdon, with a second home deep in the fen at Ramsey, a converted monastery. James VI stayed on several occasions at Hinchingbrook since he enjoyed the local hunting. The Cromwells sat in several Elizabethan and Jacobean parliaments, and served on the Huntingdonshire commission of the peace. Sir Oliver's income seems to have been around £2000, placing him in the top ten county families and top one hundred in East Anglia. Maintaining that position proved too much for him, however, and in 1628 he sold off his Huntingdonshire property and moved to Ramsey.[5]

Sir Henry had ten children to provide for; and he could not be overgenerous to younger sons. Oliver's father, Robert, was lucky to be set up as a gentleman in a town house in Huntingdon and a job lot of urban and rural property, to which he added by marriage the impropriation of a neighbouring rectory (which entitled him to collect the tithe and sell the right to present to the living). In all, his income was probably around £300 a year, just enough to secure him a place as a JP of the county;[6] and his father's influence was able to secure him a single term as MP for the borough of Huntingdon in 1597. But Robert himself had seven daughters as well as Oliver to provide for, and it is clear that the latter's inheritance from his father was a meagre one. In 1631 he was to sell up all but 17 acres of his inheritance (and all his mother's jointure) for a total of £1800, which represents an annual income of no more than £100.[7] The subsidy rolls confirm his humble circumstances. They divide taxpayers into those who paid *in terris*, on the annual value of their freehold land, and those who paid *in bonis*, on the capital value of their 'moveable goods'. All the wealthiest men paid *in terris*. Oliver's tax assessment

4. See, for example, C. Hill, *The Economic Problems of the Church* (Oxford, 1956), chs. 12–14.
5. For his family background, M. Noble, *Memoirs of the Protectoral House of Cromwell* (1787) and J.L. Sanford, *Studies and Illustrations of the Great Rebellion* (1858), ch. 4, are fullest. Abbott, I, ch. 1 summarizes but does not improve on these.
6. C.H. Firth, *Oliver Cromwell and the Rule of the Puritans* (Oxford, 1900), p. 3.
7. Sanford, *Studies*, p. 216; Firth, *Cromwell*, p. 28.

in the 1620s was £4 *in bonis*. The figure of £4 was notional, but it appears to confirm an income of no more than £100 per annum. This assessment was similar to that of another forty families at the top of a small and unprosperous market town.[8]

In 1631 Cromwell moved to St Ives. He may have been forced to sell up by financial pressures; but, as we shall see, it is more likely that he was forced out by miscalculation in local politics. At any rate, his standing in St Ives was essentially that of a yeoman, a working farmer.[9] He had moved down from the gentry to the 'middling sort'.

In 1636 his economic fortunes revived with the death of his mother's childless brother. His inheritance consisted not of freehold land but of the reversion of leases held by his uncle from the dean and chapter of Ely. He became lessee of the manor of Stuntney, to the south of the city of Ely, and lay rector (i.e. administrator) of the church lands and tithes of the parishes of Ely itself and of their outlying chapelries;[10] and he quickly extended these business interests by becoming lessee of lands owned by Cambridge colleges – Clare and Trinity Hall – near Ely.[11] By 1641 his income had probably risen to £300 per annum, and he appears on the subsidy roll as assessed at £6 *in terris*. He was eighteenth on the list. It is possible that he was invited by the bishop to take over from his uncle as JP for the Isle of Ely and that he refused.[12] In any event, his status was improving.

Despite his connections with ancient riches, Cromwell's economic status was much closer to that of the 'middling sort' and urban merchants than to that of the county gentry and governors. He always lived in towns, not in a country manor house; and he worked for his living. He held no important local offices and had no tenants or others dependent upon him beyond a few household servants. When he pleaded in 1643 for the selection of 'russet-coated captains who know what they were fighting for', and when he described his troopers as 'honest men, such as fear God',[13] this was not the condescension of a radical member of the elite, but the pleas of a man on the margins of the gentry on behalf of those with whom he had had social discourse and daily communion for twenty years.

All this makes his rise to be Head of State the more remarkable. But it may help us to understand his self-perception as Lord Protector.

8. PRO, E179/122/213, 215, 216.
9. Sanford, *Studies*, pp. 240–1.
10. R. Holmes, *Cromwell's Ely* (Ely, 1982), pp. 10–14.
11. Ibid., p. 13.
12. 'The notebook of Dr Henry Plume', *Essex Review*, XV (1906), 15. Plume, an Essex antiquary, recorded that Matthew Wren proposed to appoint Cromwell, 'but he would not act.'

The Nature of the English Revolution

In that role he never likened himself to the justice of the peace, the Christian magistrate that shaped policy and *interpreted* the law; but to 'a good constable [appointed to] keep the peace of the parish'[14] – a role that lacked initiative and executive authority, and was marked by a formal obedience to the decisions and judgements of others. Cromwell's first twenty years of adulthood were marked by a lack of formal involvement in government. Just wealthy and independent enough to escape the drudgery of parish or town government, he was not wealthy enough to *govern* in the fuller sense.

His economic background may have had one other important consequence. Both in Huntingdon and Ely his income came largely from administering tithes. The attack by Laud on lay impropriators, and specifically on the improverishment of urban clergy, would have been a particular threat to him in the 1630s.[15] Self-interest, reinforcing and reinforced by his evangelical zeal, would have drawn him to call for ecclesiastical reform. Any attack on the deans and chapters could be expected to bring him the right to preferential acquisition of the freehold of the lands he rented at Ely. On the other hand, his notorious later squeamishness about the abolition of tithes, and concern that lay impropriators should be compensated can surely be related to this aspect of his early life.[16]

Yet this does not get his social standing quite right: he *was* the grandson and the nephew of knights; he married the daughter of a substantial London fur trader and leather dresser who was establishing himself among the Essex gentry; he was in close contact with members of his family (such as the cousin married to Oliver St John, chief counsel both to Viscount Saye and Sele and to John Hampden in their ship money cases); he seems to have lived in London in the late 1610s with Lady (Joan) Barrington, another relative of his mother's; and these connections linked him into the circle of the Rich family, earls of Warwick and Holland. He also had his sons educated at Felsted School (founded and still controlled by the Riches).[17] His own education, at the local grammar school at Huntingdon and at Sidney Sussex College, Cambridge, was that of a gentleman. Following his father's death he went to London to study law. No record of his

13. Abbott, I, 256, 258.
14. Abbott, IV, 470.
15. Hill, *Economic Problems*, chs. 5, 6, 11.
16. Hill, *God's Englishman*, pp. 36, 178–9.
17. M. Craze, *A History of Felsted School* (1947), pp. 27–33, 47–50.

presence at any of the Inns of Court has been found.[18] If he stayed in London until his marriage there in 1621, he stayed far longer than those attending purely to equip themselves with a gentleman's sense of the law (i.e. not long enough to qualify to plead a cause, but long enough to know whether they had a cause worth pleading). Perhaps a career as a barrister was intended and abandoned. It would have made sense to a family in such precarious circumstances. Yet Cromwell never *sounds* or *reads* like a common lawyer. It is thus intriguing to consider the unheeded suggestion of his earliest and most reliable biographer, Samuel Carrington, writing in 1659, that 'his parents designed him to the study of the civil law'.[19] What makes this just credible is the fact that his inheritance was centred around the income from an impropriate rectory and that he already had the expectation of his uncle's extensive ecclesiastical business in and around Ely, both of which would bring him into extended dealings with the Church courts. It is also worth speculating that his later impatience with the procedural obfuscations of the common law and his preoccupations with equity might be connected with a training in civil law.

Cromwell was not, then, as he is often portrayed, the typical country squire: the secure, obscure gentleman who rose from solid respectability to govern England with all the experience and all the limitations of a godly magistrate. His economic and social standing was far more brittle than that implies: his reference to himself as being 'by birth a gentleman, living in neither any considerable height, nor yet in obscurity' takes on a tenser, more anxious patina. His cousinage flattered to deceive. Economic circumstances for much of his early manhood beckoned him to the yoke of husbandry; and political miscalculation seems nearly to have completed the task.

III

Huntingdon does not seem to have been a town much troubled by controversy or division in the decades before 1625.[20] But in the early years of Charles I a series of minor convulsions shook the town. Fragmentary evidence suggests that Cromwell was a victim of these

18. It is generally argued that he attended Lincoln's Inn; but the records (and especially the accounts) of Lincoln's Inn are very full, and he is not likely to have been a non-fee-payer or to have slipped through the accounts. The case for his being at Gray's Inn is based on the loss of its records and the presence of some cousins there.
19. S. Carrington, *The History of the Life and Death of His Most serene Highness, Oliver Late Lord Protector* (1659), p. 4.
20. W. Carruthers, *A History of Huntingdon* (1824), *passim*; P.M.G. Dickinson, *Oliver Cromwell and Huntingdon* (Huntingdon, 1981).

convulsions. The ingredients of the drama include: the departure of the senior branch of the Cromwells from Hinchingbrook House and the arrival of the Montagus; the disagreements among the leading inhabitants of the borough about the best way to spend a £2000 bequest; and (as a consequence of these changes) the grant of a new royal charter.

We know next to nothing about Oliver's role in the government of Huntingdon in the 1620s because so few borough records survive. As we have seen, he was essentially an urban landlord with a strong interest in the tithes of the parish of Hartford. He may or may not have been one of the twenty-four burgesses elected by all freemen annually to form the common council; he may even have served as one of the two bailiffs. As one of the leading subsidy-men it is to be expected that this was so; and if Hinchingbrook influence could secure his return as MP in 1628, it could surely have secured his election as a councillor.

That return as MP represents the dying embers of family interest. He was returned with and behind a member of the Montagu family who were in the process of moving into Hinchingbrook.[21] Oliver made little impact on the parliament of 1628–29. The extensive diaries for both the tempestuous sessions report only one speech by him, and the Journals record him as on few committees and never active as a teller. He made no impact at all on the first session which culminated in the passage of the Petition of Right.

His one speech was delivered on 11 February 1629 in the Committee for Religion that was investigating the spread of Arminian teaching and its protection in high places. Much of the burden of the complaint was against Bishop Neile, who had sollicited pardons on behalf both of those who had preached Arminianism (Montagu and Cosin) and those who had been imprisoned in the first session of parliament for preaching the subject's unqualified duty of obedience in the matter of the forced loan (Mainwaring and Sibthorpe). The version of the speech most readily available, and the source of much misinterpretation, has it as follows:

> *Mainwaring – who by censure of the last Parliament for his sermons, was disabled from holding any ecclesiastical dignity in the church, and confessed the justice of that censure – was, nevertheless, by this same bishop's means, preferred to a rich living. If these be the steps to church preferment, what may we not expect?* Dr Beard told me that one Dr Alabaster, in a sermon at Paul's Cross, had preached flat popery. Dr Beard was to rehearse

21. E. Griffith, *Collection of Ancient Records relating to the Borough of Huntingdon* (1827), p. 106.

[refute?] Alabaster's sermon at the Spittle, but Dr Neile, bishop of
Winchester, sent for him and charged him as his diocesan to preach
nothing contrary to Dr Alabaster's sermon. He went to Dr Felton,
bishop of Ely, who charged him as a minister to oppose it, which
Dr Beard did; but he was then sent for by Dr Neile, and was
exceedingly rated for what he had done.[22]

This account has been variously misinterpreted. The first part (in
italics above) referring to Mainwaring is specious and was not part
of what Cromwell said;[23] and the second part, which Abbott called
'a composite of three slightly different versions of the speech',[24]
suppresses the vital information that the Alabaster sermon and Beard's
row with Neile had taken place ten or twelve years earlier. Alabaster,
an unstable man who had converted to Rome *c.* 1596 and reverted
to Anglicanism *c.* 1610, was a minister in Hertfordshire.[25] Neile
was involved, as two versions of Cromwell's speech makes plain,[26]
because he was, at the time, bishop of Lincoln and therefore responsible for both preachers. Cromwell was therefore presenting the
committee with very stale beer.

By the time Cromwell returned from the Parliament following
its dramatic dissolution, Huntingdon was deeply divided over a
new issue: the Fishbourne bequest. Richard Fishbourne had been
born in the town in the 1580s and had been apprenticed into the
Mercers Company of London. He made a considerable fortune and
on his death left money for a variety of charitable uses, including a
£2000 gift for his home town.[27] It took three years for the borough's
representatives to decide whether the money should be spent entirely
for the benefit of the poor (to start a scheme to find employment for
the able-bodied unemployed) or whether it should be divided between
such a scheme and the endowment of a preaching lectureship.

22. Abbott, I, 61–2.
23. It was printed in Sanford, *Studies*, pp. 229–30. Sanford prints the italicized part
after the second half, and he gives a source which Abbott misrepresents. The
publication of W. Notestein and F. Relf (eds.), *The Commons Debates for 1629*
(New Haven, 1921) should have shown him that Sanford had a corrupt text.
Indeed, as far back as 1882, S.R. Gardiner had shown that 'the remainder of the
speech . . . relating to Mainwaring . . . is taken from another speech by another
speaker, on a different occasion' (*History*, VII, 56n).
24. Abbott, I, 62n.
25. *D. N. B.*; R.V. Caro, 'William Alabaster: Rhetor, Mediator, Devotional Poet',
Recusant History, XIX (1988), 62–79, 155–70.
26. *Commons Debates for 1629*, pp. 139, 143, both of which make explicit that the
sermon was delivered when Neile was bishop of Lincoln (1614–17) and diocesan
of both Alabaster and Beard. One puzzle is that Felton only arrived at Ely twelve
months after Neile left for Durham.
27. PRO, PROB 11/45 fos 461–5.

At the heart of the dispute was the position of Dr Thomas Beard. He is usually portrayed as a simple, devout puritan schoolmaster, devoting his life to the education of the children of a small country town.[28] In fact he was a greedy pluralist, living in grand style, ungrateful for his comfortable lot, and interfering in the secular affairs of the borough in ways no self-respecting puritan would have done.

Beard had arrived in Huntingdon as a graduate of Cambridge University, just after Oliver's birth. Within a few years he held three positions in the town, as vicar of All Saints, the central parish where most of the wealthiest inhabitants lived and worshipped, as schoolmaster and as Master of the Hospital, an imposing set of former monastic buildings at the heart of the town, close to All Saints, dominating the market square and providing him with a good income and some of the finest quarters in the town. He also held the living of Kimbolton, a wealthy parish of 600 communicants and already associated with the Montagu family. He supplied Kimbolton with a non-graduate and non-preaching curate. He held this living in plurality and in absence for fifteen years, only surrendering it, in 1610, when he had secured a second parish in Huntingdon itself, St John's, parish of the Cromwells.[29]

Beard's ambitions were clearly not satisfied by these pleasant surroundings. In 1614 he wrote to Sir Robert Cotton, complaining about 'the painful occupation of teaching' and asking for preferment to a Hertfordshire living in Cotton's gift.[30] There is not a shred of evidence that he was ever a nonconformist and his acquisition of a prebend's stall in Lincoln cathedral in 1612 and of a royal chaplaincy at some point in James's reign strongly suggest otherwise.[31] When in 1614 Bishop Barlow suppressed a combination lectureship at Huntingdon, the corporation put up the money to establish a fixed lecture every Wednesday and Sunday morning in All Saints, and

---

28. *D. N. B.*; Hill, *God's Englishman*, pp. 37–45; R.S. Paul, *The Lord Protector* (1955), pp. 24–9.
29. W.M. Noble (ed.), 'Incumbents of the county of Huntingdon', *T. Cambs and Hunts Arch. Soc.*, II (1914), 126, 130, 134, 137; C.W. Foster, 'The State of the Church in the reigns of Elizabeth and James I', *Lincs. Rec. Soc.*, XXIII (1926), 280–2; Lincs. Arch. Office, Libri Cleri, 3 (1604) and 4 (1614); *Cal. St. Pap. Dom. 1603–10*, p. 195.
30. BL, Cotton MSS, Julius c. III, fo. 109.
31. As prebend: *D. N. B.*; as royal chaplain, Mercers Hall, Acts of Court [AC] 1625–31, fo. 276v, copy of a letter from Charles I to the company.

appointed Beard to the post.[32] Although he fell foul of Neile over the Alabaster affair in or around 1617, he never seems to have fallen foul of Laud, although the latter was archdeacon of Huntingdon from 1615 to 1621.[33] At no point was his lectureship attacked, and he died in harness, as full of years as he was of livings, in 1632.

Just how 'puritan' was Cromwell's 'puritan' schoolmaster? He was fiercely anti-catholic, and wrote tracts against popery, with titles like *Antichrist the Pope of Rome;* or the *Pope of Rome is Antichrist,* and he is notorious for his providentialism.[34] But neither was a puritan preserve. His *The Theatre of God's Judgment*[35] is as much in the tradition of medieval cautionary tales as it is a self-conscious exaltation of the rewards God gives in this life to those He has saved in the next and of the foretastes of hellfire in this life to those who are to be damned. It draws far more on (pagan) classical writers and the Fathers such as Chrysostom and Cyprian than it does on post-reformation sources; it preaches against active resistance in all circumstances and for passive disobedience in terms Elizabeth and James would have approved; idolaters and upholders of ceremonies were to be found only in the Old Testament and the medieval Catholic Church. His other writings, dedicated to Cromwell's highly conformist grandfather and to Bishop John Williams, are firmly anti-catholic but show no concern at the incompleteness of the English Reformation.[36] He looks like a complacent Jacobean Calvinist conformist: not the man to ignite the fire in Cromwell's belly.

When to all this we add that Beard was quite happy to serve as a common councillor or as a JP,[37] thus mingling what to strict Calvinists had to be strictly separated, magistracy and ministry; and when we find that he was, certainly in his later years, the creature of the conformist Montagu family, his credentials as the shaper of Cromwell's puritanism appear decidely unimpressive. The apparent animosity between them in 1630 becomes easier to explain.

32. Report on 'public lectures' in Lincoln diocese, part of Neile's primary visitation in 1614, Lines. Arch. Off., Dean and Chapter MS. A4/3/43, printed in *Associated Architectural Society Reports and Papers,* XVI (1881), p. 44.
33. For Laud's appointment, see W. Bliss (ed.), *The Works of William Laud* (7 vols. 1847), III, 135; for a donation for the Huntingdon poor, see his will in ibid., IV, 445.
34. See note 27.
35. There were three editions in his lifetime, each longer than the one before (1597, 1612, 1631) and a further revised version after his death (1647).
36. *A Retractive from the Romish Religion* (1616) and *Antichrist the Pope of Rome* (1625).
37. For Beard as a common councillor, see Cambridgeshire Record Office, Huntingdon (= CRO (Hunt.), DDM/80/1983/1); as a JP, Carruthers, *Huntingdon,* appendix, unpag.

We can now return to the foundation of the Fishbourne lecture. It took more than three years for the town to find a suitable piece of land for purchase by the company.[38] There then ensued a twelve-month tussle within the borough and between the borough corporation and the company over the uses to which the endowment should be put. One party in the town, represented by Thomas Edwards, the only man rated *in terris* in the 1628 subsidy roll,[39] attended the Court of the Mercers Company in January 1630 and argued that since Beard already lectured on Wednesdays and Sundays and since there was a further lecture established in Godmanchester within half a mile of Huntingdon (this is important for Cromwell as we shall see), there was no need for any further lecture. The £100 per annum from the endowment should all be used to set the poor on work.[40] This was strongly opposed by a majority on the common council. They sent Recorder Barnard and Dr Beard to ask that £60 a year be spent on the poor, and £40 on a lectureship.[41] A committee of Mercers was sent to Huntingdon, and reported back in favour of the latter. The common council then revealed their main interest (and perhaps what underlay Edwards' opposition). The town wanted the lectureship to be awarded to Beard, thus releasing them from the burden of paying him themselves.[42] This did not impress the Mercers. This was new money and should go to a new purpose.[43] They declined and drew up a shortlist for a lecture to be held on market days (Saturday) and on Sunday afternoons in St Mary's parish at the populous and unfashionable end of town in which Fishbourne had been baptized.[44] Before they could proceed, however, they received a peremptory command to appoint Beard from King Charles I himself:

> . . . taking special notice of the good conversation and ability in learning of Dr Beard . . . late chaplain of our dear father and one whom the corporation there much desireth to supply that place . . .

38. CRO (Hunt.), Huntingdon Borough Records [H.B.R.], box 12, bundle 5, fos 9–10. This is a copy of a responsary by the Mercers, annotated by the Recorder, to a bill entered by the Corporation in 1695 alleging that the right of presentation to the Fishbourne lectureship had always lain with the town and not with the company. I have been unable to locate the original bill in the Court of Chancery.
39. PRO, E179/122/213.
40. Mercers Hall, Acts of Court 1625–31, fo. 248r.
41. Ibid., fo. 260v.
42. Ibid., fo. 268v–269r.
43. Fishbourne left money for other lectureships with the express provision that the preachers should not 'have any other benefice or church living with the cure of souls besides', PRO, PROB 11/145 fo. 461v.
44. Mercers Hall, Acts of Court 1625–31, fos 274v–277r; CRO (Hunt.), H.B.R., Box 12, bundle 5, fos 18–20.

to recommend him to their election . . . in our said town of Huntingdon, it being the ancient inheritance of our Crown.[45]

Perhaps the king was seeking to prevent the choice of an unbeneficed
lecturer; perhaps he was acting on the advice of the earl of Manchester[46] or, less likely, out of a genuine regard for Beard. In any
event, the latter was clearly no nonconformist or precisian.

The company sent a delegation (two of whose members, Mr Spur-
towe and Mr Basse, we shall meet again as friends of Cromwell)
to Nonsuch to urge the king to let them make a free choice, and,
upon an undertaking to add Beard to the shortlist, they appear to
have succeeded.[47] They considered seven candidates and selected one
Robert Procter. But they then came up against another obstacle,
the bishop of Lincoln, John Williams wrote commending Beard; he
stalled over granting Procter a licence, and he proposed a succession of
compromises. Meanwhile, the corporation prevented Procter over a
period of nine months from occupying his pulpit. Williams attempted
to persuade the Mercers to add another £20 a year to the pot and to
pay Beard and Procter £30 each. When this was rejected, he said he
would license Procter, if 'the company would bestow some gratuity'
upon Dr Beard. This was agreed, and after yet more haggling, a lump
sum of £40 was paid.[48] In mid 1631, six years after Fishbourne's death,
and six months before Beard's death, the first Fishbourne lecture was
given in St Mary's. Beard made his feelings clear by publishing a third
edition of *The Theatre of God's Judgement* with a dedication to the
mayor and aldermen of Huntingdon, who had stood by him, 'in the
late business of the lectureship, and notwithstanding the opposition
of malignant spirits'.[49]

Was Oliver Cromwell one of the malignant spirits? We do not
know. But it is tempting to think so. He and Thomas Edwards
were the wealthiest men *not* to be named as aldermen in the 1630
charter[50] (and the 'Mr Edwardes' whom Cromwell described as a
friend of twenty to thirty years' standing when he sought a position
for him as clerk (in the Prerogative Court) in 1647 is probably the

45. Mercers Hall, Acts of Court 1625–31, fo. 276.
46. As Lord Privy Seal he frequently advised the king on ecclesiastical patronage.
47. Mercers Hall, Acts of Court 1625–31, fos 275v, 277r.
48. Ibid., fos 282r–v, 286v–287r, 291v–292r, 296v, 309v, 317r–318v; Fishbourne
    Bequest, Accounts 1627–56, fo. 17r.
49. Beard, *Theatre* (1631 edn), preface.
50. For the list of aldermen, see Carruthers, *Huntingdon*, appendix 2 [unpag]; for the
    list of subsidymen, PRO, E179/122/213, 215, 216.

same man).[51] Cromwell had, or was soon to have, strong independent links with Mercers; he opposed the appointment of Beard and was subsequently a strong ally of theirs when the St Mary's lectureship came under attack and also in relation to the Godmanchester lecture (as we shall see). It seems more probable than not that the affair of the Fishbourne lecture explains Cromwell's bitter attack on the new charter in 1630 and the kick in the groin which Beard delivered him at the height of the charter dispute.

IV

In the spring of 1630, hot upon the heels of the arrival of the Montagus at Hinchingbrook and upon the snubbing of the town by the Mercers, the leading men of Huntingdon petitioned the Crown for a new charter.[52] There is good reason to believe that Cromwell supported this move.

The existing charter dated back to the reign of Richard III, and it vested power in two bailiffs and twenty-four common councillors, all elected on an annual basis by the burgesses. Now, in the words of the new charter:

> We at the humble petition of the bailiffs and burgesses of the borough aforesaid, being willing, for the better governance of the said Borough, to prevent and remove all occasions of popular tumult or to reduce the elections and other things and public business of the said borough into certainty and constant order,

reincorporated the borough with a permanent body of aldermen, to serve for life, coopting to vacancies, and a mayor to serve for a year by seniority among the aldermen.[53] The disagreements culminating in the humiliation of the borough by the Mercers must surely have had something to do with the 'popular tumults' which were to be avoided in future and the 'certainty and constant order' which were being sought.

The new charter passed the great seal just as the Fishbourne lectureship was finalized. It established a new body of aldermen, most of whom were inhabitants of All Saints parish.[54] The most

51. Abbott, I, 431–2. Cromwell speaks of his friend as having been an under-clerk 'about sixteen or seventeen years' (i.e. since 1631), suggesting that he too had left (been driven from?) Huntingdon immediately after the charter dispute.
52. Carruthers, *Huntingdon*, pp. 84–7.
53. Ibid., appendix [unpag.].
54. Based on a study of the names in the charter and of the parish registers of All Saints, St John's and St Mary's in CRO (Hunt.).

notable absentees, if we compare the list with the rankings in the 1628 subsidy roll, were Thomas Edwards, Oliver Cromwell and William Kilborne.[55] It is true that Cromwell was one of five JPs named; but the duties of a JP in a small borough did not compare with those of a county JP, especially where so much jurisdiction was exercised in the mayor's court. Had Cromwell taken up the position (which he did not) he would have had little more to do than a parish constable in the countryside.

What followed is well known. Cromwell and William Kilborne became involved in furious verbal arguments with some of the beneficiaries of the new charter, and uttered what their opponents dubbed 'disgraceful and unseemly speeches' against the mayor and the recorder, as a result of which they were reported to the Privy Council.[56] On 26 November 1630, Cromwell and Kilborne appeared before it, but were remanded in custody for six days. On 1 December 1630, the whole matter was handed over to the Lord Privy Seal, none other than the earl of Manchester.[57] On 6 December he produced a report that exonerated Barnard and the mayor, praised the new charter as 'being authorized by the common consent of the town' and required Cromwell to make an apology for words 'spoken in heat and passion'. His report makes plain that Cromwell was not complaining about the oligarchic nature of the new charter but about the intentions of the particular clique who had gained power under it. His concern, in Manchester's words, was first that

> the mayor and aldermen might now alter the rate of their cattle in the commons; secondly that the mayor and aldermen alone, without the burgesses, might dispose of the inheritances of their town lands; thirdly that it was in the power of the mayor and aldermen to fine men that might be poor £20 for refusing to be aldermen.

Manchester made it clear that 'these things . . . cannot be warranted by the new charter', but he got the aldermen to agree to uphold existing rights on the commons, to undertake not to alienate town-lands without the consent of the burgesses and to limit the fines on the reluctant to 20 marks.[58] This fits in with the idea that Cromwell

55. Kilborne was the other burgess hauled before the Privy Council for attacking the new charter (see below).
56. PRO, SP 16/186/34.
57. Abbott, I, 67–9.
58. PRO, SP 16/186/34 (full transcript in *Cal. St. Pap. Dom. 1629–31*, pp. x–xi). The extracts in Abbott, I, 69, are distorting and omit important matter. Sanford *Studies*, pp. 233–7, is also misleading. His statement (p. 233) that the charter dispute followed an electoral defeat by Cromwell is unsupported but has misled others (e.g. Hill, *God's Englishman*, p. 41).

was demoralized by the seizure of power by a clique which he saw as less paternalistic and more greedy than he and his friends were. He suspected them – following their failure to shuffle off their responsibility for Beard on to the Mercers – of trying to turn the assets of the town to their own profit. It was a personal attack, not a precocious defence of democratic principles: and he lost. Barnard showed his gratitude by having his next son baptized (in All Saints church) 'Manchester Barnard'[59] while Cromwell found his long-term position in his native town in ruins – his finances in tatters, his honour severely wounded, and his future prospects of office non-existent. What may have constituted the dregs of the bitter cup he had to drink was an affidavit sworn against him by Thomas Beard. It is to be found in the earl of Manchester's papers and it alleged that:

> Oliver Cromwell esquire and William Kilborne, gent., with a free assent and consent did agree to the renewing of our late charter and that it should be altered from bailiffs to mayor as they did hope it would be for future good and quiet of the town.[60]

The implication is that Cromwell's opposition to the charter followed his discovery that he was not to be an alderman, that he was a bad loser over a matter of personal preferment.

The likeliest hypothesis (it is hardly an explanation) of what had happened was this: that a bitter dispute over the Fishbourne bequest had led to a demand for a more settled charter; that those who had opposed Beard, including Cromwell, were ruthlessly omitted from the new, closed oligarchy, and that they responded in a bitter attack on their opponents, Robert Barnard, Thomas Beard, and behind them, the Montagus.

Within twelve months, Cromwell had sold up and moved five miles to St Ives, to begin a new life as a yeoman farmer.

V

Why St Ives? Probably because there was a suitable tenancy available, and because it allowed him to keep in touch with remaining friends in Huntingdon. He retained a nominal 17 acres of freehold there; his mother remained behind, and one of his daughters, Mary, was baptized in St John's parish church in 1636.[61]

59. CRO (Hunt.), microfilm roll 171, parish register of All Saints, baptismal entry for 22 August 1633.
60. CRO (Hunt.), Montagu MSS, DDM 80/1983/1. Abbott, I, 68, is a copy of an inadequate calendar version.
61. Sanford, *Studies*, pp. 241–4; CRO (Hunt.), St John's baptism register, 22 April 1636.

But a further reason for his move to St Ives may have been that an old Cambridge friend, Henry Downhall, had recently become vicar there. Downhall presents us with a problem. The earliest extant letter of Cromwell's is an invitation to Downhall, then a Fellow of St John's College, Cambridge, to be godfather of Richard Cromwell.[62] Downhall, however, was even less of a puritan than Thomas Beard. Although he enjoyed the patronage of the earl of Holland and of Bishop Williams (both anti-Laudians), he voted for Buckingham in the bitter contest over the Chancellorship of the University in 1625, and he was later a royalist army chaplain and was to be dispossessed of his second parish, Toft, in Cambridgeshire, for hiring a curate who 'observed ceremonies'. He was also accused of obstructing the activities at St Ives of the undoubtedly puritan lecturer, Job Tookey.[63]

This forces us back to a reconsideration of Cromwell's spiritual conversion. It is generally acknowledged that this would have occurred between 1626 and 1636, with a recent preference for a date around 1628–30.[64] A letter of October 1638 to his cousin Mrs St John is important testimony:

> . . . Yet to honour God by declaring what He hath done for my soul, in this I am confident, and I will be so. Truly, then, this I find: That he giveth springs in a dry and barren wilderness where no water is. . . . My soul is with the Congregation of the firstborn, my body rests in hope, and if here I may honour my God either by doing or by suffering I shall be most glad. Truly no creature hath more cause to put forth himself in the cause of his God than I. I have had plentiful wages beforehand, and I am sure I shall never earn the least mite. The Lord accept me in His Son, and give me to walk in the light, as He is the light. . . . You know what my manner of life hath been. Oh, I lived in and loved darkness, and hated the light. I was a chief, the chief of sinners. This is true: I hated godliness, yet God had mercy on me. O the riches of His mercy! Praise Him for me, pray for me, that he who hath begun a good work would perfect it to the day of Christ. . . .[65]

This is generally acknowledged to be a model description of a Calvinist conversion experience: 'Once a man grasped the full assurance of God's promise to him, he would pour out his heart

---

62. Abbott, I, 50–1.
63. For Downhall, see A.G. Matthews, *Walker Revised* (Oxford, 1948), p. 79 (though the original edition, viz. J. Walker, *The Sufferings of the Clergy* (1714), II, 230, is fuller); T. Baker, *History of St John's College, Cambridge* (Cambridge, 1869), pp. 199, 498, 487, 625; and C.H. Cooper, *Annals of Cambridge* (5 vols. Cambridge, 1842–53), III, 187. For Tookey, see below, p. 135.
64. Paul, *Lord Protector*, pp. 39–42; Fraser, *Cromwell: Our Chief of Men* (1973), pp. 36–40.
65. Abbott, I, 96–7.

in praise and thanksgiving for this unmerited gift; the certainty of his own salvation gave the puritan a tremendous sense of his unrepayable debt to Almighty God', as Robert Paul put it.[66] The contrast between an awareness of having been 'the chief of sinners' and a certainty of salvation despite rather than because of his nature is puritan hyperbole. It is not testimony that Cromwell was a reformed libertine and hitherto an ignorant and non-practising Christian: it is testimony to the shift from formalism and external religion to an inner certainty of a specific call from God that gave an empty life meaning and hope.

Cromwell had had that experience by 1638. It was to dominate the rest of his life. Yet our revision of Dr Beard's views challenges the assumption of a puritan schooling, and his father's will (which contains no reference at all to his Faith or Hope, and alludes only to 'man's life [being] like a bubble of water' before setting out the disposal of his property),[67] combined with the anglican-royalism of his Cromwell relatives, weakens the case for a puritan childhood still further. It is probable that he had not had that conversion experience in 1626 when he wrote to Henry Downhall asking him to be Richard's godfather in a letter utterly lacking in the biblical imagery and thankfulness to God that infused almost every letter after 1638.[68] The evidence that his 'conversion experience' occurred in 1627–9 is not as strong as the evidence that it occurred after 1630. His speech in Parliament in 1629 is explicable as the words of a pious protestant but of one not yet assured of salvation; his probable antipathy to Beard's candidacy for a Fishbourne lectureship may point to any number of personal grudges rather than to his being more precise than his old schoolmaster.

The testimony of Sir Theodore Mayerne, the prominent London physician, that he treated Cromwell for depression (*valde melancholicus*) at the time of the 1628/9 parliament, fits well with the idea of a man on the brink of a major spiritual and personal crisis.[69] Bishop Burnet, a surprisingly reliable source in such matters, reported that he had been told that Cromwell 'led a very strict life for about

---

66. Paul, *Lord Protector*, p. 37. See also pp. 399–400 where Paul analyses the biblical references and shows Cromwell to have been drawing on both the Geneva Bible and the Authorized Version. From 1640 onwards he drew almost exclusively on the Authorized Version. Perhaps he was having a flirtation with the Geneva Version in the 1630s before reverting to the text he already knew well.
67. PRO, PROB 11/130, quire 78, fo 115.
68. Paul, *Lord Protector*, p. 39.
69. Sir Henry Ellis, *Original Letters Illustrative of English History*, 2nd ser. (4 vols. 1827), III, 248.

eight years before the wars' (which would mean 1631 if Burnet – a Scot – was counting back from the Bishops' Wars, and 1634 if he was counting back from the outbreak of civil war in England).[70] If this is correct, then the man responsible for his conversion would have been either the lecturer at St Ives, Job Tookey, who was suspended by Williams in 1635[71] and whose son was immediately afterwards awarded an exhibition by the Mercers Company to complete his studies at Emmanuel College, Cambridge[72] (and we shall soon see why Cromwell is likely to have been behind this award) or Dr Walter Welles, another preacher with whom Cromwell had close ties (and, once more, someone we shall shortly meet again). If Cromwell's conversion followed rather than preceded the personal crises of 1630–31, it would not have prevented his being a conformist Christian or supporter of social discipline in Huntingdon. But it would make his outburst against Mayor Walden and Recorder Barnard a cry of baffled pain rather than the ill-considered haughtiness of a Zeal-in-the-Laud Busy.

VI

We know little about Cromwell in the 1630s. He delayed payment of the fine imposed upon him in 1631 for failing to take up a knighthood on the occasion of the king's coronation (a fine levied on all those with £40 per annum from freehold land).[73] How ironic that it should fall upon a man adjusting from gentry to yeoman status! He seems otherwise to have lived in St Ives without incident, paying his ship money, attending to family and business concerns. We get a glimpse of him from later reminiscence, attending church, generally wearing 'a piece of red flannel around his neck as he was subject to inflammation of the throat'.[74] (This story is perhaps confirmed by Cromwell's own statement, made in a law suit arising from the administration of his uncle's will in 1636 that he was 'sickly'.[75]

70. G. Burnet, *History of My Own Times* (ed. O. Airy, 2 vols., 1897–1901), I, 121.
71. *Cal. Comm. Compg. Delqts.*, II, 877–8, 1527; J. Hacket, *Memoirs of the Life of Archbishop Williams* (1715), p. 152.
72. Mercers Hall, Acts of Court 1631–37, at the General Court on 10 Nov. 1635.
73. The best account is in *Cal. St. Pap. Dom., 1629–31*, p. xiv. Abbott, I, 71 is misleading in implying that Cromwell was the last man in Huntingdonshire to comply and that 'his composition [may have been] paid by someone else'. This has misled others into even more extreme statements (e.g. Hill, *God's Englishman*, p. 43). In fact the commissioners sent down to Huntingdon summoned 35 men before them: 15 appeared, 11 failed to appear, and 8 – Cromwell probably the last of them – paid up without appearing (i.e. to avoid having to appear).
74. Noble, *Protector House*, I 105n.
75. PRO, C3/399/163.

After his uncle's death, he moved to Ely, and to the administration of dean and chapter properties. There too we only have occasional glimpses of him: a letter to London about a lectureship in 1636[76]; an account of his activities in relation to Fen drainage in 1637[77]; and the letter to Mrs St John in 1638.[78]

Too much has sometimes been made of his support for the commoners in the fens against the consortium of Dutch engineers, noble Adventurers and local gentry who were draining the Fen in a large area including Ely.[79] Those involved included at least two of his cousins. (His own immediate family had been active supporters of fen drainage around Huntingdon in his boyhood).[80] There is not a shred of evidence that Cromwell, then or later, was opposed in principle to the drainage, which would result in the creation of many thousands of acres of rich arable land at a time when many thousands of the poor elsewhere in the country could barely survive a poor harvest; but like the uncle from whom he inherited his Ely property, he was probably worried by the levels of compensation offered to the commoners whose livelihoods were threatened by the drainage. In 1653 he is reported to have said:

> the drainage of the fens was a good work, but that the drainers had too great a proportion of the land for their hazard and charge, and that the poor were not enough provided for.[81]

There is no reason to doubt that this was his attitude in 1638. His involvement is known from a single, uncorroborated aside in a paper to the privy council that discusses the deployment by a local JP of 'crowd of men and women armed with scythes and pitchforks', to oppose one of the Drainers' agents who had tried to drive the JPs cattle off the fen. The report continues:

> it was commonly reported . . . that Mr Cromwell of Ely had undertaken, they [the farmers] paying him a grout for every cow they had upon the common, to hold the drainers in suit of law for five years and that in the meantime, they should enjoy every part of their common.[82]

There is no supporting evidence that he made the offer, and none that anyone took him up on it. A report that he was also a spokesman

76. Abbott, I, 80–1.
77. Abbott, I, 102–4.
78. Abbott, I, 96–7.
79. The most reliable accounts are in M. Wickes, *Oliver Cromwell and the Drainage of the Fens* (Huntingdon 1981) and K. Lindley, *Fenland Riots and the English Revolution* (1982), pp. 95–6, 104, 115–9.
80. Sanford, *Studies*, pp. 253–6.
81. Cited in Wickes, *Fens*, p. 4.
82. Abbott, I, 103.

for commoners at a meeting with Drainers at Huntingdon comes only from a totally unreliable source.[83] His prompt action in parliament in 1641 to secure a Commons' committee investigation of a riot at Somersham and his rough handling of Montagu witnesses at the committee was probably intended not to halt the drainage but to balance a one-sided report by the earl of Manchester's friends to a Lords' committee. It may even have been a settling of the old score from 1630.[84] It was a sneer in the royalist press in 1643 that first gave him the title 'Lord of the Fens' (=a nobody).[85]

As in the case of the Huntingdon Charter, the claim that the fen disputes show Cromwell to be a precocious upholder of popular rights does not really stand up. But – by the late 1630s – he was a precocious puritan.

VII

In 1636, Cromwell wrote a letter to his 'very good friend Mr Storie, at the sign of the Dog in the Royal Exchange'. In it, he wrote that:

> Among the catalogue of those good works which your fellow citizens and our countrymen have done, this will not be reckoned for the least that they have provided for the feeding of souls. . . . Such a work as this was your erecting the lecture in our country; in which you placed Dr Welles, a man for goodness and industry, and ability to do good every way, not short of any I know in England; and I am persuaded that sithence his coming, the Lord hath by him wrought much good amongst us . . . surely, Mr Storie, it were a piteous thing to see a lecture fall [when it is] in the hands of so many able and godly men as I am persuaded the founders of this are, in these times, wherein we see they are suppressed with too much haste and violence by the enemies of God His truth. . . .[86] You know, Mr Storie, to withdraw the pay is to let fall the lecture; for who goeth to warfare at his own cost? I beseech you therefore in the bowels of Christ Jesus, put it forward, and let the good man have his pays.[87]

Who is Dr Welles and where was his lecture? He has been regularly and wrongly identified as Dr Samuel Wells, later an army chaplain.[88]

83. Dugdale, *Short View*, p. 460.
84. Abbott, 1, 130–2, is superseded by Lindley, *Fenland Riots*, pp. 115–19.
85. Ibid., p. 96; Fraser, *Chief of Men*, p. 56; The title was bestowed in the royalist newspaper *Mercurius Aulicus* in November 1643.
86. This may well be a reference to Williams's suppression, just three months earlier, of Job Tookey's lectureship at St Ives, and to the constant threat to the Fishbourne lecture in Huntingdon (see below, pp. 139–41).
87. Abbott, 1, 80.
88. As by those who follow Abbott, 1, 81n. A check of the most elementary sources would have shown that this could not be so. Samuel Welles was baptized in 1614 and was still at university without an MA, let alone a doctorate, in 1636.

It is widely and wrongly assumed that he was a lecture in Huntingdon. In fact, he was almost certainly Dr Walter Welles, lecturer in Godmanchester, just half a mile from Huntington. We know next to nothing about the lecture itself and little more about Walter Welles beyond what he tells us about himself in a flurry of letters dated from Godmanchester in 1630–31.[89] In one of these letters, Welles reveals that he studied in Leiden, and internal evidence dates his presence there to the early years of the seventeenth century. (Certainly he does not seem ever to have studied in Oxford or Cambridge.)[90] We have no idea when he arrived in Godmanchester, other than he was lecturing in the town twice a week no later than 1630, and it seems that he was still there in June 1635, when he appears as a witness on the will of a Godmanchester gentleman.[91] The letters he wrote in 1630–31 are to two interesting people: Samuel Hartlib and John Dury.[92] Hartlib was a Polish emigré who arrived in England in 1628 to set up an experimental school in Chichester based on Baconian principles, and who spent the next thirty years 'in relieving his fellow refugees, encouraging lay piety, and in disseminating useful information interfused with messianic speculations'.[93] John Dury was the son of a Scots emigré minister in the Netherlands (and a friend of Welles in his own right) who was involved in the 1620s and 1630s in a plan for pan-protestant reunion. In that connection, Hartlib arranged for him to come to England. Welles' letters show him to be close enough to the heart of this reforming group to be able to write a letter

89. G.H. Turnbull, *Hartlib, Dury and Comenius* (Liverpool, 1947), pp. 16–19, 67, 127, 134–40. I am grateful to Dr Mark Greengrass and to the Hartlib Papers Project at the University of Sheffield for a photocopy and transcript of the most important of these letters, to Hartlib, and dated 13 Sept. 1630. (Sheffield Univ. Lib., Hartlib papers 33/3/1–2.)
90. No Welles (or Wells or Weld) with a doctorate who looks plausible can be found in J. and S.A. Venn (eds.), *Alumni Cantabriensis* (4 vols. Cambridge, 1922–7) or J. Foster (ed.), *Alumni Oxoniensis* (4 vols., Oxford, 1891–92). Christopher Wells, vicar of Water Eaton in the north of Huntingdonshire, is styled 'Sacrae Theologiae Professor' (i.e. doctor of divinity) in his letter of presentation in 1629 (LAO, PD/1629/51), but he has no other link to Cromwell or the Mercers.
91. PRO, PROB 11/168 fo. 380. One further puzzle is that the Godmanchester subsidy roll for 1628/9 includes 'Job Tookey, clericus' (PRO, E179/122/216). We know that the vicar of Godmanchester was John Wybarne (*V.C.H. Hunts.*, II, 296; Noble, 'Incumbents', p. 100). The likely explanation is that Tookey owned freehold land in Godmanchester although his lecture was clearly in St Ives.
92. H.R. Trevor-Roper, 'Three Foreigners: the Philosophers of the Puritan Revolution', in *Religion, the Reformation and Social Change* (1967); Turnbull, *Hartlib, Dury and Comenius*.
93. Trevor-Roper, 'Three Foreigners', pp. 249–50. Cf. G.H. Turnbull, *Samuel Hartlib* (Oxford, 1920), pp. 16–18.

to Hartlib critical of some aspects of Dury's scheme, and able to ask for a copy of the manuscript of his commentary on St Paul's epistle to the Colossians.[94] Welles' close involvement with the Hartlib circle is also indicated by his reference to several well-wishers among the east midlands gentry, his apparent close links with the firmly Calvinist James Ussher, archbishop of Armagh,[95] and his promise to discuss Dury's scheme with Bishop Williams, 'a very wise gentleman and very able to promote this cause . . . he favours all good businesses; but how far to trust him, I know not.'[96] Williams' penchant for radical chic and for treachery was never better expressed. In the 1630s, both Hartlib and Dury caught the imagination of some of the most prominent anti-Laudian peers and gentry – prominent among them the earls of Warwick and Bedford and their clients and colleagues Oliver St John and John Pym.[97]

We do not know whether Cromwell's links with Welles preceded or followed his departure for St Ives. Nor do we know on behalf of whom he is writing. We can be fairly sure that 'Mr Storie' is George Storie, a Mercer with strong New England ties.[98] In a postscript, Cromwell asks to be remembered to 'Mr Basse, Mr Bradley and my other good friends'.[99] Mr Bradley cannot be identified, but Mr Basse is almost certainly the Mercer sent as one of the company's representatives to attend Charles I over the nomination of Beard to the Fishbourne lectureship.[100]

It seems likely that the Godmanchester lecture was tied up in some way to the Fishbourne lecture. There was a separate Fishbourne charity in Godmanchester – ten shillings a year to support four poor widows – and the revenue for this bequest came from a piece of land in the neighbouring parish of Hartford, of which Cromwell was lay impropriator.[101]

94. Turnbull, *Hartlib, Dury and Comenius*, p. 230.
95. Sheffield Univ. Lib., Hartlib MS 33/3/1b-2a.
96. Turnbull, *Hartlib, Dury and Comenius*, p. 236. For Welles' inclusion in a list of petitioners on behalf of Dury which reads like a roll-call of 1630s puritanism, see BL Sloane, MS 1465, fo. 2.
97. Trevor-Roper, 'Three Foreigners', pp. 256, 258. The links are strongest with the Warwick circle. See also BL Addit. MS 4276, fos. 176.
98. J.K. Hosmer (ed.), *Winthrop's Journal* (2 vols., New York, 1908, I, 64); *Records of the Court of Assistants of Massachusetts Bay, 1630–92* (1904), II, 117–19.
99. Abbott, I, 81.
100. Mercers Hall, Acts of Court 1625–31, fo. 275; J.R. Woodhead, *The Rulers of London* (1965), p. 25 and PRO, E179/251/22, E179/272/36, show him to be a liveryman in the company living in Cheapside.
101. *V. C. H, Hunts.*, III, 296.

There are other elusive links. Thomas Edwards referred to the Godmanchester lecture when he opposed Beard's appointment.[102] Perhaps the Godmanchester lecture was a by-product of Beard's unpopularity with some in the 1620s (Welles and Beard lectured on the same days and at the same times). More likely, individual Mercers undertook to support Welles after the threat to silence the pulpits in Huntingdon.

With the death of Beard, the All Saints lecture appears to have lapsed. That left the Fishbourne lecture on Saturday mornings and Sunday afternoons. The first lecturer, Robert Procter, died or left after only a few months and was replaced by Dionice Squire, of whom little is known other than that he was lecturer at St Leonard's, Shoreditch, in the 1620s and was left £30 in Fishbourne's will.[103] This appointment alarmed both Williams and Laud: the Mercers had set up the lecture 'with a proviso . . . that upon any dislike they have of him, he shall at a month or a fortnight's warning, give over the place, without any relation to bishop or archbishop'. Laud consulted the king who ordered the lectureship suppressed: 'for I would have no priest have any necessity of a lay dependency'.[104] Williams assured Laud that the lectureship would be suppressed until the Mercers agreed both that the bishop should approve their nominee and that the bishop alone could silence the man appointed.[105] It has always been assumed that the lecture was thereupon suppressed; but it was not so. Squire died within weeks of Williams' letter to Laud, and yet the company proceeded to a new and particularly controversial appointment, John Poynter.[106] He had been in trouble with High Commission for holding a lectureship while unlicensed in London (he was discovered soon after Laud arrived in that diocese) and he had recently been a lecturer in Warwickshire in the midst of a particularly godly circle.[107] Despite this, and despite holding a lectureship without holding a living – in direct contravention of the instructions regarding lecturers issued in 1633[108] – he remained in post until after Williams

102. Mercers Hall, Acts of Court 1625–31, fo. 248r.
103. PRO, PROB 11/145, fo. 464.
104. *Laud's Works*, V. 321.
105. Ibid., VI, 348–52.
106. His selection (on 12 August 1634) is discussed in Mercers Hall, Acts of Court 1631–37, fo. 131r. During the interval, the company paid for seven short-listed lecturers to preach to them (Mercers Hall, Fishbourne Bequest, Monies Received and Paid, 1627–56, fo. 34r).
107. P. Seaver, *The Puritan Lectureships* (Stanford, 1970), pp. 176, 179, 246–7; *Calamy Revised*, pp. 397–8; A. Hughes, *Politics, Society and Civil War in Warwickshire, 1620–1660* (Cambridge, 1987), p. 73.
108. E. Cardwell, *Documentary Annals of the Reformed Church of England* (2 vols., Oxford, 1839), II, 178.

himself had been sequestered from his bishopric and locked in the Tower in 1638.[109] Only then was the Fishbourne lecture suspended. Cromwell's continuing connection both with Huntingdon and with the Mercers is confirmed by a cryptic entry in the Mercers' register[110] for early 1640 recording a visit by Cromwell and William Spurstowe (one of those the company sent to the king to lobby against Beard in 1630, and one with decidedly puritan leanings).[111] The visit was expressly to help to get Poynter reinstated.

It seems improbable that it was purely coincidental that some Mercers were privately funding the Godmanchester lectureship when the public lecture at St Mary's was threatened with suspension; and that Cromwell's name crops up so frequently in connection with the company. But the evidence gives out on us. Too many pieces of the jigsaw are missing for its overall shape to be determined.

Cromwell's friends among the Mercers had connections into the circle of alienated magnates around the earls of Bedford and Warwick and Viscount Saye and Sele who were prominent in obstructing the Personal Rule in Church and State, who were active in puritan colonial ventures, and who were planning to bring Charles's government under strict aristocratic control if and when the opportunity provided itself.[112] Cromwell's own links look strongest with Warwick, whose power-base lay in Essex. The Barringtons (close political allies) and the Bourchiers (Oliver's in-laws and tenants of a Warwick manor) were at the heart of that circle, and Cromwell hinted to Mrs St John that family patronage had procured places for his sons at Felsted School (with its strong Warwick connections – Warwick's close personal interest in the school and other hints in Felsted sources strengthen the connection).[113] There are also links between Cromwell and

---

109. The suspensions seems to have lasted for six months in 1638 and for a further eighteen months from Michaelmas 1639 to early 1641 (PRO, SP 16/390/25 and 25.1: SP 16/540/403); and Mercers Hall, Fishbourne Accounts 1627–56, *passim*.
110. Mercers Hall, Acts of Court, 1637–41, fo. 203r-v.
111. M.F. Keeler, *The Long Parliament* (Philadelphia, 1955), pp. 346–7. Spurstowe was clearly linked to the parish of St Stephen's, Coleman Street and to its godly ministers John Davenport and John Goodwin. He was a major investor in the Massachussets Bay Company (V. Pearl, *London and the Outbreak of the Puritan Revolution* [Oxford, 1964], pp. 75, 169, 194n).
112. For a major reassessment of this question see, J.S.A. Adamson, 'The Baronial Context of the English Civil War', *TRHS*, 5th ser., XL (1990), 93–120.
113. Craze, *Felsted*, pp. 27, 50–64. Sons of tenants were given priority at the school under the deed of foundation. It seems plausible that this would be extended to the sons of daughters of tenants; the hint in Abbott, I, 97, seems to be to Masham influence.

Viscount Saye and Sele via the schoolmaster of Felsted, Martin Holbeach, and via the St Johns.[114] As John Adamson has shown,[115] that is the group with whom he was to closely associate from 1642 onwards. He may have been completely on the fringes, an obscure cousin of some close friends of great men. But, piling speculation on speculation, what has survived may just be the fragmentary remains of a more central role within one or both circles. For we have yet to confront the greatest of all puzzles of his early life: his return to parliament as burgess for the city of Cambridge in the elections of 1640.

VIII

Ever since 1558 (and probably from much earlier) only two types of men were returned as burgesses for Cambridge: the majority were senior members of the corporation, including recorders; a minority were nominees of successive High Stewards of the town, invariably the Lord Chancellor or Lord Keeper.[116] In the 1620s, for example, Lord Keepers Bacon and Coventry had nominated the clerk of the Privy Council, Thomas Meautys (and in 1626 Coventry had also secured the second seat for his secretary). More often than not the recorder held the other seat.[117]

Cromwell's return to both parliaments in 1640 – in the spring as an apparently uncontested partner for Meautys, in the autumn in a contest in which he and a puritan councilman, John Lowry, defeated the Lord Keeper's brother as well as Meautys – is thus very surprising. No evidence throwing light on this contest appears to survive in the local records.[118] We know that he was made a freeman of the borough on 7 January 1640[119] (after the election was called and before the writs arrived). But it is surely too glib to say, as W.C. Abbott did, that:

> He was now forty years old, at the height of his vigour and capacity, hardened by active outdoor life, a man of substance and position, well-

114. Ibid.; Holbeach's family came from Saye manors near Banbury.
115. J. Adamson, 'Oliver Cromwell and the Long Parliament', in J. Morrill (ed.), *Oliver Cromwell and the English Revolution* (London, 1990), pp. 55, 65.
116. P. Hasler (ed.), *History of Parliament: the House of Commons 1558–1603* (3 vols., 1981), I, 121; *V.C.H., Cambs.*, III, 68–76.
117. Ibid.; J.K. Gruenfelder, *Influence in early Stuart Elections 1603–1640* (Columbus, Ohio, 1981), pp. 5, 23n.
118. The story told by Heath, *Flagellum*, pp. 81–2, was discredited by Cooper, *Annals of Cambridge*, III, 296–304. Abbott's assertion (I, 109) that the election was 'hard fought and bitter' is pure fabrication.
119. Sanford, *Studies*, p. 267.

known in the community, with wide relationships through his family, business and church associates. He had much experience as a landowner and grazier, as a burgess of Huntingdon and a member of parliament, as a lessee of cathedral lands and in the fen dispute. He had developed his talents as a speaker . . . to this he joined a sense of leadership, deep sympathy with those who seemed to him oppressed, and confidence in his cause and himself.[120]

In fact he was an estate manager only recently recovered from a spell as a yeoman, with a troubled medical record and less credentials for eloquence and as an upholder of the oppressed than this assumes. He had neither the substance, nor the record of achievement, to be able to stand on his own account for parliament. It is hard to think of any other MP with an income as low as £300 who was not either a councilman serving for his own borough or a client imposed on a borough by a noble patron. The absence of any letters (other than those of Lord Keeper Finch) in the borough records makes it seem unlikely that he was nominated by a peer.[121] In any case the city would probably have resisted direct attempts by 'strangers' to interfere. It may just be the case that it was not the patronage brought to bear on his behalf, but the patronage that his return would bring to the town that explains his election. Cambridge had many grievances, especially against the university (for tuning its pulpits, for example). It might hope that these grievances could be addressed in parliament. If so, it would be faced by the opposition of the Chancellor of the University, the earl of Holland, no friend to the Laudians, but a courtier and a man jealous of the privileges of the university. If Cromwell was perceived as a man who could pull strings with Holland's elder brother, the earl of Warwick, his return becomes more explicable. There is one shred of evidence which, if it is reliable, gets us beyond the circumstantial into a definite connection. But it is from an unsatisfactory source, a day book compiled in the 1690s.[122] The author, a dissenter broadly sympathetic to the memory of the parliamentarian cause, recorded the following story, which he may have heard from Oliver St John in his old age:[123]

> . . . the true cause of the calling the Long Parliament thus: at the dissolution of the former short parliament the members both Lords

120. Abbott, 1, 109–10.
121. Cooper, *Annals*, III, 296–9, 303–4.
122. BL, Addit. MS 4460, fo. 74v. The catalogue describes this as 'extracts from the day books of Dr Henry Sampson, 1693–8', and gives Sampson's immediate informant as the nonconformist minister John Howe.
123. Between this and the following (connected) entry about the Attempt on the Five Members, Sampson records: 'this from my Lord Chief Justice St John's own mouth'.

and Commons had a great opinion that the king's affairs ere long would necessitate him to call them together again, therefore such as resided about London met together frequently and gave intelligence by Mr Samuel Hartlib and Mr Frost to those in the country of affairs. Ere long, they gave a more general summons to come all up, who not only came themselves but brought up also such country gentlemen as they could confide in, amongst the rest Mr Oliver St John brought with him Mr Oliver Cromwell, the first public meeting this gentlemen ever appeared at. They agreed to send down a petition to the King at York, subscribed by twenty Lords and above 40 Commons to pray him to call a parliament, that 2 Lords and 4 Commons of their number should carry it down, the Lords pitched upon the earl of Essex and Lord Howard of Escrick, the names of the Commons I have forgotten but Cromwell I am sure was the last & Essex plainly refused to go.

The late dating and the uncertain source make this highly suspect. Yet some of the detail – such as the references to Hartlib and Gualter Frost, and the unexpected prominence accorded to Howard of Escrick – gives it plausibility. The background to the petition of the twelve peers and the secret meetings that preceded the petition (in which both Warwick and Saye took leading roles) was not widely reported in the late seventeenth century. It is a tantalizing source, but can only be offered here as a spur to further thought and research: a suggestion and no more.

IX

This thesis about Cromwell's links with the leading oppositionists in the late 1630s can be taken forward by looking at his actions and contacts in the first two years of the Long Parliament. In fact, the evidence points two ways. John Adamson argues that 'there is little evidence that Cromwell was an effective collaborator, much less a client, of any major figure in either house', and he portrays him as a loner, a man who met with little success in his gauche interventions into the high politics of 1641. Such an interpretation clearly carries much weight.[124] But it is possible to put a rather different gloss upon his evidence, one which fully acknowledges Cromwell's incompetence while still seeing him as jobbing for a powerful faction.

Cromwell was immediately visible and at the heart of controversy in the Long Parliament. In its first week he presented John Lilburne's petition for a review of Lilburne's conviction and sentence for printing and distributing unlicensed (puritan) pamphlets; he was added to the powerful committee – including Pym, Hampden, Holles and St John

124. See Adamson, 'Oliver Cromwell', pp. 51–2.

– already investigating the case of the first of the 'puritan' martyrs of Star Chamber, Robert Leighton; and to a series of other committees investigating ecclesiastical tyranny and innovation.[125] In all he sat on eighteen committees in the first session of the Long Parliament.[126]

How did this come about? Why should Lilburne entrust a man who had hardly ever spoken before with his petition unless he was seen as someone with powerful friends? Was the case of so controversial a firebrand deliberately handed by someone of importance to someone not too closely identified with him? We should remember that Lilburne was flogged and incarcerated for helping to promote John Bastwicke's *Letany* and that Bastwicke's petition to both the Short and Long Parliaments was introduced by Pym.[127] Bastwicke may also have been at the centre of the struggle for power at Colchester between the factions of the earl of Warwick and Sir John Lucas.[128] Was it Cromwell's own idea to move the second reading of the annual parliaments bill (which became the Triennial Act)?[129] It also seems unlikely that a loner and a wholly unreliable member would be found so prominently involved in the bill for the abolition of episcopacy root and branch in May 1641 (he and Sir Henry Vane – another Massachusetts link and a man very close to oppositionist leaders – handed a draft to Sir Arthur Haselrig who briefed Sir Edward Dering who actually introduced it).[130] It was Cromwell who flew kites that the earl of Essex be appointed as Lord General *by ordinance* in August 1641 and October 1641 (though without getting anywhere), but whose return to the subject of parliamentary control of the militia in January 1641 led to the setting up of the committee that produced the Militia Ordinance.[131] Certainly many of his speeches were counter-

---

125. W. Notestein (ed.), *The Journal of Sir Simonds D'Ewes from the beginning of the Long Parliament to the opening of the trial of the Earl of Strafford* (New Haven, 1923), p. 19; *CJ*, II, 24, 44, 52, 54, 56. It should be added that the cases of the puritan victims of the Star Chamber were soon forgotten or laid on one side.

126. Firth, *Cromwell*, pp. 48–9.

127. J. Maltby (ed.), *The Short Parliament Diary of Sir Thomas Aston*, Camden Society, 4th ser., XXXV (1988), 109; Notestein, *D'Ewes*, p. 4. For Bastwicke's close ties with Lilburne, see F. Condick, 'The Life and Works of Dr John Bastwicke', Univ. of London PhD thesis (1984), pp. 90–4, 147.

128. Ibid., pp. 57–60, 317–26. For Bastwicke's links with Dury (from his days in Leiden), and Hartlib, ibid., p. 40.

129. Notestein, *D'Ewes*, p. 196. It had been introduced six days earlier by William Strode (ibid., p. 188n).

130. Sir Edward Dering, *A Collection of Speeches* (1642), p. 62; Abbott, I, 128–9.

131. W.H. Coates (ed.), *The Journal of Sir Simonds D'Ewes from the first recess of the Long Parliament to the withdrawal of King Charles from London* (New Haven, 1942), p. 145; W.H. Coates, (eds.), A.S. Young and V. F. Snow (eds.), *The Private Journals of the Long Parliament, 3 January to 5 March 1642* (New Haven, 1982), pp. 67, 551–5. *LJ*, IV, 625–7.

productive. His contemptuous comments on episcopacy in February 1641 almost led to him being called to the Bar of the House – a kind of parliamentary excommunication, as D'Ewes saw it, usually reserved for those who challenged the rights of the Houses to act *ultra vires*.[132] His intemperate outbursts against the Montagus' witnesses in the Fenland disputes' committee also almost led to his getting into trouble.[133] He had all the appearance of an unguided missile not really under ground control. Such a missile could be useful when ideas were to be floated: a kind of parliamentary forlorn hope. He was a man who could be trusted not to waiver on committees concerned with the destruction of Laudianism and on other issues on which the House of Commons was not divided. But, as his intemperacy in the February debates on root and branch reform made clear, he was not to be trusted when tact, sensitivity and gradualism were required. Thus on issues essential to the reformers' progress but likely to be deeply divisive, he kept (was kept?) silent. He did not speak in the debates on Strafford, on the Grand Remonstrance, on the Militia Ordinance (once it was up and running), on the Nineteen Propositions.

X

By the spring of 1642, Cromwell was one of those 'violent spirits' given to 'agitation' and 'asperity' who so alarmed the conservative, respectable puritan-parliamentarianism of Sir Simonds D'Ewes.[134] There was a notable increase in his prominence.[135] As the country slid into civil war, he was one of those who grasped nettles, took the initiative, as Austin Woolrych shows in his account of how Cromwell energized the militias of his home counties. The years of doubt and depression, impotent impulsiveness and provincial obscurity, lay behind him. In 1642 Cromwell was no republican, and probably not a religious libertarian. He would still have believed that an authoritarian national Church could be created, answerable to God's will. He could still look to the Scots as exemplars. The war was to change all that. But while other godly men who went to war to reform the Reformation fell away in despair as puritanism disintegrated and as parliamentary tyranny came to replace royal tyranny, Cromwell

132. Notestein, *D'Ewes*, pp. 339–41.
133. Abbott, I, 130–2; Edward Hyde, *The Life of Edward, Earl of Clarendon* (3 vols., Oxford, 1761), I, 78.
134. V. Snow and A.S. Young (eds.), *The Private Journals of the Long Parliament, 7 March 1642–1 June 1642* (New Haven, 1987), p. xxiii.
135. Ibid., p. xviii.

became ever clearer as to his task. If God willed the destruction, the overturning of all the landmarks of Church and State, then his trust would not be shaken. He had told Mrs St John that:

> I live in Mesheck (which they say signifies *prolonging*); in Kedar, which signifieth *blackness*: yet the Lord forsaketh me not. Though He do prolong yet He will (I trust) bring me to his tabernacle, to His resting place. My soul is with the congregation of the firstborn, body rests in hope . . .[136]

If the speculations in this chapter are at all reliable, Cromwell went through a dark night of the soul in the years 1629–31: he was stripped of all the pretensions and all the comforts of rank, honour and standing. Yet God had then shown him the purpose of that suffering, had taught him to trust Him. In a sense, what Cromwell had gone through in those vital years was what England was to go through in the years around 1649. Then, too, there was a descent into a national hell as old certainties collapsed and structures crumbled. Cromwell's view of God's plan for England was to remain malleable and ever-changing. But his knowledge that God *had* a plan for England and that he was part of that plan sustained him through war in three kingdoms and through a political career that brought him via regicide to the very edge of the throne itself. The personal faith of the man who was to be Lord Protector of England, Scotland and Ireland had been forged in the crucible of a deep personal crisis that is almost but not completely lost to us. The records of his making tell us little: but they tell us enough.

136. Abbott, I, 96–7. The reference to Mesheck and Kedar is to Psalm 120 v. 5 (biblical wildernesses) and to 'the congregation of the firstborn' is to Hebrews 12 v. 23 (in the Geneva translation) and means the elect of Christ.

CHAPTER SEVEN
The Church in England 1642–1649

I

In religion, as in politics, the Parliamentarians knew what they would not have, but not what they would have.[1] In 1640 there was a broad consensus that the Laudian experiment had to be halted and reversed, but no agreement whether to attempt to restore 'the pure religion of Elizabeth and James' or to make a fresh start. By 1642 most of those who joined the king were committed to the former, most of those who stayed at Westminster to the latter. From 1642 to 1646 the House maintained an uneasy unity. The great majority were committed to the replacement of the Anglican[2] Church by a new form of national Church and were committed to the principle of uniformity within that new Church. There were few MPs willing to concede any toleration outside the new Church to the tiny minorities of separatists or sectaries. Their uneasy unity was shattered in the course of 1646–7

---

1. Much of the expense incurred in researching this paper was met by a generous grant from the Archbishop Cranmer Fund of the University of Cambridge, which I gratefully acknowledge. Earlier versions of the essay were read at seminars in Cambridge (at Peterhouse History Society and at Professor Christopher Brooke's ecclesiastical history seminar), in (Oxford at the Stubbs Society), and in Bristol (at the Acton Society). I am grateful to the contributors to the discussion on all those occasions for their helpful comments. The final draft was read by Anthony Fletcher, Chris Haigh, Patrick Higgins and Blair Worden and gained enormously in content and presentation thereby. Several members of my own graduate seminar have generously provided me with references: Patrick Higgins, Judith Maltby, John Twigg, Tim Wales and especially Paul Gladwish.
2. The word 'Anglican' is used throughout to mean conformity to the canons and constitutions of the Church of England as they had developed since 1559. It was used in this sense by contemporaries – for example, Charles I, in a proclamation of 14 May 1644, undertook to defend 'this most holy religion of the Anglican Church'. See D. Neal, *History of the Puritans* (1822), III, 77.

by the debates which settled the new national Church. While the great majority wanted a national Church, a considerable number disliked the one proposed by the Westminster Assembly and would have preferred a settlement which gave more autonomy at parish level, or more power to the laity. This minority had to decide whether to accept defeat and submit themselves to the Presbyterian scheme, or to demand a right to opt out. By taking the latter course this large minority made the cause of toleration far more general and powerful than it had been before it changed the course of English politics.[3]

These developments have been much studied, and they are very important. But there is another side to the ecclesiastical history of the 1640s – the commitment by the majority in Parliament to eradicate Anglican worship and observance. The will of Parliament was clear and unambiguous; but the programme was a miserable failure. Within the limited space available here, it is not possible to examine the complex problem of how far the aspirations of the puritans in Parliament in the 1640s represented the articulation of a programme long cherished by puritans among the gentry, urban oligarchs, the clergy. In order to impose limits to the discussion, the principal aim here will be to examine the effectiveness of a number of specific objectives laid down by ordinance between 1643 and 1649: the suppression of the Book of Common Prayer and its replacement by the Directory of Public Worship; the suppression of the old Christian festivals, particularly Christmas, Easter and Rogationtide; the substitution of one pattern of admission to holy communion by another; the removal or destruction of idolatrous and superstitious objects and images from the churches. It is the argument of the essay that all these ordinances were not only largely ignored but actively resisted; that despite the provision of penalties for non-observance, local committees and others charged with the enforcement found themselves unable or unwilling to carry out their duties. One is reminded of the inability of bishops, archdeacons and ecclesiastical courts in general to eradicate puritanism in the half century before 1640. The tables were turned with a vengeance: puritan non-conformity under Anglican harassment gave way to Anglican non-conformity under the puritan yoke. The subject is an important one, yet historians have been so dazzled by the emergence of the radical sects (although it seems probable that at no point in the

3. For this paragraph, above all W.A. Shaw, *The History of the English Church during the Civil War and under the Commonwealth* (1900), I, 1–384; see also, A. Fletcher, *The Outbreak of the English Civil War* (1981), *passim*, and W. Abbot, 'The Issue of Episcopacy and the Long Parliament' unpublished D. Phil thesis, Oxford (1981).

critical period 1643–54 did more than five per cent attend religious assemblies other than those associated with their parish churches)[4] that they have failed to recognize that the greatest challenge to the respectable puritanism of the parliamentarian majority came from the passive strength of Anglican survivalism. If the essay ignores the radicals, it is not because they are unimportant, but because the balance needs to be redressed.

This imbalance results from the nature of the evidence: the Anglicans did not publicize their defiance – there are no tracts drawing attention to their activities; those clergy who maintained the old services and practices did not keep diaries or write autobiographies; puritan non-conformity before 1640 is recorded in the voluminous church court records while the comparable records of the 1640s, the county committee papers, do not survive. Conversely the basic sources upon which this paper is based have never been properly studied: church court records tell us about those who were disobedient, churchwardens' accounts tell us – very boringly in the main – about ordinary daily parish business and obedience. These accounts are scattered and it is only in recent years that they have been transferred in any number from vestry safes and cupboards to county record offices. Churchwardens' accounts have been used by historians of particular parishes, but not by historians of counties or dioceses, let alone historians of England. Study of them shows, however, that by 1640 most English parishes carried out the duties prescribed by law and by the Prayer Book conscientiously and often enthusiastically. The rhythms of the Anglican Year (itself deriving from more ancient custom), and the regular administration of the sacraments, were carefully observed, church ornaments and images cherished. These same accounts – even less used by historians of the 1640s and 1650s – will show the ineffectiveness of parliamentary decrees in very different regions.

Thus this essay rests upon the hypothesis that religious commitment is best observed in conditions of persecution. It is surely insufficient to portray the majority of Elizabethan and early Stuart Englishmen as wishy-washy, indolent, pale creatures besides the thrusting, vigorous puritans and the dogged, ostracized popish recusants. If three generations of Anglican practice meant anything to them, then the events of the 1640s would test their mettle. The

---

4. This is a complex and controversial point which I intend to argue elsewhere. The figure may well be too low once the Quakers emerged in the mid-1650s.

essay also grew out of the puzzle that if Anglicanism collapsed so utterly in the 1640s and 1650s, how was it that it emerged so quickly, confidently and joyfully in most parishes in 1660–2? What becomes apparent to anyone who wades through surviving churchwardens' accounts all over the country for the Civil War and for the Restoration years was the spontaneity of the response in 1660 compared with the reluctant and partial acceptance of change in the 1640s. The strength of the Anglican reaction of 1660 lay not exclusively, or even principally, in the response of a gentry who craved the return of a hierarchical Church which would shore up a hierarchical government and society, but in the popularity of traditional religious forms at all levels of society.

What follows is a five-part discussion of religious policy for and practice in the parishes in the 1640s. We will look first at the way Parliament attempted to dismantle the old Church; secondly, at the aborted Presbyterianism designed to take its place; thirdly, at the failure of king and bishops to give a lead to their flock; fourthly, at the background and experience of the parish clergy; and finally at the evidence for Anglican revival and resurgence in these unpromising conditions.

II

The old Church was dismantled piecemeal between 1641 and 1646. Laudian innovations in doctrine, government, discipline and liturgy were overthrown, and ecclesiastical jurisdiction was emasculated by the Acts abolishing the Court of High Commission and barring those in holy orders from holding secular offices. Recent innovations in church furnishing (most notably the railing of the altars in the east end) were ordered to be reversed. The Houses assumed wide-ranging powers to suspend ministers certified to them as scandalous in life or doctrine, and they deliberated over several schemes for the further reform of Church government and discipline.[5] Nothing was actually done, however, expressly to challenge the basis of the Elizabethan Acts of Supremacy and Uniformity.[6] The attack on the defining characteristics of the old Church – episcopacy, the church courts, the Prayer Book, the Anglican calendar – was undertaken step by

---

5. Shaw, *English Church*, I, 1–144; II, 295–300, J. Stoughton, *A History of Religion in England* (rev. ed., 1881), I, chs. 1–4; F.M.G. Higham, *Catholic and Reformed* (1962), pp. 181–210.
6. These Acts were not repeated until 1650 – C.H. Firth and R.S. Rait, *Acts and Ordinances of the Interregnum* (1911), II, 423.

step from 1643–6 in collaboration with the Westminster Assembly (a body of 121 divines, 10 peers and 20 members of the Commons, to whom Scots commissioners were soon added). This assembly was asked to propose a settlement of the Church 'agreeable to God's Holy Word' and to 'the Church in Scotland and other Reformed churches abroad'.[7]

Despite the mass of anti-episcopalian propaganda and the commitment of the assembly from the outset to alternative forms of government, the office, title and authority of bishops were not suspended or abolished until October 1646. In early 1643, the two Houses approved a *bill* abolishing the existing frame (archbishops, bishops, deans, chapters and so on), and this bill was sent to the king as part of Parliament's terms for a settlement, but the bill was not converted into an ordinance. It had no legal force. Fourteen of the twenty-six bishops had their temporal possessions sequestered by an ordinance of March 1643, but the remaining twelve were left free to enjoy their properties and powers; six of them were indeed invited (under their episcopal titles – for example, Dr Ralph Brownrigg, bishop of Exeter) to be members of Westminster Assembly; an ordinance for demolishing monuments of superstition in 1644 was to be superintended in the cathedrals by the deans. The most important effect of this failure to proceed to abolition was that the bishops retained sole right to ordain men to the ministry for most of the war, and those so ordained up to October 1646 (in theory) and up to mid-1654 (in practice) were deemed qualified to hold a living in the national Church. Nonetheless, the situation was a confused one: ministers were deprived in Lincolnshire in 1644, for example, in part for upholding the office of bishops since it had been 'voted down by Parliament'.[8]

The abolition and replacement of the Prayer Book (rather than its modification) seems only to have become certain after the alliance with the Scots. No formal ban on its use was attempted until January 1645 (although the two Houses ceased to use it in their own religious observances from early 1644). In January 1645 it was replaced by a new service book, the Directory of Public Worship, drawn up by the Westminster Assembly. This ordinance was almost wholly a dead

---

7. Ibid., I, 180. For its deliberations, see Shaw, *English Church*, 1. 145–384.
8. Firth and Rait, *Acts*, I, 106, 176, 180, 425, 879; Shaw, *English Church*, I, 138; J.W.F. Hill, 'The Royalist Clergy of Lincolnshire', *Lincolnshire Architectural and Archaeological Society, Reports and Papersr*, no. 2, pt I (1938), 59. See also below, pp. 161–3.

letter, and probably less than 10 per cent of parishes had acquired the new book six months later. In August, Parliament publicly acknowledged this neglect in a further ordinance which required the knights and burgesses to send down to their county committees sufficient copies of the Directory to be distributed to each parish (who had to pay for them). County committees were in return to collect in and to destroy all copies of the Book of Common Prayer. Fines and imprisonment were prescribed for the continued use of the old book.[9] Despite the survival of relevant committee and quarter sessions papers (and the reiterated commands from Parliament) there is not a single known instance of these penalties being imposed and, as we shall see, little evidence that the Directory was distributed.[10]

The doctrinal formularies of the Church of England were abrogated in 1645. Unfortunately, although many parliamentary ordinances required proof of orthodoxy from those holding parish livings, no definition of orthodoxy was ever forthcoming. A Large Catechism (of 196 questions), a small one (of 107 questions) and a Confession of Faith were drawn up by the Westminster Assembly but were never approved by the Houses and thus never published by authority.[11] The Directory did not lay down any set forms, but offered a guide to the construction of do-it-yourself services. It did not even require the use of basic formularies like the Nicene or Apostles' creeds. The nearest thing to an agreed doctrinal statement approved during the whole period was the list of elementary truths, a knowledge of which was made a condition of admission to the Lord's Supper in October 1645.[12]

On 19 December 1644 the House of Commons realized that the next monthly Fast would fall on 25 December, Christmas Day. They rushed out an ordinance smugly entitled 'for better observance of the Monthly Fast, and most especially next Wednesday, commonly called the Feast of the Nativity of Christ' on which 'men took liberty to carnal and sensual delights, contrary to the life which Christ himself led on earth'.[13] The attack on the Anglican calendar was later extended by a comprehensive ordinance which banned the observance of Christmas, Easter, Whit, Holy Days and Saints

---

9. Firth and Rait, *Acts*, I, 582–607, 755. The best brief account of the Directory is in Higham, *Catholic and Reformed*, pp. 217–20.
10. See below, pp. 164–7.
11. All three, together with other papers from the assembly, were published in a collective volume entitled *The Confession of Faith* (Edinburgh, 1885).
12. Firth and Rait, *Acts*, I, 789.
13. Ibid., I, 580.

Days, as also the Rogationtide perambulations of the bounds of the parish. Instead, the second Tuesday of every month was set aside as a day of Thanksgiving.[14] As we shall see, these decrees were widely disregarded.

Finally, Parliament set out to purify churches of popish and superstitious objects and monuments. Parliamentary orders in 1641 had already ended Laudian experiments with east-end altars, and had ordered the removal of altar-rails and the levelling of chancels. Then in August 1643 they went much further, requiring the destruction of candles, tapers and basins from the communion tables, and all crucifixes, crosses, images, pictures and superstitious objects relating to the Virgin Mary, the persons of the Trinity and the saints (though not, curiously, representations of the devil or of Old Testament figures). In 1644 a further ordinance added vestments and other popish relics such as fonts and organs. These new ordinances were directed against objects which had adorned the churches for centuries.[15]

It is instructive to compare the way the 1641 instructions were quickly and efficiently enforced by churchwardens and parish officers whereas the ordinances of 1643–4 were widely ignored until peripatetic commissioners came along. As we shall see, these commissioners often met active or passive obstruction from local congregations or parish officers.[16] The worst iconoclasm probably occurred in the cathedrals. At least fifteen of the twenty-six were seriously vandalized by detachments of the army who went far beyond the instructions of Parliament. Some cathedrals were partly dismantled and their building materials used for other projects (for example, Lichfield, Hereford). The corporation of Yarmouth petitioned that Norwich cathedral be dismantled and the stone used to build a new workhouse and to strengthen the piers of Yarmouth harbour; at Gloucester a block and tackle were mounted on the tower as the first stage of a proposed demolition; the Rump three times debated the pulling down of them all. In the event, most were taken over as preaching centres (Exeter with a central dividing wall erected

---

14. Ibid., I, 420–2, 607, 954.
15. Ibid., I, 265, 425; Shaw, *English Church*, I, p 103–10.
16. For the journal of the leading iconoclast, see *The Journal of William Dowsing*, ed. E.H. Evelyn-White (Ipswich, 1885), for his tour of Suffolk, and J.G. Cheshire, 'William Dowsing's Destructions', *Cambridgeshire and Huntingdonshire Archaeological Society Transactions*, III (1914), for Cambridgeshire. There is a good summary in A. Kingston, *East Anglia in the Great Civil War* (1897), pp. 329–32. My impressions are formed from an analysis of 150 sets of churchwardens' accounts in western and eastern England (see below note 45).

to keep apart rival Presbyterian and Independent congregations). Others were secularized: Lichfield, Durham and St Paul's were used as barracks or prisons (in St Paul's cavalry occupied the nave, but the cloisters were turned into a shopping precinct), while St Asaph was used as a wine shop and as a shippen for the local postmaster's oxen, and the font as a hog-trough (the bishop's palace at Exeter became a sugar bakery). All in all, the cathedrals suffered more than the parish churches, as we shall see.[17]

Let us conclude this section by pointing out what was not attacked: the parish system with its traditional officers (churchwardens, overseers, select and general vestries); lay impropriation (although royalists who held rights to receive tithes and to present to livings had to surrender them, albeit in return for generous reductions in the size of their composition fines); the responsibility of all to pay tithes. This is another point to which we shall return.

III

In place of the Elizabethan Church, Parliament approved a new settlement which was intended to introduce a uniformity in government, discipline and worship binding on all.[18] What emerged was a four-tier structure. The ancient parishes were to remain as the basic unit, with the minister joined in the regulation of both worship and discipline by elders elected by all those parishioners who had taken the Covenant and who were not 'servants that had no families'. Parishes were to be grouped into 'classes' (roughly the size of the old wapentake or hundred and comprising between ten and twenty parishes), and the classes in turn were to be grouped into provinces, one for each county and one for the city of London. Each parish was to be represented in the classis by its minister or ministers and by one or two lay elders, and each classis was to send clerical and lay nominees to the provincial assemblies. Finally there was to be a national synod whose actions were subject to ratification by Parliament. This scheme was a heavily modified version of the proposals which came out of the Westminster Assembly. The Houses

17. J.R. Phillips, *The Reformation of the Images* (Berkeley, 1973) pp. 192–200; V. Staley, *Hierurgia Anglicana* (revised edn., 1902–4) I, 92–101, 185–6; II, 256–70; Stoughton, *History of Religion*, I, 313–16; M.E.C. Walcott, *Traditions and Customs of Cathedrals* (1872), pp. 29–42; G.B. Tatham, *The Puritans in Power* (Cambridge, 1913), pp. 256–63; *A History of York Minster*, ed. G. Aylmer and R. Cant (York, 1977), pp. 211–15, 439–40, 503; J.F. Chanter, *The Bishop's Palace, Exeter* (Exeter, 1932), p. 93; R.W. Ketton-Cremer, *Norfolk in the Great Civil War* (1969), pp. 224–38.
18. Firth and Rait, *Acts*, I, 749, 833, 1062.

were determined to ensure that the laity were fully represented in every aspect of Church government and discipline, and they thus enhanced the power of the elders at all levels. They also weakened the power of the classes and provinces and built up the autonomy of the parishes, in which the minister could be overborne by the elders, and strengthened the power of Parliament as the ultimate source of ecclesiastical legislation and jurisdiction. These changes led the Scots to dismiss it as a 'lame erastian presbytery'. Parliament required the use of the Directory in all churches, but never ratified the catechisms or Confession of Faith.[19]

The reorganization never really got off the ground. Although it gained majority support in the Houses, there was no general support for it in the country. The problem was that the implementation of the scheme required the co-operation of local lay commissioners. The proposals allowed each county to decide for itself the most sensible way of grouping parishes into classes.[20] Groups of commissioners were expected to meet and to draw up proposals which were then vetted and approved by Parliament. It afforded massive opportunities for prevarication, for delay, and for producing unacceptable schemes. Furthermore, the will of Parliament to enforce the scheme disappeared in effect from the time of the army's first occupation of London in August 1647. Without central backing, and with the achievement of *de facto* toleration from October 1647 and *de jure* toleration from 1650, the whole rationale failed.[21] Although the ordinances enjoining the Presbyterian order remained in force from 1645 to 1654,[22] they became increasingly inoperative after the winter of 1647–8. Eight of the forty English counties (plus London) produced Presbyterian schemes and made some effort to put them into operation (Cheshire, Essex, Lancashire, Middlesex, Shropshire, Somerset, Suffolk, Surrey) and two more (Derbyshire and – much later – Nottinghamshire) appear to have established a partially operative classical system without presenting it to Parliament for approval. Six other counties

19. Shaw, *English Church*, I, 145–384. The best brief account is in Higham, *Catholic and Reformed*, pp. 213–23.
20. Shaw, *English Church*, II, 1–33, 365–400. For important modifications, see G. Yule, *The Puritans in Power*, (Sutton Courtenay, 1981), appendix II, and C.E. Surman, 'Classical Presbyterianism in England, 1643–1660', unpublished MA thesis, Manchester (1949), pp. 35–59.
21. Yule, *Puritans*, conclusion.
22. For the Cromwellian reform, see C. Cross, 'The Church in England, 1646–1660', in *The Interregnum*, ed. G.E. Aylmer (1975), pp. 104–5.

produced schemes which were never approved or implemented (Durham, Hampshire, Northumberland, Wiltshire, Westmorland, Yorkshire [West Riding]), but twenty-four counties made no formal response. Only in two areas (London and Lancashire) does the provincial machinery ever seem to have come into being, and it is probable that by the early 1650s only seven or eight of the seventy or so classes formally established in the years 1645–8 were still functioning.[23]

All was not total chaos, however. The civil power had established some supervision over aspects of parochial life pending the introduction of Presbyterianism, and much of this *ad hoc* government persisted down to the introduction of the Cromwellian reforms in 1654. Existing rights of patronage to livings were protected except where the patron was the Crown, the bishops, the deans and chapters or sequestered Royalists. In those cases patronage was exercised by the committee of plundered ministers in London, either directly or through local county committees, in response to advice from the parishes.[24] County committees – again supported by central bodies – had power to eject those whose religious practice, morals or political beliefs they found repugnant. The profits from dean to chapter and confiscated royalist impropriations were made available within each county as a fund for augmenting the stipends of ministers in the poorer parishes, and tentative beginnings were made to the rationalization of parish boundaries, large ones being broken up and small (mainly urban ones) amalgamated. Finally, much of the business of the old church courts was transferred to the JPs at quarter sessions. Much of this, however, was only formalized after 1649.[25]

This extension of lay control is one of the reasons why county committees were so reluctant to implement the parliamentary Presbyterianism. But there was another reason. The English puritan gentry had probably always preferred a looser system of church government giving effective autonomy for each parish in matters of worship

23. For the records see especially 'The Register Book of the 4th classis in the province of London', ed. C.E. Surman (Harleian Soc., LXXXII–LXXXIII, 1952–3); 'Manchester Classical Minutes', ed. W.A. Shaw (Chetham Society, n.s. XX, XXII, XXIV, 1888–91); 'Bury Classical Minutes', ed. W.A. Shaw (Chetham Soc., n.s. XXXVII, XLII, 1896, 1898), which also contains the records of the Nottingham Classis; and 'Minutes of the Wirksworth Classis', ed. J.C. Cox *Journal of the Derbyshire Archaeological Soc.*, II (1879).

24. W.A. Shaw, *The Financial Administration of the Revenues of the Disendowed Church* (Manchester, 1893); also his *English Church*, II, 175–286.

25. See e.g. A. Fletcher, *A County Community at Peace and War: Sussex, 1600–1660* (1975), pp. 113–1.

and discipline (non-separating Congregationalism).[26] This is what the stalemate of 1648–54 achieved. It was then institutionalized by the Protectorate. But such a development contains a deep irony. If each parish was allowed to decide its own patterns of worship and observance, then those who wanted to maintain the old Prayer Book and the old rhythms of Anglicanism could easily get their own way. As we shall see, the county committees, after their initial enthusiasm for ejecting scandalous and insufficient men, were unable or unwilling to stamp out the old practices.[27]

IV

The cause of Anglicanism received surprisingly little help in the later 1640s from the king and the bishops. Although the king raised himself to claim a martyr's crown, he had done very little to guide those whose religious preferences were the same as those he professed. It is amazing – in view of the apparent earlier co-operation between them – how quickly Charles abandoned Laud. He left him to rot in the Tower and made no serious attempt to prevent his trial and execution (for example, by exchanging him for important parliamentarian prisoners). By 1642, he had abandoned all the claims made for the Church by Laud and was openly identifying himself with an earlier tradition. He issued a proclamation (recording an oath he had taken immediately before receiving communion from Ussher, Archbishop of Armagh – most moderate of all the bishops, and allowed by Parliament to hold the office of chaplain to Lincoln's Inn throughout the 1640s), in which he pledged himself to maintain 'the established and true reformed protestant religion as it stood in its beauty in the happy days of Queen Elizabeth, without any connivance of popery.'[28] He nominated eleven new bishops between 1641 and 1643. Eight of them had been in trouble with Laud, and all of them were strict Calvinists in the mould of Grindal and Abbott. He also promoted several bishops, most notably Laud's arch-enemy on the bench, Bishop Williams, who was transferred from Lincoln to York.[29] Apart from a flurry of proclamations in mid 1643, denouncing the Covenant and urging loyal subjects to withhold tithes from intruded

26. See the suggestive remarks of P. Collinson, 'The Godly', paper to *Past and Present* conference on Popular Religion (1966), p. 22 (cited in Fletcher. *Sussex* p. 117).
27. See below, pp. 163–73.
28. R.R. Steele, *Bibliotheca Lindesiana: A Bibliography of Royal Proclamations of Tudor and Stuart Sovereigns* (Oxford, 1910), I, 295.
29. P. King, 'The Episcopate during the Civil War, 1642–1649', *EHR*, LXXXIII (1968), 526–48; J.H. Overton, *The Church in England* (1897), II, 95–7; *DNB*.

ministers, he did very little to advise people how to respond to the changes imposed by ordinance.[30] His attachment to the old Church was not as inflexible as hagiography maintains. At various times between 1646 and 1649 he expressed a public readiness to contemplate an abandonment of the Act of Uniformity, to reduce the number of bishops to four, or to accept a Presbyterian system experimentally for three years. However temporary he privately resolved such concessions would be, they presented a poor impression to ordinary Anglicans as they struggled to find ways of being faithful to the Church. Most remarkable of all, Charles appears to have made little effort, during his captivity with the Scots and at Holdenby, to insist on the use of the Prayer Book. When his own chaplains forced themselves past his guards at Hatfield in the summer of 1647, it was the first time for over twelve months that he received the Anglican sacrament.[31]

The bishops gave little formal lead either. They spent much of 1641–2 striving to preserve their secular powers – their right to sit in the House of Lords and to hold office – and several of them spent long periods in prison (twelve were threatened with impeachment over the canons of 1640; another, overlapping, group of twelve were imprisoned for protesting that anything done by the Lords during their enforced absence – occasioned by the presence of an angry picket-line outside the House – as invalid; Laud was in the Tower from March 1641 until his death, Wren from 1641 to 1660). In every diocese (with the partial exception of Exeter) the diocesan machinery collapsed in the winter of 1642–3, although the routine business of nominating and collating to livings did continue. It is unlikely that more than two or three bishops remained in their cathedrals, even in Royalist areas. Several were at Oxford but they made no joint statements and offered no joint advice to those troubled by the Covenant or the ban on the Prayer Book or the sequestration of their minister and the intrusion of a parliamentary nominee. Three bishops spent the war years quietly in London, two were in arms, but most retired to country livings and kept their heads low. The 1640s and 1650s may have seen a great flowering of Anglican devotional literature and doctrinal works but the leading figures were not the bishops. Such works as the bishops themselves did write were

30. Steele, *Proclamations*, I, 292–303.
31. King, 'Episcopate', pp. 54–7; Abbot, 'Issue of Episcopacy', ch. 6; A. Kingston, *The Civil War in Hertfordshire* (1894), p. 72.

personal utterances, not formal statements.[32] But the bishops made one crucial contribution: they continued to ordain.

V

In the later 1640s, the people of England had been clearly instructed by the victors in the civil war to abandon their old religious practices. The diocesan institutions which had upheld the old forms had crumbled and although no new ecclesiastical structure was operative in most areas, the civil power had assumed much of the old coercive power. They were given little help by the king or the bishops. Crucially, however, most of them still had their old clergy to lead them.

It has been reliably estimated that some 2,780 clergy (including curates, lecturers and so on) were harassed by the authorities in the period 1641–60. But of these, 400 obtained new livings, 200 were pluralists allowed to keep one of their livings, 270 managed to stay on or were reintruded into their livings despite the orders of local or central committees, and 320 were only ejected after 1649. Thus, only 1600 were dispossessed in our period – less than one in five. If there was a normal death rate of ministers in the 1640s, then between three-fifths and two-thirds of all parishes had the same ministers in 1649 as they had had in 1642.[33]

Not all vacant livings could be filled in the 1640s. There were not enough men to fill them and (until the scheme for augmenting the stipends of poor livings was brought fully into operation in the 1650s) many livings were too poor to attract qualified preachers. From 1644 onwards, Parliament made provisional arrangements for ordination (by clerical commissioners in London and Lancashire), and from 1646 permanent arrangements (all classes were empowered to ordain those properly qualified and with a call from a parish). Men from more than half of the English counties were ordained by the London classis in the years after 1646, for example. Nonetheless, the best estimate suggests that no more than 700 men had been ordained under the authorized arrangements before Cromwell introduced his Triers in

32. King, 'Episcopate', pp. 528–33; see also the chapters on ecclesiastical history in many *Victoria County History* volumes, as *Cheshire* III and *Cumberland* II; *DNB*; R. Bosher, *The Making of the Restoration Settlement* (1951), chs. 1–2; J. Packer, *The Transformation of Anglicanism* (1969), *passim*.
33. I. Green, 'The Persecution of "Scandalous" and "Malignant" Parish Clergy during the English Civil War', *EHR*, XCIV (1979), 525.

1654.[34] It is quite certain that the great majority of those who took up the ministry for the first time between 1644 and 1649 were episcopally ordained. The abolition of episcopacy did not slow down the flow of ordinands presenting themselves to the bishops in their rural retreats (at least ten bishops still held parish livings) and episcopal ordination – despite the disquiet expressed by the Lancashire province in 1649[35] – remained valid and sufficient in the eyes of authorities desperate to fill vacant livings. How utterly and ironically were the roles of Anglican and puritan reversed! In Lincoln diocese alone, official listings at the Restoration show that ninety-two men who then held livings had been episcopally ordained since 1646; the records of London and Norwich dioceses provide comparable figures. Joseph Hall, bishop of Norwich between 1646 and his death in 1654 ordained over fifty men who served in those two dioceses alone. Yet most of the ordinations were carried out by itinerant Irish and Scottish bishops. Among the English bishops, it is clear that it was the anti-Laudians who were most active, the only exception being Skinner of Oxford, probably the most energetic of all in his convenient nook close to the university city of Oxford. He is said to have ordained hundreds. Some of those ordained by the Presbyterians subsequently presented themselves for episcopal ordination. Surely the fact that – given a choice and given the legal and ecclesiastical complications – the great majority of the new clerics had sought out the bishop tells us something about the preferences of those who filled a majority of the vacant livings up and down the county.[36]

The pattern of persecution has recently been clearly established. What seems clear is that the distribution of ejections was determined less by the malignancy of the clergy than by the persecuting temper of local commissioners. Thus the highest percentage of expulsions were in solidly parliamentarian areas (London, Cambridgeshire, Suffolk and so on) and the lowest in solidly royalist areas. Often the presence of an individual hardliner could lead to differential levels of sequestration within counties (as in Cheshire and Wiltshire).

---

34. Firth and Rait, *Acts*, I, 521, 865; Surman, 'Classical Presbyterianism', chs. 2 and 3; H. Smith, *The Ecclesiastical History of Essex under the Long Parliament and Commonwealth* (Colchester, 1932), pp. 121–6; 'Register Book of the Fourth Classis of the Province of London', ed. C.E. Surman (Harleian Society, LXXXII–LXXXIII, 1952–3), xiii.

35. Ibid., p. 15.

36. Smith, *Essex*, pp. 326–30, 410; K. Major, 'Lincoln Diocesan Records' *TRHS*, 4th ser., XXII (1940), 56; King, 'Episcopate'. pp. 531–2. *DNR, Autobiography of Simon Patrick* (1839), p. 38.

Secondly (as with iconoclasm), one needs to distinguish two phases of persecution. In the first two years of the Long Parliament, the initiative was often taken by outraged parishioners. Several hundred petitions were presented to Parliament in 1641 and 1642 and formed the basis of the first 200–300 ejections. From 1643 on, however, there was a different pattern. As Dr Green says: 'there are strong grounds for thinking that it was pressure from above rather than from below that triggered off most of the ejections.'[37] Thus the instructions issued to the Lincolnshire commissioners admitted that 'it is found by sad experience that parishioners are not forward to complain of their ministers, although they be very scandalous.'[38] The stereotyping of the depositions against the clergy makes use of them difficult, but some points do emerge. Dr Green thinks that less than half of those sequestered were accused of Laudian practices or ceremonial innovation. He puts more stress on simple pastoral insufficiency and on political bias.[39] It may be, however, that he relies too heavily on an analysis of the earliest cases. A careful reading of the depositions from Suffolk, Lincolnshire, Essex and Wiltshire[40] suggests that the most important failings of those ejected after 1643 were insufficiency as preachers, Laudian practices and political unsoundness. Very few were ejected for upholding 'the true reformed protestant religion of Elizabeth and James' – for using the Prayer Book, for celebrating Christmas or Easter,[41] or for welcoming all their parishioners to the communion table – even after such actions were banned. In Dorset, for example, such ministers were remonstrated with, warned, but not suspended, and the same seems to have been true elsewhere.[42] Furthermore, although many were suspended for overt royalism, many more were suspended for refusing to take sides: for reading royalist and Parliamentarian declarations; for observing both royalist and parliamentarian fasts (and how far can one rely on depositions such as that against Mr Fisher that he read royalist declarations

37. Green, 'Persecution', pp. 509–13, 518.
38. BL Add.MSS 5829 fos 6–8.
39. Green, 'Persecution', pp. 511–12.
40. C. Holmes, 'The Suffolk Committee of Scandalous Ministers, 1644–1646', Suffolk Records Society, XIII (1970), 19–24 and *passim*; Hill, 'Royalist Clergy', *passim*; Smith, *Essex, passim*; BL Add.MSS 5829; Add.MSS 22084; Tatham, *Puritans in Power*, pp. 65–92; A. Tindal-Hart, *The Country Clergy, 1558–1660* (1958), pp. 120–5.
41. But cf. A.M. Everitt, *The Community of Kent and the Great Rebellion* (Leicester, 1966), pp. 231–2, 243.
42. *The Standing Committee of the County of Dorset, 1646–1650*, ed. C.H. Mayo (Dorchester, 1902), *passim*.

'audibly and distinctly', and parliamentary ones 'with a low voice'?).[43] Isaac Allen of Prestwich, Lancashire, affords a good example. He was sequestered in November 1643 on nine counts, including failure to instruct his parish to support Parliament, answering a royalist summons to a meeting in Manchester in June 1642, and hesitation before taking the Covenant. In each case this represents the attempts of a neutral to obey the law of the land as he understood it. His defence shows 'a man driven by force of circumstance out of the attitude of neutrality he had endeavoured to adopt'. He subsequently regained his parish and remained there throughout the Interregnum, stubbornly refusing to attend the vigorous Manchester classis within which his parish lay, yet apparently immune to its threats.[44]

Finally it should be stressed how frequently the attempt to oust a minister led to resistance from parishioners. This sometimes took the mild form of a petition, but it could also take the form of a tithe-strike against his successor, the physical protection of the parsonage against the attempts of a minister intruded by the committee of plundered ministers to take up residence, or even – after a period of disillusionment with a new minister – the violent reintrusion of a sequestered minister, usually with the Book of Common Prayer in hand. We shall return to this subject at the end of the paper.

The great majority of the clergy, then, were men who had served and conformed under Laud or who were episcopally ordained in the 1640s when the decision to seek out a bishop was a decision with very obvious political and ecclesiastical connotations. How did these men respond to the challenges and invitations laid down by Parliament?

VI

However much parliamentarians differed over the religious settlement they wanted, they were united in wanting to end the popish distractions in liturgy and observance that had marred the old Church. They explicitly set out to break men's attachment to the Book of Common Prayer, to the Anglican calendar and sacramental pattern. They created a number of offences with civil penalties sharper than those held over puritan non-conformists in the pre-war period. To find out how effectively these prohibitions were enforced, I have examined the surviving records of county committees and

---

43. BL Add.MSS 5829, fos 36–7.
44. Tatham, *Puritans in Power*, pp. 264–7; 'Manchester Classical Minutes', ed. W.A. Shaw (Chetham Society, XX, XXII, XXIV, 1888–91), 26, 32, 109, 111, 116, 208, 251–3, 284, 289, 293, 296–302.

quarter sessions, and also 150 surviving churchwardens' accounts for ten counties in western and eastern England.[45] Churchwardens' accounts record all the expenses incurred on such items as church fabric, ornaments, vestments, service books, bread and wine for communions (and much else besides). They also frequently include annual or irregular inventories of church goods. The survival of such records for the mid-seventeenth century owes most to the vagaries of eighteenth- and nineteenth-century vicars and vestries in preserving their records. There is no reason to doubt that the 150 sets of accounts are a representative cross-section.

First of all, they help to demonstrate the continued use of the Prayer Book. Inventories record their survival in more than one-third of all parishes. This is an ambiguous finding. It could be that the Prayer Book was retained but not used; or that it was used in many more parishes but prudently not recorded with other parish effects. After all, possession of it was an offence, and an ordinance had required churchwardens to surrender all copies to county committees. It is perhaps striking that most inventories continue to record the preservation of Bishop Jewel's *Apology* and Erasmus's *Paraphrases* (which were not banned) but not the *Book of Homilies* (which was). It is perhaps also worth noting that in the period up to the civil war four times as many churches possessed copies of Jewel's defence of the Elizabethan settlement as possessed Foxe's *Book of Martyrs*, with its puritanical expectation of a more perfect reformation. Certainly more churches possessed the Prayer Book than possessed the Directory: less than 25 per cent recorded purchasing the latter and less than 25 per cent of inventories record it. It seems to have widely been used only where either the classical system came into being, or where county committees made strenuous efforts to enforce the ordinance of August 1645 (as in Dorset and Gloucestershire where the travelling expenses of wardens summoned up to the committees to receive it are recorded as well as the eighteen pence or two shillings charged for copies: in contrast only one of twenty sets of accounts for Norfolk mention it).

More general evidence adds powerfully to the suggestion that the

45. I have examined all extant accounts in the following county record offices: Cheshire, Worcestershire, Herefordshire, Gloucestershire, Wiltshire, Dorset, Cambridgeshire, Norfolk and Suffolk. I have seen some Cheshire and Norfolk accounts still held by the parishes themselves. In addition, Paul Gladwish generously made available his notes and transcripts of the accounts of Shropshire and Bristol.

Prayer Book was widely used. John Evelyn had no difficulty in finding churches in London which used it throughout the 1640s and 1650s; Sir John Bramston wandered in off the street into a church in Milk Street and found the old liturgy in use. His father's carriage outside aroused interest, and soon the church was packed out. Churches in the very centre of towns continued quietly to use the Book, even in small boroughs like Abingdon, where a 'puritan' corporation failed to prevent its use in one of the two churches. In both Oxford and Cambridge colleges the old service books were in frequent use down to the summer of 1647 if not later. Fragmentary evidence from many counties suggests that prudent observance was very common. Leading Anglican moderates like Robert Sanderson and Jeremy Taylor wrote out modified versions to evade the terms of the ordinances; others memorized the common elements in daily prayer and the communion service. Even where local authorities were informed of the continued use of the Prayer Book, they were too busy with other things, too desperate to fill pulpits, too pessimistic about the effectiveness of suspensions, to take effective action. The parallels with the impotence felt and ambivalent attitudes held by pre-war bishops to puritan non-conformity are very obvious. To give an example: the Dorset committee were told in December 1647 about at least seven ministers who continued to use the banned liturgy. The seven were instructed to desist but no further action was taken against them, despite the specific penalties laid down in the 1645 ordinance. A petition of Presbyterian ministers in Essex in December 1647 spoke of the Prayer Book as being 'usually used' in the parish churches there, and a similar petition from Londoners was delivered to Parliament at the same time.[46]

Much more striking is the evidence of the continued observance of the established pattern of holy communion.[47] There are two aspects to this: the occasions on which communions are celebrated, and the rules governing admission to the sacrament.

Although customs varied from diocese to diocese, the general

---

46. *Diary of John Evelyn*, ed. E.S. de Beer (Oxford, 1955), vols. I and II. *passim*; Higham, *Catholic and Reformed*, pp. 257–8, 264–72, Overton, *Church*, II, 119–21; 'Autobiography of Sir John Bramston' (Camden Society, XXXII, 1845), 91–7; Ketton-Cremer, *Norfolk*, pp. 332–3; A.E. Preston, *The Church and Parish of St Nicholas, Abingdon* (1929), p. 97; Tatham, *Puritans in Power*, chs. 4 and 5; Neal, *History of the Puritans*, III, 365–9; CUL Baker MSS 25/167; Stoughton, *History of Religion*, II, 83, 103–4, 280–92, 322–4; Fletcher, *Sussex*, p. 111; Mayo, *Standing Committee*, pp. 318–19, 376; Smith, *Essex*, p. 84.
47. Based on sources in note 45.

pattern before 1643 was for communion to be held on the three great feasts of Christmas, Easter and Whit (sometimes as part of a monthly celebration, more frequently as part of a basically quarterly pattern). The only parishes where communion was not celebrated at the great feasts before 1642 are those with incumbents known to have been puritan non-conformists in other respects. The observance of these feasts was banned by ordinance in 1646 which reinforced the instructions of the Directory. The pattern of purchases of bread and wine suggest that in 1646 communions were still held on the major feasts in 85 per cent of all parishes; the proportion reached a nadir in 1650 when Easter communions are recorded in only 43 per cent of the accounts. From 1650 and particularly from 1657 the proportion of recorded Easter communions increases. In many places the old feasts were very publicly celebrated: in godly Gloucester, one parish held special services with guest preachers every Easter Sunday while another rang its bells for the king's birthday every year down to 1648 and continued to deck out the church with rosemary, bay and holly to celebrate Christmas as late as 1650. The annual Rogationtide perambulations of parish boundaries were banned by ordinance in 1644 but persisted in over one-third of all parishes, including two in the city of Norwich.[48]

Parliamentary ordinances did not just ban holy communions on feast days; they attempted to restrict access to the communion table to those adequately prepared morally and spiritually.[49] Anglican practice had been to admit all those not openly scandalous, unrepentant and forewarned to stay away. Puritans denounced this as a 'promiscuous' practice and preferred a 'closed' or 'railed' communion. All those who wished to take communion had to present themselves for examination by the minister and elders on specific days immediately before the celebration. Formal docquets were given to those approved. In 1645 Parliament even drew up a list of doctrinal positions, knowledge of which had to be shown by those who came before the elders. Admission was thus by ticket only.

By 1650 the pattern of holy communions at Easter and (less frequently) at other major feasts was observed in 43 per cent of the parishes. In almost every case the amount recorded as spent on bread and wine was comparable with the sums spent before the civil

48. NNRO PD 58/38 (St Lawrence); NNRO PD 59/54 (St Gregory); GRO P 154/14 CW 2/1 (St Michael); CRO P154/11 CW 2/1 (St Mary). For earlier complaints, see Staley, *Hierurgia Anglicana*, I, 257.

49. Firth and Rait, *Acts*, I, 789, 833, 852; and Neal, *History of the Puritans*, III, 245–7.

war. It seems as if the open-communion policy went along with the old pattern of celebration. Yet an alternative pattern of celebrations – at times other than the main feasts – is recorded in only 20 per cent of parishes. These celebrations were usually very infrequent – less than annually – and the Directory's recommendation of regular communions (by which was meant at least once per quarter) was extremely rare. In these 20 per cent of cases the amount spent on bread and wine was usually less than a third òf the amount spent on the pre-war celebrations. This is evidence of 'closed' communions. Yet in 38 per cent of parishes, there is no record of any communions from 1646 (and often earlier) to 1650 (and often later). This could be because the change of open to closed communion resulted in a change of practice: it may be that the bread and wine were no longer paid for out of the rates but by the communicants at a special collection. There are occasional traces of this in the records. But there is more evidence that the silence of the records results from the suspension of the Lord's Supper. Many ministers felt unable to celebrate the sacrament (indeed disqualified from doing so) because they were unable to hold the necessary preparatory meetings until elders were chosen, which, as we have seen, they mostly never were. This could be a problem even where Presbyterian classes were established. But it could also stem from another consideration: the new system was all too likely to lead to divisions in the parish, with those refused admission witholding their tithes in protest. This is expressly the reason why Ralph Josselin held no communions from 1642 to 1650, when he finally held examinations and admitted thirty-four persons, less than one-tenth of those previously eligible. In 1646 he recorded that 'speaking concerning our intermission of the Lord's Supper I told them that perhaps some feared offending people in point of my maintenance they would deny me my stipend'.[50] Similar feelings appear to have underlain the tithe strikes in 1647 against many ministers intruded in previous years in East Anglia and elsewhere.[51]

Much of this stubborn liturgical conservatism may be simply a reaction against every manifestation of parliamentarian interference in the localities. It does not necessarily indicate that long-established loyalties were being demonstrated. That it was in fact the latter could be demonstrated – if space permitted – from the evidence of the churchwardens' accounts of the period before 1640 and after 1660.

50. *The Diary of Ralph Josselin, 1616–1683*, ed. A. Macfarlane (1976), pp. 77, 96, 234–6.
51. See below, pp. 170–1.

Indeed, the increase in Easter communions as official pressure was relaxed in the 1650s is suggestive too. But the best evidence of a positive ingrained Anglicanism comes from the law courts. I have failed to find any prosecutions in the latter 1640s for use of the Book of Common Prayer: there are many indictments and presentments of ministers for *not* using it. In Norfolk at the midsummer quarter sessions of 1645, Peter Byng was presented by a grand jury for 'cutting and misusing the prayer book'.[52] There was a similar case in 1648, where the Elizabethan Act of Uniformity was invoked to enforce the use of the Prayer Book.[53] In Cambridgeshire in 1648, six ministers were indicted for 'refusing to administer the sacrament but according to the Directory'. They were convicted and had to appeal to the parliamentary Committee of Indemnity.[54] At Beeston Regis in Norfolk, according to three eye-witnesses in 1648, William Feezer arrived at the church with a group of women and an ejected clergyman intending to baptize Feezer's child. The party was met by the vicar who asked why his offer to baptize the child had been ignored. Feezer asked whether the vicar would use the font, but was told that this was contrary to the Directory. Eventually the situation deteriorated into a scuffle.[55] The Directory barred any formal liturgy for the dead: kneeling by the grave, praying beside the corpse or the grave was banned, and 'meditations and conferences suitable to the occasion' were all that was allowed.[56] An alderman of Ripon who tried in 1648 to prevent the burial of a child by a vicar using the old burial service found himself indicted and convicted of assault and subsequently outlawed.[57] As late as 1658 Richard Cromwell was to issue a proclamation recounting the difficulties of godly ministers, some of whom were still being indicted in the courts for not using the old liturgy.[58] With the law – and the ingrained sensibilities of the puritans – so widely flouted, it is clear that the yearning for a godly reformation was stillborn.

VII

It might be argued that most of the evidence for the survival of

---

52. NNRO C/53/box 37, bundle I, unfol.
53. PRO SP 24/1, fo. 187.
54. PRO SP 24/3, fos 118, 152; SP 24/4, fos 68, 77; SP 24/78, unfol.: petition of Wm Stephenson *et al.*
55. NNRO C/83/40: depositions of W. Greene, P. Rickman and A. Nicholls.
56. Firth and Rait, *Acts*, I, 604.
57. PRO SP 24/2, fos 98, 171; SP 24/3, fo. 42.
58. Steele, *Proclamations*, I, 374.

Anglican practice says more about the laziness of most parish clergy and a lack of zeal in most parliamentary agents. But there is a great deal of evidence of positive commitment to old values and practices.

Back in 1641–2, petitions in defence of the Established Church were circulated in over half the English counties (in addition to one from the six counties of North Wales). It is true that most of them were responses to anti-episcopalian petitions, but it is also true that many of the petitions were begun at, or approved by, meetings of the county community at quarter sessions or assizes. The initiative seems usually to have lain with the laity, usually with the greater gentry but sometimes with the minor gentry and freeholders who made up the grand juries. In that sense, the defence of the Church lay closer to the heart of the county communities than did the puritan critiques. There is no more (though no less) evidence that the middling sorts swarmed to sign these petitions than to sign anti-episcopal ones. Most of these petitions contained not only reasoned (and often muted) defences of the office of bishop, but also defences of the Prayer Book, as yet under no parliamentary attack. The language used in the defence of the Prayer Book was usually warmer and more positive than that used in defence of episcopacy. It is clear that some puritan petitions criticized the Prayer Book, but few or none had called for its abolition. It had been more violently attacked by itinerant preachers, or had fallen into disuse in particular parishes. Nonetheless, the threat was widely perceived and widely condemned. Finally, the petitions revealed, in Mr Fletcher's words, 'that although they show no sympathy for Arminianism, they indicate that an alternative view of the church from the puritan one was held by substantial numbers of people'.[59]

By 1645, there was widespread revulsion against the war in a great swathe of counties across the south of England and along the Welsh Marches, as men banded together to halt the effects of war, to limit the demands made by the two sides or to neutralize their region. The appeals for a return to 'normality' in these areas were frequently led and articulated by yeoman-farmers, rural craftsmen, minor gentry. These Clubman risings coincided with Parliament's first efforts to suppress the Prayer Book. The demands of most

---

59. This paragraph is based on Fletcher, *Outbreak*, ch. 9, supplemented by a reading of Sir Thomas Aston, *A Collection of Sundry Petitions* (1641) (in BL E E.201 [26]); J.S. Morrill, *The Revolt of the Provinces* (1976), p. 151; J.S. Morrill, *Cheshire 1630–1660* (Oxford, 1974), pp. 35–7; BL Add.MSS 36913 fos 136–41; CRO QSF 1642 no. 4 fos 23–4.

Clubman groups include a defence of the old liturgy. In Wiltshire, for example, many clergy who had remained politically inactive up to that point, accepting orders from whoever controlled their area, joined the Clubmen emphasizing the need to preserve the old ways in religion. Later in the year, many leaders of the 'Peaceable Army', an anti-war group in Glamorganshire who had banded together to drive out royalists seeking to create yet another marching army after the debacle at Naseby, and who had allied themselves to Pembrokeshire parliamentarians to achieve that end, broke from their new friends in part because of attacks on the Prayer Book.[60]

Positive action was often more localized still. We have already noted that in 1641–2 there was a ready compliance by churchwardens and others in the dismantling of the Laudian innovations: church-wardens' accounts record the alacrity with which altar-rails were dismantled, chancels levelled and so on (though it should be stressed that in 80 per cent of parishes they had recently been erected with the same speed – many parishes purchasing cushions or carpets to enhance the appearance of the rails or for the ease of those who kneeled at the rails. It should also be noted that rails were built in 1641–2 in some churches – including some in unlikely places like Wroxeter, the Temple Church in the centre of Bristol, Sherborne.[61] The later enforced destruction of older ornaments and images was far less frequently implemented by the parishioners themselves: rather it had to await the arrival of special itinerant commissioners like William Dowsing.[62] Occasionally, as at All Hallows, Barking, the parish did act on its own. There, churchwarden Sherman was chided for allowing a statue of St Michael to remain. On consideration, he decided that 'it stood so many years and had done no miracle, therefore he conceived it was no saint', a rather non-puritan reason for iconoclasm. The leading authority on the subject, however, gives a series of examples of churchwardens obstructing commissioners or hiding idolatrous objects ahead of their visit.[63]

It has been said that the history of the English Revolution can be written around the history of tithes. There is truth in this. But – until the rise of the Quakers, if not later – the number of tithe-refusals based on Anglican scruples, that the minister was not discharging his

---

60. Morrill, *Revolt*, pp. 92–9, 201.
61. Shropshire RO 2656/18 (Wroxeter); BRO 0065(22) Ca15(1) (the Temple Church, Bristol); DRO P 155 CW 113 (Sherborne).
62. See J.S. Morrill, 'William Dowsing, the Bureaucratic Puritan', in eds. J. Morrill, P. Slack and D. Woolf, *Public Men and Private Conscience in Seventeenth-Century England* (Oxford, 1992), pp. 178–203.
63. Smith, *Essex*, pp. 174–93, 408; Phillips, *Reformation*, pp. 184–9.

proper duties or had an insufficient title, were more numerous than instances of refusals based on a radical critique of hireling priests. By the ordinances of November 1644 and August 1647, jurisdiction in tithe disputes was transferred to quarter sessions. It is clear that the second, and probably the first, was a specific response to a royalist campaign to withhold tithes from intruded ministers. As early as May 1643, a royal proclamation had inhibited payment of tithes to anyone but ·the 'lawful incumbent', and this was much quoted in the summer of 1647. In Cheshire in September of that year the JPs, appraised that the inhabitants of Tattenhall had withheld tithes at the instigation of a group of royalist clergy, recorded that they 'conceive the Ordinance for payment of tithes cannot be put into execution without bloodshed'. A dozen intruded clergymen in Dorset between 1646 and 1649 found themselves unable to collect tithes. In Cambridgeshire in mid-1647 there were tithe strikes in favour of extruded ministers in at least four parishes. This was not just support for ejected ministers. It will be recalled that the main reason why Ralph Josselin did not celebrate the Lord's Supper in the 1640s was that he feared a tithe-strike by those excluded.[64]

But the best evidence of all of commitment to the old ways is that afforded by the reintrusion of ejected ministers in their parsonages and pulpits by their old parishioners. Many parishes lobbied so successfully that local committees dared not or chose not to enforce a planned ejection. Elsewhere men used force to keep out or to remove a nominee of the committee of plundered ministers. This could happen in the heart of London in 1647 and in Southwark in 1649.[65] As with tithe refusals, a high proportion of all reintrusions occurred in the months July to September 1647. What almost all the following have in common is that the ministers brought the Prayer Book back with them. Mobs of parishioners secured the return of ejected men in at least seven Essex parishes; at Soham in Cambridgeshire a major riot preceded the triumphant return of Richard Exeter to the pulpit from which he had been driven in 1644 for drunkenness, innovation and disaffection to Parliament. The neighbouring minister who assisted the operation kept his living up to

---

64. Firth and Rait, *Acts*, I, 567, 996; Steele, *Proclamations*, I, 292; 'Plundered Ministers Accounts', ed. W.A. Shaw (Lancashire and Cheshire Records Society, XXVIII, 1894), 185–7; Mayo, *Standing Committee*, pp. 108, 120, 353, 384, 419, 430, 438, 442, 448, 452, 453, 475, 500; *Walker Revised*, ed. A.G. Matthews (Oxford, 1948), pp. 79–84; Kingston, *East Anglia*, pp. 393–5.
65. M. Coate, *Cornwall in the Great Civil War and Interregnum* (Oxford, 1940), pp. 333–4; Tindal-Hart, *Country Clergy*, pp. 128–9; PRO SP24/77 unfol.: petition of D. Souton; BL Add.MSS 15671, fo. 240.

and beyond the Restoration.[66] There were similar incidents elsewhere in Cambridgeshire. Sometimes those who assisted a minister to regain his living were among those who had helped to get him sequestered – as in the case of Meric Casaubon in Kent.[67] In Cheshire there were six reintrusions – the initiative coming from within the parishes, and sometimes from those involved in the earlier ejection. Let us conclude with two specific examples. At Aldenham in Hertfordshire, Joseph Soane was sequestered in 1643 and the living conferred by the committee of plundered ministers on John Gilpin. When the latter tried to hold a service on Whit Sunday 1643 (perhaps omitting the usual communion?) a multitude of parishioners drove him out and reinstalled Soane. Gilpin complained to the House of Lords who had Soane imprisoned, but he quickly submitted and was released. He thereupon reoccupied his glebe and parsonage. The county committee sought to arbitrate and finally persuaded both men to withdraw. The (royalist) patron then presented a third man. So things rested until July 1647 when Soane reappeared and was reintruded by his parishioners, and despite attempts to oust him he stayed put until after the Restoration.[68]

At Bebington in Cheshire, Ralph Poole was ejected in 1646 for alehouse-haunting and preaching against Parliament, and the committee of plundered ministers nominated Josiah Clarke to take his place. In May 1647 a large number of men petitioned on behalf of Poole, and the committee suspended the payment of tithes until a decision was reached. In June, they decided in favour of Clarke. But in July, an aggressive picket-line kept the new vicar out and reinstated Poole. On 17 August the county committee admitted that they were powerless to act. The best the committee of plundered ministers could do was to refer the case to the arbitration of two MPs and the sherrif.[69] All this time, Poole had been receiving the tithes which were due.

What lay behind this surge of activity in the summer of 1647 were the rumours of an impending settlement between king and the army that would lead to the revival of episcopacy and of the Prayer Book (albeit with a freedom for tender consciences outside the restored Church). Many of those involved in the reintrusions claimed to have seen a declaration from Sir Thomas Fairfax to that effect.[70]

66. Smith, *Essex*, pp. 157–61; Kingston, *East Anglia*, pp. 326–8; Matthews, *Walker Revised*, p. 81.
67. Tatham, *Puritans in Power*, pp. 58–9, 69; Tindal-Hart, *Country Clergy*. p. 120.
68. Kingston, *Hertfordshire*, pp. 164–7.
69. Shaw, 'Plundered Ministers Accounts', pp. 175–82, 189.
70. E.g. ibid., pp. 183–9; Smith, *Essex*, pp. 162–3.

That this militant resurgence of Anglicanism was widespread is further supported by the issuance of a new ordinance on 23 August 1647 which declared that

> whereas divers ministers in the several counties of the kingdom for notorious scandals and delinquency have been put out of their livings by authority of Parliament and godly, learned, and orthodox ministers placed in their rooms . . . the said scandalous and delinquent ministers by force or other ways have entered upon the churches and gained possession of the parsonages, tithes and profits.[71]

The Prayer-Book rebellion of 1647 was the prelude to the second civil war. Several of the incidents which sparked off the provincial risings of 1648 were concerned with the suppression of Christmas or of the Prayer Book.[72]

VIII

There has been no space in the course of this essay to look at all the ecclesiastical developments of the 1640s. Instead I have concentrated on one neglected but major problem. A rounded account[73] would obviously attempt to show what happened in those parishes where the Presbyterian discipline was settled or where the old system collapsed but was *not* replaced by a Presbyterian discipline. It would have to look at the emergence and growth of the Baptist churches and of gathered congregations in towns and (to a lesser extent) the countryside; and at the peculiar religious situation in the New Model Army (which probably owed as much to the *lack* of chaplains as to the radicalism of its chaplains).[74] I have been rather vague about the social base of Anglican survivalism. It seems quite possible that this was not gentry-led but frequently owed its strength to the very middling sort who we are often told were the bedrock of puritanism.[75] If this conclusion is borne out by the case studies on which I am now engaged, it would confirm my belief that the middling sort were as deeply divided as were the gentry, though perhaps about different things.

Why does it matter that so many people *cared for* the Church

---

71. Firth and Rait, *Acts*, I, 999.
72. Everitt, *Kent*, pp. 231–40; Ketton-Cremer, *Norfolk*, pp. 337–40; Morrill, *Revolt*, pp. 125–30, 207.
73. See, e.g., Cross, 'Church in England', in Aylmer, *Interregnum*, pp. 99–120.
74. I owe this point to discussions with Dr Anne Laurence and to the paper she delivered to my graduate seminar in Cambridge in November 1980.
75. Cf. B.S. Manning, 'The Godly People', in the book he edited, *Politics, Religion and the English Civil War* (Manchester, 1973).

of England; that after eighty years of maturation, a hybrid church, thoroughly if murkily reformed in its doctrines, unreformed in its government, a mish-mash in its liturgy, had achieved not only an intellectual self-confidence but a rhythm of worship, piety, practice, that had earthed itself into the Englishman's consciousness and had sunk deep roots in popular culture? Attempts to destroy that tradition have been shown largely to have failed. One reason was that those charged to carry out the task had too much else to do. Another is that they had so little help from men and women who would voluntarily do no more than pluck off the cuttings recently grafted on to the healthy stem by Laud. Given this initial hostility to their aims, successive regimes lacked imagination. They reiterated all the 'thou shalt nots' without offering positive alternatives. In place of the old feasts, for example, they set aside the second Tuesday of every month as a day of Thanksgiving. The ordinance was almost wholly given over to proscribing forms of celebration.[76] No attempt was made to create a new public holiday to celebrate the Revolution. Throughout the 1640s and 1650s, the only event celebrated by the ringing of bells in almost all parishes was 5 November, the deliverance from popery. No attempt was made to turn, say, 3 September (Cromwell's day of providences) into such a day. Successful religious revolutions adapt themselves to popular culture just as much they change it. But the official reformation of the 1640s and 1650s was negative, sterile. As the 1650s wore on, an increasing number of parishes observed the old feasts and held open communion services. At Easter 1660, before Charles's return, there were celebrations of the sacrament in over half the parishes. During 1660 there was a spontaneity and responsiveness in the restoration of the old Church in most areas quite unlike the sloth (at best) in the previous period.

On Christmas Day 1656, John Lambert, speaking in Parliament, justified the Decimation Tax on the whole royalist party by claiming that even as he spoke, the bulk of the royalist party were in their homes, 'merry over their Christmas pies'.[77] For Lambert it was a symbol that they had not accepted the Revolution, had not turned away from old superstitions. He was right, but there was nothing he could do about it. On Christmas Day 1657, John Evelyn was at a communion service in central London when soldiers entered the chapel. They waited until the service was over, then arrested the

76. Firth and Rait, *Acts*, I, 905.
77. *Parliamentary Diary of Thomas Burton* ed. J.T. Rutt (1822), I, 240.

leaders and took note of the rest. The leaders were questioned and then released.[78] It was an act of futile bullying. Further study may well show that the more the Puritans tried to abolish Christmas, the more certain their downfall became.

78. Higham, *Catholic and Reformed*, p. 270.

PART TWO

Problems of Allegiance

Introduction: County Communities and the Problem of Allegiance in the English Civil War

I

I began to research the English civil wars in that useful ten-month gap which Oxbridge candidates used to have between school and university. The schoolmaster who inspired me to be a historian, Norman Dore, asked me whether I would like to spend time getting together some statistics on the allegiance of the Cheshire gentry in the Great Civil War to help him with a local history he was writing;[1] I was thrilled. In the ensuing months I got to know many of the printed records (such as Mrs Mary Everett Green's *Calendar of the Committee for Compounding with Delinquents*) that have been part of my life ever since. This was in the spring of 1964, and although the Gentry Controversy was no longer raging,[2] it was still the starting-point for most students of the period.

Subsequently I spent my undergraduate Long Vacations developing the work I had started in 1964 and the fruits of that further research were written up as an Oxford Prize essay in 1967, a version of which was subsequently published.[3] Looking over it again recently, I was struck at how quickly I became concerned by what I saw as the distortions of number-crunching approaches to allegiance. Two

1. R.N. Dore, *The Civil Wars in Cheshire* (Chester, 1966).
2. Those historiographically-minded enough or prurient enough to want to acquaint themselves with this academic blood-letting can approach it through L. Stone, *The Causes of the English Revolution* (1972), pt II.
3. 'The Allegiance of the Cheshire Gentry in the Great Civil War', *Trans. Lancs and Cheshire Antiq. Soc.* (1967). This was a paper written by me but carefully vetted by Norman Dore, and it appeared under our joint names, as it replaced a paper we had given to the society jointly in the winter of 1964/5.

things were very obvious to me even then: one was the problem of social specificity and social cohesiveness – the problem of deciding who was among the gentry and who was not; and the allied difficulty of seeing what a small landowner with an income of £50 per annum, with freehold in one or two parishes, had in common with the great county families with incomes well over £1,000 p.a. from land in several counties. More importantly, I became aware that political choices were frequently constrained, and that the sources for identifying and labelling men 'royalist' and 'parliamentarian' distorted more complex realities. I remember a deep sense of dissatisfaction with and revulsion against modelling of civil war allegiance on the basis of putting individuals into one of three boxes labelled *royalist*, *parliamentarian* and *other*, and then tipping out the contents of each box and looking for statistical variants between them. The essay reprinted here as chapter 9 reflects those concerns. It began life as a review of the most thoughtful and thorough of the studies based on number-crunching techniques.[4]

II

I began my D. Phil. in October 1967 just after the publication of Alan Everitt's *The Community of Kent and the Great Rebellion* (1966). It influenced me greatly, as did two other works by Everitt developing the thesis of his book.[5] Everitt disdained prosopography and distribution curves. Instead he explored the claustrophobic atmosphere of local government and politics, the self-contained worlds of local gentry who were first and foremost concerned with local issues and whose behaviour in the civil war owed little to informed choices based on the traditional 'constitutional' and 'religious' issues to be found in general studies of the period. By the time I laid down my pen and submitted my thesis in December 1970[6] I thought I had shown that in Cheshire as in Kent, there was a county community of leading families whose political behaviour was shaped by pre-existent local loyalties, and whose political culture was built around a deep loyalty to the social and administrative institutions of Cheshire and a natural suspicion of the centralizing tendencies of the Crown (before the civil wars) *and* of successive regimes after the wars.

4. B.G. Blackwood, *The Lancashire Gentry and the Great Rebellion, 1640–1660* (Manchester, 1978).
5. A.M. Everitt, *Change in the Provinces 1600–1660* (Leicester, 1969) and 'The Local Community and the Great Rebellion', *Historical Association Pamphlet* G 70 (1969).
6. Subsequently published with relatively minor changes as *Cheshire 1630–1660: County Government and Society during the 'English Revolution'* (Oxford, 1974).

I had recovered 'neutralism'[7] and I equated it with 'localism'. But I had also decided that Everitt underestimated the ideological force of religion as a solvent of local loyalties; and generally my account emphasized far more than his had the way that national events and issues of principle disrupted local patterns of behaviour. As I put it:

> local tensions and preoccupations proved more important than national issues or abstruse constitutional principles. The overriding political unit was the county community, and the particular situation in Cheshire *diffracted* the conflicts between King and Parliament into an individual and specific pattern.[8]

Thus the parties around which Cheshire politics operated and polarized in the 1640s appear first to have formed in the 1620s at a time when two groups of families, one of whom had bought baronetcies and the other Irish peerages in the expectation of achieving social primacy (e.g. in local courts and on ceremonial occasions), found that each group refused them the deference they thought they were owed.[9] This line of interpretation was followed in a number of other studies (especially in unpublished theses), most notably a study of Sussex by Anthony Fletcher which I reviewed rather ungratefully (see below, ch. 10).

These studies certainly put paid to the 'gentry controversy' and to the argument that the civil wars represented a clash between separate and opposed social groups. They drew attention to the reluctance of most men to become involved, the contingent factors that skewed the political behaviour of many individuals and families, the existence of resentment at the interference of the state in the affairs of local communities as a factor in determining political behaviour before, during and in the aftermath of the wars. In a rather trenchant review of Brian Manning's *The English People and the English Revolution* (below, ch. 10) I reiterated all these points and more, noting that his approach (that with the gentry divided against themselves, the

---

7. B.S. Manning, 'Neutrals and neutralism in the English Civil War', Oxford D. Phil. (1957), was the pioneering work. But Manning had never explored the local contexts of neutralism and he was much more concerned with popular anti-sentiment in such movements as the Levellers.
8. Morrill, *Cheshire*, p. 330. And see also how I expressed these issues in my introductory remarks to the chapter on Local Studies in J.S. Morrill, *Seventeenth-Century Britain 1603–1714* (Critical Bibliographies in Modern History, London, 1980), pp. 124–6 ('National issues took on different resonances in each local context and became intricately bound up with purely local issues and groupings.').
9. I had not established this when my first book was published. But see J.S. Morrill, 'Cheshire Parliamentary History, 1543–1974' in *The Victoria County History of Cheshire*, II (1979), 107, and below, Ch. 9, p. 198 n. 21.

radicalized middling sort were able to make a decisive contribution on the parliamentarian cause) was not sustainable.[10]

The culmination of my thinking about these issues came with the publication of *The Revolt of the Provinces* in 1976. This has been an influential book, but not in the ways I had anticipated. It has, I think, been most influential in the largely unresearched first chapter, and through its ill-thought out and misunderstood title.

It began life as a study of the workings of the committees of sequestration and compounding which administered the estates of convicted royalists. I aimed to show through this general study the complexity of allegiance and the differences, over time and in space, in the ways different bodies of parliamentarians defined royalism and treated individual royalists. I had already decided that there were committed 'neutrals' and I was keen to show how often they got caught in the net of 'delinquency' and hence into the number-crunchers' royalist box. But I then hit upon the Clubmen and through them other anti-war movements and the subject took on a life of its own. Still, the book is based on a great deal of research in the dustier parts of State Papers Office[11] and I am still broadly convinced by the lines of argument in the second and third parts of the book which deal with how the provinces were mobilized for war[12] and with how Parliament won the war but lost the peace in the provinces. The account of the period up to 1640, with its distinction between 'pure' and 'official' 'country', its account of bewildered local elites reacting against the harsh, centralist policies of Charles I was very much a lead-in only, was not intended to carry much interpretative weight and was manifestly oversimplified and at times plain wrong.

When I first sent in the manuscript to the series editor, it was in four chapters (the existing three and a fourth on the Second Civil War and its aftermath). The book was called *Conservatives and Radicals in the English Civil Wars*. The series editor (quite rightly) disapproved of

10. A new edition of this book has recently been published (Bookmark Press, 1991) with an unrepentant foreword by Brian Manning. I fear I have to say that he has not persuaded me that I was wrong in any of the counter-arguments I deployed in ch. 9 and would still write much the same review as I did 15 years ago. I would however probably indicate how well I think the last two chapters on the later 1640s and on the Levellers have stood up to the test of time.
11. Especially SP28, the Commonwealth Exchequer Papers; but also SP20 (Committee of Sequestrations), SP23 (Committee for Compounding) and SP24 (Committee for Indemnity). For some of the fruit of the latter, see below, ch. 15).
12. The only significant critique of this chapter is contained in Ann Hughes's 'The King, the Parliament, and the Localities during the English Civil War', *Jnl. Brit. Studs.*, XXIV (1985).

the title and asked me to think again. I did, and sent him other rather feeble suggestions. He phoned me in the middle of a seminar (I was then teaching at Stirling University) and on the spur of the moment I dreamt up *The Revolt of the Provinces*. I now realize that there were two things wrong with it. The first is that I think what I was trying to convey was the idea of *Revolt in the Province*. The second is that I think I saw the revolt **of** the provinces as the culmination of the process, i.e. the second civil war. This is where the second problem arose. The manuscript I had submitted contained 80,000 words rather than the contracted 70,000 and the publishers required it to go on a diet. I decided to cut the fourth part and incorporate a truncated account of the second civil war as a culmination to part 3. The two decisions – on title and how to get within the word limit – thus cut against one another. Retitled *Revolt in the Provinces*, I think the book holds up reasonably well!

Nonetheless it is now clear that the general approach adopted by Everitt, Fletcher, myself and others contained serious exaggerations. Two historians more than any other have taught us to get a more balanced view of the relationship between locality and centre. Essays by Clive Holmes[13] and Ann Hughes[14] have confronted the issues head-on, although much else has been written on the subject.[15] Holmes challenged the emphasis placed in earlier studies on the social and cultural introvertedness of 'county communities', and he emphasized that experience of the Inns of Court, of the lawcourts and fleshpots of London, and the ingrained habits of reading widened cultural horizons. He is obviously right, although there is a scale of extrovertedness and Everitt's Kent (with its geographical position and peculiar inheritance customs) and my Cheshire (a county palatine that had had no MPs – and no parliamentary taxes – and no JPs until 1543, and which still had local courts that precluded Cheshire business from the Westminster courts)[16] are obviously at one end of the scale.

13. C. Holmes, 'The County Community in Stuart Historiography', *Jnl. Brit. Studs.* (1978), 54–73. XVII
14. A. Hughes, 'Local History and the Origins of the Civil War', in R. Cust and A. Hughes (eds.), *Conflict in Early Stuart England* (1989), pp. 224–53.
15. C. Holmes, *Seventeenth-Century Lincolnshire* (Lincoln, 1980); A. Hughes, *Government, Society and Civil War in Warwickshire 1620–1660* (Cambridge, 1987); A. Coleby, *Central Government and the Localities: Hampshire 1649–1689* (Cambridge, 1987); and works referred to in the bibliographical note in Hughes, 'Local History', p. 260.
16. It even had its own judges of Great Sessions and was thus not visited by judges of the central courts on assize circuit. The Cheshire Great Sessions therefore did not 'emphasize the local magistracy's responsibility to and dependence upon, a central system of government' (Holmes, 'County Community', p. 63).

Other points are also well taken. Everitt's distinction of the 'county' gentry, whose social, administrative and cultural sphere of interest and influence was the shire, and the 'parish' gentry, whose sphere was their immediate neighbourhood, is important but perhaps overdrawn,[17] and his preoccupation with the former in writing political history is certainly limiting. Again, I was rightly criticized for bumpkinizing the gentry (and, by implication, the middling sort), misrepresenting their knowledge of what was happening in the world and understating their ability to place their knowledge within sophisticated frameworks of understanding.[18] It is also clear that I too readily equated localism and neutralism: there are connections but not coincidence in 1642.[19]

III

Although neither Holmes nor Hughes is in danger of throwing out the baby with the bathwater, some of their readers might be. I would therefore like to restate the middle ground in relation to the significance of local loyalties and the problem of allegiance in the civil wars.

As I suggested in another essay in this collection, during the period 1559–1660 and especially 1603–60 the county was a unique *locus* of power and political authority: it came between two periods when the great noble house served as a *locus* of effective regional authority and power; it was the heyday of the Lieutenancy[20] and a time when *all* the greater gentry sought admission to the county commissions of the peace; it was a time of intense status-consciousness, in which heads of families measured their standing by their position within the

17. I found it helpful in explaining the changing style of local government when the 'parish gentry' joined the commissions of the peace in the 1650s (Morrill, *Cheshire*, ch. 6).
18. Holmes' examples of Spelman's *History of Sacrilege* and Scot's *Discoverie of Witchcraft* are as extreme on the one side as examples of how members of a 'national intellectual coterie . . . could articulate their local experience and concerns, organize and explain them, and generalize from them within the framework of a common intellectual system' as my use of William Davenport was on the other side (Holmes, 'County Community', p. 59; J. Morrill, 'William Davenport and the "Silent Majority" of early Stuart England', *Jnl. Chester Arch. Soc.* (1974), summarized in Morrill, *Revolt*, pp. 19–22).
19. Fletcher, *Outbreak*, pp. 380–404; Hughes, 'Local History', 237–8.
20. But not necessarily of the Lords Lieutenant. In some counties one great family really did dominate local defence and the policing of the religious settlement. But in others effective power had shifted by the early seventeenth century to the deputy lieutenants, drawn from among the senior JPs. I owe this point, which strengthens my general argument, to a discussion with David Smith.

pecking order of *county* rankings. It is the age in which gentlemen had the coats of arms of county families painted as friezes around their walls or on their ceilings. It is an age in which the gentry measured their status by rankings within the county and in which this was *a* (in many cases *the*) determining issue when parliamentary selection went wrong and a contested election had to be held.[21]

If county government was quite diffuse, with the lathe or other petty sessional division as much the centre of practical action as the county itself, nonetheless only a grand jury at quarter sessions or assizes could draw up and endorse and present a petition in the name of the shire to king or parliament; only a grand jury serving for a whole county could impose a rate upon local communities;[22] and as I put it in 1983: 'the social and political institutions of the county were arenas within which rivalries were worked out, disputes arbitrated, prestige and honour won and lost.'[23] Ann Hughes tells us that economic boundaries do not follow jurisdictional ones, that many counties are made up of sharply contrasted farming regions or farming and industrial regions. She reports that in an unpublished paper Hassell Smith showed how MPs from the sheep-corn farming belts dominated the parliamentary representation of several counties in the early seventeenth century and uses this to suggest that counties are not homogeneous units.[24] Indeed not, but Hassell Smith's tentative but persuasive conclusion is that the electoral geography in the counties he had studied may have been dominated by the perceived inequities of the rating system at a time when all landowners paid low national taxes but high local rates. The distribution as between occupiers and owners differed sharply between farming regions and may well have been a key issue in local politics.

My conclusion from this would differ from Ann Hughes's. At this crucial stage of state formation, Englishmen had to find ways of cooperating and resolving differences at a local level, and the institutions of the county were where they primarily did so. As a result of recent work we can now see how far and how often conflict

21. M.A. Kishlansky, *Parliamentary Selection* (Cambridge, 1985), esp. chs. 3–4; see also A. Fletcher, 'Honour, Reputation and Office-Holding in Elizabethan and Stuart England', in Fletcher and Stevenson (eds.), *Order and Disorder*, pp. 92–115.
22. A point I discussed at length in *The Cheshire Grand Jury, 1525–1667: a Social and Administrative Study* (Leicester, 1978), pp. 33–7, 44–5. For the significance of the county and its institutions in the petitioning activities of the early 1640s, see A. Fletcher, *The Outbreak of the English Civil War* (1980), chs. 6, 8, 11.
23. See above, p. 48.
24. Hughes, 'Local History', pp. 229–37.

management required appeals for arbitration or confirmation of local agreement to the centre. Similarly my reading of the evidence Clive Holmes adduces for the reduction of fenland violence and which he attributes to a popular awe of statute is different from his. It seems to me that locally-arrived-at agreements in fenland disputes were confirmed and made good by the passage of local acts of Parliament (which made voluntary agreements readily enforceable).[25]

When I read studies of the fifteenth century, pre-eminently now Christine Carpenter on Warwickshire,[26] or when I read Hassell Smith on Elizabethan Norfolk[27] and Diarmaid MacCulloch on Tudor Suffolk,[28] I am struck again by the slow decline of local power structures built around the noble household, the liberty and the manor, and the gradual rise of the institutions of the shire – lieutenancy, commission of the peace, revival of the shrievalty – and of the civil parish, whose officers were supervised (unlike those of the manor) by the Crown-appointed officers of the shire. This gradual and perceptible shift in the *locus* of power reached a peak around the middle of the seventeenth century. After that the re-emergence of mega-rich families whose interests were as much metropolitan as provincial, the withdrawal of the greatest families from the tedium of local government and the bureaucratization of many sensitive matters such as tax assessment all led to a shift away from a relative county-mindedness.

The sixteenth century not only saw the development of county institutions. It saw the development of a fierce pride in local customs and local procedures. Clive Holmes suggests that what I called 'conventions and customs to meet local needs' developed only where the relevant legislation gave JPs discretionary powers. 'In fundamentals', he asserts, the English county communities were governed by a common law.[29] I do not wholly agree. There was a clear statutory duty incumbent upon JPs to raise a county rate for the

25. Holmes, 'Drainers and Fenmen: the Problem of Popular Political Culture in the 17th Century', in Fletcher and Stevenson (eds.), *Order and Disorder*, pp. 166–95. I will present my evidence for this reassessment in an essay forthcoming in a festschrift.
26. C. Carpenter, *Locality and Polity: a Study of Warwickshire Landed Society, 1401–1499*, (Cambridge, 1992), a book which self-consciously opens a dialogue with 'county community' studies of the sixteenth and seventeenth centuries.
27. A. Hassell Smith, *County or Court: Government and politics in Norfolk, 1559–1603* (Oxford, 1974).
28. D. MacCulloch, *Suffolk and the Tudors: Politics and Religion in an English County 1500–1600* (Oxford, 1986).
29. Holmes, 'County Community', p. 64.

maintenance of bridges on the king's highway. In Cheshire, the statute was ignored because the Cheshire justices preferred their own system which predated the statute. And even if the powers of grand juries were determined within local discretion they could be cherished.[30] This matters, because what was argued by Everitt and myself, and what must not be overlooked, is that the government of Charles I became clumsily interventionist, riding roughshod over such local customs and traditions in a drive for efficiency and uniformity. However much I may have filtered objections of fundamental principle out of my account of the story of Ship Money and left only localist concerns in (and I certainly did oversimplify the story),[31] it is important not to reverse the filter and return to a story of Ship Money as a tax resented essentially because it was 'unconstitutional'.[32] The Book of Orders and the exact militia (especially in the attempted use of county munitions in 1639–40), are other examples of a heavy-handed government that was far less skilful than its Elizabethan and Jacobean predecessors in using conciliar arbitration and patronage as a carrot (as well as a stick) to keep local governors on what I called 'the treadmill of endeavour'.

IV

I would still like to make the following claims for the importance of local studies of the origins of the civil war. First, that localism was an important factor in alienating many people from the government of Charles I by 1640; that it limited the support that both the king and his opponents were able to call on in 1642; and that an understanding of the ways local loyalties lie helps to an understanding of the patterning of allegiance in any part of England.

When I wrote my thesis, and when I wrote *The Revolt of the Provinces*, it never occurred to me that anyone would challenge the importance of religious passions in compelling many men to choose

30. Morrill, *Cheshire Grand Jury*, pp. 241–3, for an account of a local agreement which lasted from 1616 to 1652.
31. Morrill, *Revolt*, pp. 24–30; Holmes, 'County Community', pp. 65–9; Hughes, 'Local History', pp. 232–4; see now Alison Gill's University of Sheffield PhD thesis (1991), an exceptionally thorough and persuasive analysis of the whole question, which reaches conclusions that demonstrate that there were ideological and functional aspects to Ship Money refusal.
32. In a brilliantly playful passage in a lecture to sixth formers in March 1992 I heard Conrad Russell make some very suggestive parallels between Ship Money in the 1630s and Poll Tax in the late 1980s, resented by most, resisted by some on principle, by others on grounds of equity, avoided by many to the point of distraint but not beyond.

sides; nor did I ever doubt that at the level of high politics both the calculations and the miscalculations of the royal family, old and new councillors, peers and managers of the House of Commons were likely to result in a collapse of trust and a call to arms. I was concerned to distinguish between those people who made civil war happen and those who got drawn in to a war of other people's making. Later I became concerned with analysing the political psychology of the activists[33] but I felt then and feel now that the most important task was to look at how (unlike in 1688) the centre failed to hold in 1642. In the introduction to the new edition of *The Revolt of the Provinces* published in 1980, I noted that Norman Dore had jokingly told me I had demonstrated that the civil war had not broken out in 1642. This has been seized on by Christopher Hill and others and much used against me. It has become rather tedious. What Norman Dore clearly meant is that I had shown that civil war need not have broken out, that the forces for peace and settlement were strong; that most people were reluctant participants and warriors; and that we need to distinguish what determined the allegiance of those who made it happen from what determined the behaviour of those sucked into a war they had sought to prevent.

In the summer and autumn of 1642 men and women had to react to a series of challenges: whether to act under the parliamentary militia ordinance or under the royal commissions of array; whether to obey orders from those who had so acted; whether to respond to direct summonses from the king; whether to pay the loans which Parliament sought to *require* all landholders to pay; whether to obey orders or answer requests from local magnates. In deciding how to rsepond to this continuous stream of options, men (often after taking the advice of their wives or mothers) allowed all kinds of factors to influence them: they could put the welfare of their families first, and give aid to the side most likely to plunder them if they did not; they could behave deferentially, saying to themselves that some local magnate was more likely to understand the issues than they were; they could (for no better reasons than prudence and inertia) follow the lead of others in a local grouping which had stood together in local politics over the preceding years; they could follow short-term self-interest, seeing a way of making a bit of money by a short-term

---

33. See section A. It was Barbara Shapiro who explained to me that that was what I was about after I had given a paper in Toronto (published as 'Sir William Brereton and "England's Wars of Religion"', *Jnl. Brit. Studs.*, 24 (1985), which was said by my commentator to show I had changed my mind.

commission in a war expected to be over by Christmas; or they could decide on matters of principle (religious, constitutional) and prejudice (fear of popery, fear of religious anarchy). There would be as many patterns of choice as there were people. My earlier studies presumed that we knew what the matters of principle were, but that we needed to know what else skewed the behaviour of individuals. I also hoped that in those studies I might be able to isolate those issues of principle which proved so powerful and effective that they brought particular men to the fore. I have spent much of the past ten years working out the political psychology of those who made free choices and then compelled many others to make much more reluctant choices. If we revert to thinking that we can understand allegiance in the English civil war as being determined by simple rational choices between two party manifestoes we will not only fail to understand how it came about, but why it had the *shape* that it had, and why it had the outcome that it had.

When I first wrote about allegiance in the civil war, I was pre-occupied with questions of gentry allegiance. This was partly because I despaired of being able to find sources adequate to measure let alone account for the political choices being made at sub-gentry level, and partly because I think I underestimated the freedom of choice that existed within that society. (I will confess to underestimating it but not to discounting it.) Since then I have been taught both just how real that freedom was and how it can be studied. Derek Hirst's work on the independence of a much larger electorate was important in opening my eyes to this, even if it now seems clear that he took his case further than it can be pushed.[34] Later local studies, notably Ann Hughes's study of Warwickshire, show what could and should have been done with Cheshire sources.[35] Above all, David Underdown, in his wonderfully rich and challenging account of the political cultures of royalism and parliamentarianism[36] offers an account of an England

---

34. D. Hirst, *Representative of the People?* (Cambridge, 1975), especially chs. 6–7. Hirst certainly shows that whenever there was a contest the elite had difficulty in controlling the electorate, but he does not acknowledge how limited were the opportunities of the electorate to decide whether there should be a contest. It was almost unknown for those outside the elite to challenge the nominees of the elite. Contests only take place when the elite cannot agree how to share the representation. For a robust and more general critique of Hirst, see Kishlansky, *Parliamentary Selection*, chs. 3–4.
35. A. Hughes, *Government, Society and Civil War in Warwickshire 1620–1660* (Cambridge, 1987), chs. 1–4.
36. D.E. Underdown, *Revel, Riot and Rebellion* (Oxford, 1985).

in which men of all social groups are making free and informed political choices. My long review of his thesis is republished below as chapter 11, and my doubts and hesitations are there recorded. But *Revel, Riot and Rebellion* is undoubtedly my book of the 1980s as far as civil-war studies is concerned and it is a book which more than any other decided me not to accept an invitation to publish a new edition of *The Revolt of the Provinces*. It would require me to rethink too much. Instead I will address Underdown's agenda elsewhere and sort out what for me is the wheat from the chaff of his argument. It will be an abundant harvest.

CHAPTER NINE

The Northern Gentry and the Great Rebellion

I

The publication of *The Lancashire Gentry and the Great Rebellion, 1640–1660*[1] is a notable event. Dr Blackwood has worked on this subject for more than twenty years,[2] and the result is a book more thoroughly researched, more clearly written and more disciplined than any of its kind. The title promises both more and less than the book performs. For Dr Blackwood is concerned with people not events, groups not individuals, society and economics not politics and government. There is no account here of the civil war in Lancashire, nor of the institutions and values of the Interregnum. Dr Blackwood studies the Lancashire gentry as a group, analysing their number, their wealth, their values over the seventeenth century as a whole. Above all, he is concerned to examine what divided one group from another in 1642, to see to what extent they were divided and to find out how far the costly violence of the war changed the face of Lancashire society. To what extent did the civil wars prosper the wealth and status of the parliamentarians and damage those of the royalists? In answering this question, he has extended his researches down to the end of the seventeenth century and by straddling the Restoration settlement has broken new ground in local studies.

Those familiar with the journals and transactions of northern historical societies – including *Northern History* itself – already be

---

1. B.G. Blackwood, *The Lancashire Gentry and the Great Rebellion, 1640–1660* (Manchester: University Press for the Chetham Society. 1978).
2. He first examined the question in an Oxford University B Litt. thesis in 1956. the present work is a revised version of his Oxford University D. Phil. thesis of 1973.

familiar with Dr Blackwood's approach to the subject,[3] and some of his findings will already be familiar to them. This book, however, is more than a gathering together of his earlier articles. It offers an economical, coherent and lucid account of a society under stress. Experts will have to turn at times to the articles for a fuller explanation of his methods and of his sources, but his argument here comprehends and extends everything he has said elsewhere. The book is easy to use and every chapter ends with a splendid summary of his argument. It is a mine of useful information. But it has to be used with caution. His definition of crucial terms and compilation of particular sets of figures are open to objection. Above all, his conclusions and figures are not comparable with those of other historians of northern counties, and it will be a principal purpose of this article to show how the approaches of the leading analysts of gentry behaviour are based on such distinct presuppositions that their books cannot be used side by side.[4] Beyond that I want to withdraw some of the criticisms of this kind of approach to civil war studies which I have advanced elsewhere, and to suggest some ways forward for all local studies in this period. Let us first, however, state Dr Blackwood's conclusions.

II

Dr Blackwood's book falls into four parts, neatly summarized by the four chapter headings: Lancashire on the Eve of the Civil War – Economy, Population and Gentry; the Cavalier and Roundhead Gentry; The Roundheads in Power; the Fate of the Cavaliers. There is also a brief concluding chapter.

In his opening chapter, Dr Blackwood discusses the 774 gentry families of Lancashire in 1642. He examines their distribution within the county (finding them thicker on the ground in the arable regions

3. E.g. 'The Economic State of the Lancashire Gentry on the Eve of the Civil War', *N(orthern) H(istory)*, XII (1976), 53–83; 'The Cavalier and Roundhead Gentry of Lancashire', *Transactions of the Lancashire and Cheshire Antiquarian Society*, LXXVII (1967), 23–46; 'The Catholic and Protestant Gentry of Lancashire during the Civil War Period', *Transactions of the Historic Society of Lancashire and Cheshire*, CXXVI (1976), 1–29. These are fuller (particularly on points of methodology and definition) than comparable sections of his book, and are not rendered redundant by its appearance.
4. In particular I want to discuss Dr Blackwood's work in relation to J.T. Cliffe, *The Yorkshire Gentry* (1969); C.B. Phillips, 'The Royalist North: The Cumberland and Westmorland Gentry 1642–1660', *NH*, XIV (1978), 169–92 and Dr Phillips' thesis, 'The Gentry of Cumberland and Westmorland, 1600–1665' (unpub. PhD thesis, Lancaster Univ. 1974); and M.D.G. Wanklyn, 'Landed Society and Allegiance in Cheshire and Shropshire in the First Civil War' (unpub. PhD thesis, Manchester Univ. 1976).

than in the 'semi-industrial' south-east of the shire), he finds that the great majority were mere or lesser gentry (gentlemen) rather than county or greater gentry (esquires, knights, baronets). There was extensive mobility into and out of the lower reaches of gentry society, and an expanding number of urban gentry. He finds local political and administrative power to have been concentrated in the hands of the non-recusant half of the greater gentry. He finds them 'economically heterogeneous' but generally very poor in comparison with other northern gentry (let alone southern ones). He finds them, as a group, much less enterprising, much less well educated than the elites of other counties. Seventy-two per cent of the greater gentry were descended from pre-Tudor gentry families and eighty-one per cent had settled in Lancashire before 1485 (a higher figure than for any other recorded county). Lancashire also had an unusually high rate of gentry marriages in which both partners were born within the shire. More than ninety per cent married daughters of gentry. The other distinctive characteristic was the very high proportion of recusant gentry – almost thirty per cent.

In the second chapter, Dr Blackwood examines allegiance in the civil war. Barely one third can be classified as being either Royalist or Parliamentarian, though Dr Blackwood is less clear than he might be about whether the rest are unknown or are demonstrably non-aligned. He has, however, found fewer divided families and fewer examples of men who changed sides than Dr Cliffe found in Yorkshire. Among those who did take sides, the Royalists enjoyed a numerical superiority of 2:1. He argues, however, that they failed to take advantage of this superiority for three reasons; many more Royalists than Parliamentarians left the county to fight elsewhere; there was much popular resistance to royalist recruitment; and a higher proportion of Parliamentarians were actively committed while much of the royalism was passive. An analysis of the two groups revealed little difference between them.

> Neither in terms of age, younger sons, lineage, status, office holding or economic state does there seem to be any marked distinction between the two groups. Two significant differences alone stand out. First, the parliamentarians appear to have been better educated than the royalists . . .[5] Secondly, most parliamentarian families were puritan and most

5. He does not add that if one excludes recusants from the royalist side (they were unable to take the oaths required to matriculate) the difference vanishes. Indeed both absolutely and proportionately protestant Royalists were more highly educated than were the Parliamentarians.

royalist families were papist. There seems little doubt that religion was the issue which principally divided the two sides.[6]

In the third chapter. Dr Blackwood does two things. Firstly he examines the men who ran local government in the period 1645–60 and contrasts them with the pre-war governors. He finds that the collapse of the power of the greater gentry was more delayed and less complete in Lancashire than elsewhere. And he adds a challenging *caveat*: 'the changes in local government lose some of their social significance when one notes the large number of non-gentry officers among the Lancashire royalist forces and realises that similar changes in government may have occurred if the Cavaliers had won the civil war[7] Secondly, he studies the active land market created by the confiscation and sale of Crown, Church and royalist land in the decade after 1646. He finds very few Lancashire Parliamentarians benefiting from this bonanza. Not many bought land, and those who did usually lost their purchases in the 1660s. Virtually no new families established themselves in Lancashire as a consequence of the Revolution and the rate of extinction of parliamentarian gentry families in the late seventeenth century was similar to the extinction rate of ex-royalist families.

In the fourth chapter, Dr Blackwood considers the other side of the same problem: 'the fate of the Cavaliers'. Very few families were ruined, either by the fines levied by Parliament, or even by the forced sale of all their estates. The great majority of royalist land was bought back by the families themselves either before or shortly after the Restoration. Many families died out or faded away (more often from pre-war indebtedness than from the effects of the civil war), but others benefit from improved rents, and better estate management in which ex-royalists and ex-parliamentarians engaged equally.

These conclusions invite comparisons with the work of other historians of the northern counties, most particularly Dr Cliffe's study of Yorkshire and Dr Phillips' work on Cumberland and Westmorland (both in print), and also Dr Wanklyn's unpublished thesis on Cheshire and Shropshire.[8] But there are major obstacles in the way of such comparisons. For each historian has recognized a series of definitional and methodological problems, and each has

6. Blackwood, *Lancs. Gentry*, p. 66.
7. Ibid., p. 101.
8. See works listed in note 4.

solved them in his own way. This has affected their results and called into question the usefulness of a comparative, quantitative approach to the social history of the Great Rebellion.

III

Who were the northern gentry? This simple little question plunges us immediately into a quagmire. The problems stem from conflicts within the sources. Some.men are inconsistently titled in different classes of documents of similar date, and many men were accorded status titles by their neighbours to which they had no formal legal right. Faced by these problems, each local historian has come up with his own empirical, rather mechanistic solution. Dr Cliffe sticks closely to the heralds' visitations and admits that, if he had allowed for self-ascription, he would have increased the number of Yorkshire gentry by more than 50 per cent.[9] Dr Blackwood and Dr Phillips both opt for a wider definition, accepting all those who are *consistently* styled gentlemen in the sources they have used.[10] In many ways, this seems the more satisfactory for reasons we will explore, but it has problems of its own. The most thorough discussion of the problem is contained in Dr Wanklyn's thesis, and he presents very sound reasons for finding the sources unhelpful for modern historians. 'Landed society was not a rigid hierarchy of autonomous groups but an organic whole in which differences of rank were bridged and blurred by factors like marriage and friendship.' He proposes instead that historians draw up a series of tests based on wealth, status, title, antiquity, offices and marriage and use these as a grid which will break landowners down into four or five fairly distinctive groups. At the bottom end this excludes many mere gentlemen (particularly those with a landed income of less than £40 p.a.). This proves a most useful analytical tool in discussing differences between Royalists and Parliamentarians, but it ought not to be used as a new model for understanding the social history of the period.[11]

How can the position be clarified? It seems to me that we should

---

9. For the clearest statement of Dr Cliffe's views, see A.M. Everitt, *Change in the Provinces* (Leicester, 1966), p. 56.
10. Blackwood, *Lancs. Gentry*, p. 4; Phillips, *NH*, XIV (1978) 68. They do differ from one another, however, since Dr Blackwood places great reliance on freeholders' books and accepts their ascription of gentility without corroboration, while Dr Phillips regards such books as unreliable.
11. Wanklyn, thesis, ch. 2. I should add that Dr Wankyln's analysis is of 'landed society'. He therefore considers yeomen – and husbandmen – freeholders as well as the gentry.

stand back from the tax rolls, court records, feet of fines etc. and try to find out from literary sources and polemical writing of all kinds what contemporaries thought made a gentleman a gentleman: to examine the concept of gentility. I believe this does help to explain the problems in the source material used by these historians. What follows is impressionistic and cannot be fully documented here, though I hope to prove my assertions elsewhere. Nor is much of my evidence distinctly northern. But let us see what happens if we assume that contemporaries knew what they were doing.[12]

First of all it must be stressed that the term 'gentry' had no formal or legal authority. It was a generic term coined by sixteenth-century Englishmen to embrace a series of quite separate social groups: the knights, esquires and gentlemen.[13] These groups were discerned as having a 'quality' in common – gentility or nobility[14] – which set them apart from other status groups, notably the yeomen. It is of major importance that contemporaries neither then nor later saw any need to coin a word to conjoin the 'mere' gentry and the yeomanry despite the obvious similarity of wealth and other characteristics which they shared. Whatever united them was exceeded by what distinguished them, while contemporaries did discern something which united the £40 p.a.[15] gentleman-freeholder and the £2,000 p.a. baronet.

'Gentility' then was a concept with no legal basis. It embraced three, later four[16] groups who derived their titles by different means (knights and baronets by the direct action of the monarch:

---

12. What follows is based on a reading of a wide variety of tracts and other writings about social and political obligations and rights written in the century and a half before 1640. The stimulus, and many of the ideas, are derived from an unpublished paper on conceptions of status given by the late John Cooper at Oxford in 1972. However, that paper was mainly concerned with the period 1450–1550.
13. The earliest use of the term as one of social reference cited in the *Shorter Oxford English Dictionary* is 1585.
14. Nobility is the quality shared by the peerage *(nobilitas major)* and the gentry *(nobilitas minor)* which set both apart from the commons. The term nobility properly meant peers plus gentry, but was increasingly used simply for the peerage. One term never used for the peerage before 1640 is 'aristocracy', a term used to describe a system of government, not a social group. The best general discussion of these questions is Sir A. Wagner, *English Genealogy* (rev. ed. 1972). part IV.
15. £40 p.a. from freehold land was the requirement of a knighthood. Dr Wanklyn advances several good reasons for believing that in the north midlands by the 1630s it was the minimum required for a claim to gentility.
16. With the creation of the baronetcy in 1611. See L. Stone, *The Crisis of the Aristocracy* (short paperback edn., Oxford, 1967), pp. 43–8.

esquires by the action of the heralds, etc.). The titles themselves are all terms which had originated and had had a specific meaning within a chivalric context which had passed away. All had lost their original purpose and resonance. All had represented the right to hold blocs of land in exchange for distinctive obligations and responsibilities. All the titles survived into an age when those obligations had been extinguished. The problem faced up to by humanist thinkers in the sixteenth century was whether to abrogate those redundant titles or to reinvest them with a new meaning. They opted for the latter course. By the early seventeenth century a new conception of gentility had totally supplanted the old one. Much less emphasis was now placed on the ranking within rural society, and the new concept was intended to give a common strength and purpose to all those titles. The new conception was an adaptation of Aristotle's definition of the citizen as the man whose wealth and leisure freed him from material preoccupations for the task of equipping himself to govern the *polis*, the state. Just so, the gentry were set free from working for a living, set free to devote themselves to the common weal. The gentry were the governors. The two crucial attributes of the gentry were independence and leisure. Independence meant an adequate income to support himself and his household, and also it meant freedom from the will of others (landlords, employers, etc.). Thus a gentleman owned and derived his income from freehold land or property. Leisure was freedom *from* material concerns and freedom *for* government and the cultivation of an equitable, judicious and responsible mind and temperament. Thus the ideal form of gentry wealth came from rents. Yet gentility is not a description of social function. It was a quality, a *capacity* to govern. The actual governors were drawn from among a large reservoir of capable men, the gentry. The greater gentry (esquires and above) governed their county as justices,[17] sheriffs, militia officers, etc. The mere 'gentlemen' had lesser responsibilities as lords of manors,[18] high constables, and more arguably as grand jurymen.[19]

17. Significantly, Dr Wanklyn found that a number of 'mere' gentlemen became esquires as soon as they joined the commission of the peace.
18. Indeed I would argue that while in general one can find gentlemen who are not lords of manors. One cannot easily find lords of manors who are not gentlemen – this despite the small size and attenuated jurisdiction of many manors.
19. I have argued the case for grand jurymen elsewhere: J.S. Morrill, *The Cheshire Grand Jury 1625–1659* (Leicester, 1976), pp. 15–20. Unfortunately, the case is less strong than I supposed. Dr Wanklyn finds that a majority of my gentlemen-jurymen were still called yeomen in such sources as the feet of fines and says that the assize and quarter session ascription of gentility to them was 'a mere legal fiction'.

This was an ideal, of course, and bore only a partial resemblance to reality, but it offered a comforting explanation to rulers and ruled of the unequal distribution of wealth, and it revived defunct titles. It was excellent as a concept but was hard to apply to individuals. A man was a gentleman if he had the manner, the breeding, the bearing, the independence of means and mind, to take responsibility for the welfare of his community. Wealth, birth, cousinage, life-style, education, would all play a part: there were few preconditions, but a certain 'score' derived from the sum of the above was necessary if a man was to be accepted by his neighbours as a gentleman. Seventeenth-century Englishmen may have had difficult in articulating what made a gentleman: but they knew one if they saw one.

Contemporaries differed in their perception of gentility in individuals – as our sources reveal. But they did care passionately about it: they took one another to court to prove or disprove entitlement;[20] they disrupted local government if due precedence was not observed; they feuded over it.[21]

Thus, I believe we must begin by assuming that seventeenth-century Englishmen meant what they said when they styled one another 'gentlemen' or 'esquire'. The heralds came infrequently and applied criteria which were outmoded and only remained useful because they were applied fraudulently. But they were inefficient and should not be treated as authoritative. Drs Blackwood and Phillips are surely right to include all those 'consistently' called gentlemen by their contemporaries – or at any rate they are right to do so in most respects. But their method has two weaknesses. It does not disclose the changing meaning of 'gentleman' during the century,

20. E.g. G.C. Squibb, *The High Court of Chivalry* (1958), pp. 161–75; A. Wagner, *English Genealogy* (Oxford, 2nd edn., 1972), pp. 124–6
21. Dr Wanklyn shows how both Shropshire and Cheshire local government was disrupted in the 1620s by a row over precedence between the counties' baronets and those who had recently purchased Irish peerages. The conflicts were partly defused in 1629 by Charles I's compromise which accorded precedence to the viscounts in return for their exclusion from all future commissions of the peace (Wanklyn, thesis, p. 84). I would now see this as the cause of the divisions which played so important a part in Cheshire politics between 1639 and 1642: J.S. Morrill, *Cheshire 1630–1660* (Oxford, 1974), pp. 20–69. Failure to note this compromise was one of the things which made me misleadingly write of the 'withdrawal' of Viscounts Cholmondeley, Kilmorey, etc. from local government in the 1630s. My book on Cheshire contains a number of similar inaccuracies, many of them genealogical. One of the spin-offs of the group-biography approach advocated by Drs Blackwood, Wanklyn etc., is that they are less likely to make the kind of misidentifications which have flawed my work.

and (connected with it) it uncritically accepts the intrusion of urban or pseudo-gentry.

The right of urban oligarchs, who owned little or no freehold land, to be styled gentleman was conceded by the end of the seventeenth century, but not earlier. The new conception of gentility outlined above had been devised to shore up rural society. No account was taken of the position of borough governors, yet many of the defining characteristics of the new gentry – wealth, literacy, discretion, responsibility for the welfare of their community – were equally appropriate to their situation. Furthermore, urban elites were recruited largely from among the younger sons of rural gentry families. No wonder they clamoured for and began to ascribe to themselves the same status as their rural cousins. They became what Professor Everitt has called the 'pseudo-gentry'.[22] Both Dr Blackwood and Dr Cliffe include them in their survey (they comprise 12 per cent of Dr Blackwood's families in 1642, and a higher proportion in 1664). Dr Wanklyn rigorously excludes them and for the period up to (at least) 1650 I think he is right. For the majority of the population and most rural gentry resisted the change. Indeed as it became more and more common practice, conservative country gentry coined a new term to describe themselves and to protect their distinct identity as a *rural* group: for the first time the word 'squire' is used as a term of social reference[23]

I have dwelt at length – and have been forced to rely on *obiter dicta* – not only to suggest an alternative way in which this problem of determining gentry status might be approached (for the work of local historians hitherto has been so unimaginative – a criticism as valid for my own work as that of others) but also because it has implications for all the statistical tables upon which the local studies under discussion are based. For it is generally agreed that those at the tail of the gentry are far less likely to have been actively involved in the civil war than those at the top of the gentry. Furthermore tables for average wealth, size of holdings, etc. or of the proportion of gentry with higher education, marriages within the county and ancient gentry lineage are seriously affected by the number of minor gentry included. In other words the work of Drs Cliffe, Phillips, Wanklyn and Blackwood are non-comparable. It is unfortunate that the others did not foresee

---

22. Everitt, *Change in the Provinces*, pp. 43–6; A.M. Everitt, 'Social Mobility in early Modern England', *Past and Present*, 33 (1966), 70–2.
23. *Shorter Oxf. Engl. Dictionary*.

Dr Wanklyn's practice of producing separate tables for each of his categories or gentry. This would have minimized the problem.

IV

Once the gentry have been identified, Dr Blackwood, like Dr Cliffe and Dr Wanklyn examines the nature and scale of their wealth (including both their pattern of income and expenditure) and their other activities: education, mobility, marriage, office-holding, etc. The sources for all these are of variable quality, and it must be said that Dr Blackwood is not always clear in this book about the problems involved. However, readers can be assured that if they turn to the relevant sections of the thesis from which the book is drawn, they will find the problems fairly faced. Two of his sets of tables call for further comment, however. These are the tables of gentry income from land, and the tables listing 'Puritans'.

There has been a lively debate in the pages of *Northern History* about the possibility of using sequestration and composition records as sources of gentry income. Dr Phillips argued that – in Cumbria at any rate – the composition papers seriously understate the income of the gentry. This understatement arises from not surprisingly deceit on the part of the defeated Royalists and also from connivance in that deceit by local officials . . .',[24] and he suggested that others had placed too much reliance upon these sources. Dr Cliffe responded to this challenge by a spirited defence of his use of such sources for Yorkshire, and warned us 'to be very cautious about generalisations based on the limited evidence available for a remote and sparsely populated area of northern England'.[25] He is strongly supported in this by Dr Wanklyn, who argues that the careful scrutiny of the valuations by county commissioners who had themselves adminis-tered the estates while they were under sequestration, and the very great danger to delinquents posed by professional informers, would tend to make all but the imprudent honest in their declarations.[26]

But there is strong support for Dr Phillips' arguments in this new book. Dr Blackwood argues that 'at least 32 out of 74 compounding Royalists appear to have undervalued their lands', many of them with great deceit and by a very substantial amount. He can find only

24. C.B. Phillips, 'The Royalist Composition Papers and the Landed Income of the Gentry: A Note of Warning from Cumbria', *NH*, XIII (1977) 161.
25. J.T. Cliffe, 'The Royalist Composition Papers and the Landed Income of the Gentry: A Rejoinder', *NH*, XIV (1978) 168.
26. Wanklyn, thesis, pp. 284–7.

seven examples of accurate composition statements.[27] Furthermore, it is only fair to point out that Dr Holiday, who has subjected the Yorkshire sequestration and composition papers to a scrutiny as detailed as that of Dr Cliffe, arrived at a much less sanguine conclusion. Pointing out that 28 per cent of all active Royalists remained undiscovered and unsequestered, stressing that the inefficiency of the system was such that many Royalists were not re-sequestered when they failed to pay their fines, demonstrating how inaccurate the comparable assessments by the Committee for the Advance of Money were, Dr Holiday takes a gloomy view of the efficiency of the Yorkshire sequestrators.[28] Thus the question remains open. There is nothing in my experience of the partiality, overburdened life and chaotic record-keeping of county committees to make me believe that the system would be well-administered. On the other hand, the empirical evidence of actual correlation of compounding records and other sources presented by Drs Cliffe and Wanklyn cannot be gainsaid. The issue is still open. Here it is most important to stress that some of our local studies make extensive use of this source and others do not. And this has its effect on their comparability.

Dr Blackwood will not trust composition papers. Yet he expresses confidence in subsidy rolls. Despite the fact that fewer and fewer names appear in the rolls as we move from the sixteenth to the seventeenth century, and despite the growing inefficiency of the subsidy as a form of parliamentary taxation, Dr Blackwood believes that assessments were regularly reviewed and can be used, for the gentry at least. His defence of this source both in the book and elsewhere is rather perfunctory, and his use of a multiplier of fifty for all gentry on the basis of an off-the-cuff remark by Lord Treasurer Cranfield and of three case studies is certainly an unusually weak link in his argument. Fortunately his use of the rolls is strongly supported by the arguments of Dr Wanklyn who has examined the problems far more thoroughly. He shows – to my surprise – how much care was taken to adjust the rolls to take account of changing ranking in county society. He suggests that individual gentry would not want to be seen to have been overtaken by others in the listing (it could be added that the payment was never a heavy burden on any of them). The hierarchy of income, as expressed in the rolls, is also reflected in

27. Blackwood, *Lancs. Gentry*, pp. 115–19.
28. P.G. Holiday, 'Royalist Composition Fines and Land Sales in Yorkshire, 1645–1665' (unpub. PhD thesis, Leeds Univ. 1966), ch. 1.

the distribution of offices and positions of merit. 'Subsidy rolls reveal, in a "rough and ready" fashion, the hierarchy of landed wealth.' This seems a plausible if unexpected fact, and it is used most imaginatively by Dr Wanklyn.[29] Dr Blackwood's usage seems to be over-precise, as dangerous as the reliance of others on composition papers, and it certainly undermines the confidence with which one can compare his tables for income with those derived from other sources for other counties. But as a rough way of comparing Royalist and Parliamentarian in terms of 'were the Royalists wealthier?', his figures are still usable. That is, his statement that fifty-three Royalists and only eighteen Parliamentarians had incomes of £500 p.a. or more is unreliable and should not be used for comparative purposes. But it probably remains reasonable to say that fifty-three of the wealthiest seventy-one families in Lancashire were Royalist.

V

I shall comment more briefly on Dr Blackwood's definition of 'Puritan' gentry. He writes:

> the following may be classed as Puritans: those appointing or financially assisting Puritan ministers; builders of chapels used for Puritan worship; members of puritanical religious committees; elders of Presbyterian classical assemblies; members of Independent congregations: and finally, those shown to be Puritans by their wills, correspondence or the opinions of their contemporaries.[30]

This is quite different from and inferior to the definition offered by Dr Cliffe,[31] so that their tables for religion are not comparable. In particular Dr Cliffe (surely correctly?) only uses evidence of puritanism which can be found before 1642. Dr Blackwood's inclusion of evidence from after 1646 cannot be defended. The events of the civil war, the formal abolition of episcopacy and the Book of Common Prayer, the response to the pressure of new events, all must have had a profound effect on many of the gentry.

More generally, of course, there is the question of whether a 'Puritan movement' existed in the early seventeenth century. There is no evidence that Blackwood's 114 puritan gentlemen saw themselves as such. Religious views are not easily divided into neat compartments (Laudian/Anglican/Puritan). Religious views form a spectrum. There are issues which tended to distinguish men one

29. Wanklyn, thesis, ch. 4.
30. Blackwood, *Lancs. Gentry*, pp. 27–8.
31. Cliffe, *Yorks. Gentry*, pp. 260–2.

from another: episcopacy/the existing church courts/the lawfulness
of the Prayer Book, etc. But none of these is straightforward.
Those who wished to abolish episcopacy or to re-write the Book
of Common Prayer may be fairly described as Puritans. But what
of those who wanted bishops' powers to be reformed and reduced
only, or those who wanted more freedom for individual ministers
to omit the 'noxious ceremonies' from the Prayer Book though
not the abolition of the Prayer Book? Demands for a preaching
ministry, for a tough line with recusants, for greater lay piety and
household religion were certainly attributes of the self-appreciating
godly or puritans, but were not restricted to such men.[32]

Once more, I do not want to say that this invalidates all Dr Blackwood's findings. His 'puritan' gentry certainly include men with
a wide variety of beliefs, and many who would not have seen
themselves, or been seen by their contemporaries, as puritans. The
number and 'group profile' of his puritans differ from that which he
would have got had he used the definitions of other local historians.
But his figures, though blurred and distorted by his definition, are still
useful in their way. Within his puritan group are a significant body
of men who did want to bring the English Church into line with
Continental or the Scottish models, and their existence is important.

VI

How easy is it to decide who is a Royalist and who is a Parliamentarian? How meaningful is it to draw up two lists and to compare
the size and composition of the two groups? Drs Blackwood, Cliffe,
Wanklyn and (with reservations) Phillips, believe it is feasible and
meaningful. I have, in the past, strenuously denied it, but Drs Blackwood and Wanklyn have recently forced me to make a partial
retraction. Let me briefly summarize what I have said elsewhere.[33]

1. Because Parliament won the civil war and instigated proceedings against all their opponents, the sources are very unequal
and stronger for identifying Royalists than Parliamentarians.

2. Many neutrals and timid collaborators, and even some victims
of internal divisions within the parliamentarian cause, were wrongly

<hr/>

32. For gentry puritanism in the North before the civil war, see also R.C. Richardson,
Puritanism in North-West England (Manchester, 1972), and additional comments by
J.S. Morrill, 'Puritans and the Church in the Diocese of Chester', *NH*, VIII (1973).
145–55.
33. Morrill, *Cheshire 1630–1660*, ch. 2: J.S. Morrill. *The Revolt of the Provinces* (1976),
passim: also J.S. Morrill and R.N. Dore, 'The Allegiance of the Cheshire Gentry in
the Great Civil War', *Trans. Lancs and Chesh. Antiq. Soc.*, LXXVII (1967), 47–76.

treated as Royalists after the wars and appear in the lists of Royalists produced by recent historians. Some of these would undoubtedly have been called Parliamentarians by the Royalists had they won the civil war and instigated similar sequestration proceedings.[34]

3.   The records tell us a great deal about a man's activity, much less about his beliefs. Many men are likely to have followed the line of least resistance, accepting any command from either side which came in due form. or else doing what they were told because they were surrounded by committed supporters of one side who threatened to destroy their property or seize their family and themselves if they refused to cooperate.

All these problems exist and they weaken the case for the sufficiency of the kind of analysis presented by Dr Blackwood. But they do not make the exercise pointless. Nor should such arguments be overstressed. The sources for Royalists and Parliamentarians are not as unequal as I once supposed.[35] A more thorough and prolonged study than I attempted can produce a fairly balanced list and can minimize the difficulties raised in point (2) though it will not eradicate them. Point (3) is a substantial one and certainly affects the picture, and I shall return to it. Furthermore, whatever a man's motives, however little they had to do with actual commitment to the victory of king or Parliament, however much to do with self-preservation or the restoration of peace in his own area only, and so on, it is not necessarily valueless to examine what characteristics were shared by all those who in fact *acted* for one side or the other. Perhaps most of the gentry of northern England followed the line of least resistance. But that in itself may be significant. They could have chosen a different if more difficult path.

The conclusions reached by local historians of the North who have attempted the approach advocated by Dr Blackwood are unspectacular but important. Let me draw out the ones which seem to me unimpeachable.

1.   In every case except that of Cheshire, the number of Royalist

34. I have offered a case study in 'William Davenport and the "Silent Majority" of early Stuart England', *Journal of the Chester Archaeological Society*, LVIII (1975), 115–30.
35. I first made this statement on the basis of research I undertook as an undergraduate and uncritically retained it in my book on *Cheshire 1630–1660*, pp. 70–4. Dr Wanklyn rightly takes me to task for this overstatement in his thesis, ch. 3, where he points out the fullness of the parliamentary administrative records, particularly for Cheshire, in the 1640s. These afford information about both active and passive Parliamentarians.

gentry considerably outnumbered the number of Parliamentarian gentry.

	Royalist	Parliamentarian
Cumberland and Westmorland[36]	77	21
Lancashire[37]	272	138
Cheshire[38]	117	138
Shropshire[39]	85	64
Yorkshire[40]	242	128

2. The Royalists are particularly strong among those with the highest income, largest estates and the largest share of county offices. However, it is possible that the king's progress through the North of England and his personal appeal and commands to these leading gentry in the autumn of 1642 was responsible for this pattern.

3. The Royalists received substantial support from the Catholic community, far more than is implied by the work of Dr Lindley.[41] Over one third of the Yorkshire, and almost two-thirds of the Lancashire, royalist families were Catholic;[42] In both those counties and in Cheshire a much higher proportion of the Catholic than of the Protestant gentry were actively royalist.

4. No other county study has confirmed Dr Cliffe's finding that the prospering (as against the wealthiest) gentry tended to be parliamentarian. This has been looked for in all the other studies, but

36. Phillips, *NH*, XIV (1978), 175. I have added together the sixty-five 'Royalists' and twelve 'uncertain Royalists'. His list is of 'heads of families by allegiance as determined in 1644'.
37. Blackwood, *Lancs. Gentry*, p. 47. These figures are for all gentry, including heads of families, heirs and younger sons. In a separate table, p. 46, he divides the gentry families into 177 Royalist, 91 Parliamentarian, 24 side-changers and divided. He bases his lists on political behaviour between 1642 and 1648.
38. Wanklyn, thesis. ch. 3. He bases his tables on the allegiance of the effective head of gentry households. I have combined his totals of 'active' and 'moderate' Royalists and Parliamentarians. He only includes those whose political behaviour can be observed in the course of 1642–3.
39. Ibid.
40. Cliffe, *Yorks. Gentry*, p. 336. These figures are of royalist and parliamentarian *families* over the period 1642–8.
41. K.J. Lindley, 'The Part Played by Catholics', in *Politics, Religion and the English Civil War*, ed. B.S. Manning (1973), pp. 127–76.
42. Blackwood, *Lancs. Gentry*, p. 65; Cliffe, *Yorks. Gentry*, p. 334. Blackwood offers more precise criticisms of Lindley's work in his Oxford D. Phil. thesis, pp. 182–5. For further stress on the importance of Catholics, see P.R. Newman, 'Catholic Royalist Activists in the North', *Recusant History*, XIV (1977), 26–7; he demonstrates how large a proportion of the army officers were recusants. See, however, Phillips, *NH*, XIV, 175, where he reasserts that 'Cumberland and Westmorland were not strongholds of papist superstition' and that most papists were inactive in the war.

in vain. Dr Wanklyn finds that parliamentarianism was particularly strong among the families who had risen since 1540 (in Shropshire this was also true of cadet lines)[43] and among those just not wealthy or prestigious enough to have secured themselves in the commission of the peace and other leading positions, but this in turn has not been found in other counties (though the subtlety of Dr Wanklyn's methodology may have helped him here).

5.   No other major distinction has been found between the Royalists and Parliamentarians.

All these seem to me to be useful and viable conclusions, as long as we do not conclude that this is the only way to approach the problem of gentry allegiance, and as long as we are careful to put them in perspective. A majority of the northern gentry did help the king. It does not mean that a majority wanted the king to win an out-right victory; that is an entirely different question. A majority of the Catholic gentry did help the king and without that help the Royalists would barely have outnumbered the Parliamentarians (or would they? perhaps fewer Protestants helped the king because he gave so much power and influence to recusants). It may be that most of these studies have been comparing the wrong things. Dr Wanklyn suggests that activists on both sides had a great deal in common which distinguished them from those who stayed out of the war. Most of those with the greatest wealth, most of those who were prospering, most of those who had diversified their income by engaging in trade or the exploitation of mineral resources were active on one side or the other. The declining, debt-ridden gentry, those without such resources and those who had not done well from the buoyant land market, tended to be inactive.[44] His suggestion appears to be true of other counties, but cannot be easily extrapolated from the tables presented by Drs Blackwood and Cliffe.

One final caveat inhibits direct comparison of the tables in the several books and theses. They differ in the time-scale with which they seek out evidence of royalism and parliamentarianism. Dr Cliffe's tables 'cover the period of the two Civil Wars 1642–8'.[45] So do Dr Blackwood's. Dr Phillips produces separate tables for allegiance in 1644 and 1648,[46] while Dr Wanklyn confines himself to the period up to the end of 1643, arguing that the danger of

---

43. Wanklyn, thesis, ch. 4.
44. Ibid.
45. Cliffe, *Yorks. Gentry*, p. 336 n. 2.
46. Arguing that it was only in 1644 that the gentry made meaningful choices and that the second civil war was a new and distinct conflict.

including collaborationists as activists grows greater as the war proceeds. The assumption that the first and second civil wars can be treated as a unit is a very poor one, for the issues are arguably totally different and in some ways unrelated.[47] In this, as in many other respects. Dr Wanklyn's instincts seem sounder. Meanwhile, we find once again that it would be dangerous to attempt to use the resulting figures for anything more than the most general of purposes.

VII

The quantitative approach then, has its value. But so, I believe, does the approach I have hitherto adopted, and which is evident in my book on Cheshire in the mid seventeenth century. There I argued that the most fruitful approach to the origins of the civil war by an analysis of local government and politics in the years before 1642. I found two groups of gentry apparently antipathetic and engaged in a struggle for local supremacy. What divided the two groups were essentially local questions. The course of *local* politics between 1640 and 1642 led to one of these groups supporting the king in the civil war, while the other groups tried to neutralize the county, to keep it out of the war. This second group was split asunder by short-run factors in the autumn of 1642, an important section attaching itself to the royalist party, the majority forming the 'moderate' wing of the parliamentarian movement in the county, linking up with a radical group of minor gentry under the patronage of Sir William Brereton. I argued that the groupings in 1642 were unpredictable and unlikely and that if any deep socio-economic divisions existed within the gentry they would exist in the groupings of 1630 or 1640, not those of 1642.[48] This approach has not been attempted for any other northern county, but it was itself modelled upon Professor Everitt's study of Kent, and it has since been successfully attempted for Somerset, Sussex and the counties of East Anglia,[49] and in a

47. For recent reinterpretations of the second civil war, see Morrill, *Revolt of Provinces*, section 3, and R. Ashton, *The English Civil War 1603–1649*, pp. 317–28.
48. Morrill, *Cheshire 1630–1660*, ch. 2 particularly pp. 70–4.
49. A.M. Everitt, *The Community of Kent and the Great Rebellion* (Leicester, 1966); A. Fletcher, *A County Community at Peace and War: Sussex 1600–1660* (1975); D. Underdown, *Somerset in the Civil Wars and Interregnum* (Newton Abbot, 1972); C. Homes, *The Eastern Association in the English Civil War* (Cambridge, 1975). Two recent theses which adopt a similar approach are R.H. Silcock, 'County Government in Worcestershire 1603–1660' (unpub. PhD thesis, London Univ. 1975); and C.G. Durston, 'Berkshire and its County Gentry, 1625–49' (unpub. PhD thesis, Reading Univ. 1977), which also includes a very thorough series of about thirty individual biographies and a group profile.

second book I have proposed a scheme for the whole of England.[50]
One vital point which has emerged is the strength of neutralism in
1642. Many men subsequently to fight on different sides could be
seen making common cause to limit the spread of the war to their
area, and such men seemed to have so much in common that to see
them – once events made neutralism impracticable – as having chosen
sides by any criteria testable by group analysis seems implausible.
Since there were formal attempts at neutrality in Cheshire, Lancashire
and Yorkshire,[51] and similar sentiments were clearly very strong in
Cumberland and Westmorland (Dr Phillips sees these counties before
1644 as 'essentially a neutral area in which the royalists, rather than
the parliamentarians, tried to recruit support'),[52] this kind of approach
may appear incompatible with that adopted by Drs Blackwood, Cliffe
and Wanklyn. But the sufficiency of this approach is itself open to
question. Firstly, the Cheshire pattern (where groups of gentry
who had been allied in local politics in the sixteen-twenties and
thirties, who had made common cause in the elections on 1640,
in the campaign over episcopacy in 1640–1 and in the struggle to
neutralize the the county in 1642, split asunder at the last) may have
been untypical. Elsewhere the groupings of 1642 may well have
corresponded more closely with those of 1640. Secondly, a case can be
made (though I do not accept it) that neutralism has been overstated.
Dr Wanklyn, for example argues that the group I would call 'neutrals'
were men who 'knew which side they would join once the die was
cast, but strained every nerve to keep the peace, for fear of the effect
war might have on the traditional pattern of rural society'.[53] This is
certainly an arguable case, and one difficult to overthrow. Nonetheless
I would want to say that such men should not be placed in the same
card-index as those committed to strain every nerve to give victory
to king or Parliament. What the moderates who would join the king
and the moderates who would join Parliament shared with each other
was greater than what each shared with the committed Royalists and
the committed Parliamentarians. It is at this stage that I believe that
a model such as the one used by Drs Blackwood and Cliffe in
particular is inadequate. They define Royalists and Parliamentarians
by their actions and not by their intentions. If we could establish the

50. Morrill, *Revolt of Provinces*, section 1.
51. Ibid.: B.S. Manning, 'Neutrals and Neutralims in the English Civil War' (unpub.
    D. Phil. thesis, Oxford Univ. 1957), ch 2.
52. Phillips, *NH*, XIV, 173.
53. Wanklyn, thesis, p. 199.

names of those who believed either in the royalist cause for its own sake or in the parliamentarian cause for the achievement of a godly reformation in Church and State, then we might find clear distinctions in the profile of each group. Such listings would not be exhaustive. Their incompleteness is inevitable given that the sources are so often silent or misleading on questions of motivation. But they need not be exhaustive. A cross-section of each party is adequate. Here again, the approach pioneered by Professor Everitt and followed up by myself, Professor Underdown and others, can help. Family papers and county committee papers allow historians to identify the radical groups *within* parliamentarian movements who are dedicated to victory and to a godly reformation.[54] It would be possible to draw up lists of such men for many counties and to subject each to group analysis. Similar groups could be identified *within* the royalist parties. The remaining members of both parties could then be examined independently and together and would quite probably look very much alike and in clear contrast to the militants. In this way the quantitative and the 'localist' approaches could be harmonized. I have no doubt that in the North and West of England, the committed Royalists would appear as powerful groups of leading gentry, including dominant elements within the ruling elite bound together by a fear of social revolution from below and the need to preserve hierarchy in Church and State allied, with differing degrees of discomfort to leading recusant families; and that the parliamentarian radicals would be led by one or two leading gentry, but otherwise dominated by gentlemen of middling wealth, often kept just outside the governing circle, often of recent gentry origin, with very strong commitment not simply to a reversal of Laudian innovation, but to the radical reform of the Elizabethan settlement and to the creation of a society influenced by godly Christian values and integrity. It must be stressed, however, that such an interpretation is, in my view, likely to hold true only of the North and West.[55]

54. By this definition committed Royalists and Parliamentarians are not the same as active Royalists or Parliamentarians. Those who held office or commissions may well have been following a line of least resistance and obeying orders.
55. In East Anglia, for example, control of the parliamentarian movement remained in the hands of a moderate 'Puritan' establishment which looked initially for little social or economic reform and for a limited reform of the Church.

VIII

These 'honest radicals'[56] were drawn not only from among the gentry but also from among the yeomen and urban 'middling sorts'. And they call into question an *assumption* made by all the historians whose work has been under review here that it is the gentry alone who determine the political alignment of a county in the civil war. Such a view has recently come under attack, most notably from Dr Manning, but also from Dr Malcolm.[57] It is obviously the case that the 'middling sort' were capable of independent action and that many of them did not wait upon the gentry's decisions. Similarly, the idea that the labourers, cottagers and others blindly followed their landlords' and masters' lead needs important qualification. In my view, Dr Manning raises a legitimate question, though he does not provide a satisfying answer. Much more work needs to be done on the question of non-gentry allegiance. Meanwhile, I would be surprised if in fact the role of the 'middling sort' is decisive. For it seems likely that the 'middling sort' were as divided as were the gentry. The yeomanry, clothworkers and urban craftsmen certainly included some very highly motivated and committed radicals (particularly on religious questions), perhaps the most highly motivated groups on either side. But equally there is plenty of evidence that these very social groups contained some of the most committed neutral and anti-war sentiment. Not all grand juries were packed, yet grand juries are frequently to be found initiating neutralist positions and movements both in 1642 and 1645; the Clubmen risings of 1645, whether they are treated as crypto-royalist or neutralist were the creation of the middling sort; there is no evidence that minor officials (constables, churchwardens, etc.) obstructed royalist administration more than they did parliamentarian, and in many counties assemblies of freeholders agreed to vote extensive contributions to the royalist cause. Nonetheless, while a majority of those below the gentry probably accepted the leadership of the old elite, and while a majority probably continued to look for the continuance of known ways in Church and State, there is clearly more work to be done on the extent and nature of popular movements during and after the war. None of

56. The term is David Underdown's in his article, '"Honest Radicals" in the Counties, 1642–1649', in *Puritans and Revolutionaries*, D.H. Pennington and K.V. Thomas eds. (1978), pp. 186–205.
57. B.S. Manning, *The English People and the English Revolution* (1976); J. Malcolm, 'The English People and the Crown's Cause, 1642–1646' (unpub. PhD thesis, Brandeis Univ. 1977). A crucial part of her argument appears in 'A King in Search of Soldiers: Charles I in 1642', *HJ*, XXI (1978), 251–73.

the studies of the northern gentry so far (including my own) faces up to these problems.[58]

IX

This article has concentrated on the more debatable issues raised by Dr Blackwood's book. It is clear that I believe that its conclusions are not always convincing, and that care must be taken not to treat his conclusions as strictly comparable with those in similar studies. But it is only proper that I conclude by stressing that a great deal of his work is unexceptionable, convincing and important.

In Lancashire, as elsewhere, the old elite lost its control over county government, but only after 1649. As Dr Blackwood says, 'power shifted not from one class to another – from the gentry to the middling sort – but within a class: from the greater to the lesser gentry'.[59] The parliamentarian movement in Lancashire was not divided against itself as it was elsewhere. There is no evidence of 'war' or 'peace' parties, no major divisions over religion – the county was unique in the speed and effectiveness with which a classical presbyterian structure was created after 1646 – and no backlash in 1648 despite (or because of?) the Scots invasion to restore Charles II. Almost half the magistrates throughout the 1650s were drawn from the pre-war magisterial groups, and many of those who disappeared from government in the 1650s did so because they refused to serve. There were no major purges. Only eight men were nominated to commissions of the peace throughout the decade, less than in the comparable period before 1640 and after 1660 and a tiny number compared with the 262 nominated for Yorkshire, for example.[60] The exclusion of old families in Lancashire was of a lesser order than that of Cumberland, Westmorland or Cheshire,[61] or many counties in the South. On the other hand, there was no 'recovery' by old governing families in the later 1650s that occurred elsewhere.[62]

---

58. This takes up material from Morrill, *Revolt of Provinces* and 'Country Squires and "Middling Sorts" in the Great Rebellion', below, ch. 15.
59. Blackwood, *Lancs. Gentry*, p. 161.
60. G.C.F. Forster, 'County Government in Yorkshire during the Interregnum', *NH*, XII (1976), 102: Cf. C.B. Phillips, 'County Committees and Local Government in Cumberland and Westmorland, 1642–1660', *NH*, V (1970), 34–66: Everitt, *Community of Kent*, pp. 296–7: G.E. Aylmer, 'Who Was Ruling Herefordshire from 1645 to 1662?', *Trans. of the Woolhope Club*, XL (1972), 373–87.
61. Phillips, *NH*, V, 56–60; Morrill, *Cheshire 1630–1660*, pp. 223–5, 233–4, 256–8, 327–8.
62. See D. Underdown, 'Settlement in the Counties', in *The Interregnum*, G.E. Aylmer (ed.) pp. 165–82.

The pattern of land sales, too, is thoroughly argued and convincingly presented. Not only did few parliamentarian gentry acquire land in the 1650s, rather more suffered from the high taxation and troubled economy of those years. The largest single group of declining gentry in late seventeenth-century Lancashire were those who had held office after the Civil War and been denied it after the Restoration. The Royalists on the other hand are shown to have recovered remarkably quickly from the confiscation and/or sale of their estates. Dr Thirsk showed two decades ago that 70 per cent of the properties sold in the Home Counties under the Commonwealth were regained by the original owners or their heirs before or after the Restoration, and Dr Holiday has shown that an even higher proportion was regained in Yorkshire (82 per cent).[63] But Dr Blackwood's figures are particularly important since more Lancastrians were included in the Acts of Sale than were gentry from any other county (ninety-eight gentry and two peers). Ninety-three of these were recusants whom it might be thought had less reserves and more difficulties in raising mortgages than protestant gentry. Yet 81 per cent of all pieces of land (and over 90 per cent by value) were recovered.[64] In striking contrast, the earls of Derby lost forever two-thirds of their Lancashire holdings, principally because a great deal of it had been bought by their tenants who refused to cooperate with the 8th Earl in the 1660s.[65]

In his final pages, Dr Blackwood examines the prospering and declining gentry of the late seventeenth century. He finds that the number of gentry was declining both absolutely and as a proportion of the population and that the turnover of gentry families was greater than in the early decades of the century. What seems to have happened is that a very large number of families were extinguished by failure in the male line.[66] Furthermore there was very little movement

---

63. P.G. Holiday, 'Land Sales and Repurchases in Yorkshire after the Civil War', *NH*, V (1970), 67–92: J. Thirsk, 'The Sales of Royalist Lands During the Interregnum', *Economic History Review*, 2nd ser V (1953), 188–207.
64. In a large proportion of cases – 28 per cent of the pieces of land, 14 per cent of the value of land – it is unclear whether the property was regained before or after 1660 (Blackwood, *Lancs. Gentry*, p. 126).
65. Ibid., pp. 130–6.
66. A similar demographic catastrophe overtook the gentry of Glamorganshire, where the proportion of childless heads of families rose steeply to over one third and the average number of children per gentry family fell from 5.0 in the decades before 1640 to 2.26 in the years 1640–80 and 2.58 in the years 1681–1729: J.P. Jenkins, 'A Social and Political History of the Glamorgan Gentry, *c.* 1650–1770' (unpub. PhD thesis, Cambridge Univ. 1978), ch. 2, particularly pp. 67–8.

into the gentry from below. Most of the manors sold in the later decades were brought by existing gentry. Among the rest, pre-war indebtedness appears to have been a more significant cause of failure than the burdens of sequestrations, compositions and sale. Former royalist and parliamentarian families were extinguished at almost the same rate, but it was the minor, non-aligned families who suffered most. Only 26 per cent of the 465 families survived to the end of the century. On the other hand, there were plenty of prosperous gentry. Most of the land sold by Lancashire gentry in this period was bought by other gentry, and more efficient estate management was the key to their success. However this was less a sign of the introduction of 'progressive' farming techniques than of the ease with which entry fines could be raised in a period when population was growing. Former Royalists were at least as successful as former Parliamentarians in this respect. This is a pioneering study and raises important questions about what must be considered the dark age of English social history between 1660 and 1740. It must be concluded that while Dr Blackwood's study offers very little comfort to those who want to see the civil war as being a social revolution in its causes, it offers none at all to those who seek to portray it as one in its consequences.

Provincial Squires and 'Middling Sorts' in the Great Rebellion

In the mid-1950s Dr Manning completed a much admired and often cited thesis on neutralism in the English civil war. It has influenced the development of writing on the period in several respects: it has helped to overcome the old presumption that there was an essential division between two ideologically distinct parties; it drew attention to the existence of organized anti-war groups like the Clubmen; and, not least, it gave an enormous impetus to the study of individual county communities, since it revealed the strength of attachments to local institutions. As he wrote, 'the great importance of the county unit and the fact that it commanded a loyalty which could compete with wider loyalties is shown by the widespread efforts to keep individual counties out of the war.'[1] Mr Fletcher's book is very much an heir of the tradition which Dr Manning helped to shape. *The English People and the English Revolution* (1976) is, however, a total denial of those themes. Or rather it ignores them. There is no entry in the index of his book to neutrals or neutralism; none of the theses or books which have developed the role of provincialism in the 1640s is cited except for Professor Everitt's work on Kent, from which Dr Manning draws information without reference to, or a questioning of, Everitt's essential arguments.[2] Instead, Dr Manning sets out to re-establish the English civil war as a class struggle. The great bulk of the book consists of a narrative (punctuated by short analytical statements) of the rise of a popular movement in the years 1640–3. In these

---

1. B.S. Manning, 'Neutrals and neutralism in the English Civil War', Oxford D.Phil. thesis 1957, introduction.
2. A.M. Everitt, *The Community of Kent and the Great Rebellion 1640–60* (Leicester, 1970).

years, Dr Manning believes, the gentry-elite divided against itself and allowed the 'middling sort' to seize the initiative and to launch a revolutionary offensive 'impelled by hostility towards the nobility and gentry and richer classes, and this converted constitutional, political and religious issues into class conflict'. There is no doubt that this book will force historians to look again at the civil war. It demands that they re-examine the cosy assumptions about the gentry's control of events in the early stages and that they re-examine the aims and unity of the yeomanry and craftsmen. It is a book which shows up the unwillingness of many civil war historians to ask certain questions. But Dr Manning's answers to these questions are totally unconvincing. He is unconvincing not because there is no validity in what he wants to argue, but because he uses the wrong sources for such a study, because he handles these sources uncritically, and because there are very evident confusions in his conceptual framework.

The book is based on an impressive range of printed sources. In particular Dr Manning has an unrivalled knowledge of civil war tracts and newspapers. He could have written a superb book on civil war propaganda, that is, on the convenient half-truths set forth by the polemicists on the two extremes. But he cannot establish the actual behaviour of particular social groups on the basis of propaganda tracts and the subsequent memoirs of men all of whom looked back on the early 1640s with jaundiced eyes. This is the essential reason for the failure of this book. By ignoring the local sources, by ignoring the facts and figures about who did what which are plentifully available in local studies, and by relying on what some men wanted other men to believe, and what old men later wrote down with the wisdom of hindsight and to satisfy later objectives, Dr Manning has got at cross-purposes with himself. Certainly he has shown, more fully than ever before, the extent and vehemence of popular agitation in London in 1640–2 (this takes up five of the ten chapters). He has shown that this affected the actions and reactions of members of parliament and caused palpitations in many manor houses. He has shown that there were widespread disturbances in *some* parts of the country. It is not certain that there were more than at other times, but they were more widely reported and they did cause more alarm. But he has not shown, and on the basis of printed sources alone cannot show, that the various isolated groups had come together, seized the initiative, and established a revolutionary programme based on class interests. Similarly, an *account* of the depression in the cloth industry, virtually all the references to which are from recent secondary works, is not sufficient basis for the assertion that 'the craftsmen were politicised by their struggles against the merchant oligarchies of town and company and grew accustomed to organisation, agitation and radical notions' (p. 150). Certainly it is possible that the struggle of the peasants and craftsmen against the erosion of traditional rights may have combined with active puritanism to 'give them status and the ability to express their identity as a separate class' (p. 162), but Dr Manning must find precise evidence of this from the mouths of the men themselves. The sources for a study of popular attitudes in the 1630s and 1640s do exist in abundance in the depositions, examinations and other records of innumerable cases at quarter sessions, assizes, King's Bench and Star Chamber. The Thomason Tracts simply will not yield up answers to the questions Dr Manning wants to ask. Similarly, Dr Manning frequently cites Baxter, Corbet, Clarendon and other chroniclers without any attempt to face the harsh historiographical problems involved. Clarendon, in particular, so often demonstrably wrong in matters of fact, and writing his works for a particular purpose and in the light of experiences which affected what he wanted to believe about the course of the revolution, simply cannot be used as a spontaneous and shrewd observer of the events of 1640–2.

Similar problems arise when Dr Manning turns to analyse the outbreak of the civil war which he describes as a conflict between 'the bigger peasants and richer craftsmen [who] formed an emerging capitalist class' and the bulk of the gentry, followed blindly by their dependents. Of course he acknowledges that many gentlemen did support parliament, but in general he sees them as following behind the real revolutionaries. Thus 'in Suffolk there was a powerful popular movement that declared support for parliament, and the prominent county families, led by Sir Nathaniel Barnardiston, continued in power because they also opted for parliament in the civil war' (p. 180).[3] He also concedes that 'not all, nor a majority of the "middle sort of people" supported the parliamentarian party, but those who did were the ones whose actions and aspirations influenced events'. But he goes on 'the conflict was precipitated by popular risings against sections of the nobility and gentry' (preface). And for the greatest part

3. For an altogether more convincing and detailed view of the emergence of the parliamentarian movement in Suffolk see, C. Holmes, *The Eastern Association in the English Civil War* (Cambridge, 1974), particularly pp. 48–52, 63–8. This book appeared twelve months before the dated preface to Dr Manning's book and had existed as a widely-read thesis since 1969. David Underdown's book on Somerset, which also necessarily affects things Manning says about the west country, appeared in spring 1973 and my own book on Cheshire in spring 1974.

of the book he ignores all those of the middle sort who were not active for parliament. This super-selectivity destroys the value of his argument. It is important that parliamentary pamphleteers claimed the middling sort as their own and that, for reasons of their own, royalist pamphleteers accepted the story. But that does not make it true. On p. 18 Dr Manning says that 'some gentlemen believed that parliament had been overawed by the mob . . . but it was not just propaganda, for these lords and gentlemen became royalists precisely because they believed this'. This does not mean that the propaganda was true; just that it was successful. The pamphlets do not reveal social reality, only what people wanted to believe. Many county studies have examined the allegiance of the middling sort. They show, certainly, that a minority in many (but not all) counties were radicals who volunteered for service with parliament. In a few counties they seized the initiative (Somerset is one of them; and Dr Manning's study of Lincolnshire certainly suggests that that may be another). But in most counties they played, and were content to play, a secondary role. Furthermore, the rest of the middling sort were not apathetic: both in 1642 and again in 1645–8 many of them took the initiative in demanding a halt to the war, or at least the neutralization of their area. Clubmen risings, led by, indeed initiated by, the middling sort were more numerous and far more imposing than any provincial Leveller organizations. It was the middling sort who generally formed the grand juries at quarter sessions and assizes which were far more frequently involved in denouncing radical ideas than in promoting them.[4] It seems likely that in most counties, the proportion of royalists, neutrals and parliamentarians among the middling sorts is broadly similar to the proportion among the gentry. Different methods, more sophisticated analysis, may yet vindicate Dr Manning's argument that a minority of the yeomanry and craftsmen were impelled by class antagonisms. But local studies have not done so as yet. However, there is a little support for his case. There is evidence that the parliamentarians recruited *volunteer* soldiers more easily in 1642 than did the king.[5] Those parliamentarians committed to a vision of a godly Reformation and uncorrupt commonwealth were probably the most highly motivated men on either side, and may well have been drawn heavily from the middling sorts, but they were a tiny minority.

4. Cf. J.S. Morrill, *The Revolt of the Provinces* (1976), pp. 81–4, 125–6, and J.S. Morrill, *The Cheshire Grand Jury 1625–59* (Leicester, 1976), pp. 33–45, which includes comment on grand jury activity elsewhere.
5. See, for example, J. Malcolm, *Caesar's Due* (London, 1982), ch. 2.

Dr Manning is particularly anxious to stress the radicalism of industrial workers, and talks particularly about the clothing areas and the industrial villages of the midlands. In both cases he is highly selective. For example, although he talks about 'the midlands' for several pages (pp. 199–206) during a section headed 'the Resistance of the Industrial Districts', he deals almost exclusively with Birmingham and Coventry, relying on pamphlets written to stir the imaginations and conceits of parliament's supporters. Birmingham was indeed actively opposed to the king. So were other towns in the industrial west midlands (Walsall, Tipton, Wednesbury). But there were other Black Country towns also relatively free from guild controls and with similar economic and social organizations which were equally vehemently royalist – Wolverhampton, Handsworth, Willenshall and Bilston being clear examples. Most of the workers in the nineteen iron foundries of the area supported the king, and the colliers of Cannock Chase went off to help Rupert to mine the walls of parliamentarian Lichfield. A majority of the parishes were evenly divided in allegiance (e.g. Cannock, Sedgely, Aldridge and Shenstone). Mr John Sutton's painstaking local researches show clearly that in these villages divisions cut across 'class' lines, not along them.[6]

This book will make us question whether the middling sort meekly followed the lead of the gentry in 1640–3. It does not convince when it goes to the other extreme. Thus: 'what was happening was the people were choosing between one set of rules and another . . . and this meant that power lay with the people' (p. 180). By only looking at those of the middling sort who supported the parliamentarians, he misrepresents what happened. Since in every county the middle sort divided among themselves, that power, if it existed, was dissipated.

There is a basic conceptual confusion in the author's social analysis. It is best expressed in his own words:

> there was emerging from amongst 'the middle sort of people' a new class – a middle class or capitalist class: the bigger farmers (or yeomen) who produced primarily for the market rather than for subsistence and employed wage labourers; and the greater craftsmen who relied more on hired labour than on the labour of themselves and their families, put out work to smaller craftsmen. . . . There were inherent conflicts of interests and open antagonisms between these bigger farmers and the mass of small peasants, and between the greater craftsmen and the mass

6. I am grateful to Mr John Sutton, who has for many years studied allegiance in Staffordshire, for confirming my own impressions, for drawing my attention to additional references, and for showing me the tables and maps which conclusively demonstrate the above pattern.

of small craftsmen; but the government of Charles I and the existing social, political and religious regime antagonised these bigger farmers and larger craftsmen and led them to feel more in common with the main body of peasants and craftsmen than with the governing order and ruling class. They assumed the leadership of the 'middle sort of people' in opposition to King, lords and bishops (p. 153).

I do not wish to contest here the validity of a social analysis for the period involving the concept of class. Rather I want to stress that Dr Manning simply does not make sense of trends in social history in the hundred years prior to 1640. He adduces two kinds of evidence for his view: that the 'middle class' opposed the policies of Charles I in the 1630s (but then so did the gentry), and that 'middling and upper stratas of the peasantry suffered a reversal of their expectations in the 1620s and 1630s' (p. 117). Nothing he says supports such a view. He lists a number of factors all of which had been current since 1500 and which had resulted in continuing differentiation within the peasantry leading to the successful yeomanry and the landless labourer; and he emphasizes the depression of the 1620s: 'A succession of good harvests, which reduced the prices of corn and profits of arable farmers, was followed by a succession of bad harvests, which impoverished all who had to buy grain' (p. 118). This is having it all ways. In the handling of evidence, if not in the stating of conclusions, there is a failure to distinguish between the fate of the small proprietors who were subject to all kinds of pressures, who did suffer a catastrophic drop in their standard of living and who were expropriated, and the substantial peasants producing for the market who continued to gain in wealth and status right up to 1640. Local studies do not suggest a slowing down of mobility in the early seventeenth century. On the contrary, inter-marriage between yeomanry and gentlemen was probably on the increase. The positions of yeomen on grand juries and other intermediary institutions of local government were probably being consolidated.

Certainly the early Stuart period witnessed an assault on customary tenures (though the area Dr Manning discusses most fully, the most northern counties, was one in which the tenants remained conspicuously loyal to their landlords in the civil war). Equally there was a great deal of resistance to the rationalization of land use by enclosure of wastes and other marginal lands. But in almost every case resistance was led or passively supported by the local gentry and JPs. Is this, as Dr Manning suggests, because they feared the peasants? Or because they shared peasant outrage at the violation of customary procedures and traditional rights? It is suggestive that in almost every case that he cites, the encloser is either the Crown or an absentee landlord. Dr Manning may be right, but there are at least two alternative models which he ignores: Professor Mousnier's model for French revolts (recently and suggestively applied by Dr C.S.L. Davies to the rebellions in Tudor England),[7] and Mr E.P. Thompson's conception of the moral economy of the English crowd in the eighteenth century.[8] This latter hypothesis had been applied with great success by Mr Walter and Dr Wrightson to grain riots in the early seventeenth century.[9] To use counter-jargon, Dr Manning makes no attempt to rebut the organic-functionalist approach to English social history which is the conscious or unconscious model behind most writing on the period. Indeed, it must be said that Dr Manning never confronts any of the problems which the work of the last thirty years throws in his path. He ignores them. (A very simple example of this is the way he ignores the interpretation of the London crowd in Professor Pearl's work. There are major interpretative differences for example over leadership, which he simply ignores).[10]

It is an enormous relief to turn to the final chapters of this book. Here at last Dr Manning's sources and his purpose are compatible. Leaping forward from early 1643 and 1647–9, he offers the most stimulating and convincing reinterpretation of Leveller ideology to appear for a long time.

He shows how the well-known Leveller critique of existing economic and social conditions led them to formulate a plan for the total reconstruction of political institutions. The crucial feature of these reforms, however, was not the election of annual parliaments by manhood suffrage, but a withering away of the state. The Levellers had a conviction that all power corrupted, and they hated all forms of imposed authority. As he says 'perhaps the most striking thing about the *Agreements [of the People]* is what they omit: the lack of reference to executive government. The central government is almost eliminated' (pp. 301–2). Instead, England was to be transformed into a federation of self-governing county communities, with popular election of all local officials – justices, sheriffs, juries, etc. All central courts were to be abolished and replaced by hundredal courts under democratic

7. C.S.L. Davies, 'Peasant Revolt in France and England: A Comparison', *Agricultural History Review*, XXI (1973), 122–34.
8. In *Past and Present*, no. 50 (1971).
9. In *Past and Present*, no. 71 (1976).
10. V. Pearl, *London and the Outbreak of the Puritan Revolution* (Oxford, 1961), *passim*.

control. There would be no standing army and no centralized financial institutions. Parliaments would meet regularly, with prescribed terms of reference, to settle matters of common concern, but members would be immediately answerable to their constituents who would also elect triers to examine the members' performance. Once again I am left unconvinced how far this constituted a specific attack on the existing elite as such. But certainly Dr Manning convincingly portrays the Leveller programme as a radical extension of traditional notions of self-determination and a reinvigoration of existing institutions of local government. I am disappointed that Dr Manning assumes a continuity with 1640–3, whereas the more obvious source of these ideas lies in the experience of war: unparalleled taxation, unprecedented centralization, the virtual extinction of most of the customary, traditional elements of self-government and arbitration which had continued to mark the experience of local communities up to 1642. I am tantalized by the palpable but elusive affinity with Clubmen ideals.[11] But he has drawn attention to neglected and crucial elements of Leveller thought. He is also right, I think, to assert that the Leveller leaders, as a group, did not demand immediate 'universal suffrage, since there were unstated exceptions, for men so poor as to have to beg were excepted; rather they were assertions that poverty as such was no ground for exclusion from the franchise . . .' (pp. 310–11). It remains possible, however, to take this argument one stage further, and to see Leveller imprecision as arising from a conviction that once their economic reforms were effected, all men would be free to vote. The temporary exclusion of those dependent on the will of other men was necessary to speed up the process whereby they would recover their economic freedom and their political birthright. In the Leveller dream, there would have been manhood suffrage by 1660. This study of Leveller thought will be essential reading for students of the period and shows that when Dr Manning asks appropriate questions of his sources, he commands attention.

A. Fletcher, *A County Community at Peace and War: Sussex 1600–1660* (1976), is a splendid example of the local study which Dr Manning's earlier work did much to promote. Like other county studies (not least my own) it avoids discussing the questions Dr Manning has now shown us that we must ask. But it is a subtle, balanced, and readable account of the problems facing a gentry community in

11. Cf. Morrill, *Revolt of the Provinces*, pp. 98–111, 196–200.

seventeenth-century England. Furthermore it examines the administrative, ecclesiastical and political history of Sussex over a longer
period than any of its rivals. It is less penetrating than some, and
it integrates the various themes less successfully, but it is far more
eclectic, discussing, filtering and applying the findings of other
historians in their own counties. It is a pleasure to handle and
to read, and is almost certainly the best introduction that students
being introduced to local studies of the period could have. The book
is in five sections. The first, and slightest, analyses the lifestyle of
the Sussex gentry. The second delineates religious groupings in the
county: there is a study of the self-conscious protestant piety which
distinguished lay puritanism; a study of Arminianism strongest in
its description of clericalist pretension and the resultant gentry anger
and bemusement; a clear examination of the continuing ambiguities
of early Stuart recusancy; and a section on the ecclesiastical chaos of
1642–60 rather misleadingly entitled 'achieving the millenium'.

The third section describes the structure of local government:
separate chapters describe the framework of government, the enforcement of order, the Caroline militia reforms, and the fiscal demands of
both local and central government. It is strongest in its demonstration
of the way the Sussex Bench developed its own conventions and
practices in defiance of statute and common practice elsewhere.

The fourth section examines the rise of opposition to the early
Stuarts, contrasts the urgent parliamentarianism of east Sussex and
the corresponding paralysis and indecision of the gentry of the west,
chronicles the ebb and flow of war, and describes the increasingly
complex bureaucracy of the 1640s. Yet Mr Fletcher finds Sussex to
have been a county more marked by continuities than changes and
he attests 'the intense localism of the Sussex community'. The 1650s
are described as a period of indecision marked by 'the contortions of
men prepared to conform to, but not to create, the new regime'.

The fifth section examines 'the impact of civil war'. It is short and
oddly out of place; an anti-climax. There is nothing at all on the
Restoration period, not even a hint on how the conformists of the
Interregnum fared.

The broadly topical approach creates problems which are not fully
resolved. There are real gains in taking each topic through from
1600 to 1660, as in chapters on the personnel of local government
and on the county's political history. Indeed the book would have
gained from greater consistency in this respect. The chapter on 'the
exact militia' of Charles I is not matched by anything on the period
1643–60. The whole of part 5 would have been better if it had been

adapted to fit into part 3. On the other hand the section on the ecclesiastical changes of the 1640s and 1650s reads oddly so early in the book. It might have been better to have concluded part 2 with a section on the fate of the Anglicans and Catholics and incorporated the material on the more positive proposals for religious change in the 'Quest for Settlement' chapter in part 4.

This is essentially a work of political and administrative history: there is little here for the economic historian, though the increased length which a section on the economy would have involved would have driven the price to unimaginable heights. I was only concerned by the lack of any mention of the effect of land sales in the 1650s. I was more concerned that in his laudable attempt to apply the insights of others in their own communities, Mr Fletcher may have lost something of the uniqueness of the Sussex community. At certain points he misses the full significance of local developments. The petitions of the autumn of 1645 against the activities of the county committee point to a situation in Sussex only superficially similar to that prevalent elsewhere (p. 272). Similarly, the distinctiveness and importance of the Sussex petitions of the summer of 1648 are missed. At other times, the book is let down by an uncritical eclecticism: incompatible definitions of puritanism are used side by side (pp. 84–5); the notion of millenarianism is taken up over-enthusiastically and made to cover all forms of quest for a godly commonwealth; definitions of Court and Country inappropriate to local studies are adopted and applied (pp. 239ff.).

Yet in the end it is the book's virtues which linger: it is well written, it displays great sensitivity and subtlety in its portrayal of the complexities of life in a local community, and Mr Fletcher has a splendid eye for the apt illustration, the precise detail (like the guest lists at Lord Dacre's dinner parties in the 1640s which reveal the gentry's 'reluctance to face the stark fact of allegiance which the war posed'). The book deserves a wide readership, even if, at this price, the publishers do seem likely to make most of us read it in copyright libraries.

CHAPTER ELEVEN

The Ecology of Allegiance in the English Civil Wars

I

David Underdown tells his readers in the preface to *Revel, Riot and Rebellion* that my scepticism over a cup of tea in the Institute of Historical Research was one of the things that led him to write the book.[1] It is, of course, true that many books have been conceived in that tearoom, but this must be one of the few of them not to have been stillborn. Alas, he and I have too few occasions to debate such issues over tea; this review is thus in essence an open letter to tell him whether he has now persuaded me that he is right about patterns of allegiance in the civil war and whether my scepticism was misplaced. The answer, I suppose inevitably, is yes and no.

II

It is necessary to begin by stating the thesis that is the core of his argument. This is a rich book, remarkable for its eclecticism of knowledge and approaches. But everything revolves around one central hypothesis:

> The division in the English body politic which erupted into civil war in 1642 can be traced in part to the earlier emergence of two quite different constellations of social, political and cultural forces, involving diametrically opposite responses to the problems of the time. On the one side stood those who had put their trust in the traditional conception of the harmonious, vertically-integrated society – a society in which the old bonds of paternalism, deference, and good-neighborliness were expressed in familiar religious and communal rituals – and wished

---

1. D.E. Underdown, *Revel, Riot, and Rebellion: Popular Politics and Culture in England, 1603–1660* (Oxford, 1985). Specific references will appear in the text. I am grateful to Anthony Fletcher, Glenn Burgess, John Walter, Keith Wrighton, and especially, Tim Wales for discussions about this book.

to strengthen and preserve it. On the other stood those – mostly among the gentry and middling sort of the new parish elites – who wished to emphasize the moral and cultural distinctions which marked them off from their poorer, less disciplined neighbours, and to use their power to reform society according to their own principles of order and godliness. These two socio-cultural constellations can be observed in all parts of England, but in varied strengths in different geographical areas: the former more conspicuously in arable regions, the latter in the cloth-making wood-pasture districts. [p. 40]

This general hypothesis is tested against a mass of evidence from the counties of Wiltshire, Dorset, and Somerset. The book falls into three main sections. The first establishes the context: it identifies the two main farming regions and looks for evidence of a contrast between 'the "traditional" areas of open-field, sheep-corn husbandry in the nucleated villages of the chalk downlands, and the more individualistic economies and settlement patterns of the North Somerset and Wiltshire cheese and cloth-making regions; and the less industrially developed pasture regions in south-east Somerset and Blackmore Vale representing an intermediate type in respect of both economic and settlement patterns' (p. 6). This leads into a discussion of social relations, patterns of protestantization, and elements of order and disorder in each region. The second section examines the evidence for patterns of popular allegiance in the civil war, relying principally on two forms of evidence – lists of 1,142 maimed Royalist soldiers who received pensions in the early years of the Restoration and lists of 3,264 'suspected persons' required to give bonds of good behavior to the major generals in 1655. The final section examines the failure of puritanism in the 1640s and 1650s in its confrontation with 'popular culture', the disintegration of puritanism after the Restoration and the long-term emergence of dissent, and the pyrrhic victory of an Anglicanism that sought to assimilate rather than to challenge popular culture.

What follows is a critique of this thesis. I want both to acknowledge my indebtedness to the book and to challenge some of its conclusions. I have *not* set out to offer an alternative hypothesis. My reasons are simple and twofold: the space I am permitted is limited; and I want David Underdown to defend himself and his book – he must not be allowed off the hook by my setting up nice soft targets for him, which could take up the space he is allowed in reply!

III

Five features of the book seem to be major contributions to the on-going struggle to make sense of seventeenth-century English history.

First, this thesis is in every way more sophisticated and interesting than the old account of the patterning of allegiance that pitched a conservative North and West against a progressive South and East, an account time and again discredited by detailed local studies.[2] Furthermore, such an interpretation was predicated on the assumption that the civil war was a contest between a reactionary Crown (upholding the feudal order, paternalistic economic values, and residual Catholic elements in the Church) and a dynamic Parliament (representing liberal political, religious, and social values). Such assumptions have now been largely discredited. It is now widely accepted that the civil war represented a conservative reaction by sections of the gentry and others against the innovative policies of the Stuarts in church and state. In fact, while Underdown's hypothesis can accommodate such a view, it can also suggest the possibility that both sides represented alternative progressive tendencies, while the mass of the population was conservative in its reflexes and neutralist in its response to the outbreak of war. Thus the Crown can be seen as in the forefront of rationalizing land use, sponsoring capital-intensive development of fen and forest (which, in consequence, made it possible to feed the pauperized sections of the community); it can be seen as seeking to reinvigorate the Church as an institution and to increase its appeal to those who had largely ignored it and its teachings. On the other hand, the Crown's leading opponents can be seen as men who felt that their interests were threatened and as men who were obstructed as they sought to challenge in their own way the ignorance, superstition, idolatry, and worldliness that kept a majority of the nation from owning their Christian duty. It reminds me of nothing so much as Malcolm Wanklyn's unheeded suggestion that the civil war was fought not between 'rising' gentry on the one side and 'declining' gentry on the other side (*pace* Tawney, Stone, Trevor-Roper, etc.) but between two groups of rising, prosperous, activist gentry, with those who were economically passive or declining tending to be neutralist and inactive and pushed around by events.[3]

Second, this book is by far the best attempt yet to examine 'popular' allegiance in the civil war. As Underdown says, this is a problem usually approached in one of three ways. The first way is to assert that

2. For the old account, see, e.g., J.E.C. Hill, *The Century of Revolution* (rev. ed. London, 1968), pp. 111–13. For a review of several of the local studies, see, 'The Northern Gentry and the Great Rebellion,' above, ch. 9.
3. M.D.G. Wanklyn, 'Landed Society and Allegiance in Cheshire and Shropshire in the First Civil War' (PhD, thesis, University of Manchester, 1976), ch. 4.

mass illiteracy and economic dependency rendered those below the gentry impotent to make autonomous political choices. The second is to assert that many were (though in varying degrees) free agents but that their first priority was to protect their homes, families, and communities from the armies of both sides – the wider issues did not touch them. The third is to assert that 'many of the common people *did* take an active part in the civil war, *did* have a real preference for one side or the other, and that the side they overwhelmingly preferred was that of Parliament' (p. 2.). What this book does is to make it quite clear that the first view is wholly inadequate, that the second is much more complicated than it has usually seemed, and that the third is not so much too simple as too rigid.[4] Underdown's own approach is both pioneering and represents of the most sophisticated general discussion of the problem currently available. It creates a sense of the contexts within which yeomen, rural and urban craftsmen, husbandmen, and laborers struggled to make choices. It demonstrates how they could express those choices, and it draws on sources not hitherto adequately studied by historians of allegiance. I shall argue later that we can readily go along neither with much of Underdown's methodology nor with some of his specific conclusions. But he has changed the agenda of civil war studies.

Third, one particular consequence of this attempt to elucidate the problem of popular allegiance can be recognized and separately applauded; this is the recovery of popular royalism. Those who have argued for a popular dynamism in the civil war have stressed not only the existence of popular puritanism/parliamentarianism but also the disproportionate contribution of popular parliamentarianism to the defeat of the king. With the peerage and gentry split down the middle, it has been asserted, it was middling-sort militants who settled the issue.[5] It has always seemed to me that this is a distortion that is the result of certain built-in assumptions and a reliance on particular kinds of evidence. It rests on giving credence to the convenient half-truths put out by propagandists of both sides. It rests on misplaced assumptions that the Royalist armies were conscripted at best among

---

4. The second view is probably more complicated than it was made to seem in J.S. Morrill, *The Revolt of the Provinces* (London, 1976). Underdown's analysis of neutralism is close to that presented in such recent work as A. Fletcher, *The Outbreak of the English Civil War* (London, 1982), ch. 12, and 'The Coming of War', in *Reactions to the English Civil War*, ed. J.S. Morrill (London, 1982), pp. 29–50.
5. B.S. Manning, *The English People and the English Revolution* (London, 1976), pp. ix–x and *passim*.

the dependent tenantry, at worst among a feudal host. It is predicated on the idea that the Crown was vainly propping up a decayed social, political, and religious order against dynamic and progressive social, economic, and religious forces. It takes no account of the existence of popular Anglicanism.[6] Despite all these caveats, I will not deny that a case can be made for the view that the people were more strongly in favour of Parliament than of the king. One cannot find much evidence of popular royalism to match the writings of Nehemiah Wallington or the petition of William Davenport's tenants.[7] Probably the strongest case, however, is that made by Joyce Malcolm.[8] She has claimed that the royalists had, from the outset, greater difficulty than the parliamentarians in raising infantry. This she attributes directly to the king's unpopularity among those beneath the gentry. However, even her argument creates major difficulties, both evidential and conceptual.[9] If, as the argument goes, Parliament had more success with the middling sorts (yeomen, skilled craftsmen, etc.), then one would expect the king to have had great difficulty in raising junior infantry officers and cavalry troopers. Infantrymen were most likely to come from lower in the social scale. Yet the evidence of Peter Newman and Ronald Hutton suggests that the Royalist armies were at least as thick with nongentle junior officers as were the Parliamentarian armies; and one thing that no one disagrees with is that the Royalists had no difficulty filling cavalry regiments.[10] The Royalists had problems, it seems, in mustering those beneath the parish elites to serve as pikemen and musketeers.

Fourth, this book addresses one of the central issues in early modern historiography and adds significantly to it. How protestant was England by the early seventeenth century? The traditional answer has been that it was largely protestant. Either as a result of the sustained will and authority of Crown, Parliament, and church, or as a consequence of the successful campaign of a grass-roots movement

6. For a full critique of Manning's thesis, see 'Provincial Squires and "Middling Sorts" in the Great Rebellion', above ch. 10.
7. P. Seaver, *Wallington's World* (London, 1985). See the petition in J.S. Morrill, 'William Davenport and the "Silent Majority" of Early Stuart England', *Journal of the Chester Archaeological Society*, 58 (1975), 128–9.
8. L. Malcolm, *Caesar's Due* (London, 1982), and 'A King in Search of Soldiers: Charles I in 1642', *HJ* 21, no. 2 (1978), 251–68.
9. For a telling critique of her empirical study see M. Wanklyn and P. Young, 'A Rejoinder', *HJ* 24, no. 1 (1981) 147–54.
10. See P.R. Newman, *Royalists Officers in England and Wales, 1642–1660: A Biographical Dictionary* (New York, 1981); R. Hutton, *The Royalist War Effort, 1642–1646* (Oxford, 1982).

(itself predicated on lay reaction against priestcraft, hocus-pocus, and depredations of late medieval Catholicism and allowed to prosper by regimes divided against themselves), the mass of the population had come in varying degrees to conform to the practices and to embrace the values of a rather diluted version of the Continental Reformation.[11] Such views allow for the survival of a minority clinging to the old religion (or a refurbished version of it) and allow for the development of a hotter sort of protestantism among those who were zealous for the fullest implementation of the more rigorist practices of the new religion. For the past decade, the work of Keith Thomas has demonstrated the fragility of all such accounts that assume that all Englishmen were members of some church or other – Catholic, Anglican, Puritan-Anglican, or Separatist.[12] Thomas's insights have now been powerfully challenged by scholars like Jack Scarisbrick and Christopher Haigh, who have argued for a rather different trajectory of religious change.[13] Although there are significant differences between them, Scarisbrick and Haigh agree that the state was not powerful enough or stubborn enough to do much more than inhibit and destroy the old structures, and certainly was not powerful enough to destroy patterns of belief, and that the teachings, values, and practices of the established church made little headway among the mass of the people, who may (or may not) have conformed outwardly on Sundays but who otherwise found the Jacobean church irrelevant or else a nuisance. For Haigh, this led to a widespread de-christianization of the population; for Scarisbrick, it led to the survival of a sort of folk Catholicism, cut off from the structures of the church but inoculated against the commands of Anglicanism. Both see Laud as appealing to widespread surviving conservatism. Underdown seems to me to give such interpretations a considerable boost, though he is closer to Haigh than to Scarisbrick (pp. 66–72). My personal view is that such interpretations make very good sense for the Tudor period but that they understate the comfortable conformism of the generations

---

11. C. Haigh, 'The Recent Historiography of the English Reformation', *HJ* 25, no. 4 (1982) 995–1008.
12. K.V. Thomas, *Religion and the Decline of Magic* (London, 1971), esp. ch. 2, 3, and 6.
13. J.J. Scarisbrick, *The Reformation and the English People* (Oxford, 1982); C. Haigh, 'The Church of England, the Catholics and the People', in *The Reign of Elizabeth I*, ed. C. Haigh (London, 1984), pp. 195–220. I have also had the benefit of hearing several papers by Haigh that form part of his forthcoming book on religion in England, 1558–1642.

born and brought up under the 1559 settlement, specifically after 1598. Nonetheless, there is something very satisfying about Underdown's interpretation, which sees Laudianism and Caroline puritanism as rival and conflicting evangelisms, one seeking to assimilate the residual expressions of a traditional faith and practice and the other to suppress such expressions the better to expose the people to the teachings and values of the Reformation. I find both this conceptualization of the problem and the evidence for this trajectory helpful.

Fifth, and consequent on this, Underdown argues powerfully and effectively that the Restoration was a popular event, especially in the short term, precisely because the puritans, having gained power in the later 1640s, failed in their attempt to impose their values and beliefs. The internal divisions and tensions within puritanism weakened its ability to impose itself, and the depth and strength of the cultural norms and practices that puritanism sought to supplant was simply too strong even for a succession of revolutionary regimes, especially when those regimes could sustain themselves in power only by the adoption of military, fiscal, and institutional structures that violated deeply cherished norms of civil liberty. This is so close to what I have myself argued over the years that I found myself reading the final chapters of the book with no intellectual discomfort whatsoever.

IV

These are the book's major achievements. They make it an important book to read by all those interested in the period. There are, however, major problems with other, and central, features of the book, including what for David Underdown is its central argument – the cultural differences beneath the sheep-corn and wood-pasture regions that underpinned patterns of allegiance. I wish to challenge a series of assumptions behind this thesis and aspects of the methodology deployed to demonstrate it.

I need to start with recording my agnosticism with the appropriation of distinctive 'cultures' to the sheep-corn and wood-pasture regions. Underdown is not, of course, producing this distinction as a new insight. It was the basis of the work of Joan Thirsk and Alan Everitt in the 1960s, for example, although its deployment is far more circumspect in Thirsk's recent work.[14] More important, the thesis has

14. J. Thirsk, *The Rural Economy of England* (London, 1984), chs. 12 and 13; *The Agrarian History of England and Wales*, vol. 4, 1500–1640, ed. J. Thirsk (Cambridge, 1967), ch. 1, sec. A: A.M. Everitt, *Landscape and Community in England* (London, 1986), chs. 1–3, and *Change in the Provinces* (Leicester, 1969). Compare *The Agrarian History of England and Wales*, vol. 5, *1640–1750*, pt 1, *Regional Farming Systems*, ed. J. Thirsk (Cambridge, 1985), pp. xix–xxxi.

been most effectively worked out for areas of the Midland Plain and Anglia.[15] While some of the topographical characteristics of those regions can be found in the West Country, many others cannot be, a fact borne out recently as I travelled from arable (and very flat) East Anglia to arable (and very rolling) Dorset. After all, there are some sheep-corn regions with highly dispersed patterns of settlement.[16] I was not persuaded that Underdown had here produced sufficient evidence that there were markedly different patterns of landholding between the two regions, or that nucleated settlements predominated in the arable regions but did not predominate throughout the wood-pasture regions, or that gentry settlement was denser and gentry control more effective in the arable regions (scatter maps of gentry and of magistrates' seats are needed), or that parish churches and resident clergy were more concentrated in the arable regions. I have always felt that the contrast is better expressed as arable and non-arable rather than as sheep-corn and wood-pasture since the latter were so various in structure. In some wood-pasture regions, especially where there had been dramatic clearance and enclosure, the concentration of land and wealth was more extreme than in sheep-corn regions, whereas in others it was far less concentrated. It is as difficult to find common links within wood-pasture regions as between wood-pasture and sheep-corn regions. This is not, of course, to deny that there may have been rough-and-ready distinctions between the cultural patterns of arable and non-arable regions (or arable and some non-arable regions), but it does call into question the social basis of many of the cultural patterns observed. Reading and rereading this book did not in the end persuade me that the full variety of patterns in the non-arable regions had been sufficiently clarified and applied. All this makes me queasy about building too much on these topographical distinctions. Frankly, it seems to me that Underdown states all the objections to the topographical survey and then proceeds willy-nilly with tempting and intriguing passages like the following:

> Put simply, the typical team sport of the south Wiltshire downlands was football; the typical sports of the North Wiltshire cheese country were variants of bat-and-ball games, of which stoolball was in this

15. See, e.g., W.G. Hoskins, *The Midland Peasant* (London, 1957); M. Spufford, *Contrasting Communities* (Cambridge, 1975), pt 1.
16. One obvious example is the Chilterns (a sheep-corn area with a highly dispersed pattern of settlement, irregular field systems, and extensive commons). I was emboldened to make this point (not one within my main areas of competence) by hearing a paper by T. Williamson, 'The Origins of Regions in Lowland Britain', at a conference of regional and local historians at the University of East Anglia in September 1986.

period by far the most popular. . . . Football . . . [was] a more or less
ritualized combat between communities, often represented by almost the
entire young male population of whole parishes. It was an appropriate
expression of parochial loyalty against outsiders, in which the identity of
the individual was totally submerged in that of the group. Its disorderly
violence made it an inevitable target of moral reformers; Laudian clergy,
by contrast, encouraged it as a harmless reinforcement of feelings of
neighborhood. . . . Football was less popular in the cheese country,
but bat-and-ball games were more widely played. Stoolball's popularity
might be ascribed to the fact that its structure expressed, better than
football, the more individualistic nature of the wood/pasture community
(pp. 75–6).

Those willing to accept this will probably also be willing to accept
Underdown's account of distinctive patterns of disorder in the two
farming regions – the concentration of charivari in wood-pasture
regions: 'In these unstable wood/pasture villages, economic change
and geographical mobility had weakened the ability of neighbours
and kinsfolk to maintain order in the old informal ways. Different
social groups had correspondingly different responses; puritanism
for the middling sort, skimmingtons for the lower orders. But
though the responses were different, they were provoked by the
same problem' (p. 103). However, this distinction leaves us with a
further problem. What do we mean by 'popular' allegiance? Clearly,
in the model that Underdown erects, the harmonious communities of
the sheep-corn regions are likely to be solidly royalist since the elite
have the middling and lower orders under control and do not feel
especially threatened by the religious policies for which Charles stood
(especially in 1642). In the wood-pasture regions, however, the social
imperatives would point in different directions. On the one hand,
there would presumably be regions where the puritan strivings of the
middling sort alienated the proponents of 'popular' customs such as
'skimmingtons'.[17] Such men and women would presumably not wish
to support a movement closely associated with the puritan cause. Yet
in other wood-pasture regions where puritanism had triumphed and
skimmington had been extinguished, one would expect the populace
to be parliamentarian. Thus we would have solidly royalist regions
(arable), solidly parliamentarian regions (some wood-pasture), and
some regions with middling-sort parliamentarians and lower-sort
royalists and neuters. I do not think that this is thoroughly worked

17. It is worth stressing that charivari (like church-ales) are fairly regionally specific
and are not characteristic of pastoral regions elsewhere in the country. This has
implications that I would suggest are not spelled out.

through in the book. In part this is because we never get the evidence of how puritans set about confronting popular culture. We really can expect to be given evidence of a group of active puritan commissioners of the peace applying relentless pressure on parish officers, both in and out of sessions. Even in what looks like a clear example – the *cause célèbre* of church-ales in Somerset in 1633 – Underdown does not contradict Tom Barnes's view that the magistrates were seeking not to suppress church fetes but to keep them within bounds.[18] Even more vital, of course, is the need for detailed case studies for particular villages, such as Wrightson and Levine have attempted for Terling.[19]

Here, Martin Ingram's work is especially challenging, both in general and insofar as it grows out of many years' study of Wiltshire, in Underdown's heartland. Ingram has denied the necessary connection between the economic forces at work in the period 1540–1640 (and the consequent social differentiation and strain) and a 'puritan' cultural response as identified and studied by Wrightson and Levine in Terling in Essex. He has, in 'Religion, Communities and Moral Discipline in Late Sixteenth- and Early Seventeenth-Century England', argued that 'while the[ir] study proposes two main engines of change, economic and cultural-religious, their relative importance in influencing the various strands of development remains unclear' (p. 180). More important, he has offered a parallel study of Keevil, on the edge of the Wiltshire clothing area. There he has found most of the economic disruptions seen in Terling and most of the social responses, but he finds no specific 'puritan' moral underpinning. 'Compared to Terling, the religious life of Keevil appears less polarized in terms not only of horizontal social divisions, but also of the general quality of religious observance and commitment, and less change is visible over time. The village had its pious members and its profligates: but the majority of the people appear to have been neither' (p. 189). In relation to the 'reformation of manners', Ingram suggests that 'economic factors were of greater importance. In the absence of a strong Puritan religious drive in Keevil, a harsher attitude to those offences nonetheless developed' (p. 190). This is dynamite indeed. What is more, he has planted other land mines along the track Underdown chooses to take. In his detailed study of Wiltshire

18. T. Barnes, 'County Politics and a Puritan *cause célèbre*: Somerset Churchales, 1633,' *TRHS* 5th ser, 9 (1959), 103–22.
19. K. Wrightson and D. Levine, *Poverty and Piety in an English Village: Terling, 1525–1700* (Toronto, 1980).

charivari, he challenges the notion of an organized puritan campaign against popular culture. Stressing the consonance of elite and popular attitudes and the connivance of many gentry in popular 'shame sanctions' that echoed and were very similar to those prescribed by official agencies, Ingram, in 'Ridings, Rough Music and the "Reform of Popular Culture" in Early Modern England', characterizes opposition to charivari as 'infrequent and muted'. 'They were at least one form of popular custom, and an impressive one, which escaped any really serious attempt at repression' (pp. 110–11). These are surely challenges that can be met only by detailed local studies that identify puritan elites and describe their campaigns.[20] In the absence both of knots of militant magistrates and of studies revealing the contests between puritans and others in the context of particular local communities, the case for a puritan crusade cannot be said to have been achieved. At the most, there is *some* evidence of cultural conflict but nothing on its dynamics. I was left with one further anxiety. If there are two regional cultures (as laid out above in the quotation from Underdown (pp. 75–6), can we be sure that we are witnessing 'Anglican' and 'Puritan' responses? To put it bluntly, what did Anglicans think of stoolball? Arable regions have a 'communal' ethic and pastoral regions an 'individualistic' ethic. But do Laudian Anglicanism and puritanism not both espouse a nostalgic attachment to the crumbling sense of community? It is at least arguable that both could engage with and seek to exploit aspects of 'arable' culture and that both would wish to challenge the values of wood-pasture. Perhaps we are looking not at an arable Anglicanism and a pastoral puritanism but at shared Anglican and puritan responses to contrasting popular cultures.

Thus, even if we grant that there are two farming regions each with a distinctive culture, we are left with many problems about how we proceed to a discussion of religious allegiances and hence political allegiances.

In the end, the whole apparatus of the arable/pastoral debate seems unnecessary to elucidate such wider questions, for the discussion

---

20. M. Ingram, 'Religion, Communities and Moral Discipline in Late Sixteenth and Early Seventeenth-Century England', in *Religion and Society in Early Modern Europe*, ed. K. von Greertz (London, 1985), and 'Ridings, Rough Music and the "Reform of Popular Culture" in Early Modern England', *Past and Present*, 105 (1984), 79–113. I find the former more telling than M. Spufford, 'Puritanism and Social Control', in *Order and Disorder in Early Modern England*, eds. A. Fletcher and J. Stevenson (Cambridge, 1985). The book on which Ingram is commenting is Wrightson and Levine.

of allegiance demonstrates that parliamentarianism is distinctively strong only in the clothing regions and towns. None of the statistical evidence supports the broader generalization that the wood-pasture culture led either to strong parliamentarianism or the kind of highly polarized middling-sort puritanism/lower-order royalism that his cultural argument leaves room for. Indeed, the game is largely given away at one point in the book when Underdown accepts that most of the non-clothing wood-pasture regions 'were as culturally conservative as the downlands' (pp. 103–4). Surely there are simpler ways to explain the concentration of puritanism in clothing regions than to see it as a particularly intense example of wood-pasture culture? Surely the instrinsic appeal of puritan discipline and biblicism within the context of cloth working, the greater openness of clothing regions to wandering evangelists moving with the lines of trade and even with the line of the main roads, perhaps simply the greater contact with London, all go a long way to explain the phenomenon without recourse to the broader cultural analysis.

V

I am, then, unhappy with Underdown's spatial distribution of royalism and parliamentarianism. I am also worried by his account of the social distribution of puritanism and Anglicanism and therefore of royalism and parliamentarianism.

The notion that puritanism has a particular appeal to the middling sort has, of course, a strong pedigree. It is central to the work of Christopher Hill, of course, and has recently been strongly endorsed by Keith Wrighton, William Hunt, Brian Manning, and others.[21] I am drawn to it myself. A religion that is Bible-centred is likely to be a religion of the literate; a religion of sheep and goats is likely to appeal to those differentiating themselves from their fellow peasants and assimulating themselves economically and culturally to an established elite. Such a view can be challenged in several ways. Puritanism is certainly characteristic of the cloth-working districts and of some urban centers, though I have to say that Underdown does not provide direct evidence that it consolidated itself among the wealthier farmers and craftsmen before disseminating downward. I cannot say that the book provides much evidence that puritanism was generally stronger in wood-pasture regions than in

---

21. J.E.C. Hill, *Society and Puritanism: Pre-revolutionary England* (London, 1964); K. Wrighton, *English Society, 1580–1680* (London, 1981), ch. 6; Wrightson and Levine, chs. 5 and 6; Manning (n. 5 above), esp. ch. 7.

sheep-corn regions. Certainly, historians of East Anglian puritanism, such as William Hunt, have not suggested that puritanism there is concentrated away from the arable regions.[22] More important, several scholars, including Patrick Collinson, Margaret Spufford, and Eamon Duffy, have recently suggested that puritanism was not as socially specific as Underdown assumes and that it did not necessarily disseminate downward.[23] There are some problems of definition involved, however, especially in the formulations of Spufford and Duffy, in that they conflate all protestant enthusiasm under the catchall title 'puritanism', citing Anabaptists, Quakers, separating Congregationalists, and other sectaries as if they were merely offshoots of predestinarian Calvinism. If we see such movements as being as much reactions against puritanism as extensions of it, then the dilemma might be resolved. Those who had seen little of 'prayer book Anglicanism' and were confronted by prating puritan divines whose stereotype of the saint involved Bible reading, worldly success, and self-conscious charity in measures unattainable by the humble and illiterate poor might reject Christianity and retreat into paganism, or they might turn to those who offered a more convincing gospel. This might result in a socially specific, semi-Pelagian, radical Arminian, Pentecostal, or Pietistic sectarianism hostile to mainstream Calvinist dogma and ecclesiology that would help to resolve the apparent contradictions in existing literature. It might help Underdown's case. As it is, I fear his rather static account of a popular culture waiting to be overborne or assimilated takes no account of it.

It is implicit in what I have just said that this book proceeds at times from assumption to evidence rather than the reverse. Most of the exercises for quantifying 'Anglicanism' or 'puritanism' are, of course, treacherous (presentments in church courts for non-conformity, petitioning for and against the prayer book and the bishops, etc.), but they are not attempted here.[24] Patterns of ecclesiastical patronage, perhaps the most fruitful avenue of inquiry, together with patterns of clerical

22. W. Hunt, *The Puritan Moment* (Cambridge, Mass., 1983), esp. ch. 6.
23. P. Collinson, *The Religion of Protestants* (Oxford, 1982), ch. 5; Spufford, 'Puritanism and Social Control', ch. 1; E. Duffy, 'The Godly and the Multitude in Stuart England', *Seventeenth Century*, 1, no. 1 (1986), 31–55.
24. J. Maltby, in an almost completed Cambridge PhD thesis, will release some telling figures on the social distribution of support for episcopacy and the prayer book in a number of Cheshire parishes in rather different farming regions.

persecution in the 1640s, are also ignored.[25] Instead, Underdown suggests that working conditions, the absence of strong informal controls, the lack of 'brokers', and the rugged individualism of the wood-pasture region left those who wished to impose protestantism little option but to fall back on a confrontation with popular culture. However plausible, I have to record that I felt this was more asserted than demonstrated.

The point has to be labored because it threatens Underdown's central thesis about the distribution of allegiance. The fundamental patterns of thought that determined allegiance are, ultimately, religious. He is well aware of the impact of Charles's secular oppressions and gives weight to elements of class animus, but neither is seen as being capable of sparking the conflagration of the 1640s and creating the distinctive patterns of allegiance in different farming regions, although a model in which they did so could be constructed.

There is, then, some fuzziness in the social and religious analysis, and there are problems with the spatial analysis. For me, the most worrying aspect of this book is the lack of a grid of elite allegiance for the western shires. Underdown shows that many below the gentry were free agents. But their freedom also included the right to follow the line of least resistance. Men of strong preference and conviction might still prefer inactivity to suicidal commitment (or might not), while men of little or no conviction might find that obeying orders was the simplest line of conduct. This might lead to enlistment or to minor office holding. In my view, we will never be able to quantify the number of militants on either side – that is, those who followed personal conviction and commitment whatever cost. But very careful source criticism should allow us to identify *some* of the militants on both sides. The militancy of many will lie hidden, but we will recover enough individuals to be able to say something about its nature. Such an exercise would, however, rest on four exercises not attempted in this book.

First, a painstaking, retrieval of the recruitment of soldiers, especially at the outbreak of war, and the movement of armies and stationing of garrisons throughout the war would help us to establish how far the distribution of known soldiers follows a purely military logic. We must never forget that many signed up after the harvest

---

25. I. Green ('The Persecution of "Scandalous" and "Malignant" Clergy in the English Civil War', *EHR*, 94 [1979], 507–31), suggests that most Wiltshire ejections took place in the (puritan) southern deaneries. For remarks on the ejections in Somerset, see D.E. Underdown, *Somerset in the Civil Wars and Interregnum* (Newton Abbott, 1973), pp. 154–5.

of 1642 for a war that was to be over by Christmas and before the next demand for agricultural labor.[26] Second, we need maps of gentry allegiance (royal/parliamentarian seats and manors), with subsets for the most active gentry on each side. Third, we need maps of the residences of army officers on both sides. Peter Newman has identified eighty-six royalist field officers from Wiltshire, Dorset, and Somerset; he has also identified no less than 521 junior officers who claimed to be indigent at the Restoration and who were at that time resident in Wiltshire, Dorset, and Somerset.[27] It would be possible to produce fairly full and comparable lists for parliamentarian armies. Fourth, we need a full discussion of clerical allegiance. What was the pattern of persecution? Who was ejected, and what was the geographic pattern?[28] Many ministers appear to have been 'Anglican conformists' in the later 1640s. Were they topographically concentrated?[29] How many were committed to a non-episcopalian state church?[30] Such a study must have implications for popular allegiance. The aim of all this would be to help to identify those probably outside the elite who swam against the tide, the likely hardliners. What was their background?

VI

When we come to the detailed analysis of the distribution of support, we need to stress (as Underdown, of course, does) that it is one-sided. We have lists of maimed royalist soldiers but only vestigial lists of maimed parliamentarian soldiers, and we have lists of suspects

26. Underdown, in *Somerset in the Civil Wars and Interregnum*, provides the basis of a narrative for that county; for Wiltshire, see G. Harrison, 'Royalist Organization in Wiltshire, 1642–6' (PhD thesis, University of London, 1963), chs. 1–3; for Dorset, see A.R. Bayley, *The Civil Wars in Dorset* (Dorchester, 1910).
27. P.R. Newman, 'The Royalist Officer Corps, 1642–1660', *HJ* 26, no. 4 (1983), 953, and 'The 1663 List of Indigent Officers Considered as a Primary Source', *HJ* 30(1987), 885–904.
28. For a general discussion, see Green; for Wiltshire, there is an especially valuable collection of papers relating to the investigation of civil war clerical activities in BL, Additional MS 22084.
29. There is much useful material in B. Williams, 'The Church of England and Protestant Nonconformity in Wiltshire, 1645–1665' (M. Litt. thesis, University of Bristol, 1963), chs. 3 and 4. Among other things he discusses the identity of those who preached the combination lectures set up by Parliament in 1642 at Warminster. He also establishes that there were five working Presbyterian classes in Wiltshire by the late 1640s and not just one, as has been widely supposed. Williams also offers a pioneering study of the relation between ecclesiastical patronage and civil war allegiance.
30. Use might also have been made of the eighty-four signatures to the *Concurrent Testimony to the Solemn League and Covenant* (London, 1648).

rounded up by the major generals in 1655–6 but no comparable list of parliamentarians. This is what Underdown wishes to claim for this analysis:

> Taken together, the pension lists and the Major Generals' returns confirm the existence of widespread popular royalism, and indicate that it was distinctly regional in character . . . [It was most widespread] in Blackmore Vale,[31] south-east Somerset, the chalk country. In the downlands, to be sure, the smaller villages show no impressive indications of active royalism. But the towns in and around the chalk country include some of the most royalist places. . . . On the other side, we have found fewer royalists in the north Somerset and north-west Wiltshire clothing districts (pp. 206–7).

Might not the lists of maimed soldiers tell a different story? Might it not tell us something more about the social and political history of poor relief? Maimed soldiers could be relieved on the parish poor rate, out of charity funds, or out of a county fund. Perhaps some towns were quick to put responsibility off on to a county rate. It may also be that maimed soldiers moved after the civil war to an area more likely to grant them parish relief. What had disabled ex-royalists done in the 1650s when they were specifically excluded from county relief? If there had been a large number of poor royalist soldiers in Dorchester, is it likely they would have returned after the war to face the wrath and the absence of charity in the hearts of the ruling puritan clique? Maybe royalist gentry in the sheep-corn areas were better able to offer protection to ex-soldiers. Maybe some JPs in the 1660s were happier to grant disability certificates to the maimed. That there was a strong element of choice and deliberation about who was to receive relief is suggested by Underdown's study of the different patterns in Wiltshire and Dorset. Perhaps different patterns exist within counties as well.[32] Nor should we assume that all the maimed soldiers are best described as 'royalist'. Some may have served in the trained bands; some certainly served in the regiments sent by king and Parliament (really Parliament) to Ireland in 1642. Some are almost certainly drawn from 'foreign' regiments who served in the county during the war and chose to settle there afterward. For example, Malcolm Wanklyn has suggested to me that many of the maimed soldiers around Devizes came from a Denbighshire regiment garrisoned there during the war. He has also pointed out that some regiments saw

---

31. Blackmore Vale is more pastoral than arable, more royalist than parliamentarian, and, to be blunt, a thorn in the flesh of the argument from first to last.

32. My thoughts on this subject owe much to Tim Wales, whose pioneering work on poor relief in Norfolk is full of kindred points.

more active service and sustained far higher casualties than others.[33] All these factors make the use of this source far too problematic to carry the weight imposed on it in this book.

Similar doubts assail the use of the lists of suspected persons drawn up by and for the major generals. We do not know that the suspects were all or even primarily ex-royalists. Between 1646 and 1656, a large proportion of the population had been alienated from its neutralism or conservative parliamentarianism by the Regicide, by military rule, and by religious liberty run to licence. It is clear, for example, that in the North Midlands Major General Worsley bound over all alehouse keepers afresh to ensure that they kept sedition and immorality at bay. Furthermore, the major generals depended on the cooperation of commissioners who may have been more zealous in some areas than others.[34] Underdown has to admit that returns from some areas were wholly deficient. But that does not mean that we should exclude those and accept the rest as equally reliable. Once one admits that there were likely to have been differences between counties, the value of the exercise loses its force.

VII

At the end of the day, I think these sources are too flawed to demonstrate that the pattern of civil war allegiance was determined by a clash of regional cultures. My scepticism over the teacups has not been overridden. Underdown does persuade me that parliamentarians were strongest in cloth regions and clothing towns and that puritanism was more characteristic of that region than others. But that owes little to the argument that cloth-working took place in wood-pasture regions. It has to do with other factors mentioned above. That Anglicans and puritans had different evangelistic strategies in dealing with the poor, the illiterate, and the ignorant can be readily granted. But I would prefer to see this as the product rather than the source of other attitudinal differences. I cannot accept that it was cultural strategies that determined political responses. Puritans hated Charles I and William Laud only in part because the latter obstructed the puritan attack on church-ales, football, and alehouses.

33. Private communication, based on M.D.G. Wanklyn, 'The King's Armies in the West of England' (MA thesis, University of Manchester, 1965).
34. See the discussion of these points in J.S. Morrill, *Cheshire, 1630–1660* (Oxford, 1974), pp. 281–3, and the maps in the thesis on which it was based: J.S. Morrill, 'The Government of Cheshire during the Civil Wars and Interregnum' (D. Phil. thesis, University of Oxford, 1971), map iv following p. 484. Keith Wrightson and Derek Hirst pointed out that many of Worsley's sureties in Lancashire were taken from alehouse keepers.

They hated them principally because they represented a compromise with popery, a disparagement of preaching, a commitment to a centralizing theocracy, and ultimately a false account of the relations of God and man. These convictions were sufficient unto themselves.

I have learned enormously from this book. I believe everyone who studies the seventeenth century will be wiser for reading it. But it would take something stronger than the tea at the Institute of Historical Research to make me accept its central argument.[35]

35. David Underdown replied to this review in *JBS*, 26 (1987) 468–79.

PART THREE

The Nature and Consequences of the English Revolution

CHAPTER TWELVE

Introduction: Britain's Revolutions

The third part of this collection of essays is more varied and diffuse. It consists of a series of essays written over twenty years on aspects of the period 1640–90. I am not going to try to impose a rationalized unity upon them, beyond saying that I suppose they reveal a concern with the law of unintended consequences, the escalation of events out of control once civil war broke out, and the long shadow cast by the events of the 1640s over the rest of the century.

I have included my review of Christopher Hill's collected essays (chapter 14) because he is read nowadays far less than he was and should be – I am constantly dismayed that my new graduate students are unlikely to have read more than one or two works by him. For twenty years his was the interpretation that dominated the grammar school classroom. For those of us over the age of 40 he was, during our student days, *the* historian of seventeenth-century England. We were not necessarily brought up to accept his view of the period; but we were expected to define ourselves in relation to his powerful views.

He should still be read. *Society and Puritanism in Pre-Revolutionary England*, *The World Turned Upside Down*, *God's Englishmen* and innumerable essays are simply the most vital of his remarkable stream of publications. Anyone trying to see what created the agenda for many of the articles that follow should realize how much I owe to him and how discovering my own truth in the seventeenth century has caused me to wrestle with his ideas. It seems only right therefore to reprint my fullest published appreciation of his work and contribution. It appears as chapter 14. My main criticism has to do with sources; but there is another which is not perhaps sufficiently brought out in that essay. My centre of gravity has always been in the 1640s. I have been concerned to show how a generalized alarm at misgovernment in 1640 turned into a focussed militarized struggle in 1642 over limited objectives; and how *that* limited conflict turned into Revolution by 1649. Christopher Hill's interests have been fairly broad-brush down to the civil war and then an intense focus on the writings of the post-civil-war years, 1647–60. He has not concerned himself with the nature of the crisis of 1642 nor with how we get from there to 1649. But he has (far more than I have) thrown a powerful spotlight on the writings made possible by the teeming liberty inaugurated by the overthrow of those great landmarks, Church, Crown and House of Lords.

I have included another review essay at the head of this section. Conrad Russell's eloquent voice has been a distinctive one within the revisionist ensemble of the 1980s. His ideas and mine have developed very much side-by-side, emphasizing the importance of central-local relations in the 1970s, religion in the early 1980s, and the British dimension in the later 1980s and early 1990s. I have included this review largely to illustrate how important I now think the British dimension to be, and why I am rather more radical than is Russell about where I would want to take the argument. For the past five years Brendan Bradshaw and I have been running a final-year Cambridge undergraduate course entitled *The British Problem: England, Ireland, Scotland, c.1534–1707*. It has led me to see that we have here something more than three separate histories colliding, and to call for a holistic approach to the history of the British Isles. Thus I have described Russell's approach as 'enriched English History' rather than 'British History'. It will, however, be some time before the full fruits of this new approach become apparent.[1] Rereading that review after a few months leads me to one other conclusion. I have just said that my centre of gravity has always been the 1640s as against Christopher Hill's 1650s. In relation to the outbreak of the civil war, it seems to me that Conrad Russell's recent books concentrate on explaining what happens between the spring of 1640 and the summer of 1641. By then he sees the momentum to polarization and war as unstoppable. By contrast my own work is less concerned with

---

1. My preliminary attempt to write a British History appears above, chapter 5. A more developed account was given at a Conference at the University of Illinois in April 1990 and as a James Ford Special lecture in Oxford in November 1991 under the title 'A British Patriarchy? Ecclesiastical Imperialism under the early Stuarts', and it is now in press in a festschrift. I am currently researching a book which will explore the interactions of the Reformation processes in England, Ireland and Scotland over the period 1559 to 1689.

that period than with the events of the period November 1641 to August 1642. I think I have had an oversimplified view of the events of 1641 but can offer a more open-ended account of 1642, with neither king nor parliament able to command the loyalty of the mass of backbenchers or of the provinces and with many possible outcomes other than a nation by the sword divided.

I twice tried to write a book to be called *England's Wars of Religion*. The first version (twelve chapters written, four unwritten) was abandoned in 1981. It was ultra-revisionist, and its early chapters were entitled 'the strength of early Stuart monarchy', 'the weakness of early Stuart monarchy', 'the decline of early Stuart monarchy' and 'the fall of early Stuart monarchy'. The second version, written in 1987, was even less complete. But it began with four chapters entitled 'The Social Context of the English Civil War', 'the political context . . .', 'the religious context . . .' and 'the British context . . .' The religious context would have been a revised version of what appears as chapter 3 above. The 'political context' would have been an alternative version of chapter 15 here. It explores the reticence of the constitutional rhetoric of 1641–2, the deafening silences, the inhibition. In an early incarnation the paper was entitled 'circumspection and circumscription' and it was an attempt to show that not only was there reticence in the rhetoric; there was an ensuing reticence of action. The purpose, of course, was to strengthen the claim that only the heady language and the imperative call to action contained in puritan rhetoric could break down 'resistance to resistance theory' in 1641–2. There were secular constitutional reasons for preferring the parliamentarian to the royalist cause; but only an additional injection of zeal turned armchair preferences into a determination to use force to press them home. With the caveats mentioned in ch. 2, pp. 36–8, in mind, I would still feel that that was a case worth arguing.

My views on the war years themselves are still very much as laid out in *The Revolt of the Provinces*, chapters 2 and 3.[2] I have not found any reason to change my mind on the major points made in that book, although historians like Ann Hughes and David Underdown have taught me to qualify some of the balder claims – about the nature of 'parliamentary tyranny', for example, or about the high-

---

2. But see also my introductions to *Reactions to the English Civil War* (1982) and to *The Impact of the English Civil War* (1991).

minded neutralism of the Clubmen.[3]

As far as this volume is concerned, the next theme is that of army radicalism in the later 1640s. Chapter 16, my first publication, is an article which grew out of a paper given to Keith Thomas's seminar in Oxford at about the time I completed my D.Phil., with shavings from it and some of the preparatory research for what turned into *The Revolt of the Provinces*. It was, I suppose, revisionism *avant la lettre*, with its attempt to put the Army Revolts of 1647 into perspective and to contextualize them so as to emphasize bread-and-butter complaints at the expense of Leveller constitutionalism. This was taken a stage further by chapter 17, a piece which began life as a conference paper in 1976 and which sought to analyze the debates within the New Model Army in the summer and autumn of 1647. Once again I was exploring and challenging the view that the radicalization of the New Model was the product of Leveller infiltration and of tensions between the Grandees and the rank-and-file. The first essay ('Mutiny and Discontent in English Provincial Armies') still seems to me a sound piece of empirical research. The second ('The Army Revolt of 1647') is a piece I have mixed feelings about. The deep ambivalence among the Leveller leaders about the army and the ambivalences within the army (among rank-and-filers as well as officers) about the Leveller programme needed exposing; as did the importance of the papers of the Committee of Indemnity, hitherto little used.[4] It is an essay that has never quite convinced me. I felt the themes needed airing, and I cannot fault the logic. But somehow my historical intuition tells me I did not get it quite right. One day someone will spot the flaw. Meanwhile, it remains a piece that does present a challenge to traditional views about the radicalization of the army.[5] Meanwhile I would like to float an idea I had in 1976 and was

3. In general support of what I argued see the chapters by Pennington and Ashton in Morrill, (ed.) *Reactions*; and for telling qualifications see A. Hughes, 'Parliamentary Tyranny? Indemnity Proceedings and the Impact of the Civil War: a case study from Warwickshire', *Midland History*, XI (1986), 49–78; A. Hughes, 'The King, the Parliament and the Localities during the English Civil War', *Jnl. Brit. Studs.*, 24 (1985), 236–63; D.E. Underdown, 'The Chalk and the Cheese: Contrasts among the English Clubmen', *Past and Present*, 85 (1979), 25–48.
4. I was assisted in my work on these papers (class SP24 in the Public Records Office) by reading an unpublished paper on indemnity by Gerald Aylmer. Since then several historians have explored them, no-one more successfully than Ann Hughes, 'Parliamentary Tyranny?'.
5. Since I wrote that article there has been much written on the army and the Levellers, notably by Mark Kishlansky, *The Rise of the New Model Army* (Cambridge, 1979), esp. chs. 7–8; A. Woolrych, *Soldiers and Statesmen: The General Council of the Army and its Debates 1647–1648* (Oxford, 1987), *passim*; I. Gentles, *The New Model Army in England, Ireland and Scotland 1645–1653* (Oxford, 1991), chs. 6–8.

too timid to advance then, although its plausibility was reinforced for me by reading Austin Woolrych's *Soldiers and Statesmen* ten years later. What do we take to be the significance of the term 'agitator', used of those who represented the rank-and-file of the army on the General Council? And in what sense were they 'elected'? According to the *Oxford English Dictionary*, the linkage between agitator and agitation or political plotting is a late eighteenth-century usage. With respect to 1647, the *Dictionary* rightly sees it as 'varied with adjutator, a corruption infl[uenced] by *adjutant* or *adjutor*'. Indeed, in a sample I made of thirty newsletters and pamphlets from 1647, 17 used 'adjutator' and 13 had 'agitator'. The definition of 'adjutator' is 'helper' or 'assistant'. It leads me to speculate that the 'adjutators' chosen in the spring of 1647 were not 'elected' by their fellow soldiers but coopted by the officers. What evidence is there for either view? Which is the more likely to have traces in the political record?

Perhaps I should also add that although these essays (and chapter 18 – 'Order and Disorder in the English Revolution') play down the significance of Leveller ideas as the basis of popular politics in the later 1640s, I take the Levellers very seriously. It has been a long-term private commitment on my part to write at length about Leveller ideas and what they tell us about the later 1640s.[6] Two essays, by Colin Davis and Brian Manning,[7] would be my starting point. But I would want to examine how Leveller pamphlets and petitions combined deeply regressive economic and social ideas with a core commitment to religious liberty and to a political doctrine born of experience in Independent churches, all bound together in an innovative natural rights framework.

Chapter 18 ('Order and Disorder in the English Revolution') is also about the limits of the radical challenge. It was written jointly with John Walter and was very much more than the sum of our parts. Unlike chapter 17, I always felt that this essay did hit the nail on the head, and I have been surprised and disappointed that it has not received more attention than it has. I think it is certainly a better and truer piece of history than chapters 2 or 3, for example. The argument about the trajectory of violence, with a peak in 1641, or the argument about the threat of disorder being more important than the reality,

---

6. The nearest I ever got was in a very revisionist (3,000-word) essay on John Lilburne in R. Greaves and R. Zaller, (eds.) *Dictionary of British Radicals: the Seventeenth Century* (3 vols., 1982), II, 185–90.
7. J.C. Davis, 'The Levellers and Christianity' in B. Manning (ed.), *Politics, Religion and the English Civil War* (1972), pp. 225–50; B. Manning, *The English People and the English Revolution* (1976), ch. 10.

did need saying. We were more speculative about the 1650s, but in general I would not wish to change much in this article, although Bill Cliftlands, in a rather unstructured but intellectually powerful PhD on the middling-sort activists of Essex and Cheshire in the 1640s certainly taught me a lot about the dynamics of protest.[8]

The last two chapters are fairly recent, and they stand here as examples of my thinking about the consequences of the Revolution of 1649. Chapter 19 ('A Glorious Resolution?') began as a paper to a conference in Los Angeles in 1988. A heavily truncated and revised version was published in *History Today*. I hesitated about which version to publish. The longer version is certainly flawed: I am far from clear that what I say about Locke is fair to Locke or even to Locke scholarship; and at the Conference in Los Angeles John Pocock certainly showed that the links I had tried to make between Locke's prescriptions and the actual ills of the English polity in the 1680s could not take the strain I had placed upon them. This version therefore incorporates some changes to deal with that problem and it draws on the wise advice of Norma Landau, the commentator, who concentrated on my argument about the weakening ties of the centre over the provinces. It remains flawed, but I prefer it to the shorter version because it attempts more of an overview than the *History Today* version does.

The final essay in the volume ('The Sensible Revolution') has a clear message: that G.M. Trevelyan's analysis of the significance of 1688, however little he researched it, still has much to teach us. But there is a clear subtext which I became aware of as I was writing it. It was my liberation from some of the failings of revisionism. Faced by a revisionist historiography of 1688 in which I had no investment, I could see its limitations: I recognized the force of the historical law of unintended consequences; I recognized how certain kinds of narrative foreclosed any recognition of underlying causes; I applied to the Revolution of 1688 the distinction between 'weak' and 'strong' teleology which Glenn Burgess has so fruitfully explored for the early seventeenth century. Burgess has argued that all history must be written with an end (*telos*) in view, an end determined by historians before they complete their writing in order that they can structure and convey their thoughts to their readers (weak teleology); but they do not have to believe that such an end is inevitable and

---

8. W. Cliftlands, 'The Well-Affected and the Country', Religion and Politics in English Provincial Society, c.1640–c.1654, Univ. of Essex PhD thesis (1988), esp. chs. 3–4.

predetermined (strong teleology). Revisionism, he suggests, rejects strong teleology, and with it anachronism, the use of present-day standards and concepts to organize our study of the past or to judge the past; and it rejects the idea that one can deduce the motivation of historical actors by looking at the consequences of their actions. Revisionists, he suggests, have confused their antipathy towards anachronism with an unrealistic rejection of all forms of teleology[9] I plead guilty to having suffered from that confusion and hope chapter 20 represents a healthier reinstatement of 'weak' teleology into my writing.

This final essay allowed me to see more clearly some aspects of the earlier crisis. Discovering so many resonances of the 1640s in the 1680s helped me to get the continuities of the century into focus – whether about parliamentary history or the nature of anti-catholicism. Most important was the recognition of a key difference between 1642 and 1689: in both there was a vast middle ground of men who disagreed on a range of issues which mattered deeply to them but who wanted to believe that these differences were negotiable, and in both there were activist minorities ready and willing to resolve the differences by force. The difference between 1642 and 1689 is that *in 1689 the centre held*. The implications of this statement for the 1690s and beyond are spelt out in chapter 20. The implications for our understanding of the 1640s of the centre not holding will be found in my forthcoming work on the civil war. But it put a lot of my earlier thinking into perspective. It remains to be seen whether I can apply the lessons I learnt from this therapeutic exploration of the events of 1688–90 to my future writing about the nearly-parallel events of 1640–2.

9. G. Burgess, 'On Revisionism: an Analysis of Early Stuart Historiography in the 1970s and 1980s', *HJ*, 33 (1990), 614–16.

CHAPTER THIRTEEN

The Causes of Britain's Civil Wars[1]

I

Three books from Conrad Russell in a six-month period is a feast indeed.[2] Russell combines a keen intelligence with an out-of-the-ordinary ability to ask startling and challenging questions and to approach issues from new and refreshing angles. His eye for the apt and telling quotation is second to none.

As *Unrevolutionary England*,[3] a collection of his essays, makes clear, Russell's principal research interests have been in the 1620s (and especially in the parliamentary history of that decade[4] and in the years 1637–42.[5] Several of the essays have acquired classic status, including 'Parliamentary History in Perpective, 1604–1629' (first published in *History*, 1976), the clarion call to revisionism and the precursor of *Parliaments and English Politics 1621–1629* (Oxford, 1979), which set the agenda on the 1620s for the 1980s. Another essay reprinted in *Unrevolutionary England*, his inaugural lecture as Astor Professor, 'The British Problem and the English Civil War', is an equally important harbinger of his two brand-new books.[6] Both of these argue that in order to understand the collapse of Charles's power in England, we

---

1. I am grateful to Colin Davis, Jonathan Scott and David Smith for their helpful comments on drafts of this essay a shortened version of which appeared in *Jnl. Eccl. Hist.*, 43 (1992).
2. *The Causes of the English Civil Wars. The Ford Lectures delivered in the University of Oxford, 1987–1988* (Oxford: Clarendon Press, 1990), pp. xv + 236; *The Fall of the British Monarchies 1637–1642.* (Oxford: Clarendon Press, 1991), pp. xx + 550; *Unrevolutionary England, 1603–1642.* (London: Hambledon Press, 1990), pp. xii + 286.
3. This reprints sixteen essays published over the past 25 years.
4. Five of the sixteen essays are on this subject.
5. Eight of the sixteen essays are on this subject.
6. First published in *History*, LXXII (1987).

have to recognize the effect on English politics of the prior collapse of his power in Scotland and Ireland and the interaction between the events in all three kingdoms.

The two works are intimately connected. As Russell puts it:

> My order of researching, and of writing, has been to compose a three-kingdom narrative of events, *The Fall of the British Monarchies 1637–1642*, and only then, when I decided what I needed to explain, to consider *The Causes of the English Civil War*. . . . I hope the two books will be taken as a single corpus of work, and judged as a whole.[7]

Each book – and not just *The Fall of the British Monarchies* – is certainly fully comprehensible on its own. Readers of *The Causes of the English Civil War* who want to see the evidence rather than follow the argument will, however, frequently need to cross-refer to the much larger work, *The Fall of the British Monarchies, 1637–1642*.

II

The Causes of the English Civil War has not been well served by the publicity department of Oxford University Press. It is a published version of his Ford Lectures at Oxford in 1988, and it has the scintillation and challenge appropriate to such a series of lectures. It is not, however, a *vade mecum* for undergraduates or sixth-formers coming to grips with this period for the first time. It presumes a great deal of background knowledge, and it offers only occasional and limited commentary on the vast corpus of modern writing on the issues with which it is concerned.[8] One chapter does engage in an argument with the writings of Johann Sommerville,[9] but much of the best and most influential writing on the period goes unmentioned.[10] This would not matter if O.U.P. had not attempted to promote this book as though it was the replacement for Lawrence Stone's *Causes of the English Revolution*. It isn't, although it is a great deal more. As an *introduction* to the period and its problems, the book by Ann Hughes, which shares its title with Russell's Ford Lectures, has to be preferred. By contrast, Russell's *Causes* is an advanced and very

---

7. *Causes*, p. ix. cf. *Causes*, p. 2.
8. See, for example, the statement that 'it is unnecessary to dwell on the changes produced in the Church of England by the triumph of the Arminians after York House. What this book would say on that subject would follow Dr Tyacke very closely, and perhaps we may take that as read' (*Cause*, p. 109).
9. J.P. Sommerville, *Politics and Ideology in England, 1603–1640* (1986).
10. None of the work of Anthony Fletcher, Brian Manning, David Underdown or myself is referred to in *Causes*, and it is hardly ever referred to in the text or footnotes of *The Fall*.

powerful presentation of a particular vision of a subject at the heart of English and of British History.

III

The Causes of the English Civil War consists of eight chapters and a brief conclusion. The first chapter ('The Corpus Delicti') identifies various unhelpful approaches to the problem (arguing that it was not a 'clash of clearly differentiated social groups or classes' [p. 2]; that it was not 'a conflict between a court and a country, or a government and an opposition' [p. 4]; and that 'there is little evidence to suggest that the more extreme radical ideas originated before the crisis of 1637–42, rather than as a response to it' [p. 8]. Russell then develops his thesis that the English civil war was only made possible by the prior revolts in Scotland and Ireland: 'what we should be explaining is not why revolutionary propensities in England were so strong, but why [in comparison to those in the outlying kingdoms] they were so weak' (p. 11). The ensuing discussion identifies seven effects of this reorientation, and the problem of their conjunction. These are not '"causes of the civil war"; but . . . causes of the events which led to civil war'. They were: 'the Bishops' Wars, England's defeat in the Bishops' Wars, the failure to reach a settlement [between November 1640 and May 1641], the failure to dissolve or prorogue the Parliament, the choice of sides, the failure to negotiate, and the problem of the King's diminished Majesty' (p. 24). Collectively, these were 'causes of the events which led to civil war . . . the removal of any one of [which] could have prevented the Civil War as we know it'. These seven 'causes of the events' act as leitmotifs running through the whole book. Readers need to dwell on this chapter. For if Russell's characterization of what it is that needs explaining does not convince, the rest of the book loses much of its potency. My own view is that these are – within limits to be discussed below[11] – very helpful ways into an analysis of the crisis of 1640–2. I find little to disagree with in Russell's characterization of these points, and his use of them to prise open the politics of 1638–42 is fruitful. I have to say that, as Blair Worden has pointed out, they cannot logically be *the* seven indispensable 'causes of the events'.[12] Many other things caused events without which there could not have been civil war or

---

11. See pp. 271–2.
12. Blair Worden's review based on a careful reading of the two books lays down a powerful challenge to the self-sufficiency of these seven 'causes of the events' and to the illogicality of Russell's reliance upon them (Blair Worden, 'Conrad Russell's Civil War', *London Review of Books*, 29 Aug. 1991, pp. 13–14).

that civil war. Furthermore, while Russell's general thesis underlies the narrative of *The Fall of the British Monarchies*, these seven are not really any more evident than a host of other 'causes of events'.

Chapters 2 ('The Problem of Multiple Kingdoms, c. 1580–1630') and 5 ('Religious Unity in Three Kingdoms . . . 1625–1642') develop the thesis that the English civil war was the culmination of a crisis of multiple kingship, of the constant 'billiard-ball effect of each of the kingdoms on the affairs of the others' (p. 27). Emphasis throughout both chapters is on the tensions between the Reformations in England, Ireland and Scotland, and on the contrast between James VI and I's skill in managing those tensions, and the folly of Charles I in exacerbating them.[13]

Between these chapters come two discussing the developing religious crisis in England. Chapter 3 ('The Church, Religion and Politics: the Problem of the Definite Article') analyzes why and how religion proved the greatest divider of the English nation in the years 1640–2. Distinguishing those who were to take sides 'because of religion' from those who took sides 'for religion' (p. 62), Russell places great emphasis on the fact that the civil war began 'not as an uprising in the provinces but with breakdown in the centre'; and he argues that religion is crucial in explaining not only the origins and outcome of the Bishops' Wars but in creating the pro- and anti-Scottish factions in 1640–1 which he believes were to form the kernels of the royalist and parliamentarian parties in 1642. He also suggests that it was the pursuit of root-and-branch and other religious issues (the price English politicians paid for maintaining the military pressure of the Scots) that was to make settlement with the king impossible, and that was to generate epidemics of distrust on both sides.

In the three remaining chapters, Russell moves on from his twin and intertwined themes of the collapse of British monarchies and the derailing of the Jacobethan religious settlement. In chapter 6, he examines the limited contribution that rival conceptions of sovereignty played in causing the breakdown. In a rebuttal of the work of Johann Sommerville (pp. 144–50)[14] and in a careful discussion of the failure of the parliamentarians to develop resistance theory in the

---

13. Cf. A. Macinnes, *Charles I and the Making of the Covenanting Movement 1625–1640* (Edinburgh, 1991), and essays by Macinnes, E.J. Cowan, and others in J.S. Morrill (ed.), *The Scottish National Covenant in its British Context 1638–1651* (Edinburgh, 1991). Perhaps I should add that I myself am sympathetic to Russell's emphasis on religious factors if not wholly to his characterization of them (see J.S. Morrill, 'A British Patriarchy? Ecclesiastical Imperialism under the early Stuarts', forthcoming).

14. Sommerville, *Politics and Ideology.*

years and months before the king raised his standard (pp. 132–5, 150)[15] Russell narrows down the secular constitutional issues that compelled men to take sides, although he does offer an elegant discussion of the drift by Charles's opponents into arguments from necessity and into a widespread perception of a growing *parliamentary* tyranny, and he shows how 'during 1642 argument came to concentrate on how far the authority of the Crown could be separated from the King's person' (p. 159). He also takes up the argument that the events of 1640–2 should be seen largely as a failed baronial coup in a tradition stretching back to the fourteenth century and beyond.[16]

In chapter 7 ('The Poverty of the Crown and the Weakness of the King'), Russell looks at the crisis of royal finances over the half century before 1641 ('the painful death of [a] system the Stuarts inherited [from] the fourteenth century' [p. 166]) and at the particular problems that the reforms of 1641 created for those involved in finding a new basis for settled government. He concludes that 'the links which lead from financial breakdown to civil war are in all cases indirect', and that although we should not suppose 'that financial breakdown by itself was ever likely to lead to civil war, it did make it very much more likely that the upheaval precipitated by the Scottish invasion of 1640 would do so' (pp. 183–4).

The final chapter looks at 'the Man Charles Stuart'. It is a finely-nuanced portrait, recognizing Charles's unfitness for government (as shown in his personal responsibility for initiating and largely for defeat in the Bishops' Wars, his major contribution to the failure to find a settlement in 1641, and inability to shake himself loose from the Long Parliament). Russell also stresses Charles's 'tunnel vision' – albeit one which was mirrored by that of Pym; his incomprehension of views different from those of his own; and his utter inflexibility in 'the area where religion and his authority' met. But he also praises Charles's ability to form and to nurture a party in 1641; and he is more sympathetic than most recent commentators in identifying the intolerable demands of Charles's opponents:

> One reason for the intransigence of Charles and Henrietta Maria which is not generally appreciated, and which makes their position appear less irrational . . . is the resolute refusal of Pym and his fellow-Parliamentarians to allow Henrietta Maria her Mass, or the services of any priest whatsoever (p. 193).

15. For a fuller discussion of this point, see J.S. Morrill, 'Charles I, Tyranny and the English Civil War', below, ch. 15.
16. J.S.A. Adamson, 'The Baronial Context of the English Civil War', *TRHS*, 5th ser., vol. 40 (1990). The influence is even stronger and more pervasive in *The Fall of the British Monarchies*, as at pp. 151–2, 274–7, 365–6.

This concluding chapter is one of the most persuasive, and it ends with a pleasing paradox: 'perhaps the real lesson of 1641 was that Charles was incompetent, but not quite incompetent enough to leave the kingdom free from civil war'.[17]

IV

I have dwelt at length on the argument of the *Causes* because it gives coherence to the great body of work Russell has published over the past decade, as represented in the essays in *Unrevolutionary England* and as the underpinning of the *Fall of the British Monarchies*. What those books add is a mass of illuminating detail, and an endless succession of fresh epigrams and startling connections. Right at the beginning of *The Fall of the British Monarchies*, there is a succession of thumbnail sketches showing how those who were offended by what Charles and his ministers were doing were preoccupied with finding ways of bringing about changes of policy, ways which fell short of a resort to violence. Throughout the discussion of the events of 1640–2 there is a vivid recreation of the web of connection among the parliamentary 'managers' and between them and the Scots. For this reviewer, the analysis of the projected settlement of 1641 (chapter 6) was the high point of the book, equally important in its analysis of religion, finance and the storming of the closet. Arising from this chapter, but powerfully followed through later, is Russell's analysis of the fading prospects of a moderate church settlement (cf. *The Fall*, pp. 249–51 and 342–5). In just the same way as Russell was the first historian to unravel and make sense of the complexities of the First Army Plot,[18] so now he is the first to explain convincingly the Incident, the Scottish dress rehearsal for the Attempt on the Five Members (*The Fall*, pp. 322–8). However, the book is less fertile in new ideas as we move beyond the summer recess of 1641. It is striking that Russell devotes 250 pages to the first ten months of the Long Parliament (up to the autumn recess) and only 120 pages to the 10 months after it (down to the raising of the royal standard). However, what I am saying is that while the big book is intended as the narrative that demonstrates in practice the concepts of the pithier

17. There are many further insights into the mind and personality of Charles in *The Fall*, including a striking section at pp. 50–4, and an illuminating discussion of how Charles and Pym came to misread the same situations in psychologically similar ways at pp. 444–6.
18. Reprinted in *Unrevolutionary England*, pp. 281–302, and see now *The Fall*, pp. 291–4.

book, there is in it much to deepen our understanding of the *why* questions as well as the *how* questions.

Cumulatively, these books will set an agenda for debate among historians in the 1990s. Russell has achieved many things which will surely become normative. It is unlikely that anyone will henceforth see the crisis in England as other than part of a crisis throughout the British Isles, or will fail to recognize the force of Russell's billiard-ball conceit. Among the arguments likely to carry many but not all with Russell, I would include: his characterization of the Laudian challenge; his picture of a country badly governed after 1625 and as less governable than it had been though certainly not ungovernable; and his insistence on much greater precision about what it is that needs to be explained and (even more important) his insistence on a very precise sense of the chronology of crisis. Many readers, furthermore, will be at least as much instructed by the brilliant aphorisms,[19] the wonderful eye (or is it ear?) for the apt quotation,[20] the ability to make vivid a particular incident or person,[21] the startling counter-factual speculation,[22] the ability to take in the broad sweep of English history.[23]

V

I was left with three main areas of dissatisfaction. I will discuss first the way in which he treats the problem of multiple kingdoms. I will argue both that he does not go far enough in seeking to develop a holistic approach to British History and that he overstates the importance of Scottish pressure in explaining religious polarization in England. I will seek to demonstrate that this allows him to concentrate too much on the high political intrigues of the king and Juntos in all three kingdoms, and that he fails to give sufficient weight to what is happening in the English provinces. And I will conclude that he

19. E.g., of the memorandum of Lord Herbert of Cherbury at the time of the making of the Scottish canons, a memorandum resting on scripture rather than statute: 'it is a claim to supremacy *iure divino*' (*Causes*, p. 114).
20. Impossible to document out of context. For some favourites of mine, see *Causes*, p. 115 (Robert Baillie on Charles's ecclesiastical authoritarianism in Scotland); or the French ambassador's characterization of Charles's unrealistic search for '*parlement a sa mode*'.
21. For example, nothing has brought home to me so clearly the dilemmas of the elite in the 1630s as the case studies of 1637 in *Fall*, pp. 2–8.
22. For example, the speculations about what would have happened if James had been succeeded by his daughter and not his son; or if it had been Charles not Bedford who had died in May 1641 (*Causes*, p. 212).
23. E.g., that the war of 1639 was 'the first war to be fought without a Parliament since 1323' (*Causes*, p. 12).

understates the explosive power of English puritanism to generate a national movement ready to fight the king, and, in direct response to puritan militancy, a national movement ready to join a discredited king.

VI

There is a tension between the titles of Russell's two books: *The Causes of the **English** Civil War*; *The Fall of the **British** Monarchies*. In fact in both cases his concern is to explain the course of **English** history. Russell argues that to understand what happens in England in 1642 we need to see what happened first in Scotland and Ireland, so that we can see how that allows us to understand English history. Thus we do not hear about the non-religious background to the Scottish revolt. We are not invited to consider the causes of the events that led to the 1638 rebellion, that wider alienation of the greater part of the Scottish elite. Neither book discusses or evaluates the Act of Revocation or the reorganization of Scottish government, for example. The Fall of the Irish Monarchy in 1641 is treated as even more of a *diabolus ex machina*, a bolt out of the blue that matters because it destroyed lingering hopes of a settlement. Even though Strafford's fall on charges connected with Ireland revealed a reconfiguration of Irish politics as a result of his adamantine authoritarianism in Ireland, there is no analysis of events in Ireland in *The Fall of the British Monarchies* until page 373.

This matters. Russell is interested in explaining England's collapse into civil war. He says that it could not have happened (at least as it did) without the prior collapse of royal authority in Scotland and Ireland. He offers three main reasons for this. Firstly, he suggests that whatever the financial and military frailties of the English state, the elite was sufficiently in control and the vested interest of the elite too tied into the existing structures for any successful rebellion to be feasible. There may have been combustible material around, but spontaneous combustion was impossible. Secondly, the violence in Scotland created conditions for the recall of the English Parliament in circumstances in which uniquely the king lost the initiative; and the violence in Ireland created an issue (control of the army of reconquest) that forced a politically divided elite to arms. Thirdly, the Scottish rebellion caused leading members of the English political elite to commit treason. Ever thereafter they were compelled by fear for their own survival to make demands of the king which he simply could not be expected to concede.

All this is true. But why did Scotland and Ireland rebel? Here

Russell is in difficulties. For by not examining the 'causes of the events that led to' those rebellions he leaves open the possibility that there are common causes of all three rebellions. The causes of the events *may* have been local and specific. But it is equally possible that they were interconnected. Russell's billiard-ball effect requires an equal and equally full analysis of the preconditions of the collapse of the Scottish, Irish and English monarchies. What we are offered in these books is not a holistic approach to British history but an enriched English history. What we do not get, and yet what the logic of Russell's argument and the detail of his researches demand, is a study of *The Causes of the **British** Civil Wars*. We need to know the causes of the events that led to a British civil war rather than an account of how events in two became causes of the event in a third kingdom.

Allied to this is a second concern: Russell's characterization of royal ecclesiastical policy in Scotland. He writes:

> Charles and Laud [sought] to construct a new programme of British uniformity. Since their major commitment was to those features of the English church which were conspicuously absent in Ireland and Scotland, this programme for British uniformity inevitably turned into one for English hegemony. (*Causes*, p. 111)

But was it a programme of 'British uniformity'? It is striking that despite the widespread discussion in intellectual circles in the 1630s about the Patriarchies of the ancient Church, and of the Patriarchy of Britain in particular, Laud never resurrected the claims of Canterbury to jurisdiction over the Church in Ireland, nor of Canterbury and York to jurisdiction over Scotland. Nor did Charles seek to transform the nature of episcopal authority in Scotland into that held by English bishops, and even if he could not bring himself to enshrine presbyterian forms in the Scottish canons, the polity of the Church of Scotland remained episcopacy-in-presbytery. When Charles came to provide a liturgy for Scotland, he did not impose the English Prayer Book, but one which both respected many Scottish customs and imposed ceremonies which were not permitted by the English Prayer Book. The Scots case in 1637–8 was not that they were being anglicanized, but that they were being subjected to something worse than the English Prayer Book. The Churches of Scotland and Ireland were not being subordinated to the jurisdiction of the Church of England nor was there a straightforward English acculturation of Scotland. What Scotland and Ireland experienced was nothing as straightforward as a drive for uniformity; rather each was subject to a naked royal authoritarianism that followed overlapping but distinct objectives in each kingdom.[24] This was, indeed, in Russell's evocative phrase, royal supremacy *iure divino*, but it was constrained in each kingdom only by the limits of the king's ignorance of local law and custom. I would suggest, then, that we need to distinguish between a policy *common to* all kingdoms and a policy *for* all three kingdoms.

Furthermore, Russell surely does not get the nature of the Scottish response quite right. He characterizes this as a *Scottish Imperial* policy,[25] a determination to safeguard true religion in Scotland by imposing their own ecclesiology on England (and on Ireland) and (since Charles could not be trusted to honour concessions extorted from him) this had to be secured 'by constitutional arrangements which deprived him of the power to reverse them' – a triple emasculation to be effected by the Parliaments of England, Scotland and Ireland.

Now I have to say I think his notion of a 'Scottish imperial vision' has serious distorting effects. It is true that from at least the time of the second Bishops' War, the Scottish Junto (to coin a phrase) headed by Argyll and Wariston were determined to redefine the religious and constitutional relationship between the three kingdoms. But that was to be by a federal structure not by institutional uniformity, let alone integration. And there is nothing the English Junto were less interested in than in federal union.[26] A full discussion of Anglo-Scottish relations in this period would require an analysis of the deteriorating relations between English and Scottish Juntos as the indifference of the former to the political vision of the latter became painfully obvious. This of course explains why the Scots are so uninterested in making common cause with the Junto in the summer of 1642 or again until Charles's dealings with the Irish Confederates in 1643 drove them to it. But these themes are not explored.

Russell needs the Scottish Imperial vision to explain the rapid radicalization of the Long Parliament in matters of religion. His account of the English Reformation process as one of continuous tension plays down puritan militancy in the period 1625–41 while stressing the offensiveness and the dynamism of Laudianism. Russell does not accept that there is sufficient puritan militancy around in the 1630s to explain the polarization in 1641 and 1642. Here the Scots are indeed a *diabolus ex machina* and time and again in *The Fall of the British*

---

24. See J.S. Morrill, 'A British Patriarchy? Ecclesiastical Imperialism under the early Stuarts', forthcoming.
25. B. Levack, *The Formation of the British State* (Oxford, 1987), pp. 108–11, 128–9.
26. As in P. Donald, *An Uncounselled King* (Cambridge, 1990), chs. 5–7.

Monarchies, Scots ministerial pressure is seen as the engine behind the Junto's religious policy.

The Scots (or at least many of them) did indeed come to believe that the Scottish revolution of 1639–41 would need to be secured by constitutional arrangements that deprived Charles of the power to reverse them. But they had no desire for an integration of the English and Scottish states. In 1641 the Scots wanted two of everything: two Parliaments, two Councils, two legal systems, two Churches; and they wanted means to coordinate them – joint commissions of parliamentarians, *conservatores pacis*, etc. In religion they wanted an end to episcopacy throughout the British Isles, but not a mega-kirk.

Nothing interested the English Junto less than a federal union with Scotland. The Union of 1603 had suited the interests of the English well enough and the only alternative worth considering by English politicians in 1641 as in 1606 was incorporative union. Their indifference to Scottish federal unionism is demonstrated by the Long Parliament's refusal to negotiate seriously over it in 1641, their failure to develop the institutional arrangements which the Scots assumed to be part of the package negotiated as the Solemn League and Covenant, and the hash English politicians made of Anglo-Scottish relations in 1648–50. In fact their relations with the Scots were always more ambivalent than Russell allows. The English wanted to use the Scots rebellion to cantilever themselves into power in 1640. It is not clear that they would not have been willing to pay for the conquest of Scotland in the summer of 1640 if they could thereby wring the concessions they most needed out of Charles. Sympathy for the plight of the Scots did not create a blood bond between Saye and Argyll or between Pym and Wariston.

The Scots ministers in London were certainly active in 1641, promoting the cause of godly reformation and presbyterian discipline. Russell demonstrates that the pace and timing of the progress of ecclesiastical activity in the Long Parliament was shaped in response to that Scottish pressure. But at times Russell seems to let the Scottish tail wag the English dog. This is most obvious when he says that 'the 1707 solution, allowing two churches within one united kingdom, was not one that was conceptually possible in the middle of the seventeenth century' (*Fall*, p. 170). But surely it did prove conceptually possible for anyone who saw forms of church government as adiaphoristic (most of the constitutional royalists and those who refused to take sides in the ensuing war); it proved possible for the primitive episcopacy party among the future parliamentarians and for those who were drawn to the New England way as a blueprint for England without considering it necessary to impose it on Scotland. It is equally true for the little Scotlander groups among the Scottish peerage who were increasingly impatient with Argyll's will to determine the outcome of the crisis in England. Other examples of what may be exaggerations of the Scottish dynamic of religious policy include the statement that 'the [etcetera] oath and the canons [of 1640] generally were probably intended to isolate and reveal the pro-Scots' (*Fall*, p. 139) and the account of Scottish pressure behind the root and branch petitions (*Fall*, pp. 180–1).[27] Although Russell has strengthened our awareness of the nature and extent of Scottish ministerial pressure, it has been at the expense of other pressures. As I have suggested elsewhere, those seeking to marshall the voices of protest against recent misgovernment of church and state in 1641 were visibly shaken by the scale and virulence of the demands for reformation and renewal coming up from the provinces (almost all of it unorchestrated from the centre). Just as important were the alternative intellectual pressures on the Junto. For 1641 saw not just the arrival of a handful of Scottish ministers but the return of many of the exiles from New England and the Netherlands; and the voices of such men – such as Jeremiah Burroughs, Samuel Eaton, Hugh Peter – were (as events amply proved) far more influential in shaping the plans of those who determined to withstand Charles by force than were Scottish voices.

Finally, while the presence of the Scots helped to shape the course of events during the first session of the Long Parliament, the withdrawal of the Scottish army in the summer of 1641 and the signing of the Treaty of London removed that influence. The drift to war after the summer recess, and the drift towards an ever-harder commitment to the abolition of episcopacy, has to be explained in other terms. Russell believes that by the summer of 1641 the Junto was so deeply compromised by their actions that unless Charles I remained manacled to the wall he would seek to destroy them, and he believes that the

---

27. I would like to add a caveat about another potentially misleading statement on a matter of some importance. In *Fall*, p. 189, Russell writes that 'we are given a rare glimpse of the advance planning behind these petitions and also of the irritation Scottish pressure could cause for their English friends, in a letter written by Lord Howard of Escrick.' But the following discussion does not demonstrate the former point (and even the latter is not straightforward). His subsequent gloss, that 'central prompting [*of which there is no evidence adduced in this case*] was not a sufficient condition for the presentation of this petition' is nearer the mark. See now J.D. Maltby, 'Approaches to the Study of religious conformity in late Elizabethan and early Stuart England', University of Cambridge PhD thesis (1991), chs. 3 and 4.

treasonous correspondence with the Scots in 1639 and 1640 was a principal reason for the great gulf of trust between king and Junto. This is fair enough.

As a result, the events of the period from the first Bishops' War to the recess are exhaustively treated (the one startling, even deafening, silence being the mysterious episode of the letters between Lord Savile and the Scots in the summer of 1640).[28] In contrast we whizz through some of the major turning-points in the second session: the concessions that had to be made to get the Grand Remonstrance through; the narrow majorities achieved by Pym in a shrinking House of Commons (if only Charles had ordered his supporters to remain at their post after he had deserted his . . .); a very abbreviated account of the struggle to determine the precise content of the Nineteen Propositions; a failure to examine the possibility that the peace party, combined with neutralist sentiment among anxious backbenchers, might have stopped the Junto in their tracks.

Let me give one example of how, just occasionally and mainly after the summer recess of 1641, Russell does not follow through his own arguments as far as he might. One of his seven 'causes of the events' is 'the failure to dissolve or prorogue the Parliament' (*Causes*, pp. 16–17, 187). Yet any attempt on Charles's part to be rid of Parliament would both come up against the limiting Act of May 1641 and leave him in a hopeless financial position. What Charles needed, then, was a Parliament in which a majority had looked into the abyss and was reacting against what they had seen. Such a situation was

28. See S.R. Gardiner, *History of England 1603–1642* (10 vols., 1884), IX, 179–81. His lengthy footnote discusses the correspondence of leading English peers and the Scots allegedly culminating in Lord Savile's forgery of the signatures of six other peers alongside his own to a letter inviting the Scots to invade England and promising them military aid if they do so. Gardiner believed on the basis of the later memoirs of (he supposes) the 2nd earl of Manchester both that such a letter was sent and that it was Savile's forgery. (Clarendon tells substantially the same story in his *History*, in his book II, para. 107.) Peter Donald, *An Uncounselled King* (Cambridge, 1990), pp. 246–7, has cast doubts on the reliability of these memoirs. The behaviour of those implicated in treason by Savile in remaining his friends helping him to fulfil his ambitions for high office (Russell, *Fall*, p. 263), and even meeting at his house to coordinate with the Scots the drawing up of the Root-and-Branch petition (Donald, *op. cit.*, p. 281) deepens the mystery. It is possible both that the letter was sent but was not a forgery so that Manchester, fearful the Scots might reveal earlier treasons, sought to lay blame on Savile; or that he made up the whole episode. It is possible that the author of the memoirs was not Manchester but Falkland (or someone else). Less controversial is the status of the earlier correspondence between Savile and his fellow peers and the Scots (as published in Oldmixon, *History of England during the Reigns of the Royal House of Stuart* [1730], pp. 142–4). The episode ought to be central to Russell's theme, yet it is completely bypassed.

developing in the late summer of 1641. It is worth considering what would have happened if Charles had sent an order from Edinburgh in early October 1641 asking his Parliament to reconvene at York, away from the plague (he would have said), and where he could complete the deferred parts of Scottish treaty more easily (he would have said); and where (in fact) he could have removed the threat of mass picketing and the consequent intimidation of MPs. This would have put the Junto into a terrible quandary. Can it seriously be doubted but that much the greater part of the members would have accepted such a summons? If he had been lucky, many Junto leaders would have sulked and stayed away. Alternatively, what if Charles had instructed loyalist MPs to remain at Westminster in the spring of 1642? One of the striking things about parliamentary divisions in the months after the Attempt on the Five Members and the (surely a critical error?)[29] royal retreat from London is the way Pym's majority remained constant in a rapidly dwindling House. If half of those who had voted against the Grand Remonstrance and who subsequently abandoned London with the king had stayed put, it is unlikely that any of the major escalations towards war could have been put through the House of Commons.[30]

Russell's account thus becomes deterministic from the summer of 1641 on, when he falls victim to the belief that because the Junto could not afford to make peace, the Houses could not make peace. In explaining how they gained control of the Lords by the expulsion of the bishops, he fails to consider how easily they could have have lost control of the Commons. It may be that having so effectively argued against the teleological assumptions of earlier historians who treated the events of 1603–42 as leading naturally to the civil war of 1642, Russell has fallen into a high political teleology for the years 1641–2. Charles and the Junto were locked into a situation on which neither could avoid a head-on collision. But they were not the only players, and where king and Junto led others were not bound to follow.

VII

By asking much more sharply focussed questions about the dynamics of politics at Westminster and even more at Whitehall, and with the help of his 'causes of the events that led to civil war', Russell has aided

---

29. Were Charles and his family in real personal danger if he stayed? If the king had sent Henrietta Maria away (in case of her impeachment), was there any real chance Essex would have failed to defend the king's person from mob violence, assuming that that violence was not itself controllable by Junto leaders?
30. For an inkling of this point, see *Causes*, p. 124.

our understanding of how the king blundered away the initiative, and of how a powerful and supple Junto surprised and dismayed themselves into turning to an extra-constitutional form of redress: rebellion. For he has reinforced (especially in the early pages of *The Fall of the British Monarchies*) the view that the early seventeenth-century English political system and English political culture was a mature and highly sophisticated one in which political dissent and passionate debate were natural and inevitable, in which debate and dissent were both permitted within clearly recognized limits, and was a system and a culture in which various means of redress (in Court, Council and Parliament, by lobbying, petitioning, by acts of passive disobedience and so on) were both widely recognized and – at least until 1641 – assumed by almost everyone to be sufficient unto the task of bringing an end to misgovernment. Russell both captures the essence of this middle ground between revisionism and post-revisionism, and offers a persuasive account of how and in what stages that comforting belief that the political system contained the remedies to its own diseases collapsed and how the hundred or less men who took the initiatives at Westminster came reluctantly but grimly to call the nation to arms in defence of its liberties.

But in reaching that grim conclusion, that constitutionally-validated modes of redress were insufficient to secure religious and civil liberties, Russell may have distorted the story in two ways. The first is that he underestimates the pressure the Junto was under from what was happening in provincial England, and the second is that it does not fully explain the behaviour of that great majority of MPs who were independent of the clusters of peers and their commoner allies who set the agendas and dominated the procedure of the two Houses.

If the likes of Bedford, Warwick, Essex, Pym, Hampden, and St John felt under pressure from the Scots in 1641 and (supposedly) in 1642, how much more, surely, were they under pressure from the evidence of polarization, especially over religious issues in the provinces? The piling of horror story upon horror story of Laudian excesses,[31] the unmanageable press of writs of error from several hundred individuals claiming miscarriages of justice (many of them grotesque) in Caroline lawcourts,[32] the huge and geographically widespread petitions demanding the abolition of bishops and the

---

31. J.S. Morrill, 'The Attack on the Church of England in the Long Parliament', above, ch. 4.
32. J.S. Hart, *Justice upon Petition* (1991), pp. 64–105.

Prayer Book, the renewed iconoclasm (the first popular explosion of religious violence in living memory), the mushrooming of gathered churches. All this has been painstakingly chronicled by historians, especially by Anthony Fletcher,[33] and it is very hard not to believe that this was a cause of the events that led to civil war. The civil war may not have begun as a collapse of government in the provinces, but I would argue that fear of and belief in an imminent collapse into anarchy was a far more important conditioner of the Junto's responses to developments in high politics than was looking kindly on Scottish demands, certainly after the parliamentary recess of 1641.

A great majority of all members of the House of Commons were middling gentry and urban patricians who were unconnected with any great Lord and his political retinue. They rarely spoke, they rarely took initiatives, and yet they were not lobby fodder. They had minds, consciences, voices and votes when the House divided. Many of them were impressionable, liable to be swayed by what the weight of opinion revealed in the hundreds of petitions laid before the House, subject to intensive lobbying by their constituents and friends back home. Their story needs to be told too.[34]

Thus Russell's preoccupation with the breakdown at the centre represents the concern of an investigator who concentrates on understanding the detonator that caused an explosion and not on the form and amount of explosive material. For it does not explain how the king and the Junto mobilized cross-sections of the nation. Were Russell's 'causes of events that led to civil war' directly relevant to the decisions tens of thousands of individuals took about how to respond to the calls to arms coming (often within days of one another) from king and Parliament? Here Russell's brushing aside of the political sociology of early Stuart England is unfortunate. The war may not have been 'the clash of two clearly differentiated social

---

33. A. Fletcher, *The Outbreak of the English Civil War* (1981); J.S. Morrill, *The Revolt of the Provinces* (1980); above, chs. 3 and 4. But see *The Fall of the British Monarchies*, p. 455 n. 3, where Russell writes that 'the absence of a full discussion of the petitions is because I have very little to add to Prof Fletcher's account'. This is does not absolve him from an obligation to discuss the implications for his very different thesis of this massive external pressure.

34. In *Parliaments and English Politics* (Oxford, 1979) Professor Russell is above all concerned to see parliamentary history in the perspective of provincial realities: 'the difficulties of the early Stuarts were not, in the first instance, difficulties with their parliaments; they were difficulties which were reflected in their Parliaments' (p. 417). It is a great pity that he has completely bypassed this perspective in his new books.

groups or classes' (*Causes*, p. 2) but that does not mean that we have no need of a social history of its origins.[35]

As has been widely demonstrated, the descent into civil war in the provinces was neither straightforward nor inevitable once there had been a breakdown at the centre.[36] At the centre, the ancient nobility may well have been replaying the constitutional games of past centuries, and the king may well have been willing to play those games, but once that game led to fighting one should not assume that it was a war fought between baronial retinues. Many hundreds of officers and many thousands of common soldiers were volunteers making choices that were free political choices (even if that freedom of choice often caused individuals to follow the line of least resistance and join their local social leaders). Those political choices include active and passive resistance to the build up of armed force and they could have prevented a war. The creation of a parliamentarian movement and even more the phoenix phenomenon,[37] the ability of the king to get an army of volunteers together – something surely unthinkable in 1640 – rested upon events that had separate causes from those considered in this book. In other words, a crisis in the centre formed a detonator, but the political sociology of England in 1642 represented a quantifiable amount of semtex, and an analysis of both is necessary to any full understanding of the nature of the explosion. It is of little value to explain how England came to have a civil war unless we can also explain why it had a particular kind of civil war, of a type that could not have happened fifty, one hundred or three hundred years before. On several occasions, Russell fails to allow for the dynamic changes in English society and political structures which explain what was happening in 1642. Thus he writes that following the battle of Newburn:

> a new political settlement, with scapegoats and an afforced Council, was
> *a normal result* of such political crises, and the belief that one was in
> the offing accounts for much of the belief that November 1640 was the
> beginning of a 'golden age'. It was notoriously difficult to make such

35. It is particularly unfortunate that Russell fails anywhere to address the implications of David Underdown's *Revel, Riot and Rebellion* (Oxford, 1985), which posits by far the most suggestive and challenging account we have of the sociology and ecology of civil-war allegiance.
36. R. Hutton, *The Royalist War Effort 1642–1646* (1982), chs. 1–3; Fletcher, *Outbreak*, chs. 9–12; J.S. Morrill (ed.), *Reactions to the English Civil War* (1982), chs. 1–2; and in many local studies such as those of C. Holmes, *The Eastern Association in the English Civil War* (Cambridge, 1974), ch. 3, and A. Hughes, *Politics, Society and Civil War in Warwickshire 1620–1660* (Cambridge 1987), ch. 4.
37. I owe this phrase to Colin Davis.

settlements stick, as in the cases of 1216, 1261, and 1397 showed very clearly, but the failure in 1641 to conclude one at all was *highly unusual*. (*Causes*, pp. 13–14)[38]

What had been the normal result in the fourteenth century was no longer appropriate to the socio-political conditions of seventeenth-century England. There is nothing unusual about the failure of aristocratic constitutionalism to provide a solution to a political crisis affecting the political culture in the years 1641 and 1642.[39]

VIII

Many of these points come together in one other point: the failure to come to terms with puritan dynamism. In chapter 4 of *The Causes of the English Civil War*, Professor Russell offers an account of English Church History from 1559 to 1640 which is overwhelmingly (and most persuasively) concerned to demonstrate the dynamism of the reforms introduced by Charles I and Laud. It is true that he speaks of the Church as having been always divided between 'rival criteria of orthodoxy' (*Causes*, p. 84), but the thrust of the chapter is to stress the dynamism of Laudianism and to imply the static or regressive nature of early Stuart puritanism. In chapter 3, Russell makes useful, helpful distinctions about how men chose to fight because of religion as well as for religion, and his discussion of the negative religious reasons and antipathies driving men like George Digby is especially valuable. He also attempts to capture what he terms the 'philosophical underpinnings' of seventeenth-century intolerance and to measure the passions that the trappings of worship could arouse. This certainly allows him to demonstrate that 'many people, and very many of the first activists, did fight for religion' (*Causes*, p. 62). But he remains convinced that since religious division was long-standing it will not explain the timing of the civil war. He could have done more to demonstrate the *psychological* underpinnings of puritanism, and the way that parallel to (and in some measure responding to)

38. My italics.
39. Russell himself clears the way for this argument by showing that in 1640, the peerage needed Scottish arms to be able to impose their constitutionalism; they were no longer in a position to raise private armies to intimidate the Crown. No wonder their programme was not sufficient to solve the crisis they had created. This is an argument he develops further in his inaugural lecture to the Chair of History at King's College London, published late in 1991 under the title *The Scottish Party in English Parliaments 1640–1642 or The Myth of the English Revolution*. This was published after the completion of this review.

Laudian dynamism we need to understand an equally dramatic puritan dynamism. Gone by 1640 were comforting thoughts of a Laodicean compromise; and gone was the willingness to tarry for the magistrate. Whereas for the godly James had been moving the English Church all too slowly in the right direction, Charles was frogmarching it away from reformation. Armageddon on the Continent, and a reinvigorated notion of Antichrist no longer manifesting himself as Pope, foreign prince and domestic fifth column, but as a hideous and largely concealed conspiracy at the very heart of government,[40] created a new urgency and a new set of imperatives. There was in the 1630s, I would suggest, a bitterness, anger, willingness to contemplate fundamental change in the English Church which had not been seen since the 1580s and perhaps not even then. There was by 1640 a 'coiled spring' of godly zeal. Evidence for it can be found in William Hunt's study of 'the Puritan Moment' in Essex;[41] Ann Hughes's study of Thomas Dugard, closing ranks with his fellow godly ministers and withdrawing from the company of the wider brotherhood of Warwickshire ministers;[42] John Fielding's study of Robert Woodford, a man without patrons to look after him, a godly man forced to bow the knee to Laudian ritual to protect his family and livelihood, pouring out into a diary his bile against his own weakness and the wickedness of those who forced his conscience;[43] Peter Salt's study of Edward Dering, re-examining the scriptures and the Fathers in the late 1630s in order to gain greater understanding of his own acute anxiety at what he termed with bitter irony 'the piety of the times'; and many others. From the opening of the Long Parliament, a growing number of MPs were convinced that removing the Laudian bishops and getting back to 'the pure religion of Elizabeth and James I' was not enough. Zion was not to be built on to the structures of the Elizabethan Church, but on a site levelled and flattened. And this was not just desirable; it was God's will. If the opportunity was not taken, then God would punish the English as He had punished the Israelites when they had disobeyed, by a Babylonian or Egyptian slavery. 'When John Dod spoke of Jeroboam setting up "infectious idols" he was not speaking metaphorically' (*Causes*, p. 78). Indeed,

---

40. See now Peter Lake, 'Anti-popery: the structure of a prejudice', in R. Cust and A. Hughes (eds.), *Conflict in Early Stuart England* (1989), pp. 72–106.
41. W. Hunt, *The Puritan Moment* (Cambridge, Mass.,1983), part 3.
42. A. Hughes, 'Thomas Dugard and his Circle', *HJ*, XXIX (1986), 771–94.
43. J. Fielding, 'Puritan Opposition to Charles I: the diary of Robert Woodford, 1637–1641', *HJ*, XXXI (1988), 769–88.

And in the same way, preachers too who promised a new subjection under the Babylonian yoke if the corruptions of religion were not utterly purged out were not speaking metaphorically.[44]

Russell relies heavily, and rightly so, on the work of Nicholas Tyacke in his reconstruction of the dynamics of Laudianism. Ironically, at the very moment that *The Causes of the English Civil War* appeared, Tyacke delivered a most impressive lecture on *The Fortunes of English Puritanism, 1603–1640*.[45] He has demonstrated the continuing and vital history of 'a radical puritan continuum' (*Fortunes*, p. 20); he has examined the networks of patronage and connection; he has traced the important shifts and changes in the financing, organization and ideology of early Stuart puritanism. He has concluded that 'the religious opponents of Charles in both kingdoms [i.e. England and Scotland] made common cause, but the English were never less than equal partners' (p. 20). Scottish arms allowed members of the Long Parliament to dictate terms to Charles for ten months; but it did not need Scottish zeal to put the government, discipline and worship of the English Church near the top of the political agenda or to make such issues the most divisive and explosive of all.

IX

These books will henceforth be indispensible reading for anyone undertaking advanced study of the civil war. *The Fall of the British Monarchies* provides a narrative framework for the twenty-four months down to September 1641 which is richer and carries more narrative conviction even than Gardiner.[46] For the period from September 1641 to August 1642 it is less effective than, and certainly needs to be read alongside, other narratives, as subsidiary to Anthony Fletcher's *The Outbreak of the English Civil War*, for example. Meanwhile *The Causes of the English Civil War* offers a series of challenging and rewarding contextualizations of the background to the events of 1637–42. Russell's seven 'causes of the events that led to civil war' are all important but, as I said earlier, they cannot logically be *the* seven indispensable 'causes of the events'. I would suggest that at least as important as some of

44. S.P. Salt, 'The Origins of Sir Edward Dering's Attack on the Ecclesiastical Hierarchy', *HJ* XXX (1987), 21–52.
45. Nicholas Tyacke, 'The Fortunes of English Puritanism 1603–1640', *Friends of Dr Williams Library, 44th Annual Lecture* (1990).
46. S.R. Gardiner, *The History of England . . . 1603–1642* (10 vols., 1892), vols. 9 and 10.

them are an understanding of the changed political sociology of early Stuart England which shaped the way that the collapse of the centre led to a particular sort of civil war: the way the perceptions of MPs were changed by patterns of political protest and unrest in the provinces (cumulatively more important in determining the behaviour of MPs than the furtive pressure applied by the Scots to particular groups); and an understanding of the imperatives to reformation which was particular to the godly of the early 1640s. Russell defends his seven causes by saying that 'the removal of any one of these seven things could have prevented the Civil War as we know it'. I would suggest that exactly the same applies to these three additions. Reading Conrad Russell's new books has, then, stimulated me to think thoughts I would not have thought without engaging with his work. I am wiser as well as better informed than I was. But I am not persuaded that we have here discovered the early modernists' Holy Grail – the efficient cause of England's (though actually Britain's) civil wars.

CHAPTER FOURTEEN

Christopher Hill's Revolution

My love of seventeenth-century history was nurtured by a particularly gifted schoolmaster and a brilliant Oxford tutor. But among those books I was given to read, none had more influence on me as a student, and none deepened my passion for that century of revolution more than those of Christopher Hill. When I went away from Oxford for five days of peace and rest immediately before my Honours School in 1967, I took one history book with me for company and last-minute inspiration: *Society and Puritanism in Pre-Revolutionary England*. It is difficult now to recall the impact of the magisterial series of books which Hill produced between the late 1950s and the early 1970s that fired a generation of budding scholars and broke down so many barriers in the way seventeenth-century history was done: above all the interpenetration of religious, constitutional, social and scientific ideas; the social context of religious radicalism; the importance of 'literary' sources as historical documents; the *vitality* of the English revolutionary decades. Hill never convinced everyone of his view of the Oliver Cromwellian Revolution any more than Geoffrey Elton ever convinced everyone of his view of the Thomas Cromwellian Revolution. But each achieved an astonishing dominance of his field; each produced an account of his century that everyone else had to define themselves in terms of; each set the agenda of study; and each inspired an army of research students who went out in the days of the Robbins Revolution to spread the message. Neither produced a team of yes-men and yes-women (as the *Festschriften* of their graduate pupils show). But each had a dominance of his field that is unusual and unlikely to be repeated. The appearance of a convenient paperback edition in three volumes of Hill's essays, and of a volume which seeks to 'reaffirm the interest and importance of Christopher Hill's own body of work' is an excellent moment to reassess the continuing importance of his work.[1]

I

I have fifteen books by Christopher Hill on my shelves. Two of them collect his most important articles, one from the period down to the early 1960s and the other from the early 1960s to the late 1970s. Now come three more volumes containing no less than 44 essays, mainly items first published within the last fifteen years, a few longer ago. Some of the essays began life as lectures, some as reviews of the work of others, some as journal articles. Some are thoroughly reworked, some tidied, some left as they were. The first volume is the most compact: twelve items considering the ideas of individual writers – the cavalier journalism of Sir John Berkenhead, the polemic of Defoe's *Robinson Crusoe*, eight poets from Milton to Rochester, via Marvell, Quarles and Traherne, two diarists (Evelyn and Pepys), and more; set between new essays on the hermeneutics of censorship and a conclusion on the 'literary revolution' which Hill sees as part and parcel of the English Revolution. The second volume looks at the relationship of religious and social change over the period from the Henrician Reformation to the Puritan Revolution. Once again the familiar ('From Lollards to Levellers', 'God and the English Revolution') mingles with the recycled (one good example is a 24-page article wrought from four separate reviews of the major books of Patrick Collinson), and with hitherto unpublished (including four general essays under the head 'The First Century of the Church of England' first given as a course of lectures). Amongst items previously published in difficult-to-get-hold-of places is a study of a pre-civil war 'Antinomian' (no Ranter he) Tobias Crisp, a study of the roots of occasional conformity and a short piece on the perils of name-calling in religious history. The third volume is much more of a miscellany, with some rather slighter pieces alongside some of Hill's most provocative recent reformulations of major themes: 'Parliament

1. *The Collected Essays of Christopher Hill: Volume One: Writing and Revolution in 17th Century England* (Brighton, Harvester Press, 1985), xi + 340 pp., £28.50.
   Volume Two: Religion and Politics in 17th Century England (Brighton, Harvester Press, 1986), xi + 356 pp., £28.50.
   Volume Three: People and Ideas in 17th Century England (Brighton, Harvester Press), xi + 340 pp., £28.50.
   All three volumes reprinted 1988 in paperback, £15.95 per volume.
   Reviving the English Revolution. By Geoff Eley and William Hunt (London, Verso, 1988), viii + 356 pp., £24.95.

and People in 17th-century England' and 'A Bourgeois Revolution?' prominent amongst them. I will explore some of the major themes of these three volumes after considering the argument of a book about Hill rather than by him.

II

Reviving the English Revolution is a disappointing book with some redeeming things in it. It falls into four parts. The first, to be discussed in the next paragraph, consists of essays reviewing aspects of Hill's method. The second consists of 'further explanations' of the relationship of society and puritanism that Hill has so fruitfully explored over the years (a fifth chapter in this section, a reprint of the unworthy review of Colin Davis's book on the Ranters by Edward Thompson, should certainly have been omitted, especially as another essay in the book, by Barry Reay, engages more intelligently with Davis and makes a case that it is worth Davis's while to answer). Only Buchanan Sharp's essay is of real substance. The third section of three essays examining themes in American History on Hillite themes is hardly germane to the editors' expressed aims. The fourth section on 'the future of the English Revolution' consists of two essays by Lawrence Stone and Cynthia Herrup easily available elsewhere, both slight and unrepresentative of their authors' powerful intellects; a piece by William Hunt on 'legitimation crisis in early Stuart England' which is the pilot for what looks like an interesting project but which is still at too early a stage to warrant publication; and an excellent piece by David Underdown which belonged in part I.

In that first section C.H. George reviews Hill's career and major writings; Mary Fulbrook examines his historical sociology; Barry Reay considers the lasting merit of 'The World Turned Upside Down'; and Margot Heinemann considers Hill's contribution to literary studies – his role in combatting elitism in the selection and evaluation of 'texts'. David Underdown's essay offers a typically shrewd and courteous critique of Hill's conceptualization of the English Revolution. George, Fulbrook, Reay and Underdown all offer firm criticism within broadly sympathetic essays. George identifies difficulties in Hill's account of puritanism, Fulbrook in his analysis of social structure. Both would argue that they have identified the stress points in a massive and heroic intellectual structure. Stress points need not cause collapse; but they need reinforcement. I will examine their points later.

Despite the interest of these essays, it has to be said that the volume does less for Hill's reputation than the *Festschrift* presented to him in

1982. That collection, by his pupils, addressed the agenda he had created. If many of the essays in it reached conclusions different from his, they addressed the issues he had highlighted, they examined the connections he had posited, they endorsed the concept of the English Revolution. *Reviving the English Revolution* lacks the vibrancy of *Puritans and Revolutionaries*; for the most part it lacks the freshness and precision and adventure of Hill's own scholarship and of the *Festschrift*. Far worse, it does him a disservice by exaggerating the collapse of his reputation. Eley's introduction to the new volume is in fact a grossly unfair and unjust one. His characterization of 'revisionism' ought to become a case study of how to misrepresent those you wish to criticize. It is true that revisionists have challenged the *inevitability* of the collapse of the political system in the mid-century: for them England is not so much ungovernable as badly governed. It is also true that they have sought to set the ideological conflicts and the social conflicts into perspective: since every mature political culture will be characterized by debate and argument about the locus of power and the legitimation of authority, it is important to look at continuing areas of agreement and consensus as well as at areas of contention. If at times revisionists have seen the war as a squabble amongst the nobility and gentry about access to the honeypot, it must be remembered that revisionists were reacting against the body of work which treated ideology in a crudely positivist fashion. If revisionism was provoked by any particular work, it was not one of Hill's so much as Lawrence Stone's *Causes of the English Revolution*. At times revisionists' wilful refusal to set their explanations into broad social and intellectual contexts has been blinkered and unsophisticated. But to say, as Eley does, that 'the connections which Hill explores among the social, the political and the ideological have been placed beyond the boundaries of most present discussion' is monstrous (*Reviving* p. 4). It is the *nature* of the connections which have been argued for in the work of Kevin Sharpe, Anthony Fletcher or Conrad Russell that have challenged Hill's interpretation, rather than any unwillingness on the part of such scholars to consider the connections. My own work suffers particularly harshly at Eley's hands. He sees *The Revolt of the Provinces* as 'the reduction of the mid-century crisis to a narrowly circumscribed process of political manoeuvre, from which Hill's distinctive concerns – the social, cultural and ideological determination of political conflict, in all their multiform complexity – have been systematically left out' (*Reviving*, p. 4). The one thing my book is *not* about is processes of political maneouvre. It is about a political and religious culture that spawned not only militant puritan-parliamentarianism and militant cavalierism, but various forms of popular neutralism and anti-war sentiment. My book is a guarded compliment to Christopher Hill. It says in effect, 'we have good work on puritan militancy and need not explore it afresh. So let's look at that great mass of people – gentry and commons – who did not want war, did what they could to stop it and to end it, who rose up in 1648 in a revolt of the provinces against centralism and religious zealotry, and who lost. Theirs is a vital part of the story too.'

Then there is Eley's comment about my recent work and Blair Worden's that it comes as 'something of a surprise to find two of the most inveterate revisionists . . . rediscovering the centrality of religion . . . the irony is worth savouring' (*Reviving*, p. 9). It is inconceivable to me that anyone who has read any of the early work of Blair Worden could say that. As for myself, I have to confess that I must have been less clear than I intended, for others have made similar jibes. My early work was about the uncommitted and about the victims. But I hoped I had explained in my work on Cheshire that I saw the conflict in that county as centred around a royalist party which grew out of a defence of episcopacy and a parliamentarian movement led by a devout puritan who reached across social barriers to assemble a coalition of the godly. And *The Revolt of the Provinces* (1976) states categorically (p. 47) that 'What emerges quite clearly from a study of the activists in the summer of 1642 . . . is that, for them religion was the crucial issue.' Christopher Hill has never, and would never, mistake the extent to which revisionism sets his work in context with a charge that it ignored or rejected it. Indeed, I would argue that no-one who has read Hill's work could write the kind of impoverished history Eley writes about. Other contributors to *Reviving the English Revolution* and Hill's three volumes of essays allow us to reassess his importance.

First, he has played a fundamental role in breaking 'religious' history and especially the history of religious ideas free from 'denominational' history. (Just look at the Ecclesiastical History chapter in G. Davies and M. Keeler, *Bibliography of British History: Stuart Period* for the state of play as late as 1960. Only Geoffrey Nuttall had really done work which prefigured Hill's subtle interplay of ideas and contexts.) Hill has written: 'environment is more important than heredity in the evolution of ideas' (*Essays*, II, 4–51). He has posited a subtle and convincing account of the social reasons for which men could hold many of the traditional puritan beliefs. . . . To understand Puritanism we must understand the needs, hopes, fears and aspirations of the godly artisans, merchants, yeomen, gentlemen, ministers and their wives, who gave their support to its doctrines. . . . Puritanism was valid for them only when they felt it in their pulses. It seemed to point the way to heaven because it helped them to live on earth.

As Mary Fulbrook says:

such an approach does not try to 'reduce' the reality of the religious ideas, but does try to render them intelligible to later observers in terms of their relationships with other aspects of social experience. Whether consciously aware of it or not, people found that certain religious ideas 'made sense' (or, in the Quaker expression, 'spoke to their condition') because they related to real, material experiences of life, in the context of a particular social environment' (*Reviving*, pp. 39–40).

Secondly, who has done more than Christopher Hill to make us aware of 'literary' texts as historical documents, to see Milton, Bunyan and a host of other poets and writers as sources for understanding the anxieties, aspirations and self-delusions of the epoch? We do not have to agree with Hill that 'there was a revolution in English literature as well as science', politics, economics and society (*Essays*, I, 3), to agree with him that developments in the form and content of fictional writing are part of the warp and woof of our subject and our understanding of that age. Kevin Sharpe's *Criticism and Compliment* (1988) or *Politics of Discourse* (1987) or Blair Worden's brilliant exegesis of Marvell's Horation Ode are part of an intellectual endeavour made possible by Hill's pioneering studies that have placed us light years beyond the flatulent 'Arts and Culture' chapters of the older textbooks. In these three volumes of essays, Hill again and again stresses the uniqueness of individual responses to the pressured world of the 1620s and 1630s, and the post-diluvian world of the Restoration. Volume I in particular is a cave of delights: Francis Quarles' Collinsonian protestantism, Thomas Traherne's low-church arminianism, Samuel Pepys's residual puritanism, Rochester's railing against his own and his age's puritan past.

Hill's third and most problematic achievement has been to set the *nature* of the English revolution at the heart of the historical agenda. This contribution is the crucial one to which I shall devote the rest of this article. In doing so, I will dwell on what I see as the main weaknesses of methodology and argument. So let me state clearly what I see as his enduring achievement. He, together with Lawrence Stone, has established the paradigms with which we work, but his own work on the interplay of societal development and the history of ideas is far subtler. He has done more than anyone else to evoke the pain and striving and to recreate the mental world of the revolutionary decades. His later work on the restoration leaves us in no doubt that the mid seventeenth century is a climacteric, after which everything was different. If we can be sure that the seventeenth century changed England and Englishmen more than any century bar the present one, we owe that recognition to him more than to any other scholar.

III

For all that Eley might think, my major criticism of Hill is not that he is wrong about the nature of puritanism, the extraordinary excitement of the freeing of minds and pens in the 1640s and 1650s, or even about the extent to which the convulsions of those decades transformed the ways that Englishmen and women viewed their world; but rather that the dynamics of that process require a more balanced assessment of other groups, a less sentimental attachment to some victims and a less harsh view of others, and the kind of awareness of nuance in social history that he has developed in religious history. But above all, my critique would be methodological. It would have to do with sources.

At the beginning of the first volume of his collected essays, Christopher Hill rightly castigates those who concentrate on parliamentary debates, state papers and the correspondence of the gentry to the exclusion of other sources. Indeed, I once heard a colleague say of a PhD thesis on the Exchequer that the candidate had 'pulled Petty Bag firmly down over both ears and subjected the contents to intense scrutiny from within'. A certain perspective was missing. My D. Phil. thesis, subsequently my first book, *Cheshire 1630–1660* is of a type with that (though myopic books are not valueless books and county studies, when undertaken with the help of corrective spectacles, as by Ann Hughes in her recent study of civil war Warwickshire, remain a vital part of our understanding of the nature of the English Revolution). But Hill's own work suffers from a defect as great in its way: the reliance, indeed the total reliance, on printed sources. Throughout his career, Hill has built up a massive knowledge of printed material. The overwhelming majority of his references are to works printed in the seventeenth century. There are no references in any of these three volumes nor, I think, in any of his previous books, to manuscript sources. This has to be a significant handicap the more general and ambitious his work becomes. At its simplest, this leads to such serious lapses as 'censorship made it difficult for lower class viewpoints to come across. The nearest we can get to

these is through literature . . . [as in] the city comedies by Dekker
and Middleton' (*Essays*, I, 14). In the wake of much recent work
being done with a variety of manuscript sources – depositions in
church courts, for example – this is a serious mis-statement and
betrays a myopia as great as that of county-community truffle-pigs.
Hill wants to look at the social history and intellectual history of early
modern England, and at their interconnections. I would suggest that
the limitations that his concentration on certain types of evidence has
placed on the 'social history' side of his work have become more
evident as more and more sophisticated work has been attempted
with new and unprinted sources. His social history has not matured
and deepened at the same rate as his intellectual history.

More generally, concentration on printed sources has led to a
comparative weakness in his understanding of political and legal
process. He has, for example, consistently maintained that the severity
and ubiquity of censorship in seventeenth-century England both
drove 'subversive' ideas underground and caused the courageous
few to encode and disguise their protest. Yet he has never described
the nature of the censorship laws; *how* they were enforced; *in what
circumstances* they were enforced; *how often* they were enforced. A
list of books written but not printed in the decades before the civil
war (*Essays*, I, 39–40) is no substitute for a systematic study of this
problem. Sheila Lambert has recently thrown down a fundamental
challenge ('The Printers and the Government, 1604–1640' in *Aspects
of Printing since 1600*, eds. R. Myers and M. Harris, [Oxford, 1987],
pp. 1–29). There were virtually *no* prosecutions under the Star
Chamber Decree of 1638 (which was, in any case, issued to suit
the business interests of the printers not the security concerns of
the state). Blair Worden has also recently suggested (in an essay in
Censorship and the Press in Britain and the Netherlands, eds. A. Duke
and C. Tamse [1988]), that 'the government's principal concern
in the exercise of censorship . . . was evidently to forestall not
criticism but disorder'. These works, together with that of Annabel
Patterson (especially *Censorship and Interpretation* [1984]) have shown
that the state was not efficient enough, determined enough, worried
enough to punish more than a tiny minority of the unlicensed
items or to remove every potentially subversive statement from
the items submitted for licensing. I am *not* saying that there was
freedom of expression in Stuart England, still less that we should
take all pamphlets or parliamentary speeches at face value; but I
am suggesting that we cannot so readily treat the almost complete
absence of calls for resistance to Charles I or the absence of evidence

for widespread popular heresy as the result of ubiquitous and effective state censorship.

At the end of the day, no account of any major event in world history will be convincing unless all *types* of evidence have been explored. I do not consider it romantic but commonsense to say that unless one has dirtied one's hands with the grime of the Commonwealth Exchequer Papers, and unless one has ploughed through a cross-section of the surviving Assize Files and county committee papers, the nature of the revolutionary experience will remain elusive. At the heart of the revolution is a desperation bred of seeing an orderly search for liberty turning into something vicious, without an obvious end, a monster devouring its young. Christopher Hill has written movingly of the victims of the Revolution and of those who constituted its epiphenomena. Their story needed to be told. *The World Turned Upside Down* is about the sparks that fly when the chisel strikes the turning grindstone. He has never really explained those who held the chisel, who sought to control the forces unleashed by the descent into total war. His work, so strong on the period up to 1642 and after 1649, is notably thinner on the years 1642–9. In my view the sects of the 1650s make more sense in the context of 'real, material experiences of life' in the 1640s than as creatures rising from a subterranean deep where they had lurked, out of scholarly sight, for generations. Environment is more important than heredity in the evolution of ideas. Hill knows this. My point is that he cannot and has not fully 'felt the pulse' of his sectaries because he has not fully shared their sense of what it was to live through the civil war.

IV

David Underdown puts his finger on what, for me, is Hill's other major methodological weakness. On picking up the latter's review of his book on civil-war Somerset, Underdown tells us that he expected to find (*Reviving*, pp. 338–9):

> some comments on the chapters dealing with the risings of the Clubmen. . . . Here were men living their own history, plebeians who could not be written off as obedient pawns of the élite, because they were in fact revolting against the authority of the leading gentry of their shires. . . . Alas, the review . . . did not mention the Clubmen, who, like the middling and lower-class people who made up the rank and file of the King's army (and who were by no means all recruited under compulsion), are difficult to fit into Hill's general conception of the Revolution. For him, Puritanism and the Parliament were the causes of the middling and industrious sorts, and when we find great masses of people from these groups espousing a different ideology – of conservative localism they create a problem. What can we make of

a popular leader like Humphrey Willis, spokesman for the Somerset Clubmen, who supported Parliament but used the 'world turned upside down' image only to deplore the fact that it had happened. So while Hill's work casts plenty of light on the social and intellectual formations promoting change in seventeenth-century England, that light leaves the conforming majority still largely in the shadows. Yet we need to understand these people if we are to realize the limits as well as the achievements of the English Revolution, the reasons for its failure (to the extent that it failed), and why it was possible for so much of the old society to survive the years of upheaval.

I agree with this diagnosis. Ultimately, for me, Hill's account of the revolution is one-sided: the royalists remain in the shadows. He can certainly be illuminating on individual royalists (his study of Francis Quarles is a case in point). But on his large canvasses, the civil war remains a struggle between the forces of progress and the forces of reaction. Although, throughout the continent, monarchical centralism, absolutism, the dilution of particularist and prescriptive rights represent the dynamic forces of the century, Hill insists that the early Stuart state was engaged in propping up a decayed political order: 'by 1640 the social forces let loose by or accompanying the rise of capitalism, especially in agriculture, could no longer be contained within the old political framework except by means of a violent repression of which Charles' government proved incapable' (*Essays*, III, 96). The weight of recent scholarship – both from those who believe in the civil war as the culmination of a long drawn-out structural crisis, and those who see it as a strong but vulnerable political system badly managed by a perverse monarch – is either to see the civil war as a struggle between two dynamic and rival authoritarianisms, or else as a Caroline social, political, religious, cultural dynamism confronting a conservative puritan/particularist aristocratic parliamentarianism. Hill has never given the royalist *mentalité* the close and sympathetic investigation it needs if he is to sustain his argument. Furthermore, in constantly commending the thesis of Brian Manning in his *English People and the English Revolution* (1976), Hill has still to confront the claims of Manning's critics, much strengthened by David Underdown (especially in *Revel, Riot and Rebellion* [1985]) that (a) there is no evidence that the middling sort were more parliamentarian than royalist, or (b) that the gentry lost control in 1642 and that the parliamentarian movement was a popular revolt led by an intimidated nobility and gentry. The limited social revolution of 1646–60 and the greater freedom of expression for all social groups in those years can be explained as the product of war and its multiplex demands and tyrannies.

The century 1540–1640 witnessed massive changes in the economic, social and cultural structures, and the consequences for England of a breakdown of order in the 1640s were very different from those that would have resulted from a breakdown of order in the 1540s. But that does not make collapse probable, let alone *necessary*. The Stuarts in my view were, with difficulty, riding and taming the tiger of social and cultural change, and could have promoted the 'modernization' of the economy. They did so in fact after 1660 and not just and not primarily because of their memory of 1649.

I will make one final point. Who were the bourgeoisie? Hill has long retreated from the view that the civil war was a clash between feudal and bourgeois forces, with proto-capitalists pushing their way past an impotent and reactionary monarchy in a carefully and long-planned push for political dominance and economic liberalism. In his most recent formulation, the English Revolution was caused by 'the breakdown of the old society; it was brought about neither by wishes of the bourgeoisie, nor by the leaders of the Long Parliament. But its *outcome* was the establishment of conditions far more favourable to the development of capitalism than those which prevailed before 1640' (*Essays* III, 95). His heroes are the 'middling sorts, the yeomenry and market-oriented craftsmen and traders'. They were the groups who had kept faith with radical values in the days of oppression, they were the victims of Tudor and early Stuart persecution and harassment, which forced them into but silent witness. When their chance came in 1642, Hill argues, with the elite fatally divided and mutually hostile, the middling sort were able to demand and to impose as a condition of selling their labour in arms, that their interests were taken up alongside those of the elite who turned to them. As the war dragged on, their determination gave them ever-greater say, as the many vacillating and fearful nobles and gentry fell away. It was the middling sort who came to see the need for revolution. I have problems with the logic of this. Was this the bourgeoisie (let alone was it the members of the 'third culture' of radical sectaries), who were the beneficaries of the revolution? By 1700 the yeomanry were in terminal decline; the bigger the landholding, the greater the prosperity; it was rentiers not smallholders who led the agrarian revolution. The collapse of guild regulation helped not the independent small producer but the merchant and distributor, subordinating the producer to his will and reducing him wherever possible to a wage-earner or dependent. The bourgeoisie who benefitted were not the bourgeoisie to whom Hill has devoted his life. All too many of them had been cavaliers.

In my view, three things transformed England in the seventeenth century. One owed nothing to the revolution: the demographic turnaround in mid-century which changed the whole economic, social and political context. A second was the recognition by governors that they could solve their financial problems by encouraging and then by taxing progress rather than by inhibiting it. The early Stuarts were halfway there (realizing that there was money to be made from encouraging progressive economic activity and rationalization such as fen drainage, woodland clearance, new draperies etc. as well as from propping up vested interests and from the inhibitory aspects of fiscal feudalism). Indeed the early Stuarts were more the champions of capitalist enterprise than they were obstructors of it. It did not take a civil war to turn ambivalent attitudes into positive ones, especially when the demographic turnaround made state intervention in the food market, internal trade, etc. in the interests of public order largely unnecessary. The third factor was the creation in the late seventeenth century of a new cultural climate, rationalistic, empirical, pragmatic. Religious issues dominated politics, but religious values were far less pervasive, and economic, scientific, even social discourse was increasingly secularized. The Millenium vanished, Antichrist faded, Zeal cooled. The new climate was a reaction against Puritanism at least as much as it was a permanent consequence of the check the Revolution gave to state assertiveness and belief in its right and duty to impose belief. But it is undeniably tied up to the upheavals of the mid-century. It was a revolution in the consciousness of those who lived through it, and it was transmitted to their children and their children's children. Christopher Hill has dwelt on the way some vital groups worked out their destiny in those desperate days. He may have illuminated part of the picture and left other parts in the shade. But as we all struggle to make sense of the English Revolution, we will for a long time yet owe him a massive debt. Because of him, I know many vital things about the English Revolution; but for him I might never have wanted to know anything about it.

CHAPTER FIFTEEN

Charles I, Tyranny and the English Civil War

This is a paper about intellectual reticence and circumspection. It is about the way the critics of Charles I perceived his government, or rather, it is about the way in which they chose to articulate their perceptions about his misgovernment during the paper war of 1641 and 1642. It attempts to set into context the account which the members of the two Houses gave of their improvised actions and longer-term settlement proposals as the country lurched towards civil war. At its core is a discussion of the forty-three formal declarations, remonstrances, and open letters which passed between the king and the two Houses from the introduction of the Grand Remonstrance to the outbreak of hostilities between the field armies commanded by the king and the earl of Essex.[1] The evidence of this material is complemented by an analysis of the semi-official pamphlets licensed to be printed by the Houses,[2] and a reading of printed and unprinted

---

1. [Edward Husbands], *An Exact Collection of all Remonstrances, Declarations, Votes, Orders, Ordinances and Proclamations, Petitions, Messages and Answers . . . between the King's Most Excellent Majesty, and his High Court of Parliament from his Return from Scotland, Being in December 1641 and Continued until March . . . 1643* (1643). I have found this a far more satisfactory source than the more usual John Rushworth, *Historical Collections* (7 vols., 1659–1701) because it is more complete and more accurate in its texts and prints things chronologically rather than in 'subject clusters', such as the defence of Hull or the Nineteen Propositions. But I have not relied entirely upon Husbands. I have checked the texts in Husbands against copies in the Cambridge University Library or on the microfilms of the British Library, Thomason Tracts.
2. S. Lambert, 'Printing for Parliament, 1641–1700', *List and Index Society*, special series, no. 20 (1984). This is a remarkable and invaluable aid to scholars. It was vital for this paper since I wished to distinguish material put out with the knowledge and consent of the two Houses (or at least of the Commons) from what every crank and those with an eye solely to the market managed to put out.

parliamentary diaries for the period.[3] But I have tried to set this material into the general context of the political history of the reign as a whole and to make comparison with the largely uninhibited and uncircumspect religious rhetoric of the same period. The argument will be that there are some very surprising and startling silences, omissions, and confusions in the case the Houses presented in their attempt to persuade the English people to defend themselves against the misgovernment of Charles I.

In an earlier paper, I claimed that:

> A reading of the pamphlets and debates, at least up to the battle of Edgehill, tells not of a radical group leading a quailing majority onward, but of a leadership picking its way through a minefield, full of self-doubt, seeing the hazards of turning back as worse than the perils of pursuing their passage,

a view which I defended by arguing that the logic of

> events forced the Houses to make claims and *then* to justify them [and that] the constitutional issues of 1642 were means to an end, not ends in themselves. They were a controversial means to protect the uncontroversial settlement of 1641 and to deal with a king no longer trusted to keep his word.[4]

In turn I argued that that lack of trust grew out of religious perceptions.

To sustain this thesis, I will pay especial attention to the avoidance of all charges in official parliamentary statements in the twelve months up to the raising of the royal standard in mid-August 1642 that Charles I was a tyrant. The air was thick in 1640 and 1641 with allegations of royal tyranny and arbitrary government, although the word 'tyrant' itself was little used. But as the prospect of civil war came closer, more and more care was taken to avoid the use of the term. What makes this startling is that by all contemporary understanding of the term, the *prima facie* case against Charles was very strong. So strong, in fact, that Charles came very close to confessing it both at the time and, more particularly, on the eve of his execution.

3. W. Notestein, *The Journal of Sir Simonds d'Ewes from the Beginning of the Long Parliament to the Opening of the Trial of the Earl of Strafford* (1923); W.H. Coates, *The Journal of Sir Simonds d'Ewes from the First Recess of the Long Parliament to the Withdrawal of the King from London* (1942); W.H. Coates, et. al., *The Private Journals of the Long Parliament, 7 March 1642–1 June 1642* (1987). I have read the journals of Sir Simonds d'Ewes (BL, Harl. MSS. 162–64) for the periods not covered by the above, and Christopher Thompson's transcript of the diary of Walter Yonge for the period after 1 September 1642.
4. J.S. Morrill, 'The Religious Context of the English Civil War', above pp. 59–60.

The charge of tyranny was the one on which Charles was eventually to be tried and executed. The indictment drawn up in January 1649 was uncompromising:

> That the said Charles Stuart . . . out of a wicked design to erect and uphold in himself an unlimited and tyrannical power to rule according to his will, and to overthrow the rights and liberties of the people, yea, to take away and make void the foundations thereof . . . hath traiterously and maliciously levied war against the present Parliament, and the people therein represented . . .[5]

For reasons which would require a separate paper, it is striking that the examples of tyranny contained in the charge dated from after 1642.[6] Charles I, of course, contemptuously dismissed the charges as the malicious inventions of unprincipled adventurers – 'private men's covetous and ambitious designs'[7] he called them – but the letter that he wrote to the Prince of Wales on the eve of his execution does contain an interesting confession. The letter itself is little more than a sequence of poignant platitudes, but it can also be read as a covert confession, a plea to his son to govern in the ways he wished he himself had ruled. For the most part he accused himself of weakness, of surrendering in 1641 the powers with which he was entrusted by God, of betraying his servants, above all the earl of Strafford, and of compromising his commitment to uphold the Church of England, 'as coming', he said, 'as close [as any] to God's word for doctrine, and to the primitive examples for government', by his various concessions throughout the 1640s, above all in his unworthy compact with the Scots in 1648. But then he made a very startling statement. He wrote 'your prerogative is best showed and exercised in remitting rather than in exacting the rigour of the laws; there being nothing worse than legal tyranny'.[8] What might he have had in mind?

<hr/>

5. S.R. Gardiner, *Constitutional Documents of the Puritan Revolution* (3rd ed., 1906), p. 372.
6. The charges actually begin with the raising of the standard at Nottingham in August 1642 and the battle of Edgehill in October 1642 and dwell on the events of 1648. My own view is that the case for executing Charles arose from what his opponents in the army came to see as his *sacrilege* in seeking – in the second civil war – to overturn the judgement of God in giving the Parliament victory in the first civil war. I shall be arguing this case at length elsewhere. Meanwhile, see Sarah Barber, 'The Moral Case against Charles I: Regicidal and Republican Thought, 1647–1651' (PhD thesis, Trinity College, University of Dublin, 1988).
7. Ed. C. Petrie, *The Letters of King Charles I* (1935), p. 262.
8. Ibid., pp. 263, 265.

The concept of tyranny was one widely used and understood and yet fuzzily defined in the early seventeenth century.[9] Both in its classical usage by Aristotle and in its medieval adaptations, it represented a corruption of monarchy. Tyrants were typically divided into those who usurped their thrones and those who acquired their titles legitimately but who used their power arbitrarily. Most of the time, the term 'tyranny' was used as a rather loose term of condemnation – immoral government. When it was more tightly defined to describe unjust forms of government, the emphasis tended to be on the ends to which power was used rather than the means by which it was exercised. A tyrant was a ruler who put self-interest above national interest, whose actions benefitted himself and the clique with which he surrounded himself at the expense of the interests of his subjects, whose liberties and property he trampled underfoot. Most of the exegeses of the careers of classical tyrants – Caligula and Nero – or biblical tyrants – Saul and Rehoboam – stressed a corruption of the will, an indifference to legality, an arbitrariness of behaviour which suggested that tyranny infected the means as well as corrupting the ends of government; and for many authors the terms 'tyranny' and 'arbitrary government', are interchangeable. But there is no necessary connection. Attentive readers of Bodin were aware that 'the true greatness of a ruler was to behave justly even when it was not illegal to behave unjustly.'[10] Perhaps that is what Charles had in mind when he told his son that he would rather be remembered as *Charles le bon* than as *Charles le grand*.[11] And certainly it is what Sir John Eliot had in mind when in 1631 he wrote in *De Iure Majestatis* that the difference between a lawful king and a tyrant was that a lawful king 'will not do what he may do'. As Bill Hinton argued thirty years ago, 'when Charles I did only what the law allowed, this does not mean that he acted correctly'.[12] When Charles governed *pro bono suo* and not *pro bono publico* his subjects were justified in calling him a tyrant.

9. For what follows there is a host of familiar authorities on early modern thought. Good introductions to early modern discussions of tyranny against their classical and medieval background include O. Jaszi and J.D. Lewis, *Against the Tyrant* (1957), pt. 1; R. Mousnier, The *Assassination of Henrie IV* (1973), pp. 63–105; W.A. Armstrong, 'The Elizabethan Conception of the Tyrant,' *Rev. Eng. Studs.*, 22 (1946). Those looking for something fresh and stimulating on the subject should not overlook Glenn Burgess, 'Theories of Tyranny in England, 1603–60' (MA Thesis Victoria University of Wellington, 1982).
10. R.W.K. Hinton, 'Charles I and Tyranny', *Review of Politics*, XVIII (1956), 70–2.
11. Petrie, *Charles I*, p. 262.
12. Hinton, 'Charles I', 87.

Eliot's rueful gloss on Bodin was written while he languished in the Tower. Most of those imprisoned with him for participation in the angry scuffles at the end of the third parliament of the reign secured release by making tacit acknowledgement of their wrong-doing; but Eliot, along with Strode and Valentine, refused to do so. For Eliot, surely, the lesson of the previous six years had been precisely that Charles had sought to do all that which he might do: he had used emergency powers with which he was entrusted by custom and law to preserve the commonwealth from external threat and internal subversion in what most of his subjects believed to be a non-emergency situation or to get his own way where the public interest required him to seek consent and where that consent was not forthcoming. Three recent studies by Richard Cust, John Guy, and John Reeve all demonstrate Charles's legal tyranny in the years 1626–9. Let me give five examples drawn from their work.

The first is the personal order from Charles to Attorney-General Heath to change the ruling entered by the officers of the Court of King's Bench on the face of the writ of habeas corpus brought by the five knights. Charles was determined not to have the judges adjudicate his right to imprison for refusal to pay the forced loan and was equally determined to secure a full and binding precedent for his claim to imprison at will where he alleged reason of state. The hedged interim order of the court did not give him that binding precedent. Buckingham's unequivocal statement in the House of Lords that Heath was carrying out express orders when he had sought to alter the ruling entered on the writ was a stunning exposure of the king's authoritarianism.[13]

The second example comes from the beginning of the 1629 Parliament, when the House of Commons set out to investigate why the printed form of the Petition of Right differed from the one approved by the two Houses. The Petition of Right had originally been assigned a statute number by the king's printer, but this had been effaced by a pumice stone so as to make its statutory force less certain, and its status had been further complicated by the insertion of the unsatisfactory first royal answer into the body of the text. It became clear that both changes had been personally authorized by the king.[14]

Thirdly, during the 1629 session the House of Commons investigated the action of customs officers in seizing the goods of Rolle

---

13. J. Guy, 'The Origins of the Petition of Right', *HJ*, 25 (1982), 289–312.
14. *Ex info.* John Guy.

for refusing to pay tonnage and poundage. They claimed that the customs officers had exceeded their authority. But Charles stepped in and stated that everything they had done was by his express authority. [15]

Fourthly and following the dissolution of the third Parliament, several MPs were imprisoned for their parts in the incidents that took place on 2 March 1629. The king, not wishing to repeat the furore that followed his use of prerogative imprisonment in 1627, accepted Heath's advice that they show some cause of their imprisonment. However the king did not wish to show the full nature of their offence (and specifically where it took place) lest they plead parliamentary privilege. The attorney general therefore returned 'sedition' as the cause, but without stating the precise nature of the sedition. The prisoners then sought bail on the ground that sedition was a misdemeanor and not a felony, and the judges on the eve of the vacation privately informed the king that they would grant bail the next day unless further grounds for the detention of the prisoners were given. To give himself time to meet this challenge, Charles personally ordered the prisoners to be moved overnight to a different prison and ordered them not to be brought to court. This gave the law officers the vacation to find new arguments for keeping the prisoners locked up. This they succeeded in doing. The prisoners were offered bail under letters patent but on humiliating and self-incriminating conditions which they had little option but to reject; but that rejection was used to persuade the judges that the prisoners' plea to them for bail was bothersome and unnecessary, since bail was available already. [16]

Fifthly and more generally, there were constant leaks about Charles's general highhandedness of manner. For example, when he first heard of the widespread refusal to pay forced loans in 1627, he personally authorized the drawing up of letters from the council to the lords lieutenant and their deputies instructing them to impress loan refusers into the royal army and to quarter royal troops on the homes of better-off refusers. He was talked out of these manoeuvres by the majority of the privy council but not before his proposals had been leaked by the earl of Pembroke

---

15. J. Reeve, *Charles I and the Making of the Personal Rule* (Cambridge, 1989), 32–3.
16. J. Reeve, 'Arguments in King's Bench in 1629 Concerning the Imprisonment of Members of the House of Commons' *Jnl. Brit. Stud.* 25 (1986).

to foreign ambassadors and by them to the newsmen of St Paul's Churchyard.[17]

Such behavior surely constituted a formidable *prima facie* case of legal tyranny; and some of Charles's subjects agreed. An anonymous tract from the Midlands in 1627 likened Charles to Rehoboam, the Canaanite king who levied arbitrary taxation upon the tribes of Israel,[18] and the paranoiac Thomas Scott, alderman and MP for Canterbury, likened Charles to Saul and Buckingham to Agag, whom Saul had protected after he committed atrocities against Saul's people and whom Samuel, acting as a lesser magistrate, slew in defiance of Saul's orders.[19] The revival of plays concerned with classical tyrants, while never crudely adapted to make parallels with Charles's government, surely also represents an implicit comment on contemporary preoccupations with the rights and the tribulations of a people experiencing a mild form of tyranny. If the plays did not provide easy answers, they at least heightened awareness of difficult choices.[20]

The 1630s sustained if they did not intensify levels of anxiety. A study of ship-money collection reinforces the points I have already made. Charles maintained that he could raise money without formal consent for naval defence in a national emergency, that he was sole judge of what constituted an emergency, and that there was in fact a sustained state of emergency. Counsel for Hampden maintained that there was no emergency, that even if there was it would only validate the initial writ, since in subsequent years the king had ample time to gain relief from Parliament, and the king's use of his discretionary powers was subject to judicial review. The judges by a large majority, if with varying degrees of enthusiasm, ruled for the king. In the perception of most of his subjects, the king was misusing his emergency powers. The consequence was

17. R. Cust, *The Forced Loan and English Politics* (1988), pp. 39–82; for an example of Charles's vindictiveness, see PRO, SP16/89 no. 4., printed in C. Daniels and J.S. Morrill, *Charles I* (1988), p. 25.
18. PRO, SP16/54 no. 821, in Daniels and Morrill, *Charles I*, p. 23.
19. Ibid.
20. This is a theme at the centre of much discussion in a variety of works: M. Heinemann, *Puritanism and Theatre* (1980), ch. 12; M. Butler, *Theatre and Crisis* (1984), ch. 4; and K. Sharpe, *Criticism and Compliment* (1987), ch. 1, give a good cross-section of views.

widespread distrust.[21] By 1639 the instinctive response of many of Charles's subjects to his policy initiatives was one of suspicion and alarm. His actions thereafter confirmed their worst fears: the levying of coat and conduct money; the welcoming of loans from English papists; the modifying of the Oath of Allegiance tendered to Catholic officers in the English army; the negotiations for military support from Highland and Irish Catholics to ram religious change down the throats of Scottish Protestants; the negotiations for loans from Philip IV and the pope; the precipitous dissolution of the Short Parliament and the provocative arrest of members of both Houses and ransacking of their studies;[22] followed, in the course of the Long Parliament, by all-too-plausible suspicions of the king's personal complicity in the army plots, the Irish rebellion and the Incident in Scotland, and the all-too-palpable responsibility for the attempt on the five members and the military provocations and escalations from January to August 1642.[23] The evidence for labelling Charles I a tyrant was very palpable, and one tract in September 1642 made that case emphatically and ruthlessly. Entitled *King James his judgment of a king and a tyrant*, it used the distinction in James I's speech of March 1610 between the unlimited nature of royal power in the abstract and the limited nature of royal power in settled kingdoms to indict James's son of tyranny. At the end of his discussion of James's speech, the author lists '28 questions, worthy due consideration.' They rehearse the major misuses of power by Charles since his accession – ship money, forest fine, the book of sports, the army plots, etc – and culminate and fulminate with 'whether the setting up the king's standard against the Parliament, and the best subjects

---

21. I have been criticized by, amongst others (but most directly), my old friend Johann Sommerville ('Ideology, Property and the Constitution,' in R. Cust and A. Hughes (eds.), *Conflict in Early Stuart England* [1969], pp. 63–4) for concentrating on the theme of the misuse of agreed powers. I am afraid I am unrepentant. John Cooper taught me long ago that a close reading of the legal judgements showed that the frustrating thing for the critics of the Crown in all the big set-piece arguments was precisely that: how to control the king's use of discretionary powers, not to deploy *pro bono suo* powers he ought to enjoy *pro bono*. Sommerville's position (in this matter) seems to me over-logical.
22. These are all points discussed in C. Hibbard, *Charles I and the Popish Plot* (1983), ch. 5–9.
23. R. Ashton, *The English Civil War* (1978), ch. 6, and D. Hirst, *Authority and Conflict* (1986), ch. 7, are the best introductory accounts; A. Fletcher, *The Outbreak of the English Civil War* (1981) is the best recent analysis of the politics of the Parliament. Conrad Russell, 'The First Army Plot of 1641', *TRHS* (1988), pp. 85–107, is important and a foretaste of his important forthcoming study of the parliamentary background to the outbreak of civil war.

of the kingdom, be not an actual unkinging of him . . . to set up tyrannical government over his land'.[24]

Significantly, the author of the pamphlet proclaims himself to be a Scot, and internal evidence confirms that he was one.[25] Much more significant is that this pamphlet has no parallel in the first eight months of 1642. I want to suggest that the most deafening in a series of deafening silences in the twelve months up to the raising of the royal standard is the absence of accusations of tyranny against Charles I. To call him a tyrant would have unlocked the principal arguments for resistance in early modern Europe; not to call him a tyrant made justification of resistance far more difficult. The air was thick with anticipation of the charge, but it never came. It was clearly a charge which the royalists anticipated, as in a tract published in September 1642 entitled *The Definition of a King with the Cure of a king Willfully Mad and the Way to Prevent Tyranny*.[26] This was a defence of passive resistance and a reassurance that what the reforms of 1641 had not accomplished, prayer could perfect. This royalist tract does not deny that the king may be seen as mad or tyrannical, and the implication must be that it was seeking to foreclose the options of those who had persuaded themselves that he was one or the other.

If we move back to the first twelve months of the Long Parliament, we find that charges of arbitrary government were being levied against the king's ministers and especially against the bishops. Typical early examples were the speeches of Sir Francis Seymour and John Pym in the early days of the Long Parliament. Sir Francis Seymour asserted that 'None can say he is a freeborne subject, things inforced of will more then of our lawes, noe: by no lawe'; and Pym, more explicitly, spoke of 'arbitrary proceeding of Courts of Justice: lawe and presidents were nothing.'[27] Such statements went unreproved, and similar sentiments can be found echoing through the impeachment of Strafford and the debates on the protestation oath in May 1641.[28] As far as I can see, however, the word tyranny is reserved

---

24. BL, Thomason Tract E111 (20), query 28.
25. Ibid., query 12, 'we poor harmless Scots are proclaimed rebels'.
26. BL, Thomason Tract E118 (18).
27. Ed. Notestein, *d'Ewes*, p. 7; Rushworth, *Historical Collections*, p. 4. See also d'Ewes's note of the 'petition against the archbishops, bishops, deans etc and their tyrannical government', in Notestein, *d'Ewes*, p. 138 (for 11 Dec. 1640). For the willingness of those in the 1610s and 1620s to bandy around notions of tyranny, see T.K. Rabb, 'Revisionism Revised: the Place of the Commons', *PP*, 92 (1981), pp. 69–70; Cust, *Forced Loan*, pp. 151–86.
28. C. Russell, 'The Theory of Treason in the Trial of Strafford', *EHR*, 80 (1965); J.H. Timmis, *Thine Is the Kingdom* (1977), *passim*.

exclusively to describe the bishops in their government of the church and in their usurpation of the king's authority. We will examine this shortly.

All such accusations, however, remain unsystematic and are more part of an abusive rhetoric than of a developed charge. They do, however, make the more dramatic the abandonment of all such usage, focussed or unfocussed, after the summer of 1641. The more MPs and others sensed the proximity of civil war, the more careful they were with their words. And tyranny was a term to be avoided. This can be clearly seen from the debates on the Grand Remonstrance, that great catalogue of royal misdeeds, in which not only are the words 'tyrannical' and 'arbitrary' absent; we know that they were cut out from the drafts drawn up before the recess.[29] Thus the clause which had originally described the judgements of named conciliar courts as 'arbitrary and unjust in their proceedings' was changed to read that 'they have been grievous in exceeding their jurisdiction'.[30] This leads us to a neat irony: in 1642 almost the only Englishman publicly to refer to the government of the 1630s as 'arbitrary' or 'tyrannical' was Charles himself. In *His Majesty's Declaration to all his loving subjects*, published on 12 August 1642, Charles acknowledged the charge in order to highlight the benefits that his subjects had derived from the reforms of 1641. He, or his ghost writers, spoke of the king as having taken

> a full clear prospect of the inconveniences and mischiefs which had grown by the long intermission of Parliaments, and by departing too much from the known rule of law, to an arbitrary power.[31]

Later in the same document, the king acknowledged that there had been 'the exercise of an arbitrary power' by the courts of Star Chamber and High Commission.[32]

How can we explain the reticence of those who took up arms against the king? The task of the draftsmen of the official and semi-official declarations, remonstrances, and other tracts of 1642 had, after all, to justify resistance to an anointed king. They had to justify the removal from the king of the authority to appoint lords lieutenant and to deploy the militia; to justify Parliament's representatives' refusal

---

29. The most recent full discussion is in J.S. Hart, 'The Origins of the Grand Remonstrance' (MA thesis, Portland State University, 1979), a good study of the obvious sources only.
30. Coates, *d'Ewes*, pp. 185–6 and nn.
31. Husbands, *Exact Collection*, p. 515.
32. Ibid., p. 518.

to admit the king to the city of Hull and access to the supply of ordnance and armaments stockpiled there for his army during the second Bishops' War; they had to justify the making of ordinances without royal assent; they had to justify the Nineteen Propositions which denied the king freedom to choose his own councillors and ministers; and they had to justify the appointment of the earl of Essex to raise an army to defend the Parliament and people from the power of the king and indeed to call the nation to arms against him.

What I want to suggest is that they chose not to use what must seem the most obvious arguments. I will show that they did not use history as their justification; nor Charles's record down to 1641; nor did they adopt the most straighforward and highly developed justification for resistance, the right of the subject to withstand a tyrant. In the event, I will suggest, it was a religious case for resistance, not the case from secular tyranny, which mobilized men against Charles I.

Why the reticence and the deafening silences? We do not have direct evidence. We cannot even be certain whether those who organized the paper war believed their own arguments. Did their public rhetoric mask their private perceptions? Did many MPs privately believe that Charles I was a tyrant? I suspect – though I cannot prove it – that some did and would suggest that the likeliest candidates are Viscount Saye and Sir Harry Vane. But I also suspect that many more did not – perhaps dared not – think through the implication of that charge. I cannot find a great gap in most of the private papers I have seen between the public and private language of key figures in the debates of 1642. Of course even if there were such a gap, we must conclude that it is highly instructive that there was such overt reticence. Clearly those in charge of parliamentary propaganda in 1642 used the arguments they believed would rally support. They would not use arguments they believed would be counter-productive. Their circumspection and circumscription may be grounded, then, less on the way MPs viewed Charles I than on their perception of how the people at large viewed him. But I suspect there are other factors at work. I do not myself think their caution resulted from a desire to bring him to the conference table. Their actions and ferocity of their language and behavior in relation to religious reform suggest otherwise. But there are at least three other reasons why a majority of those who were to fight for the Parliament could not bring themselves to take up the argument.

The first relates to the history of the argument in English thought. While the Calvinist tradition which had played so prominent a part in

European and Scottish history in the sixteenth century had, of course, its English antecedents in Goodman and Ponet, English Protestantism had been for the fifty years up to 1640 staunchly upholding the rights of the English Crown in the face of radical Catholic theories of resistance to heretical and tyrannical rulers. Furthermore, the debates on resistance, like popular chess openings, were so fully explored that the counter-arguments were known in advance. MPs in the early 1640s did not relish having their faces rubbed in the very arguments that they had been ramming down popish throats for half a century.

Secondly, to label the king a tyrant was to invite remedies which went far beyond what they were willing to contemplate, and here I do mean privately as well as publicly. The precedents for restraining tyrants were not encouraging, whether in scripture, in classical times, or in English history. Attempts to restrain the wilfulness of Edward II and Richard II in 1310, 1322, 1388, and 1397 had all failed, and those monarchs had been deposed and killed. The example of King John, who was restrained by what Stuart legal theorists took to be statute, was available; but most other precedents were too gloomy to contemplate. For those who wished only to compel the king to honour his promises and abide by the reforms of 1641, then, the argument that Charles was a tyrant was a remedy likely to be more terminal than the disease. Such arguments could only alienate those very people they wanted to attract: sober, god-fearing, conservative gentlemen.

The third reason for the failure of parliamentary publicists to accuse the *king* of tyranny was that they had committed themselves to the view that archbishop Laud and the papalists for whom he was interchangeably the agent and the dupe had usurped royal power and exercised it tyrannically. This was the essential message of the Grand Remonstrance, for example. The Commons expunged references to arbitrary actions by the secular arm in order to pin it on the bishops. Thus the convocation of 1640 was said to have 'imposed a new oath upon divers of His Majesties subjects, both ecclesiastical and lay, for maintenance of their own *tyranny*'. It also spoke of 'the inordinate power, vexation and usurpation of the Bishops'. The whole frame of the remonstrance was to document 'the roote of all mischiefs . . . a malignant and pernicious designe of subverting the fundamentall laws and principle of government'.[33] The charge was made with ever greater precision as the winter wore on. One of the most dramatic

---

33. Gardiner, *Const. Docs.*, pp. 218–19, 206.

charges was contained in a speech by Oliver St John in January 1642 in which he claimed that

> so high and proud were these prelates grown that they dare adventure to abridge and abrogate the king's royall prerogative in issuing forth warrants and proces in their severall courts which ever was used to read *Carolus Dei Gratia Rex* now must read *Gulielmus divina providentia dei archiepiscopus.* In their names must writs and process run, and not in the kings.[34]

This was a charge taken up and developed by other pamphleteers, notably by Henry Parker in *The True Grounds of Ecclesiastical Regiment.*[35]

By the winter of 1641–2, therefore, the Houses were saddled with an interpretation of the causes of political instability which they could not, or did not, jettison. They had set out a program of constitutional reform intended to amend or abate those powers which had been abused and to truncate those institutions which had upheld abuses, and they had come increasingly to account for those abuses not by accusing the king of tyranny but of abdication and weakness.

This central perception was, of course, very closely bound up in 1642 with the fear of popery and belief in popish plot to subvert monarchy and the protestant religion. I see no reason – especially in the wake of recent work by Caroline Hibbard, Anthony Fletcher, Paul Christianson, William Lamont, and others,[36] to doubt that men like John Pym were genuinely convinced both of the reality of the plot and of the need to take up arms to defend the nation from it. In their account of the plot, the radicals around Pym saw Charles as a man whose mind had been so poisoned by the lies and deceptions of the papists and their fellow-travellers that he was no longer capable of defending his office or his realm. He was guilty not of tyranny but of abdication, not of over-mightiness but of supineness. It is a theme of Pym's speeches from 26 January 1642 on, of several other MPs, most notably Peter Wentworth in the autumn of 1642, and is one of the charges against which the anonymous royalist pamphleteer of September 1642 set out to defend the king.[37]

34. *Master St John His Speech in Parliament on Monday, the 17th of January, Concerning the Charge of Treason Exhibited against the Bishops* (1642), p. 3.
35. H. Parker, *The True Grounds of Ecclesiastical Regiment* (1641), p. 12.
36. Hibbard, *Popish Plot*; Fletcher, *Outbreak*; P. Christianson, *Reformers and Babylon* (1978), ch. 5; W. Lamont, *Godly Rule* (1970), ch. 1–2.
37. *LJ*, 4, 540–3, 5 p. 201–2; C. Thompson (ed.), *Walter Yonge's Diary of Proceedings in the House of Commons* (1986), p. 34. J.S.A. Adamson, 'Pym as Draftsman: an Unpublished Declaration of March 1643', *Parliamentary History* 6 (1987), 137, for Pym's willingness to make use of the charge well into the war.

The argument from incapacity and abdication provided the Houses with an alternative justification for taking up arms in 1642: the argument from necessity. If the king failed in the essential task of protecting the people from antichrist, then the people must look to their own defence. Such arguments permitted a limited program of constitutional change and avoided the risk of either contemplating the deposition or execution of the king. It involved putting him in a decontamination chamber surrounded by soothing protestant-nationalist noises until he was detoxified, which might take twenty years.

Let us draw together the threads. The reforms of 1641 – the removal of evil counsellors, the abolition of conciliar jurisdictions and prerogative revenues – were essentially negative acts. Only the Triennial Bill was a constructive reform. Furthermore, the bulk of the 'remedial' measures were traditional in form – i.e., king-in-parliament using the omnicompetence of statute to remedy grievance – and they were agreed with little dissent.[38] The Grand Remonstrance was certainly more aggressive in nature and content, but thereafter the Houses' defence of their constitutional demands can only be described as reactive, a series of *ad hoc* responses to royal escalations.[39] Charles was portrayed as the aggressor, seeking to overturn the settlement arrived at by consent or by traditional means in 1641; necessity and the irreducible rights of every free man to protect his life and liberties from the collapse of government were the grounds of taking up arms.[40] If the king failed to mobilize his people against the threat of popery at home and abroad, the people must be instructed by their representatives in Parliament to take the necessary steps to protect themselves. But the rhetoric remained reactive and was unfolded reluctantly as new aggressions were added to existing ones. Constitutional demands were arrived at hesitantly piecemeal, and justifications, often half-hearted ones, were found after the event.[41] Lois Schwoerer has shown this in her case study of the making of

---

38. The major acts are listed in Gardiner, *Constit. Docs*, nos. 27–31, 33–8. Let me stress: these are not 'revolutionary' or innovative in *form*: they are enacted by king-in-parliament. For the comparison between this constitutional propriety and the willingness to appropriate powers not hitherto claimed in order to bring Laudianism crashing down, see J.S. Morrill, 'The Attack on the Church of England in the Long Parliment', above ch. 4.
39. Cf. Morrill, 'Religious Context', pp. 58–60.
40. E.g., Husbands, *Exact Collection, passim,* though for good examples see the undated declaration (2 August 1642?), pp. 461–4, and the Declaration of 8 August 1642, pp. 491–9.
41. Morrill, 'Religious Context', above, pp. 58–61.

the Militia Ordinance,[42] and I have suggested elsewhere that what is remarkable about the ordinances Parliament issued in the months before the outbreak of the civil war is the fact that they were non-coercive.[43] However desperate Parliament's desire, in the face of royal aggression, to gain control of the militia and of the purse-strings, they could not bring themselves to give their ordinances the force of law: they were morally but not legally binding.

Before I draw my conclusions, I want to develop two final and broad points about constitutional reticence. I want to discuss the striking failure of the Houses to draw on precedent and on English history in their defence of their actions in 1642, and I want to relate that to the kind of peace that their waging of war was intended to make possible.

It is a commonplace of Tudor and early Stuart scholarship that lawyers and antiquarians felt no inhibition about exploring and applying precedents of innumerable kinds; and that this was a growth industry in the 1620s. The extraordinary absence of such references from the polemic of 1642 is thus all the more remarkable.

On reflection, perhaps absence is too strong a term; perhaps it would be more accurate to speak of the presence of only muffled and opaque references. Let us take the case or the Nineteen Propositions.[44] At one level, they seem little more than an attempt to appropriate for Englishmen what the king had already conceded to his Scottish subjects.[45] Yet there are some tantalizing glimpses of fourteenth century parliamentary documents contain within it, perhaps most notably the ordinances of 1311 and the *Modus Tenendi Parliamentum* of 1322.[46] I am puzzled by the particular list of royal officials whom the Houses were to approve. Note the prominence of the constable, the lord high steward and the earl marshall, the three officers empowered within the *Modus* to establish a commission of estates in the event of an irreconcilable dispute between the king and the magnates.[47] The

42. L. Schwoerer, '"The Fittest Subject for a King's Quarrel:" an Essay in the Militia Controversy', 11 (1971).
43. See the important speech by d'Ewes, BL, Harl. M.S., 163 fol. 427.
44. See above, pp. 10–13.
45. A point made by David Stevenson, *The Scottish Revolution* (1973), ch. 7; P. Donald, 'Charles I's Scottish Policy' (PhD thesis, University of Cambridge 1987), chs. 5–6; C. Russell, 'The British Problem and the English Civil War', *History*, 72 (1987), 395–415.
46. N. Pronay and J. Taylor, *Parliamentary Texts of the Later Middle Ages* (1980), pp. 13–117; M.V. Clarke, *Medieval Representation and Consent* (1936), esp. pp. 188–93.
47. Pronay and Taylor, p. 87.

presence of the constable is especially remarkable, both because the constable was held by many antiquaries to have the authority, *in extremis*, to arrest the king and because the office had been in effect vacant since 1521 or even earlier[48] The connection remains elusive and was never spelled out, perhaps deliberately so.

A further tantalizing resonance in the Nineteen Propositions is with the fifteenth- and early sixteenth-century debate on the nature of counsel, recently discussed by John Guy.[49] The tension between an 'aristocratic' and a 'bureaucratic' council, that is, whether the king should be advised by representatives of the estates who could inform him of the needs and grievances of the commonwealth or by his own chosen servants, was one of the central themes of the later middle ages; and the case for the former was pressed not only by baronial interests, but by loyalist writers such as Fortescue, St German, Elyot, and Starkey, all of whom believed that king and realm would benefit from a scheme in which the royal council was appointed or at least approved by representatives of the estates.[50] Despite these comfortable precedents, let alone the many uncomfortable ones, however, the Parliamentarians of 1642 argued for their right to veto councillors on grounds of necessity and not of history, as guards against popery and the king's blindness to the evils of the counsellors around him in on the eve of the war.[51]

More interesting is what must have been a conscious decision not to argue the case for the constitutional reforms envisaged by the leaders of the two Houses in 1642. For all the populist agitation of 1641, the extraordinary thing about the constitutional deadlock in 1642 was that it concerned issues not of parliamentary sovereignty, still less of popular liberties; it was concerned with the restoration of the ancient peerage to its dominant role around the Crown. The civil war began as an aristocratic coup.[52]

Parliament's war aims were set forth in two documents: the Militia Ordinance and the Nineteen Propositions. The Militia Ordinance certainly appropriates to the two Houses the right to nominate lords

48. T. Hearne, *A Collection of Curious Discourses*, 2 vols. (1771), 2, 65–9, 265–7.
49. J. Guy, 'The King's Council and Political Participation', in. A. Fox and J. Guy, *Reassessing the Henrician Age* (1986), 121–51.
50. Important authors in this connection include Fortescue, see C. Plummer (ed.), *The Governance of England* (1886), app. B, pp. 348–53; and K.M. Burton (ed.), *A Dialogue between Reginald Pole and Sir Thomas Lupset* (1948), pp. 155–66.
51. E.g., Husbands, *Exact Collection*, pp. 92, 96–103, 195–214, 491–9.
52. This will shortly be the subject of a major study by John Adamson, who will develop and demonstrate this point at length.

lieutenant – but it merely names the men who were to control local defence forces throughout England. In almost every case the lord, lieutenant was to be a peer of the realm.[53] Those newly appointed included twice as many men whose titles had been created before 1558 as there were in the group they replaced.[54] Almost no men with post-1603 titles were newly appointed. It was these peers, not Parliament, who were to choose the deputy lieutenants, and together they were given greater freedom and responsibility for the training and deployment of the militia than existed before 1640.[55] The Nineteen Propositions laid out terms for ensuring that Charles stayed within the framework agreed in 1641. It claimed for the two Houses the right to veto all royal appointments to his council and to named senior offices; it made ministers accountable for the advice they gave; it allowed parliamentary vetting of those appointed to educate the king's children; it strengthened the laws against Catholics; and it committed the king to accept whatever reform of the Church was proposed by an assembly of puritan ministers and laymen to be established by Parliament.[56] No attempt was made to formalize Parliament's role in the administration of the country: to make permanent that range of duties which they had assumed on an *ad hoc* basis during the crisis of 1641 – supervising the levying and disbursement of taxes, direct involvement in the negotiation of treaties and alliances – or to institutionalize the standing committee of estates between parliamentary sessions and so on.[57] Instead, the Houses sought the right to approve appointments principally to major offices. This has normally been seen as aiming to enhance the authority of Parliament. In so far as it did so, it was simply the lever by which an aristocratic coup could be completed. These proposals were not designed disingenuously, in a void. Those who proposed them knew

53. The List is in *LJ*, 4. 587.
54. For royal appointees hitherto, see J.L. Sainty, *Lords Lieutenants of English Counties 1559–1642* (List and Index Society, 1970).
55. Gardiner, *Const. Docs.*, pp. 245–7, gives the text but not the names. This is symptomatic of all editors of 'constitutional documents' from the nineteenth century on. The same thing happens with the Oxford, Uxbridge, and Newcastle Propositions and the Heads of the Proposals. We will never understand the political responses to peace proposals unless we realize that Charles had to decide not on (and sometimes, as in 1647, between) sets of proposals but at the same time on a slate of names of those he would have to be counselled by.
56. Gardiner, *Const. Docs.*, pp. 249–54.
57. For which see D.H. Pennington, 'The Making of War', in D.H. Pennington and K.V. Thomas (eds.), *Puritans and Revolutionaries* (1979). S. Lambert, 'The Opening of the Long Parliament', *HJ*, 27 (1974), is also important.

just who they wished to see placed in each of the major offices. It is noteworthy that the first nine offices named in the propositions were those traditionally held by the peerage. Furthermore, as we have already seen, the Nineteen Propositions attempted to reestablish a medieval doctrine of council and the primacy of the ancient nobility. While a majority of all peers supported the king, a clear majority of the peers whose titles were pre-Elizabethan supported Parliament. Yet at no point did the Houses, in any of their 'official' defences of the Militia Ordinance or Nineteen Propositions, make the connection with the precedents that they must have had in mind.

These unsystematic evocations apart, the exchanges between king and Parliament in 1642 addressed specific historical precedents on only three occasions, and on two of those it was the king's side that took the initiative. The first occasion was when the king applied the Treason Act of 25 Edward III and the De Facto Act of 11 Henry VII to prove his case against Sir John Hotham, a case which the Houses only partially addressed in their reply.[58] The second was the king's reliance on 5 Henry IV to justify the issuing of the Commission of Array, a use which was fully and quite effectively challenged by the Houses,[59] and the third was the House's own citation of the preamble to the Statute of Provisors, by which they claimed 'the obligation that lyeth upon the kings of this realm to pass such bills as are offered unto them by both Houses of Parliament'.[60] The king gave a reply which the Houses found it impossible to counter, and he added salt to the wound by offering a translation of the relevant section of the preamble together with the observation that the Houses had published it only in Latin which 'they knew many of our good subjects could not and many of them do not understand'.[61]

The paucity and shallowness of such exchanges contrast with the detailed and assured way that the debate on episcopacy and on the temporal authority of ministers was fought out in the House and in print with relation to scripture, to the primitive Church and with relation to statute. Perhaps they were deterred by the fact that even generally sympathetic antiquarians like Selden and d'Ewes were always likely to denounce specious use of precedents, as Selden did during the attainder of Strafford and during the passage of the Militia

58. Husbands, *Exact Collection*, pp. 154–5.
59. Ibid., pp. 372–5, 386–95.
60. Ibid., p. 268.
61. Ibid., p. 291.

Ordinance.[62] At any rate, their failure to demonstrate that they were acting within established constitutional procedures created mounting problems for them. They had campaigned fiercely in 1641 to represent Charles's government as innovative. They held all innovations to be wrong. Yet by the summer of 1642 they stood accused of precisely the same practices themselves and they found themselves asserting that

> if we have made any precedents this Parliament, we have made them for posterity, upon the same or better grounds of reason and Law then those were upon, which our predecessors first made for us, and some presidents ought not to be rules for us to follow; so none can be limits to bound our proceedings and must vary according to the different conditions of times. . . . If there were never any example . . . it is because there were never any such Monsters before, that ever attempted to disaffect the people from their Parliament.[63]

Ill-considered and undefended statements like this gave the king his greatest propaganda coup. With the Houses too inhibited to pin the label of tyrant on the king, they were all too vulnerable to having him pin the label of tyranny on them. In August 1642 he alleged that the faction which had mystified and manipulated the House of Commons had set out to create conditions of anarchy the better to secure themselves as tyrants.[64]

The title of my lecture was, then, profoundly ironic. Although in January 1649, Charles I may, ruefully, have looked back on his shipwrecked fortunes and recognized that he had perhaps contributed to his undoing by misuse of power, a limited legal tyranny, and although by the conventions of the day, he could certainly have stood accused of that charge, it is Charles who began the civil war very precisely sticking the label on his enemies and gaining support throughout the country as a result.

I have been arguing for several years that the best title for the crisis in mid-seventeenth century England is 'England's Wars of Religion'. This title locates the civil wars in an early modern context rather than as the precursor of the revolutions of the modern world; it reminds us that England's wars in the 1640s and 1650s were wars with Scotland and Ireland as well as with itself. It does not mean that the crisis in England, any more than the earlier religious wars in France, the Netherlands, and Germany were only about religion. The

---

62. C.V. Wedgwood, *Thomas Wentworth, First Earl of Strafford* (1961), p. 366; BL, Harl. M.S. 163, fol. 254v.
63. Husbands, *Exact Collection*, p. 265.
64. Ibid., pp. 514–15, 528–62.

swirling cross-currents of social change and the structural problems associated with the growth of the state both contributed to the nature and outcome of the wars of religion. Yet most historians would see confessional polarities as exercising the single most powerful pull and I would claim no more for England in the 1640s and 1650s.

Once the will to defy the king and take up arms against him had been formed, many other considerations determined how individuals decided to respond. Many followed the line of least resistance, or followed material self-interest; many more tried to opt out; many just did what they were told. Those who committed themselves to one side or the other often allowed their assessment of the king's record of secular misgovernment or parliament's usurpation of his hitherto unquestioned prerogative to sway them. But in my view, very few men opted for war, made war happen, determined that there should be a war, if their preoccupations were primarily secular and constitutional. If there were constitutional radicals who were religious moderates, I have not discovered them. Those who, on the parliamentary side, made things happen, were those who, whatever their views on the best way to preserve a balanced constitution, felt passionately about religion. Fearful of a popish takeover, persuaded by the preachers that God was offering them a stark choice between on the one hand a greater obedience to Him and on the other hand the erection of a church more congruent with His commands or subjection to popery and superstition, the religious hard-liners sought not conservation but reformation, not checks and balances but dynamism and experiment.

What I am trying to suggest is that the constitutional case for Parliament was muddled and avoided the most obvious and potent traditions of argument, while the religious case was argued powerfully and divisively. From the moment the House of Commons agreed to consider the Root and Branch petition, they were on the offensive with regard to religion; the suspension and deprivation of ministers, the impeachment of bishops, the licensing of iconoclasm, the appointment of ministers, the vetting of religious treatises, all by the Houses and their committees, all backed up the determination to change things, while the popish plot created a belief that if no reformation was completed, then God would permit the subjugation of his disobedient people to the yoke of antichrist.[65] More than 75 per

65. Morrill, 'Attack on the Church', above, ch. 4.

cent of all published parliamentary speeches and more than 75 per cent
of all tracts on public affairs in the years 1640–2 were concerned with
the matters of church government and liturgy – the percentage would
be higher if sermons are included. This literature served to polarize
opinion and not to create consensus. In contrast virtually no MP
published his speech or speeches on the Grand Remonstrance, the
Militia Ordinance, the Nineteen Propositions.[66] Anthony Fletcher's
work on county petitioning would suggest that after the summer of
1641, petitions on religion tended to polarize opinion, petitions on
constitutional issues tended to reinforce peace and consensus. Where
are the mass petitions for the Nineteen Propositions to compare with
the mass petitions for and against bishops?[67]

Thus my analysis of the political polemics of the Long Parliament
does not shift me from seeing religious issues as being those which
made civil war happen. Political issues help to explain what many
men do once a state of war exists. But the political crisis of 1641 led
on to a particular kind of war because a minority of zealots believed
there would be no resolution of the political impasse which would
safeguard true religion unless they took up arms to bring it about.

In January 1642, Francis White, MP, accused the bishops of being

> the prime authors of all the troubles we are now encumbered withall
> . . . by innovating religion, joyning with the Church of Rome, ap-
> proving as well of the doctrines as the ceremonies thereof . . . to
> raise divisions between the king and his subjects, king and Parliament,
> between Lords and Commons and between the Commons themselves;
> to raise mutinies, insurrection, rebellions among his Majesty's king-
> doms, one against another, and all under pretence of religion.[68]

Seven months later, on 12 August 1642, the Lords and Commons
declared that:

> by the concurrence and assistance of the papists, an ambitious and
> discontented clergy, delinquents obnoxious to the Parliament, and some
> ill-affected persons of the nobility and gentry; who out of their desire
> of a dissolute liberty, apprehend and would keep off the reformation
> intended by the Parliament . . . [their aim was] that so men's minds
> made poor and base, and their Liberties lost and gone, they might be
> ready to let goe their religion, whensoever it should be resolved to alter

66. The whole subject of the printing of parliamentary speeches in the years 1640–2
   is dealt with by A. Cromatie, 'The Printing of Parlimentary Speeches, November
   1640 to July 1642', *HJ*, XXXIII (1990), pp. 23–44.
67. Fletcher, *Origins*, chs. 6, 8, 10–12.
68. *Mr White's speech in Parliament on Monday the 17th of January, Concerning the Triall
   of the XII Bishops*, pp. 4–5.

it, which was, and still is, the great designe, and all else made use of, but as instrumentary and subservient to it.[69]

Many things weakened Charles I's hold on the affections of his subjects. But it was that perception and belief which made civil war necessary and which was ultimately to bring him to the scaffold.

69. Husbands, *Exact Collection*, p. 492.

CHAPTER SIXTEEN

The Army Revolt of 1647

I

In order to win the civil war, Parliament had to trample on those very susceptibilities and conventional political wisdoms which it went to war to protect. The parliamentarian propaganda of 1642 is drenched in the language of civil liberties: of freedom from arbitrary taxation; from arbitrary imprisonment; from misguided paternalism; and from the centralizing tendencies of early Stuart monarchy. The dream-world of many Parliamentarians, particularly in the provinces, was of a well-ordered state comprising semi-autonomous local communities meeting common problems, and seeking powers to answer local needs, through free parliaments under the general regulation of a monarch whose role was that of chief justiciar and arbiter. Instead, more and more as the years passed, Parliament was forced to break with all the cherished nostrums conjured up by their propaganda. They fought to protect a herd of sacred cows each of which was slaughtered to propitiate the god of war. Unprecedented fiscal demands were met by a massive invasion of property rights; rights of habeas corpus and trial by jury were swept aside by a massive introduction of *droit administratif*; billeting of troops, free quarter, martial law were soon widely in force. Unlike the king, Parliament abandoned all pretence of respecting the traditional modes of consultation with and delegation to the particular institutional bodies which had evolved in each county and borough. Indeed, every article of the Petition of Right, the most cherished statement of the rights of the subject drawn up in the early seventeenth century, was broken by Parliament in the course of the war. And I have argued that, as a result, there was a great revulsion against the wars in 1645 and 1646 which took two forms: the militant neutralism evident in such movements as the

Clubmen, who demanded a return to the old institutions and ways, and an end to centralization and government unresponsive to local needs and sensibilities, and the radicalism of the Levellers, again demanding an end to the powers assumed by Parliament, but seeking a massive democratization as well as a massive decentralization of power and justice. They are closely related movements, both earthed in the mythology of local community consensus government, and both created by the harsh facts of war. Neither could ultimately cope with the continuing existence of the New Model Army.[1]

In 1647 the Houses of Parliament were trapped between incompatible objectives. They were committed to a settlement with a king who was committed not to agree to a settlement; they were conscious that the continuing fiscal and administrative burdens threatened a further outbreak of provincial rebellions; they were also conscious of the continuing existence of an army owed £3m in arrears – this in the context of a kingdom whose royal revenues before the civil war had never approached £1m p.a.[2] The apparent folly of the Parliament in attempting to disband the Army without settlement of its grievances must be weighed in that context. The struggle between Parliament and Army in 1647 is the history of two groups who ultimately needed one another but who long failed to recognize the fact.[3]

Recent work has made the policies of the Presbyterian alliance in Parliament more comprehensible. It has also emphasized that the Leveller ideas penetrated the Army rather later than had been thought.[4] My task here is to examine those bread-and-butter grievances of the Army with which they were exclusively concerned until the end of May 1647, and to see how far those grievances were subsequently redressed. Historians have too often presumed that once the Army was politicized, made aware of its political destiny and constitutional responsibilities by the Levellers, its material grievances became unimportant. Far from it. I want to argue that from early June onwards Parliament was providing remedies to those grievances, but that those remedies required an extension of the very administrative

---

1. J.S. Morrill, *The Revolt of the Provinces* (London, 1976), sections 2 and 3.
2. I. Gentles, 'The Arrears of Pay of the Parliamentary Army at the End of First Civil War', *Bulletin of the Institute of Historical Research*, XLVIII (1975), 52–63.
3. V. Pearl, 'London's Counter-Revolution' in *The Interregnum* (ed. G.E. Aylmer, London, 1972), pp. 29–56; I. Gentles, 'Arrears of Pay and Ideology in the Army Revolt of 1647', in *War and Society* (eds. B. Bond and I. Roy, London, 1975), pp. 44–66.
4. Gentles, ibid.; J.S. Morrill, 'Mutiny and Discontent in English Provincial Armies', below, ch. 17.

and legal abuses against which the Levellers railed. By the end of 1647, the Leveller programme looked in many respects unsatisfactory to the rank and file, and this helped the Grandees to re-establish their control and put a brake on army radicalism.

II

In February 1647 the Scots army was paid off and returned home. The way was now clear for the Presbyterian leaders at Westminster to win the support of the many backbenchers eager to see an end to the burdens, fiscal and administrative, imposed by the civil war. It was this motive, rather than a prescient fear of army radicalism, which led the Presbyterians to call for the reduction of the Army to 5,400 men in England; the remainder were to be disbanded or sent to Ireland.[5] Between the end of February and the end of May, the increasingly sour exchanges of views between the Houses and the officers of the New Model Army centred around the arrangements for the Irish expedition and around the safeguards of the rights of soldiers which should be enacted before the disbandment.[6] The demands of the Army which gradually emerged during these months related almost entirely to the soldiers' rights as soldiers. There is little evidence that Leveller ideas, or any conception of the Army's responsibilities to promote broader political objectives, had emerged at this stage. On 20 May, for example, the agitators wrote to the Northern regiments[7] counselling them to do 'nothing but what is relating to them as soldiers'.[8] But the best and most comprehensive evidence of this comes from the Army's debates at Saffron Walden in the middle of May. At these, the Council of Officers asked every regiment to draw up a list of its own grievances. The Council of Officers then made a digest of the demands of the soldiers, and presented it to Parliament under the title the *Declaration of the Army*. An analysis of the original

5. S.R. Gardiner, *History of the Great Civil War* (4 vols, London, 1894), III, 212–30; M.P. Mahony, *The Presbyterian Party in the Long Parliament, 2 July 1644 to 3 June 1647* (Oxford D. Phil. thesis, 1972), chs. vii–ix.
6. The New Model was all too well aware that promises, subsequently ignored, had been made to other units which Parliament had disbanded (e.g. Massey's Western Brigade in the summer and autumn of 1646).
7. The Northern regiments contributed a separate force of 12,000 men under the command of the (Presbyterian) Major-General Poyntz until he was overthrown in a mutiny in July 1647. They were then merged with the New Model; Morrill, *Mutiny*, pp. 69–71.
8. *The Clarke Papers. Selections from the Papers of William Clarke* (ed. C.H. Firth for the Camden Society, 4 vols, 1891–1901), I, 91.

papers presented by eleven of the regiments is given in appendix II, below.[9]

These petitions show that while the language and the precise problems of every regiment were quite distinct,[10] there was a general consensus about what were the main concerns, and a very clear agreement on priorities. Almost all the petitions begin with, and devote most space to, problems relating to arrears and indemnity. These are the two major problems to which we shall turn in a moment. But it is also important to emphasize that the *Declaration of the Army* is a very fair reflection of the demands of the rank-and-file. As the officers said, some of the regiments were 'confused and full of tautologies, impertinences or weaknesses answerable to the Soldiers' dialects'[11] but it is the language, not the specific demands, which they smoothed out. The only substantial issues referred to in more than two petitions to be omitted by the officers were enforced service in Ireland and the charges of corruption wildly brought against committees of the Houses and in the counties. On the former issue, at least, the views of the officers had often been heard at Westminster.[12]

Two issues, however, stand out above the rest: arrears and indemnity. While Professor Gentles has done much to elucidate the nature of the former,[13] the latter has received little attention, and it is with this matter that I propose to begin.

Many of the principal military and fiscal ordinances passed by Parliament since 1643 had contained clauses freeing the agents of Parliament from any legal liability for actions undertaken on parliamentary authority. There were, however, two main problems: the ordinances did not extend to protect officers and soldiers who

9. The originals are in the library of Worcester College, Oxford, Clarke MS. 41, fos. 105–25. I am grateful to the Provost and Fellows for their permission to consult and cite these papers, and to Miss L. Montgomery, custodian of the MSS, for her kindness and help. The eleven regiments included are those of Rich, Disbrowe, Ireton, Whalley, Boteler, Fairfax (foot), Hewson, (Hardress) Waller, (Robert) Lilburne, Harley and Lambert.
10. The exception to this is that Fairfax's foot regiment and Hewson's regiment presented identical petitions.
11. Cited in Gentles, 'Arrears of Pay and Ideology', p. 49.
12. Professor Gentles claims that 'a comparison between the Declaration of the Army and the individual regimental papers bears out the officers' claim to have exercised a moderating influence'; Gentles, ibid., 50. He gives four examples. Two of them were matters raised only by one regiment, one by two regiments. The fourth complaint was taken up by the officers using more moderate language. The Officers' Declaration was not intended to include every item included by every regiment, but to reflect fairly general issues. The real difference is one of tone.
13. Gentles, 'The Arrears of Pay of the Parliamentary Army', *passim*.

had assumed emergency powers in prosecuting the war, and the enforcement of the indemnity clauses was in the hands of men determined to ignore them. Colonel Rich's regiment described 'the sad complaints & the miserable sufferings of many of our fellow soldiers who now suffer, and the recalling to our serious meditations the miserable imprisonment and ignominious death of many who were real and faithful to the service, all which they have undergone for acting things which the exigency of war constrained them to do'.[14] Thus, several regiments demanded an extension of indemnity to cover 'all things done as soldiers in relation to the war', or 'that which they have done in time and place of war'.[15] The fact remained for others, however, that 'we conceive, that upon every trespass, or other thing done in the war (which we may be questioned for) it will be very chargeable and difficult either to derive a clear authority for the same from the Ordinances of Parliament, or to bring proofs sufficient to make up such a constructive conclusion'.[16] This also led on to a second and more far-reaching demand. The end of the civil war and the restoration of the normal processes of law (quarter sessions, assizes, borough courts) had led very many civilians to bring actions against soldiers alleging civil damage or criminal acts. Juries and justices were totally disregarding even existing indemnity rights, and were convicting soldiers or awarding damages against them. Thus Colonel Harley's regiment demanded that Parliament 'preserve us from the common law'.[17] It is also clear that many county committees, in pursuing local interests, had arbitrarily imprisoned many men, and the regimental petitions are bitterly hostile to county committees.[18] The soldiers demanded institutional protection from existing committees and courts.

From late April onwards, Parliament was prepared to make concessions over indemnity. On 30 April, even before the regimental petitions were drawn up at Saffron Walden, but in response to an earlier army petition, the Commons resolved to press ahead with a Bill of Indemnity. By 21 May, this Bill had passed both Houses and had been published.[19] Its central provision, however, was ambiguous,

---

14. Clarke MS. 41, fos. 113–14.
15. Ibid., fos. 105, 119.
16. J. Rushworth, *Historical Collections* (8 vols., London, 1659–1701), VII, 508; cited in Morrill, *Revolt*, pp. 175–6.
17. Clarke MS. 41, fos. 120–3.
18. Ibid., fos. 108, 119; see also British Library (hereafter BL), Thomason Tracts E 392(9) and Rushworth, *Historical Collections*, VII, 505–10.
19. *CJ*, V, 158, 166, 174, 181; *LJ*, IX, 201.

and certainly did not go as far as the soldiers wanted: 'that no person or persons whatsoever, who have since the beginning of this present Parliament, *acted or done*, or commanded to be acted any act or thing whatsoever, *by authority of this present Parliament, or for the service or benefit thereof*, by Sea or by Land, ought to be sued, indicted, prosecuted or molested for the same'. Unfortunately the precise meaning of the phrase 'for the service or benefit' of Parliament was left unexplained. Did it include the many acts of military requisition, often in the grey area between distraint and plunder, sanctioned not by a warrant derived from an ordinance but by the exigencies of war?

The much more radical claims of the 21 May ordinance came in the second half, and showed the extent to which, even at this stage, Parliament was willing to accommodate the Army. Any soldiers or civilians who believed themselves protected by the ordinance, and who were 'not able to defend a suit at common law, or may find themselves aggrieved in the proceedings thereof' were granted the right of appeal to a new standing committee of Parliament (comprising fifty-two members of the Commons and twenty-six of the Lords) who were given swingeing powers (a) to stay proceedings before all courts and commissioners, (b) to imprison plaintiffs who continued actions against those under the protection of the Indemnity commissioners, (c) 'to receive, hear and determine such aforesaid complaints, and to that end to examine witnesses upon oath', (d) to annul any verdict, sentence or judgement made elsewhere and to award triple damages to the complainant, (e) to inhibit all lawyers from acting on behalf of plaintiffs continuing their actions at common law or initiating collateral actions, including the power to commit any lawyer who took instructions 'to safe custody'. The ordinance clearly conceded that judges and juries, especially in the boroughs, were not honouring, and were not expected to begin honouring, rights of indemnity.[20]

This ordinance did not satisfy the soldiers who demanded, in a petition of 4 June, a clarification of the indemnity clauses; indeed, a blanket protection for all things done in time and place of war, sufficient 'to meet all the evasions and elusions of a subtle lawyer or to convince the senses of a Country Jury'.[21] Within three days the soldiers' demand was satisfied by a new ordinance that distinguished their indemnity 'for all such acts as the exigency of war hath

---

20. C.H. Firth and R.S. Rait, *Acts and Ordinances of the Interregnum* (3 vols, London, 1911), I, 936–8.
21. Rushworth, *Historical Collections*, VII, 508.

necessitated them unto' from that of civilian officials, only indemnified for actions clearly derived from parliamentary ordinance.[22]

On 4 June the Army did indeed express regret that their indemnity
should be 'the occasion of setting up more arbitrary courts than there
be already' but the actual operation of the committee soon won them
over and by December, the Army actually demanded an extension
of the system with the creation of county committees of indemnity
chosen jointly by the Army and Parliament under the control of the
central committee.[23] In December the Army also asked that these new
indemnity committees should be made responsible for the raising and
disbursing of local rates for the relief of maimed soldiers and widows
– powers which had always resided with the Justices of the Peace. At
first sight this is a surprising request. What was the connection with
indemnity? In fact it would have been only one of several radical
extensions of the jurisdiction of the indemnity commissioners which
were assumed by the committee in the course of 1647 and 1648. One
of the demands made by several regiments in May was that royalists
and neuters should be excluded from office. As Hardress Waller's
men put it:

> faithful, cordially, godly men some whereof related to this army . . . are
> discountenanced, distrusted, and put out of office and places of authority
> and others ambidexters and neuters &c, are preferred to places of trust,
> yea some [who] were apparent malignants are made tryers and judges of
> those who have been and still are faithful and cordial in the behalf of
> the kingdom's good.[24]

The problem was greatest in the boroughs over whose governors
Parliament often had restricted control. On 9 September Parliament
passed an ordinance disabling from office all those who had ever
been sequestered as enemies of the Parliament. Those who had
wriggled back to power were also to be heavily fined. A second
ordinance on 4 October extended the prohibition to all borough
electors. Both these ordinances were to be enforced by the Indemnity
Commissioners. Within a few weeks, they received complaints about
the town governments of Maidstone, Stamford, Carlisle, Wigan,
and elsewhere, and had launched investigations which led to heavy
purges.[25]

22. Firth and Rait, *Acts*, I, 953–4.
23. *LJ*, IX, 556–63.
24. Clarke MS. 41, fos. 117–18.
25. Firth and Rait, *Acts*, I, 1009, 1023; Public Record Office (hereafter PRO) SP 24/1,
   passim.

Several regiments had also asked that apprentices who had enlisted for Parliament during the war should, upon disbandment, be made free of their trades or crafts as though they had completed their apprenticeships.[26] Legislation already existed to protect them in this respect,[27] but enforcement lay with the local courts and it is clear that local governors were simply refusing to implement it. Parliament soon granted power to enforce these ordinances to the Committee of Indemnity.[28]

The papers of the Indemnity Committee confirm the extent to which the soldiers' demands had been gratified by 1647. The committee, meeting on three or four days each week, soon came under the control of a small number of men. None of the peers and only a minority of the Commons attended the committee. Almost all the most active members in 1647–8 were future Rumpers, and several of the most assiduous were among those who withdrew to the Army during the counter-revolution in July. Only two men associated with the Presbyterian leadership (John Birch and John Swinfen) were at all active on the committee. More characteristic of the leadership in 1647 were men like Miles Corbett, Humphrey Edwards, Michael Livesey, William Purefoy, John Weaver and John Lisle. It was not so much the Independent leaders as their second-ranking supporters who led the way.[29]

The total number of cases heard by the committee is difficult to determine, since many were heard on several dispersed occasions. But Professor Aylmer has estimated that more than 1,000 were begun by the end of 1648, about a third of which were brought by soldiers.[30] The great majority of these were quite straightforward. Quartermasters who had taken up quantities of military supplies

26. Clarke MS. 41, fos. 108–10, 112–15.
27. Firth and Rait, *Acts*, I, 37.
28. Firth and Rait, ibid, I, 1054.
29. The Committee of Indemnity Papers (PRO SP 24) fall naturally into two main groups. The first series of sixteen volumes comprises the fair copy order books arranged in chronological order from 1647 to 1655. The main series (more than fifty volumes) comprises the original petitions presented to the Commissioners. These are arranged in alphabetical order. For the purposes of this paper I examined the first three order books, covering the period up to the middle of 1649, and a random sample of twelve boxes of petitions. I am most grateful to Professor G.E. Almer for allowing me to read and use his unpublished paper, 'Indemnity and Oblivion, 1647–1659'. I consulted the petitions in the PRO, but the order books form part of the collection of microfilms recently issued by Harvester Press, under the title 'Unpublished State Papers of the English Civil War and Interregnum', and it is in this form that I consulted them.
30. Aylmer, unpublished article.

(food, clothing, colours, carts, boats) sought protection from actions for payment brought by their suppliers.[31] Soldiers sought protection from men requiring payment for board and lodging;[32] and from those suing them for having distrained goods or seized arms.[33] Many other soldiers had become involved in brawls or skirmishes with civilians while executing warrants or while simply on the march.[34] Perhaps the commonest petitions of all relate to the seizure of horses. But in many of these latter cases, no authority derived from an ordinance was alleged. They had simply commandeered horses when the old ones had died, gone lame, or were about to foal.[35] In some cases the situation became even more deeply confused. Thomas Smallwood, a common soldier, commandeered a horse at the battle of Rowton Moor, and subsequently sold it to an Elizabeth Kent. The latter was later sued at common law by the original owner, who was awarded £8 damages and £5 costs. But the ordinance was held to protect not only the soldier who seized the mare, but the person who subsequently acquired it, and Mistress Kent got her money back on appeal to the Commissioners.[36]

John Carpenter of Culham, Oxfordshire, was another beneficiary of this loose interpretation of the ordinance. He was taken prisoner by the royal garrison at Oxford, and only released on payment of a ransom of £60. Major-General Browne, parliamentarian governor of Abingdon, responded by taking prisoner an Oxford man, from whom he similarly demanded a £60 ransom which, with the consent of his council of war, he handed over to Carpenter. However the Oxonian 'hath since sued your petitioner for the said 60li & at Oxford Assizes last obtained a verdict for the same against your petitioner'. Carpenter was rescued by the Commissioners.[37]

Readers of Professor Holmes' study of the truculent, uninhibited Lincolnshire parliamentarian, Colonel Edward King,[38] will be unsurprised to learn that he appears in the papers of the Indemnity Commissioners both as petitioner and as defendant. In July 1647 he sought redress against the action of Nehemiah Rawson who had sued him in the courts for seizing and selling wool valued at £440

---

31. E.g. PRO SP 24/1 fos. 54–5, 131.
32. E.g. PRO SP 24/1 fos. 6, 13; SP 24/70 unfoliated petition of Richard Price.
33. E.g. PRO SP 24/1 fos. 20, 143; SP 24/31, petition of Richard Aylesworth.
34. E.g. PRO SP 24/1 fos. 77, 133.
35. E.g. PRO SP 24/1 fos. 18, 32.
36. PRO SP 24/1 fo. 9.
37. PRO SP 24/38, petition of John Carpenter.
38. C. Holmes, 'Colonel Edward King and Lincolnshire Politics', *HJ*, XVI (1973), 451–84.

from the Parliamentarian garrison at Tattershall castle (part of his feud with parts of the local Parliamentarian establishment?). Since he had deployed the money 'for the good of the state' he was indemnified, but the county committee was ordered to repay Rawson out of county funds. Yet at the same time King was himself being brought before the same committee by Thomas Wallett, high constable of Elloe hundred, who claimed that King had fined him £100 for failing to call a general meeting of all the inhabitants of his hundred. Four months later, King was vindicated in a report from Lincolnshire Members of Parliament Sir Anthony Irby and Sir Edward Aiscough. Yet Wallett 'hath been faithful to the Parliament & constantly performed his duty to them for their service', and the county committee was again ordered to reimburse him. The commissioners trod carefully in the shark-infested waters of Lincolnshire politics.[39]

Many of the petitions reveal that the soldiers had pleaded the Ordinance of Indemnity in the common law courts, but that the judges or juries had ignored it. In one case at York assizes, for example, both counsel for Sir Edward Rhodes, an officer in Lord Fairfax's army, and the Justice of Assize had argued for an acquittal on the ordinance, but the jury had convicted.[40]

Furthermore many cases surely fell outside the scope of the ordinance. One soldier who was being sued for a pre-war debt owed to a royalist was protected by the commissioners.[41] But perhaps the most important creative extension of the ordinance came with the willingness of the commissioners to act on behalf of parliamentary soldiers who found on their return to their tenancies that their landlords were determined to evict them or convert their copyholds to rack rents.[42]

Several important points can be made about the working of the indemnity ordinances as they affected soldiers: (1) They were very broadly and generously interpreted by the commissioners. (2) They were willing to extend its scope to give protection to soldiers in their non-military problems. (3) In the years 1647–8 they almost invariably protected soldiers. The only exceptions involved soldiers who refused to submit themselves to the committees for taking accounts. The ordinances had specifically excluded such actions from the jurisdiction of the Indemnity commission. Other groups of

39. PRO SP 24/1 fos. 21, 71.
40. PRO SP 24/71, petition of 30 November 1647.
41. PRO SP 24/5 fo. 137.
42. E.g. PRO SP 24/38, petition of Richard Caswall.

petitioners (notably excisemen) were quite often refused protection from the courts. (4) The tough action of the commissioners in awarding triple damages against those harassing soldiers may have greatly reduced the number of soldiers taken to court and may have strengthened the resolve of judges to implement the ordinances in the courts. (5) The petitions do confirm the deep hostility felt towards the Army by large sections of the civilian population. It underscores all the other evidence recently presented that there was a very real threat of the collapse of order in the summer of 1647. But the greatest threats came not from the Levellers but from the clashes of soldiers and civilians in many garrison towns, in the fresh wave of Clubmen or neutralist risings, in the activities of mysterious brigand groups like the Dalesmen and the Mosstroopers of the Scots Border Counties or the Moorlanders of north Staffordshire.[43] This also gives credibility to the desperate attempts of the moderate majority in Parliament in the summer to cut the Gordian knot by disbanding the Army as the probable prelude to a sell-out to the king. (6) And finally, the evidence powerfully suggests that only strong, effective executive action by a centralized, bureaucratic body exercising *droit administratif* could protect soldiers and civilians from a backlash in the provinces. Indemnity had not only to be pronounced but effected, and it could only be effected by action at the centre.

III

Parliament's response to the Army's other major concern, the question of arrears, may have taught the soldiers the same lesson. For from the outset the Army's demands were moderate and realizable. The problem was not so much one of principle as of enforcement. The total volume of arrears was in the region of £2.8m; arrears for service in the New Model were about £1.2m.[44] As late as early June, Fairfax's foot regiment, one of the most militant, declared that it would accept four months' arrears in cash and the rest in debentures. Four months' pay for the whole army would have cost less than the amount Parliament borrowed in order to raise a force to get rid of the New Model.[45] In the Saffron Walden petitions, the regiments

43. Morrill *Revolt*, pp. 125–6; D.E. Underdown, *Pride's Purge* (London, 1970), pp. 38–44, 90–5.
44. Gentles, 'Arrears of Pay of the Parliamentary Army', pp. 54–55.
45. Bodleian Library, Tanner MS. 58 fo. 129. See Gentles, 'Arrears of Pay and Ideology', p. 50. At the end of May Parliament increased its cash offer from six to eight weeks.

concentrated on two other points. Firstly, they demanded a far more effective method of establishing the arrears of each soldier. At that time each soldier's claim had to be established by his presentation of proof of his length of service in each of several armies (perhaps those of Lord Grey, Lord Manchester and the New Model). And he had to certify the extent of his obligations to civilians for free quarter during his service. Most regiments demanded revised, speedier procedures and a guarantee that no soldier was to be disbanded until his accounts had been audited and arrears certified.

Secondly, the regimental papers demanded that Parliament should specify and secure future sources of revenue adequate to pay off the remaining bulk of their arrears.[46] In the event, the problem for Parliament was not to specify which revenues should be attached; it was to collect any revenue at all.

Nothing could be done to reduce the volume of arrears. If anything they were greater in December 1647 than in May.[47] Yet by December Fairfax was asking for a reduction of 18,000 men, and nearly half the army did submit to disbandment uncomplainingly.[48] It is crucial to remember that in the Saffron Walden petitions, the soldiers asked not for full payment, but for speedy and effective statement of accounts, and for guarantees of future payment. Parliament concentrated on meeting these conditions.

Ordinances in June and December 1647 radically changed and simplified accounting procedures as they affected the Army.[49] In particular, the slow and cumbersome methods whereby every soldier received a debenture only after proving the precise extent of his obligations for free quarter was abandoned in favour of standard reductions from the arrears of everyone (e.g. three shillings per week for foot soldiers, or six shillings and eight pence in the pound for all cavalry officers).[50]

In an attempt to create resources to pay the Army, the monthly assessment was extended, reformed, and attached firmly for the pay of the Army (23 June), both the excise and customs machinery was overhauled, action was taken against royalists who had not paid the

---

46. Two clear statements of these points come from the regiments of Colonels Whalley and Boteler; Clarke MS. 41, fos. 112, 115.
47. Gentles, 'Arrears of Pay of the Parliamentary Army', pp. 56–7.
48. I am grateful to Professor Gentles for drawing my attention to this point and for allowing me to read his unpublished paper 'The Army and the City of London, 1645–8', in which it is discussed.
49. Firth and Rait, *Acts*, I, 940–8, 956–7, 1051–2.
50. Firth and Rait, ibid., I, 940–8.

second half of the fines which they were required to pay once their lands had been restored, and the Army was voted money from the sale of episcopal lands.[51] On paper, Parliament had made adequate provision for the Army. What went wrong was simply the refusal or inability of the county committees to raise the money voted or at least to hand it over. The City of London in particular collected during 1647 none of the money voted on the monthly assessments.[52] As a desperate measure to meet this crisis, Parliament created on 23 September a new Committee of the Army, consisting of most of the New Model's friends in the Houses. This committee was given unprecedented powers to oversee the action of the county committees with respect to assessments. In particular they were given direct powers to fine and imprison defaulting assessors and collectors. An ordinance of 12 October extended to this committee power to collect arrears from two wartime assessment ordinances.[53] The qualified success of these measures may well account for the quiescence of the Army in the face of the disbandments of February 1648.

Almost all the other grievances included in the regimental petitions in May resolved themselves. The soldiers' right of petitioning was vindicated and the 'Declaration of Dislike', Parliament's denunciation of that right, was expunged from the Journals;[54] following the collapse of the counter-revolution, eleven leading opponents of the Army were expelled from the Commons.[55] Major new ordinances secured the position of ex-apprentices who had served in the Army,[56] extended Elizabethan legislation to give succour to war invalids, widows and orphans,[57] and restricted the freedom of boroughs to elect or coopt into office former royalists or neutrals.[58] Above all, the problem of the relief of Ireland was completely shelved until 1649, and (except for money voted in December 1647 at the Army's request), nothing was done to help the depleted and demoralized forces which had already served there for years. At no time between July 1647 and the execution of the king did Parliament authorize impressment, and even in 1649 there was no return to the general powers of impressment exercised between 1643 and 1646.

---

51. Firth and Rait, ibid., I, 958–84, 1004–7, 1025–6, 1032–42, 1049–51.
52. Gentles, unpublished article.
53. Firth and Rait, *Acts*, I, 1025–6.
54. *CJ*, V, 202; *LJ*, IX, 247–8.
55. Gardiner, *History*, III, 334–52.
56. Firth and Rait, *Acts*, I, 1054; *LJ*, IX, 610.
57. Firth and Rait, ibid., I, 938–40, 997–8, 1055–6; (based on 43 Eliz. c. 3).
58. Firth and Rait, ibid., I, 1009, 1023–4.

Thus between June and December 1647 a programme of action was worked out which went a long way towards meeting the demands of the soldiers as expressed in all their petitions up to early June 1647, when parliamentary action precluded a partnership of the two. At no time did Parliament refuse to meet the soldiers' demands. But in May and June they did insist on an immediate disbandment before the details of the programme had been settled. Nonetheless a series of concessions in those very months (above all in the setting up of the Indemnity Committee) prepared the way for the main series of reforms introduced in August–September and then December 1647. The central feature of this programme was a recognition of the hostility of the provincial communities both to the Army and to existing fiscal burdens. Yet the consequent centralization and extended executive action was totally incompatible with Leveller demands and preconceptions. By the time of the Putney debates both officers and rank and file had to make a painful choice.

IV

Colonel Hewson's regiment summed up its grievances thus:

> that unless we be relieved in these our grievances and answered in our just desires before we are disbanded, we fear that we should be hanged like dogs for the good service that we have done this kingdom as many of our fellow soldiers have been already since they were disbanded even for that which they have done in time and place of war and in obedience to the Parliament's commands.[59]

The Army was hated by the local communities. Even the radical county bosses were opposed to a standing army which drained local resources. Petitions against free quarter, against the burden of taxation, against religious libertinism in the Army, poured into Parliament in the early months of 1647. For example, a petition from the previously very Parliamentarian county of Essex expressed the fear of being 'eaten up, enslaved, and destroyed by an army raised for their defence'.[60] Above all, the Army was faced by the bitter hostility of the authorities in the City of London, who several times demanded its immediate disbandment, most notably in the Common Council's *Humble Representation* of December 1646.[61] A

59. Clarke MS.41, fos. 119–20.
60. Gardiner, *History*, III, 220.
61. Gentles, unpublished paper, emphasizes the religious motivation behind the Corporation's opposition to the Army. He cites City of London, Guildhall MSS Journal of Common Council 40, fos. 199–200. See also the Remonstrance of May 1646 (ibid. fo. 168) and a contemporary comment on its aims, 'in plain terms the disbandment of the army' (BL Thomason Tracts E 340 (20)).

wave of fresh mutinies across the provinces both heightened anti-military feelings and reflected the existing poor relations between soldiers and civilians.[62] The army leaders had no illusions. If they were to receive their arrears, gain effective indemnity, return to their trades or to husbandry, the soldiers had to rely on a strong central authority and upon determined executive action. This is precisely what the Levellers could not provide. Leveller pamphlets in late 1646 and early 1647 were implicitly anti-army. They railed against the inherent evils of the new, corrupt, centralizing bureaucracy which had broken the old legal restraints provided by the jury system and by community involvement in the dispensation of justice. The Levellers emphasized the enormous costs of the war: overtaxation, arbitrary methods of taxation and collection, etc. The Army, if not the cause of the oppression of the artisans, craftsmen and tenant-farmers who formed the Levellers' principal constituency, was the main occasion of it. The Army might have experienced the same spiritual liberation as the Levellers, but it was seen as part of the bloated, usurping, centralized power which fed on the lifeblood of the people. The *Large Petition* of March 1647, rightly seen as the most important summary of Leveller objectives up to that time, completely ignored the Army.[63] Indeed the thrust of Leveller thought was incompatible with the attainment of the Army's material ends. Here I am saved from false emphasis by the work of Dr Manning, whose excellent recent account of Leveller ideas, devised to argue a very different case, makes my point for me.[64] He shows how the well-known Leveller critique of existing economic and social conditions led them to formulate a plan for the total reconstruction of political institutions. The crucial feature of these reforms, however, was not the election of annual parliaments by manhood suffrage, but a withering away of the state. As he says, 'perhaps the most striking thing about the *Agreements* [*of the People*] is what they omit: the lack of reference to executive government. The central government is almost eliminated.' Instead, England was to be transformed into a federation of self-governing county communities, with popular elections of all local officials – justices, sheriffs, jurors etc. All central courts were to be abolished and replaced by hundredal courts under democratic control. There would be no standing army

---

62. Morrill, *Mutiny*, pp. 53–68; Underdown, *Pride's Purge*, pp. 38–44.
63. D.M. Wolfe, *Leveller Manifestoes of the Puritan Revolution* (New York, 1944), pp. 138–41.
64. B.S. Manning, *The English People and the English Revolution* (London, 1976), chs. ix and x.

and no centralized financial institutions. Parliaments would meet regularly, with prescribed terms of reference, to settle matters of common concern, but members would be immediately answerable to their constituents who would also elect triers to examine the members' performance. It is true that this radical programme of decentralization was played down in the *Case of the Army Truly Stated*, the central text of the Army-Leveller dialogue, but then the whole document is extremely evasive about how the Army's needs could be met. A great deal of the document consists of a confused rhetoric about arrears, and it does concentrate on describing how corruption in the central organs of power was responsible for the Army's plight. Yet it demanded the abolition or curtailment of precisely those sources of revenue most likely to meet the immediate financial needs of the Army. It called for an end both to excise and sequestrations, and for a moderation of composition fines, for example. The Levellers' main solution to the intractable problem of arrears was the sale of bishops' lands (the profits from which had already been fully allocated) and a fresh sale of dean and chapter lands. In addition, the receivers of customs and excise were to be made to disgorge 'their excessive fees and profits', and the London companies to hand over sums tied up in 'dead stocks in . . . the halls and companies'. Even more impracticably, there was to be an immutable Act of Indemnity and Oblivion but no central committee to enforce it.[65] As we have seen, the problem was not to enact indemnity, but to force local courts to acknowledge it. The most direct and imposing Leveller programme for solving the Army's problems, however, was not the *Case of the Army*, but Richard Overton's *Appeal From the Degenerate Representative Body of the Commons of England . . . to his Excellency Sir Thomas Fairfax and All the Officers and Soldiers under his Command* (July 1647). This contained a pungent attack on *droit administratif*, and demanded the abolition of all central courts and offices. In particular,

> That all Courts which are not established by the just old Law of the Land: and all illegal offices, and Officers, belonging to the same, and all other vexatious and unnecessary Courts, be abolished by act of Parliament. And that provision be made that for time to come, no Courts or Offices whatsoever may be obtruded upon the free commoners of England, either by Royal Grant, Patent, Act of Parliament, or otherwise contrary to the Old Law of the Land. That according to the old Law and custom of the Land, long before, or sometime after the Conquest, there may be Courts of Judicature for the speedy trial

65. Wolfe, *Leveller Manifestoes*, pp. 198–222.

322

and determination of all causes, whether Criminal or Civil, erected and
established in every Hundred . . . to be holden once or twice every
month . . . [and] that all such officers . . . to be chosen by the Free
Commons, as Mayors, Sheriffs, Justices of Peace etc. may be left to the
free election of the . . .

No institution or person, not even Parliament itself could imprison
without cause shown and speedy recourse to trial by jury.[66] Nothing
could have been further from the minds of those who formulated the
demands for indemnity in the regimental petitions in May.

This is not to deny that Leveller influence had penetrated deeply
into the Army in May, June and July. But let us recall the context.
Until 25 May, the soldiers were only concerned with their grievances
as soldiers. Their regimental petitions at Saffron Walden were almost
exclusively concerned with pay, conditions of service and guarantees
of security for disbanded men. There was little difference in the
demands of the regiments and of the controlling group of officers.
It is true that a large minority of 'moderate' junior officers at Saffron
Walden were opposed to the articulation even of those demands, but
these officers were hopelessly out of touch with rank-and-file feeling
and quickly deserted their regiments, or were dismissed, at Saffron
Walden or in the following weeks. Perhaps one hundred and sixty
'Presbyterian' officers were replaced in the next four weeks. The
result was an army in late May united behind Fairfax, Cromwell
and Lambert. When Cromwell reported to the Commons that the
Army was firmly under the officers' control, and would peacefully
disband if the grievances expressed in the *Declaration* were satisfied,
he was being perfectly truthful.[67] As we have seen, these demands
were in fact met in the following months: they were not unattainable.

It was Parliament's decision to confront rather than to conciliate
which transformed the situation. That decision clearly involved a
calculated risk of an army revolt. But it was not totally unreasonable.
Politically, the Presbyterian leadership was bidding for the support
of the great many 'backbench' Members of Parliament (including a
majority of the recruiters) whose primary interest lay in a reduction
of the tensions and conflicts in the provinces, exacerbated as they were
by the continuing fiscal burdens and continued existence of quartered
troops. The disbandment of the New Model would consolidate the
support of such Members of Parliament behind the Presbyterians

---

66. Printed in G.E. Aylmer, *The Levellers in the English Revolution* (London, 1975),
   pp. 83–4.
67. Gardiner, *History*, III, 257–8.

and isolate the Independent caucus further. Subsequently this would aid the Presbyterians in their attempt to reach agreement with the king on their terms. Beyond this, the Presbyterians were themselves genuinely fearful of a counter-revolution in London and the provinces and believed that to give in to the Army would be more likely to produce such a revolt.[68] Furthermore their success in disbanding other parliamentarian armies in 1646 suggested that the New Model might be peacefully reduced.[69] Finally they were not wholly vindictive in their behaviour towards the Army. In late May and early June they did make some concessions to the Army: they increased the amount of money payable on disbandment; they went some way to modify the methods for auditing soldiers' accounts; they made major concessions over indemnity; and on 21 May they made promises that no man who had volunteered should be forced to serve abroad, they promised additional help for maimed soldiers, widows and orphans, and they re-emphasized that soldiers could count time spent in the Army towards their period of apprenticeship. But they insisted on immediate disbandment before these concessions had been embodied in ordinances; they declined to meet the other grievances; and they made it clear that they were prepared to use force to dissolve the New Model if necessary.

For the time being, the option of an alliance with the legislature and central executive was denied to the Army. Not surprisingly, the New Model turned with far greater attention and sympathy to the Levellers, who offered a friendly hand, a rhetoric of support (we understand your problem, we are all the victims of the same corrupt power) and a doctrine of popular sovereignty which justified the Army's defiance of Parliament. It explained how the existing legislature had become as corrupt and tyrannical as the king had been, and it suggested that power had to be taken away from all future governments, to prevent both kingly or parliamentary tyranny. It was not only the rank and file who were taken up with Leveller ideas. The officers' own ideas, as reflected in the petition of 14 June or in the terms which they offered to the king, the *Heads of the Proposals*, represent a diluted but recognizable Leveller inspiration. The demands for Parliaments of fixed duration, and for the decentralization of local and judicial offices come straight from earlier Leveller tracts. In particular, the statement in the Declaration of 14 June that 'all authority is fundamentally seated in the office and but

68. Mahony, thesis, chs viii and ix; Underdown, *Pride's Purge*, pp. 76–81.
69. Morrill, *Mutiny*, *passim*.

ministerially in the persons' is related to the crucial Leveller claim that all representatives were directly answerable to a sovereign people.[70] Thus in the ensuing weeks, there was no prospect of a compliant Parliament, and both officers and men were obsessed with the need to destroy the power of the existing body. The Levellers had not split the Grandees from the rank and file.

The resolution of the crisis by the military *coup d'état* in early August transformed the situation. Almost immediately, Parliament resumed redressing the original grievances of the Army, particularly by the creation of the new Committee of the Army. The Indemnity Commissioners were beginning to gain a reputation for their resolute protection of soldiers hounded by civilian enemies. Now the ambiguities of the Leveller programme began to appear. Neither the Grandees nor the agitators were pressing on with the demands for political reform. They looked increasingly content with the activities of the purged and chastened Parliament. In mid-October, the civilian Levellers returned to the offensive by issuing the *Case of the Army Truly Stated.* How was it issued? Not by the existing agitators, who never subscribed it, but by agitators newly elected for just five regiments.

This raises a question which has never been answered. These new agitators acted alongside the old ones, and there were allegations that they were unrepresentative even of the regiments they served.[71] It is far from clear whether the other regiments and the older agitators ever wholeheartedly supported or subscribed to the *Case of the Army.* The officers agreed to a series of debates on the gist of this document (the *Agreement of the People*), but it is worth speculating whether their agreement to do so was based not so much on a fear of the Levellers as on a belief that they could regain majority support. Certainly their decisive and successful actions after the Putney debates reveal few signs of weakness or lack of confidence. It may be that they simply allowed themselves, briefly, to be out-manoeuvred tactically. I am not suggesting that Leveller support had entirely evaporated among the rank and file, simply that the officers had other reasons for fearing the implementation of the Leveller programme beyond their genuine aversion to particular aspects of its constitutional provisions. That is, they could see that the implementation of the *Agreement of the People*

---

70. BL, Thomason Tracts E 409(25) 39.
71. Gardiner, *History*, III, 378. I am grateful to Blair Worden for pointing out to me how little is known about the activities of the different groups of agitators who seem to have coexisted for some months.

would destroy all the achievements of the previous six months in reducing the material problems of the Army. Thus they sought on the first day of the debates to counter Sexby's demand for an end to the 'rotten studs – I mean the Parliament' by ponderous talk of the Army's commitment to honour existing engagements.[72] On this interpretation, their great error of judgement was to allow the debates on the second day to centre around the question of the franchise, possibly because they hoped to exploit the divisions on this question within the Leveller-inclined members of the Council. They had misread the situation, for this proved to be an emotive issue on which they could not retain the initiative. But note what happened: in Ivan Roots' words, 'the debates went on . . . and discussion went into side issues and dead ends. One senses something of Cromwell and Ireton's satisfaction at this'.[73] The debates fizzled out. Furthermore, the Grandees' subsequent actions reveal little evidence of anxiety. They ordered a series of separate rendezvous to sound out rank-and-file opinion (a repeat of the Saffron Walden procedures). When two regiments attempted to join a rendezvous to which they had not been summoned (carrying Leveller emblems and papers in their caps) Cromwell dispersed them with ease and subsequently had one leader shot. But note several points normally overlooked. The several rendezvous of the Army were held and did accept the officers' proposals for a new petition to be presented to Parliament; there were no more mutinies and no protest after the execution of Arnold, the mutineer; the permanent exclusion of the agitators from the Council of Officers was barely questioned; and within eight weeks 18,000 men quietly disbanded, many of them (those who volunteered during the July crisis) receiving no payment beforehand.[74] I find it hard to believe but that the rank and file were reluctantly behind their officers throughout the crisis: that at the Putney debates the Levellers were trying to regain lost ground among soldiers who as individuals both felt the force of Leveller ideology, and yet were aware that their essential interests were now being safeguarded by the existing institutions. Of course there was a clash of ideals at Putney; of course the debates witnessed some of the most invigorating and moving moments in the course of the whole Revolution; of course the Levellers were proposing a massive redistribution of power, were

---

72. A.S.P. Woodhouse, *Puritanism and Liberty* (London, 1938), pp. 2ff.
73. I.A. Roots, *The Great Rebellion* (London, 1965), pp. 119–20.
74. The decision to merge the New Model with other regional forces had swollen the number of men under Fairfax's command to at least 36,000 men.

demanding the establishment of civil rights and economic freedoms which struck sympathetic chords in the hearts of many soldiers. But their minds and pockets were telling them, day in, day out, that the existing system was now benefiting them; that the urgent needs and requirements discussed earlier in the year had not gone away, but were now being met by strenuous legislative effort and determined executive action. By the time that Fairfax presented the *Humble Representation* to Parliament on 8 December, I would suggest that it reflected the agreed interests of the whole of the Army as surely as did the officers' petition after Saffron Walden. The *Humble Representation*, longest of all the army declarations, was exclusively concerned with bread-and-butter questions.

The great bulk of it is concerned with arrears. It accepts the need for a reduction in the size of the Army, but insists that the grievances of the soldiery be met before the disbandment. Although it complains about 'the difficulty and delay of getting things passed in Parliament', it is more critical of 'the neglect or slowness of County committees, assessors, or collectors . . . and through the general backwardness of all (especially in the city of London)'. It next proposed an extension of the powers of several existing committees. Above all, it 'propounded a way whereby all the soldiery of the kingdom may be instantly put in a condition of constant pay . . . all free quarter (with the abuses, exactions, annoyances and unequal pressure that accompany it) immediately taken off, no further debts of arrears incurred upon the kingdom and that which is already incurred put in a way to be recovered and overcome in time'. These measures included a temporary increase in the monthly assessment from £60,000 to £100,000, and an increase in the power of the Committee of the Army to supervise collection, with additional local commissioners to be nominated by the Lord General and the army council. Every regiment was to be allocated the revenues of stated counties with power to 'assist' in the collection. Recently introduced procedures for stating accounts were to be continued and extended. For the securing of future payment of arrears, more money should be allocated from the composition fines (they ask for two-thirds of all receipts), and dean and chapter lands should be sold. The petition acknowledged that the only secure form of indemnity was for soldiers to 'fly to some committee or commissioners for relief': and they asked for an extension of the system which had been in operation since June. Local committees were to be created under the control of the Grand Committee, the new commissioners to 'be such as ordinarily reside in the respective counties and mixed of such as have been military officers of Parliament together with such as have appeared active and faithful for the Parliament in the late War, for which purpose we shall (if admitted) offer names'. The petition also seeks the transfer of responsibility for the relief of maimed soldiers, widows and orphans from the Justices of the Peace to the commissioners for indemnity; tougher action to secure the rights of apprentices who had served in the Army, and fresh guarantees against the future impressment of men who had served in the first war. The rights of ex-soldiers were clearly distinguished in this clause from the rights of others.[75]

By early December, the Army was asking for more of what it had already been given. This programme is totally incompatible with Leveller objectives. Furthermore, Parliament passed a series of measures on 24 December which went a long way towards meeting these demands. It launched a fresh and largely successful incentive scheme to bring in arrears of assessment; the Army was voted additional money from the excise (the tax most hated by the Levellers); the demand for two-thirds of all composition fines was conceded; more money was allocated from the sale of episcopal lands (though no move was yet made to sell the capitular lands); the Army's desire for the auditing of soldiers' accounts to be undertaken by the Committee of Army was gratified, and the rates of deduction for free quarter lowered; a fresh ordinance for the relief of war victims was passed (though it did not go so far as the petitioners had asked) and the Indemnity Committee was empowered to enforce the ordinances regarding former apprentices. Parliament accepted the Army's suggestion as to the reduction in the number of soldiers.[76] Within two months 18,000 men had quietly disbanded – some of them[77] receiving no arrears, others precisely the amount parliament had offered at the end of May 1647. There were no mutinies.

Throughout the spring and summer of 1648 the Army was quiescent. Yet succeeding events went some way to vindicate the fears of the Presbyterian caucus in the spring of 1647. The alliance of Parliament and Army required an extension of fiscal demands and further extensions of centralized institutions running roughshod over customary local institutions and practices. They helped to provoke the counter-revolution which Presbyterians had always feared. The aims of most of those groups whose revolts are given the collective title 'the

75. *LJ*, IX, 556–63.
76. Firth and Rait, *Acts*, I, 1048–62.
77. Gentles, unpublished paper, citing BL, Thomason Tracts E 419(17), E 420(2), E 421(13), E 429(10), E 520(11 and 14).

second civil war' had much less to do with the restoration of the king than with the reassertion of provincial independence and a shedding of the burdens and bureaucracy of war. The second civil war came closer to expressing the Clubmen philosophy than the royalist one. Or so I have asserted elsewhere.[78] Parliament received little *active* support except from the Army. Passivity and reluctant collaboration were more characteristic of the response of local communities than was resolute enthusiasm.

Everywhere we are forced back to the problems of the relationship between the centre and localities. Everywhere we find evidence that this tension provides a context within which historians must examine the Army revolt of 1647. By separating out the particular problems posed by this context I have doubtless distorted the over-all picture. For too little has been said about the king; parliamentary politics and groupings within the Army have been over-simplified; the appeal of the Levellers to the economic interests, even perhaps (though I doubt it) to the 'class' interests of the common soldier, has been ignored. Yet I hope that in addition to drawing attention to a neglected aspect of the Army's history in 1647, I have shaken a few assumptions. Above all, I have sought to challenge the assumption of a self-evident identity of interest between civilian Leveller and soldier. Parliament, with its newly developed structure of centralized, executive committees with paralegal powers and unchecked jurisdictions was offering the Army its bread and butter. The Levellers offered them ideological jam. The Army could not have both. It had to choose. Would it be surprising if the great majority chose bread and butter? Soldiers may not live by jam alone.

---

78. Morrill, *Revolt*, pp. 125–31, 206–8. See also A.M. Everitt, *The Community of Kent and the Great Rebellion* (Leicester, 1966), pp. 231–70.

APPENDIX I

THE ARMY REVOLT OF 1647

February: Scots paid off and go home.
Initial parliamentary decision to reduce army to 5,400.

March: Parliament plans to send part of army to Ireland, part to be disbanded.
Declaration of Dislike passed (ban on army petitions).

April: London militia remodelled as start of counter-revolution.
Army agitators elected.

May: Leveller interest in the Army begins in earnest.
Army Debates at Saffron Walden lead to full statement of material grievances. Officers report Army under control and willing to disband if concessions are made.
(25) House of Commons vote immediate disbandment.

June: (4) Army seizes the king.
(14–23) Leveller-influenced general political demands by the Army.
(23–7) Conciliatory moves by Parliament forestall confrontation.

July: Counter-revolution in London forces Parliament's hand.
Army debates at Reading again postpone confrontation.
Radicals in Parliament flee to the Army.

August: Army occupies London.

September: Army and Parliament cooperate to resolve original military grievances.

October: Levellers denounce backsliding by the Grandees (*Case of the Army Truly Stated*, and a digest of its constitutional provisions, *Agreement of the People*).

November: Army debates on the Leveller Proposals (The Putney Debates). Agitators subsequently silenced. Army council reconstituted without them. Mutiny by two regiments easily suppressed.

December: Grandees present fresh Remonstrance restating the original material grievances of the Army. Parliament acquiesces.

February: 1648:   18,000 soldiers peacefully disband.

APPENDIX II

ARMY GRIEVANCES AT SAFFRON WALDEN, MID-MAY 1647

Based on the returns of eleven regiments. The number of regiments including each item is given in the right-hand column. Each item taken up in the Report of the Council of Officers is indicated by the symbol@.

	Nature of Grievance	Number of Regiments
1	*Arrears.* Demands for new accounts procedures/for 12–16 weeks cash/for guaranteed future payment of residue.	10 @
2	*Ireland.* Resistance to conscription for service there/and to serving under officers nominated by Parliament.	5
3	*Indemnity.* From prosecution in the courts for actions done 'in time and place of war'	9 @
3A	The particular case of Ensign Nicholls.	7 @
4	*Impressment.* Freedom from, for men who had freely enlisted in the past.	6 @
5	*Petitioning.* Vindication of the soldiers' rights to/ denunciation of the parliamentary 'Declaration of Dislike' and censure of particular officers.	11 @
6	*Purge.* Of all ex-royalists and neutrals still in office, particularly in the towns.	7 @
7	*Free Quarter.* Clearer regulation of.	7 @
8	*Corruption.* Demand for investigations of misuse of public funds by civilian commissioners. General hostility to county committees.	4
9	*Pensions.* For maimed soldiers, widows and orphans of parliamentarian soldiers.	4 @
10	*Apprenticeships.* Ex-apprentices who have served in the Army to be granted full freedom of their trades or crafts.	5 @
11	*Religion.* Demand for freedom of worship/denunciation of the Covenant/attack on the works of Thomas Edwards and other vituperative Presbyterians.	3 @
12	*Law Reform.*	2
13	*Others.*	2

CHAPTER SEVENTEEN
Mutiny and Discontent in English Provincial Armies, 1645–1647

In the spring of 1647, Parliament faced up to the enormous problem of how to pay off an idle, discontented army, whose arrears were continuing to grow despite the fact that the civil war had been effectively over for twelve months. A recent estimate of the arrears of the Army in March 1647 is two and a half million pounds,[1] which would be several times the annual sum which Parliament had allocated to it. Other revenues were already attached for the repayment of massive loans to the City of London and other creditors. Since the monthly assessment ordinance had expired in September 1646, and the House of Lords was obstructing its renewal, and since collection of the Excise had virtually ceased, the situation was deteriorating rapidly. Furthermore the Parliamentarian cause was losing ground in Ireland. A partial solution to these problems was to persuade large sections of the New Model to cross the Irish Sea, but, according to most authorities, this part of Parliament's programme, like the rest, was mishandled and only served to exacerbate relations between Commons and Army. The story of the breakdown of two sections of the Parliamentarian movement into open hostility is well enough known in outline, although there remain many outstanding problems of interpretation.[2] But virtually nothing has been written about the

I am grateful for the helpful advice and criticism offered by Mr J.P. Cooper, Mr D.H. Pennington and Dr M. Mahony on an earlier draft of this article.

1. I.J. Gentles, 'The Debentures Market and Military Purchases of Crown Land 1649–60' (Univ. of London PhD thesis, 1969), pp. 16–46. This gives a clear discussion of the crisis over arrears in 1647–8, though the author confines himself to the New Model.
2. Notably the extent to which the officers led, or were led by, the agitators and common soldiers, or the exact stages by which simple army grievances led to an irrevocable commitment to a wider programme of political and constitutional reform.

crisis in many parts of the country during 1645–7 in which mutinous troops confronted their officers or civilian committees. As a result the struggle between Army and Parliament in the months February to November 1647 has been largely misunderstood.

To begin with, it is important to realize that probably as late as September 1647 there were more men in arms outside Fairfax's command than there were under him. Most of these were scattered among numerous garrisons, but until the summer of 1647 the Northern army under Poyntz was maintained at two-thirds the strength of the New Model, while Massie's Western army was only disbanded in October 1646. Between them Poyntz and Massie (both of whom were closely linked to the 'Presbyterian' leadership in July 1647) led forces numerically much stronger than the New Model.

Furthermore, it is extremely likely that arrears in these other armies and in the other garrisoned towns were greater than those of the New Model; but this is impossible to determine with any certainty.[3] For example, the Cheshire forces under Sir William Brereton were £80,000 in arrears in March 1646, while the monthly assessment to maintain them was well below £1,000 per month at that stage.[4] The corrected accounts of several of Brereton's officers show that their regiments and troops were owed up to or more than half the total owing to them since their enlistment.[5] One result was the wave of mutinies taking the different forms defined below in at least thirty-four English counties and in most of Wales. The extent of these mutinies, and their degree of organization, cast shadows over some of the statements frequently made about the nature of the New Model protests in 1647, and in particular about the importance of the Levellers as the directors of army unrest into constructive modes of protest.

But just as important is the evidence that the continued existence of provincial armies created extreme tensions within local communities

---

3. In March 1647, the arrears of the New Model were reckoned at forty-three weeks for the horse, eighteen weeks for the foot. But these figures include neither deductions for free quarter (in many cases substantial) nor arrears still owed for service before the creation of the New Model. Similar difficulties apply in working on the accounts of provincial armies.
4. See J.S. Morrill, *Cheshire 1630–1660: Government and Society during the English Revolution* (Oxford, 1974), ch. 3.
5. E.g. Colonel Duckenfield's regiment received a total of only £5,444 by the summer of 1647; £3,557 remained outstanding. Colonel Bromhall's regiment, had, in the summer of 1645, had only £909 out of a total of £6,880, and Colonel Venables's only £560 out of £2,113 up to January 1647. PRO, SP 28 (Commonwealth Exchequer Papers), vol. 128 unfoliated; BM, Harl. MS. 2128 (Randle Holme MSS.), fos. 20–33; ibid., 1999, fos. 62–3.

and threatened to produce extensive conflict between troops and the rural population. It is a pity that this phenomenon has not been noted in recent local studies. Thus Professor Everitt ignores several references to unrest in Kent in mid-1647, such as the report of the County Committee in June that the effects of quartering troops in Kent was leading to a backlash in the countryside which 'may be means to make this county the seat of a new warre'.[6] He also ignores evidence that the Canterbury riots of January 1648 were caused not only by the Committee's religious policy but also by fresh violence in the garrison there.[7] Throughout 1646–7 there was very real fear that the Clubman mentality – the determination of local communities to drive out predatory forces of both sides – might return more virulently than before.

During 1645–7 at least twenty-five counties petitioned that they were unable to bear the burden of maintaining their forces at their current strength. These petitions *can* be dismissed as unnecessarily alarmist and exaggerated, but frequently their claims are substantiated by independent evidence.[8] The report of William Ball in March 1646 is typical in its description of the situation in the provinces, but more objective than most – as the work of an agent sent down specially from parliament to Berkshire to investigate one such complaint.

> That wch exceedingly afflicts mee is the continuall clamour of the soldiers of Newbery & countrie people thereabouts, the soldiers having almost starved the people where they quarter & are half starved themselves, & for want of pay are become very desperate, raunging about the country & breaking and robbing houses and passengers & driving away sheepe & other cattell before the Owners faces.[9]

Professor Everitt has also recently attempted to minimize the economic effects of the civil wars.[10] But this appears to be based on the misconception that the taxation records for the civil war years give a full impression of the financial burdens borne by the countryside, since physical damage during the wars was limited to a few areas and was no more disastrous than the periodic ravages of plague and fire

---

6. A.M. Everitt, *The Community of Kent and the Great Rebellion* (Leicester, 1966), pp. 219–40, and Bodl. Lib., Tanner MS. 58 (Lenthall Papers), fos. 181, 211.
7. Ibid., fos. 645, 653, 657.
8. For some good examples, see Bodl. Lib., Tanner MS. 60, fo. III; ibid., MS. 59, fos. 195, 392; *LJ*, VIII, 135, IX, 72 (Lancashire, Dorset, Yorkshire, Cumberland, Essex).
9. Bodl. Lib., Tanner MS. 60, fo. 491. This general point is substantiated by detailed discussion and examples.
10. A.M. Everitt, 'The Local Community and the Great Rebellion', *Historical Assoc. Pamphlet* (London, 1969), pp. 24–6.

experienced by many towns and villages. Thus he has calculated that
the weekly and monthly assessments – mainstay of Parliamentarian
war finance – was only equivalent to an income tax of two shillings
and sixpence in the pound for Kent, and Dr Johnson has suggested
a similar figure for Buckinghamshire.[11] This ignores the question of
free quarter and other substantial financial side-effects of war. Thus in
Buckinghamshire, where the total amount levied in war taxation up
to the end of 1646 was about £65–70,000, returns from thirty-eight of
the two hundred and ten townships in the county for the same period
show that £17,636 was provided in free quarter. It seems probable
that over the county as a whole, the cost of quarter would exceed
the amount levied in taxation.[12] In this context, it should be stressed
that the civil war was the first occasion in English history that troops
had been kept at nominal full strength for years on end. Indeed with
the exception of the campaigns in the Netherlands at the end of the
sixteenth century, this feature is new to European warfare as a whole
in the seventeenth century. Previously armies were disbanded during
the winter months. Certainly Professor Everitt has failed to learn the
lesson of historians of the Thirty Years' War who agree that the major
economic cost of that war came from billeting and free quarter.[13]

Similar figures are available for other counties. In Cheshire, several
villages kept complete accounts of all expenditure during the war,
and it is again clear that even in areas remote from the fighting,
as much again was paid out in quarter and in the forcible distraint
of provisions by soldiers on the march, as was paid in taxation.[14]
Only occasionally did an enterprising local Committee find a way
round the impasse. The Lancashire Committee short-circuited the
sequestration machinery by leasing royalists' estates to leading officers
– thus providing supplies for their men, in return for a nominal rent
which was to be remitted against arrears, a plan whose legality was
queried by both the local and the central accounts committees.[15] It is

11. Everitt, *The Community of Kent* . . ., p. 159; A.M. Johnson, 'Buckinghamshire 1640–60' (Univ. Coll. of Swansea MA thesis, 1963), pp. 117ff.
12. Johnson, 'Buckinghamshire', pp. 142–5. Dr Johnson does not break down his figures year by year. I have tried to form estimates on the basis of his totals for 1643–8.
13. E.g. J.H. Elliott, *The Revolt of the Catalans* (Cambridge, 1963), pp. 387–417; R. Mousnier, *Fureurs Paysannes* (Paris, 1967), *passim*, particularly pp. 309–12; V.J. Polišenský, *The Thirty Years War* (London, 1971), *passim*.
14. See my thesis, loc. cit. pp. 142–6. Some figures for other counties are given in C. Holmes, 'The Eastern Association 1642–6' (Univ. of Cambridge PhD thesis, 1969), ch. 5. For some examples, see PRO, SP 28 vol. 23, fo. 149; vol. 24, fos. 85–8, 96, 569; vols. 148–51, 171–3, 219–21, *passim*.
15. *Cal. State Papers Dom.*, 1645–7, p. 553.

not, therefore, altogether surprising that the crisis over pay should be a national issue rather than the straightforward conflict between New Model and Parliament which it has usually been represented to be, and makes it correspondingly strange that it has been ignored by modern historians, despite the copious evidence available.[16]

As we shall see later, discontent took several distinguishable forms. In fact there are signs of increasing organization and control as time went by. From the systematic looting and desertion endemic to seventeenth-century warfare and widespread throughout the early years of the war,[17] there developed effective strike action by the troops, threats of mass disbandment unless grievances were met, and later the seizure and ransoming of officers and civilian officials. Superimposed on these developments was a further pattern. Mutinies were concentrated into two periods. The first was in the months May to September 1646, the second in the months April to August 1647.

The first coincided with the return of peace. The troops had no fighting or danger to preoccupy them and became increasingly listless. Yet without settlement of their arrears there was little prospect of disbandment, and the financial exhaustion of the countryside prevented an early solution. Indeed, arrears were mounting rather than falling. By the late summer of 1646, Parliament was faced with reports of mutinies in at least twenty-two English counties and several Welsh counties.[18] Hitherto, neither of the Houses had found any convincing solution to the problem. They had coped piecemeal with each crisis, sending off small sums from their depleted treasuries to ease the immediate situation. But from the beginning of July, they began to rationalize the chaotic spread of idle garrisons and quartered troops across the country. Money was diverted from Goldsmiths Hall (from royalists' compositions) and from the Excise

16. A recent exception to this stricture is Professor Underdown's *Pride's Purge* (Oxford, 1971), pp. 39–40, 76–8. But he does not go far beyond listing (far from exhaustively) the areas of unrest, without analysing its nature or bringing out its full significance.
17. This is of course true for both sides in the civil wars: see, for example, J. Adair, *Roundhead General: a Military Biography of Sir William Waller*, (London, 1969), *passim*, where the point is stressed in explaining successive failures by both sides. Sir William Brereton, the Cheshire commander, claimed that Parliamentarian success in the north-west was largely the result of greater discipline on their side which had won over the country people: BM, Add. MS. 11331, fo. 25.
18. Bedfordshire, Cambridgeshire, Cheshire, Derbyshire, Dorset, Essex, Gloucestershire, Hampshire, Herefordshire, Hertfordshire, Lancashire, Leicestershire, Lincolnshire, Monmouthshire, Oxfordshire, Shropshire, Somerset, Staffordshire, Suffolk, Warwickshire, Wiltshire, Yorkshire.

(locally collected) for partial settlement of arrears, early provision of the rest being promised. The House of Commons then set to work to decide which garrisons were to be maintained, and undertook to make regular provision for them.[19] These measures led to an immediate reduction of tension, but the ensuing failure to honour their promises to the reduced troops was to lead to fresh violence in 1647. Even more serious was that, having made temporary arrangements for the remaining garrisons, parliament never provided adequate machinery to ensure that its orders were implemented. Thus the gentry of Yorkshire petitioned that the failure to renew the Northern Association Ordinance had resulted in the collapse of local government.

> In this intervall of power to order the affaires both Militarie and Civile, wee doe plainely foresee very daungerous Inconveniences like to ensue, wch perhapps may not soe easelie be apprehended in such multiplicitie of weightie affaires at such a distance. The countrie wee observe takinge notice of the cessation of Authoritye refuse, or at leaste are extremely backward to paye the Arrears of Assessments and civil officers there not forward to collect eyther those or any other monies that should helpe towards a meane subsistence for the souldiers, while they were continewed in paye. . . . The souldier wee finde growe discontented, and high in their deportment towards those from whom they were wonte to receive enterteinement. A little time wee much feare will produce those sadd and mischievous effects wch a greate deale of care and time will not probablie redresse.[20]

Similarly at Plymouth fresh trouble broke out in the summer of 1647 when the ordinance providing the garrison with pay out of the local Excise lapsed and Parliament omitted to renew it.[21] A major mutiny in Cheshire resulted from Parliament's failure to send down money for four months after taking over direct responsibility for paying the garrison from the county committee.[22] These administrative blunders – no doubt partly caused by preoccupation with the New Model – contributed greatly to serious mutinies in at least seventeen counties in the summer of 1647.[23]

Nonetheless, the short-term benefits of Parliament's actions in the

19. These debates can be followed in *CJ*, IV and V, particularly IV, 633–4 and V, 96–104.
20. Bodl. Lib., Tanner MS. 59, fo. 399.
21. For the Plymouth mutiny, see below, pp. 352–3 and notes 93, 97 and 98.
22. See below, pp. 346–7.
23. Cheshire, Devon, Dorset, Essex, Hampshire, Herefordshire, Kent, Lancashire, Leicestershire, Norfolk, Northumberland, Oxfordshire, Somerset, Sussex, Westmorland, Wiltshire, Yorkshire.

autumn of 1646 are clear, and can be exemplified by the disbandment of Massie's brigade in the West Country. The complaints against these forces which had poured in from Dorset, Wiltshire, Somerset and Gloucestershire throughout the spring and early summer of 1646 made its disbandment essential,[24] though the religious (and increasingly the political) views of its commander made its retention attractive to the 'Presbyterian' party in the Commons. But their attempts in mid-June to make the New Model the main recruiting ground for fresh Irish regiments were deflected by the 'Independents', and attention centred on Massie's forces.[25] As late as early August, the Irish Committee were asked to decide how many of his men were to be sent there.[26] The initial terms – £20,000 cash and the discharge without arrears of all those enlisted since 1 January 1646 – were highly unfavourable to his troops,[27] whose behaviour had deteriorated yet further.[28] But with the central political issue settled,[29] the Commons now settled down to solve the problem more fairly, and the aid of Sir Thomas Fairfax was enlisted. At the end of September, he went down to the West Country with additional cash (which averaged out at six week's pay per man) and assurances about the rapid provision of the rest. Most importantly, he divided the troops and regiments into separate bodies[30] and disbanded each separately, his own horse standing by in case of trouble. Douceurs notwithstanding, few would enlist for Ireland (not enough to make up one troop, according to Fairfax), but the Commons wisely decided not to press the matter, and the immediate crisis was resolved.[31]

Unfortunately, once it became clear that Parliament could not honour its promise to pay off remaining arrears, the disbanded soldiers crowded to London and protested about their betrayal.

24. A few examples: *CJ*, IV, 581, 615, 649; BM, Thomason Tracts, E511(12), *Perfect Occurrences*, 13–19 June 1646; E511(13), *Perfect Diurnall*, 15–22 June 1646; E341 (18), *Mercurius Civicus*, 18–25 June 1646; B. Whitelocke, *Memorials of English Affairs*, 4 vols. (Oxford, 1853), II, 33, 58; Bodl. Lib., Tanner MS. 59, fos. 247, 330, 353, 392.
25. *CJ*, IV, 631; *The Memoirs of Edmund Ludlow*, ed. C.H. Firth, 2 vols. (Oxford, 1894), I, 141–2.
26. *CJ*, IV, 638.
27. Ibid., p. 615.
28. Bodl. Lib., Tanner MS. 59, fo. 444.
29. Except for a futile attempt by the House of Lords to prevent Fairfax from taking the initiative on the instructions of the Commons: *LJ*, VIII, 531.
30. A device used successfully elsewhere, and soon made a regular feature of Commons orders: e.g. Derbyshire, *CJ*, IV, 656–7.
31. See the letters of Fairfax, Bodl. Lib., Tanner MS. 59, fo. 573, and J. Sprigge, *Anglia Rediviva* (Oxford, 1854), p. 314; and of Ludlow and Allen (who assisted Fairfax), in Ludlow, *Memoirs . . .*, i, 480–1.

This was in February 1647, just as the New Model was about to be disbanded on similar terms.[32]

The pattern of unrest can be most clearly shown by means of a case study. Although there is ample evidence from several counties (e.g. Yorkshire, Leicestershire, Montgomeryshire), I shall take Cheshire as my example both because of my closer acquaintance with the sources, and because of its particularly clear demonstration of the main trends observable elsewhere.

Available funds there had always fallen far short of commitments, of course, and this had contributed to a continuous problem of pilfering and theft from villages in which troops had quartered or through which they had passed. However, the emptiness of their bellies was not the only need of the soldiers satisfied by these means. One inhabitant of the township of Over reported that troops had seized 'clothes, [a] byble and other necessaries', and his complaint could be multiplied hundreds of times over from the sources.[33] Sometimes these thefts were committed by individual soldiers, but frequently a whole unit would systematically plunder a village of its provisions, while the officers stood by hopelessly, or even joined in, preferring to ensure orderly pillage than face a mutiny from their hungry, ill-clad troops.[34] At times, plundering expeditions from friend and foe alike covered a wide area. One such, when Cheshire forces stationed beyond the Dee went on an extended raid into Wales (April 1645), led to retaliatory action from Brereton, after protests from parliament, alerted about the raid by Sir John Trevor, Parliamentarian MP, whose house had been among those sacked. Brereton said of the activities of his forces,

> There is nothing accompanieing this service hath more afflicted mee then to see those insolencies that are sometyme committed by the soldiers and not have power wholy to restraine them.

He announced stringent measures to ensure the return of or compensation for goods taken from Welsh Parliamentarians, and sought out those involved for punishment. For example, all common soldiers sleeping on new sheepskins were immediately suspect.[35] Indiscriminate raids on friends and foes alike were periodically reported within Cheshire, particularly during 1644 and 1645; only occasionally were junior officers associated with them.[36]

32. E.g. *CJ*, V, 75, 82.
33. BM, Harl. MS. 2126, fo. 16.
34. See my thesis (cited note 4), pp. 227–9, 252–5.
35. BM, Add. MS. 11331, fos. 20, 25, 26, 30, 63–4, etc.
36. E.g. BM, Harl. MS. 1999, fo. 70; Harl. MS. 2018, fo. 69.

After the fall of Chester in February 1646, the Committee of Both Kingdoms was quick to realize the dangers of indiscipline among troops whose task was accomplished, and who were beginning to brood about their arrears. They

> desired the House [of Commons] that money may be provided for the Payment of those Forces, both in regard of the Poverty of their Country, and that the Soldiers, through want of Pay, may not disaffect the Inhabitants; and thereby hinder their submission to the Parliament.[37]

Nothing was done. At the time of the final negotiations for the surrender of the City, Brereton revealingly told Parliament that the large number of negotiators

> was proposed by them, and was the rather assented to by us, to the end, better satisfaccon might bee given to ye common Soldyers, when some of their owne officers were intrusted and imployed in Treating & makeing compositions for them, that they might thereby bee alsoe obliged to restraine their soldyers from plunder and vyolation of what is concluded and agreed upon.[38]

On the whole Brereton refused to act in a repressive manner. He sought to control excesses, but, faced by the impossibility of solving the problem while county finances remained so inadequate, he undoubtedly turned a blind eye to many incidents. Seizure of food and clothing might be the only answer when men

> have not wherwthall to cover their nackedness nor a penny mony in their pockets; truely I confess, if I had not bin an eye witness I should hardly have believed it. . . .[39]

Organized plunder was the most elementary form of unrest. More direct were the concerted efforts of bodies of men to exact their arrears. Thus on several occasions troops refused to march to fresh quarters or into action until grievances had been redressed. The most serious mutiny of this kind occurred when Yorkshire troops refused to advance to the siege of Chester from Macclesfield hundred (where their military value was negligible) in the spring of 1645.[40] But the Cheshire forces themselves refused to serve on several occasions, notably during Brereton's absence in London following the Self-Denying Ordinance.[41] It was this which persuaded parliament to grant him a commission of martial law – a right they were always

---

37. *CJ*, IV, 443.
38. Bodl. Lib., Tanner MS. 60, fo. 393.
39. BM, Add. MS. 11332, fo. 107.
40. BM, Add. MS. 11331, *passim*, e.g. fos. 32, 56, 75, 95.
41. E.g. BM, Add. MS. 11332, fos. 14, 15, 23–4, 30.

most reluctant to grant – on his return to the county.[42] In fact one general feature of the increase in the seriousness of army unrest across the country in 1646–7 was the marked rise in the number of these commissions granted to provincial commanders.

Distinct from these mutinies were threats by whole regiments to disband themselves. A steady trickle of deserters was inevitable, but the decision of a whole body of troops to desert was a more serious matter. The clearest example is that of Colonel Duckenfield's men, who on several occasions threatened to disband themselves, and on at least one occasion did so. In their case arrears were secondary. As Duckenfield told Sir Thomas Fairfax in 1644,

> I have endeavoured (since I knew your pleasure) to get my soldiers into order fit for service, to advance to Nantwich, but they have disbanded themselves, and are following the plough, and from thence they will not be drawn. Yet upon the receipt of your letter yesterday, I sent to the captains to join with mee presently, to call their companies together, to march with them and mee to Nantwich; but they refuse to stir yet. They pretend that the dragoons are so uncivil, that they plunder the country extremely, and they dare not leave their houses for fear of them.[43]

The same complaint is recorded during their later mutinies. Henry Bradshaw, a Major in the regiment, stated that 'whilst they themselves are upon dutie here [at Chester] and have notheing: that straingers haveing pay and doeing no service devour that wch should sustaine both them and theirs at whome'[44], and one of the arguments put to the Yorkshire commanders to induce them to force their men up to the siege was that 'if yor Regiment would draw more this way it would prevent ye disbandeing of coll Duckenfeild's Regiment of foote'.[45]

Two petitions from the common soldiers to their officers have survived from the last months of the war. The first, from Duckenfield's men, dealt with this last grievance and with arrears. The other, addressed to Colonel Michael Jones, is marked with bitterness at the trail of broken promises made by the County Committee. The soldiers called upon Jones to intervene on their behalf, they 'haveing long waited with patience the performance of the Gents Engagements (which wee now see are not to be confided in)'. They

42. BM, Add. MS. 11332, fo. 29.
43. BM, Add. MS. 18979 (Fairfax MS.), fo. 147: printed in R. Bell, *Memorials of the Civil War, Comprising the Correspondence of the Fairfax Family*, 2 vols. (London, 1849), I, 79–80.
44. BM, Add. MS. 11331, fo. 70. The 'straingers' were the Yorkshire horse.
45. Ibid., fo. 75.

warned him that necessity might 'constraine us to dispose otherwayes of ourselves'.[46]

Both the refusal to perform duties and organized desertion lost their effectiveness once the king had been defeated. As a means of exacting arrears, the latter in particular was actually self-defeating.

As a result affairs reached a climax in the summer of 1646, when officials were seized by troops and held to ransom. Even this had been foreshadowed. Reluctant to mulct the countryside further, infuriated by the delays and false hopes created by vain promises, the troops began to threaten and extort money from any official reputed to be holding cash. In the sequestrators' accounts there were about thirty reports of the following kind: 'pd to quiett soldiers when they came tumultuously to the sitting of the committee for sequestr' twice . . .'; or 'spent when Colonel Booth soldiers came for the first time for monies to Moberley and toke me with them to bowden and kept mee there two daies a prisoner'.[47] The sums involved were usually very small.

For most of 1646, leading gentlemen in the country were aware that a major crisis was looming.[48] Tensions were heightened by the return of forces from service in Staffordshire and Wales, and by a fresh attempt to settle the Excise on the county – earlier attempts during the war having been abandoned. The proceeds of the Excise were intended for the soldiers, but it was hated by them as much as by the townspeople of Chester and Nantwich. Several writers agree that it was one of the major sources of the ensuing mutinies.[49] In a letter to three Cheshire gentlemen in London, the rest of the Committee pitch the case very high.

> . . . the Souldiery take great dislike at the Excise, the Citty and County almost gennerally distaste it, the gentlemen that are imployed have carryed themselves very well in it and endeavour by all fayre means to effect the same but our feare is that will not perfect the businesse but some constraint must be used, otherwise little will bee made of it to prevent present evill, Wee have tould the souldiers, that they are to bee payd forth of it, and if that take not there is noe way left to satisfye them. . . . Wee extreamely feare, if the souldiery joyne not in ye Tumult yet all or most of them will stand apart and will not assist theire

46. Ibid., fo. 94; BM, Add. MS. 11332, fo. 103.
47. BM, Harl. MS. 2018, fo. 106; Harl. MS. 2126, fo. 103.
48. BM, Thomason Tracts E511(17), *Perfect Occurrences*, 27 June–3 July, 1646; Bodl. Lib., Tanner MS. 59, fos. 230, 232, 426.
49. BM, Thomason Tracts E511(24), *Perfect Occurrences*, 18–24 July 1646; Bodl. Lib., Tanner MS. 59, fo. 442; *Hist. MSS. Comm.*, Portland MSS., i, p. 390. As far as I can determine, the Committee had made this promise without consulting the central government.

officers and what greater evill will come thereof more then the damage
in the excise in this cittye which hath cost much blood wee know not,
but leave to your serious consideracon.[50]

There was a preliminary crisis at the end of June among the newly
returned forces at Chester. According to a newsletter of the 29th:

> Sir William Brereton, Coll George Booth, Henry Brooke esq High-
> shreiffe; and the rest of the Deputy Lieutenants of the County, and other
> Gentl of quallity, were forsed to ingage themselves for 18,000[1] at the
> le[a]st (under their handwriting) about the businesse of Chester (besides
> other ingagements since) which somme was expected out of Delinquents
> Estates but now fayles by reason of Compositions, so that the souldiery
> have but a small part of what they expected, and was promised, and
> being sencible of the fayling therein; they are in a way to fall into the
> Estates of the Gentry.[51]

Significantly the Sequestrators and Excise men were also attacked.[52]
The mutiny was, however, quietened down by extensive borrowings
and the promise of £2,000 from London.[53]

More serious was the mutiny in Nantwich on 14 July, when
about five hundred of the garrison, defying their officers, seized the
Nantwich sequestration committee and held them prisoner for two
days. The victims later reported that

> ffyve Companyes of our Garrison Soldyers of Namptwich, being about
> ffive hundred unreasonable men without either Captyns or Comanders,
> in a most outragious maner fell upon us and with great fury (wherefore
> wee know not) did throwe us into the Comon prison amongst pris-
> oners, Cavaliers and Horstealers, neither sufferinge any to relieve us
> with meate drinke or any necessaryes but what the parsons or some
> weomen did privatlie convaye unto us, where wee (being Ancyent
> men) did lye upon the boards, not sufferinge our friends to bring us
> Quyssions nor any Comforde the[y] cold hinder us from for the space
> of 54 howers, neither would they be perswaded to gyve us better
> Quarter although the Heughe Sherryff Mr Brooke and most of the
> Deputie Lieftenants and Justices a peace of the Countie were then in
> Towne sitting in Quarter Sessiones did there best and moved for us and
> the Governor of the Towne and his man they wounded and abused
> most cruelly. Soe that the shereff, Governor and all the Justices went fro
> the Towne not able to suppresse that greate multitude beinge all men
> and armed, and lefte us in prison to the mercy of those wicked and
> unreasonable men, wee gyving them noe occasion att all.[54]

50. Bodl. Lib., Tanner MS. 59, fo. 442.
51. BM, Thomason Tracts, E511(17), *Perfect Occurrences*, 27 June–3 July 1646.
52. Ibid., E349(7), *Scottish Dove*, 29 July–5 August 1646.
53. Ibid.; also E349(4), *Kingdome's Weekly Intelligencer*, 28 July–4 August 1646.
54. Transcribed from the composition papers of Sir Thomas Smyth and published
    in F. Sanders and W. Fergusson Irvine (eds.), *Cheshire Sheaf*, 3rd ser., (1896),
    91–2.

Other contemporary accounts bear out their story,[55] emphasizing that the officers were not involved, that Thomas Croxton (the town Governor) was attacked and wounded when he tried to intervene, and that the Justices were forced to flee from the town. Again the question of Excise appears. One report speaks of the collectors being beaten out of the town.[56] It is in fact surprising that they and the sequestrators should again be singled out. As Malbon said

> they knew that the same Committee for Sequestrations never paid theim or noe other soldyers . . . for they receyved their paye alwayes from the Treasurer by warrant of the deputie lieutenants. But as some of theim said, they wolde beate Jacke for Gill[57]

A more startling feature was that, at the height of the mutiny, the soldiers, still acting independently of their officers, sent representatives to put their case before the County Committee. The report of their meeting shows that their demands were moderate, but they ended with a veiled threat. They hoped to 'bee prevented of takeing any unusuall course to supply our wants, but may bee enabled to behave themselves'.[58]

However, according to one London report, the soldiers were forced to capitulate without achieving their demands because troops from Lichfield had been despatched against them. They had to rest content with a promise from the Committee and Governor not to prosecute them, and the contents of a chest of money – rumoured to contain £500 – which they had seized.[59]

The gentry's problems were not yet over. At the end of the month two troops of horse marched over to Peover and Alderley and quartered themselves on the homes of two of the leading deputy lieutenants, Philip Mainwaring and Thomas Stanley; when no money was immediately forthcoming they broke down the doors of the houses and forced each of the gentlemen to pay them £50–60.[60] Philip Mainwaring hurriedly sent off warnings to his fellows telling them that troops stationed at Congleton and Chester intended

> to falle upon theire howses in the like kind & this they profes to act in imitacon of the Nampwchians their brave exployte the last quarter

55. E.g. T. Malbon, *Memorials of the Civil Wars in Cheshire* (Lancashire and Cheshire Rec. Soc., 1889), pp. 208–11; BM, Thomason Tracts, E511(24), *Perfect Occurrences*, 18–24 July 1646.
56. Ibid.
57. Malbon, *Memorials*, p. 210.
58. Bodl. Lib., Tanner MS. 59, fo. 412.
59. BM, Thomason Tracts, E511(24), *Perfect Occurrences*, 18–24 July 1646.
60. BM, Thomason Tracts, E513(3), *Perfect Occurrences*, 8–14 August 1646.

sessions if some very speedy course be not taken to prevent theis thinges & from above, by hastning down moneys (the onely way to do it).[61]

Parliament reacted slowly, but in the short term successfully. Nantwich was disgarrisoned, and all the forces in the county disbanded except for a residual garrison of six hundred at Chester. £12,000 was eventually provided from London towards arrears, and a compromise agreement on the scale of payment at disbandment reached at a meeting of the officers and Committee on 2 November. By February 1647 the situation appeared under control.[62] But unfortunately the Commons had taken upon itself the responsibility of paying the remaining garrison and, although some pay arrived on 25 March, no more was seen until a fresh and even more alarming mutiny in July 1647.[63]

The immediate cause was a rumour that there was £3,000 in the city intended for the troops in Ireland. But by the time the troops acted it had already been despatched.[64] They now adopted a fresh course, marching to Nantwich where they seized a group of deputy lieutenants at a meeting there, while others arrested several gentlemen in their homes about the county, driving them to Chester 'like rogues and theeves in a base and disgraceful manner'. According to Sir George Booth, elder statesman of county politics, those arrested included deputy lieutenants 'together with Colonell Massey the Governor of the city and a captaine with some of the committee and sequestrators and Commissioners of Excise'. Nine of the prisoners wrote a long plaintive account of their predicament on 3 July, mentioning that fifteen of them had been locked in a single room.[65] Plague was rife in the city, yet they were left there without food, drink or 'accomodacon for nature but publiquely like beasts amongst ourselves'. As in 1646, the officers had been powerless to prevent the arrests, and stood by during the first days of the mutiny. Eventually they prevailed upon the troops to move the prisoners 'into a house where wee have two or three roomes & necessary

61. Bodl. Lib., Tanner MS. 59, fo. 448; see also, ibid., fos. 426, 436.
62. For details, see my thesis, loc. cit., pp. 263–6.
63. Bodl. Lib., Tanner MS. 58, fo. 323.
64. This account is based on four letters: Bodl. Lib., Tanner MS. 58, fos. 323, 326, 429 and PRO, SP. 28, vol. 208 (blue packet marked 'Chester 208'), unfoliated letter dated 25 June 1649. William Massey, the Governor, was the brother of Edward Massie, commander of the Western Army which had caused so much trouble in 1646.
65. This letter was addressed to Parliament and begged the Houses to speed up the flow of money. The names of those arrested, and their significance in local politics, are given in my thesis, loc. cit., p. 267.

accomodation to preserve our lives'. This time the soldiers were determined not to let their prisoners go until they had their arrears in their hands. Their demands were simple. Four thousand pounds in cash and an engagement from the prisoners 'that the citizens would be satisfied for the quarter of the souldiers'. With parliament dithering, the imprisoned gentry managed to raise the money by extensive loans – from 'our friends and welwishers' who still exacted 'strikkt bondds for the repayment of it'.[66] The letter announcing their release was dated 30 July, and in the absence of other evidence, it seems likely that the imprisonments had lasted for over four weeks. Parliament, preoccupied with other problems, sent neither money nor troops to restore order, and postponed giving advice four times before setting up a committee which failed to report back to the Commons. The only subsequent action taken by Westminster was a halving of the garrison to three hundred men.[67]

As in 1646, the soldiers had shown themselves capable of quite complicated operations in defiance of their officers. Although there is no evidence that on this occasion elected representatives had argued the soldiers' case before the County Committee as in 1646 (eight months before the election of agitators in the New Model), the 1647 mutiny involved coordinated marches over considerable distances by separate bodies of troops. But the mutineers' aims remain local and personal: there is no evidence of Leveller involvement in the planning or execution of any of the unrest in Cheshire.

One or more of the organized patterns of unrest can be found in counties across the country. There is evidence of systematic plundering for thirty counties, of refusal to obey orders until grievances had been redressed for eighteen counties, threats of mass disbandment for ten, and the seizure of officials or officers for fourteen. Thirty-six of the forty English counties were involved, and for twenty-eight of them there is evidence of two or more of these forms of protest. The whole of north-east and parts of south Wales were also affected.[68]

66. These loans were a source of persistent rancour and bickering in the county for the next four years.
67. See my thesis, loc. cit., p. 268 and n. 1 for details.
68. Furthermore this article is not exhaustive. It is based on the main printed and some general MS sources, but, except for the north midlands, hardly at all on local sources. Above all, painstaking examination of the vast and uncalendared Commonwealth Exchequer Papers (PRO, SP. 28) would probably yield plentiful additional information. However, the aim of this article is simply to draw attention to the need to take the problems raised by the continuing existence of provincial armies into consideration for the years 1645–7, and I believe it fulfils this aim.

Since in most respects there was a common pattern to these mutinies, I shall simply draw attention to the most important distinctions and similarities between Cheshire and the rest of the country.

It is clear that the demands of the soldiers were almost invariably about arrears. This might take a more complex form than a simple cash demand (for example, it might result from the unfair distribution of available resources between different regiments, or a protest against inadequate quartering),[69] or it might extend to cover other personal grievances (just as Colonel Duckenfield's regiment mutinied over the presence of 'foreign' forces in East Cheshire, so Yorkshire troops mutinied over the Scottish quartering on their own homes),[70] but there is no evidence that any provincial army questioned the political structures which were in part responsible for the deteriorating financial position.

It is not, of course, as though provincial armies, remote from London, were unaware of the factional struggles that bitterly divided local Parliamentarian Committees. Troops were frequently employed in the course of these disputes. Thus, late in 1645, Sir William Brereton's forces were employed to seize control of the town of Stafford and to arrest several members of the County Committee who had consistently supported the earl of Denbigh in the bitter feuding within the Parliamentarian movement in Staffordshire.[71] Mr Pennington, in his brilliant unravelling of the records of the Committee for Taking the Accounts of the Kingdom, has shown how troops were frequently employed by local subcommissioners of accounts or by their opponents in the struggle for control of county finances.[72] In the most spectacular case, Montgomeryshire in the last months of 1646, both sides enlisted the aid of different regiments to arrest or harass their opponents.[73] Although these are certainly not mutinies in the clear sense of the Cheshire troubles, they are important in that they revealed to the soldiers both the political disunity of their leaders, and the effectiveness of violence.

In discussing the general types of unrest, there is little to add to

69. M.A.E. Green (ed.), *Cal. Comm. for the Advance of Money*, 3 vols. (London, 1888), I, 48 (Lancashire); Bodl. Lib., Tanner MS. 60, fos. 127–8 (Wiltshire).
70. Ibid., fo. 216.
71. D.H. Pennington and I.A. Roots, *The Committee at Stafford 1643–5*, (Manchester, 1957), pp. lxxiv–lxxxiii and references there given.
72. D.H. Pennington, 'The Accounts of the Kingdom', in F.J. Fisher (ed.), *Essays in the Economic and Social History of Tudor and Stuart England in Honour of R.H. Tawney* (London, 1961), pp. 182–203.
73. *Cal. State Pap. Dom., 1645–7*, pp. 441, 458–9; PRO, SP. 28, vol. 256, *passim*.

what I have said about Cheshire. But, as the history of the Clubman movement showed, civilian resistance to plundering could be highly organized and lead to an extension of violence. Unlike the forces in Cheshire, soldiers in many counties were accused, even after the end of the war itself, of murder, violence and destruction as well as of seizing goods, though this was frequently occasioned by civilian resistance. A good example of this was the fight at Midbourne in Leicestershire between villagers and troopers of Major Babbington's troop (apparently without an officer in charge) in April 1646 which resulted in 'divers Murders, Maims and other violent outrages committed by divers soldiers . . . upon the Minister and other honest men . . .'.[74] Similarly in June 1647, a commission of oyer and terminer was granted in Kent to try soldiers charged with 'divers murders and other outrages' while forcibly quartering themselves near Maidstone. As elsewhere the Kentish gentry saw this not only as a short-term threat to persons and property but as a challenge to the whole basis of settled government.

> Here are Blows struck, here is Bloodshed; the Lord Direct the Parliament, and the city, and the Army, to study how to compose these fresh Divisions lest poor England be overwhelmed in the Red Sea of Subdivisions.[75]

The most remarkable series of complaints were against Massie's Western army in the spring and summer of 1646. Complaints and pleas to halt the violence poured in from Wiltshire, Dorset, Somerset and Gloucestershire.[76]

As in Cheshire, mass desertion lost its attractiveness once the fighting was completed. It became self-defeating, since the authorities would then have even less reason to find extra money. But it was fairly common during the last months of the fighting. One example also serves to indicate the different financial situation in neighbouring counties. Massie complained in April 1645 that

> Our troupers dayly leave me & now they see the Warwicke troupes so well cloathed, horsed & armed, & soe well payed I feare I shall not keepe one quarter part of those I have if a very speedy course be not taken for us.[77]

The most frequent form of mutiny in the years 1646–7 was for the

74. *LJ* VIII, 265–6; *CJ*, IV, 504.
75. J. Rushworth, *Historical Collections* (London, 1701), VIII, 741; see also ibid., VII, 575; *CJ*, V, 215; Bodl. Lib., Tanner MS. 58, fos. 181, 211 etc.
76. See p. 338, n. 24.
77. Bodl. Lib., Tanner MS. 60, fos. 127–8.

troops to refuse to obey the orders of their officers. This might take the form of a refusal to move from their quarters, or a deliberate march to fresh quarters against orders. Thus the Wiltshire horse rode over the Devon border in March 1647 and settled down there, refusing to heed the pleas of the Devon Committee that they remove themselves. The Devon Committee sought unavailingly for Parliament's assistance, since 'wee are not able to force them hence'.[78] When the Gloucestershire Committee ignored a parliamentary order allocating the assessment from six hundreds for the pay of Bristol garrison, several regiments marched into the area, quartered themselves and refused to return to the city.[79] In Newcastle, the garrison rescued some of their comrades from prison and marched from the town in defiance of the Governor. Four days later they returned on receipt of the fourteen days' pay they had demanded.[80]

The gravest of these mutinies took place in Dublin in July 1647, when Colonel Kinaston's company mutinied, 'beat and abused their field officers', and occupied the College Green for several hours, while Michael Jones, the Governor, parleyed with them (fearful to use his other troops lest they should join the mutineers). Once again, serious consequences were avoided by the capitulation of the officers (this time enemy forces were nearby).[81]

At the same time, Thomas Hogan was returning from London to Lyme Regis with an order to pay the garrison £500 from the Customs House there. Which

> immediately at my comminge home I sent for, but could not receive it, beinge disbursed by him [the High Collector], and much more upon former orders. The Soldjers in the Guarrison havinge intimation of it, ranne into a mutiny on Friday last sayinge they would have all their pay to a day, declaringe they would goe to the Army.[82]

As a result Hogan and the mayor had to raise the money by personal loans. The mayor of another town, King's Lynn, wrote to Lenthall at the same time, revealing a further local response to the troubles.

> The miserie of our Towne is growne unto such a highet, and our

78. Ibid., 59, fo. 805.
79. Ibid., fo. 247.
80. BM, Thomason Tracts, E396(2), *Mercurius Britanicus*, 24 June–1 July 1647.
81. Ibid., E398(13), *Moderate Intelligencer*, 8–15 July 1647; E518(6), *Perfect Diurnall*, 12–19 July 1647; *Hist. MSS. Comm.*, Portland MSS., I, 429–30; *Hist. MSS. Comm.*, Egmont MSS., I, part ii, 425. Even the New Model was not free from such unrest. Several regiments deserted their quarters in July 1646 and met at a rendezvous at St Albans, but the situations was saved by the swift action of their officers as Parliament dithered: *CJ*, IV, 625; Whitlocke, *Memorials*, II, 53.
82. Bodl. Lib., Tanner MS. 58, fo. 335.

souldiers for want of pay are growne so mutinous as here wilbe noe livinge for us. . . . Sr I am confident yf the House would be pleased to order their disbandinge, the Towne wilbe kept closer to ye Parlament by the Townsmen themselves then by the Souldiers, for the Townsemen have heretofore ingaged themselves & their whole estates by a former peticon to keepe that Towne for kinge and parliament against all opposers. . . .[83]

From this it was but a small step to the ultimate outrage, the arrest of prominent committeemen or officers. Major-General Poyntz was arrested at York by dissident members of his army and removed to Pontefract, his wife telling the Commons that he was 'carried away in his slippers, not suffered to Express any congugall comefort or courtesie to me his wife at his departing, & what wilbe ye doome they will passe on him I cannot tell. . . .'[84]

Also in July 1647 several members of the Leicestershire Committee were arrested at a meeting in Leicester and locked up at Lubenham. The soldiers demanded 'five shillings sixpence weekely more than the Twelve shillings a weeke alreadie paid unto them' – an inflationary wage claim by any standards.[85] Officials were also seized in Westmorland, Lancashire and Dorset that month.[86]

Three months earlier, it had been reported that

the Mutiny of the Souldiers in North Wales for Arreares continues; they still hold in Prison several committeemen in Richam (Wrexham) church, Colonel Mitton is gone for Shrewsbury, Colonel Alderson is come to this Town; other chief men in the country, not in their hands, have taken refuge in Conway Castle, which they threaten to Besiege, and say they will have money before Disbanding.[87]

An earlier series of similar arrests in July 1646 is mentioned in the weekly papers as having occured in Suffolk, Montgomeryshire, Radnorshire, Derbyshire, Lancashire, Cheshire and Staffordshire. As *Perfect Occurrences* commented: 'The like is in divers other places, and they are set on by malignants to set us into new Combustion, some must be made examples, or else we shall be in danger of a new warre'.[88]

83. Ibid., fo. 343.
84. Ibid., fo. 363; see below, pp. 353–6.
85. Ibid., fo. 329.
86. Underdown, *Pride's Purge* p. 77; BM, Thomason Tracts, E518(17), *Perfect Occurrences*, 6–13 August 1647.
87. Rushworth, *Historical Collections*, VII, 455, 496–7. See also the reports in BM, Thomason Tracts, E384(15), *Kingdome's Weekly Intelligencer*, 13–20 April 1647; E388(6), ibid., 11–18 May 1647; E387(5), *Perfect Occurrences*, 7–14 May 1647; and Whitlocke, *Memorials* II, 131.
88. BM, Thomason Tracts, E511(24), *Perfect Occurrences*, 18–24 July, 1646.

Many of these mutinies involved large numbers of men and coordinated, or at least well-organized, marches. They also involved conferences between officials and the soldiers concerned. It is therefore obviously of great importance to discover the extent to which these mutinies were organized or carried through independently of the officers. In one of the cases I have quoted above, the refusal of the Wiltshire force to return out of Devon, some officers were clearly involved at a later stage, and probably from the beginning, and there is evidence that elsewhere officers were helping to foment discontent. According to Edward Harley, Captain Milward (of Thomas Birch's regiment in the garrison of Hereford)

> used speeches tending to the prejudice of the Committee with the soldiery, saying that they would not look upon soldiery and that he would endeavour to be a committee man and to examine their actions. The same night these speeches were used there was a mutiny in the garrison, the soldiers crying out 'money, money'.[89]

Similarly in February 1645 Colonel Montagu reported 'a Mutiny that was amongst some companies of his, upon their drawing out to be mustered at Henley, occasioned, as is conceived, by Captain Taylor and Lieutenant Rowse'.[90]

But against this, there is strong evidence, as I have shown, that almost all the major mutinies were controlled and organized from within the ranks. Often, as in the Welsh mutiny of April 1647,[91] the Hull mutiny of June,[92] or the Plymouth mutiny of August, the case for arguing from silence or from the tone of the description is a strong one. Thus the Governor of Plymouth, Ralph Weldon, while not speaking about the leadership of the mutiny there, said

> Souldiers who were to relieve the guards came to the Parade on Satterday morning last but absolutely refused to goe uppon duty and would also forcibly have carryed away their colors. Amonge whome I resolved to make some Examples, but well veining them, Famine seemed to appeare in most of their faces . . . uppon weh grounds I forbore to proceed against them and to allay this mutiny I was inforced to take five

---

89. *Hist. MSS. Comm.*, Portland MSS, III, 145 (the incident took place in Feb. 1646).
90. *CJ*, IV, 60. Here the issues were clouded by the general political crisis of early 1645. The two captains had been cashiered from the army of the Eastern Association, but later reinstated by Manchester. Montagu, on the other hand, was a noted opponent of the Earl, having given evidence to the Commons about Manchester's deportment at the siege of Donnington Castle. I am indebted to Mr M. Mahony for this point.
91. See above, p. 339.
92. Bodl. Lib., Tanner MS. 58, fo. 261.

hundred pounds out of the Custome howse for their present supply with bread.[93]

In any case the Cheshire example in itself demonstrates what could be achieved.

The exact role of the Levellers in fomenting and organizing the New Model unrest in March to November 1647 has yet to be fully analysed. Clearly, in view of what has been said above, the old view that, without Leveller organizational ideas, discontent would have remained ineffective, spasmodic and inchoately violent, must be modified. Elaborate movements of troops to back up specific objectives had been possible in many provincial armies – not famed like the New Model for their professionalism and discipline – as early as the summer of 1646, and were to follow parallel but distinct courses to the New Model throughout 1647. On the other hand, only in the New Model did personal, immediate objectives become underpinned by an ideology which saw that grievances were the inevitable result of a corrupt and unconstitutional political system and lead to a fundamental attack on the government. As one writer said in April 1647, 'Lilburne's bookes are quoted by them as statute law . . . though the army differ in judgement about religion, yet they all agree in ther discontented speeches agaynst the parliament.'[94]

The role of the Levellers in provincial unrest was both delayed and limited in importance. I have already pointed out that there is absolutely no evidence of outside influence in the Cheshire mutinies of 1646–7. Nor is there any suggestion of it in any other area before July 1647. Thus the major mutiny in North Wales took place three months before the agitators of the New Model wrote to the regiments there calling for their support and clearly introducing themselves and their proceedings.[95] More suggestive was the circular sent out in early August, in which the agitators called upon every county which had petitioned the Army to elect two or more agitators to represent them at Army Head-Quarters.[96] It seems that at the end of June and in early July, the Levellers, having won their immediate aims within the New Model, were seeking to extend their pressure on Parliament to the

---

93. Ibid., fo. 439.
94. *Hist. MSS. Comm.*, Portland MSS, III, 155–6.
95. C.H. Forth (ed.) *The Clarke Papers*, I (Camden Soc., new ser., 1891), 158–60. See also the approach made to the Lancashire forces reported in BM Thomason Tracts, E518(17), *Perfect Occurrences*, 6–13 Aug. 1647, and ibid., E397(24), *A Copie of a Letter out of Lancashire*, 12 July 1647.
96. *Hist. MSS. Comm.*, Portland MSS, I, 432–3.

whole country. Since this coincided with Parliament's attempts to purge the London militia and the clear intention of the Presbyterians to discover their own military strength, this became fused with the demand for the whole army, including Poyntz's Yorkshire forces and all remaining garrisons, to acknowledge the authority and command of Sir Thomas Fairfax. Since Parliament could not be relied upon to give way, active steps were taken to ensure that commanders hostile to the New Model were removed. At the height of the Plymouth mutiny,[97] the harassed Governor, Ralph Weldon, arrested an agent of the army, Daniel Lewes, who had made approaches to a Lieutenant in neighbouring Saltcombe and offered him a Captain's place in the New Model and his arrears to a farthing if he would deliver the fort into Lewes's hands in the name of the Army. When arrested he was engaged in subverting the Plymouth garrison.[98] Furthermore, Lewes had come from Lyme, where a few days earlier the mutiny had occurred during which the soldiers had said 'they would have all their pay to a day, declaringe they would goe to the army'.[99] At the same time *The Kingdome's Weekly Intelligencer* reported that in South Wales, six mutinous companies had stated their intention 'to be readmitted into his Excellencyes army'.[100] The Venetian ambassador wrote home about Fairfax's demand for absolute control over all garrisons and ports in the country and noted that 'the fortress of Dover and the county of Kent refuse to obey the army, and other governors of fortresses claim to be neutral, and to look after themselves'.[101]

This evidence is not by itself particularly convincing. Events in Yorkshire, however, reveal the pattern far more clearly. Yorkshire forces had always been among the most restive and mutinous in the kingdom. Perhaps their needs were greater than most; certainly the complaints of the Yorkshire Committee about the impoverishment of their county were more eloquent than those from elsewhere. There were constant reports of systematic plundering throughout 1646, and by June 1647 there had already been three major mutinies. The first, in August 1645, centred in Doncaster, saw the arrest of the commander, threats to the Committee and demands for a full month's pay;[102] the

---

97. For the involved mutiny at Plymouth, see Bodl. Lib., Tanner MS. 58, fos. 380, 382, 427, 439, 444, 448, 476, 482, 507.
98. Ibid., fo. 382.
99. Ibid., fo. 335.
100. BM, Thomason Tracts, E394(13), *Kingdome's Weekly Intelligencer*, 22–9 June 1647.
101. *Cal. State Pap. Ven.*, 1647–52, pp. 9, 16.
102. *Hist. MSS. Comm.*, Portland MSS, I 252.

second, in November 1646, saw the arrests of Poyntz and the mayor of York by separate companies, both being dragged from their beds and threatened with cocked muskets and lighted matches (a situation saved, according to Whitlocke, by Poyntz's conspicuous courage);[103] and the third, in May 1647, when the sequestrators were seized and only ransomed after handing over all the money in their hands.[104]

It was soon after this that the first letter from the New Model agitators arrived in Yorkshire, explaining their proceedings 'to the end you may have right apprehensions of our candid intentions and actions'.[105] A week later representatives from the New Model were at York headed by Major Henry Lilburne, newly returned from Ireland. According to a newsletter, they were soon 'engaging souldiers heere'.[106] Hearing of this, Parliament ordered Poyntz to arrest those involved.[107] But Poyntz, though 'according to the rule and discipline of warre, if any comes into another's Quarters to inveagle or perswade Souldiers from their Superiours hee is to be punnished with death', did not feel strong enough to take any action without further parliamentary support.[108]

While he dithered, the agitators seized the initiative. A surgeon in Colonel Copley's regiment marched the Colonel's own company to a rendezvous near Leeds where others were gathered and read out letters from the South which called on them to join with the New Model and demand their just arrears and a proper indemnity. They returned in greater strength the next day; after further discussions some returned to their quarters wearing blue and white emblems in their hats, while others marched to Pontefract, recently disgarrisoned, and installed themselves there. In the following days they were joined by other dissidents.[109]

Poyntz meanwhile had been desperately trying to get Parliament to help him undo Leveller propaganda (for example by sending down copies of the Indemnity Bill), but Fairfax's letter approving the activities of the Pontefract mutineers further undermined his position.[110] He now made a fresh bid to seize the initiative, sending a safe-conduct to Pontefract requesting Henry Lilburne and agitators

103. *CJ*, IV, 723; Whitlocke, ii, 85–6.
104. Ed. Bell, *Memorials . . .*, I, 335–6; Bodl. Lib., Tanner MS. 58, fol 113.
105. *Clarke Papers*, I, 89–92.
106. Ibid., pp. 121–2.
107. *CJ*, V, 219.
108. *Clarke Papers*, I, 142–4.
109. Bodl. Lib., Tanner MS. 58, fo 188.
110. *Clarke Papers*, I, 46–7.

of the five regiments now gathered there to come to a conference in York, and taking steps to remove unreliable officers (notably one of Fairfax's relatives who had been in charge of Clifford's Tower in York).[111] At the conference, Poyntz felt it best not to reject the agitators demands outright but to play for time, as he told Lenthall:

> Theire maine desire is to associate these forces with his Ex[cellen]cies' army, resolving to stand or fall with them in their just request, as they say. To this purpose they have selected two out of every assenting Troope & Companie, who reside at Pontefract, advisinge & actinge (with some come from the Southern Army) what they think fitt in pursuance of the aforesaid aim.[112]

Poyntz's own view is made clear in a letter to Colonel Copley,

> I would faine knowe why they should make their grievances knowne to Sir Thomas more then they have done formerly. And why to Sir Thomas? they all knowing these forces are a distinct Army and not under the command of Sir Thomas. . . .[113]

The failure of Poyntz to commit himself to the New Model, his dismissal of Captain Fairfax, his continued attempt to prevent further desertions to Pontefract, and his correspondence with Parliament during the crisis over the Eleven Members, led to his arrest and imprisonment at Pontefract. There is no evidence that any part of his army tried to prevent his seizure or later tried to rescue him.[114]

After a few days he was escorted south to the Army Headquarters, where Fairfax secured his release. He made his way to London and played a leading part in the Presbyterian bid to prevent the Army's reinstatement of the MPs forced to withdraw in late July.

In the north, his army declared its conjunction with the New Model.[115] By October, Cromwell and Fairfax were corresponding about the disposition of troops and the appointment of new garrison commanders in the area.[116]

---

111. Ibid., pp. 167–9.
112. Bodl. Lib., Tanner MS. 58, fo. 311; see also Poyntz'sletter of 2 July in BM, Add. MS. 18979, fo. 242.
113. *Clarke Papers*, I, 144. Poyntz goes on to claim that he believes Farifax will denounce the mutiny. Ironically Sir Thomas's letter approving the actions of the Pontefract forces was signed that very day at Windsor.
114. See above, p. 350, and Bodl. Lib., Tanner MS. 58, fos. 363, 366; H Cary, *Memorials of the Civil War*, 2 vols (Oxford, 1842), I, 293; *Clarke Papers*, I, 163–4; *CJ*, V, 245. For the charges made against him by the northern agitators, see *Clarke Papers*, I, 167–9.
115. BM, Thomason Tracts E398(II), *Perfect Weekly Account*, 7–14 July 1647; ibid., E398(6), *Kingdome's Weekly Intelligencer*, 6–13 July 1647.
116. E.g. Cromwell's letter to Fairfax about the garrison at Hull, 22 Oct. 1647; BM, Sloane MS. 1519 (Fairfax Correspondence), fo. 164.

The scope of this article has not permitted me to examine the effect of this pattern of unrest on the course of the struggle between Parliament and the Army. But perhaps in conclusion I might go beyond summarizing the above argument and suggest some of the ways in which the existence of provincial armies was important in determining the course of events at Westminster. Traditional explanations of the crisis have laid emphasis on the tensions and conflicts between the 'Presbyterian' and 'Independent' parties; these are largely seen in terms of the religious question and the problem of the guarantees necessary for any settlement with the king, though the existence of disputes over the sale of or composition for Crown, Church and Delinquents' lands, relations with the City of London and the priority repayment of loans has also been noted. But the work of historians undertaking local studies has not been absorbed into the thinking of historians of events at Westminster. That the logic and dynamics of political affiliations were bound up with the tensions and pre-existent conditions in each county community has now been widely accepted. But that local developments could in turn affect politics at Westminster has not been properly acknowledged.[117] The parties in 1646–7 were not merely concerned with the narrow range of issues mentioned above, however important these may have been. Thus, the course of disbandment in the autumn and winter of 1646, although an essential response to the mutinies of the summer, became a clearcut and divisive party issue within the house of commons, since decisions over which garrisons to retain and the choice of commanders vitally affected the balance of power in the localities. Behind this struggle remained a much deeper one. What was to become of the structures of local government constructed to win the war? How much of this was to remain, and how far should the central government exercise control in local affairs? The dispute was sharpened, but not created, by the knowledge that in most parts of the country, power had been seized from the hands of the traditional, moderate county leaders and now lay with more radical men of lesser birth.[118]

---

117. An exception must be made in favour of Professor Underdown.
118. Underdown, *Pride Purge* pp. 29–39, 76–8. Excellent local studies are provided by Everitt, *The Community of Kent . . .*, ch. 5, and Johnson, 'Buskinghamshire' (for Buckinghamshire). But the linkage between the localities and Westminster has yet to be exhaustively examined. The outline of the struggle to suppress county committees can be found in the Journals of the two Houses, and the weekly newspaper, *The Scottish Dove*, led a prolonged attack which can be followed in its numbers for 1646–7.

Just as important, Parliament in February 1647 was not merely faced with the specific question of how and when to disband the New Model (with the allied question of Ireland). It was faced by the much wider question of how to prevent the country dissolving into a second civil war. One lesson taught by all local studies is that the fear of a collapse of civil order was ever-present throughout the civil war and was particularly acute in 1641, 1645 and 1647. In 1646 it was probably exaggerated, though understandable; in 1645 the Clubman movement, though posing a political threat to the parliamentarian cause, had, in most areas, fallen safely into the controlling hands of neutralist or crypto-royalist gentry. But the unrest in 1646–7, which developed in the face of the continuing existence of restive troops across the country, aggravated by a food crisis and massive rise in prices and leavened by extremist propaganda from the Levellers and other sectarian groups, seemed likely to go further. In several counties – as far apart as Leicestershire and Northumberland, Yorkshire and Hampshire – fighting broke out between soldiers and armed civilian bands. From many other parts of the country, Radnorshire, Northamptonshire, Cheshire, Kent, pleas poured in to Parliament speaking of the imminence of a new and more terrible war. County Committees were more divided than ever; in Buckinghamshire two Committees claimed authority, one issuing warrants for the maintennace of a garrison at Aylesbury, the other cancelling the warrants and ordering the troops to disband.[119]

All this vitally reduced Parliament's room for manoeuvre. Fighting to solve the question of how to pay off bodies of troops whose arrears were ever growing, considerable headway had been made by the beginning of 1647. Many of the recalcitrant provincial armies and garrisons had been disbanded; the royalists seemed resigned, were flooding in to compound, and were settling down to restore their shattered fortunes; the Scots had been paid off and were disbanding. The case for a large military establishment was not strong. Party-political issues were integrally involved, but were not all-embracing. Furthermore the dangers of a major political stance being adopted by the Army was unthinkable in February, and only clearly emerged in May and June. In the circumstances, the Commons set out to dissolve the New Model using extremely similar means to those that had been tardily but effectively employed elsewhere, notably against Massie's brigade. Indeed, over the question of indemnity, Parliament's

119. E.g. Bodl. Lib., Tanner MS. 59, fo. 406.

policy, though fatally vacillating, constituted an astonishing reversal of thought for a party which had gone to war in defence of the absolute supremacy of the common law. By a process parallelling that of the royal dispensing power, the Presbyterians were prepared to remove a wide range of issues from the competence of the courts, and to deprive the population of redress for wrongs which were unquestionably *mala in se*.[120]

If the growth of political consciousness within the New Model made it unique, it has been one of the aims of this article to suggest that the development of organised and effective resistance to the orders of officers and civilian officials was not in itself remarkable or startling. The existence of provincial armies in 1646–7 both broadened the problems facing parliament, forced it into premature – though not vindictive – attempts to settle the question of the New Model, and finally afforded the radicals an opportunity to extend their campaign against Parliament and the Army moderates to a national level. But above all their importance must lie in the extent to which they were responsible for the widespread conviction among the gentry and Members of parliament that

> As affairs now stand, I am sure it will concern both parliament and the army to make a speedy closure, both of the differences betwixt them, and likewise of the settlement and peace of the kingdom; for otherwise clubs and clouted shoes will in the end be too hard for them both.[121]

120. See above, ch. 16.
121. Cary, *Memorials*, I, 293: Sir Henry Cholmondely to Lenthall, 8 July 1647.

CHAPTER EIGHTEEN
Order and Disorder in the English Revolution

Despite the hopes of a few (like the Somerset man who declared that there was now no law in force) and the fears of many more, Charles I's execution was not to be the signal for the collapse of that social order whose keystone he had claimed to be. Previous 'interregnums' had seen an outbreak of rioting prompted by the belief that the law died with the monarch, but the 'year of intended parity' saw no popular rising emerge to take advantage of such beliefs; the intention remained unrealized.[1] Indeed, an examination of disorder in the 1640s and 50s might suggest that the possibilities of an 'intended parity' were greater in the fantasies projected by the fears of the propertied classes than in the reality of popular disorder in the period. There exists a notable discrepancy between both the character and level of disorder generated by the 'moral panic' that gripped propertied contemporaries and the evidence recoverable in the historical record. While the Revolution imposed new sources of conflict on pre-existing social and economic tensions, it failed to produce that popular explosion, fear of which ran like a red thread through the political history of the period.

Measuring disorder is at the best of times a difficult (and even questionable) exercise. To the familiar problems of the under-reporting of riot and patchy record survival, the Revolution added its own obstacles. That what the people said and did continued to be less often witnessed to by themselves, than reported by men of property who 'talked of the danger of a popular uprising in

This essay was co-written with John Walter, with whose kind permission it is reprinted here.

1. Somerset RO Q/SR 81/47; *The Souldiers Demand Shewing the Present Misery, And Prescribing a Perfect Remedy, Printed at Bristoil in the yeare of intended Parity*, BL, Thomason Tract E555(29), a reference we owe to the kindness of Margaret Sampson.

order to discourage each other from taking up arms',[2] makes even harder the Solomon-like task of disentangling reality from rumour and the paranoia of the propertied. The cessation of judicial activity for a time in some areas, and at the centre the collapse of those prerogative courts preoccupied with the punishment of riot compounds the problem.[3] While this might have had the effect of understating the level of disorder, the switch to other courts, and notably Parliament, probably had the opposite effect. Both as the focus of contemporary concern with civil conflict and as an institution that has left full documentation, Parliament's assumption of the prosecution of various forms of riot may have served to inflate both contemporary and historical perceptions of the scale of disorder in the Revolution.[4] At the same time, the collapse of censorship and the emergence of unprecedented forms of communication reporting riot – pamphlet, broadsheet and newspaper – would have had the same effect.[5] The immediacy of this reporting was in stark contrast to the muffled, delayed and confused reports by which one region had heard of disturbances in other regions in preceding decades. Furthermore, there was an extensive correspondence between MPs and others in London and their families and friends in the provinces in which reports and rumours of disorder featured prominently.[6] Even if there had not

2. L. Stone, *The Causes of the English Revolution 1529–1642* (London, Routledge, 1972), p. 77.
3. J. Mather, 'Parliamentary Committees and the Justices of the Peace, 1642–60', *American Journal of Legal History*, XXIII (1979), 122–3, 133n.
4. That the House of Lords assumed the judicial business of Star Chamber (whose records exist mainly in manuscript and are largely missing, reports excepted, for the reign of Charles I) not only assured that evidence of disorder would be easier to recover by historians, but also that MPs would be made continuously aware of riots in the provinces and reflect this awareness in letters to friends and family.
5. J. Frank, *The Beginnings of the English Newspaper* (Cambridge, Mass., Harvard University Press, 1961), pp. 19–31. For general comments on the astonishing growth of publications at this time, see P. Zagorin, *The Court and the Country* (London, Routledge, 1969), pp. 203–5; G.K. Fortescue, *Catalogue of the Pamphlets of George Thomason* (2 vols., London, 1908), I, xx–xxiv. The total number of known publications between 1640 and 1660 exceeded the total number from 1485 to 1640. Thomason collected 721 items in 1641 and 2104 in 1642. S. Lambert, 'The Beginnings of Printing for the House of Commons', *The Library*, 6th ser., III (1981), 45n., suggests that in these years, Thomason may have collected less than half the items actually published. We know that these publications were distributed very widely and passed from hand to hand: R. Cust, 'News and Politics in early seventeenth-century England', *Past and Present*, CXII (1986), 60–90; Morrill, *Cheshire 1630–1660* (OUP, 1974), pp. 39–42.
6. For some examples, see D. Hirst, 'The Defection of Sir Edward Dering 1640–41', *HJ* XV (1972), 193–208; D. Gardiner (ed.), *The Oxinden Letters, 1607–1642* (London, Constable, 1933).

been an actual increase in the incidence of disorder, these changes in the manner of reporting and recording riot would have inflated contemporaries' perceptions.

All this, we would wish to argue, has contributed to a tendency by some historians to misread the trajectory of disorder in the 1640s and 1650s. While this period witnessed an undoubted increase in disorder, it also registered important discontinuities with an earlier pattern of disorder and in the forms and levels of riot within the Revolution itself. The potential for some important forms of popular disorder (enclosure and grain riots) had been removed from some areas before 1640; within the Revolution there were two separate peaks of disorder, the early and late 1640s, with little continuity, and some surprising breaks, in the forms of riot. These discontinuities challenge the accepted wisdom of an interpretation that sees popular disorder growing throughout the period.

Disturbances were undoubtedly at their greatest in the first peak of disorder in the early 1640s. Enclosures were thrown down, altar rails torn out. Elections, both municipal and parliamentary, had seen the unwelcome and sometimes tumultuous intrusion of 'fellowes without shirts'. In the provinces, crowds attacked and pillaged the houses of recusants and malignants; in London, they pressed round Parliament. And all this took place against a clamour of unemployed clothworkers and multiplying evidence of a breakdown of the traditional bulwarks of church and state.[7] Aggregating the various disturbances thus catches contemporaries' uneasy perception of what seemed to them a social order in dissolution. But to disaggregate these various disturbances is to question the accuracy of that contemporary perception upon which historians have sometimes placed overmuch reliance as evidence of the *actuality* of disorder.

As MPs nervously debated and argued, it could indeed appear that their disagreement with the king might let loose a popular movement for 'Lex Graria', the confiscation and redistribution of their estates.[8] There was a notable increase in the number of agrarian riots in the early 1640s. To see these as the culmination of a *rising* trend of agrarian protest is to ignore the contradictory evidence of the changing geography of disorder. The classic locus of earlier enclosure riot and rebellion, the fielden Midlands, remained remarkably still. For the most part, enclosure riots were restricted to areas where the

---

7. B. Manning, *The English People and the English Revolution 1640–1649* (London, Heinemann, 1976) gives a vivid sense of these years.
8. Manning, *English People*, p. 58.

radical challenge of enclosure to local economies prompted, and local social and economic structures permitted, the persistence of active, collective resistance. It was in the western forests and eastern fens and the larger estates whose royal, aristocratic and episcopal owners were associated with a discredited regime that most riots were to be found.[9]

In the charged political atmosphere of the 1640s, the tendency to equate the levelling of enclosures with the threat of levelling in society became more pronounced. As a description of the politics of agrarian disorder this reveals more about the propertied classes' fears than the rioters' intent. While recent assessments of agrarian disorder as non-ideological or apolitical are too cut and dried (it is possible to reconstruct the politics of enclosure rioters in contexts other than those of class or party allegiance),[10] it remains the case that agrarian crowds were intent on a recovery of rights that involved the righting, not the transformation, of a world turned upside-down. The not unsurprising decision of the House of Commons (whose earlier attack on enclosure in the Grand Remonstrance had raised popular hopes) to throw their weight behind enclosers after 1643 ensured that enclosure rioters did not form a radical agrarian wing of the parliamentarian cause. Land and liberty was not to be the cry of the English Revolution. But this failure to meet popular expectations did not lead to a radicalization of agrarian disorder. At its greatest in the early 1640s, agrarian disorder became progressively restricted. It remained a problem in forest and fen or flared up when new owners of confiscated estates attempted to enclose. There was, however, to be no revolution in the countryside. The passivity of the Midlands (outside of its forests) suggests that the possibilities of a revolt of the fields may already have been undermined by the very changes in social

9. The discussion of agrarian disorder is based on systematic research on a wide variety of sources, including *State Papers; Journals of the Lords and Commons*; Main Papers, House of Lords RO; PRO, King's Bench; *Historical Manuscripts Commission* and Quarter Sessions Record for a large number of counties. Further discussion of, and further references for, the points raised in the following discussion will be found in J. Walter, 'The Poor Man's Friend and the Gentleman's Plague: Agrarian Disorder in Early Modern England' (forthcoming paper). A. Charlesworth (ed.), *An Atlas of Rural Protest in Britain, 1548–1900* (London, Croom Helm, 1983), pp. 16–22, 39–42, provides a good, concise discussion. See also B. Sharp, *In Contempt of all Authority: Rural Artisans and Riot in the West of England, 1580–1660* (Berkeley, University of California, 1980); K. Lindley, *Fenland Riots in the English Revolution* (1982).
10. Some preliminary comments on the politics of riot in early modern England are to be found in J. Walter, 'Reconstructing Popular Political Culture in Early Modern England' (forthcoming).

and economic relationships which provoked popular discontent, an important point to which we later return.

What made agrarian disorder more threatening was the simultaneous occurrence of other disturbances. Popular iconoclasm was probably more common than the destruction of hedges; in Essex, for example, the authorities needed to hold a special court to deal with those who broke down altar rails.[11] A reaction to Laud's 'beauty of holiness', such riots nevertheless could seem to presage a more general toppling of traditional structures. Some contemporaries saw iconoclasm as 'abolishing superstition with sedition'.[12] It might involve the riotous destruction of altar rails and images, but iconoclasm had its own sources of legitimacy (parliamentary declarations and preaching) and discipline. Not infrequently, it involved the tacit cooperation of local elites.[13] Events like those at Chelmsford in which the royalist clergyman and polemicist, Bruno Ryves, drew a direct link between religious and social radicalism were, if true, an exception.[14] Popular iconoclasm was at its height in the early 1640s; after 1643 it became the prerogative of reforming parliamentary troops at whose hands many cathedrals suffered.[15]

More alarming were the attacks on recusants and malignants. Here could be seen more direct evidence of the people taking advantage of the times to challenge their 'betters'. According to Clarendon, malignants' goods were seized 'by the fury and license of the common people, who were in all places grown to that barbarity and rage against the nobility and gentry (under the style of *Cavaliers*) that it was not safe for any to live at their houses who were taken notice of as no votaries to the parliament'.[16] The focus on the riots in the

11. J.R. Phillips, *The Reformation of Images* (Berkeley, University of California, 1973); J.S. Morrill, 'The Church in England, 1642–9' above, ch. 7; Morrill, *Cheshire*, pp. 36–7; D. Underdown, *Somerset in the Civil War and Interregnum* (Newton Abbot, David and Charles, 1973), pp. 27, 38, 44, 78; W. Hunt, *The Puritan Moment: The Coming of Revolution in an English County* (Cambridge, Mass., Harvard University Press, 1983), pp. 285–6; J. Sharpe, *Crime in Early Modern England* (1984), pp. 84–6; [Bruno Ryves], *Mercurius Rusticus, or the Countries Complaint of the Sacriledges Prophanations and Plunderings*.
12. Manning, *English People*, pp. 32–45.
13. See, for example, J.T. Evans, *Seventeenth-Century Norwich: Politics, Religion, and Government, 1620–1690* (OUP, 1979), pp. 128–9; House of Lords RO, Main Papers, 30 June 1641; *HMC Buccleuch Mss.*, III, 415–16; PRO, SP 16/460/31.
14. [B. Ryves], *Mercurius Rusticus* no. 3, pp. 17–21.
15. Above, pp. 154–5. I. Gentles, 'Conflict between Soldiers and Civilians in the English Revolution, 1640–1655'. We are grateful to Professor Gentles for allowing me to read this valuable unpublished paper.
16. Clarendon, *The History of the Rebellion and Civil Wars in England*, W.D. Macray (ed.) (6 vols., OUP, 1888), II, 318–19.

Stour Valley in 1642 (on whose example Clarendon drew) in which crowds looted gentry households has, however, obscured the more general point that only a tiny minority of recusants were attacked. Even in the Stour Valley riots local evidence suggests that some victims owed their selection to a previous history of conflict with their local community; at Colchester, Sir John Lucas was in conflict with the corporation and popularly detested for his enclosures.[17] Attacks were concentrated in the period before the onset of armed conflict when official licence, rather than the collapse of political authority, made Catholic and 'malignant' gentry legitimate targets. With the exception of those Catholic officers murdered by troops raised to fight the Scots, violence when it did occur was directed against property and not persons. The outbreak of war saw a decline in this form of disorder which coincided with an end to the panics and alarums over supposed 'Popish plots'.[18] Where such attacks persisted it was the work of parliamentary troops who had been often at the heart of earlier crowds. But the English Revolution was not to be stained by the bloody violence that marked religious conflict on the continent.

What gave these generally distinct forms of disorder in the early 1640s their menace was the political context in which they took place. In London, sullen crowds jostled members of both Houses and prevented them from taking their seats in Parliament, while the lord mayor found his authority flouted.[19] The worst actual violence occurred in May 1640 when rioters swarmed around the archbishop's palace at Lambeth but they failed to carry out their threat to burn it down. When some of the leaders were seized and imprisoned, rioters broke open the gaol and delivered the prisoners, for which they were tried for treason.[20] Thereafter the London crowd demonstrated

17. C. Holmes, *The Eastern Association in the English Civil War* (CUP, 1974), pp. 35–6, 43–4; CUL, Add. MS 33, fols. 19–21; *HMC Braye Mss.*, pp. 147–8; PRO, SP 16/458/12 and 13; House of Lords RO Main Papers, 5 August 1641; R. Clifton, 'The Popular Fear of Catholics during the English Revolution', *Past and Present*, LII (1971), 23–55, reprinted in P. Slack (ed.), *Rebellion, Popular Protest and the Social Order in Early Modern England*, (CUP, 1984), pp. 129–61.
18. Clifton, *Past and Present*, LII (1971), 32ff. A. Hughes, 'Politics, Society and Civil War in Warwickshire 1620–50', unpublished PhD thesis (University of Liverpool, 1979), p. 265; Manning, *English People*, pp. 165–6; PRO, SP 16/491/119, 133, 138; 492/2, 11; *LJ*, V, 294–5; N.Z. Davies, 'The Rites of Violence: Religious Riot in Sixteenth-Century France', *Past and Present*, LIX (1973), 51–91.
19. V. Pearl, *London and the Outbreak of the Puritan Revolution* (OUP, 1962), pp. 212–16 and *passim*.
20. S.R. Gardiner, *History of England from the Accession of King James I to the Outbreak of the Civil War* (10 vols., London, 1884), IX, 133–5.

against and intimidated churchmen, politicians and the royal family.[21] These examples in the capital of crowds who showed scant regard for established authority and of the coercive petitioning of Parliament gave provincial disorders a threatening and unfolding unity they perhaps did not merit seen in isolation and in their local context. In the provinces, exaggerated reports of events in London had the same effect.

In reality, however, there was a failure to link radical ideas with popular grievances in the collective action of the early 1640s. Even in London the crowds often embraced substantial citizens and were well disciplined; there were few attacks on property or persons. As Valerie Pearl has written of events in the capital, here was

> a striking phenomenon . . . unknown in the rest of Europe: the rise of mass political activity of a new kind, accompanied by demonstrations in the streets and petitions . . . the absence of attacks on private property contrasts sharply with the behaviour of eighteenth-century city mobs. . . . London remained without a popular uprising, even without significant bloodshed, during some of the most disturbed years in English history. . . . The point was not lost on the French ambassador: blood would certainly have flowed in the streets of Paris, he wrote in 1642, if similar events had happened there.[22]

A third, popular force did not emerge from the widespread disorders of the early 1640s. There was, in fact, discontinuity in the patterns of disorder carried into the civil war. Much of the force of this earlier popular political initiative had been dissipated. It had been alienated by the failure of Parliament, a body of landowners, to respond to their appeals, sublimated in the wider military conflict between Crown and Parliament or ultimately turned against both by the costs of the war.

It was the strains of the civil war and the politico-religious conflicts accompanying it that explain the second peak of disturbances in the later 1640s. The armies became the major direct and indirect source of disorder. Plundering troops prompted conflicts between civilians and the military that culminated in the Club risings in south and south-west England.[23] Ill-paid troops became themselves a source

21. Manning, *English People*, pp. 71–98.
22. V. Pearl, 'Change and Stability in Seventeenth Century London', *London Journal*, IV (1979), 5.
23. J.S. Morrill, *The Revolt of the Provinces: Conservatives and Radicals in the English Civil War 1630–1650* (London, Allen and Unwin, 1976), pp. 98–111; J.S. Morrill, 'Mutiny and Discontent in English Provincial Armies 1645–1647', above, pp. 356–8; D. Underdown, 'The Chalk and the Cheese: Contrasts among the English Clubmen', *Past and Present*, LXXXV (1979), 25–48; R. Hutton, 'The Worcestershire Clubmen in the English Civil War', *Midland History*, V (1979–80), 39–49.

of disorder, staging mutinies in at least thirty-four English counties and in most of Wales in the years 1645 to 1647.[24] The excise, a new form of indirect taxation introduced to meet the costs of the war, occasioned riots in both the larger cities (London, Norwich) and smaller communities. Though we lack a full study of excise riots, this form of disorder seems to have been at its height when the harvest failures of the later 1640s made the collection of a tax imposed on the consumption of basic commodities (but not bread) especially resented. While some areas may have been relatively untroubled by such riots, others might experience considerable disorder.[25] In 1647 there was a further outbreak of religious disorder, but this time associated with counter-revolution. In the Revolt of the Prayer Book, large crowds reinstated ejected ministers or compelled the use of the Book of Common Prayer. These disturbances, spontaneously occurring in different regions, were linked to rumours that the army was negotiating with the king for the restoration of the old Church.[26]

But while the pressures of civil war conflict produced a second peak of disorders in the later 1640s, these riots against specific grievances did not become the occasion for rebellion. Conflict over the tithe resulted in some riots for example (but how many precisely we have yet to discover) and more tithe-strikes probably, but the politics of the tithe never initiated disorder on the scale that it did in continental Europe.[27] And if the riots of the later 1640s challenged the exercise of authority, they did not automatically signal popular support for a radical attack on the social bases of authority. The largest popular movement of these years, the Clubmen, did not seek to threaten that social order whose hierarchies were seemingly well observed within its ranks.

Ironically the discontinuities between the two peaks of disorder in the early and late 1640s suggest that the emergence of more organized

---

24. Above, pp. 333–43, 346.
25. C.H. Firth and R.S. Rait (eds.), *Acts and Ordinances of the Interregnum 1642–1600* (3 vols., London, 1911), I, 916–19, 1004–6; D. Underdown, *Pride's Purge: Politics in the Puritan Revolution* (OUP, 1971), pp. 90, 298; Evans, *Norwich*, pp. 170–1; Morrill, *Cheshire*, pp. 195–6. The geography of the excise riots awaits systematic study. While a large number of counties experienced disorder and opposition could be a particular problem in an area like the West Country, some counties seem to have been largely untroubled: J.S. Cockburn (ed.), *Western Circuit Assize Orders, 1629–1648: A Calendar* (Camden Society, 4th series, XVII, 1976), 254, 276, 280; PRO SP 25/169, fols. 5–6; Wiltshire RO, Q/S Gt. Roll, Michaelmas 1659, 10 May 1659; Sharpe, p. 79.
26. Above, ch.17, p. 346.
27. Morrill in *Reactions to the English Civil War*, p. 110; cf. H. Kamen, *The Iron Century* (London, Weidenfeld, 1971), ch. 10.

radical groupings, like the Levellers and Diggers, coincided with a decline in those forms of disorder which should have provided them with potentially their best opportunities for proselytizing. By the later 1640s agrarian disorder had become even more confined to specific areas. The earlier attacks on recusants and malignants had not developed into the feared attack on 'Protestants as well as Papists'. There are isolated examples of attacks by tenants on manor houses and detailed local research may provide more, but the frequency with which a few familiar examples are cited raises doubts as to how common these were.[28] Sequestration and confiscation may have tilted the balance of power in favour of tenants (as incomplete evidence on rent-strikes and arrears suggests) and afforded the odd opportunity for riot, but they did not provide the legitimation or pretext for wholesale popular plunder.[29] In the English Revolution (some) manorial records were burnt, but not chateaux. For reasons that we look at more fully later, this period did not witness an English rising against seigneurialism.

In the towns, economic discontent provoked tax riots and prompted some to support the radical groups, but harvest failure and popular chafing at the attempted puritan 'reformation of manners' persuaded others to join in the counter-revolutionary political demonstrations that took place in London and other cities.[30] As Peter Clark and Paul Slack note, political upheaval at the centre, popular opposition to high taxation and extreme religious radicalism in many towns meant that the new civic rulers, often differing but in degree from the social composition

28. See, for example, I. Roy, 'The English Civil War and English Society', B. Bond and I. Roy (eds.), *A Yearbook of Military History*, 1 (1977), 34–5. This is a subject crying out for systematic study. Most of the known attacks on muniment rooms seem to have occurred just after a fortified manor house was taken over by besieging parliamentary troops.
29. Charlesworth (ed.), *Atlas of Rural Protest*, p. 41; L. Stone, *Family and Fortune: Studies in Aristocratic Finance in the Sixteenth and Seventeenth Centuries* (OUP, 1973), p. 151; A.L. Hughes, 'Politics, Society and Civil War in Warwickshire, 1620–1650', unpublished PhD thesis (Liverpool University, 1980), pp. 220, 421–2; Manning, *English People*, p. 194; Gardiner (ed.), *Oxinden Letters*, pp. 67–8; B. Schofield (ed.), *The Knyvett Letters, 1620–1644* (Norfolk Record Society, xx, 1949), 134, 137; *HMC 5th Report*, MSS E. Field, p. 388.
30. P. Clark and P. Slack, *English Towns in Transition 1500–1700* (OUP, 1976), pp. 99, 135–6; V. Pearl, 'London's Counter-Revolution' in G.E. Aylmer (ed.), *The Interregnum: The Quest for Settlement 1646–1660* (London, Macmillan, 1972); Underdown, *Pride's Purge*, pp. 323–4; Manning, *English People*, ch. 10; Gentles, 'Conflict between Soldiers and Civilians'; A. Everitt, *The Community of Kent and the Great Rebellion 1640–1660* (Leicester University Press, 1966), pp. 231–59; *VCH Suffolk*, II, 192.

of their predecessors, were as anxious as their predecessors to exert their authority over the 'meaner sort'.[31]

And despite the tensions and sufferings caused by successive poor harvests in the later 1640s, the urban poor were not brought to the barricades by the demand for Bread and Justice. In fact, grain riots were not only noticeable by their continued absence from the capital; sensitive and previously much troubled areas, like Kent and Essex, also escaped the food riot. While the clothing districts of the West Country continued to experience grain riots, there seems to have been a contraction in the geography of the food riot.[32] Famine, even in the conditions of the later 1640s, never became the spur to popular risings.

After the king's execution, social hierarchies trembled but ultimately held firm. Charles's execution had coincided with a third year of harvest failure. Wildman, for the Levellers, had tried to draw on the evidence of food riots in Wiltshire to urge on a reluctant parliament the necessity for reforms to stave-off 'the many-headed monster'.[33] But after 1649 the harvests improved and, despite fears that military provisioning might provoke further disorder, grain riots faded away. Opposition to enclosure continued to flare up in those areas of forest and fen where disorder had been previously pronounced. In parts of the fens, notably Hatfield Chase, running warfare continued between drainers and commoners.[34] There were occasional riots in the western forests where communities of commoners continued the defence of their rights. Where a financially hard-pressed republic attempted to continue the royal policy of disafforestation on former crown lands, their efforts met similar resistance: there were riots in the later 1650s in the forests of Needwood and Sherwood and at Enfield Chase.[35] Elsewhere, attempts at piecemeal enclosure continued to prompt minor disorders.[36] But the overall impression is that the Interregnum witnessed a contraction in the pattern of disorder prompted by traditional popular grievances. Even in forest and fen, riots were less frequent, a silent testimony perhaps to the temporary victory of the commoners. Similarly, what is so far

31. Clark and Slack, *English Towns*, p. 136.
32. J. Walter, 'The geography of food riots, 1585–1649' in Charlesworth (ed.), *Atlas of Rural Protest*, pp. 72–80.
33. J. Wildman, *Truth's Triumph or Treachery Anatomized* (London, 1648), pp. 3–4.
34. Lindley, chs. 4–6.
35. *CSPD 1658–9*, pp. 152, 328; *VCH Staffordshire*, II, 353; D.O. Pam, *The Rude Multitude: Enfield and the Civil War* (Edmonton Hundred Historical Society, Occasional Papers, NS, XXXIII, 1977); Sharp, ch. ix.
36. For examples of minor riots prompted by enclosure in the 1650s, see Somerset RO, Q/SR 90/67, 93.2/72; Coventry RO, City Annals F, fol. 46v.

known about the collection of the excise suggests that it occasioned fewer confrontations in the 1650s than in the period 1645–9.[37]

In the 1640s, the Army had been both source and focus of disorder because of its indiscipline: in the 1650s it became a cause of resentment and complaint but rarely of disorder, for it was orderly and effective. There were at most times between 10,000 and 14,000 men in active service in England, scattered in garrisons mainly in London and around the coast and the Scots border.[38] Garrisoned troops were irritants in various ways: they asserted themselves over and against local governors, demanding custody of the town keys or insisting that senior officers be allowed to attend meetings of the corporation;[39] they frequently set up their own gathered church and welcomed citizens to it;[40] or they protected local separatist groups in the face of civilian hostility – one notable example being the Bristol garrison's succour of the Quakers in 1654–5.[41] Sometimes they intervened to carry out the suppression of popular festivities that the reformation of manners demanded.[42] Occasionally garrisons intervened in local elections.[43] But, despite the barrage of complaints against troops, there is little evidence of street fighting or other violent clashes between soldiers and civilians. Those that did occur, like the events at Enfield Chase, were well reported.[44]

In fact, the existence of well-disciplined and professionally led troops gave governments of the 1650s the opportunity to deal with riotous expressions of dissent by brute force. Agrarian rioters felt the full weight of a military presence when government desired it. Thus troops were used to put down disturbances in the Forest of Dean and Lincolnshire and Cambridgeshire fens.[45] They were called in by the corporation of Newcastle to break a strike by the keelmen;[46] and they enforced sequestration orders.[47] In the summer of 1649, one troop was quartered in each of the five lathes of Kent

37. G.E. Aylmer, *The State's Servants* (London, Routledge, 1973), p. 299.
38. H. Reece, 'The Military Presence in England, 1649–60', unpublished D. Phil thesis (University of Oxford, 1981), p. 287.
39. Reece, 'Military Presence', pp. 126–76.
40. At Hull, the parish church was divided by a wall, the garrison worshipping on one side and the citizens on the other: *CSPD 1650*, p. 452.
41. T. Birch (ed.), *Thurloe State Papers* (7 vols., London, 1742), III, 170–2.
42. Gentles, 'Conflict between Soldiers and Civilians'.
43. *CSPD 1654*, pp. 331–2.
44. Pam, *The Rude Multitude*, pp. 10–11.
45. *CSPD 1649–50*, p. *316; 1651*, p. 286 (and cf. *1656–7*, p. 80); *1650*, p. 218.
46. *Weekly Intelligencer* for 22 August 1654, cited in Reece, 'Military Presence', p. 182.
47. *Calendar of the Committee for Compounding*, 1, 186, 222, 361, 366.

as a direct response to the reports of the meeting of 'disaffected persons'.[48] It established a pattern. Occasionally, insufficient force was applied and disturbances continued, especially where there was considerable community support for the rioters and a difficult terrain for the troops. At Swaffham Bulbeck (Cambs.) in 1653, the failure of stationed troops to prevent rioters from destroying the drainage works led a frustrated commander to recommend that a hundred or so inhabitants be pressed for naval service *in terrorem*.[49] But in general, the arrogant order represented by the army inhibited popular resistance as it did royalist resistance. It was not used all the time; that would have strained resources. Troops could maintain order but only while they remained on permanent standby. This probably explains why many scandalous ministers remained in their parsonages despite streams of orders from local and national committees dismissing them. Where they had the support of their congregations, it would have taken a permanent military presence to evict them and to sustain a successor. Only in 1659, as a lack of pay again began to lead to a collapse of discipline, did the army become again a force of disorder rather than of resentment.[50]

If the 1650s saw a contraction in the scale and scope of popular disorder, the government's sense of its own insecurities encouraged it to read into reports of often minor disorders 'the beginnings of insurrection'. To the hyperbolic language of its predecessors, the republic added a new political vocabulary which spoke of often minor riots as evidence of 'designs against the Commonwealth'.[51] Men of property continued to fear 'an intended parity' that hurried them into a *de facto* acceptance of republican government. Their fear was less an accurate pointer to the possibilities of popular revolution from below than a reflection of the continuing failure to achieve a political settlement and the emergence of more organized forms of popular radicalism. Caught in a 'moral panic' and witness to many petty acts of insubordination,[52] they could only regard any evidence of disorder as the preliminary rites to the popular rising they had always feared.

48. *CSPD 1649–50*, pp. 253–4.
49. PRO, SP 18/39/96.
50. See below pp. 388–9.
51. See, for example, the attitudes to disorder expression in PRO, SP 25/194, fols. 43–4; SP 25/195, fol.11; SP 25/196, fol. 287.
52. What probably alarmed gentlemen as much as evidence of collective action by the poor was the growing evidence of plebeian disregard for the niceties of social and religious hierarchies, of which the Quakers' use of 'thou' to address superiors is only the best-known example. This is a subject calling for more investigation; see K.V. Thomas, 'The Place of Laughter in Tudor and Stuart England', *Times Literary Supplement*, 21 Jan. 1977, pp. 77–81.

From the very outset this 'moral panic' had been fuelled by the unprecedented availability of information about the activities of the 'many-headed monster'. The collapse of censorship and the rapid growth of newspapers and pamphlets at a time of political uncertainty would by themselves have fed this panic. That much of the reporting was just good copy directed at an anxious public fearfully greedy to learn about new disturbances only exacerbated the situation. Never hitherto could gentlemen buy hot from the presses tracts with such titles as *The Last Tumult in Fleet Street Raised by the Disorderly Preachment, Pratings and Pratlings of Mr Barbones the Leatherseller and Mr Greene the Feltmaker.*[53] Such alarmist writings could colour responses to more sober accounts of the marches of thousands of countrymen to present petitions at Westminister, or of disturbances in the provinces. In late 1641 and early 1642, the tempo of such publications quickened,[54] with lurid accounts of atrocities in Ulster spilling over into circumstantial accounts of plots in England and even into plausible but fabricated narratives of popish uprisings.[55] The reality of the early 1640s was bad enough; rumour made it worse. One prebend of Hereford, preaching on 17 April 1642, solemnly told his congregation that he had certain knowledge that sectaries now controlled London and had forced the king to flee to the north.[56]

Both sides in the developing political conflict made deliberate and propagandist use of this alarmist literature. The royalists had the easier task, indicting the House of Commons of 'traitorously endeavouring to subvert the fundamental laws and . . . to deprive the king of his royal power',[57] and claiming that this occasioned a breakdown of order. The royalists specifically accused the Commons of wilful encouragement of popular violence and iconoclasm, or more generally of wilful indulgence of them. Only the restoration of royal authority could lead to a restoration of order. It became a central

53. BL, Thomason Tracts, E 180 (26).
54. See n. 6 above.
55. J. Rushworth, *Historical Collections* (7 vols., London 1659–1701), IV, [398]–[416], 385–421 (page numbers 385–416 are used twice in this edition); K.J. Lindley, 'The Impact of the Irish Rebellion in England and Wales', *Irish Historical Studies*, XVIII (1972–3), 143–76; Clifton, *Past and Present*, LII (1971), 25–55; R. Clifton, 'Fear of Popery' in C.S.R. Russell, *The Origins of the English Civil War* (London, Macmillan, 1973), pp. 144–67. For an example of a fabricated papist rising, see 'A True Relation of a Bloody Conspiracy in Cheshire Intended for the Destruction of the Whole County' in J. Atkinson (ed.), *Civil War Tracts of Cheshire* (Chetham Society, 2nd series, 65, 1909), 2–4.
56. BL, Loan MS 29/173 173, fols. 237–8.
57. Rushworth, *Historical Collections*, IV, 473.

prop of royal propaganda in 1642, most famously in the *Reply to the Nineteen Propositions*,[58] but even more pointedly elsewhere:

> We complained . . . of the multitudes of seditious pamphlets and sermons. And the declaration tells us, they know we have ways enough in our ordinary courts of justice to punish those: so we have to punish tumults and riots, and yet they will not serve our turn to keep our towns, our forests and parks from violence. And it may be, those courts have still the power to punish, they have lost the skill to define what riots and tumults are: otherwise a jury in Southwark legally impanelled to examine a riot there, would not have been superceded, and the sheriff enjoyned not to proceed, by virtue of an order from the House of Commons.[59]

Equally, however, the managers of the Long Parliament were using the very threat of a collapse of order to advance the case for an imposed political settlement. Throughout the winter of 1641–2, the managers whipped up the hysteria about the massacres in Ireland, and the plans of the papists to spread their campaign to the mainland. They have been shown to have distorted the information flowing into them to that end.[60] Besmirching the king as deranged, incapable of governing, and arguing that anarchy was developing from the king's incapacity,[61] Pym and his colleagues used the existence of popular disturbances to illustrate the results of misgovernment and to justify further remedial legislation. Thus on 25 January 1642 Pym picked up a theme from a petition of the clothworkers of Essex, which had included the failure to crush popery among the causes of the depression,[62] when he predicted an insurrection of the poor if there was no political reform or religious renewal.[63] Five months later, crowds of clothiers sacked the houses of 'papists' and 'malignants', accusing them of being 'the cause of the present troubles and distractions'.[64] Here and elsewhere – in their response to iconoclasm, to lay preaching, even to enclosure riots – there was an ambivalence in parliamentarian attitudes to popular disturbances: they were understandable if reprehensible, to be met not by repression but by the prospect of reform.[65]

58. J.P. Kenyon, *The Stuart Constitution* (CUP, 1962), pp. 21–3.
59. Rushworth, *Historical Collections*, IV, 711.
60. M. Mendle, 'Mixed Government, The Estates and the Bishops', PhD thesis (Washington University, St Louis, 1977), pp. 396–432.
61. J.S. Morrill, 'The Religious Context of the English Civil War', above, p. 62.
62. Hunt, *Puritan Moment*, pp. 293–4.
63. BL, Thomason Tract 200 (21).
64. See note 17 for sources.
65. J.S. Morrill, 'The Attack on the Church of England in the Long Parliament, 1640–1642', above, pp. 73–5.

That Parliament was aware of the damage royalist propaganda could inflict can be seen in the Houses' attempt on 19 May 1642 to vindicate the intimidation of MPs the previous December. Its speciousness stands out:

> We do not conceive that Numbers do make an assembly unlawful, but when either the end or manner of their carriage shall be unlawful. Divers just occasions might draw the citizens to Westminster, and other causes were depending in Parliament, and why that should be found more faulty in the citizens than the resort of great numbers every day in the term to the ordinary courts of Justice we know not . . . [66]

Throughout the 1640s and the 1650s the same pattern was to recur. It was always in the interests of newsmen to report in exaggerated detail all manifestations of disorder; and it always suited the polemical purposes of government to exaggerate and to draw lessons from threats to the peace. The manipulation of 'Leveller' plots, of army mutinies, of Quaker plots are the most obvious examples. Historians who rely entirely or principally upon the press give us a reliable guide as to how contemporaries were led to believe in the imminent disintegration of the rule of law. But reality was only in part as it was portrayed at the time.

Propaganda was all the more readily believed, since it not only confirmed gentlemen's beliefs about the real nature of the many-headed monster, but because it also spoke to the deepening social divisions that pre-dated the Revolution. D'Ewes touched on a common fear among the propertied classes when he reminded his fellow MPs that, 'all right and property, *meum et tuum*, must cease in a civil war and they knew not what advantage the meaner sort also may take to divide the spoils of the rich and noble among them, who begin already to alledge that all being of one mould they saw no reason why some should have so much and others so little'. This was a common theme, given a popular (and deliberate) echo in petitions to parliament: 'Necessity dissolves all laws and government, and hunger will break through stone walls', asserted one such petition. [67] In the conditions of the 1640, the gentry needed little reminding of such proverbial lore.

The real threat of the political conflict was, as D'Ewes observed,

---

66. Rushworth, *Historical Collections*, IV, 695.
67. BL, Harleian MS 163, fol. 541; 'The mournfull Cryes of many thousand poor Tradesmen, who are ready to famish through decay of Trade' in D.M. Wolfe (ed.), *Leveller Manifestoes of the Puritan Revolution* (New York, Thomas Nelson, 1944), p. 278.

that it threatened to explode the deeper tensions latent within a situation of accelerating social and economic differentiation. But, as we have seen, in reality there was a notable discrepancy between actual and projected levels of disorder. This discrepancy suggests the need for a re-evaluation of the traditional view of the civil war period as one which saw a paralysis of political order permitting latent social conflicts to become manifest. We would wish to argue that the breakdown in order was less marked at the level of the local community than at Westminster and that the potential for widespread popular mobilization in the social and economic changes preceding the Revolution was less great than has been assumed. This resilience of local structures of authority and the containment of disorder have common roots in the pattern of shifting social relationships. Economic change undoubtedly prompted greater popular discontent, but ultimately it created new structures which made possible the containment and even appeasement of that discontent.

If economic changes led to growing popular discontent, it did not of itself create a revolutionary potential. England's earlier omission from the roll-call of European rebellions in the extremely difficult conditions of the 1590s should caution against too facile an equation of economic distress with disorder.[68] A more sensitive assessment of the process and progress of economic change would suggest that there were limits (geographical as much as ideological) to the disorder that popular grievances might prompt. Enclosure could promote riots which in areas with common grievances might achieve extensive coverage, but its ability to prompt a revolt of the countryside was questionable. England remained a society that was local and regional; there seems little evidence to suggest that rural rioters any more than sixteenth-century rebels could have burst the 'natural' boundaries to collective action that this imposed. Moreover, to the extent that agrarian grievances seem to have needed the physical evidence of hedges as a goad to riot, then enclosure's patchwork geography and piecemeal timing imposed further limits.

This is not to argue that these limitations were insurmountable. Famine, an effective collapse of local order which permitted the wider dissemination of destabilizing rumours, a growing belief in the imminence of a radical millennium or an effective political lead by radical 'vanguard' parties – any of these might have broken down the ideological and physical restraints on wider popular political action.

68. J. Walter, 'A Rising of the People? The Oxfordshire Rising and the Crisis of 1590s', *Past and Present*, CVII (1985).

But the fear of popish plots never became the Great Fear of the French Revolution[69] and a radical millenarianism (for reasons which cry out for investigation) never mobilized the rural poor.[70] The bad harvests of the later 1640s led to a heightening of tensions but not to a breakdown of social order. The demographic evidence suggests that by the 1640s England (including previously vulnerable regions like the north-west) had slipped the shadow of a crisis of subsistence.[71] Increased agricultural output, achieved at the cost of heightened potential conflict where it required enclosure and engrossing for its achievement, not only prevented widespread famine but also made possible the continuing effectiveness of crisis relief which made grain available to the poor. These policies seem to have held up well in the later 1640s.[72] As we have already noted, there was a contraction in the areas scarred by food riots at the end of the decade. Despite worries expressed in the economic crisis of the early 1640s, necessity never became great enough in the English Revolution to impel the poor to break *en masse* through the walls of society.

Nor was there a breakdown of order at the level of the local community. There was within seventeenth-century England a process of growing social differentiation.[73] At one extreme this saw the growth in poverty that so alarmed contemporaries (though there is evidence to suggest that historians have perhaps exaggerated its depth and character).[74] But the corollary of this was the consolidation of the smaller landowner and the growth of the 'middling sort', the

69. Clifton, *Past and Present*, LII (1971), 159–60; G. Lefebvre, *The Great Fear of 1789* (London, NLB, 1973).
70. The Fifth Monarchists were predominantly an urban movement dominated by London: B.S. Capp, *The Fifth Monarchy Men: A Study in Seventeenth-Century English Millenarianism* (London, Faber, 1972), ch. 4.
71. E.A. Wrigley and R.S. Schofield, *The Population History of England 1541–1871: A Reconstruction* (London, Edward Arnold, 1981), pp. 332–55 and appendix 10; R.S. Schofield, 'The Impact of Scarcity and Plenty on Population Change in England, 1541–1871', *Journal of Interdisciplinary History*, XIV (1983), 265–91; A. Appleby, *Famine in Tudor and Stuart England* (Liverpool University Press, 1978), ch. 10; A. Appleby, 'Grain Prices and Subsistence Crises in England and France', *Journal of Economic History*, XXXIX (1979), 865–87.
72. J. Walter and K. Wrightson, 'Dearth and the Social Order in Early Modern England', *Past and Present*, LXXI (1976), reprinted in Slack (ed.), *Rebellion, Popular Protest and Social Order*, pp. 124–6.
73. W.G. Hoskins, *The Midland Peasant* (London, Macmillan, 1957), chs. VI–VII; Spufford, pp. 46–167; J. Thirsk (ed.), *The Agrarian History of England and Wales*, IV (CUP, 1967), 301–6, 396–465; F. Hull, 'Agriculture and Rural Society in Essex, 1500–1640', unpublished PhD thesis (University of London, 1950), pp. 74–81.
74. J. Walter, 'Social Responses to Dearth in Early Modern England', in R.S. Schofield and J. Walter (eds.), *Dearth and the Social Order* (1988).

yeomen and richer husbandmen in the countryside. The effect of this growing differentiation was to question the validity of the unitary description of those below the level of the gentry as 'the people'. For as a counterpoint to the better-known political conflict between royalist and parliamentarian, there was a developing conflict at a lower level between the beneficiaries and victims of economic change.

As a consequence of this conflict there was a subtle shifting of alliances in the countryside which pre-dated the Revolution. Those groups whose combination of wealth, status and local parish or manorial office allowed them to dominate local communities had provided the backbone of many earlier rebellions.[75] But potential conflict with their poorer neighbours had encouraged them to align themselves with the state in a common attack on a developing 'culture of poverty'. Denied the earlier use of more informal ties of patron and client by their growing pursuit of 'possessive individualism',[76] they turned to local office and an alliance with the gentry as magistrates. This was an alliance eased by an identity of economic interests in service of the market, facilitated by the trend towards enclosure by agreement and cemented where there occurred a shared religion and literate culture. Increasing mobility from the ranks of the yeomen over time and through the avenue of university education had helped to blur the social distinction between parish gentry and wealthy farmers.[77]

Developing political and religious conflict between crown and political nation, therefore, placed the 'middling sort' in something of a dilemma. Like their betters, they resented many royal policies in the 1630s, especially where these seemed to endanger their attempts to impose greater controls over the poor. In the early stages of the Revolution they probably found some forms of crowd action (for example iconoclasm) not unwelcome. But, since the broader political conflict might offer the occasion for popular attacks on

75. C.S.L. Davies, 'Peasant Revolt in France and England: a Comparison', *Agricultural History Review*, XXI (1973), 130–2.
76. For the concept of 'possessive individualism', see C.B. Macpherson, *The Political Theory of Possessive Individualism: Hobbes to Locke* (OUP, 1964), pp. 52–61.
77. The best general discussion of this process is to be found in Wrightson, chs. 6 and 7; for a detailed local study, Wrightson and Levine, chs. 5–7; see also Walter, *Past and Present* (1985); M. Ingram, 'Religion, Communities, and Moral Discipline in Late Sixteenth and Early Seventeenth Century England' in C. von Greyertz (ed.), *Religion and Society in Early-modern England* (1985). We are very grateful to Dr Ingram for allowing us to see this paper. R. Smith, '"Modernization" and the Corporate Medieval Village Community in England: Some Sceptical Reflections' (forthcoming).

them,[78] they offered only very reluctant endorsement. Those who sided with Parliament (and we should not assume that there was a natural identity between the 'middling sort' and support for Parliament) wished for political and religious reform, not least to strengthen their position over their poorer neighbours. But they did not seek the radical social and economic reforms that the poorer sort might have sought. To challenge the drift of agrarian capitalism would have been to bite the hand that fed them their profits.

In the English Revolution, therefore, the yeomanry and richer husbandmen were not to play the vital role they had in sixteenth-century rebellions. Rather than use their considerable local power to mobilize a popular movement, they were more likely to use their power to stifle local grievance. Only where these local elites continued to find themselves in conflict with their landlord (or in the Revolution, with army or regime) would they be likely to organize popular action. Thus, the one major area where the 'middling sort' continued to give a lead to popular opposition to enclosure was that of forest and fen. Here imposed enclosure continued to challenge their interests. This was the more so, since the proposed conversion from pastoral to arable economies struck at the pursuit of their market interests which were best served within the context of regional specialization by their ability to over-exploit the waste and commons. It is their willingness to continue to oppose enclosure that helps to explain the persistence of agrarian disorder in these areas.[79] Some historians have argued that the immediate decades before the Revolution saw a deterioration in the position of the yeomanry that gave them a common interest with the poorer tenants. Much of the evidence for this comes from regions with a history of poor landlord/tenant relationships.[80] But in southern and eastern England the evidence seems to point to growing cooperation between landlord and yeomen.[81]

---

78. See, for example, the comments of Thomas May in his *History of the Parliament of England* (London, 1647, repr. Oxford, 1854), p. 112. For popular attacks on puritans in response to their attempt to discipline the poor, see B. Manning, 'Religion and Politics: The Godly People' in Manning (ed.), *Politics, Religion and the English Civil War* (London, Edward Arnold, 1973), pp. 92–3, 102–3.
79. Historians have perhaps been too ready to accept the argument of Buchanan Sharp, based on a simple counting of heads from lists of rioters known to authority, which downplays the role of the yeomen in the western forests, ch. 5. For evidence of the 'middling sort's' role in the fens, see Lindley, p. 256; C. Holmes, 'Drainers and Fenmen' in A. Fletcher and J. Stevenson (eds.), *Order and Disorder in Early Modern England* (Cambridge, 1985), p. 84.
80. B. Manning, 'The Peasantry and the English Revolution', *Journal of Peasant Studies*, II (1975), 134–8, where much of the evidence comes from the north of England.
81. Charlesworth (ed.), *Atlas of Rural Protest*, p. 17.

The incorporation of the 'middling sort' into a state whose presence was becoming more effective at the level of the local community ensured the maintenance of order at a local level. Their presence served not only to suppress disorder but also to ensure that the traditional policies for coping with the problem of the poor did not collapse. In the English Revolution they, not the gentry, became the garrisons of good order. Where local elites succeeded in imposing tighter controls (and we have as yet an incomplete knowledge of the geography of these new patterns of order)[82] they doubtless denied radical groups, if not radical ideas, a toehold in their local communities. Thus, though there is sufficient evidence of popular grievances in outbursts of sedition to give some credence to the threats made in radical petitioning,[83] the possibilities for the collective expression of that discontent in riot were being narrowed rather than extended by social and economic change. Roger Crab's 'labouring poor Men, which in Times of Scarcity pine and murmur for Want of Bread, cursing the Rich behind his Back; and before his Face, Cap and Knee and a whining countenance' were those who had had to accommodate themselves to these changed realities.[84]

Not enough is known about the impact of the Revolution on social and economic relations at a village level to make generalizations safe or secure. But what is known suggests that it might be the case that increases in levels of disorder arose less from conflict *within* local communities than from pressure from without. While we would emphatically reject the view that the English village 'was a place filled with malice and hatred, its only unifying bond being the occasional episode of mass hysteria, which temporarily bound together the majority in order to harry and persecute the local witch',[85] we would not want to go to the other extreme. Divisions of many kinds could create tensions and create disorder within particular communities. Disputes over land, over common rights, over local rates, over religion, over the performance of social duties could create brief or prolonged disagreements and conflict.

82. Much of the best evidence for this pattern of changing relationships of authority in the local community comes from a relatively few (and mostly southern) counties.
83. For some examples of popular discontent, see Wiltshire RO, Q/S Gt Roll Hilary 1647/8, petition of the inhabitants of Westbury; Essex RO, Q/SR 332/106.
84. Roger Crab, *Dagon's Downfall*, quoted in C. Hill, *Puritanism and Revolution: Studies in Interpretation of the English Revolution of the 17th Century* (London, Secker and Warburg, 1958), p. 307.
85. L. Stone, *The Family, Sex and Marriage in England, 1500–1800* (London, Weidenfeld and Nicolson, 1977), p. 98.

Our concern is not with the existence of such tensions so much as with their prevalence during the 1640s and 1650s in comparison with the previous period. This, above all, is impossible to quantify. But despite the existence of new potential sources of internal conflict, our impression is that communal life was not generally more torn by dissension and disorder in the mid-century.

There were three potential new sources of conflict. The first was a direct result of the 'puritan' victory, which brought a renewed drive towards a 'reformation of manners', the imposition of more sober and self-disciplined ways of life: the regulation of alehouses and gaming, of sabbath observance and sexual relations. Pressure for the enforcement of existing legislation and for the introduction of additional ordinances in all of these areas was a constant feature of the period 1640–60, and was dear to the heart of Oliver Cromwell himself. Court records suggest patchy increases in prosecutions and magisterial initiatives. This was not merely an imposition from outside. In this instance, the survival of petitions from parishes calling for magisterial action is clear evidence of divided attitudes which led to the godly seeking external assistance. But we must beware of making too much even of this evidence. Concern for 'the reformation of manners' was nothing new; most of the specific demands of its proponents derive from legislation unanimously agreed in Parliament and consonant with, growing out of, the canon law of the Church; pleas for enforcement were characteristic of puritanism, but not their preserve alone; the apparent increase in secular court business may in large part reflect a transfer of business from the defunct church courts.[86]

The second and connected source of additional strain on parishes was the stillborn puritan church order.[87] The old Church – its government, liturgy, even the rhythms of its calendar (the celebrations of the great Feasts) – was abolished and proscribed, but nothing was put in its place. A new system, replete with disciplinary procedures, service books, catechisms, etc., was legislated for, but the political will at the centre to enforce it crumbled. In the 1650s, successive regimes in practice allowed local self-determination in matters of worship.[88] This led in many – probably most – parishes to the restoration of a watered-down Anglican worship, built around parts

---

86. The fullest study is in K. Wrightson, 'The Puritan Reformation of Manners', unpublished PhD thesis, (University of Cambridge, 1973), *passim*; the main points are taken up in Wrightson, pp. 168–170, 181–2, 199–219.
87. Above, pp. 160–73.
88. C. Cross, 'The Church in England, 1646–1660' in G.E. Aylmer (ed.), *The Interregnum*, pp. 99–120.

of the Prayer Book and Christmas and Easter communions. But in many parishes, godly minorities fought to impose the new order or at least to resist the (illegal) restoration of the old order. Yet all the signs are that violent confrontation between 'anglican' and 'puritan' parties were concentrated in the years 1646–8 when there was some political will at Westminster to introduce the new system. Thereafter, accommodation and compromises were reached: in market towns, the minister in one church would use the Prayer Book and in another the new services;[89] in the countryside, ministers would hold no holy communions at all, an unpopular decision but less inflammatory to the conservatives than of following puritan prescription and opening the communion table only to the godly, and less inflammatory to the godly than a 'promiscuous' communion of all but notorious sinners on the Anglican pattern.[90]

The third new source of conflict arose from the sequestration of the estates of many – perhaps a quarter – of the gentry for having served the king during the wars. This potentially gave an ideal opportunity to tenants and neighbours to settle scores, by denouncing them to parliamentary authority, uncovering lands which the delinquents were seeking to conceal, spoliating their homes and demesnes. Yet this happened remarkably rarely. Committeemen seem to have relied far more on professional informers than on tenants; looting and mean acts of vandalism cannot be found on any scale. There is plenty of evidence to suggest that successive regimes were concerned to minimize the degree of political ostracism and social humiliation of their defeated opponents. Although ex-royalists were, at least in theory, disfranchised and barred from public office, there was no wider proscription: ex-royalists continued to sit on juries, serve as churchwardens, overseers, constables. Nor is there evidence of political discrimination against ex-royalists in the administration of the poor laws (except that maimed royalist soldiers could not receive state pensions).[91]

89. For an example, see A.E. Preston, *The Church and Parish of St Nicholas, Abingdon* (Abingdon, 1909), p. 97. It is widely true of the towns in at least the south-west and the Welsh borders. We are grateful to Paul Gladwish, Patrick Higgins and Nick Marlowe for advice on this point.
90. Morrill in *Reactions to the English Civil War*, pp. 105–9.
91. This is based on a reading of printed quarter sessions records and committee papers and of several unpublished dissertations, as listed in G.E. Aylmer and J.S. Morrill, *The Civil Wars and Interregnum: Sources for Local Historians* (London, Bedford Square Press, 1979), appendices 4, 5, 7. See particularly S.K. Roberts, 'Participation and Performance in Devon Local Administration 1649–1670', unpublished PhD thesis (University of Exeter, 1980), chs. 4–5; J.S. Morrill, *The Cheshire Grand Jury* (Leicester University Press, 1976), *passim*.

In general, these potential new sources of conflict were most likely
to divide the 'parish aristocracies' – literate, schooled in Christian
teaching, independent proprietors – from labourers, artificers, the
poor. In the 1640s and 1650s, as before, relations between the
two were uneasy, ambivalent. On the one hand, the latter were
dependent upon the former for employment, credit, relief, mediation
with county or national authorities; on the other hand, they might
find themselves the victims of the former's strengthening relations
with the gentry in the extension of agrarian capitalism. Here we
would stress that if in the 1640s and 1650s some magistrates and
parish notables were increasing the pressure on the poor to conform
to their idea of Christian duty, these same magistrates and parish
notables were increasing their efforts to provide relief and succour
in times of hardship. During the years 1647–9 when grain deficiencies
were probably the worst of the century, the full battery of controls
on the grain market were employed and a forthcoming study will
argue for significant changes in the administration of poor relief in
these years.[92] What evidence has been looked at makes the point
just as clearly for the towns.[93] While the poor had grounds to
be more in conflict with parish elites, they were also becoming
ever more dependent upon them; and paradoxically while parish
aristocracies felt more vulnerable, it increased their vested interest
in the maintenance of order and it may well have increased their
solidarity against outside pressures and demands. In stark contrast
to the findings of historians of the French, the Russian, the Chinese
Revolutions, in England the impression is that the civil war neither
created nor fuelled vendettas or blood feuds. We are not aware of
more than a handful of cases of inhabitants fighting one another over
the issues dividing king and parliament, though many communities
sent forth men to opposing armies; and after 1642 divisive actions
such as the ejection of a minister most usually followed the arrival of

92. T. Wales, 'The Structure of Poverty in Seventeenth Century Norfolk', PhD
thesis (University of Cambridge, forthcoming) and his important article,
'Poverty, Poor Relief and the Life-Cycle: Some Evidence from Seventeenth-
Century Norfolk' in R.M. Smith (ed.), *Land, Kinship and Life-Cycle* (CUP,
1985), pp. 351–404; Morrill, *Cheshire*, pp. 247–52; J.P. Cooper, 'Social and
Economic Politics under the Commonwealth' in Aylmer (ed.), *The Interregnum*,
pp. 125–9.
93. V. Pearl, 'Puritans and the Poor: The London Workhouse 1649–1660' in
D. Pennington and K. Thomas (eds.), *Puritans and Revolutionaries* (OUP,
1978), pp. 206–32; see also R.W. Herlan's various articles on poor relief in
London parishes during the English Revolution, *Guildhall Studies in London
History*, II (1976), 43–53; III (1977), 13–36, 179–99.

'foreign' commissioners with interrogatories rather than an initiative from within.

It is our impression, then, that increased levels of disorder owed less to intra-communal strife than to the intrusion of 'outsiders'. The most obvious flashpoints were the arrival of garrisons or the passage of troops; the impositions of new types of taxation; and externally imposed religious change. These were often linked: it was the use of troops to destroy religious images, stained-glass windows, altar rails, service books, or to requisition horses and supplies or to support tax-gatherers, which provoked some of the greatest scenes of violence.[94] Such interventions were especially likely to reinforce local solidarity against the intruders rather than to polarize the community.

Such demands varied, of course, from place to place and from time to time, and there is no simple relationship between the scale of demands and the likelihood of violent resistance. In part this was because the proximity of overwhelming physical force would act as a deterrent. The remarkably low level of violence in London in the 1650s probably owed much to the constant quartering of 3,000 or more troops in the centre.[95] But here and elsewhere it also owed something to the ability of 'passive resistance' to limit or to avoid the burdens. Local courts could be used to uphold religious practices banned by the Long Parliament; to indict soldiers for requisitioning horses and supplies and to secure recompense; to undo the work of excisement.[96] The explicit orders of county committees or parliamentary committees could be flagrantly ignored in the knowledge that there was insufficient political will or physical force available to implement the original order.[97] Although the civil wars and Interregnum threw up new bureaucratic bodies with wide powers, most of the fiscal demands were enforced by existing local officials. Such men could get caught in the middle, but they could also

94. For iconoclasm, see n. 11 above.
95. Reece, 'Military Presence', ch. 1.
96. Aylmer, *State's Servants*, pp. 13–14, 299–302; J.S. Morrill, 'The Army Revolt of 1647' in A. Duke and C. Tamse (eds.), *Britain and the Netherlands*, VI (1977), 59–64. We are grateful to Bill Cliftlands for help with this and many other questions, and for allowing us to see his valuable unpublished paper on the working of indemnity commissioners who investigated these cases.
97. E.g. W.A. Shaw (ed.), 'Manchester Classis Minutes' (Chetham Society, 2nd series, XXII, 1891), 375–95, supplemented by the *CSPD 1650*, p. 442; and W.A. Shaw (ed.), 'Plundered Ministers Accounts' (Lancashire and Cheshire Record Society, XXVII, 1894), 185–7. This is not inconsistent with the point about 'overwhelming physical force'. To be effective, the force had to be at hand and in strength. In many parts of the country it was neither.

mediate or mitigate the burdens, or negotiate distributions of taxation in ways felt to be as equitable as possible. It is surely no accident that there are many more reports of disturbances involving excise (assessed by itinerant agents) than assessment (handled by village constables). Once again, it may be noteworthy that those disorders which produced violence against persons and property were those in which there was direct conflict between local communities and outsiders where the scope for local mediation was very limited – particular military/civilian skirmishes, excise riots, the imposition of a minister in place of one forcibly sequestered. The apparent decline of these disorders in the 1650s may be related to the state's relaxation of earlier burdens, and willingness to work through local elites: for example, in at least some areas, parishes 'compounded' with the excisemen and paid a local rate in lieu of the previous assessments backed up by house-searches and distraint; while Cromwell preferred to fill vacant livings in the church with men chosen by the parishioners themselves.[98]

We must not, therefore, exaggerate the extent to which government broke down at a local level. After the war years, when county institutions were suspended for up to four years, there was a return to the old ways and old officers: assizes, quarter sessions, grand juries, churchwardens, overseers. But on top of these familiar institutions and practices were laid new layers of bureaucracy and new forms of control: sequestration committees, assessment committees, commissioners for ejecting scandalous ministers, excisemen.[99] In general, the rhythms of administration at a village level were quickened rather than transformed, reinforced rather than abandoned. Successive regimes from 1646 to 1660 worked through existing structures in their concern with markets and with the poor; they created new structures when they made new demands. It is not surprising that provincial reaction was to cling to the familiar and to reject the unfamiliar which offered nothing and took much.

The resilience of local relationships of authority imposed constraints on the poor's ability to combine which perhaps only leadership from outside would have broken. But effective leadership was not available. Hugh Peter's wish that the army be used to teach the peasants liberty

98. E.g., PRO, Chester 24/129 no. 2, grand jury petitions of 27 October 1651, speaking of a 'composition' for the excises on ale made by the jury.
99. Mather, *American Journal of Legal History* XXIII (1979), 122–3, 133n. For the 1640s, Morrill, *Revolt of the Provinces*, pp. 52–72; for the 1650s, Aylmer, *State's Servants*, pp. 9–17, 305–16.

was never realized.[100] The radical sects made too little headway, though exaggerated estimates of their size and militancy created great fear of disaster. Despite the attention paid to them at the time, they constituted a tiny minority of the population. Probably less than 5 per cent attended religious assemblies other than those in their parish church.[101] The flamboyant evangelism of some of the tiny fringe groups provoked responses from their orthodox neighbours.

It is not clear how far the subversive ideas advanced by the sects and taken up, at different times, by groups within the army were responses to the events of the 1640s or the surfacing of subterranean traditions from previous decades and centuries, and irretrievable by us for lack of surviving evidence.[102] It hardly matters. It is hard to be evangelical and secretive. Clearly there was considerable momentum behind the radical ideas during the Revolution. Most striking is the rejection of Calvinist notions of Man and of Grace, an insistence on the dignity rather than on the degradation of Man, of universal access to Grace, and of the need for all men to be free to seek out that Grace without the intervention of church or state; and the political and economic extensions of that liberated doctrine of Man. Yet, powerful and moving as the polemics of the new creeds were, they had very limited impact. In terms of membership, organization, integration and ability to implement their ideas, they were much less impressive. Violence played little part in their history.

In the 1640s and 1650s, of course, many groups formulated, articulated, disseminated ideas which were profoundly subversive of the social, political and religious order. But those who had subversive *ideas* were not necessarily committed to the use of subversive *means* to impose those ideas. In general, the more subversive the ideas, the less violent the attempt to impose them. Tiny splinter groups like the Ranters and Muggletonians whose ideas were religious and/or individualistic showed little concern with the political implications of their beliefs or for their political implementation.[103] The Fifth

---

100. Quoted in C. Hill, *The Century of The Revolution 1603–1714*, 2nd edn (London, Nelson, 1980), p. 161.
101. A figure proposed in ch. 7, pp. 149–50.
102. B. Reay, 'Early Quaker Activity and Reactions to It', unpublished D.Phil. thesis (University of Oxford, 1979) pp. 8–112. C. Hill, 'From Lollards to Levellers' in M. Cornforth (ed.), *Rebels and Their Causes* (London, Lawrence and Wishart, 1978), pp. 49–67.
103. J.F. Macgregor, 'Seekers and Ranters' in B. Reay and J.F. Macgregor (eds.), *Radical Religion in the English Revolutions* (OUP, 1984), pp. 121–39; C. Hill, W. Lamont and B. Reay, *The World of the Muggletonians* (London, Temple Smith, 1982), *passim*.

Monarchists generally eschewed violent preparations for the Second
Coming of Christ, and the breakaway group under Venner who tired
of waiting passively and planned an insurrection in April 1657 appear
to have numbered no more than twenty (Venner did only slightly
better in 1661).[104]

The Diggers, too, had only a sketchy organization and hence little
ability to proselytize their programme for the communal cultivation
of the wastes and commons. The programme, in any case, while
it might appeal to the rural poor (cottagers and landless labourers)
jarred with an earlier tradition of agrarian protest in which the defence
of the commons had been undertaken in support of diminishing
individual holdings whose viability only common rights guaranteed.
This had led to a growing clash between indigenous communities and
squatters. Where the Diggers appeared as outsiders to a community
(as in Surrey and Northamptonshire, though not at Iver in Buckinghamshire) they risked incurring the traditional hostility towards
strangers. The Diggers' natural allies, the labourers and cottagers,
were the groups with least scope for independent action, and therefore
the most difficult to mobilize.[105]

These groups all derived their unity from the labelling of opponents, but even so, should be numbered in scores or hundreds rather
than thousands. The most highly 'politicized' of the radicals were,
of course, the Levellers. Growing out of the campaign for religious
freedom, and coming to believe that there would be no religious
liberty until there was political liberty, the Levellers articulated
a radical doctrine of political obligation which held that moral
authority had been forfeit by all existing political and ecclesiastical
institutions. The three leaders at some point in 1646–7 declared
the social contract null and void and the nation returned to a
state of nature.[106] What was needed was a new social contract, an
Agreement of all the People, to put all men under a new, just
and accountable government. This was heady stuff, movingly and

104. Capp, *Fifth Monarchy Men, passim*; C.H. Firth, *The Last Years of the Protectorate* (2 vols., London, Longmans Green, 1909) II, 208–18. While only twenty took part, over 4,700 Quakers were arrested in the wake of the rising.
105. C. Hill (ed.), *Gerrard Winstanley: The Law of Freedom and Other Writings* (Harmondsworth, Penguin, 1973), pp. 26–31; K. Thomas, 'Another Digger Broadside', *Past and Present*, XLII (1969), 57–68; J. Walter, 'The Poor Man's Friend and the Gentleman's Plague' (forthcoming).
106. For example, see J. Lilburne, *Jonah's Cry form the Whale's Belly* (London, 1647); R. Overton, *Rash Oaths Unwarrantable* (London, 1647); W. Walwyn, *Outcryes of the Oppressed Citizens* (London, 1647).

extensively canvassed in several hundred tracts, and there was some ability to gather together thousands of supporters and a penumbra of sympathizers willing to petition and to lobby parliament.[107] In London, much of the activity seems to have been organized through (until 1649) sympathetic Baptist churches, although on occasion they canvassed through *ad hoc* and ephemeral committees in the wards of the city.[108] But they never appear to have contemplated raising their supporters in armed insurrections; their 'crowds' above all others seem to have been disciplined and orderly; and even their campaigns of civil disobedience may have been limited to encouragement of those who obstructed the collectors of the excise.[109] For the critical periods of mid- to late 1647 and late 1648 there is no indication that they appealed to the rank and file against the officers, rather than attempting to persuade both of the justice of their programme. They called upon the rank and file to disarm the Grandees in 1649, but they did not explain how they should do so; the agitators had long since lost their power; and there is little evidence that either the so-called Ware mutiny (which was not a mutiny) or the Burford mutiny (which was a mutiny but one disowned by Leveller leaders) were attempts to overthrow the authority of the officers, let alone of the state.[110] There was certainly a rhetoric of violence at times, but the principal thrust of all the leaders (and so unstructured a movement depended upon the decisions of the handful of leaders) was to emphasize 'moral force' rather than 'physical force'. They believed in the self-evident justice of their cause, and assumed that it would capture the hearts and minds of all whose attention could be attracted. There was a potentiality for violence in Leveller determination, but it was never realized. The only exception to this general point is the involvement of Lilburne and Wildman in the fenland disturbances in and around the Isle of Axholme in the early 1650s. Lilburne was certainly not averse to breaking the heads or burning the houses of hapless foreign settlers on drained fen. But *pace* Professor Holmes, their role remains

107. The best of many books remains J. Frank, *The Levellers* (Cambridge, Mass., Harvard University Press, 1958); G.E. Aylmer, *The Levellers in the English Revolution* (London, Thames and Hudson, 1975) is an excellent introduction and collection of key texts.
108. M. Tolmie, *The Triumph of the Saints* (CUP, 1977), pp. 138–55, 169–72, 181–4; N. Carlin, 'Leveller Organisation in London', *Historical Journal*, XXVII (1984), 955–60.
109. See e.g. J. Lilburne, *England's Birthright Justified* (London, 1645).
110. M. Kishlansky, 'What Happened at Ware?' *Historical Journal*, XXV (1982), 827–40, sorts out that episode. The traditional view of the Burford mutiny was challenged in a paper by Brian Manning at a seminar in Cambridge in 1980.

mysterious. The fenmen may have paid (and paid lavishly) for the expertise of the Levellers in taking on the enclosers and the law courts, but the ex-Leveller leaders appear neither to have used their presence in Axholme to organize a rural campaign for the Agreement of the People, nor to raise the whole of the fens, and their lasting contribution to the shaping of fenmen's understanding of their plights appears, on present evidence, to be very slight.[111]

Because their organization was ephemeral, the disillusion and disarray of the leadership in 1649 led to the evaporation of the 'Levellers' as a visible force. Unlike revolutionary movements in sixteenth-century Europe, they never evolved a cellular structure that could take on a will of its own. So far as our present state of knowledge allows us to determine, the Levellers made little impact beyond London, except in small patches, notably in the Home Counties, and where army garrisons acted as carriers to separatist congregations. It would seem that they failed to make headway in the countryside. Perhaps they never found a way of making their tracts available there; perhaps countervailing propaganda inoculated their natural constituency against their ideas; perhaps they failed adequately to integrate their agrarian programme into their political and religious eschatologies, and into their moving vision of restored human dignity. Their pamphlets do make reference to enclosure, but they never give this important issue the attention it deserved if they were to have hopes of mobilizing the rural poor.[112]

The Levellers were a phenomenon of the late 1640s. Although their name and some of their ideas flickered on through the 1650s, it was then much more as a bogey, a phantom menace, than as an actual force. However, the most substantial and, as it turned out, the most enduring of the sects, the Quakers, only emerged in 1652–3. Although, like the other sects (other than the Baptists), their membership was amorphous, casual, it has been plausibly suggested that there were about 40,000 active Quakers by 1660. Once more their ideas were more subversive than their actions, but there was nothing quietist about the early Quaker leaders. Their calculated disrespect for rank and degree, their disturbance of the worship of 'steeple houses' and of the preaching of 'hireling priests', their encouragement of tithe-

---

111. Lindley, ch. 6; C. Holmes, *Seventeenth Century Lincolnshire* (Lincoln, History of Lincoln Committee, 1980), pp. 198–9, 210–3; PRO SP 18/37/11; Holmes, in Fletcher and Stevenson (eds.), *Order and Disorder*, pp. 166–95.
112. Above, pp. 352–5; BL, Stowe MS 189, fols. 52–5; C. Hill, *The World Turned Upside Down* (London, Temple Smith, 1972), p. 96.

strikes aroused fear and bewilderment. Among orthodox puritans, their dethronement of scripture and proclamation of the universality of grace created bitterness and resentment. But they did not burn down steeple houses, assault hireling priests, organize themselves nationally either in self-defence or to confront the Commonwealth. In fact they were more the victims of violence than the source of it. They were prosecuted under a wide variety of statutes, notably the late Elizabethan vagrancy laws and (ironically) under Marian legislation against field conventicles.[113] But many individual Quakers were set upon and beaten up and some of their larger meetings were broken up by angry crowds, as in Bristol by armed apprentices in 1654.[114] As James Powell told Secretary of State Thurloe on 24 February 1655:

> The other cause [of tension] is the comeinge of the Quakers, who with their franticke doctrines have made such an impression on the mindes of the people of this cittie and places adjacent that it is wonderfull to imagin, and hath also made such a rent in all societies and relations, which, with a publique afront offered to ministers and magistrates, hath caused a devision . . . and consequently many broyles and affronts; these quakers being countenanced by the officers of the garrison . . .[115]

Nothing illustrates better the principal theme of this paper: if we must beware of exaggerating the scale of disorder, we must also beware of underestimating how the fear of disorder filled the minds and affected the actions of those in authority. By 1659, the Quakers had become, in Barry Reay's words, 'the apotheosis of the ecclesiastical and social upheaval that was anathema to the provincial traditionalists who hearkened back to the old order.'[116]

The regimes of the 1650s survived because they had the perceived power to maintain order. Disheartened, divided, unconfident, the royalists licked their wounds and sought to restore their shattered finances. The lesson of the Penruddock rising was that thousands of royalists could have foreknowledge of a royalist rebellion without disclosing it to the authorities, but only a few hundred would take to arms. Royalist plotters in the 1650s made no effort to harness social and economic ills as part of a broad insurgency.[117] But such

113. Reay, 'Early Quaker Activity', ch. 3.
114. Reece, 'Military Presence', p. 152.
115. Birch (ed.), *Thurloe State Papers*, III, 170
116. B. Reay, 'The Quakers, 1659 and the Restoration of the Monarchy', *History*, LXIII (1978), 212–13.
117. D.E. Underdown, *Royalist Conspiracy in England* (New Haven, Yale University Press, 1962); P. Hardacre, *The Royalists in the Puritan Revolution* (The Hague, Nijhoff, 1955); A. Woolrych, *Penruddock's Rising* (Historical Association Pamphlet G. 29).

acceptance of the Commonwealth and Protectorate *de facto* rested upon a perception of the unity and purpose of the army. In 1659 army unity crumbled. This was in part due to the failure of the late Protectorate to keep expenditure under control: for the first time since 1641–9 army pay was falling seriously into arrears creating indiscipline and rank-and-file restiveness.[118] But it was also due to a bankruptcy of ideas once Richard Cromwell had fallen. From May 1659–60, there was an inexorable withdrawal of cooperation by the gentry as JPs, commissioners, etc. With taxes unpaid and orders from Whitehall unheeded, government fell to pieces. Yet still, in the vacuum of power in the winter of 1659–60, there was astonishingly little disorder. Booth's rising was on a bigger scale than Penruddock's but it was still localized and quickly snuffed out by Lambert. In London, apprentices 'did very much affront the soulders as they went up and down the street'[119] and greeted a proclamation on 5 December by pelting the soldiers accompanying the serjeant-at-arms with tiles and lumps of ice.[120]

Yet again, however, the actual disorder and the perceived imminence of the total collapse of order are quite different. The political vacuum, the yearning for a restoration of 'the old parliament and a new king' tantalizingly just out of reach, the machinations of a divided and mean army leadership, all made for a total sense of insecurity. In 1640–2 this sense of dread, of the overturning of the natural order, led to the widespread 'catholic' panics and fears. There was no 'papist' conspiracy to slaughter protestants in their beds, despite all the apprehensions of the gentry and others. In 1659–60 there was a precisely similar Quaker panic. Across the country there were rumours of huge marauding bands of Quakers and fears of a God punishing the nation by allowing England 'to be transformed into a Munster'.[121] A central feature of Booth's rising was his proclamation that he was organizing a pre-emptive strike against Quakers and Anabaptists.[122] As Barry Reay says, 'The king came back on the crest of a wave of reaction against the "immense and boundless liberty" of 1659.'[123]

---

118. Reece, 'Army Presence', pp. 45–8.
119. W.L. Sachse (ed.), 'The Diurnall of Thomas Rugg' (Camden Society, 3rd series, XCI, 1961), 13, 16, 34–5.
120. A. Woolrych, introduction to R.W. Ayres (ed.), *The Complete Prose Works of John Milton*, (8 vols., 1955–82), VII, 145.
121. Reay, *History*, LXII (1978), 205.
122. Ibid., pp. 198–201, 206–9; 'The Life of Adam Martindale' (Chetham Society, IV, 1845), 135–9.
123. Reay, *History*, LXIII (1978) 212.

This essay should not be read as arguing that the English Revolution produced little disorder. We are concerned only to suggest that a number of easy assumptions have been made by many scholars, and a number of false claims made. As we said at the outset, the disappearance of familiar sources, and their problematical replacement by new types of evidence makes the whole question a treacherous one. No two scholars can claim to have looked at more than a fragment of the sources, certainly not in the light of the conceptual framework developed here. No careful, analytical studies have been attempted of landlord–tenant relations in the wake of the abolition of the prerogative courts and the humiliating sequestration of a quarter of the landlords; of the nature and extent of tithe disputes; of the impact of military service and discipline on one in five of the adult male population; and many similar questions. In an overambitious and doubtless overschematic essay, we have attempted to record our impressions based on independent research which has led us to look at different aspects of these problems from very different angles and for different regions.

But if the violence of civil war led on to an uneasy but far less violent peace, there was no easy return to 'normality'. If scholars have assumed too readily that the English Revolution saw a collapse of order, it is because they have believed the testimony of the governors who were caught up in it. Christopher Hill has rebuked historians of order for falling for the 'illusion of the epoch . . . accepting the standards of the articulate and uncensored classes as though they represented "truth"'.[124] It is a warning which historians of disorder must also beware. We have seen that there were good reasons why contemporaries persuaded themselves that they lived on the brink of anarchy, in the face of a disintegrating social and legal order. Back in 1641, Sir Thomas Aston wrote that he

> looked upon the nobilitie and gentry of this Isle . . . situate as the Low Countries, in a flat, under the banks and bounds of the Lawes, secured from that ocean, the Vulgar, which by the breach of those bounds would quickly overwhelme us, and deface all distinctions of degrees and persons.[125]

The political elite was unsure of itself, unbelieving in the strength of ubiquitous and formalized arbitration procedures, unrecognizing the decline of public violence, unaware how deeply (though not

124. C. Hill in a review article in *Analytical and Enumerative Bibliography*, IV (1980), 270.
125. Sir Thomas Aston, *A Remonstrance Against Presbytery* (London, 1641), sig. A13.

universally) ideologies of acquiesence and order had penetrated. Over the next decade they saw most of the landmarks of an ordered society destroyed: monarchy, House of Lords, the *ecclesia anglicana*. It seemed inconceivable that there would not be a descent into chaos. Their preachers anticipated it; their newspapers reported manifestations of disorder (but not of order). Minorities whose rhetoric and inspiration was indeed subversive talked openly about their dreams. Men steeped in classical literature knew that great empires could fall to the vandals; men steeped in the Old Testament knew that God's chosen people were not only led to the land of Canaan but were also made bondmen in Egypt, made captive in Babylon, scattered to the corners of the earth. Such fears prospered, even in the 1650s when Oliver Cromwell, seeing himself as a 'good constable set to keep the peace of the parish',[126] maintained an order more abrasive than, but as effective as, that of the 1630s.

The 'moral panic' of political elites was, in the event, one of the most enduring legacies of the Revolution. It is a generalization worth pondering that the later a memoir of the Revolution was written by someone living through it, the greater its memory of the disorders. Just as Sir John Oglander, Richard Baxter, Edward Hyde, Denzil Holles retrospectively got it wrong when they spoke of those who ruled as being drawn from the dregs of the people, so they remembered in exaggerated fashion their own anxieties and terrors as the familiar landmarks of their ordered universe were knocked away. Fear of impending anarchy made them give glum recognition to the Interregnum as *de facto* government forestalling chaos, and later inhibited them from a return to arms against their kings and encouraged them to vindictive repression of groups who disturbed their peace of mind. There was disorder in revolutionary England. But there was less than contemporaries anticipated and less than they led themselves and us to believe to have taken place.

126. A phrase from Oliver Cromwell's speech of 13 April 1657; T. Carlyle (ed.), *Letters and Speeches of Oliver Cromwell*, III (1871), 248.

CHAPTER NINETEEN

A Glorious Resolution?[1]

I

Thinking afresh about the political and religious ethos of the period from the 1670s to the 1690s, the period of Locke's major political and religious writings, I was struck again by the basic continuity of seventeenth-century English politics and the discontinuity of seventeenth-century English religion. The crises of 1678–81 and 1688–9, beneath their particularities, are variations on the themes of early Stuart politics; whereas the religious issues see a new tune counterpointed above the familiar ground base of anti-popery.

Reading Locke again, what struck me was a precisely parallel point. Here was Aristotle, as filtered through Hooker, but with Locke asking the questions about the limits of obligation that Hooker had not had to ask himself and tease out of his thinking. Here was a clear view that royal authority must be exercised in ways defined by, and redefinable by, Parliament à la Parker, but with none of Parker's naïveté about the inability of Parliament to err. Here was the Levellers' sense of the space, physical, mental, spiritual that each person had, of (natural) right, to explore and to develop his or her own worldly possessions, mind and conscience. As with the Levellers (especially Overton), we find Locke developing a sense of every human life being held as a leasehold from God.[2] One can even see in both a reaction against the

---

1. This paper began life as a paper given to the Joseph Cassassa Conference at Loyola Marymount University in Los Angeles in 1988, on the theme of the Legacy of John Locke. My brief was to examine the historical context within which his political thought was formed. It is not supposed to be a study of Locke himself. In preparing it for publication, I have incorporated material from the excellent commentary by Professor Norma Landau. I also record my gratitude to Colin Davis and Jonathan Scott for their firm advice on drafts of this paper.
2. J. Tully, *A Discourse on Property* (1980), pp. 35–8, 167–70 and *passim*. Cf. R. Tuck, *Natural Rights Theories Before Locke* (1979), pp. 149–50, 154–5, 172–3.

authoritarianism of Renaissance church and state, the reflex against
the claims of government (parliaments as much as princes and priests)
to omnicompetence and to a duty of Regiment – the imposition of
obedience to God's law on an unregenerate. In what follows, I want
to explore two themes: first and more briefly, how Locke articulates
a second-generation commitment to religious liberty; secondly, and
more fully, the search for a new equilibrium in seventeenth-century
government, the restoration of a lost harmony of interest between
governors and governed. I shall focus on the history of Parliament
in the sixteenth and seventeenth centuries, but will seek to relate
that history to broader changes in English politics and religion.
I will compare the failure of the Restoration to reestablish a lost
equilibrium with the eventual success of the 1688 settlement. In some
senses at least, my title suggests, the Glorious Revolution proved to
be a Glorious Resolution.

II

I can still remember how stunned I was years ago when, already
someone immersed in the 1640s and 1650s. I read Locke's *Letters
Concerning Toleration*. I entered a world remote indeed from that of
that other proponent of religious freedom, Oliver Cromwell. What
most stunned me was Locke's definition of a Church:[3]

> A Church, then, I take to be a voluntary society of men, joining
> themselves together of their own accord in order to the public worship-
> ping of God in such a manner as they judge acceptable to him, and
> effectual to the salvation of their souls.

At one level (as when he argues that the state should no more concern
itself with when individuals sit or kneel in church than it does when
they are at home), he is saying that worship is what consenting
adults get up to in private, and is no concern of the state. It is
something unthreatening, which need not impinge upon, or have
implications for, those not directly involved. This is startling enough.
But at another level, he is specifically talking about 'public' worship
and asserting that not everything that is *public* is the concern of the
state: that there may be a plurality of 'publics'. This was to prove
a powerful solvent of conventions of political argument grounded
on organic analogy. This is not, of course, what the champions of
toleration during the Revolution had in mind. We must remember
that only a tiny proportion of the nation had considered religious

---

3. J. Locke, *A Letter Concerning Toleration*, J.W. Gough (Ed) (3rd edn., 1966), p. 131.

toleration as an option, let alone a desirable option, before 1646. Neither the New England Fathers nor those who took up arms against Charles I in 1642 believed in religious pluralism. They simply believed in forms of religious authoritarianism different from that currently enforced upon them.

Perhaps the most extraordinary development of the 1640s and 1650s is how a civil war that began as a struggle between two authoritarianisms became a revolution for religious liberty. This is what Cromwell meant when he said that 'religion was not the thing first contended for, but God hath brought it to that issue at last'.[4] But the dynamics of the trek towards that belief in religious freedom are very different from the cool rationalism of Lockeian ecclesiology. For Cromwell, above all, religious toleration was a means to effect a deeper and elusive unity which was part of his fierce vision of England as the new Elect Nation being led on by God to a new Promised Land.[5] Man, fallen, depraved – morally and intellectually – could achieve nothing in this world, and could stake no claim to salvation in the next, by himself. All existing human institutions were 'dross and dung in comparison with Christ'.[6] Cromwell was not, in his own words, 'wedded and glued to forms of government'.[7] Just as the civil war had discredited monarchy, existing parliamentary forms and ancient constitutionalism, so no one group of Christians could claim a monopoly on the Truth. Instead Cromwell identified 'the various forms of godliness in this nation',[8] ranging from ex-bishops like James Ussher to the Quaker George Fox – each of whom had been vouchsafed a fragment of God's truth. Cromwell saw his task as to create a context within which each of the godly could contribute to the building of a mosaic of truth: a new unity in the True Church of Christ. Such adaptations of Old Testament eschatology, God working through his people to create his Temple here on earth, is characteristic of mid-seventeenth-century Enthusiasm. In many ways, Cromwell's

---

4. T. Carlyle (rev. S.C. Lomas), *The Letters and Speeches of Oliver Cromwell* (3 vols., 1895), II, 417.
5. See the innumerable biographies of Cromwell for this theme; but see especially two articles by A.B. Worden: 'Toleration and the Cromwellian Protectorate', in W. Sheils (ed.), *Studies in Church History*, 21 (1984), 199–233; and 'Providence and Oliver Cromwell', *Past and Present*, 109 (1986). Also W.M. Lamont, 'Pamphleteering, the Protestant Consensus and the English Revolution', in R. Richardson and G.M. Ridden (eds.), *Freedom and the English Revolution* (Manchester, 1986), pp. 72–92.
6. Carlyle/Lomas, *Cromwell*, I, 373.
7. Ibid., I, 362.
8. Ibid., II, 538.

view of the godly magistrate and of his role is conventionally Calvinist in its notions of Election, of magisterial Regiment and of God's intrusive providentialism. It is not characteristic of the late seventeenth-century pleas for toleration of which Locke is an exemplar.

Locke is the product of what Robert Beddard has called the emancipation of dissent:[9] the abandonment by the godly of the itch to impose what has been vouchsafed to them as the Will of God for all Men. Nothing was so much at a discount in the Restoration as enthusiasm, as zeal. The sheer despair of the godly at the fact of the Restoration, the shattering experience of seeing a God who through His providences had 'blasted the very title of king' as well as the office, permitting the return of all that which he had destroyed and lain in the dust',[10] induced a psychological and intellectual quietism. It was not possible to perfect or to improve men and women by perfecting or improving human institutions; in this broken and fallen world, Man could only come to God through building a temple of Grace within himself. Dissenters gathered to share an experience of personal spiritual growth, not to experience the warmth of the spiritual greenhouse before being disseminated as germinated seed in a barren landscape.[11]

The end of chiliasm, the moral imperative upon the godly to impose order upon the ungodly, was based partly upon the 'experience of defeat' of which Christopher Hill has movingly written.[12] But it is also grounded upon a fundamental shift in theological views. Whatever stance one takes in the scholarly debate about the rise of 'Arminianism' in the early seventeenth century, one thing is plain: bitter disputes about Grace take place within the context of a firm commitment on all sides to a Pauline-Augustinian view of Man. Laud and his friends in the Durham House Group were as persuaded as were their critics of the inability of men and women, by *their own*

9. R. Beddard, 'Vincent Alsop and the Emancipation of Restoration Dissent', *Jnl. Eccl. Hist.* XXIV (1973).
10. Carlyle/Lomas, *Cromwell*, III, 71.
11. The best general works on Restoration Dissent remain G.R. Cragg, *Puritanism in the Age of the Great Persecution* (Cambridge, 1957); M.R. Watts, *The Dissenters* (Oxford, 1978); C.G. Bolam (ed.), *The English Presbyterians* (1968); N. Keeble, *The Literary Culture of Non-Conformity in Restoration England* (Leicester, 1987). (Since I wrote this I have come to realize how wrong-headed it is to turn Locke into a Dissenter. But the point retains diluted force even if we see him as amongst those claiming a personal space within a capacious church.)
12. C. Hill, *The Experience of Defeat* (1984); also C. Hill, *Some Intellectual Consequences of the English Revolution* (1978), esp. pp. 53–74.

efforts, to rescue themselves from the depravity of their nature. They may have differed about whether salvation came by the action of God, in choosing to redeem some men and women despite their nature, or through the grace of the sacraments and through obedience to the teachings of the Church; but they retained a profoundly pessimistic view of Man.[13] Outside clerical and university circles, it is true, some statesmen operated on more politique principles grounded upon a neo-stoic philosophy: but theirs was a lack of persecuting spirit based not in the confidence that each human creature was capable of rational conduct and care of his or her own conscience, but rather on scepticism about the capacity of any church to be sufficiently confident about more than a few basic axioms of Christianity to dictate to others: and their concerns were latitudinarian rather than tolerationist.[14] Both they and that much smaller number of speculative minds who did espouse the cause of liberty of conscience more completely, of whom Milton and Viscount Say and Sele[15] come most readily to mind, were much more convinced of the intellectual capacity of a minority of trained and leisured minds, than by a more general rational capacity in all men. Locke's *Letters Concerning Toleration* reflect a new but widespread confidence in human nature, a selective memory of the responsible uses of religious freedom (in Locke's case clearly strengthened by his visit to Cleves in the mid 1660s and exile in Holland in the 1680s),[16] a forgetfulness of how liberty had run to license in the Interregnum, and a confidence in a world whose rules were being laid bare by scientific enquiry. As Man became less vulnerable to and incomprehending of the forces of nature, so he needed less regimentation by churches and

13. There is a massive literature on this, of which the following are fundamental: N.R.N. Tyacke, *Anti-Calvinists* (Oxford, 1987); P. Lake, 'Calvinism and the English Church, 1570–1635', *Past and Present*, 114 (1987); P. White, 'The Rise of Arminianism Reconsidered', *Past and Present*, 101 (1983); H.R. Trevor-Roper, 'William Laud' in his book of essays, *Puritans, Anglicans and Catholics* (1987), pp. 40–114. J.S. Coolidge, *The Pauline Renaissance in England* (Oxford, 1970), is an important and little-cited book on this aspect of the subject.
14. This too requires a bibliographical essay rather than a footnote. I find G. Oestreich, *Neostoicism and the Early Modern State* (Cambridge, 1982) and H.R. Trevor-Roper's essay on 'Great Tew' in *Puritans, Anglicans and Catholics*, pp. 166–230, especially illuminating.
15. The pertinent scholarship on Milton is boundless. I find accounts that stress his humanism rather than his puritanism, his elitism more than his populism, his basic consistency rather than his inconsistency the more persuasive. There is no good study of Viscount Saye and Sele, but his elitist ideas are clearly laid out in *Two Speeches of the Right Honourable William, Lord Viscount Say and Sele* (1641).
16. For which see R. Ashcraft, *Revolutionary Politics and Locke's Two Treatises of Government* (Princeton, N.J., 1986), pp. 92–101.

states. When Locke argued that 'the Commonwealth seems to me to be a society of men constituted only for the procuring, preserving, and advancing their own civil interests',[17] he was articulating a dis-aggregation or dis-integration of religion and politics that has been a dominant trait in English thought ever since.

III

It is often thought that the document that best sums up the Restoration Settlement of 1660 is the King's Declaration from Breda.[18] I would dissent from that view. That Declaration is no more than a parroting back to Monck of a message he had sent to Charles via Sir John Grenville.[19] Within weeks, Monck's primacy was broken. I would propose that any discussion of the Restoration should begin from consideration of the Declaration which the Convention Parliament found itself – to its own amazement – issuing, *nemine contradicente*, on 8 May 1660:[20]

> It can no way be doubted but that His Majesty's right and title to this Crown and Kingdom is and was every way completed by the death of his most royal father of blessed memory, without the ceremony or solemnity of a proclamation.

The two Houses (the Commons largely, and the Lords at this stage wholly, made up of those who had fought against Charles I or collaborated with Cromwell), had been expecting to recall Charles II on terms derived from the Treaty of Newport which his father had accepted on the eve of the Army coup that led on to his trial and execution. It is probable that what underlay the unanticipated and unconditional restoration of Charles II was first and foremost a yearning for the stability represented by forms of government rooted in history. The debates of 1657 in which Cromwell was offered the Crown had demonstrated a revival of belief in forms of government 'known to the laws'.[21] It is not that the proponents of Cromwellian monarchy had forgotten how difficult it had proved to bind Charles I to acknowledge and to abide by 'the rule of law', and to restrain him by the sheet anchors of precedent and custom. But

17. J. Locke, *A Letter Concerning Toleration*, p. 128.
18. S.R. Gardiner, *Constitutional Documents of the Puritan Revolution* (3rd edn., Oxford, 1906), pp. 465–7.
19. R. Hutton, *The Restoration* (Oxford, 1984), pp. 106–9.
20. *Commons Journal* (henceforth *CJ*), VIII, 16.
21. For the kingship debates and the background, see C.H. Firth, 'Cromwell and the Crown', *EHR*, 17 (1902), 429–42, 18 (1903), 52–80. My views are explored in 'King Oliver?', *Cromwelliana* (1983).

they recognized the even greater failure of attempts to prevent abuses of power by governments that were grounded in, and legitimized by, appeals to the present (i.e. consent) or to the future (that God was guiding his new Elect Nation, the English, towards a new Promised Land, and that anything done by the Elect to bring closer the attainment of God's will was thereby justified). The latter was Cromwell's philosophy. The offer of the crown in 1657 reflected a recognition that not even Charles I had ever behaved as arbitrarily as the Lord Protector had in establishing the regime of the major generals, in levying decimation tax without parliamentary assent,[22] in imprisoning Cony and his lawyers[23] and preventing a trial of the issues. Nor had pre-war parliaments ever acted as the second Protectorate Parliament had done in proceeding to order the physical mutilation of James Nayler by an order neither legislative nor judicial in character.[24] The doomed Interregnum search for religious liberty and regiment had two lasting consequences. One was to deliver a grievous blow to this-world millenarianism, to politics unrestrained by Hope rather than restrained by Law; and the other was that it caused Englishmen to lose faith in paper constitutions and in shuffling sovereign power between the executive and legislative branches of government. Indeed, the institution of Parliament came out of the mid-century crisis severely blighted. The assumption of 1641–2 (still shared by a majority of the king's opponents in 1647–8) that the way to restrain untrustworthy kings was to increase the power and authority of the two Houses had been shaken by widespread experience of parliamentary tyranny.

Tudor distaste for overmighty subjects gave way to a new distaste for overmighty parliaments. There arose a perception shared by those who had gone to war to preserve rather than to extend liberties and by those in the army and the sects who experienced the arbitrariness of a parliament which had to lurch from one expedient to another in order to sustain the war effort, of assemblies more out-of-control than the king had been in the 1630s. Hence the demands from the 'Country', from the army and from the Levellers that parliaments sit for maximum as well as minimum terms; for a rigid separation

22. S.R. Gardiner, *History of the Commonwealth and Protectorate* (4 vols., 1903), III, ch. 40 and IV, ch. 42; and in C.H. Firth, *The Last Years of the Protectorate* (2 vols., Oxford, 1909), I, chs. 4–5.
23. There is a brief analysis in most Cromwell biographies, but no full study. The clearest introduction is probably D. Hirst, *Authority and Conflict* (1985), p. 334.
24. Firth, *Last Years*, I, 84–106; F. Wilson and T. Merli, 'Nayler's Case and the Dilemmas of the Protectorate', *Univ. of Birmingham Historical Journal*, 10 (1965–6); W.G. Bittle, *James Nayler, 1618–1660* (1986), chs. 5–6.

A Glorious Resolution?

of powers; and for restrictions on the scope of statute. Mechanisms were sought to prevent legislation against the natural rights of those whom parliaments represented.[25] That bedrock of country gentry who dominated the Convention Parliament of 1660 had no intention of enhancing the authority of the Houses as a check and balance on the Crown, for that would be merely to shuffle the potential for tyranny from one arm of the body politic to the other.

Since the natural rights theorists of the mid-century, left, like so many Cheshire cats, a smile behind them, Restoration political thinkers had to define what natural rights might be and how on earth they were to be protected. The problem for the future was no longer how to place limits on royal discretionary power (− prerogative) but on the omnicompetence of statute. In a sense the futility of the extreme constitutional contrivances of the Harringtonians made the problem even harder to solve, driving Locke among others into a camouflaged but ultimately traditional resistance theory.

It is perhaps worth mentioning here that while Locke – at least by the late 1670s – did not share this view in its entirety, he did not shed it in its entirety either. In his scheme of things, legislatures were to be free from executive manipulation and control, and were indeed solely responsible for the form and nature of the executive arm of government. But parliaments were not to engage directly in the tasks of executing and enforcing law. Locke's principle of the separation of powers did cut both ways.

He argued that there was 'no need that the legislative should be always in being' and that 'it may be too great a temptation to human frailty apt to grasp at power for the same persons who have the power of making laws to have also in their hands the power to execute them, whereby they might exempt themselves from obedience to the laws they make.' But he also argues that when the people 'shall find the Legislative act contrary to the trust reposed in them . . . the trust must necessarily be forfeit. . . . The community perpetually retains a supreme power of saving themselves from the attempts and designs of any body, even of the legislators.[26]

25. J.S. Morrill, *The Revolt of the Provinces* (1976), ch. 2; R. Ashton, 'From Cavalier to Roundhead Tyranny' in J.S. Morrill (ed.), *Reactions to the English Civil War* (1983); B.S. Manning, *The English People and the English Revolution* (1976), ch. 10. All the Agreements of the People restricted the lives of parliaments and contained 'reservation', areas within which parliaments could not legislate. There are echoes of these proposals in most planned paper constitutions of the Interregnum.
26. J. Locke, *Second Treatise*, para. 143 and para. 149 (and cf. para. 153). See also the discussion in R. Ashcraft, *Locke's Two Treatises on Government* (1987), pp. 182–7, and in Ashcraft, *Revolutionary Politics*, esp. pp. 304–9.

Set unattributed, as a gobbet, this would surely be identified as from a Leveller tract.

At first sight the Declaration of 8 May 1660 was an act of prostration before divine-right monarchy. Charles II was said to have been king since the moment his father's head was parted from his shoulders, and parliament could neither prevent his son's accession nor claim any authority in making good his title. One very firm demonstration of this was the dating of the reign from 30 January 1649, making 1660 Charles II's 12th regnal year. Charles II rapidly moved to reinforce the image of himself as the divinely-appointed and instituted king, touching for the Evil more than any of his predecessors, except, possibly, Henry VI. More generally, he set out jealously to guard – if only occasionally to deploy – those royal prerogatives that Charles I had failed to misuse and which therefore the Long Parliament had not thought fit to abrogate – the suspending and dispensing powers, the pardon and, above all, the royal supremacy in matters ecclesiastical.[27]

The historical-rootedness of the Restoration was no capitulation to royal absolutism. The presumption was that the coral reef of precedent, custom and statute that had grown up to define the powers of the Crown would protect the liberties of the subject more than any alternative solution could. Thus, while every ordinance enacted since 1642 (lacking the royal assent) was null and void, and while it was a source of reassurance that anomalies such as peculiar jurisdictions should be restored, nonetheless the reform legislation of 1641 (which had received the royal assent) was in force, and the context within which Charles II was to govern would be very different from the one which had prevailed in the 1630s. Charles II had no conciliar courts to enforce his will; he had none of the discretionary powers that his father had abused in order to enhance his revenues; and the Privy Council itself lost its institutional muscle. The Tudor Council, Sir Geoffrey Elton has taught us, was unique among Renaissance royal councils in that it was not simply a deliberative, advisory body: it did things.[28] The 1641 reforms stripped it of its judicial power and left it

27. P. Birdsall, '"Non-Obstante": a study of the Dispensing Power', in *Essays in History and Political Science in Honor of Charles Hamilton McIlwain* [no editor given] (Cambridge, Mass., 1936); A.F. Havighurst, 'Charles II and the Judiciary', *Law Quarterly Review*, 66 (1950), 62–78, 229–52; A.F. Havighurst, 'James II and the Twelve Men in scarlet', *Law Quarterly Review*, 69 (1953), 522–46.
28. G.R. Elton, *The Tudor Constitution* (2nd edn., Cambridge, 1982), ch. 8; G.R. Elton, *Studies in Tudor and Stuart Politics and Government* (3 vols., Cambridge, 1974–83), II, chs. 21, 22; III, chs. 331, 34, 35.

less capable of policing, or even monitoring, what local governors got up to.[29]

Historical-rootedness was then, to some extent, a king-yoking policy. And as such this historical-rootedness was to prove a formidable bulwark against the intellectual assaults of Charles's critics in the 1670s; and although it was breached by the events of 1688, it was to afford some shelter to many for at least another generation. But the Restoration settlement was also erected upon two other pillars which were to prove shakier and more problematical. The first was the victory of the gentry-out-of-parliament; and the other was the incomplete drive for political and religious comprehension, a settlement designed to incorporate and to offer power-sharing to all those groups willing to accept the fact of the Restoration.

The Restoration was predicated upon a massive decentralization of power.[30] In the shaping of the financial settlement, in the militia acts, in the Corporation Act, and in the ecclesiastical settlement, the gentry-in-parliament devolved upon themselves in the localities largely unsupervised responsibility for the implementation of policy. Compared with the period 1540–1640, the Crown in the 1660s possessed little capacity to monitor or to enforce – or to arbitrate disputes in relation to – excise, hearth tax, and assessment;[31] the Militia Acts combined unparalleled concessions to the Crown with regard to the right to raise, train and deploy the militia, with equally unparallelled decentralization of its day-to-day control and administration.[32] The Crown employed country gentlemen to undertake, largely unsupervised, unparallelled purges of the boroughs and to intrude their own interests. Never had the boroughs been so

---

29. For the reforms, see *Statutes of the Realm*, V, 110–2 (16 Car. I, cap. 10); for the effects, E.R. Turner, *The Privy Council of England* (1927) remains fundamental. See also J.R. Jones, *The Restored Monarchy* (1981), chs. 3–4.
30. This next section contradicts some of the arguments of A. Fletcher, *Reform in the Provinces* (New Haven, 1986), itself heavily influenced by A. Coleby, *Central Government and the Provinces: Hampshire 1649–1688* (Cambridge, 1987). This latter is surely right to emphasize the considerable trend towards centralization in the 1670s and 1680s. In my judgement, however, it misrepresents the situation in the early Restoration.
31. Much of the story can be traced through C.D. Chandaman, *English Public Revenues, 1660–1689* (Oxford, 1975). Crucial to an understanding of how the state was able to tax more effectively will be M.J. Braddick, *The Roots of the Tax State* (1993).
32. In addition to the works mentioned in note 30, and in J.R. Western, *The English Militia in the Eighteenth Century* (1965), see the statutes themselves and the five speeches of Sir John Holland, *BIHR*, 28 (1955), 189–202.

comprehensively subordinated to rural elite control as in the early Restoration.[33]

Whatever the religious character of the ecclesiastical settlement,[34] we should note its extraordinary erastianism. The autonomy of the Church so striven for by Laud was destroyed utterly: High Commission, the only church court with claws, was (uniquely) abolished anew at the Restoration. Convocation ceased to meet after 1664 until after the Glorious Revolution.[35] The House of Commons built in to the Act of Uniformity that Parliament, and not the Church, had the right to determine every detail of the prescribed liturgy;[36] and nothing was so tenaciously restored as the rights of lay patrons to impropriations and other church property.[37] The major acts reshaping the Church and imposing conformity – Prynne's Bill relating to advowsons,[38] the Act of Uniformity, the Conventicle Acts and the Five Mile Act, were all to be enforced by Justices of the Peace, for the most part working singly or in pairs and without accountability.[39]

The final part of the Restoration settlement that we need to discuss is the attempt at comprehension, to share power broadly accross the political elite. In the distribution of office and favour, Charles set out – unlike Cromwell – to accommodate his former enemies more than his former friends. Almost half of the privy councillors in 1660–1 were enemies of his father, several active supporters of the Protectorate.[40] Among the royalists those who stayed at home and acquiesced under Interregnum regimes did better than those who

33. J. Miller, 'Borough Charters and the Crown in the reign of Charles II', *EHR*, 84 (1984), is an important corrective to earlier work. But the work of Patrick Higgins on the Corporation Act, nearing completion, offers important new perspectives.
34. R. Beddard, 'The Restoration Church', in Jones (ed.), *The Restored Monarchy*; R.S. Bosher, *The Making of the Restoration Settlement* (1961); I. Green, *The Re-Establishment of the Church of England* (Oxford, 1978); G.R. Abernethy, *The English Presbyterians and the Stuart Restoration* (Philadelphia, 1965); A.O. Whiteman, 'The Worcester House Declaration' in G. Nuttall and W.O. Chadwick (eds.), *From Uniformity to Unity* (1962).
35. The best account of the temporary demise of Convocation is still N. Sykes, *From Sheldon to Secker* (Cambridge, 1959), pp. 36–7.
36. See the resolution of the House of Commons in *CJ* VIII, 408.
37. This also involved the voiding of scores of sensible ordinances passed by Protectorate parliaments uniting tiny and dividing unmanageably large parishes.
38. *Statutes of the Realm*, V, 12 Car. II, cap. 17). This Act of the Convention Parliament restored ministers ejected from livings to which they had been lawfully presented by those with rightful patronage, but protected all other ministers in possession.
39. A. Fletcher, 'The Enforcement of the Conventicle Acts', in W. Sheils (ed.), *Studies in Church History*, 21 (1984), 235–46.
40. The clearest discussion is in Hutton, *The Restoration*, pp. 139–42.

had gone into exile. A clear majority of the paid civil servants of the 1650s were retained, especially in the middle ranks. More than half of the colonels in the Restoration Army and Navy and one in three of the judges had served in the 1650s.[41] About thirty per cent of all JPs had served under the Protectorate; and a further thirty per cent had identified to some extent with the parliamentarian cause in the 1640s, while distancing themselves from the Interregnum. In a majority of counties only a minority of the JPs in the early years of the Restoration had suffered for their royalism.[42] When these findings are combined with the extraordinary leniency of the Act of Indemnity and Oblivion[43] and with the final form of the land settlement that gave no relief to most ex-royalists, and possession if not title to many purchasers of Crown and Church lands,[44] the political basis of the Restoration becomes very clear. Charles II believed that it was better for him to offend his friends (who would not send him on his travels again) than his erstwhile opponents (who might do so, if sufficiently provoked).

The greatest source of weakness in the Restoration settlement was that while Charles created a comprehensive political settlement, he failed in his attempt to create a comprehensive religious settlement. His ecclesiastical patronage in the early months – at parish, capitular and episcopal levels – make his desire for such a settlement clear,[45] and on balance it seems that the Worcester House Declaration represents his true intentions for a religious settlement.[46] The terms of membership of the established Church were to be relaxed so that all but a few thousand diehards among the laity and perhaps two hundred or so of the clergy could accept it, and he intended to grant even that dissenting rump a share in the general toleration which was intended

41. H. Tomlinson, 'Financial and Administrative Developments', in Jones (ed.), *The Restored Monarchy*, pp. 24–6.
42. Full details will be set forth in a table for 15 English and four Welsh counties in J.S. Morrill, *New Oxford History of England: England 1643–1689* (forthcoming).
43. *Statutes of the Realm*, V, 226–34 (12 Car. II, cap. 11).
44. A vast literature is summarised by Hutton, *Restoration*, pp. 132–6. It should also be noted that most ex-royalist land was restored after local arbitration and again not to the satisfaction of those who had been the victims of the Acts of Sale of 1650–2. Paul Gladwish, 'Aspects of the English Revolution in the Four Shires', Cambridge PhD thesis (forthcoming), will be the first comprehensive regional study of all land transfers in this period.
45. See the discussion in Green, *Re-establishment*, pp. 37–99.
46. On this issue, I prefer the readings of Abernethy and Whiteman (note 34) to others. Accepting the central thrust of Abernethy's reading does not mean accepting all of it (for example I believe that Clarendon consistently favoured comprehension and equally consistently opposed toleration).

mainly to help the Catholic recusants of whose political loyalty he had no doubt and with whose religious beliefs he was almost certainly privately deeply sympathetic.[47]

In the event, these plans for religious comprehension collapsed.[48] In part this was because of Charles's own miscalculations; in part it was due to inexorable pressure from the Anglican gentry who, for short-term reasons, found themselves in a dominant position in the Parliament of 1661; in large measure it was due to the intransigence and inflexibility of the leading 'presbyterian' negotiators at the Savoy Conference of 1661, and in their attack on Charles's plans for toleration. Whatever the cause, the outcome was a disaster for the king and for the prospects of a stable settlement: the Act of Uniformity drove one in four of the clergy and perhaps between five and ten per cent of the laity into actual or mental dissent from the established Church. It also meant that there was a fundamental imbalance and contradiction between the basis of the political and the religious settlements. It created immense problems over the next thirty years.[49]

Locke's political thought cannot be said to have taken account of these pillars of the Restoration settlement, although he did confront (and overreact to) some of the stress fractures that resulted from the structural weakness in these pillars. This is not to belittle his achievement in the long run, but to point out that he did not address the preoccupations of his contemporaries rather than the preoccupations of his coterie in 1682–3.

The problem of historical-rootedness is confronted in only a limited way. Locke is at his best ambivalent about scriptural history (as used by Filmer and others) as a basis for political authority, and for anyone who has encountered the richness and subtlety of pre-1640 ancient constitutionalism, Locke's mythic anthropology is frankly disappointing (abeit increasingly characteristic of natural law

47. Charles's own religious position remains a matter of controversy, recent views ranging from seeing him as a precocious deist to a long-time closet Catholic. I lean towards the latter interpretation, and argued for it in a Radio 3 talk in February 1985, a version of which will appear in *England 1643–1685*.
48. Once more I prefer the reading of Abernethy, *English Presbyterians*, chs. 3–4, to the views of others.
49. This comes through clearly in several recent studies, including T. Harris, *The London Crowd in the Reign of Charles II* (Cambridge 1987) and Coleby, *Central Government*. For the legislative framework which was to create endless problems of enforcement, see P. Seaward, *The Cavalier Parliament and the reconstruction of the Ancien Regime* (Cambridge, 1989). This point was forcefully made by the late G.V. Bennett in his Birkbeck Lectures at Cambridge, sadly unpublished.

theorists). Nor does Locke address the tension of centre and locality, or recognize the crunch issue in that relationship: for to succeed on a European – let alone a world – stage the *state* had to be strengthened. How was this to be achieved without the creation of an absolutist state? And how was the absolutist state to be prevented without bossy and blinkered Parliaments hobbling external expansion? At the end of this paper I will remind readers how it *was* done. It owed nothing to Locke's thought. He does, as we will see, have things to say about the third of the pillars of the Restoration settlement – its muddled comprehensiveness – but he had more to say about the unravelling of that settlement, especially in the years after 1675 in which he wrote his major tracts.

IV

In at least two ways, the problems of the later Stuarts were different from and less stressful than those which had afflicted their immediate predecessors. They had a less intractable financial problem and needed to be less concerned with central executive regulation of the economy and society.

The financial settlement of 1660–2 was quite generous to the Crown. Provision was made for a standing income of £1.2 million a year (and indeed over the reign as a whole the average yield exceeded this sum).[50] If there were budgetary problems in the Restoration, they were caused by mild fiscal incontinence which caused far fewer problems than the stubborn fiscal constipation that beset the early Stuarts.

Furthermore, the stabilization of population levels and of prices, linked to the disappearance of grain shortages (crowned by the introduction of export bounties in 1674) and of the chronic problem of underemployment, reduced significantly the need for the Crown (or at least for ministers and the Council) to be constantly monitoring and enforcing the great body of legislation designed to ease the effects of economic and social dislocation. Just as the sixteenth century saw a general decline in royal and conciliar day-to-day monitoring of the enforcement of justice (just compare the 1470s and the 1570s, the decline of special commissions of oyer and terminer and the disappearance of the monarch leading judicial review bodies around the provinces), so the seventeenth century sees a decline of hands-on *central executive* control of the local administration and the rapid development of more passive and impassive forms of judicial review.

50. Chandaman, *Public Revenues*, ch. 6 and appendix.

From 1660 on we see what Norma Landau has called 'new uses for an old writ – the writ of *certiorari*'. In relation to the poor laws and the settlement laws for example, the Court of King's Bench accepted responsibility for hearing appeals from the orders and decisions of local government, and, if it thought fit, to quash those orders and decisions. No longer was the intervention of the Privy Council necessary to settle disputes about the activity of local government. Similarly, the development of the writ of *mandamus* allowed King's Bench to order local governors to do what was statutorily required, such as to make a poor rate.[51] By the late seventeenth century a period of institutional construction introduced as a piecemeal kind of crisis management had given way; in Landau's words, 'there were now institutions whose activities were impelled by the logic of their own structures, and instead of appeal to the Privy Council, there was now appeal against the decisions of local government under the common law.'

The Restoration Settlement was also designed to repudiate the failed values of the Puritan Revolution that had led to the collapse of the early Stuart state. We have already seen how Enthusiasm and political eschatologies (the creation of a New Jerusalem in England's green and pleasant land) was abandoned by the Crown as well as by the heirs of the Puritans. Laudian visions were as much at a discount as Cromwellian ones.

But the 1660–2 settlement had fudged other long-standing problems and they were to run as a *leitmotif* through the later as through the early seventeenth century. In my view the three central ones are: fear of popery, the nature of counsel and the freedom of Parliaments. They are at the heart of the political crises of the period 1678–89 and of the thinking of John Locke.

Between the 1580s and the 1630s anti-popery shifted from being a fear of external threat, of invasion by Spain and a linking up with the dissident, alienated, marginalized Catholic subjects of a Protestant monarch, to become a fear of a cancer in the very bowels of government.[52] It became a fear of an insidious plot

51. E.G. Henderson, *The Foundations of English Administrative Law* (Cambridge, Mass., 1963), pp. 127–159. I am deeply grateful to Norma Landau for allowing me to quote from her commentary on the original version of this paper.
52. For Elizabethan anti-popery, see C.Z. Weiner, '"The Beleaguered Isle"', *Past and Present*, 81 (1976); P. Christianson, *Reformers and Babylon* (Toronto, 1978); for the early Stuart period, G. Albion, *Charles I and the Court of Rome* (1934); C. Hibbard, *Charles I and the Popish Plot* (Chapel Hill, 1983); R. Clifton, 'Fear of Popery' in C. Russell (ed.), *The Origins of the English Civil War* (1973).

designed in Rome and the Escorial (as later at St Germain and Versailles) to infiltrate agents into the very heart of government in order to subvert it from within. This has been shown to be a crucial feature of the perceptions of those who took up arms against Charles I in 1642.[53] It is also the very core of the Whig perception of misgovernment in 1678 and, with fuller reason, in 1688.[54] It cannot be said firmly enough that the so-called[55] Exclusion Crisis is not about popery to come: it is about popery already here. It is already evident in *A Letter From a Person of Quality*, in the writing of which Locke was surely implicated in 1675.[56] By 1678 it is the dominant fear. Why else should Shaftesbury's obsessive concern in the early months of the crisis have been not with the succession but with the destruction of Danby?[57] And why else should the impeachment articles against Danby allege that he was 'popishly affected'?[58] The comment of Sir Henry Capel: 'lay popery flat and there is an end of arbitrary government'[59] is often quoted but never fully explicated. It was not just a demonstration of anti-popish venom: it draws attention to a perceived symbiosis between popery and arbitrary government. End popery and end arbitrary government. Therefore *where there is arbitrary government, there must be popery*. This solves the puzzle of Danby's fall. Here was a minister who was apparently pursuing firmly Anglican-Protestant policies at home and abroad, who was committed to budgetary equilibrium and a more friendly relationship between Crown and Parliament. And yet here also was the minister who was destroyed on a charge of promoting popery and arbitrary government. The answer is that the arbitrariness of his government

---

53. E.g. A. Fletcher, *The Outbreak of the English Civil War* (1979); J.S. Morrill, 'The Religious Context', above, ch. 3.
54. J. Miller, *Popery and Politics, 1660–1688* (Cambridge, 1973); Harris, *London Crowd*, chs. 5–6. This is especially important for its discussion of *two* anti-poperies – a Tory anti-popery that blamed the Dissenters for splitting and weakening Protestantism and letting popery grow; and Whig anti-popery that blamed the established Church for persecuting fellow-Protestants and being soft on Catholics.
55. See the two books by J. Scott: *Algernon Sidney and the English Republic* (Cambridge, 1987) and *Algernon Sidney and the Restoration Crisis* (Cambridge, 1991); and his article 'Radicalism and Restoration', *HJ*, 31 (1988).
56. See Ashcraft, *Locke's Revolutionary Politics*, pp. 120–3; K.D.H. Haley, *The First Earl of Shaftesbury* (1968), pp. 391–3.
57. Shaftesbury initially believed that the Popish Plot allegations of Oates and others had been manufactured at Court to justify the retention of the army raised on the pretext of war with France. He even sounded out the Duke of York about the prospects of an alliance to prevent the court scheme.
58. W.C. Costin and J.S. Watson, *the Law and Working of the Constitution* vol. I, *1660–1783* (Edinburgh, 1961), 181.
59. Quoted in Miller, *Popery and Politics*, p. 172.

was seen precisely in the partisan Anglicanism of his domestic policies, in an anti-French foreign policy which came to appear as no more than a screen for creating a standing army, and in his corrosion of the independence of Parliament. And because all this was experienced as arbitrary government, he *had* to be a closet papist. This is a classic example of paranoid logic. The Test Acts had flushed out and revealed some very surprising papists: but the persistence of misgovernment led all too many to believe that the worst papists were still in the woodwork. The more someone proclaimed his protestantism but acted in an arbitrary way, the more certain it was that he was at the heart of a popish conspiracy.

Following the collapse of the anti-Dutch, pro-toleration policies (Charles's preferred lines) in the early 1670s, the king gave Danby the brief of sorting out the fiscal mess left behind by the war and of giving him a quiet life.[60] If that meant following anti-French and Anglican policies, so be it. To achieve this, Danby embarked on a programme which built on one of the three pillars of the Restoration Settlement (the Divine Right of Kings, Church and gentry) but undermined the others (decentralization and political comprehension). His programme systematically built up the central government's interference in local affairs, above all efficient tax collection, which resulted in a striking financial improvement.[61] It also rested upon an ever-greater willingness to rely upon men from one background in local government: the Cavalier-Anglicans.[62] There were (minor) purges of living justices in more than half of the English shires.[63] More importantly, those JPs from old parliamentarian/Cromwellian backgrounds who died between 1675 and 1678 were replaced not by their sons and men of like mind.[64] There was an inexorable move on hand to shift the balance towards the loyalist sons of loyalist Anglican families. There was nothing on the scale of the purges of the 1680s, of course, but it was enough for powerful local groups of 'Country' and pro-Dissenting gentry to see the writing on the wall.[65] The emergence of the very phrase 'the Country Lords' at this juncture

---

60. A. Browning, *Thomas Osborne, Earl of Danby and Duke of Leeds* (3 vols., 1944–9), remains authoritative.
61. Chandaman, *Public Revenues*, ch. 6.
62. This is based on further work on the material referred to in n. 42.
63. L. Glassey, *Politics and the Appointment of Justices of the Peace, 1628–1721* (Oxford, 1979), pp. 32–6.
64. As in n. 42.
65. For the 1680s, see Glassey, *Justices*, chs. 2–3 and N. Landau, *The Justices of the Peace* (Berkeley, 1984), ch. 1.

is telling enough.[66] At the grassroots, 'Whiggery' frequently grew out of those who could see their heirs and their values being squeezed out of power. And they saw it as a betrayal of the Restoration Settlement.

The most damaging and alarming of all Danby's policies was his attempt at parliamentary management. Here a point needs making unequivocally. Too often historians have assumed that absolutism is government outside Parliament, at the expense of Parliament; that the ultimate aim of Stuart kings was to be rid of Parliaments.[67] This may be true of the early Stuarts. But it is categorically not true of the later Stuarts. There were periods of English history (mainly within the period 1340–1450) when the exercise of royal authority was closely controlled by Parliaments (essentially as an instrument of aristocratic control). But the more recent Tudor experience was different. Faced by the memory of fifteenth-century anarchy occasioned by weak government, by the sight of religious wars abroad and by the social and economic dislocations occasioned by demographic and inflationary forces, Tudor Parliaments – Crown-in-Parliament – collaborated to develop the authority of the state. Sixteenth-century Parliaments did not reduce royal power: they shaped its growth.[68] Tudor Monarchs-in-Parliament were more powerful than any other European rulers, with an instrument – the omnicompetent statute – which could sheer through prescriptive right and natural law like a scalpel through flesh. By statute, Henry VIII was allowed to intrude his bastards into the line of succession and to extrude legitimate lines. By statute, Henry VIII could abrogate all irrevocable grants of jurisdiction granted away by his predecessors (Franchises Act, 1536). By statute successive rulers were accorded unrivalled control over the minds and consciences of their subjects. By statute the Crown secured a ubiquity and universality for its writs unparalleled elsewhere. In fact, by statute the Plantagenet patrimonial state became the Tudor Empire. By statute *rex* did indeed become *imperator in regno suo*.[69]

---

66. E.g. *A Letter from a Gentleman of Quality*, p. 211.
67. J. Miller, 'Charles II and Parliament', *TRHS*, 32 (1982), 1–24 is a clear guide to the existing literature but seems to me to miss this essential point. For the traditional view, see also Jones (ed.), *Restored Monarchy*, ch. 2.
68. Fundamental is the work of Sir Geoffrey Elton, notably in *The Parliament of England, 1559–1581* (Cambridge, 1986); *Studies in Tudor and Stuart Politics and Government*, II, chs. 21–2; III, chs. 33–6; *The Tudor Constitution*, ch. 8. It is instructive to compare this last with the comparable chapter in the first edition (1960). Nowhere is the revolution in scholarship on this subject so visible.
69. Much of the debate on Elton's thesis rests on the significance of this phrase. Of great importance, but frequently overlooked, is the article by W. Ullmann, '"This Realm of England is an Empire"', *Jnl. Eccl. H.*, 30 (1979), 175–204.

Parliament was a unique instrument in shaping the growth of royal power, and it chose to shape the growth of that power by requiring the Crown to exercise it through members of those elites whose representatives served in Parliament.

Under the early Stuarts the monarchy was unable to sustain that identity of interest with the other estates. The Houses lost their bargaining power and their willingness to solve the Crown's problems by the grant of further powers.[70] But while the Houses prevented the expansion of royal authority, they could do little to reduce it. The failed Act of Union of 1606–7[71] and the Great Contract (1610)[72] were arguably missed opportunities; the Statute of Monopolies of 1624 a futile gesture;[73] the Petition of Right (1628) the one half-effective measure.[74] But the Crown retained the veto and the power to summon, prorogue and dissolve Parliament at will; and the decline in the value of subsidies reduced the Houses' bargaining position considerably. Thus the total proportion of the royal budget provided by parliamentary grants fell from 17 per cent under Elizabeth to 7 per cent under the early Stuarts before rising to 22 per cent under Charles II and James II.[75] In these circumstances, the Crown was not threatened by a parliamentary takeover: it simply lost the capacity to rely on statute to solve its and the nation's problems. It had to fall back on its residual and underdeveloped discretionary and prerogative powers. The paradox is that governing without Parliament made the Crown far weaker than governing with Parliament. The monarchs of the early seventeenth century resemble executives who had driven to work for thirty years in smart cars who suddenly discover that they have to get about on a rusty bicycle. While it was tempting for Charles I to attempt to govern without

---

70. Hirst, *Authority and Conflict, 1603–1658*, pp. 33–42, 126–60, is a good introduction to this large topic.
71. B. Galloway, *The Union of England and Scotland, 1606–1608* (Edinburgh, 1986).
72. A.G.R. Smith, 'Crown, Parliament, and Finance: the Great Contract of 1610', in P. Clark et al. (eds.), *The English Commonwealth 1540–1640* (Leicester, 1979), is the best introduction to this.
73. R. Ashton, *The City and the Court 1603–1643* (Cambridge, 1979), pp. 106–20.
74. J. Reeve's remarks on the aftermath in 'The Legal Status of the Petition of Right', *HJ*, 29 (1986), 275–7, are less controversial than his account of the statutory nature of the Petition. C. Russell, *Parliaments and English Politics 1621–9* (Oxford, 1979), ch. 6, is also important.
75. These are provisional figures calculated from what are recognized as inadequate figures in F.C. Dietz, *Receipts and Issues of the Exchequer* (Northampton, Mass., 1928) and from the better figures in Chandaman, *Public Revenues*, appendix 3.

calling Parliaments, it also revealed the weakness of early Stuart rule and not its strength.[76]

Against this background, we can see that the later Stuarts recognized the folly of governing without Parliament. Their aim was to govern by more effective and directive management.[77] In the later 1680s this amounted to a fundamental perversion of parliamentary independence;[78] but, as with manipulation of local government, that which became a reality under James II had been feared and suspected over the last eight years of Charles's reign. We should not underestimate the Crown's potential: the House of Lords throughout this period was dominated by first generation peers and bishops. It was steered through its business by the judges and law officers who sat as advisors and who influenced much of the work of the House. Although after 1678 the Crown lost control of the appointment of the Speaker of the Commons, it still appointed the clerks and their ability to use their office to steer business towards or away from matters of concern to the Crown is much underrated, as was their selective deafness when it came to hearing the names of those proposed as members of key committees.[79] Negatively, the Crown's broad powers to summon, prorogue, adjourn and dissolve remained vital (as Charles showed in 1679–81),[80] as indeed was his right to determine

---

76. One of the curiosities of this is that both James I and Charles I were adept at 'managing' the Scottish and 'Irish' Parliaments in some of the ways that Charles II and James II attempted to 'manage' the English Parliament in the later seventeenth century.
77. For James II's attempts to manage Parliament, J.R. Jones, *The Revolution of 1688 in England* (1972) remains the best introduction. For the more complicated story of 1681–5, the standard work of Ogg, Western and Sacret has been supplanted by R. Pickavance, 'The Crown and the Boroughs, 1681–5', Univ. of Oxford D. Phil. thesis (1975), which argues that Charles's campaign was more concerned to root out Dissenters than pack Parliament. This in turn is being subject to modification in the forthcoming Cambridge PhD by Patrick Higgins and by C. Lee, '"Fanatic magistrates": Religious and Political Conflict in Three Kentish Boroughs', *HJ*, 35 (1992), 43–61.
78. Jones, *Revolution of 1688*; Miller, *Popery and Politics*; and Landau, *Justices of the Peace*, are all excellent on this.
79. A full study of the working of Parliament in the late seventeenth century is still needed. The account given by Elton, *Parliament of England*, still holds in many respects a century later. See also, S. Lambert, 'Procedure in the House of Commons in the Early Stuart Period', *EHR*, 95 (1980), 753–81; E.R. Foster, *The Painful Labor of Mr Elsynge* (Philadelphia, 1972) and *The House of Lords, 1603–1649* (Chapel Hill, 1983) are also important. That such procedural points remain important can be seen from the biographical entries in *The History of Parliament: the House of Commons 1660–1688* (3 vols., 1983).
80. E.g. in the constant prorogation of the second Exclusion Parliament until the storm of popular alarm had blown itself out: Charles neither refused to meet the Houses, nor did he do so.

where Parliaments should meet (as he showed when he summoned it to Oxford in 1681; it makes one wonder what might have happened if Charles I had reconvened the Long Parliament in late 1641 in York or Oxford instead of London).[81] None of this secured a quiet life for the Crown in the parliamentary sessions of 1661–74, though the extent to which jurisdictional disputes between the Houses and personal rivalries vitiated the smooth passage of Crown Bills should not be understated.[82] The ineffectiveness (from the Crown's point of view) of those sessions was by no means always due to the unpopularity of the Crown or its policies. But from 1675 to 1678 Danby set out to 'manage' Parliament. This meant careful distribution of secret service money and of the loaves and fishes of office to sympathetic members.[83] It was not buying consciences; it was buying the attendance of the naturally but lazily loyal backbenchers. It also involved Charles in adopting policies that he did not really believe in: but then the policy that mattered above all was an untroubled life. We must remember too that this management took place in a Parliament that had been elected in 1661 and seemed set to see Charles's reign out.[84] Many MPs had largely lost touch with their constituencies and now resided semi-permanently in London. This appeared to some to mean that they were easier to buy. As MPs died off, they were replaced at by-elections, and while the government had mixed fortunes in controlling those by-elections without the kind of gerrymandering of franchises that was attempted after 1681,[85] it is clear that government involvement in by-elections was far more intrusive and effective than it could ever hope to be in general elections. The obsessive concern of Shaftesbury in the mid-1670s was to have the Cavalier Parliament dissolved and fresh elections held.[86] Otherwise, Parliament would become a rubber stamp of the royal will, and king-in-Parliament would become the most authoritarian government in Europe. Here

81. Parliament had, of course, met all over England in the fourteenth and fifteenth centuries; only in Westminster in the sixteenth and seventeenth centuries except for sessions in the plague years 1625 and 1665, held at Oxford. A session of the Long Parliament made up of royalist members had also met at Oxford in 1644 and 1645.
82. The discussion of such disputes as *Skinner vs the East India Company* (which stymied the Lords' attempts to develop instance jurisdiction) and *Shirley vs Fagg* (which confirmed the Lords' appellate jurisdiction) too often assumes that disputes were used 'politically' to frustrate Crown business. There are major issues in these cases sufficient to create deadlock.
83. Browning, *Danby*, I, 185–246; III, appendix iii, b–f.
84. The cavalier Parliament sat in 17 sessions over 18 years.
85. For electoral matters, see *History of Parliament 1660–1690*, vol. I.
86. Haley, *Shaftesbury*, pp. 403ff.

412

the memory of parliamentary tyranny of the 1640s and 1650s proved an ironic precedent. Hence the furore when Charles and Danby tried to impose a Non-Resistance Test (similar to that already imposed on the clergy and the boroughs) on MPs; and hence the furore over the standing army in 1678.

The catalogue of parliamentary tyrannies in *The Letter from a Gentleman of Quality* and in Marvell's *Account of the Growth of Popery and Arbitrary Government* take up these themes. And, as Professor Ashcraft has so well reminded us, Locke's analysis of Stuart tyranny recognizes that Parliaments can be corrupted, their independence subverted, and converted into tools of the royal will.[87] The truth fell far short of Shaftesbury's imaginings. Danby was simply trying to ensure a smoother ride through the Houses of limited and traditional Crown business. Charles was no visionary king. He had no fire in his belly other than to see his days out in peace. The burning ambition of his youth had been to acquire his throne, not to do anything with it. But the jolt which the crisis of 1678–81 gave him turned his mind to bolder strokes and to careful preparations for unprecedented royal manipulation of the 'Tory reaction' Parliament (the fruits of the campaign can be seen in the elections after his death in 1685). This in turn gave way to the grotesque manipulations planned and executed by James II in 1687–8. No wonder the scattered Whigs maintained such a deafening silence about Charles's failure to honour the Triennial Act in 1684. Despotism was unthinkable in the absence of Parliament: all too feasible once a monarch had a rubber stamp in St Stephen's Chapel.

I want to add one final piece to the jigsaw. One of the major themes of England's constitutional government from the fourteenth century (and perhaps earlier) to 1689 was the debate about the nature of counsel. Here I would like to remind you of John Guy's recent work which examines the tension in the period 1450–1540 between two concepts of counsel: the 'bureaucratic' model in which the king is advised by his personal and personally selected servants, and the 'aristocratic' model in which the king is advised by his 'natural' counsellors from among the peerage and perhaps from among the other estates.[88] Many loyalist writers, such as Fortescue, St Germain and Starkey not only favoured the latter, but favoured parliamentary involvement in the selection of these counsellors, believing that both

87. Ashcraft, *Locke's Two Treatises*, ch. 7.
88. J. Guy, 'The King's Council and Political Participation', in A. Fox and J. Guy (eds.), *Reassessing the Henrician Age* (Oxford, 1986), pp. 121–50.

Crown and realm would benefit from such a scheme. In the period 1536–40, however, the issue was decisively settled in favour of the 'bureaucratic' council by Henry VIII's and Cromwell's reforms.[89] This reorganized Privy Council dominated English government from 1540 to 1641. But then the whole issue was reopened. In an article to appear elsewhere, I am arguing that to describe the Nineteen Propositions as attempting to establish 'parliamentary government'[90] is misleading. Rather it is an attempt to revive fourteenth-century notions of 'aristocratic' counsel. Parliamentary vetting and approval is but the mechanism towards the end of aristocratic control of the executive.[91] It was to remain the central obsession of Charles's opponents throughout the 1640s. The divisions among them are as much about *who* is to control Charles as about *how* he is to be controlled.

The problem of counsel became both less and more acute in the Restoration: essentially because of the fragmentation of decision-making. The Privy Council had been, as we have seen, largely shorn of its power to monitor and to cajole local governors; but it also very rapidly grew to an unmanageable size and ceased to be an effective deliberative body. Policy-discussion and decision-making passed to formal and informal committees and, increasingly, to wholly private, unminuted meetings of the king and a handful of ministers in the king's private quarters.[92] There was far less direction. Since, as the 1660s and especially the 1670s progressed, individual offices of state, notably the royal secretariat and the Treasury, developed extensive networks of information, patronage and authority of their own, new anxieties grew up about how and by whom the king was being advised.[93] This became critical in the face of the heightened fears of popery which we have already discussed.

When I was in China in 1987 I heard a fascinating paper from a Chinese scholar on state formation in Europe and in China.[94] Whereas western scholars automatically classify state systems in Aristotelian categories (monarchical/aristocratic/democratic, or as blends of these),

89. For other recent accounts of the Council, see D. Starkey and C. Coleman (eds.), *Revolution Reassessed* (Oxford, 1986), chs. 2–3.
90. See above, ch. 15.
91. See above, pp. 11–13.
92. Turner, *Privy Council*, pp. 371–408.
93. Coleby, *Central Government and the Localities*, ch. 6; Jones (ed.), *Restored Monarchy*, *passim*. It is also a central theme of Dr Alan Marshall's forthcoming study of intelligence services of Charles II.
94. Liu Xinyang; abstract available in 'Papers presented to the International Symposium on British History' (Nanjing, 1987).

Chinese scholars categorize state systems as monotonic, diatonic or multitonic according to whether the locus of power is centralized, or balanced between two or more institutions or places. England is viewed as a clear diatonic system, as having, from early in its development, dual *loci* of authority in the royal court and in the shires (with their distinctive patterns of officers, courts, juries and so on). Parliament arose as an institution to coordinate these two distinct centres of power. By the seventeenth century both institutional bifocation and the political need for integration were at their height.

Such an approach is immensely fertile although it has its difficulties. Certainly it helps us to pull together the strings of my argument. In a state in which the Crown could only govern with the consent of social elites whose primary sources of wealth and status derived only indirectly from the Crown, it was essential that there should be a perceived identity of interest between the Crown and those elites and institutions which could mediate between them. The English system had developed a whole series of checks to allow that to happen. First, there was no hereditary caste of families like the French *noblesse de robe* surrounding and sheltering the Crown. In every generation the great majority of senior civil servants and household officials were the sons of 'mere' country gentry, clergy, lawyers or urban oligarchs. *Their* sons were more likely than not to return to the shires to plant new landed dynasties. Secondly, the Crown was not compelled in central or local government to work with and through *all* members of those social elites. It could and did marginalize groups whose values and beliefs it felt it could safely ignore (as Elizabeth slowly squeezed out Catholic recusant families in the late sixteenth century, and the Hanoverians squeezed out Tory families, or some kinds of Tory families in the eighteenth). Thirdly, as we have seen, the Crown allowed itself to become more and more dependent upon parliamentary statute to create law, to shape the growth of its institutions and to finance its activities. For much of the time, these mechanisms secured cooperation and stability. England was, after all, the most law-abiding, the least violent, the most orderly state in Europe for most of the seventeenth century. But when there was a succession of monarchs whose preferred lines of policy was significantly different from the spectrum of views held by groups within the elite, there was bound to be tension within the system. How and how far could the monarch overcome the reluctance of legislators to fund and to give legal force to their policies? How far could the legislators call the king and his servants to account for proceding beyond or failing to carry out their legal duties? When king and the representatives of the local communities were in conflict, who was to decide between them?

Here at last we can locate Locke's contribution to the resolution of the tensions in England's constitutional development; and can weigh the successes and failures of that contribution. In the narrow, theoretical sense, James II's flight and William's accession could not be demonstrated to the satisfaction of anyone but the already converted to be an act of deposition, the removal of a king who had violated and put himself outside the Contract and into a state of nature, or to be a parliamentary redefinition of the nature of executive power in the English Commonwealth. Those who preferred to treat James as a man who had deserted his kingdom and left a vacuum that William occupied and to whom obedience was due *de facto* but not *de iure*, could not be made to see it otherwise. Even when the tragically unanticipated inability of Anne to provide for the succession gave the Whigs a further chance to establish their principles, Lockeian views, although, of course, deeply influential, were far from dominant in determining recognition of Hanoverian claims.[95]

In a more pragmatic sense, however, Locke's attempt to exalt the independence of executive and legislature, and to make the former accountable to and ultimately replaceable at the will of the latter, foundered. We can see what happened by dividing the period 1530–1730 into four:

(1)   Between 1530 and about 1603 there was an equilibrium in which the Crown and the other estates worked in general harmony to expand the power of the state and to grant to the Crown extensive and increasing power which it was to exercise through officials drawn from old and new political elites: as social and economic power was redistributed, so, through Parliament, political power was redistributed.

(2)   Between about 1603 and 1640 there was a steep decline in the perceived identity of interest between the Crown and political elites which drove a particularly wayward and maladroit King, Charles I, to govern outside, and independently of, Parliament. This necessarily made him weaker than his predecessors and (not inevitably, but as a

---

95. J.P. Kenyon, *Revolution Principles* (Cambridge, 1977), pp. 1–2, 7, 35–7, and J.C.D. Clark, *English Society 1660–1832* (Cambridge, 1985), pp. 45–50, are amongst the main detractors. In the introduction to the revised edition of *British Politics in the Reign of Anne* (1986), pp. xxxii–xxxiv, Geoffrey Holmes has sensible things to say in redressing the balance.

result of continuing incompetence and lack of judgement) it created conditions in which the whole political system collapsed.

(3) From 1660 to 1689 a further failure to create an identity of interest between Crown and political elites continued to weaken government. (The blunt fact was: neither Charles II nor James was a Tory Anglican.) The Crown now tried an alternative strategy: it intervened in the selection of MPs, manipulated its powers to determine the times and places of meetings, and sought to influence the business and procedures of the Houses so as to create an artificial cooperation of Crown and Parliament. The Crown continued to assert that *it* was the ultimate arbiter of what was for the general good. In response to this challenge, those whom we know as the Whigs developed a precise mirror-image policy: cooperation had to be achieved not by the executive reshaping the legislature, but by the legislature reshaping the executive. Locke was an influential proponent of that view.

(4) From 1689 to 1730 and beyond, we see the reestablishment of equilibrium between Crown and Parliament, and (or is it through?) a new dominance of the centre over the provinces. The wars of 1689–1714 more than the settlements of 1688–9 (let alone the half-abandoned settlement of 1701) created two new contexts: the primary one was that Britain was faced – for the first time since the 1590s – with invasion and conquest. As a result, the political elite acquiesced in the transference to the state of the bureaucratic, fiscal and military resources necessary to see off French absolutism and Catholic monarchy. This proved to be an irreversible transfer of resources. It strengthened the office of monarchy more than the persons of the monarchs, but it was a fundamental switch. It permitted Britain to emerge as a formidable naval and colonial power and proved self-extending.

Alongside this, however, was a second and more unexpected development: a new, delicate but effective interdependence of legislature and executive. The formal mechanisms for government by a Council nominated by or accountable to the legislature were supplanted by a cabinet council comprising those who could command a majority in both Houses on bills crucial to the Crown, and many combinations of ministers were normally in a position to deliver those goods. At times, too, the electorate could deliver such a rebuke to the Crown and its ministers that adjustments were necessary. But behind the ministers and the independent squires and men of property in the Houses sat a new ballast, the career civil servants and placemen (or Court and Treasury party) whose votes could normally stabilize the government in all but the most violent of political squalls. This 'ballast' was made possible by the vast expansion of patronage resulting from the mobilization of resources for global war. And the Crown more generally held elections to strengthen the ministers in Parliament than it held an election and then had to change its ministers as a result.

Parliament in early modern England was crucial not only because it was such a powerful instrument for making law and approving taxation; but also because it demonstrated to the Crown the limits of its enforceable will. The Stuarts forgot that lesson and it cost them dear: but for the eighteenth century as for the sixteenth, this was to be the true bedrock of Liberty and Property. It is not really what Lockeian separation of powers and the subordination of governors had striven for: but, as usual in British history, the resolution of political crisis owed less to political precept than to muddling through.

CHAPTER TWENTY
The Sensible Revolution, 1688

I

Back in 1938, on the 250th anniversary of the Glorious Revolution, it all seemed very straightforward. The English had opted for compromise, common sense, the abandonment of extremism and of enthusiasm:

> The element of 'moderation' which the Revolution enthroned . . . was, in its essence, the chaining up of fanaticism alike in politics and in religion. Religion in those days was the chief motive of politics, and after the Revolution a movement towards Latitudinarianism in religion enveloped first England and then for a while all Europe.[1]

These were the confident words of G.M. Trevelyan, concluding his commemorative volume, *The English Revolution, 1688–1689*. His book is unhesitating in its judgement that the Revolution was a good thing, that the institutions and values which emerged from it were those that lay at the foundations of England's greatness as a world power and as a liberal state in the succeeding decades and centuries. It is written with such a transparent insouciance, such a lightness of touch in its laying out of evidence, and with such a fluency of style, that as I struggled through the confusing and hesitant writings of recent years, reading Trevelyan felt like a glass of glycerine and honey slipping down a sore throat. It momentarily eased the inflammation; but was it a cure?

Trevelyan was Whiggish in his approval of the Revolution as a progressive event that contributed much to the advance of modern

I am grateful to Julian Hoppit, Jonathan Israel, David Smith, and Bill Speck for some deservedly heavy criticism of drafts of this article.
1. G.M. Trevelyan, *The English Revolution, 1688–1689* (Oxford, 1938), pp. 240–1.

and advanced values. This is perhaps at its most exposed in his peroration:

> The great emollient of the common ills of life, the humanitarian move-
> ment in all its aspects, began in the eighteenth century before the issue
> of democracy was aroused . . . This great humanitarian movement to
> whose sphere of operations there is no limit, was a new birth of time. It
> arose in the milder atmosphere of the great religious and party truce
> which the Revolution settlement had ushered in. It could not have arisen
> if the feuds of the Stuart era had been carried on in their full intensity
> into later generations.[2]

But Trevelyan saw this effect of the Revolution as neither willed nor inevitable. The outcome was, for him, a classic example of the law of unintended consequences: 'in the affair of the Revolution, the element of chance, of sheer good luck, was dominant'.[3] Much of his book is concerned with might-have-beens. Furthermore (as his very choice of title makes clear), Trevelyan was not concerned to endorse the events of 1688–9 as a 'Glorious Revolution'. In his view '"the Sensible Revolution" would have been a more appropriate title'.[4] Thus: 'the true glory of the Revolution lies not in the minimum of violence which was necessary for its success, but in the way of escape from violence which the Revolution Settlement found for future generations of Englishmen'.[5] The elements of his argument were straightforward: England had an intrinsically unstable form of government, and had oscillated dangerously between royal absolutism and the growing power of Parliaments, 'chary of supply to governments whose policy they could not continuously control'.[6] James II's grotesque despotism constituted 'the accident . . . that gave our ancestors the opportunity to right themselves'.[7] By his overt popery and clumsy tyranny, he did what even Charles I had avoided doing: he united his subjects in a desire to be rid of him. As a result,

> wise compromise . . . staunched for ever bloodfeud of Roundhead and
> Cavalier, of Anglican and Puritan, which had broken out first at Edge-
> hill and Naseby, and bled afresh four years back at Sedgemoor. Whig
> and Tory, having risen together in rebellion against James, seized the
> fleeting moment of their union to fix a new-old form of government,
> known in History as the Revolution Settlement.[8]

2. Ibid., pp. 243–4.
3. Ibid., p. 240.
4. Ibid., p. 7.
5. Ibid., p. 9.
6. Ibid., pp. 17–18.
7. Ibid., p. 240.
8. Ibid., p. 10.

The outcome was a firm subordination of monarchy to the law, an 'agreement between parties and churches to live and let live', a supple but durable balancing of the interests of the three estates, 'an ordered and legal freedom [which gave England] her power'.[9]

> She often abused her power, as in the matters of Ireland and the Slave Trade, till she reversed her engines; but the whole of mankind would have breathed a harsher air if England had not grown strong. For her power was based not only on her free constitution, but on the maritime and commercial enterprize of her sons, a kind of power naturally akin to freedom, as the power of great armies in its nature is not.[10]

This essay will explore just how much of Trevelyan's confident celebration of the 'Sensible Revolution' has stood up to the corrosive effects of empirical research and, more recently, of 'revisionist' method. I certainly do not wish to deny that Trevelyan's lightness of touch overlays a thinness of research that would forbid publication nowadays. But I find judgements such as Jonathan Clark's to be too harsh (he is writing of the work of both Trevelyan and Basil Williams): 'Whatever their professional gifts it is now impossible to examine their narratives without a mounting sense of frustration at their shallowness, the superficiality and glibness of much of their writing, their willingness to skate over ignorance with a commonly received form of words, and to evade important problems with well-turned generalizations.'[11] What struck me on re-reading it after many years was its startling quality, not its pleasantries and platitudes. Trevelyan is concerned to show that _despite_ the confusions and fudges, the Revolution came to have unanticipated and unsought-after consequences. The book as a whole lacks the apparatus, the thorough immersion in the sources, to command scholarly reverence. I am not trying to rehabilitate it as a standard textbook. In deciding to write this essay around a series of quotations from _The English Revolution_, I was doing no more than seeking a framework (I originally intended a series of Aunt Sallies) within which to meet my brief from the editor: to summarize recent historiographical trends in relation to the Revolution of 1688. I came to the view that in his counterpointing of the confusions of the actors with the unintended consequences of their actings, Trevelyan had set up a number of challenging and shrewd assertions which have been subsequently not so much demolished as ducked.

The tactical decision to structure a review of recent literature around passages of Trevelyan has, it is hoped, advantages. It creates a natural

9. Ibid., pp. 11, 62–3, 175, 240.
10. Ibid., p. 240.
11. J.C.D. Clark, _Revolution and Rebellion: State and Society in England in the Seventeenth and Eighteenth Centuries_ (Cambridge, 1986), pp. 18–19.

agenda and allows for greater clarity of argument. It has the drawback that certain major new approaches are hard to accommodate within that agenda. Trevelyan was concerned with two things: with the short-term causes and immediate nature of the Revolution; and with its long-term consequences. He was not concerned with explicating the medium-term effects and developments – and he ignores or glosses over the rage of party, the nature and extent of Jacobitism, the constitutional and ecclesiological debates over the twenty-five years after 1689, indeed the whole question of how sustaining myths about the Revolution emerged from the ideological tongue-biting of 1689. Something will be said about these issues towards the end of the essay. But first we will pursue Trevelyan through the agenda he created.

In turn we will review recent work concerning the nature of James' government and the political context of his downfall; the circumstances of his flight; the significance of the dynastic change; the political aims of William himself; the significance of the Declaration of Rights and the relationship between the Declaration and the offer of the Crown; the significance of the Toleration Act; the impact of the Revolution on Scotland and Ireland; the political and constitutional impact of the wars of the decades after 1689; and the long-term consequences of the Revolution settlement.

II

Since Parliament would not alter the laws, James could only attain his ends by regarding the law as a restriction on the royal will. The prerogative of the kings of England, their ancient claims to an undefined residuary power, had sometimes in the course of our history swelled to monstrous proportions, and sometimes shrunk back to little, but never quite to nothing. Prerogative was now to be conjured up once more and fashioned into the one substantial reality of a new constitution. This vital change in the royal authority must be effected by pronouncements from the judicial Bench. . . . James, in short, in his desire to restore Romanism in England, found it necessary to become an absolute monarch like the Princes of Europe. The absurd medieval shackles on the royal power, peculiar to our retrograde island, must be removed. . . . James, though he was most imprudent in making such an attempt, had at least some reason to hope for success. He had complete control of the executive power, he could dismiss and nominate every servant of the State, and the higher Church patronage was in his hand. Above all he had a large army. . . . James proceeded to break law on law. Prerogative was to be everything, statutes nothing, if they were not to the liking of the King.[12]

12. Trevelyan, *The English Revolution*, pp. 62–4.

This passage raises a whole series of points which have been much debated since 1938. Was the crisis of 1688 the crisis of a system of government or of a particular man? Is it correct to describe James's government as a despotism or an absolutism or neither? Could James have succeeded in his aims (whatever those were)? Was James seeking to 'restore Romanism'?

Trevelyan's discussion of the origins of the Revolution focuses on the misdeeds of James II. The crisis of 1688–9 was a crisis of confidence in a particular king more than with a system of government.[13] There was an inherent instability in the system of government, a lack of precision in the locus of sovereignty which gave the people of England little protection against a man like James II. But it was the particular way in which power was abused, and the particular circumstances of James's rule that determined the nature and outcome of the crisis. Trevelyan began his account with a discussion of 'the provisional compromise between kingly and parliamentary power',[14] but the pre-1685 section is by way of preamble only, to explain how it was that James was able to erect such a despotism. Most of the writing on the Revolution in recent years has followed Trevelyan's lead. J.R. Jones and W.A. Speck in the two most thorough and comprehensive surveys[15] both adopt the same approach as he did – a survey chapter of the Restoration settlement and then an account of the destabilization of politics once James was on the throne. J.R. Western, who was concerned to see 1688 as a counter-revolution, treated the crisis as dating from the early 1680s, and both the Tory reaction of 1681–5 and James's reign as part of a process with a unifying underlying theme – a bid to establish the autonomy and pre-eminence of royal prerogative.[16] The different ends of Charles and James were seen by Western as subordinate to a common purpose as to means – the establishment of royal absolutism. There never has been any serious attempt, however, to see the crisis of 1688 as the culmination of a gradual process of disintegration, in the sense that many scholars from the 1950s to the 1970s saw the collapse

---

13. This is, of course, precisely parallelled by recent concentration by historians of the English civil war on the iniquities of Charles I, who, it is said, inherited and threw away an essentially strong position.

14. Trevelyan, *The English Revolution*, p. 22. The difference between this shallow compromise of 1660 and the sensible compromise of 1688 was, of course, that in 1688 the location of sovereignty was not fudged, although everything else was.

15. J.R. Jones, *The Revolution of 1688 in England* (London, 1972); W.A. Speck, *Reluctant Revolutionaries* (Oxford, 1988).

16. J.R. Western, *Monarchy and Revolution: The English State in the 1680s* (London, 1972).

of Charles I's government in 1640–9 as the culmination of a century of decline and atrophy.

There are no serious adherents to the view that the settlement of 1660–2 was so inherently unstable that the further collapse of royal authority was only a matter of time. There is no reason to disturb the central claims of Trevelyan that what happened in the Revolution resulted from the actions of a particular king following particular policies.

Trevelyan clearly believed that James could have succeeded – especially once he had a son and (presumably Catholic) heir to succeed him. The above passage describes James's promotion of 'Romanism' as 'imprudent', but the drift of the book as a whole is to see James as all too likely to succeed. This view has been sharply contested. John Miller, for example, has argued that such freedom of action as the Crown possessed was quite inadequate to the task of establishing an authoritarian state. There was no alternative to a reliance upon Parliament for taxation and for the creation (rather than the modification or abrogation) of law, and neither Charles II nor James II believed otherwise; the ubiquity of jury trial was a major safeguard against royal diktat; the Crown continued to rely upon unpaid local elites to supervise tax-collection, enforce law, regulate much social and economic activity, and any attempt to bypass that elite would lead to a rapid decline of efficiency and an eventual collapse of royal authority. Many historians have agreed with Miller that both Charles and James were well aware of these constraints, and that neither had any intention of erecting a royal absolutism.[17] It is now widely accepted that Charles was too lazy, too easy-going, too unsystematic to be a threat to liberties. He might turn a blind eye to the assassination of some, and the continuing harassment of many other, former republicans, he might for short-term political advantage seek to bend his prerogative to help or strain due process to disrupt the lives of Protestant Dissenters, but the anxieties genuinely felt and exaggeratedly expressed in the 1670s about popery *now* and arbitrary government *now* were a chimera.[18] It has been pointed out that for much of his reign, James expected to be succeeded by his Protestant

---

17. This is a theme which can be found in much of John Miller's extensive writing, but perhaps most succinctly in 'The Potential for Absolutism in Later Stuart England', *History*, 69 (1984), 187–207.
18. The best recent biography of Charles II is by J.R. Jones, *Charles II: Royal Politician* (London, 1987); others by Ronald Hutton and John Miller are imminent. From the papers deriving from these biographies which I have heard, neither is likely to challenge the view expressed here.

daughter and her Dutch husband. Why should he seek to establish an absolutism for their benefit? Rather, he was a man in a hurry, trying to secure full civil and religious equality and liberty for his co-religionists. He was sufficiently bigoted to believe that once those rights were established, the self-evident truth and majesty of the Roman Catholic faith would impress itself upon a people who had never had a chance to study or experience it. There would be widespread conversions and no future monarch would be able to suppress the devotion of a largely convert nation. Thus, the emphasis in much recent writing has been on James' genuine commitment to religious toleration; and his single-minded determination to create the conditions within which this counter-reformation would develop the necessary free momentum was political folly but not a despotic design.[19] In that sense at least Trevelyan now appears to be the victim of the seventeenth-century conviction that popery and absolutism were indissolubly linked.

Yet, somehow a lot of recent writing has missed the point. James may not have been absolutist in the technical sense that he imitated the methods of continental absolutisms. He may have misused agreed powers more than he claimed novel ones. But there is no denying his natural authoritarianism. He was like his father only more so. He examined his conscience, he satisfied himself that what he was doing lay within the discretionary area allowed to the king under the law, and he acted. He could not accept that criticism of his policies was principled or sincere. Any protest was of its nature seditious, the questioning of the superior (in every sense) wisdom of the king. And W.A. Speck reminds us that 'the exercise of absolutism across the Atlantic was not merely the means to an end of religious toleration; it was an end in itself.'[20] It should be said, furthermore, that perhaps not enough attention has been paid to the fact that, in English conditions, royal absolutism would have to be erected not outside and at the expense of Parliament as an institution, but *through* a packed and

19. This is the view of J. Miller, *James II: A Study in Kingship* (Hove, 1978); M. Ashley, *James II* (London, 1977); and Jones, *The Revolution of 1688*, ch. 5; and more recently of J. Miller, 'James II and Toleration', in E. Cruickshanks (ed.). *By Force or by Default: The Revolution of 1688–89* (Edinburgh, 1989), ch. 2.
20. Speck, *Reluctant Revolutionaries*, p. 12. James suppressed representative assemblies throughout New England, and created a highly authoritarian viceroyalty. For Trevelyan's awareness of the implications of James's New England policies, see *The English Revolution*, pp. 204–5. The fullest recent accounts are D.S. Lovejoy, *The Glorious Revolution in America* (Middleton, Conn., 1972), and J. Sosin, *English America and the Revolution of 1688* (Lincoln, Nebr., 1982). See also James's policies in Ireland, as discussed in J. Miller, 'The Earl of Tyrconnel and James II's Irish Policy, 1685–1688', *HJ*, 20 (1977), 803–23.

managed Parliament. What made the period of Danby's rule in the mid-1670s so much more threatening than the extra-parliamentary tinkerings of 1670–3 to many both within and without the elite, and what made the whole of the manipulation of borough charters in the 1680s more menacing still, was this apparent attempt to subvert the independence of Parliament. The buying of MPs' votes or the rigging of elections could be seen as an effort to transform the Houses into a rubber-stamp of the royal will. Given the omnicompetence of statute, and the absence of all checks against legislative tyranny, this was a palpable danger. Professor Jones has suggested that James could have brought this off in 1688, and gained a House of Commons willing to repeal the Test Acts and penal laws. If this is so, then it has to be admitted that the Revolution settlement did little to prevent further gerrymandering. The pious and vacuous hope of the Bill of Rights 'that elections ought to be free' did nothing in itself to protect the realm from executive subversion of the independence of Parliament. Pragmatism and not prescription ensured that nothing like the methods employed by Sunderland and Brent were attempted again; but it must be remembered that opportunities were created and ruthlessly exploited from the 1690s onwards to secure the return of 150 placemen to the House of Commons which were largely responsible for the effectiveness of ministerial control of Parliament in the succeeding decades.[21]

James may well have been genuinely tolerant, but it was surely for complacent, cynical, and shallow reasons and it was not the product of precocious Enlightenment. Toleration would unleash the fissiparous tendencies within Protestantism; there would be a reversion to the chaos of the 1650s and a consequent demoralization amongst Anglican leaders; the scandal of Protestant disunion would itself turn men and women to the order, cohesion, and authority of the Catholic religion. One does not have to agree with Halifax's dictum that James was hugging the Dissenters now the better to squeeze them thereafter to see that his alliance with them was a patronizing expedient.

21. Jones, *The Revolution of 1688*, pp. 127–75. Several historians have doubted that James could have persuaded even a packed Parliament to do his bidding (see the comments of Speck, *Reluctant Revolutionaries*, pp. 131–2). Two things are worth noting about James's obsession with the repeal of these laws. One is the recognition that he had to secure repeal. Suspension would make Catholics dependent upon his prerogative for protection and that protection would die with him. Full equality for Catholics rested upon full statutory protection. More importantly, James believed/recognized that he could only secure the repeal of those Acts in a Parliament made up of Protestants. He acknowledged that he could not suspend the second Test Act and thereby pack the Commons with Catholics. It is a telling illustration that he was a constitutionalist, albeit a warped one.

More problematic is quite what James meant when he called for the establishment of full civil and religious rights for Catholics.[22] It is true, as has been often pointed out, that in 1688 still less than one quarter of the army and naval officers and of the JPs were Catholic. But in a nation in which rather less than one in twenty overall were Catholic, James's appointments since 1685 still represented an affirmative action programme with a vengeance! And what of James's plans for the full establishment of the Catholic Church on an equality with the Church of England? He had made no progress by 1688 in his plans to appoint diocesan bishops for the Catholic Church in England, and his willingness in 1688 to establish four vicars-apostolic with authority over the Catholics in the four quarters of England indicates at least a medium-term abandonment of the hope of having diocesan bishops appointed.[23] Yet there are suggestions that he had previously been thinking much more in terms of diocesan bishops and the delay in introducing even the compromise of vicars-apostolic was the result not of James's concern for Anglican scruples as of the refusal of the pope to accept James's first nominees. He would not, for example, appoint Fr Petre because of an objection to the consecration of Jesuits to the episcopate.[24] It can hardly be imagined that James would want to see England in a subordinate 'missionary' status for more than a limited time. The establishment of equality for Anglicans and Roman Catholics would involve the establishment of diocesan bishops, who would necessarily have their own courts (it is unthinkable that James would long continue to allow Catholics to be subject to Anglican church courts in such matters as marriage litigation, defamation, or the transmission of property by will). The envisaged wholesale conversions would lead to a massive demand for priests. Where were they to be trained? Surely a full equality for Catholics would entail a sharing of the resources of the universities. Indeed, had not many of the colleges been founded centuries before to train up the administrative elite of the Catholic Church and to combat heresy? Is this not what ultimately lay behind the Catholic takeover

---

22. There are clear and consistent accounts of James's aims in each of the following: Miller, *James II*, pp. 125–8; Western, *Monarchy and Revolution*, pp. 185–210; Jones, *The Revolution of 1688*, pp. 80–6.
23. For the appointment of vicars-apostolic, see R. Beddard, *A Kingdom without a King. The Journal of the Provisional Government in the Revolution of 1688* (Oxford, 1988), p. 15. The four appointees were, of course, all bishops *in partibus infidelium*.
24. For the general question of James II's poor relations with Innocent XI, see J. Miller, *Popery and Politics in England 1660–1688* (Cambridge, 1973), ch. 12, and B. Neveu, 'Jacques II, médiateur entre Louis XIV et Innocent XI', *Mélanges d'Archéologie et d'histoire de L'Ecole Française à Rome*, 79 (1967), 699–764.

of Magdalen College, Oxford,[25] and the proposed takeover of other colleges at both universities? Particularly sinister was the launching of an enquiry into the management of college property, especially of charitable funds. This raised the spectre of the security of the former monastic lands.[26] Would they not be needed for the re-endowment of Catholic churches? And would not the tithes of the Catholics need to be appropriated for the maintenance of a Catholic clergy? Little of this had materialized by 1688, but it fuelled Anglican fears for the future. If these speculations are right, then James's aim of achieving a full civil and religious equality for Catholics was *not* a moderate programme. James was an authoritarian bigot utterly determined to destroy not only the Anglican control of evangelism but the structures of its material and jurisdictional pre-eminence. Furthermore, the intimidation of the judiciary, the unprecedented reliance upon a supposed suspending power, dubious redefinitions of the dispensing power and the host of other misuses of prerogative power complained against in the Declaration of Rights did happen, and even as means to other ends in James's mind are frightening enough in themselves for his unbigoted or differently bigoted subjects. Trevelyan's harsh view still has something to commend it.

III

If James had remained in England and submitted to be King under the tutelage of Parliament, it is probable that the change made by the Revolution in the forms of our Constitution would have been greater than it actually was. James would not have been trusted again, without defined limitations on his power. But since William was put on the throne, it was not thought necessary to tie his hands by quasi-republican restrictions on his free action. . . . We were saved by James's flight to France from the necessity of making such formal change in the law of the constitution, which would have proved in practice a very clumsy and possibly a disastrous experiment.[27]

There are many layers of irony in this passage. First, the appropriation by some scholars of the Bill of Rights as a dummy run for the American Revolution is challenged by Trevelyan's almost contemptuous dismissal of paper-constitutionalism with its built-in rigidities.

---

25. G.V. Bennett, 'Loyalist Oxford and the Revolution', in L.S. Sutherland and L.G. Mitchell (eds.), *History of the University of Oxford*, V (Oxford, 1986), 16–19.
26. Western, *Monarchy and Revolution*, p. 202. Speck, *Reluctant Revolutionaries*, pp. 144–5, has an important discussion of the perceived threat of James seeking the wholesale recovery of monastic lands.
27. Trevelyan, *The English Revolution*, pp. 129–30.

Secondly, the flight of James, the offer of the Crown to William and Mary, and the legislation of 1689–90 are seen as leading to a minimalist settlement. Since the problem was more with a particular king than with a system of government, the departure of the particular king lessened the need to change the system. In re-examining the claims of historians like Lois Schwoerer that those 'men who endorsed the Declaration of Rights did . . . want to change the kingship as well as the king',[28] we should bear Trevelyan's counter-factual speculation in mind: the way in 1688 to change kingship was *not* to change the king.

But there is another layer of irony too. Much recent work has suggested that William was soon seen as anything but the deliverer hailed in 1689. Although Angus MacInnes has characterized him as 'the betrayer of English absolutism', a man 'far less tenacious of the Crown's prerogatives than any of his predecessors had been',[29] much recent work has emphasized the ruthlessness with which William subordinated the scruples of his English subjects to his drive to mobilize resources against Louis XIV. The standing army controversy of 1697–1700 is but the most prominent example of this. We must never forget that what we now call the Act of Settlement of 1701 was officially entitled 'An act for the further limitation of the Crown and better securing the rights and liberties of the subject' – the better securing of them, that is, against the practices of William III. Only the securing of the tenure of judges was present in that Act as a hangover from 1689. The bulk of the clauses relate to the perceived malpractices of the new king.[30] Trevelyan's sense of the complaisance of the political elite at having a Protestant king clearly smoothed over a rather more unsettling tale.

28. L.G. Schwoerer, 'The Glorious Revolution as Spectacle: A New Perspective', in S. B. Baxter (ed.), *England's Rise to Greatness, 1660–1783* (Berkeley, Calif., 1983), pp. 127–8.
29. A. MacInnes, 'When was the English Revolution?', *History*, 66 (1982), 376.
30. R.J. Frankle, 'The Formulation of the Declaration of Rights', *HJ*, 17 (1974), 275–9; J. Childs, '1688', *History*, 73 (1988), 415–24; S.B. Baxter, *William III* (London, 1966), chs. 18–22; J. Carter, 'The Revolution and the Constitution', in G. S. Holmes (ed.), *Britain after the Glorious Revolution 1689–1714* (London, 1969), pp. 39–58; Edmund Ludlow, *A Voice from the Watch Tower*. ed. A.B. Worden (Royal Historical Society, Camden, fourth series 21, London, 1978), 38–55 (Worden rightly commends us to look still at the 23rd chapter of Macaulay's *History*); H. Horwitz, *Parliament, Policy and Politics in the Reign of William III* (Manchester, 1977), chs. 4, 9, 13; L.G. Schwoerer, '*No Standing Armies!': The Anti-Army Ideology in Seventeenth-Century England* (Baltimore, 1971), ch. 6; P. Hopkins, 'Aspects of Jacobite Conspiracy in England in the Reign of William III', Univ. of Cambridge PhD thesis (1981), esp. pp. 244–64.

IV

The dynastic change . . . coloured everything.[31]

Coloured, Trevelyan writes, not determined. At the heart of the resolution of the political crisis of 1688–9 are two ineluctable facts: an *Interregnum* and the curious arrangements made for the dual monarchy of William and Mary.

The fact of an Interregnum was probably more important than the breach in the line of succession. The legitimate line had been broken at almost half the accessions between 1066 and 1685, and several 'usurpers' were further removed from the natural line of succession than was William III from James II. Neither was there anything in the fact that a living monarch was superseded by a rival following a military coup. The period 1327–1485 saw more irregular than regular transmissions of the kingly office, with kings regnant being deposed on no less than seven occasions. Parliament had more than once been called upon to arbitrate the right to the Crown, most notably in 1460 when, by the Act of Accord, Richard of York was granted the reversion of the Crown ahead of Henry VI's own son Edward. Some historians have seen the titles of both Henry IV and Richard III as being as fully 'parliamentary' and 'constitutionalist' as those of William and Mary.[32] More importantly, Henry VIII had used statute to alter and determine the line of succession, incorporating his bastards at law (Mary and Elizabeth) and excluding and barring a legitimate line (the heirs of his sister Margaret).[33] In the mid-1580s, no less a personage than William Cecil had seriously canvassed the proposal that an act be passed whereby when Elizabeth died, there should be a thirty-day Interregnum during which anyone who asserted his or her title would be debarred, and at the end of which the members of the last sitting Parliament should meet together with a Great Council of dignitaries, to consider the claims to the throne

31. Trevelyan, *The English Revolution*, p. 133.
32. G. T. Lapsley, 'The Parliamentary Title of Henry IV', *EHR*, 44 (1934), 423–49, 577–606; W.H. Dunham and C.T. Wood, 'The Right to Rule in England: Depositions and the Kingdom's Authority', *American History Review*, 81 (1976), 738–61; cf. J.W. McKenna, 'The Myth of Parliamentary Sovereignty in Late-Medieval England', *EHR*, 99 (1979), 481–506, which argues against any of the parliamentary acts beings more than declaratory or confirmatory in nature. It seems to me by extrapolation, that if Dunham and Wood are right, William and Mary's title derived from the same principles as these fourteenth- and fifteenth-century precedents; if (as is more likely) McKenna is right, then his arguments reduce the 1689 settlement to the last in a long sequence of *confirmatory* acts.
33. G.R. Elton, *The Tudor Constitution* (2nd edn., Cambridge, 1984), pp. 2–3.

submitted to them, and to determine the succession. Here indeed are pre-echoes of 1689.[34]

Yet the events we are considering were 'coloured' by the dynastic change. The period between 11 December 1688[35] and 13 February 1689 was deemed to be legally and actually an Interregnum. Although from the eleventh to the fourteenth century, kings dated their reigns from their coronations and not from the date of the death of their predecessors, it had become fully established since the accession of Richard II that the throne was never vacant. The regnal years for all legal purposes began at the very moment when the previous reign ended.[36] Thus Charles II was proclaimed by his Convention in 1660 to have been king since 30 January 1649. The Cromwellian Interregnum was deemed not to have been an Interregnum. Although the historical situation was not straightforward, therefore, it is clear that the transition of authority in 1689 did constitute a discontinuity. England could be, in the full legal sense, a monarchy without a monarch.

Various options were logically open to those for whom the flight of James II required a transfer of title: some form of regency, Mary alone, William alone, or some form of joint or dual monarchy of William and Mary. The decision was effectively William's. He would settle for nothing less than full executive power; but recognized the value of keeping wavering Tories in line by granting Mary a share in the title. The result was a unique and purely parliamentary creature: a dual monarchy totally unlike anything that had preceded it. The offer of the crown, the acceptance of it and the formal investiture of William and Mary in Westminster Abbey in April all represented

---

34. P. Collinson, 'The Monarchical Republic of Elizabeth I', *Bulletin of the John Rylands Library of Manchester*, 69 (1987), 419–23.

35. None of the constitutional documents of 1689 specify the date of his presumed abdication. *DNB*; E.B. Fryde *et al.* (eds.), *Handbook of British Chronology* (Royal Historical Society Handbook, 3rd edn. London, 1986), pp. 44–5; and C. Cheney (ed.), *A Handbook of Dates* (RHS Handbook, London, 1978), p. 27, all give 11 December as the effective date for his abdication. I have not had an opportunity to confirm this date although various commissions and patents would need renewal from the end of the reign and James's grants made during his brief return to London from 16 to 22 December might well have been subject to judicial investigation. If the reign was deemed to have ended with his formation of the intention to desert his charge and not from when he actually did so, it could be argued that Whig views had prevailed over Tory ones.

36. Fryde *et al.* (eds.), *Handbook*, pp. 30–1, 34–45. Henry VII, in order to convict of treason those opposed to his conquest of treason, dated his reign from the day *before* the death of Richard III at the battle of Bosworth. Mary I dated her reign from the moment of her brother's death, not from the moment she was proclaimed against Jane Grey.

an equal share in the dignity of the title. In that sense, there are real differences between their situation and that of Philip and Mary.[37] For example, it was made clear that when one of them died, the other would become sole ruler. This had been excluded by the Act making Philip King of England in 1554. Yet – in the words of the Declaration of Rights – 'the sole and full exercise of regal power'[38] resided, during his lifetime, with William alone. Only on his death did Mary have the right to issue writs, assent to acts, grant pardons by her own authority. This was an intellectually confused but practical solution to the need to keep very different groups happy in 1689. It did not of itself guarantee that a parliamentary title would thereafter govern the succession. Acts of the Convention declared that once William was dead the hereditary order of succession would be resumed. It was a major victory for Tory scruples that William's heirs by any marriage he might make after Mary's death should take their place in the order of succession *after* Anne and her heirs.[39] Setting aside James's right and that of the son he presented to the world in June 1688 (on the grounds that there were sufficient doubts as to the Prince's actually being James's son to make his accession unsafe), Parliament was in fact seeking to reinstate the hereditary principle. It is unlikely, had Anne left a son or daughter to succeed her, that the dynastic hiccup of 1689 would of itself be now proclaimed as of fundamental importance. The replacement of James II by William and Mary is itself of far less constitutional significance than the enforcement of the 1701 Act of Settlement and the bringing in of the Hanoverians. Trevelyan was right: the dynastic change coloured but did not dominate everything.

V

William did not come over for love of England or for pity of her misfortunes. Neither the country nor its inhabitants made any appeal to his affections, which were all centred in Holland. . . . In his cold judgment, Holland could only be saved from ultimate conquest by France if England was brought in as an active partner of the anti-French alliance which he had painfully built up in Europe. If he could himself become King of England that object could certainly be secured. Failing that, the object might still be attained if the policy of James were subjected to the will of a freely elected Parliament.[40]

37. D. Loades, *The Reign of Mary Tudor* (London, 1979), pp. 121–2, 219, 223–6.
38. The phrase was an amendment proposed in the Lords at the last minute, replacing the words 'administration of the government' which had appeared in the Commons draft (*CJ*, X, 24, 25, 29).
39. 1 William and Mary 1, s. 2 c. 2 (the Bill of Rights).
40. Trevelyan, *The English Revolution*, pp. 101–2.

This generally harsh view of William has been endorsed by most recent scholars. Far from being the champion of English liberties, he is now generally portrayed as a cold, ruthless politician who used the resources of the English state as an arsenal for his continental ventures. As we have already seen, by the mid-1690s many leading Whigs and Tories regretted placing William on the throne. Many of them even opened secret negotiations with James to find out the terms on which he would come back.[41] Certainly a majority of recent scholars would concur with Geoffrey Holmes that:

> too often a convenient blanket [is] thrown over a whole series of changes affecting government, finance, the judiciary and the Church between 1689 and 1701 . . . [which] consequently conveys an entirely false idea of the grievances and aspirations of those who chased James II from the throne . . . The Act of Settlement provides a perfect illustration of this confusion. Its celebrated restrictive clauses . . . reflected dissatisfaction not with James but with William.[42]

In other words, if the Bill of Rights 'gave the throne to William and Mary on condition that they did not behave like James II,'[43] then the Act of Settlement promised it to the Hanoverians on condition that they did not behave like William III.

The above extract also reveals the conundrum of William's initial purpose. Like Monck in his invasion of England in 1660, it is impossible to penetrate the mask to see whether there was a set purpose beyond the remedying of a great evil. Was he expecting to have to settle for less than the Crown? His purposes down to James's flight from Salisbury surely remain as inscrutable in 1988 as they did in 1938. But his purposes thereafter can now be read much more clearly, as a result of the brilliant reconstruction of his reactions to the unfolding of events on a day-by-day basis recently offered by Robert Beddard. He has shown that by early December at the latest, William would settle for nothing less than the Crown, but that he had the patience of Job in working and waiting for it to fall into his lap.[44]

If Trevelyan had a suitably tart view of William, he also had a sense of William's priorities: continental war. He does not develop this at any length in *The English Revolution*, however. Books like John Carswell's *The Descent on England* and Stephen Baxter's *William*

---

41. Hopkins, 'Jacobite Conspiracy', esp. ch. 5; J. Israel (ed.), *The Anglo–Dutch Moment: Essays on the Revolution of 1688* (Cambridge, 1991), pp. 7, 82.
42. Holmes, 'Introduction', in Holmes (ed.), *Britain after the Glorious Revolution*, pp. 7–8.
43. Carter, 'The Revolution and the Constitution', p. 42.
44. Beddard, *A Kingdom without a King*, pp. 25–41.

III^{45} have fleshed out what Trevelyan alluded to, but only recently has the co-equal responsibility of the States of Holland and the States General of the United Provinces with William become clear. This was less a dynastic adventure on William's part than a Dutch invasion intended to appropriate English resources for a live-or-die struggle against Louis XIV. If Trevelyan had read Jonathan Israel's introduction to *The Anglo–Dutch Moment*, there would have been some entries in his index under 'Netherlands', which in 1938 there were not. Perhaps we should see the events of 1689 less as the imposition of terms upon invited rulers than as the granting of concessions to a conquered people by a new William the Conqueror.

VI

> Here then lay the revolutionary and extra-legal basis of all that was done in 1689. It was impossible to avoid a flaw in the legal title of a Parliament summoned and chosen during an Interregnum, for the English constitution cannot function legally without a King. None the less, the Revolution settlement was first and foremost the establishment of the rule of law. . . . Apart from the dynastic change, which coloured everything in the new era, there were only two new principles of any importance introduced in 1689. One was that the Crown could not remove Judges, and the other was that Protestant dissenters were to enjoy toleration for their religious worship. Almost everything else was, nominally at least, only restoration, to repair the breaches in the constitutional fabric made by the illegalities of James II.[46]

> William and Mary were not made King and Queen without conditions. The instrument by which the Convention raised them to the throne was the famous Declaration of Right. . . . It required the acceptance of these limitations [in the Declaration] as a condition of their elevation to the throne . . . The Declaration of Right was, in form at least, purely conservative. It introduced no new principle of law . . . for the Convention had wisely decided that alterations in existing laws would require time for debate, and that not another day could be spared before the throne was filled, without great risk to the public safety.[47]

> The settlement of 1689 was not . . . a mere party or sectarian triumph, but an agreement between parties and Churches to live and let live.[48]

We have already considered the dynastic points. Here we must ponder the following arguments of Trevelyan: that in its conception and

45. J. Carswell, *The Descent on England* (London, 1969); Baxter, *William III*; and more generally, see W.A. Speck, 'The Orangist Conspiracy against James II', *HJ*, 30 (1987), 453–62.
46. Trevelyan, *The English Revolution*, pp. 133–4.
47. Ibid., pp. 149–50.
48. Ibid., p. 175.

execution the settlement of 1689 was conservative; that William and Mary were made King and Queen upon conditions but that those conditions were that they did not behave like their predecessor; that what mattered was that the parties sank their differences and agreed not to ram their beliefs and philosophies down one another's throats. Let us take each of these propositions in turn.

Trevelyan's cool assessment of the Convention of 1689 seems just about right. By comparison Lois Schwoerer's description of it as 'a revolutionary tribunal' seems inapposite.[49] It differed in hardly any significant way from that of 1660. If anything it was less of an aberration, because the Convention of 1660 was elected on writs issued by a body at least as irregular as that which summoned the Convention of 1689, and writs which placed political constraints on those allowed to be elected. The nervousness of the 1689 Convention at its own legitimacy is seen in the Act which it passed once William and Mary were safely on the throne retroactively confirming the propriety of its summons, and, more importantly, by the Act passed by the Parliament summoned upon royal writs in 1690 which again confirmed everything done by the Convention. The meetings of Caroline MPs and of the Great Council of Peers were indeed irregular, but James's flight created a situation which was wholly without precedent, and for which there was no provision. Nothing was done to give bodies of that kind any standing in any foreseeable future crisis. They were part of the constitutional black hole that separated the 'flight(s)' of James from the proclamation of William and Mary.

The nub of the claim that 1689 created constitutional monarchy is, of course, the status of the Declaration of Rights and the Bill of Rights. Here two points need to be more starkly distinguished than they usually are: first, whether the Declaration actually placed any effective constraints upon William's freedom of action; and secondly, whether it was, as Trevelyan unambiguously argued, a condition of the offer of the Crown, a form of contract between king and people.

In relation to the former, the weight of modern opinion is with Trevelyan: the Declaration looked at those actions of James II (and, to a much lesser extent, those of Charles II in the years 1681–5)[50]

49. Schwoerer, 'Revolution as Spectacle', p. 111. But see also her important discussion of 'The Transformation of the 1689 Convention into a Parliament', *Parliamentary History*, 3 (1984), 57–76.
50. Most prominently in the clauses against abuses in treason trials (which looked back to the trials of the Rye House plotters) and the levying of excessive fines (principally referring to the 1682 fine on Sir Thomas Pilkington and the 1684 fine on Sir Samuel Barnardiston). See Speck, *Reluctant Revolutionaries*, pp. 147–8, 162.

which were in breach of existing law, and confirmed the illegality of those royal acts. More importantly, it has been argued that the major constraints on the Crown in the eighteenth century, the effective parliamentary power of the purse, the consequent necessity for annual sessions of Parliament, the accountability of the executive to the legislature, and the ending of the Crown's ability to remove judges at will and hence to secure an intimidated (or at any rate compliant) judiciary,[51] were all the consequences of the wars that followed the Revolution and not of the Revolution itself.[52] To this, an essay by Jonathan Israel powerfully retorts that war was the purpose of the invasion and conquest of England and was not an optional or unnecessary extra.[53] But it is no longer sensible to predicate whatever new form of monarchy one wants to see in the eighteenth century upon the *content* of the Declaration of Rights. Fourteenth-century kings had been bound in tighter swaddling bands than bound William in 1689 but had escaped from them soon enough.

The best argument against what I take to be this majority view is that of Lois Schwoerer and Howard Nenner, who concur that 'it was a time-honored tactic in seventeenth-century England for parliamentmen to win new rights by claiming to recover old ones'. Lois Schwoerer's careful study of the text and context is the best and most persuasive account we have for any seventeenth-century document of the methodological and evidential problems of sorting out whether we can determine what politicians meant from what they said.[54] This raises fundamental problems of hermeneutic and exegesis which have bedevilled historical discussion of the 1620s, 1640s, and 1670s as well as the years around 1688 – and for none

---

51. This in turn disallows Trevelyan's assertion that the loss of the right to remove judges was one of 'the two new principles of any importance introduced in 1689'. It was introduced – and only partially as an afterthought from 1689 – in 1701. See D. Rubini, 'The Precarious Independence of the Judiciary', *Law Quarterly Review*, 83 (1967), 1–19.

52. The classic statement of this case is Carter, 'The Revolution and the Constitution', pp. 39–58; see also C. Roberts, 'The Constitutional Significance of the Financial Settlement of 1690', *HJ*, 20 (1977), 59–76.

53. See J. Israel, 'The Dutch Role in the Glorious Revolution' in J. Israel (ed.), *The Anglo–Dutch Moment*, pp. 119–21, 134–5.

54. This is a principle theme of L.G. Schwoerer, *The Declaration of Rights, 1689* (Baltimore, 1981), and more specifically in L.G. Schwoerer, 'The Role of the Lawyers in the Revolution of 1688–9', in R. Schnur (ed.), *Die Rolle der Juristen bei der Entstebung des modernen Staates* (Berlin, 1986), p. 484. Howard Nenner's important discussion of this point (which has important implications for early Stuart historians) is in *By Colour of Law: Legal Culture and Constitutional Politics in England, 1660–1689* (Chicago, 1976), pp. 63–70.

of these periods can it be said that historians have really come to grips with this question.[55] I would here try to side-step the issue by saying that – as Trevelyan realized – it did not matter what those who drew up and passed the Declaration intended. The historian of 1689 needs to know who was responsible for the draft finally agreed, but the historian of the consequences of the Revolution is concerned more with the crucial ambiguities which everyone acknowledges to have been left in the text. There was enough of a fudge for everyone to believe what they wanted. Furthermore – and more crucially – the Declaration of Rights could not and did not have the power or the authority to bind kings, however much a majority of those who proferred it on 13 February may have believed that William and Mary were bound to observe it. It did not compel anyone else to accept that there was now a contract between king and people, and it did not help those who believed that there had been and should be a contract to make such contracts easier to enforce.

Many historians, like contemporaries of the Declaration, can and do argue whether the offer of the throne was conditional upon the acceptance of the Declaration.[56] Trevelyan certainly argues too readily that it was. But even if it had been a condition, how could it be enforced? Unlike the Petition of Right of 1628 it was not assented to by the king using a formula of assent known to the law. It was not a statute, and its engrossment on parchment and enrolment in Chancery could not and did not give it any status as a statutory instrument that could be pleaded in court. It did not bind the judges. It was not even in any tangible form incorporated into the new coronation oath. What redress did the subject have if he or she believed a future monarch had violated it? That subject could not plead protection under it in court, but would have to cite the statutes and precedents which the

---

55. I have attempted some discussion of these questions with relation to the early 1640s in 'Charles I, Tyranny and the Origins of the English Revolution', above, ch. 15.

56. For four attempts to show it *was* a condition, see L. Pinkham, *William III and the Respectable Revolution* (Cambridge, Mass., 1954), pp. 234–5; Frankle, 'The Formulaiton of the Declaration of Rights', p. 270; H. Nenner, 'The Convention of 1689: A Triumph of Constitutional Form', *American Journal of Legal History*, 10 (1966), 295, and 'Constitutional Uncertainty and the Declaration of Right', in B. Malament (ed.), *After the Reformation* (Philadelphia, 1980), pp. 291–308; Schwoerer, *Declaration of Rights*, esp. pp. 281–91. For a more convincing denial, see Carter, 'The Revolution and the Constitution', pp. 40–4; Horwitz, *Parliament*, pp. 10–14. Most of these are discussed by Schwoerer in 'Revolution as Spectacle', pp. 127–31. A close consideration of the meaning to those engaged in the debates of the crucial words 'abdicate' and 'contract' is to be found in a sequence of articles by Thomas Slaughter and John Miller in *HJ*, 24 (1981), 25 (1982), and 28 (1985).

Declaration itself claimed to have been violated. The Declaration laid down no new procedure for investigating violations of those laws and precedents. There was no attempt to revive constitutional forms that could call the king to account. The subjects had no way to remove an arbitrary king in the aftermath of 1688 other than the ways they had to remove an arbitrary king before 1688: by parliamentary pressure, by passive disobedience or by rebellion.[57]

The Bill of Rights was a diluted version of the Declaration. It was indeed an Act which had received royal approval, it was enrolled in Chancery, it was pleadable. But it was a statute only in the normal sense, revocable by the simple act of any future Parliament. It was a part of the fabric of the law, not a yardstick by which other laws could be judged. And it is certainly not part of a contract between king and people. By the time William assented to it, he and Mary had been crowned.[58]

The final point Trevelyan makes about the settlement of 1689 is that it was 'an agreement between parties . . . to live and let live'. He was well aware that this truce of the parties was of short duration. I doubt whether he would have quibbled with the phrase 'the rage of party' so favoured by more recent historians of the period 1694–1715. But in his keenness to see the Revolution as ending the sectarianism of Roundhead and Cavalier, Anglican and Puritan, and so on,[59] he certainly smoothes out the bitterness of the following decades. If Toryism is equated too much with the temporizings of the likes of Nottingham and Danby, then Whiggism is also assumed too readily to be reborn in 1688 fully formed in the shape of the Venetian oligarchs of the eighteenth century.

57. L.G. Schwoerer makes a further important claim when she draws attention to the wording of the proclamation issued following the *offer* of the Crown to William and Mary and their acceptance of it. She writes: 'the text they finally agreed upon is significantly different from that of the documents proclaiming earlier Stuart kings. The Privy Council is not named, but the House of Commons and "others of the commons of the realm" are specifically mentioned along with the Lords Spiritual and Temporal and the Lord Mayor and Citizens of London as persons proclaiming the new monarchs' (Schwoerer, 'Revolution as Spectacle', pp. 113–14). There was no Privy Council capable of proclaiming William and Mary in February, and the Londoners and Commoners are pointedly not mentioned in the first half of the proclamation which describes how the Crown came to be offered and accepted; they are simply mentioned as those who sought to broadcast news of an accomplished fact (*CJ*, X, 28).
58. The date of the coronation was 11 April 1689 (Baxter, *William III*, p. 248) and of the royal assent to the Bill of Rights was 16 December 1689. For an admirable discussion of the *content* of the Bill of Rights, see L. G. Schwoerer, 'The Bill of Rights: Epitome of the Revolution of 1688–9', in J.G.A. Pocock (ed.), *Three British Revolutions: 1641, 1688, 1776* (Princeton, 1980), pp. 224–43.
59. See above, pp. 419–20.

Trevelyan's account can be faulted on all sorts of levels. We are by no means as sure as we were that we can speak of Whig and Tory parties with a continuous history from the 1670s to the 1700s and beyond. The coherence of the Whigs in the great crisis of the Restoration is coming in for attack.[60] The continuities from the 1670s to the 1690s are looking increasingly hard to find. Certainly once one has read Geoffrey Holmes's masterpiece *British Politics in the Age of Anne*,[61] one is in no doubt that the structure of 'party' and the existence of party organization is neither present in nor a necessary consequence of, the events of 1688–9. The 1690s remain the most difficult and incoherent of all decades to narrate precisely because of the lack of strong party identities.[62] It is not just that Whig and Tory groupings are political invertebrates in the 1690s; fundamental shifts were to occur in the way most groups conceptualized and articulated their view on the nature of the state and the polity. Most Whigs had to decide whether to abandon their roots as a natural 'Country' party, suspicious of, even hostile to, the pretensions of the executive; and the Tories, upholders of strong but responsible government, had, though a politics of regret, and for some a politics of nostalgia, to adjust to perpetual exile from power and disdain, even contempt, for the burgeoning apparatus of an expanding state.[63] Particularly important on the Whig side is the way in which initially dangerous, subversive, destabilizing political philosophies which played a minimal part in the making of the Revolution itself were appropriated by later Whigs but reinterpreted so as to draw their sting. Above all the eighteenth

---

60. See J. Scott, *Algernon Sidney and the Restoration Crisis, 1677–1683* (Cambridge, 1991), part I.
61. G. Holmes, *British Politics in the Age of Anne* (rev. edn., London 1987).
62. Horwitz, *Parliament*, has three excellent analytical chapters (4,9, and 13), but the narrative is impossible to follow. B.W. Hill, *The Growth of Parliamentary Parties, 1689–1742* (London, 1976), comes into its own after 1700 and especially after 1715, while D. Rubini, *Court and Country 1688–1702* (London, 1968), flounders completely. Two articles provide the best context for understanding what was happening: H. Howitz, 'The Structure of Parliamentary Politics', in Holmes (ed.), *Britain after the Glorious Revolution*, pp. 96–114, and D. Hayton, 'The "Country" Interest and the Party System', in C. Jones (ed.), *Party and Management in Parliament, 1660–1784* (Leicester, 1984), pp. 37–86. J.C.D. Clark, 'A General Theory of Party, Opposition and Government', *HJ*, 23 (1980), 295–325, is one of that author's most thought-provoking pieces.
63. The best discussion of the tergiversations and transmutations of party ideology in the years after 1689 is J.P. Kenyon, *Revolution Principles* (Cambridge, 1977), but there is a great deal of value (and which has not appeared in his stream of influential articles) in Mark Goldie's unpublished 1978 Cambridge PhD thesis, 'Tory Political Thought in England, 1688–1714'.

century was to lionize the thought of Locke and Sidney but only after emasculating the one and sanitizing the other.[64]

What Trevelyan's account even more fatally obscures is the fissiparous tendencies of the Revolution settlement. Because Jacobites and Nonjurors died out eventually, there is no reason to discount their anguish and the threat they constituted, or were believed to constitute, to those who, however frigidly, embraced the Revolution.[65] I doubt whether there is any livelier debate at present over the political aftermath of the Revolution than that over the nature and significance of Jacobitism. Both as a real threat to the survival of the 1689 settlement, let alone the settlement of 1701/14, and as a tantalizing option which in the 1710s bankrupted politically if not intellectually the lives of many of those Tories who had gone along with William and (with a sigh of relief) with Anne, it certainly disturbs the irenic atmosphere conjured up by Trevelyan.

Curiously, while the radicals of the 1640s and 1650s enjoyed a heyday in the historiography of the 1960s and 1970s, the radicals of the period around and after 1689 received little attention. We certainly know less about them than about the Jacobites. Their religious ideas are finally receiving the attention they deserve.[66] But the importance of republican thinking at the heart of the Revolution has been glanced at more often than confronted head-on. Recently, however, Mark Goldie has – better than anyone else – retrieved for

64. R. Ashcraft, *Revolutionary Politics and Locke's Two Treatises of Government* (Princeton, 1986); J. Scott, *Algernon Sidney and the English Republic 1623–1677* (Cambridge, 1988), esp. ch. 1; Kenyon, *Revolution Principles*, pp. 17–19, 63–4; J. Dunn, 'The Politics of Locke in Eighteenth-Century England and America', in J.W. Yolton (ed.), *John Locke: Problems and Perspectives* (Cambridge, 1969), pp. 45–80.
65. For a cross-section of the large-scale recent rediscovery of Jacobitism, see B. Lenman, *The Jacobite Risings in Britain, 1689–1746* (London, 1980); E. Cruickshanks (ed.), *Ideology and Conspiracy: Aspects of Jacobitism, 1689–1759* (Edinburgh, 1982); Hopkins, 'Jacobite Conspiracy'. Clark, *Revolution and Rebellion*, appendix 2, is a bibliography of recent Jacobite writings. M. Goldie, 'The Nonjurors, Episcopacy and the Origins of the Convention Parliament', in Cruickshanks (ed.), *Ideology and Conspiracy*, pp. 15–35, is an important study of the 'clerical counterpart of Jacobitism'.
66. The classical texts on post-1688 republicanism are C. Robbins, *The Eighteenth-Century Commonwealth men* (Cambridge, Mass., 1959), and J.G.A. Pocock, *The Machiavellian Moment* (Princeton, 1977), esp. ch. 13. An important recent contribution is M. Goldie, 'The Roots of True Whiggism', *History of Political Thought*, 1 (1980), 195–236. On the religious radicalism of the 1690s, all previous accounts are supplanted by J. Champion, 'The Ancient Constitution of the Christian Church: The Church of England and its Enemies, 1660–1730', Univ. of Cambridge PhD thesis (1989), chs. 4–6.

us the 'roots of true Whiggism', the frustrated republican hopes of a broad, radical grouping in 1689 who had to be rudely shoved aside.[67] Goldie's article makes ever greater sense as a far more complex picture is being painted of politics of the 1670s, and as intellectually much tougher and more ruthless republican strands of thought and activist groups are identified.[68] What seems to have happened is that in 1688–9 the more moderate of the Tories made common cause, albeit very briefly, with the more moderate of the Whigs to produce a centrist compromise and constitutional blur to the frustration of significant numbers of principled men on both wings, a centrist compromise more enduring than the alliance of moderates. It is as though neutralism had triumphed in 1642 to the rage, discomfiture, and frustration of Cavalier and of Puritan bigots.

All this admitted, the absence of any pogroms, the informal oblivion if not a formal indemnity for all indiscretions up to the moment of William's landing, the willingness by the parties to the Declaration, especially the Whigs, not to make others devour their own vomit, all suggest that Trevelyan is right in essence. And his transcription of the crucial words with a running gloss that sums up the spirit of compromise clinches it.[69]

As a coda to this section, I will just add a few further observations about Trevelyan's view of the constitutional harmony engendered by 1689. The first is a paradox in relation to the Catholic community. The right of free assembly conferred upon Protestant Dissenters under the Toleration Act was not, of course, extended to Roman Catholics, but this was just part of a general reinforcement of anti-papal legislation – most notably by the extension of the Oath contained in the Second Test Act to the monarch in the Act Settling the Succession of the Crown and by the clauses of the Act of Settlement debarring Catholics from the throne. It was – a point often missed – the former Act, not the latter, that produced a contract limiting the

67. Goldie, 'True Whiggism', pp. 195–236. This point is powerfully reinforced by the essay by A.B. Worden, 'The Revolution and the English Republican Tradition' in J. Israel (ed.), *The Anglo–Dutch Moment*, pp. 255–67.
68. Scott, *Sidney and the English Republic*; Scott, *Sidney and the Restoration Crisis*; Ashcraft, *Revolutionary Politics*; Ludlow, *Voyce from the Watch Tower*, ed. Worden, introduction.
69. Trevelyan, *The English Revolution*, p. 146: 'That King James the Second, having endeavoured to subvert the constitution of the Kingdom, by breaking the *original contract* between the King and people [a Whig remark], and by the advice of Jesuits and other wicked persons having violated the fundamental laws and withdrawn himself out of the kingdom, hath *abdicated* the government [a concession to the Tories] and that *the throne is thereby vacant* [a Whig conclusion].'

throne to non-Catholics.[70] At least as significant, however, is the fact that while the settlement did not overnight destroy the anti-popery of the mass of Englishmen, it transformed it. Before 1603 and after 1688 fear of popery was a fear of an external threat, of foreign rulers (Philip II and Mary Queen of Scots, Louis XIV and the Stuarts) working with a fifth column in the English provinces and, of course, in Ireland. The nation sought to rally around a Protestant ruler against this double threat. Between 1603 and 1688 the threat was very different: the threat of an insidious conspiracy at the heart of government, the poisoning of the king's mind, the weakening of the state's defences against the international popish conspiracy.[71]

A final comment upon the constitutional settlement: it was clearly intended to prevent any further attempt at executive tyranny, at least in the form which, it was believed, James had practised it. But it did nothing to prevent any further legislative tyranny. For the Dissenters in particular, measures like the Second Conventicle Act of 1670 (which subjected them to invasions of their property and to severe penalties without trial by jury) demonstrated that Parliament could as readily set aside natural rights as could a popish king. The readiness of the Convention, almost as soon as it had proffered the Declaration of Rights to William and Mary, to suspend rights of *habeas corpus* and to allow William, upon his request, 'in this conjuncture of affairs, and for the public safety, [to] secure some persons as dangerous to the government and [if] it might be convenient to secure more',[72] did not augur well. Given the ease with which Charles II and James II had sought to subvert the independence of the Houses, and the absence of safeguards in 1689 to prevent a return by the Crown to that policy at a later date, this is a glaring omission.[73] Here, above all, it was not the bloodlessness of the Sensible Revolution so much as the bloodiness of the wars against Louis XIV which reduced the

70. 1 William and Mary 1 s. 2, c. 2. This was a *quid pro quo* for the Tory concern, expressed in the bill, that the natural line of inheritance should reassert itself no later than at the death of William: the succession was to lie with Mary's heirs, then Anne and her heirs, then Williams's heirs by any second or further wife.
71. Compare C. Wiener, 'The Beleaguered Isle: A Study of Elizabethan and Early Jacobean Anti-Catholicism', *Past and Present*, 51 (1973). P. Lake, 'Anti-Popery: The Structure of a Prejudice', in R. Cust and A. Hughes (eds.), *Conflict in Early Stuart England* (Harlow, 1989); and J. Scott, 'England's Troubles: Exhuming the Popish Plot', in T. Harris, P. Seaward and M. Goldie (eds.), *Liberty and authority: The Politics of Religion in Restoration England* (Oxford, 1990).
72. *LJ*, XIV, 135. It is, however, a point not missed by Henry Horwitz, '1689 (and All That)', *Parliamentary History*, 6 (1987), 25–31.
73. For fuller comments on this, see J.S. Morrill, 'The Later Stuarts: A Glorious Restoration?', *History Today*, 38 (July 1988), 8–16.

risk of legislative tyranny. The risk was reduced but never (down to this day) removed.

VII

The Ecclesiastical Settlement of 1689 was a compromise inclining to the Church and Tory side of things, whereas the Dynastic Settlement had inclined to the Whig side . . . The success of the Toleration Act was in part due to its limitations. It had been drawn up with great practical skill and prudence, so as to win the consent of all parties, to relieve the timid and to placate the prejudiced. Its limitations, its illogicality, its want of theoretical principle which made it acceptable in a bygone age, amuse or irritate the modern student. . . . No general principle of Toleration is announced. Indeed the suspected word 'Toleration' is nowhere to be found in the measure. . . . The Clarendon code of persecuting laws is not repealed but certain classes of people on certain conditions are allowed to claim exemption. . . . In fact, by this careful picking of steps along a slippery path, England advanced further towards Toleration in practice than any other European country except Holland.[74]

Trevelyan's discussion of the Toleration Act and of its consequences is one of the most remarkable and most perceptive sections of his book. To show why I think this is so, it is necessary to digress a little.

Patrick Collinson once drew an exceptionally helpful distinction between two types of ecclesiastical history; but the distinction holds for all kinds of history. It is between the vertical approach, which he associated with 'denominationally committed historians' isolating and tracing the developments of those characteristic values, beliefs, structures which came to characterize their sect; and the horizontal approach, which seeks to recreate the particularity of the subject studied in time and place. William Lamont, in developing this distinction, describes the vertical approach as an attempt to discard the 'dross, the prejudices and contentiousness of the age . . . and to extract the residual gold'.[75] Horizontal history, by comparison, gives the contingent, the idea which withered and perished, the dross, equal importance in recapturing the particularity of the past. In many ways the search for a fuller *horizontal* history is the story of 'revisionism'. 'Revisionists' refuse to use the historical filter, to

---

74. Trevelyan, *The English Revolution*, pp. 173–5.
75. P. Collinson, 'Towards a Broader Understanding of the Early Dissenting Tradition', in C.R. Cole and M.E. Moody (eds.), *The Dissenting Tradition* (Ohio, 1975), pp. 1–38; W. M. Lamont, *Richard Baxter and the Millennium* (Brighton, 1979), pp. 19–22.

highlight or emphasize those events, values, structures which were to persist, endure, *win out*. The hazard with 'revisionism' is a kind of nominalism. Every event, every idea is over-contextualized and over-particularized. By looking at the short-term and often muddled or unprincipled actions of those involved, particular Acts, actions, judgements, can be stripped of their role in changing things. It has led to the not wholly unjustified complaint that early Stuart historians have demonstrated that there was no need for a civil war; that there was no deepening crisis in the hearts and minds of those living through the reign of a man whose notion of his own powers and of their liberties was fundamentally different from their own. A lesser quantity of less critical ink has been devoted to showing that the offer of the Crown to William and Mary along with the Declaration of Rights, the later Bill of Rights, and the Toleration Act were all muddled compromises, most things to most men, and were not, could not be, the foundation of a new order. The immense value and importance of Trevelyan's book was that it accepted all the contingency, all the dross, all the unsatisfying and irritating compromise of the settlement, and then shows how despite that (even because of it) English history took a new course.

Modern scholarship has amply demonstrated the niggardly aspects of the Toleration Act, how narrowly it was conceived, how limited were the rights conferred.[76] But modern scholarship has also shown what a body-blow it came to be to the Church of England. The limited rights accorded to the few who set up in competition with the Church created a space to be taken advantage of by the many who chose to ignore all organized religion. The collapse of ecclesiastical discipline and the ability of the church courts to enforce moral and spiritual norms was far steeper in the decades after 1688 than in the previous period. What modern scholarship would modify in Trevelyan's account would be the way he underestimates the bitter feuding over the next thirty years occasioned by the ambiguities in the Act, feuds which reached a height in the years 1702–5 and 1709–13 and which culminated in the passage of the Occasional Conformity

---

76. It is difficult to think of a reliable and full account of the making of the 'Toleration Act' (or *An Act for exempting their Majestyes Protestant Subjects dissenting from the Church of England from the penalties of certain laws* as it was properly called) – 1 William and Mary 1 c. 18. H. Horwitz, *Revolution Politicks* (Cambridge, 1968), pp. 87–94, and G. Holmes, *The Trial of Doctor Sacheverell* (London, 1973), pp. 23–36, are as clear and straightforward as any. But see the important article by John Spurr, 'The Church of England, Comprehension and the 1689 Toleration Act', *EHR* CIV (1989).

and Schism Bills. In the search for long-term benefits, he smooths over medium-term perturbations.

Yet the Toleration Act *was* a bi-partisan measure, introduced by the Tory earl of Nottingham. It satisfied no one, but that was its merit. It caused the corrosion of Anglican triumphalism; it recognized, and in the decades that followed it inculcated the recognition, that it was no longer possible for English governors to seek to recreate a confessional state. Thus, like the Tories after the Great Reform Act of 1832, the Tories of the eighteenth century continued to regret that fundamental changes had taken place, but they could not seek to reverse them. They could seek to interpret the Toleration Act as narrowly as possible; but they could not think of repealing it, even with the majorities of 1710 or 1713. On the other hand, the Act's meanness and pettiness meant that membership of dissenting churches remained unattractive, inducing most respectable Dissenters into the dreary compromise of occasional conformity, a blow to self-esteem and to the holier-than-thou side of the Puritan tradition. The effect again was to accelerate change. Trevelyan was able to discern the link between these changes and the death of Enthusiasm, of Zeal – 'the chaining up of fanaticism', as he put it.[77]

It could be argued that the experience of defeat in 1660, the shattering experience of abandonment by God of the people He had led and caused to overthrow both monarchy and idolatry in the 1640s, had already transformed English Puritanism. The persecution of the 1660s completed what the catastrophe of 1660–2 had not achieved. William Lamont, among others, has suggested that it was not as straightforward as that.[78] Self-confidence, self-assurance (I use the latter term conscious of its theological ambiguity) drained after 1660; but it is not clear that the belief in a New Jerusalem, the perfection of human institutions under divine guidance so that all men could be brought to an understanding of and disciplined obedience to the revealed Will of God, vanished so quickly. Equally, it is not at all clear that the bishops and their apologists would agree that their version of a godly symmetry of church and state working together to bring

---

77. See above, pp. 419–20. For Anglican triumphalism in the period 1660–1714 see especially the work of Mark Goldie, as in 'John Locke and Anglican Royalism', *Political Studies*, 31 (1983), 65–85, and 'The Political Thought of the Anglican Revolution', forthcoming, a marvellous reconstruction of the foiled 'Anglican' coup against James in the second half of 1688. For the shriller Anglicanism of the twenty-five years after 1688, see G.V. Bennett, *The Tory Crisis in Church and State 1688–1730* (Oxford, 1975).

78. Lamont, *Baxter*, ch. 4, 'Baxter and the Non-Emancipation of Restoration Dissent'.

imperfect men and women to a perfect obedience was unrealizable, however much in practice it seemed further from realization than before the civil wars. The Toleration Act, by its humbling of everyone's pretensions, by being 'a compromise inclining to the Church and Tory side of things',[79] but only just, completed the disillusionment with using perfected institutions to perfect Man. Instead, those forms of pietism came to predominate which accepted the world as a broken and fallen place and sought only to use religious institutions as forms within which individuals could find the means to build Temples of Grace within themselves. Of course, this is only part of the picture: one cannot see the Toleration Act as achieving this of itself. Deeper intellectual currents were flowing and creating new imperatives. The late seventeenth century saw the rise of more optimistic accounts of human nature and above all human reason. In these new accounts all men and women – not just a clerical elite or a Cosy coterie of intellectuals gathered at Great Tew[80] – were invested with reason enough to make sense of the Christian message and of its moral demands, with the final dethronement of Calvinism as one outcome. But Trevelyan's point that the Toleration Act made fanaticism and persecution *impracticable* remains one of his most important insights.

VIII

The Revolution had its consequences in the other lands ruled by James, on the English colonies, on Scotland and on Ireland[81]

Ireland had to be reconquered before she would submit to the change of sovereigns. To the Roman Catholic majority of her inhabitants the Revolution meant not political and religious freedom but foreign domination and religious persecution.[82]

The new spirit of independence that the Revolution had breathed into the Scottish Parliament made it impossible to preserve the system of Dual Monarchy. Either England and Scotland must again have separate kings, or else they must cease to have separate Parliaments[83]

Trevelyan devoted almost one fifth of his book to the differing patterns of Revolution in the three kingdoms and casts a sideways

79. Trevelyan, *The English Revolution*, p. 153.
80. As captured in the splendid essay on 'The Great Tew Circle' by Hugh Trevor-Roper, in *Catholics, Anglicans and Puritans* (London, 1987), pp. 166–230.
81. Trevelyan, *The English Revolution*, p. 203.
82. Ibid., p. 205.
83. Ibid., p. 220.

glance across the Atlantic as penetrating as any general study since of the English Revolution of 1688. While the historiography of early modern Scotland and Ireland has been transformed in the past two decades, scholars have generally failed to reach 1688. Whereas the major convulsions in Scotland around 1560 and 1637 have received several extensive treatments, and whereas the historiography of Tudor Ireland and of mid-seventeenth-century Ireland is in uproar,[84] not one major study of the events of 1688–9 in either has been published since 1938.[85]

The situation could not be more grave. In his standard textbook *The Stuart Age*, Barry Coward does not deal with the settlements in either Scotland or Ireland.[86] In J.R. Jones' more advanced survey *Country and Court*, covering the period 1658–1714, there is no entry in the index under 'Scotland', 'Covenanters', 'Parliament, the Scottish', or any other clue to a Scottish dimension, despite a preface which speaks of the author having 'inhabited the strange world of late-Stuart *Britain*'.[87] The index entry in J.R. Western's *Monarchy and Revolution* rather promisingly offers us 'Scotland, Revolution of 1688 in, 376ff' but this leads us merely to a one and a half page coda to a fifty-five-page chapter on the aftermath of the settlement in England.[88] In his recent book *Reluctant Revolutionaries*, Bill Speck has one index entry to Scotland, which explains why he has not been able to write about it.[89] No major biography of James II offers a serious consideration of his government of Scotland; there is no researched study of the Argyll rebellion to set alongside the many serious studies of the Monmouth rebellion. I will not labour the point. Yet in evaluating the nature of the English settlement, the kind of comparisons Trevelyan attempted

---

84. For Scotland, one only has to look at the catalogue of the splendid Edinburgh publisher John Donald or the bibliographies in J. Wormald, *Court, Kirk and Community 1461–1625* (London, 1981), and R. Mitchison, *Lordship to Patronage* (London, 1983); for Ireland the many works of Brendan Bradshaw, Ciaran Brady, Nicholas Canny, Aidan Clarke, Steven Ellis, and others.

85. The best introduction (which covers 1680–1750) now is by Daniel Szechi and David Hayton, 'John Bull's Other Kingdoms: The English Government of Scotland and Ireland', in Clyve Jones (ed.), *Britain in the First Age of Party 1680–1750: Essays Presented to Geoffrey Holmes* (London, 1987), pp. 241–80. There is much of importance on Scottish politics in the aftermath of the Revolution in P.W.J. Riley, *King William and the Scottish Politicians* (Edinburgh, 1979), and P. Hopkins, *Glencoe and the End of the Highland War* (Edinburgh, 1986), but neither offers an analysis of the nature and consequences of the settlement. The same can be said of J. G. Simms, *Jacobite Ireland 1685–91* (London, 1969).

86. B. Coward, *The Stuart Age: A History of England, 1603–1714* (London, 1980).

87. J.R. Jones, *Country and Court* (London, 1978), p. x.

88. Western, *Monarchy and Revolution*, index.

89. Speck, *Reluctant Revolutionaries*, pp. 14–16.

are invaluable. In Scotland, there was an explicit forfeiture of the Crown, predicated not upon James's flight and desertion of his realms but upon his 'subversione of the protestant religione, and the violation of the lawes and liberties of the Kingdome, inverting all the Ends of Government'.[90] There was a totally different religious settlement, the substitution of a Presbyterian for an episcopal Church, a purge of those held responsible for past persecutions, and the creation of two religious groups on either wing – Jacobite episcopalians and Cameronian Covenanters who were denied religious freedom as well as civil rights. Even in books unashamedly concerned with *English* affairs, it is surely essential to look at the destabilizing effects of the Scottish settlement on Scotland and hence on England, just as in calculating how the English settlement changed attitudes in the long term, the Scottish settlement acts as an important control.

The state of Irish historiography is even less satisfactory. Basic questions about the transfer of sovereignty, and how it was perceived by different groups in England and in Ireland, have not been addressed. That the Irish gained little of what the historians of England see as the benefits the world derived from the placing of government under law needs constant reiteration.

There are broader points which could be made about the *British* dimension of the Revolution of 1688. In a sense it marks a fundamental shift in the relationship between Britain and Europe. Recorded British history can be divided essentially into four periods. In the first all parts of Britain, but especially England, were repeatedly invaded, colonized, conquered. This phase culminated in the Norman Conquest of and after 1066. The second phase, from 1066 to 1453, saw the creation of an Anglo-Norman state in the south and east of England straddling the Channel and extending through much of south and western France. There was a subsidiary Anglo-Norman kingdom in the Lowlands of Scotland, but broadly speaking the Gaelic/Celtic Highland regions of northern and western England, Wales, Scotland, and Ireland were only periodically and incompletely the central concern of Norman and Plantagenet kings. This phase abruptly ended with the loss of France by Henry VI and the treaties of 1453. From 1453 to 1688, English monarchs were less active in European wars, less important certainly in the calculations of continental rulers, for the most part reacting to, and on the defensive about, events abroad. But the period saw sustained attempts to subordinate the outlying parts of

90. From 'The Claim of Right', printed in *Acts of the Parliament of Scotland* (11 vols., Edinburgh, 1844–75), IX, 37–40.

England, the principality of Wales and the kingdoms of Ireland and (to a lesser extent) Scotland to the bureaucratic-centralist concerns of a London-based government. This activity created the greatest strains on the resources of the state from the 1530s to the 1630s, was in large part responsible for the War in Three Kingdoms which lasted from 1637 to 1651, and certainly had important consequences for the shape and outcome of the three-nation civil war of 1688–91. But thereafter, the central preoccupation of Crown and ministers reverted to the continent and to Britain's role within it. The uneasy compromises of British and federalist structures which were the product of Tudor and Stuart aggrandizement were firmed up by the Treaty of Limerick and its betrayals and by the 1707 Act of Union. With the major exception of the events leading up to the 1801 Act of Union, the dynamic elements in the geopolitics of the eighteenth and the first half of the nineteenth centuries relate to England-in-Europe rather than England-in-Britain.[91]

IX

William and Anne, because they were trusted and supported by Parliament, were able to fight a long and ultimately successful war against the great strength of France. England's efficiency was doubled by the Revolution, without that loss of our domestic liberty which had been the price of Cromwell's power in the counsels of Europe . . . The financial system that arose after the Revolution was the key to the power of England in the eighteenth and nineteenth centuries. . . . It was also the chief sanction of the revolution . . . With all its disadvantages and dangers, party spirit at least served to mitigate corruption. Whigs and Tories, each with their one-sided idealism and factious loyalty preserved an incorruptible core of zealots ready to bribe but not to be bribed.[92]

Stripped of its unfashionable value judgements, this could almost be a blurb for John Brewer's book *The Sinews of Power*, published in 1989. He too sees the growth of the state, especially its ability to tax and to borrow, its increased efficiency of operation, and its imperviousness to the more crippling forms of corruption, as 'the direct consequence of the political and diplomatic crisis which surrounded the Glorious Revolution'[93] It was war which was the engine of change, but it

91. This paragraph draws heavily on conversations with Dr Steven Ellis. See also on neglected aspects of the first and final forms of the Treaty of Limerick, W. Troost, *William III and the Treaty of Limerick (1691–1697): A study of his Irish Policy* (Lieden, 1983).

92. Trevelyan, The *English Revolution*, p. 179.

93. J. Brewer, *The Sinews of Power: War, Money and the English State* (London, 1989), dust jacket.

was the political settlement of 1689 which gave the political nation the confidence to entrust itself and its resources to governments which were more accountable and more securely Protestant. Brewer's work is important as a synthesis of much preceding work. It is original principally in its study of the working of the Excise, and in its suggestion (not quite a demonstration) that it is the ability to tax rather than the ability to sustain an immense burden of debt at controllable levels of interest that was crucial to the success of the extended military and naval operations.[94] On the growth of the civil service,[95] on the rise of permanent standing armies, on the politics of 'big government', he draws together a mass of work that in fine confirms the general judgement that Trevelyan more by intuition than research summed up in the above. Insofar as it is possible to criticize Trevelyan, it would have to be for the reasons that one might criticize Brewer: that while they are not unaware of the prehistory of much of the administrative revolution in the decades before 1688, they yet understate it. A series of studies of the army and navy, and the administrative departments behind both, and recent work on taxation, show that the mechanics of achieving higher tax yields without provoking serious popular resistance, and the increasing role of government contractors and others involved in generating credit for the state, owed much to the Interregnum and the period following the Restoration.[96] The sheer scale of warfare and the financial and bureaucratic efforts needed to sustain that warfare after 1689 did see an irreversible shift of resources from the nation to the state: but almost all the techniques were tried and tested. Let me give

94. The latter was the major and important conclusion of P.G.M. Dickson, *The Financial Revolution in England 1688–1756* (London, 1967); and is powerfully reinforced by D.W. Jones, *War and Economy in the Age of William III and Marlborough* (Oxford, 1988), essentially a study of the logistics of paying armies, the formidable task of maintaining the flow of bullion to the armies, navies, and their suppliers.
95. The work which itself subsumes and transcends a whole literature on this subject is G. Holmes, *Augustan England: Professions, State and Society, 1680–1730* (London, 1982) which has a particularly helpful bibliography.
96. On the army, see the three volumes of John Childs: *The Army of Charles II* (London, 1976); *The Army, James II and the Glorious Revolution* (Manchester, 1980); *The British Army of William III, 1689–1702* (Manchester, 1987). See, too, H. Tomlinson, *Guns and Government: The Ordinance Office under the Later Stuarts* (London, 1981). On the navy, all previous work has been supplanted by D. Davies, 'The Seagoing Personnel of the Navy, 1660–1689', Univ. of Oxford L. Phil thesis (1986). Much of the groundwork for efficient tax collection was laid between 1640 and 1689: see M.J. Braddick, 'Parliamentary Lay Taxation, c. 1590–1670: Local Problems of Assessment and Collection with Special Reference to Norfolk', Univ. of Cambridge PhD thesis (1987).

one little known example. The state's reliance upon the assistance of major gentry families for the enforcement of government policy in the localities is well known.[97] Equally well known is how before 1640 the Privy Council, through a complex application of sticks and carrots, persuaded and cajoled often reluctant elites into cooperation in the collection of taxes and non-statutory rates, in the regulation of society and of the economy, in maintaining order, and so on. It is widely recognized that the collapse of the prerogative and conciliar courts and the demise of the Council as a manageable administrative overseer in 1660 reduced the Crown's (and ministers') ability to monitor, let alone to control, the work of local governors. The complaisance of the gentry at the Restoration, the real reason why they did not need to place firm statutory controls on the king's freedom to hire and fire members of the executive was that the gentry were immune from central diktat.[98] This is what I used to argue myself. But Norma Landau pointed out to me[99] – and I hope she will publish more on this – that the Crown had far less need to exercise personal, administrative oversight of the work of JPs and other local commissioners. A study of King's Bench records reveals that lazy, negligent or obstructive commissioners were proceeded against in increasing numbers by judicial process, the Assize judges hauling them up to London to answer charges under writs of *mandamus* and *certiorari*. Just as personal royal surveillance of justice in the late fifteenth century gave way to an impersonal supervision by conciliar and the central law courts, so the supervision of local government became a routine judicial matter in the late seventeenth century. A major development in administrative law preceded the Revolution of 1688 and made much possible after it.[100]

In a more general sense, however, Trevelyan's account, like most recent accounts, finds little evidence of a *social* revolution in 1688–9.

97. A. Fletcher, *Reform in the Provinces: The Government of Stuart England* (New Haven, 1986), esp. chs. 1 and 10, subsumes a mass of earlier works.
98. I will defend this proposition in a forthcoming study. It is rather at odds with the attractive thesis of Andrew Coleby, *Government in the Localities: Hampshire 1649–89* (Cambridge, 1987); but see P.J. Norrey, 'The Restoration Regime in Action: The Relationship between Central and Local Government in Dorset, Somerset and Wiltshire', *HJ*, 31 (1988), 789–812.
99. When she was a considerate commentator on a paper entitled 'A Glorious Resolution?', which I gave to the Joseph Cassassa Conference on the theme of 'John Locke and the Glorious Revolution' at Loyola Marymount University, Los Angeles in April 1988,
100. E.G. Henderson, *The Foundations of English Administrative Law* (Cambridge, Mass., 1963) and reprinted here as ch. 19.

The most interesting challenge to this view has been that of J.R. Jones, who sees James as abandoning the Crown's natural alliance with the gentry and making a deliberate bid for the support of new and prosperous social groups business and professional men. An attempted alliance of James and the bourgeoisie led to a feudal reaction in 1689.[101] But Jones does not make too much of this point. It is more of a suggestion than a principal plank in his argument. Other historians have been quick to describe the events of the winter of 1688–9 as an aristocratic coup.[102] Like the similar claims made for an aristocratic coup of 1640–2, this is an important dimension long played down too much. Yet most nobles in 1688–9 were paralysed by a commitment to passive obedience or by sheer fright,[103] and it took the willing and free actions of men of all social groups to see the crisis resolved.

X

The Sensible Revolution of 1688–9 was a conservative Revolution. It did not create damaging new rifts in the English nation, although it did sharpen and to some extent extend divisions in Scotland and Ireland that were of lasting consequence. The constitutional settlement and the ecclesiastical settlements were both fudges. It was possible in 1689 for all kinds of people to continue to believe all sorts of contradictory things.[104] I will give just two examples. First, that James had been lawfully resisted by his subjects because he had violated their civil rights and threatened the true religion; or that there had been no resistance in 1688, only passive disobedience, and that William's expedition had been intended merely to remonstrate with his uncle about the violations of Englishmen's rights and to secure his wife's rights to the succession in the face of a possible dynastic fraud. Second, that England had an elected king contractually bound to his subjects; or that it had a caretaker ruler – to whom no allegiance was due other than as to one who maintained a bare order – because the rightful, anointed king had abandoned his responsibilities by desertion, but that the true succession would in due course be restored. Such ambiguities kept the peace (more or less) in 1688, were productive of much political disagreement in

101. Jones, *The Revolution of 1688*, pp. 13–15, 130–75.
102. See the discussion in Speck, *Reluctant Revolutionaries*, pp. 6–7.
103. J.P. Kenyon, *The Nobility in the Revolution of 1688*, University of Hull Inaugural Lecture (Hull, 1963); cf. D.H. Hosford, *Nottingham, the Nobles and the North* (Hamden, Conn., 1976).
104. J.G.A. Pocock, 'The Fourth British Civil War', *Government and Opposition*, 23 (1988), 151–66.

the decades to come, and gradually hardened into alternative myths of the Revolution that became normative in the eighteenth century. Trevelyan's argument was that it was this triumph of particular myths that contained glorious benefits for the British people. There has been some vigorous 'revisionism' that shows (and to my mind conclusively) that more than one myth survived and prospered in the eighteenth century.[105] But one myth, the Whig myth, legitimated the possession and retention of power by one group and one politico-religious vision predicated upon a particular view of liberty. It is possible for historians to recognize that this is what happened without saying that it was a good thing. What makes Trevelyan read oddly now is not his subtle distinctions between what was intended in 1689 and what eventuated; not his uncomplicated application of the law of unintended consequences; but his approval of particular forms of development. Revisionist historians – like many intellectuals in many fields – have tended to confuse *actus rea* and *mens rea*. Intention is all. If the actors in 1689 were confused, largely unprincipled, living from day-to-day and scrambling for solutions, then there can be no turning-point, no great divide. The 'revisionist' question precludes the Whig answer. In establishing a new pattern of constitutional relationships (many of them unanticipated); in creating a new context within which men and women had to make sense of spiritual and moral imperatives; in crystallizing out the two great parties which, in constant evolution, would dominate English politics for the next 200 years; in forcing a redefinition of England's relationship to Europe and the world, thereby bringing on administrative and institutional change already slowly gestating, and (just as importantly) in reformulating the relationship between the constituent kingdoms of the British Isles, the events of 1688–9 quickened and nurtured a distinctive phase in British historical development. Whether this process is called Glorious, Respectable, or just plain Sensible, it is certainly a Revolution.

105. J.C.D. Clark, *English Society 1688–1832* (Cambridge, 1985). I have no argument with Jonathan Clark's recovery of the survival and resilience of both patriarchalism and Divine Right ideas well into the eighteenth century. But why do we have to wait until the fourth of the six sections, over halfway through, to reach 'the self-image of the state: the case for the establishment' and then for the period 1760–1815? Did not the state have a self-image before that?

Major Publications by John Morrill, 1967–1992

BOOKS

1. *Cheshire 1630–1660: Government and Society during the 'English Revolution'* (OUP, 1974).
2. *The Revolt of the Provinces: Conservatives and Radicals in the English Civil Wars, 1630–1650* (Allen and Unwin, 1976; rev edn., Longman, 1980).
3. *The Cheshire Grand Jury, 1625–1659: a social and administrative study* (Leicester UP, 1976).
4. (with Gerald Aylmer) *The Civil Wars and Interregnum: Sources for Local Historians* (Bedford Square Press, 1979).
5. *Seventeenth-Century Britain* (Dawson/Archon, 1980).
6. *Reactions to the English Civil War* (Macmillan, 1982). My essay on 'The Church in England 1642–1649' appears here as chapter 7.
7. (with Gerald Aylmer) *Land, Men and Beliefs* (Hambledon Press, 1985, 312 pp.). I wrote an introduction and prepared for publication unpublished papers by my former tutor, J.P. Cooper).
8. (with Christopher Daniels) *Charles I* (CUP, 1989).
9. *Oliver Cromwell and the English Revolution* (Longman, 1990). The Chapter on 'The Making of Oliver Cromwell' appears here as chapter 6.
10. *The Scottish National Convenant in its British Context, 1638–51* (Edinburgh University Press, 1990). The title essay appears here as chapter 5.
11. *The Impact of the English Civil War* (Collins and Brown, 1991).
12. *The Consequences of the English Revolution* (Collins and Brown, 1992).

CHAPTERS IN BOOKS

13. 'The Army Revolt of 1647', in A. Duke and C. Tamse (eds.), *Britain and The Netherlands*, vol. 6 (Stenfert Kroese/Martinus Nijhoff, 1977). See here, chapter 16.
14. 'Cheshire Parliamentary History, 1543–1974' in the *Victoria County History of Cheshire*, vol. II (1979).
15. 'The Stuarts', in K.O. Morgan (ed.), *The Oxford Illustrated History of Britain* (OUP, 1984).
16. 'The Attack on the Church of England in the Long Parliament', in D. Beales and G. Best (eds.), *History, Society and the Churches* (CUP, 1985). See here, chapter 4.
17. (With John Walter) 'Order and Disorder in the English Revolution' in A. Fletcher and J. Stevenson (eds.), *Order and Disorder in Early Modern Britain* (CUP, 1985). See here, chapter 18.
18. 'Buckinghamshire Contributions for Ireland, 1642', in J. Wilson (ed.), *Bucks. Rec. Soc.* (1983), introduction.
19. 'The Nature of the English Revolution' in Wang Jue-Fei (ed.), *Proceedings of the Sino-British Historical Congress of 1987* (Nanjing, 1989) – in Chinese! But here as chapter 1.
20. 'Charles I, Tyranny and the English Civil War', in W. Lamont, (ed.), *Religion, Resistance and the Civil War* (Folger Institute Publications, 1990). See here, chapter 15.
21. 'The Sensible Revolution, 1688' in J. Israel (ed.), *The Anglo-Dutch Moment* (CUP, 1991). See here, chapter 20.
22. 'William Dowsing, the Bureaucratic Puritan', in J. Morrill, P. Slack and D. Woolf (eds.), *Public Men and Private Conscience in Seventeenth-Century England* (OUP 1992).

ARTICLES IN REFEREED JOURNALS

23. 'The Allegiance of the Cheshire Gentry in the Great Civil War', *Trans. Lancs and Cheshire Antiq. Soc.* (1967).
24. 'Mutiny and Discontent in English Provincial Armies', *Past and Present* (1972); reprinted in P. Slack (ed.), *Popular Protest and Social Order* (CUP, 1984). See here, chapter 17.
25. 'William Davenport and the Silent Majority of early Stuart England', *Jnl. Chester and N. Wales Arch. Soc.* (1974).
26. 'King Oliver?', *Cromwelliana* (1981–2).
27. 'The Religious Context of the English Civil War', *Trans. Royal Historical Society* (1984). See here, chapter 3.

28. 'What Was the English Revolution?', *History Today* (1984).
29. 'Sir William Brereton and England's "Wars of Religion"', *Journal of British Studies* (1985).
30. 'Microform and the Historian', *Microform Review* (1987).
31. 'Restoring the Balance: the Later Stuarts and the Glorious Revolution', *History Today* (1988). This forms the base of chapter 19.
32. 'La Revolucion Inglesia', *Historia* (1987).
33. 'Tempered Steel: The Conversion of Oliver Cromwell', *Cromwelliana* (1989–90).
34. 'Charles II, Cromwell and Cicero', *Connotations* I (1991).

REVIEW ARTICLES

35. 'Puritans and the Church Courts in the Diocese of Chester', *Northern History* (1976).
36. 'Country Squires and "Middling Sorts" in the Great Rebellion', *Historical Journal* (1976). See here, chapter 10.
37. 'In Search of Popery and Arbitrary Government', *Historical Journal* (1977).
38. 'English Local Government in the early modern period', *Archives* (1977).
39. 'French Absolutism as Limited Monarchy', *Historical Journal* (1979).
40. 'The Northern Gentry and the English Civil War', *Northern History* (1979). See here, chapter 9.
41. 'The English Civil War: A Bibliographical Survey', *History Today* (1982).
42. 'Seventeenth-Century Scotland', *Jnl. Eccl. Hist.* (1982).
43. 'The recent Historiography of the early modern period, part IV, England 1603–1750', *Tijdschrift voor Geschiedensis* (1984).
44. 'Between Conventions: the Members of the Restoration Parliaments', *Parliamentary History* (1986).
45. 'The Ecology of Allegiance in the English Civil Wars' *Journal of British Studies* (1987). See here, chapter 11.
46. 'Christopher Hill's Revolution', *History* (1989). See here, chapter 14.
47. 'Textualizing and Contextualizing Cromwell', *Historical Journal* (1990).
48. 'The Causes of the British Civil War', *Jnl. Eccl. Hist.* (1991). See here, chapter 13.

Index

457

The Nature of the English Revolution

Privy Council (English), 11, 118, 400, 405, 406, 414, 438n; (Scottish), 6, 93n, 99n
Procter, Robert, 129, 140
Protestation (1641), 293
providence, 58
Prynne, William, 41n, 57, 79, 402
Purefoy, William, 314
puritanism, defined, 202–3, 278; culture of, 229–37, 240–1, 273–7, 379–80; and the reform of the church, 10, 14–16, 61–4, 70–90, 148–58, 255–6, 269–71, 276–8, 363–5; political radicalism and, 3, 21, 363–6, 382; disunity of, 25–9, 383–9; and antichrist 64–6; Cromwell and, 124–30, 133–5, 144–6, 393–5; and the Hartlib circle, 138–40
Putney Debates, 320, 326
Pym, John, 63, 64, 65, 80, 81, 139, 144, 256, 262, 265, 266, 293–4, 297, 372
Pyne, Hugh, 5n
Pyne, John, 78

quakers, 25–6, 28, 150n, 170, 236, 369, 371n, 373, 387–90
Quarles, Francis, 274, 278
Quarter Sessions, 157, 216, 311, 343, 383

Radnorshire, 350, 357
Ramsey (Cambs), 120
Ranters, 274–5, 384
Rawson, Nehemiah, 315–16
rebellion, 5
regicide, 22
Rehoboam, 288, 291
republicanism, 22–5
Rex vs Darnell, 289
Rex vs Hampden, 291
Rhodes, Sir Edward, 316
Rich, Henry, 1st earl of Holland, 94, 122, 133, 143
Rich, Nathaniel, 311
Rich, Robert, 266
Rich, Robert, 2nd earl of Warwick, 122, 139, 141, 142, 143, 145, 266
Richard, duke of York (d. 1461), 430
Richard II, King, 62, 296
Richard III, King, 431; charters of, 130
Rigby, Alexander, 66
riots, 361–4, 366–71, 382–3
Ripon, 168
Rolle, Henry, 289
Root and Branch Petition, 61, 77, 264n
Rotherthorpe (Northants), 86
Rothes, earls of, *see* Leslie

Rous, Francis, 74
Row, John, 101
Rowton Moor, battle of, 315
Rubens, Peter-Paul, 96
Russell, Francis, 4th earl of Bedford, 139, 266
Rutherford, Samuel, 111
Rye House Plot, 435n
Ryves, Bruno, 363

sabbatarianism, 14, 74, 379
sacrilege, 21
Saffron Walden, army debates at, 309, 311, 317, 323
St Andrews, 112
St Asaph, 155
St German, Christopher, 13, 300, 413
St Ives (Cambs), 121, 132–3, 135
St John, Mrs, 133, 141, 147
St John, Oliver, 122, 139, 143, 144, 145, 266, 297
St Paul's Cathedral, 158
Salisbury, 55, 433
Saltcombe, 353
Sampson, Dr Henry, 143n
Samuel, 291
Saul, 288, 291
Savile, George, 1st marquis of Halifax, 426
Savile, Thomas, Lord, 264
Savoy Conference, 404
Saye and Sele, Viscount, *see* Fiennes
scandalous ministers ejected, 74, 160–1, 383
Schism Act, 445
Scone, coronations at, 42, 93
Scot, Reginald, 184n
Scotland, 6, 10, 15, 20, 35, 38, 42, 62, 68, 91–117, 246, 255–65, 292, 422, 446–8, armies of, 211; religion in, 203; border violence in, 317
Scott, James, 1st duke of Monmouth, 447
Scott, Thomas, MP, 291
Selden, John, 65, 66, 302
Self-Denying Ordinance, 340
separatists, 229, 369
sequestrations, 200, 335, 342, 344, 367
Sexby, Thomas, 326
Seymour, Sir Francis, 293–4
sheep-corn Husbandry, 225, 230–2
Sherborne, 170
Sherwood Forest, 368
ship money, 17, 47–8, 187, 291, 292
Shrewsbury, 350
shrievalty, 47